THE TALE OF GENJI

THE
Tale
OF
Genji

TRANSLATION,
CANONIZATION,
AND WORLD
LITERATURE

Michael Emmerich

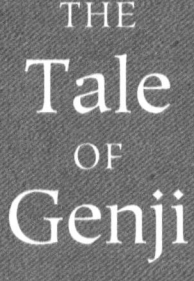

COLUMBIA UNIVERSITY PRESS
NEW YORK

Columbia University Press wishes to express its appreciation for assistance given by the
Hellman Family Foundation and the Association for Asian Studies toward the
cost of publishing this book.

Columbia University Press
Publishers Since 1893
New York   Chichester, West Sussex
cup.columbia.edu
Copyright © 2013 Columbia University Press
Paperback edition, 2015
All rights reserved

Library of Congress Cataloging-in-Publication Data
Emmerich, Michael.
The Tale of Genji : translation, canonization, and world literature /
Michael Emmerich.
pages cm
Includes bibliographical references and index.
ISBN 978-0-231-16272-2 (cloth)
ISBN 978-0-231-16273-9 (pbk.)
ISBN 978-0-231-53442-0 (e-book)
1. Murasaki Shikibu, b. 978? Genji monogatari. 2. Japanese literature—
Heian period, 794–1185—History and criticism. I. Title.
PL788.4.G43E45 2013
895.6'314—dc22
2012048514

COVER IMAGE: (*Main image*) Utagawa Kunisada, *The Courtesan Takigawa of the Kukimanjiya
Reading Inaka Genji* (*Kukimanjiya nai Takigawa*), *uchiwa-e* (fan print), 1838
(Publisher: Iseya Ichiemon) (from the Paulette and Jack Lantz Collection);
(*inset panel*) unidentified artist, cover of [Murasaki Shikibu,] *Genji Monogatari:
The Most Celebrated of the Classical Japanese Romances*, trans. Suyematz Kenchio
(London: Trübner, 1882) (courtesy of the author)
COVER DESIGN: Milenda Nan Ok Lee

Or maybe it's that we do not live in the present,
which is the rock in the stream
that splits us as we flow around it.

> James Richardson,
> "How Things Are: A Suite for Lucretians"

Contents

Acknowledgments
ix

A Note to the Reader
xiii

Introduction
Replacing the Text
1

PART I
Ninety-Nine Years in the Life of an Image

TOUCHSTONE 1
Reimagining the Canon
43

CHAPTER 1
A *Gōkan* Is a *Gōkan* Is a *Gōkan*
Inaka Genji Beyond Parody
47

CHAPTER 2
Reading Higashiyama
Image, Text, and Book in *Inaka Genji*
109

CHAPTER 3
Turning a New Page
Bibliographic Translation and the *Yomihon*ization of *Inaka Genji*
171

PART II
In Medias Res

TOUCHSTONE 2
The Triangle
229

CHAPTER 4
The History of a Romance
Genji Before Waley
237

CHAPTER 5
From the World to the Nation
Making *Genji* Ours
315

CHAPTER 6
"*Genji monogatari*:
Translation and Original"
363

Conclusion
Turning to Translation, Returning to Translation
383

Notes
405

Index
469

Acknowledgments

Fourteen years of learning, crystallized in the pages of this study, means fourteen years of gratitude: I have more thanks to say than a second volume of equal heft could hold. That book would be redundant, however, since this one—the product of innumerable debts—is also my best attempt to repay them. Appreciation infuses every word. These acknowledgments are a partial, inadequate index.

Eleven years after I first struggled to read his smudged scribbles on an essay about Suematsu Kenchō's *Genji Monogatari*, Haruo Shirane continues to be more generous, caring, and prudent than the best adviser or mentor I could have imagined. Tomi Suzuki and Paul Anderer were patient and strict throughout my years at Columbia University, and have been unfailingly supportive ever since. Ellis Tinios and Lawrence Venuti provided comments on my dissertation that helped me realize what it should have been about. Royall Tyler invited me to present some of my work at a conference while I was still in my first year as a graduate student, and was the first person aside from me to read the finished manuscript. My fellow students in the Department of East Asian Languages and Cultures made life as a student and beyond both comfortable and stimulating. Francesco Brindisi revealed that not all roommates are nuisances, by becoming a treasured friend.

When I was an undergraduate, the late H. Richard Okada first demonstrated to me how inspiring and gloriously inconclusive the study of literature could be. He also introduced me to Nakagawa Shigemi, who was my sponsor as a master's student at Ritsumeikan University in Kyoto. In a way, this book is an outgrowth of those years: I encountered Masamune Hakuchō's writings on *Genji* then, and bought the lacquer-boxed copy of

Kogetsushō that became my guide to the value of reading *Genji monogatari* in the least approachable form one can manage. The students in my department at Ritsumeikan gamely endured my enthusiasms, and my limitless ignorance.

During a second extended period of studying in Japan, this time at the National Institute for Japanese Literature, I benefited from the kindness and guidance of Suzuki Jun, Ōtaka Yōji, Katō Masayoshi, Itō Testuya, and Yamashita Noriko. Professor Ōtaka's graciousness over the years has been humbling. I was also assisted in various ways by scholars at other institutions, including Chiba Shunji, Satō Satoru, Shibata Motoyuki, and Gaye Rowley. Dr. Rowley kindly introduced me to Ibuki Kazuko, who shared her memories of Tanizaki Jun'ichirō over a delicious lunch.

After I graduated from Columbia, I had the extraordinary good fortune to spend two years as a fellow at the Society of Fellows in the Liberal Arts at Princeton University. Among those who made my tenure there as productive as any paradise could be are Leonard Barkan, Mary Harper, Carol Rigolot, Cass Garner, Lin DeTitta, Susan Coburn, Penny Stone, Christine Hollendonner, and Jay Barnes—and, above all, my fellow fellows. Tom Hare was a generous mentor, letter writer, and friend. Martin Kern, Benjamin Elman, Susan Naquin, Seiichi Makino, Joy Kim, Stephen Chung, Wang Ping, David Leheny, Ueda Atsuko, and H. Richard Okada assisted and inspired me in ways large and small. The late and much lamented Jim Clark read parts of my manuscript and pointed out that the introduction was a lost conclusion. Yasuko Makino and Gonul Yurdakul were assiduous in tracking down obscure publications. Indra Levy invited me to write the essay that would become the core of chapter 5, and then astutely pressed me to elaborate key points. Chiba Shunji arranged for me to have an office in the library at Waseda University during my first summer as a fellow.

Joining the Department of East Asian Languages and Cultural Studies at the University of California, Santa Barbara, was like being chased out of one paradise into another. I am deeply grateful to everyone in the department, but especially to Kate Saltzman-Li, John Nathan, Michael Berry, Sabine Fruhstuck, and ann-elise lewallen. I won't say more, because momentum would lead me to say too much, especially about all that Dr. Saltzman-Li has done for me. Thank you, thank you. Thanks, too, to Suk-Young Kim. And to Cathy Chiu, Lisa Blanco, Shubra Agrawal, Vera Reyes, Terri Dunson, and everyone else in the HASC office who has made it easier to find time to do research. In the summer of my first year at UCSB, Kamioka Nobuo was instrumental in arranging for me to spend a happy summer at Gakushūin University as a guest of the Department of English Language and Cultures. Katō Norihiro helped me obtain housing and a library card at Waseda two summers later.

In collecting images and acquiring rights, I had help from the staff at the Art Research Center at Ritsumeikan University, the National Diet Library, Waseda University Library, the Princeton University Rare Books and Special Collections Department and the Cotsen Children's Library, the New York Public Library, Kawanabe Kusumi at the Kawanabe Kyōsai Memorial Museum, Ikeda Kenji at the Hokusai Museum, and Andreas Marks. Peter Lang, Taylor and Francis, and the *Review of Japanese Culture and Society* kindly allowed me to reprint parts of chapters that they had first published in a different form.

The research that allowed me to write this book was sponsored over the years by grants from the Itō Foundation for International Education Exchange; the Andrew W. Mellon Foundation; the Fulbright Foundation; the University Committee on Research in the Humanities and Social Sciences, Princeton University; the William Hallum Tuck Memorial Fund, Princeton University; Gakushūin University; the University of California, Santa Barbara; the Northeast Asia Council of the Association for Asian Studies; and the Hellman Family Foundation. The Hellman Family Foundation not only funded research, but also generously subsidized the publication of this image-laden book, as did a smaller grant from the Association for Asian Studies.

The process of turning the manuscript into a book was made as smooth as it could possibly be by two anonymous reviewers, who read the text attentively and made excellent suggestions, and by everyone at Columbia University Press, beginning with Jennifer Crewe and Kathryn Schell. Kerri Cox Sullivan edited the text with a meticulous, surgically precise touch; Irene Pavitt approached the final stages of editing and proofing with what I can only suppose is a bionic eye. Milenda Nan Ok Lee made the book beautiful, inside and out, and Alex Trotter did a masterful job with the index. Jack and Pauline Lantz generously allowed the use of a fan print from their collection on the jacket.

Among the many friends and mentors to whom I am indebted in ways that are not limited to any single place or time are Elmer Luke and Robert Seward, Alfred Birnbaum and ThiThi Aye, Toeda Hirokazu and Tanaka Yukari, and Katō Norihiro and Katō Atsuko. I am so much more than privileged to know them all.

Itō Kiyo has been like family since I first lived in her house as a student at the Kyoto Center for Japanese Studies. Her knowledge, curiosity, and wisdom are infectious and inspiring.

And then there is family. Ikeda Teiichi, Ikeda Mieko, Shimazaki Fumio, Shimazaki Kiyoko, and Shimazaki Akiko have all been incredibly supportive over the years, as was Shimazaki Yuki. My parents, David and Helen Emmerich, have always been encouraging, patient, warm, willing to let me drift off into other languages, other worlds—knowing, no doubt, that however far I went, I always carried my love and respect for them with me. I dedicate this study to them. (That doesn't mean they have to read it again.) Karen Emmerich is not only the best sister I could have wished for, she was also my second-most critical reader. Her advice improved this book enormously.

And then there is Satoko. Thank you, always, always.

A Note to the Reader

In the following pages, I cite terms and passages from a number of languages, most often in English translation but sometimes in romanized form and occasionally in non-roman scripts. For the sake of simplicity in a book that quotes writings from the eleventh to the twenty-first century, I have consistently romanized Japanese words in accordance with their contemporary pronunciation. The only exceptions to this policy are when Japanese words appear in quotations, in which case the original romanizations are maintained, even when they are clearly erroneous.

All translations are my own, except when otherwise noted.

Since this book deals with *Genji monogatari*, its translations, and discourse about its translations, I have had to adopt a rather unusual nomenclature to distinguish the various *Genji*s I write about. Generally speaking, I use *Genji monogatari* to denote the tale in Japanese, including the original classical text and all manner of later translations and adaptations. I use *Genji Monogatari* to refer to Suematsu Kenchō's 1882 partial translation into English, and *The Tale of Genji* to refer to all subsequent translations into English. The abbreviation *Genji* is used to refer ambiguously to either the original or a translation, or to an image or a vision of the tale in which original and translation seem, on some level, to have fused.

In order to make this study accessible to as wide an audience as possible, the titles of only a few particularly important Japanese works have been presented throughout in romanized form; most often, an English translation has been used. Titles of writings in European languages have been given first in their original languages, followed by translations. The titles of Japanese periodicals have been left in romanized Japanese, since they reveal little about the articles they contain.

In citing premodern Japanese books, I have followed the standard procedure: each leaf is counted as one page with two sides. The "first page" of a book is 1 *omote* (obverse), the "second page" is 1 *ura* (reverse), and so on. Names are presented in the order preferred in the language in which their owners have most often published; most Japanese names appear family name first, and given name second. I have followed Japanese convention, as well, in referring to certain authors, often but not always those who published under noms de plume, by their (adopted) given names. Birth and death dates are provided only when they are known, and when it seems germane.

Full citations have been provided in the notes. In the interest of preventing an already lengthy book from becoming even longer, a complete list of works cited is on the page for this book at the Columbia University Press Web site (http://www.cup.columbia.edu/static/emmerich=bibliography).

Titles of frequently cited books are abbreviated in accordance with the following list. Note that the abbreviation SNKBT occurs twice; it will be clear from context which book is being cited.

GM [Murasaki Shikibu.] *Genji Monogatari: The Most Celebrated of the Classical Japanese Romances.* Translated by Suyematz Kenchio. London: Trübner, 1882.

GMK [Murasaki Shikibu.] *Genji monogatari kogetsushō: Zōchū.* Annotated by Kitamura Kigin. Edited by Arikawa Takehiko. Kōdansha gakujutsu bunko 314. 3 vols. Tokyo: Kōdansha, 1982.

GN [Yoda Gakkai.] *Gakkai nichiroku.* Edited by Gakkai Nichiroku Kenkyūkai. 12 vols. Tokyo: Iwanami Shoten, 1991-1993.

KGS [Murasaki Shikibu.] *Genji monogatari kogetsushō.* Annotated by Kitamura Kigin. 60 vols. Kyoto: Murakami Kanzaemon, colophon 1673.

MHZ Masamune Hakuchō. *Masamune Hakuchō zenshū.* 30 vols. Tokyo: Fukutake Shoten, 1983-1986.

NMIG Ryūtei Tanehiko (text) and Utagawa Kunisada (pictures). *Nise Murasaki inaka Genji.* 38 volumes in 76 fascicles. Edo: Senkakudō, 1829-1842.

SNKBT [Murasaki Shikibu.] *Genji monogatari.* Edited by Yanai Shigeshi et al. Shin Nihon koten bungaku taikei 19-23. 5 vols. Tokyo: Iwanami Shoten, 1993-1997.

SNKBT   [Ryūtei Tanehiko.] *Nise Murasaki inaka Genji*. Edited by Suzuki Jūzō. Shin Nihon koten bungaku taikei 88–89. 2 vols. Tokyo: Iwanami Shoten, 1995.
SNKBZ   [Murasaki Shikibu.] *Genji monogatari*. Edited by Abe Akio et al. Shinpen Nihon koten bungaku zenshū 20–25. 6 vols. Tokyo: Shōgakukan, 1994–1998.
TG   Murasaki Shikibu. *The Tale of Genji*. Translated by Royall Tyler. 2 vols. New York: Viking, 2001.

THE TALE OF GENJI

Returning to *Genji*

The late Mitani Kuniaki, one of the most astute contemporary readers of the early-eleventh-century classic *Genji monogatari*, or *The Tale of Genji*, once suggested that no first experience of the tale will ever be more than preliminary; that in order to begin making sense of all it presents to us we must, having finished it, return to the beginning. "*Genji monogatari*," he observes, "is literature that demands to be read again."[1] Reading *Genji* now, at this juncture, prepares us for some potential future rereading; and by the same token,

Introduction

Replacing the Text

Every reading of a classic is in fact a rereading.

Italo Calvino,
"Why Read the Classics?"

each subsequent rereading is an elaboration of those that came before. The tale unfolds in time. "Sense, in *Genji monogatari*, is suspended," Mitani continues: our first, straightforward reading is fractured by contradictions that surface the second time around, inspiring us to doubt the very telling of the tale, "relativizing the narrators."[2] Like Ukifune, adrift in the omnipresent present, we are pulled, as we read, in many directions. At any given instant, as the text streams through us or as we stream around it, we are like Genji gazing across "the great expanse of ocean I had not known" twelve days before he makes the all-important crossing from Suma to Akashi: "The ocean, its surface unperturbed, stretched off into an unfathomable distance, calling up thoughts of how he had come, and where he was headed."[3]

This is the kind of reading experience *Genji* offers us—or perhaps demands of us. But if an individual reader's first reading is, in this sense, ideally no more than an extraordinary prelude, the first tick of a clock whose hands do not so much mark time as reel it in, the same first reading is also, in another sense, a culmination of centuries of earlier readings. Even before she opens the book and encounters those famous first words—*Izure no ontoki ni ka*, "In which reign might it have been?"—the history of all the things people have said and thought and written about *Genji* is there, but almost invisibly, hanging over her head. This, too, is the kind of reading experience *Genji* offers us, or perhaps demands of us: reading within a history of reading, within a community of readers to which first-time readers—and even non-readers near enough to the world of *Genji* discourse to feel its gravitational pull—already unknowingly belong. *Genji* is literature that can only ever be *read again*.

It is easy to forget how enmeshed in the histories of reading and textual transmission we are, and it is not easy to recognize the ways in which, and the extent to which, such histories shape ostensibly private reading practices. Still more difficult is the task of learning to see that earlier readers, and above all non-readers, were not guided by our own transparent assumptions. This book, *The Tale of Genji: Translation, Canonization, and World Literature*, traces a portion of the vast sweep of *Genji*'s history that is deeply, immediately relevant to the present and that has had a profound impact on the myriad forms in which contemporary readers, and non-readers, encounter *Genji*. But while the history it explores is unmistakably our own, and while we are unquestionably part of that historical flow, it is not necessarily something we share with our predecessors. The things we have inherited from them are not the things they left behind. Neither is this history something that *we*, today, whoever we are, will share.

If there is no objective history, then neither are there objective readings of histories. This study is itself swept up in the histories of reading and textual transmission it relates—and so am I, its author, and so is whoever reads it. This is a history of *Genji*, yes, but it is also implicated in the ongoing process it examines: it maps the very conditions that enabled it to be written, it is a chapter in its own story, and this will affect the ways in which it is read. The global community of *Genji*'s readership, and of its non-readership, is ultimately linked—translingually, transnationally, transhistorically—by something its members do not hold in common: *Genji*. This is a book about precisely that *Genji*, a product of translation, global circulation, and mass-media discourse. It seems appropriate, then, to begin by marking the contours of this study in terms not of its subject matter, but of certain constitutive structures that make it possible for it to have a subject at all: the English language, the practice of translation, and the discipline of English-language Japanese literary studies.

On Writing in English

This book began to crystallize into its current form in 2008, a year celebrated worldwide as the approximate millennial anniversary of *Genji monogatari*'s composition. Presenting portions of my research to academic and lay audiences in English and Japanese, I found that I was more than usually sensitized to the social and political valences that speaking about *Genji*, and doing research on *Genji*, can have. At the same time, I also felt more acutely the significance of how and in what context one writes about *Genji*. It is not only what we say, but also the language we use. This study is a history, in part, of the emergence of the conditions that enable a scholar to conceive a history like it *in English*, in an English-language academic context.

Genji is now perceived, both in Japan and abroad, as one of the most potent emblems of the imagined community of the Japanese nation; as a masterpiece of world literature for which, and to which, Japan, its language, and its citizens are somehow responsible. Ed Fisher captured this in an amusing cartoon published in the *New Yorker* on May 20, 1991: two socialites stand in the foyer of a glamorous New York apartment, welcoming a Japanese couple to a party glimpsed through the doorway behind them. "I'm so glad to meet someone Japanese," the hostess croons, extending her hand. "I loved 'The Tale of Genji'!" (figure 1). The joke, it seems, is on the wealthy white woman, who is cultivated enough to have read the tale, or at least to recall its title, but has no sense that anything might separate it and its author from her guests. In her mind, the Japanese visitor whose hand she is about to shake is a modern stand-in for Murasaki Shikibu, an avatar of that fantasy Japan, the country of *The Tale of Genji*. Cosmopolitan readers of the *New Yorker* are expected to chuckle at the hostess's gracious ignorance, perhaps putting themselves in the Japanese couple's shoes and imagining their puzzled bemusement.[4]

"*I'm so glad to meet someone Japanese. I loved 'The Tale of Genji'!*"

Figure 1 A cartoon by Ed Fisher from the *New Yorker*, May 20, 1991. (Courtesy of the *New Yorker*)

But there is more to the exchange than that. The most crucial element in its humor is, indeed, all too easily overlooked—it is the language in which the hostess is speaking: the English language. Even if the caption were to be translated into Japanese, even if it had originally been written in Japanese, it would still be *almost* indubitably apparent that the words are spoken in English—not, at any rate, in Japanese. When the Japanese woman replies, she too will speak in English. And if she says anything about *Genji*, her hostess will interpret her words in light of her own memory of the English-language translation that she has read. We have no idea who the people in this cartoon are, or what they do, or how they are related to one another as individuals; we do know, however, that they have come together in the wake of English's emergence as a global language, and that this process was tied not only to the rise of the United States as a military and economic superpower, but also to the smaller phenomenon of the postwar popularization of Japanese literature in English translation—and, in a distant way, to the establishment of Japanese literary studies as an academic field in the United States. The joke, perhaps, depends less on a wealthy white woman's blithe ignorance of Japan than on her sense of entitlement, and on *our* awareness of the history of relations between the United States and Japan, and of the history of English-language knowledge about Japan.

English matters in Ed Fisher's cartoon. English matters, too, in this study, and not only in the self-evident manner—as a figure in the transnational, translingual, translational history it traces. The medium, here too, is a crucial part of the message. It is significant that this book was written and published in English by a scholar of Japanese literature who received much of his training in the United States. These facts are themselves implicated in the sprawling story the book relates—or, rather, in the different stories that may be read into it, each enmeshed in its own history.

Translation, too, is central to this book. And so it seems fitting, here at the outset, to call on the practice of translation to mark the historicity of the act of writing about *Genji* in the English language—the manner in which the now global field of Japanese literary studies is bound up, for instance, with the history of European, American, and Japanese colonialism. On June 23, 1888, *Yomiuri shinbun* (*Yomiuri Newspaper*) printed an editorial titled "On Writing in English" (Eibun o motte chojutsu suru koto) that pointed, with a sort of pessimistic hope, toward a future that is now *our* past. It is impossible to read it today without remembering the history it presages, and without feeling—to echo Mitani Kuniaki's description of *Genji*—that it is "relativizing" us. We, too, are figures in a narrative that may appear very different one day, when it is revisited in the future, read again from some other, as yet unfathomable perspective. In a sense this editorial, and its translation into English, serve as a touchstone for the rest of the book, and so I present it here in its entirety.

ON WRITING IN ENGLISH

Recently the phrase "preserving the national essence" has acquired a certain prominence in public discourse, and evidently many have adopted this as a doctrine; it would appear, however, that no one is yet advocating the *propagation* of the national essence. Perhaps it is assumed that there is an appropriate order to things, and one must first of all preserve the essence and only then see to its propagation, but insofar as we have now recognized that the national essence exists, it seems only fitting, I would suggest, that we should not rest content merely to strive for its preservation, but rather desire to disseminate it far and wide among the various countries of the West. In my own view, there is no shortage of things that might be described with reference to the national essence: we should apply the term to more than Mount Fuji and Lake Biwa. It appears that the field of literature, above all, is rife with candidates. I submit that in all the world, there is hardly a single novel that can be said to rank with Murasaki Shikibu's *Genji monogatari* in loftiness and elegance. George Eliot, Madame d'Arblay . . . how could they ever hope to equal it? Indeed, even among the mustachioed sex, men such as Dickens and Thackeray, she is quite without parallel. That such a celebrated novel as hers appeared some nine hundred years ago is truly a matter for national pride; and if this is not what we mean by the national essence, I do not know what it could be. Or, again, take a novel like Bakin's *Chronicle of the Eight Dogs*, which is on a par with Walter Scott and greatly surpasses him in the richness of its imagination. While it is said that where dramatic works are concerned none can excel Shakespeare, surely it is false to suggest that no one in the age of Chikamatsu Monzaemon and Takeda Izumo could hold his own against the other playwrights active in the Elizabethan age, coming before and after Shakespeare and Ben Jonson. Thus while any number of celebrated writers have appeared in our nation over the centuries, they are famous only within the borders of this land, at the easternmost limit of the world, and remain unknown, not only in Western nations, but even in China; while, in contrast, the glory of the great writers of England, America, Germany, France, and so on, shines brightly throughout Europe and America, so that even we Japanese find ourselves, at last, struck with reverence for them. The gap between their profits and our losses in this matter is by no means slight. And is this not a truly regrettable circumstance? I am told that in recent years a growing number of Westerners has finally begun to take pleasure in our Japanese art, and they have even recognized that Japan has masters superior to Michelangelo and Raphael. This is because art appeals to the eye by means of its form, and a man may appreciate an artwork even if he and it hail from different nations. The situation is not at all the same where works of literature are concerned: when countries possess different national languages, it is, in the final analysis, impossible for a person from one country to be awakened to the true beauty of a work from the other. In consequence, while the fame of an artist is capable of crossing boundaries, an author's renown rarely penetrates beyond them. To be sure, nations such as England, Germany, and France have different languages, but in the beginning these languages arose from the same root, and as such it is possible to translate works of literature between them, and to savor the works through their translations. Examples of this include, for instance, the rendering of Shakespeare into French and German, or of Schiller and Goethe into English and French. But this is only practicable among countries possessing similar languages, such as England, Germany, and France; no matter how ingenious the translator, it is impossible to translate Shakespeare's plays or Milton's poetry into Japanese, and however accomplished one may be at writing in English, to translate *Genji monogatari* or *Chronicle of the Eight Dogs* into English would be difficult indeed. Anyone who tried would be condemned, no doubt, compared to "the blind man, unafraid of a snake."

Ah, to think that the literary genius of Murasaki Shikibu and Kyokutei Bakin will be praised through the ages, but only by us Japanese! I cannot believe that Westerners will ever read their works, and reading them, come to see that the East has great novelists of its own. And this is the case not only with literary figures from our past such as Shikibu and Bakin; however great our future writers may be, their fame will never succeed in crossing beyond our borders. If we ever hope to see our writers celebrated beyond our borders, the Japanese Empire will have to make of itself a nation as powerful as those others: England, France, Germany, and America. If Japan were to become as powerful a nation as England, France, Germany, and America, then foreigners would study the Japanese language, and they would begin to read *Genji monogatari* and *Chronicle of the Eight Dogs*, and they would be awakened to the true excellence of these works. Judging from the contemporary situation, however, one must admit that this seems an unreasonable hope.

There are many things apart from literature that we might speak of in terms of national essence, and they are sure to grow more numerous over time. Among them, there will be some, and surely not a small number, that it will be impossible to propagate abroad without having recourse to the medium of language. It will not be any less difficult to disseminate knowledge of these things, which demand that we have recourse to the linguistic medium, than it is in the case of literature. And so I would like to suggest to the public-spirited men of the world that they engage themselves in the writing of English. If Japan were a great and powerful nation, foreigners would study Japanese, and there would be no need of our taking the trouble to write in English; but as that is not yet our situation, we must ourselves make the effort to learn to write in English, and compose books that will show them just how skilled we are. Some may protest that it will be difficult for a man who is not English to learn to write in English, and wield the language freely, but considering the long history we Japanese have of writing in accordance with classical Chinese grammar, it will in fact be quite simple; there is no comparison, even, to the old scholars of Chinese learning, who learned only by translating prose in the classical style, without studying the pronunciation, since nowadays paths have been established for the study of English writing along with pronunciation. In this day and age, it is self-evident that a man with great ambitions should study English writing. Study it, and strive, by using the language, to make his glory shine abroad. There is nothing great about a fame garnered solely in the context of this pathetic string of islands.

One would be hard-pressed to find a more explicit, clear-sighted expression of the feeling of utter powerless, voicelessness, and exclusion that plagued Japanese intellectuals in the first decades of the modern period—and that still remained relevant in the 1950s, the decade in which this book winds up, when the author, playwright, and critic Masamune Hakuchō (1879–1962) imagined Murasaki Shikibu being awarded a Nobel Prize for an English translation of *Genji monogatari*, but never for the original text. Indeed, a similar awareness of "the gap between their profits and our losses" continues to resonate even today in, for instance, Mizumura Minae's *The Fall of the Japanese Language in the Age of English* (*Nihongo ga horobiru toki: Eigo no seiki no naka de*), a book published the very same week that *Genji monogatari*'s millennial anniversary was observed.[5]

And yet, skeptical as the editorial's author was regarding the "unreasonable hope" that Japan might one day "become as powerful a nation as England, France, Germany, and America" with the consequence that "foreigners would study the Japanese language, and they would begin to read *Genji monogatari* and *Chronicle of the Eight Dogs*," this is exactly what happened. In 1895, Japan took over Formosa and the Liaodong Peninsula; in 1910, it annexed Korea; in 1931, it invaded Manchuria; in 1941 and 1942, it seized Hong Kong, British Malaya, the Philippines, Singapore, and Burma. As the empire expanded, Japan did indeed strive to propagate the national essence, and over time foreigners began to take notice. As we will see in the second part of this study, the slow process of *Genji*'s dissemination had already gotten under way in 1882 when a young Japanese named Suematsu Kenchō (1855-1920) translated part of the tale into English; it would continue with the publication of Arthur Waley's (1889-1966) six-volume translation *The Tale of Genji* from 1925 to 1933. My own interest in *Genji monogatari*, and my authorship of this book in English, are a direct extension of this history.

The editorial in *Yomiuri shinbun* anticipates the *New Yorker* cartoon—the woman extending her hand to a Japanese guest, welcoming her into a privileged, powerful circle—even as it draws our attention to the history of violence and inequality that underwrites that gesture of friendship and the expression of admiration, in English, that accompanies it. At the same time, the editorial is also prescient in its questioning of the notion that "there is an appropriate order to things, and one must first of all preserve the [national] essence and only then see to its propagation." One of the points this study will make is that even within Japan, the canonization of *Genji monogatari* as a national classic—the "preservation" of an image of *Genji* as the fountainhead of a traditional, unified Japanese culture and aesthetic sensibility—was a by-product of the foreign "propagation" of the tale, above all through the vehicle of the English language. This study, written in English, is thus both part of the legacy of Japan's colonialist history and an attempt to create a perspective from which we might see *Genji monogatari* in a manner less deeply colored by that history.

Replacing Reception

We—whoever we are—read and talk and write about *Genji* for many reasons, in many forms, in many contexts, in many ways. But in the contemporary world, it is difficult to imagine anyone encountering the tale as anything other than a classic of both Japanese and world literature; and it is nearly impossible to imagine anyone reading it in a form that is not some form of translation—transcription, Jerome McGann suggests, is already a type of "type-translation."[6] Any academic study of *Genji* will inevitably connect, then, in one way or another, to the fields of canonization and translation studies, and to the recent burgeoning interest in world literature. This is as true of scholarship in Japanese as it is of work in other languages. This book, tracing the history of the early modern and modern re-creation of *Genji* as a classic of Japanese and world literature that is widely read in translation, engages actively with these fields. It does so, however, in a manner that contrasts markedly with the approach that is generally favored.

Perhaps the best way to suggest the broad outlines of the theoretical channel that guides my analysis is through considering the title of this introduction: "Replacing the Text." Research on canonization has focused, by and large, on particular canonical texts or groups of canonical texts, and on what is described as the history of their "reception." The notion of audience reception, which has been a feature of literary studies and cultural studies more generally since the late 1960s and has crystallized into an approach called "reception theory," remains influential even today, even in cases where the term "reception" seems subtly wrong. This is evident in two major, pathbreaking volumes that together can be seen as inspirations for this study: *Inventing the Classics: Modernity, National Identity, and Japanese Literature*, edited by Haruo Shirane and Tomi Suzuki, and *Envisioning The Tale of Genji: Media, Gender, and Cultural Production*, edited by Haruo Shirane.

Shirane opens his introduction to *Inventing the Classics* by offering a list of canonical titles and authors, including *Genji*, and suggesting that while "these texts and authors are repeatedly anthologized in textbooks in Japan and abroad," their contemporary status "is as much a result of reception in the medieval period, when the vernacular canon was first formed, as it is of the radical configurations of literature and learning that occurred in the nineteenth and twentieth centuries."[7] He begins his introduction to *Envisioning The Tale of Genji* with the observation that "the history of the reception of *The Tale of Genji* is no less than a cultural history of Japan."[8] In both cases, the key term is "reception." In this respect, both *Inventing the Classics* and *Envisioning The Tale of Genji* can clearly be situated in the larger movement of reception studies. And yet it seems to me that part of the value of these two collections, particularly when read in tandem, lies in the trajectory they trace *away from* reception. It is telling that Shirane's introduction to *Envisioning The Tale of Genji* is titled "*The Tale of Genji* and the Dynamics of Cultural Production" and that "cultural production" appears in the book's subtitle. We are not only looking backward, here—interacting with a given textual product of the past—but also, and more crucially, creating new images of the past for the present and for the future.

Drawing on Serge Gavronsky's notions of "pietistic" and "cannibalistic" translation, Shirane proposes that we interpret the history of *Genji* culture in terms of pietistic and cannibalistic modes of reception: "The medieval commentaries of *The Tale of Genji* . . . closely resemble the pietistic model in that they attempt to preserve and transmit the original text, while writerly and media modes of reception often follow the cannibalistic model, in which the writer, artist, or filmmaker uses the source text (an adaptation or a digest) to produce something unique and contemporary."[9] But one might also argue that the invention of the idea of "the original text" of *Genji monogatari* and of the importance of its preservation and transmission was itself the medieval commentators' most significant accomplishment. The pietistic stance, too, is productive. And so I have come to believe that studies of canonization, or at least the field of canonization studies, would do well to dispense with the inherently passive word "reception." There is a need for a new terminology more in tune with the shift that has already occurred, away from a focus on supposedly stable classic texts themselves and toward an interest in the mutable history of books and other material forms, in the processes by which new *images* of texts are produced. I propose that we think in terms not of reception, but of a more engaged notion of *replacement*.

Replacing *Genji monogatari*

Even in Japan, it is abundantly clear that the eleventh-century classical text itself, composed in classical Japanese, has little to do with the prestige *Genji* continues to enjoy as a canonical work. A casual survey I conducted a few years ago of library catalogs and other online databases turned up over ninety partial or complete modern-Japanese translations of the tale published between 1888—the year in which "On Writing in English" was published—and the present. (Here I define translation in a narrow, conventional way from an English-language perspective but broadly and eccentrically from a Japanese-language viewpoint, since in Japanese one usually distinguishes between "translations" [*hon'yaku*] and "modern-language renderings" [*gendaigoyaku*].) And that figure does not include annotated editions, whose notes consist largely of renderings into modern Japanese of words and passages expected to pose difficulties even for reasonably fluent readers of classical Japanese. Some of these editions go so far as to provide running translations of the entire classical text, which is at any rate a transliteration, or type-translation, of a calligraphic or woodblock-printed manuscript, indecipherable to anyone without the requisite linguistic training, into the standard, contemporary, typeset Japanese of novels, newspapers, and restaurant menus. More important, the figure of ninety-plus translations does not include *manga* versions of the tale such as Yamato Waki's famous *Who from a*

Restless Dream (*Asaki yume mishi*, 1979–1993), which could be considered a translation; or Murasaki Shikibu and Egawa Tatsuya's *Genji monogatari* (*The Tale of Genji*, 2001–2005), which was marketed explicitly as a translation.[10]

In short, the text of *Genji monogatari* itself—as though we could even begin to imagine the existence of a text we might describe as "*Genji monogatari* itself" when we know from Murasaki Shikibu's diary that she herself was involved in the preparation of at least three versions of parts of the tale, if not the whole thing—is not really being "received" all that much even in Japan.[11] Vastly more important than "the text" and its reception are its replacements: translations, broadly defined to encompass all the varieties of books just mentioned and more, that literally take the place of *Genji monogatari*, texts that are read instead of the (unknown and unknowable) original. This is what I mean, first of all, by "replacing" a text: canonization as the continual replacement of canonical texts by new, different versions of themselves that answer to the needs not only of authoritative institutions intent on preserving and propagating their own values and ideologies, but also of their consumers; the literary canon as an enormous gallery of look-alikes, a string of placeholders.

Indeed, in the real world, replacements need not be word-for-word translations or even image-for-word translations at all: just about any text or object will do, so long as it enables its readers or consumers to participate in the communal act of valuing the story it was made to represent. The famously bulky *Genji monogatari* can be whittled down until it sits comfortably in the palm of the hand, as in *The Palm-Size Tale of Genji* (*Shōchū Genji monogatari*, 1837), a guide to the tale, its author, its chapter titles, and its characters published especially for poets that is less than three inches high and just over six and one-half inches wide. It can be reduced still further, turned into a bit of an image and a few chopped-off lines of text on a publication that is about the same size as *The Palm-Size Tale of Genji* but consists of only one sheet, and artfully symbolizes *Genji*'s value as what Pierre Bourdieu called "cultural capital": the 2,000-yen banknote, issued in the year 2000, whose verso features a scene from the twelfth-century *Tale of Genji Picture Scroll* (*Genji monogatari emaki*).[12] The classic, we might say, is gold in a world of fiat currency. And there is no need to stop there—no size is too small where replacements of the masterpiece are concerned. In 1749, a publisher in Kyoto named Yoshidaya Zengorō issued a "bean-size" illustrated guide in twenty-eight volumes, including one for the table of contents and a "Complete Overview" (*sōtaii*), each two and three-quarter inches high and just under two inches wide (figure 2). These volumes, though legible, were not necessarily meant to be read: they served as pieces in a game in which the numbers of the volumes, marked on the covers, were translated into points.

And even this is only the beginning. Once you have stripped away this much of the text, it is a simple matter to dispose of the rest. *Genji monogatari* is replaced (rather than received) in any number of other forms. This became strikingly clear in the year 2008, November 1 of which was declared the tale's millennial anniversary—rather randomly, on the basis of a reference in *The Diary of Murasaki Shikibu* (*Murasaki Shikibu nikki*, 1008–1010)—providing an excuse for a dizzying explosion of *Genji*-related events, reportage, and paraphernalia.[13] Much of this activity was supported by the Committee for the Thousandth Anniversary of *Genji monogatari*, whose slogan, "Purple Affinities, Once Again" (Murasaki no yukari, futatabi), came to seem, in its almost inescapable ubiquity, like a translation of the vision of *Genji* as "literature that demands to be read again" into the hollow language of commercialism.[14]

Between November 2, 2006, and March 7, 2009, no fewer than 2,247 articles relating in one way or another to the madcap millennial celebrations ran in newspapers around Japan. NHK, the public television and radio organization known in English as the Japan Broadcasting Corporation, covered topics relating to the anniversary in its television news programs some seventy-six times in 2008 alone, and broadcast several dozen special programs ("Begin Japanology: *Genji monogatari* 1 & 2," "Sunday Forum: From *Genji monogatari* to the Future of the Classics," "Night Essay: *Genji monogatari* as Argentine Tango") on its various channels and stations. The popular music group Rin' released an album called *Genji Nostalgia* in December 2007. The main Kyoto branch of the delivery company "Black Cat" Yamato Transport created two special packing labels using pictures from the Uji City The Tale of Genji Museum's *An Illustrated Mirror of The Tale of Genji in Album Form* (*Genji monogatari ekagamichō*, early seventeenth century), selections from which were also reproduced in a set of ten postage stamps and on two Surutto Kansai Miyako bus and subway cards. I counted nine varieties of millennial saké, a startling array of sweets and snacks—including *Genji monogatari* Millennial Anni-

Figure 2 The cover, in actual size, of the "bean-size" guide to *Genji monogatari* (Kyoto: Yoshidaya Zengorō, 1749). (Courtesy of Cotsen Children's Library, Princeton University)

versary Matcha Baumkuchen and Matcha Bread with Sweet Beans (both baked by Yamazaki Baking Company); even the familiar and unrelated Genji Pie carried "*Genji monogatari* Fortune-telling" games on its packages.[15] There were millennial postcards; incenses; Beware of Fire posters; signs on toilets; lottery tickets; ads on buses, trains, and taxis; a new mural in Kyoto's underground shopping mall Zest Oike; concerts; conferences; symposiums; plays; a picture of Murasaki Shikibu kneeling at her desk and a woman in a Heian-style twelve-layered kimono leaping into the arms of a man in a hunting outfit that appeared one day above the Google logo on the search-engine's homepage; packed exhibits in department stores; a 570-square-foot rice paddy in Uji planted with a bright green millennial Murasaki Shikibu logo; readings; lectures; festivals; a *Genji*-themed "Work-Life Balance Promotion Forum"; fireworks; dances; *kamishibai* (paper theater); a special issue of *Han'ei* (*Flourishing*), the newsletter of the Kyoto Chamber of Commerce and Industry, on "How Small to Mid-Size Businesses Are Using the *Genji monogatari* Millennial Anniversary"; and an e-text of the poet Yosano Akiko's (1878–1942) modern-Japanese translation of *Genji monogatari* produced for the Nintendo DS handheld game system's "Let's All Read Together" (*minna de dokusho*) series of miscellaneous games. The game has the charming title "*The Tale of Genji* + A Little Bit of Literature" (*Genji monogatari* + chottodakebungaku).[16]

The *Genji monogatari* Millennial Anniversary Symbol Mark and Hikaru Genji and Murasaki Shikibu, the two *Genji monogatari* Millennial Anniversary official characters commissioned by the Committee for the Thousandth Anniversary of *Genji monogatari*, were used—in accordance with the licensing regulations, which stipulated the payment of 10,000 yen or 1 percent of a marked item's pre-tax retail price multiplied by the quantity produced, whichever value was higher—155,622,690 times from the beginning of the licensing period until March 31, 2009, when it ended; these images were utilized for developing products and stimulating sales, in mass media, at events, and in other ways by public and private organizations and even by some private individuals.[17]

By my calculations, between March 24, 2007, and February 28, 2009, some 156,470,443 people—a figure about one-quarter again as large as the entire population of Japan in 2008—participated in events with which the Committee for the Thousandth Anniversary of *Genji monogatari* was in some way involved, and even this dizzying figure includes only those at which someone was actually counting. Events ranged from the tiny, such as a five-part seminar on "The World of *Genji monogatari*" at Kyōritsu Women's University that drew just nine participants, to the huge: an estimated 300,000 people visited an exhibition called "A *Tale of Genji* Picture Scroll: From the Old Capital to the Future" in Porta, the underground shopping area in Kyoto Station.[18] On November 1, 2008, an estimated 2,400 people attended the *Genji monogatari* Millennial Anniversary Memorial Ceremony in the main hall of the Kyoto International Conference Center. At lunch, those of us who were there to participate in the Second *Genji monogatari* International Forum, which was to begin the following day, were given seventeen-ounce bottles of "Celebrating the *Genji monogatari* Millennial Anniversary Uji Tea (With Tencha)," decorated with a detail of the picture for the "Hashihime" (The Maiden of the Bridge) chapter in *An Illustrated Mirror of The Tale of Genji in Album Form*. I still have the bottle, which retains its celebratory air even now that it is empty.

This is the simple, almost obvious point I am making: canonization is not really a function of the historically changing *reception* of old texts, although we have gotten into the habit of talking as though it is, but of the production and the circulation of new *replacements* of old texts. Even my necessarily circumscribed account of the efforts of the Committee for the Thousandth Anniversary of *Genji monogatari* to recanonize or, perhaps, hypercanonize *Genji* between 2007 and 2009 should make this clear. To be sure, certain texts and objects stand in a closer relationship to the (unknown and unknowable) original text of *Genji monogatari* than others. A fifteenth-century calligraphic transcription of the tale is undoubtedly closer than a typeset annotated edition, which is closer than a translation into modern Japanese, which is closer than an animated film, which is still a good deal closer than *Genji monogatari* Millennial Anniversary Matcha Baumkuchen. But each of these objects holds out the promise, however tenuous, of an indirect connection to *Genji monogatari* and its canonical prestige. Indeed, if we were to interpret the fees collected by the Committee for the Thousandth Anniversary of *Genji monogatari* for the use of its logo and official characters as approximate indications of the value of each replacement's contribution to *Genji*'s recanonization—well, the old calligraphic text itself, squirreled away in some collection, would bring in only 10,000 yen if it were stamped with a logo. Surely the Baumkuchen was worth much more.

And come to think of it, from the perspective of the organization that devoted itself over the course of two years to the elaboration of *Genji*'s canonicity, what value could the actual *original* text of *Genji monogatari* itself possibly have? Even imagining that a single perfect, authoritative original ever existed—and as I noted earlier, Murasaki Shikibu herself appears to have overseen the preparation of at least three versions of the tale, or some portion of it—that text has been lost. The canonization of *Genji* does not, because it cannot, in any way depend on an original text. And yet that is not to say that the original text of *Genji monogatari* itself, illusory though it may be, is ever made irrelevant by its replacement. There is a crucial difference between an original text, or the idea of an original text, that has been reinvented as a classic and one that has been allowed to languish. If the former has managed to survive in the form of successive replacements of itself, each shaped by the vagaries of its historical moment, the latter has disappeared, temporarily or permanently, from human memory.

Each time a text is recanonized by being replaced, having a new stand-in created and circulated, it is *re-placed* within the contemporary sociocultural field. Each new image of *Genji* relates in some way to earlier images and is caught up in the ebb and flow of life in its moment—in the social, cultural, economic, and political currents into which it is set adrift; each new replacement, in its consumption, pulls the old text into a new articulation with the present, or at least anchors some conception of the original in a new position within a system of relationships to other texts, real and imagined, and to social, economic, political, and cultural conditions that are endlessly contemporary, but also always split by history—by thoughts of how we have come, and where we are headed. The *manga* that Egawa Tatsuya says he co-authored with Murasaki Shikibu includes excerpts of a text of *Genji monogatari* in classical Japanese, penned so as to recall a calligraphic manuscript. This almost fetishistic attachment to the concept of the original created by medieval scholars—above all, Fujiwara no Teika—is a perfect instance of the complex forward- and backward-looking dynamic of replacement in the second sense in which I use the term.

Earlier I mentioned the *Genji monogatari* Millennial Anniversary Memorial Ceremony, held on November 1, 2008, in the cavernous main hall of the Kyoto International Conference Center. The highlight of this event, extensively covered in the news, was the proclamation of "Classics Day." The actress Shibamoto Yuki, clad in a Heian-style twelve-layer kimono—presumably she was meant to represent Murasaki Shikibu, although in news reports she was identified simply as "the millennial anniversary image-character"—shuffled slowly to the center of the stage and read out, as the emperor and empress listened from a raised platform at stage left, one of two texts of the proclamation that had been prepared and distributed to the audience. The text she read was in Japanese; the other, quoted here, was in English.

PROCLAMATION OF "CLASSICS DAY"

The Tale of Genji is a Japanese classic. It is also a world classic.

This novel, born a thousand years ago in the Heian capital with its "lavender hills and crystal streams," has exerted a profound influence not only on literature but on the arts, craftwork and on stage works of many kinds, and has long been considered the origin of the Japanese sense of beauty. It was translated into English during the 1920s and 30s and, in recent years, it has been translated into over twenty other foreign languages. It has given pleasure to readers in every part of the world and has deeply impressed them. On this day, a thousand years ago, this work was mentioned by Murasaki Shikibu, the author, in her diary. We, celebrating the thousandth anniversary of *The Tale of Genji*, would like henceforward to call November 1 "Classics Day."

A classic, though rooted in the climate and history of a particular country, is something that can be widely appreciated, transcending time and place. It is a "crystallization of the wisdom" of humanity and, by the strength of its insights into human nature and the beauty of its expression, deepens our thought and enriches our hearts. Even now, it stirs our souls and brings us back to the eternal questions of "What is a human being? What is life?" This is what it means to be a classic.

It is precisely because we are in a world in constant fluctuation that we study the classics and embrace them firmly in our hearts. With them as our support, we will share our hearts more deeply than ever before, with the peoples of the world.

We have decided, on this thousandth anniversary of *The Tale of Genji*, to take a first step in that direction.

November 1, 2008
Promoters of the Commemoration of the Thousandth Anniversary of
   The Tale of Genji
Committee for the Thousandth Anniversary of *The Tale of Genji*

It is hard not to see in this proclamation the fulfillment, all but unimaginable 120 years earlier, of the dream that inspired the 1888 *Yomiuri shinbun* editorial "On Writing in English." The crucial point, however, is that all the pageantry of this proclamation centered on an attempt, admirable in its way, to open up a new space in contemporary Japan, and in the lives of Japanese citizens, for classical Japanese texts, with *Genji monogatari* figured as their representative. The classical text, imagined as something stable and unchanging, capable of transcending history—as something that can be *received*, in a word, even if its reception changes—was being called to serve "as our support" in a world that is otherwise "in constant fluctuation." Assuming that the proclamation achieves its goal, which is the designation of "Classics Day" as a national holiday, this, too, will stand as a perfect instantiation of the second sense in which I am using the word "replacement," to describe the creation of a new "place" in the present for the imagination of a canonical work, and to describe the realignment of textual relationships that occurs as a new image of the original settles into the contemporary literary field. The application of the concept of reception to a book or a text, in other words, is itself an instance of replacement.

The Imagined Text

So far I have focused on the double meaning of the term "replacement" in my conception of canonization. I would now like to turn to the word "text," which I also use in more than one sense. First of all, the "text" in the phrase "replacing the text" refers to the original, the idea of the original, or the embodiment of the original or the idea of the original in some prior replacement—in most cases it will, in fact, be an intricate layering of these—that is canonized, recanonized, or decanonized by being replaced. Second, it refers to the term "text" as it has come to be used in literary criticism and cultural studies more generally to mark the subjectivity of the interpretive experience, the process of reading. And third, it denotes the portion of the object indicated by this abstract, catchall term that is actually composed of words.

In the first instance, the text is something understood to have existed prior to a given material replacement, but that is imagined through that replacement; in the second, the text consists of an experience of the material replacement, and is thus understood as something that arises from it. It will be helpful to consider each of these meanings separately to clarify the distinction, to the extent that one can be made: the first meaning might, after all, be considered a subset of the second. For the time being, the third sense—text as writing—can be interpreted straightforwardly with a minimum of fretting, although, as we will discover in chapter 2, the notion of replacement I am advocating here (with Jerome McGann, D. F. McKenzie, Peter Shillingsburg, and others) involves seeing text as inextricably fused with other elements of the page on which it is printed, and the book in which it is bound. In the case of the notion of text as an imagined original, which will be the focus of this section, I will tease out the significance of "replacing the text" by exploring specific examples, at the same time highlighting a crucial replacement that occurred near the end of World War II and marks the transition from the early modern to the contemporary textual world of Genji monogatari—the endpoint toward which this study progresses.

Earlier I mentioned a "bean-size" illustrated guide to Genji monogatari published in Kyoto in 1749 whose twenty-eight volumes were intended to be used in a game. It goes without saying that this book played a role, however small, in reinforcing Genji monogatari's canonical status, and as a guidebook it can be understood as pointing back, across the centuries, to an original text that it purportedly explicates. At the same time, it took the particular material form of an early modern woodblock-printed book whose blue covers called to mind other, more recent printed texts of Genji monogatari, as well as digests of the tale. The bean-size guide is not so much a representation of some abstract notion of "the text" of Genji monogatari, in other words, as it is a miniaturized emblem of a very particular type of text of Genji monogatari that had first appeared in the early seventeenth century and became firmly established almost exactly a century before the miniature guide was created, with the publication of the hugely influential An Illustrated Tale of Genji (Eiri Genji monogatari, postface 1650), illustrated by Yamamoto Shunshō.

The specificity of the visual allusion here is evident from a comparison of the guide's covers to those of the 1673 edition, which remained one of the most widely circulated, and widely replaced, texts of Genji monogatari through the first half of the twentieth century: Kitamura Kigin's Kogetsushō (The Moon on the Lake Commentary) (figure 3). The books have identical plain blue covers, centered title slips, and ordinary four-hole bindings. This is not necessarily to say that the bean-size guide was intended to look like a miniature Kogetsushō, since none of these bibliographic features was unique; the point is that while the guidebook can presumably be understood as gesturing back toward some notion of the original text of Genji monogatari, it gestures *through the medium of the early modern printed edition*. It replaces both an imagined original, in other words, and a more narrowly defined set of existing editions of the tale that one might actually have found at a bookstore, of which Kogetsushō was the most famous.

Perhaps it will seem inappropriate to speak of "texts" when I have compared only two covers, but in fact the bean-size guide's close resemblance to Kogetsushō marks their co-participation in a world of early modern textual transmission of Genji monogatari that constituted the essential framework for the vast majority of readings of the tale until

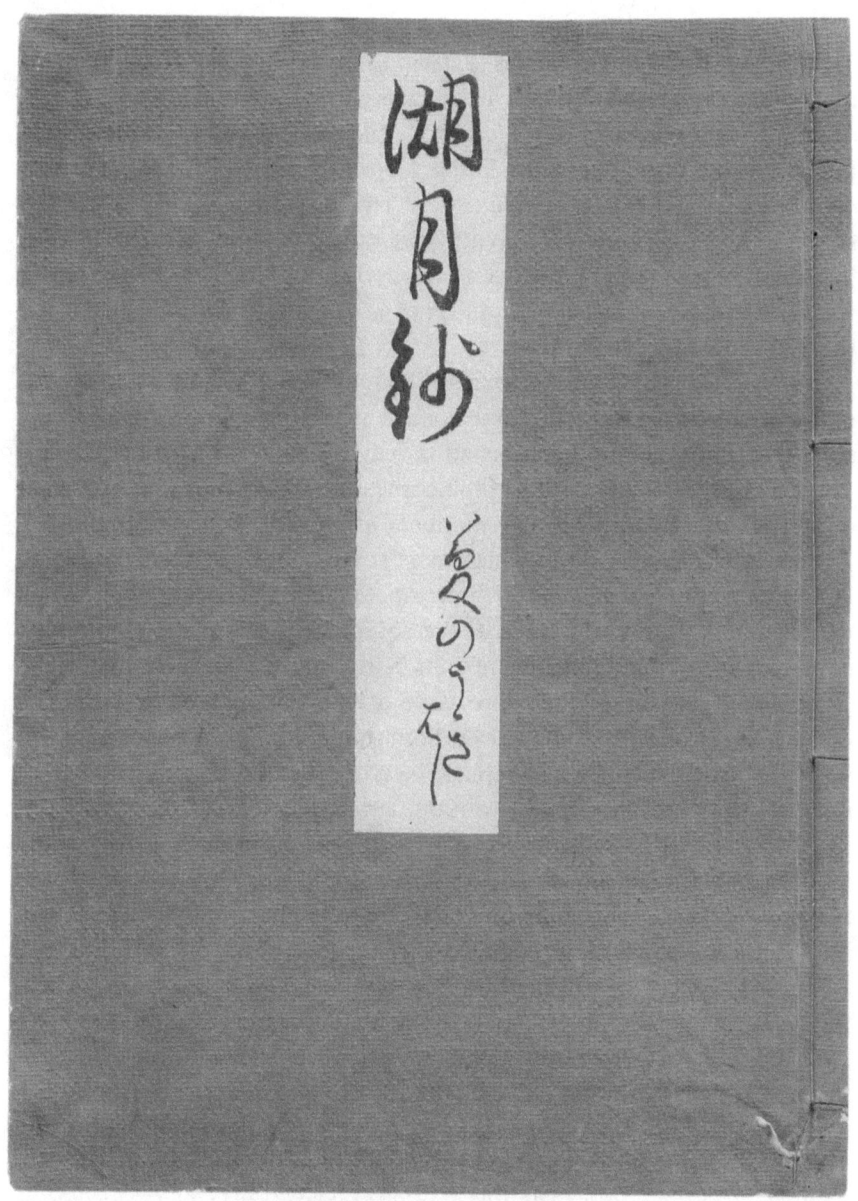

Figure 3 The cover of one of the sixty volumes of Kitamura Kigin's *Kogetsushō*. (Courtesy of the author)

the postwar era. As Shimizu Fukuko has shown, both *Kogetsushō* and *The Tale of Genji with Headnotes* (*Shusho Genji monogatari*, 1673), the two most widely read and copied early modern annotated texts of *Genji monogatari*, were based on *An Illustrated Tale of Genji*, which was largely based on an edition published in the very early years of the seventeenth century using wooden movable type.[19] This early movable-type edition seems to have drawn largely on an unidentified calligraphic text in what is now known as the "Blue-Covers" (Aobyōshibon) lineage—the group of texts from which almost every edition of *Genji monogatari* published since the 1960s also derives.

But here we encounter a significant textual break: while these more recent editions derive from the same lineage as their early modern predecessors, they have usually been based *directly* on what are considered particularly authoritative calligraphic copies of "Blue-Covers" texts, most often the late-fifteenth-century manuscript known as the Ōshimabon.[20] The specific *textual* world in which most contemporary readers, and even non-readers, of *Genji monogatari* participate came into being, then, when the Ōshimabon took the place of the seventeenth-century movable-type edition as the dominant source text for new editions of the tale, and in the process also supplanted the entire world of texts and replacements of texts of *Genji monogatari* that had arisen from that edition.[21] It makes sense to view the bean-size guide as a replacement of the early modern *texts* whose outward trappings it mimics—even though as part of a game it was primarily meant to be recognized, not to be read, and even though early modern non-readers imagined *Genji monogatari* first and foremost as a *book*, not as a text—because on some level the guide did implicitly refer back to those texts and, through them, to the idea of the original that they embodied. When the Ōshimabon was established as the new best text, the bean-size guide, too, was part of the textual world it replaced.

It is hard to overstate how momentous this replacement was, as it overturned three and a half centuries not merely of textual criticism, but of the history of images of *Genji monogatari* in the popular imagination. The book that prompted it was Ikeda Kikan's (1896–1956) magnificent five-volume variorum edition *The Tale of Genji Collated* (*Kōi Genji monogatari*)—first published in 1942 and revised and reprinted in eight volumes between 1953 and 1956 as *The Tale of Genji Compendium* (*Genji monogatari taisei*)—and it was clear the moment it appeared that it would profoundly alter the way people viewed *Genji monogatari*, and do so by "replacing" all previous texts. We see this, for instance, in a touching passage from a 1957 review of the revised edition in which the author recalls his reaction to the publication of the first edition:

It was during the Great War, at a time when it was particularly difficult to get one's hands on academic books, and though I traipsed all around downtown Osaka looking for a copy not a single bookstore would even allow me to order it–in the end, they just laughed. So I was absolutely mad with joy when, through the good offices of Yoshinaga Minoru, I was able to acquire a set. . . . Previously, I'd had no alternative but to depend on *Kogetsushō*, the *Headnotes* [*Shusho*] text, the *Illustrated* [*Eiri*] text, and *Ten-Thousand Waters in a Drop* [*Bansui ichiro*, 1652]. . . . And then *The Tale of Genji Collated* came out, and it was like "the sight of clouds and rainbows during a time of great drought," as they say. To be able to consult at a glance, at my desk, all the best calligraphic texts–just like that, it swept away all the uncertainty and the futility of dealing with early modern editions. I remember once a student came to me and said, "There's something I don't understand in the 'Yūgao' [The Twilight Beauty] chapter, it's part of my assignment," and sure enough, when I checked a movable-type edition I had on hand, I couldn't make sense of it either. The passage made perfect sense in *The Tale of Genji Collated*. And nothing like the phrase that had puzzled the student appeared among the collations. I glanced into *Kogetsushō* to see what it had, and realized that it was a mistake in the early modern printed texts. I found it puzzling that anyone in this day and age would think he could research *Genji* without consulting *Genji Collated*.[22]

Once Ikeda Kikan's extraordinary collation became available, "just like that, it swept away" the old early modern editions, replacing them by making it possible for readers to access, through it, in an easily legible type-translation, "all the best calligraphic texts." All of a sudden, when people thought about *Genji monogatari*, they were imagining a very different sort of text.

Except that I am simplifying matters. The process of replacing the text of *Genji monogatari* in 1942 was actually more complex. First of all, the rise of the Ōshimabon by no means rendered irrelevant early modern commentaries based on early modern texts, including most famously Motoori Norinaga's (1730–1801) *The Tale of Genji Jeweled Comb* (*Genji monogatari tama no ogushi*, published 1799), the main source text of which was *Kogetsushō*. And then there are the circumstances of the publication of *The Tale of Genji Collated*: the book was issued as a sort of sequel or companion to the first of novelist Tanizaki Jun'ichirō's (1886–1965) three modern-Japanese translations of *Genji monogatari*, which became a huge best seller from 1939 to 1941.

In an announcement printed in the last of a series of educational pamphlets distributed with Tanizaki's translation, the publisher noted that *The Tale of Genji Collated* would be "an unprecedented and unsurpassable *Genji* text for anyone with any interest in looking into *Genji monogatari* as a student of Japanese literature," and then explained that "if the 'Tanizaki Genji' is a work of pure art, this book [*The Tale of Genji Collated*] can only be described as a work of pure scholarship."[23] As it happens, Tanizaki used *Kogetsushō* as the main text for his translation, and just as the bean-size commentary gestured back toward *Kogetsushō* and other early modern editions of *Genji monogatari*, so too did the covers of Tanizaki's version—although somewhat ambiguously, since the decorative cover might also suggest a calligraphic text (figure 4).[24] Indeed, Tanizaki was still using *Kogetsushō* when he did his second translation, published from 1951 to 1954, and his third was really only a superficial retooling of the second.[25] Thus while *The Tale of Genji Collated* revolutionized scholarly notions of how the original text of *Genji monogatari* might best be imagined, and while this new understanding would gradually radiate into the popular sphere, the commercial success of Tanizaki's popular replacement of *Kogetsushō* is what enabled this larger textual replacement in the first place, and in the world of "pure art," at least for the time being, one could still remain faithful to an old text of the sort *The Tale of Genji Collated* made academically obsolete.

When I speak of replacing the "text," then, I am referring first of all to the complex process by which the continued relevance of the idea of a canonical work's original text is maintained by the production of new images of it. Some of these images will themselves be texts, and over time the fortunes of these texts will rise

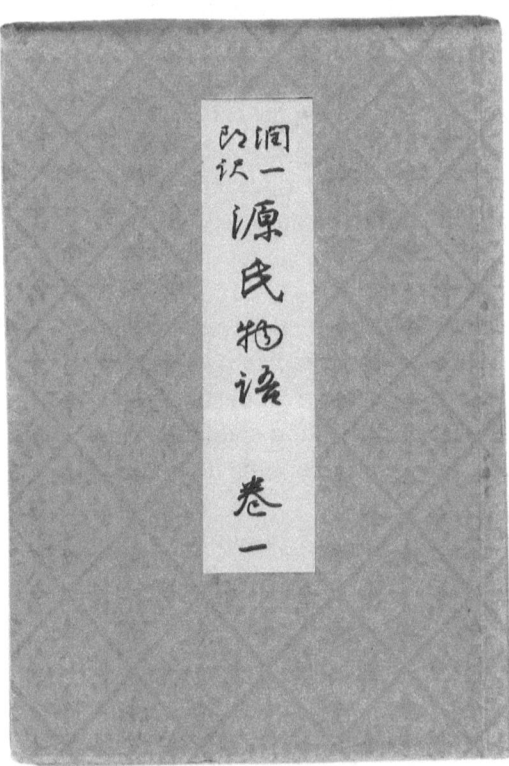

Figure 4 The cover of one of the volumes of Tanizaki Jun'ichirō's *Jun'ichirō-yaku Genji monogatari*, his first translation into modern Japanese of *Genji monogatari*. (Courtesy of the author)

and fall as new competitors appear, each one prompting a shift in the tangled web of relationships that define the position and authority of each individual text and edition vis-à-vis the others. Some of the images will be texts that stand more obviously at a remove from the idea of the original: these include translations, in the ordinary sense of the word, which are replacements of replacements. And then there are those knickknacks I touched on—the bean-size guide, the plastic-wrapped package of *Genji monogatari* Millennial Anniversary Matcha Baumkuchen on the convenience-store shelf—which may well seem ridiculous or trivial but whose contribution to canonization is extremely important, and which, irrelevant though they may appear, nevertheless participate in a world of textual transmission and presume a particular understanding of what the canonical text is like. The design for the Baumkuchen package did not have to feature the picture from *An Illustrated Mirror of The Tale of Genji in Album Form* that it did, but it could not have been created in the form of a blue book with a white title slip intended to resemble *Kogetsushō*, because for the contemporary consumer *Kogetsushō* no longer stands as a recognizable image of the tale or as a symbol of its canonical value.

Indeed, one of the most compelling representations of the value *Genji monogatari* had as an imagined text in the early modern period appears in a context that has little more to do with *Genji* than Baumkuchen. It figures in a beautiful picture that Katsushika Hokusai (1760–1849) prepared for a collection of "crazy poetry" (*kyōka*) called *Spring Dawn* (*Haru no akebono*, 1796) (figure 5). In the picture, we see three women gazing out at the early-morning sky, a tall lacquer box bearing the title *The Spring Dawn Commentary* (*Shunshoshō*, 1674) positioned conspicuously behind them. *The Spring Dawn Commentary* is an edition of Sei Shōnagon's *The Pillow Book* (*Makura no sōshi*, ca. 1005), annotated by Kitamura Kigin, the same man responsible for *Kogetsushō*. But while *Kogetsushō* was published in sixty volumes, *The Spring Dawn Commentary* consists of only twelve, and in some printings even fewer: if the box in this illustration is really the book it claims to be, it is mostly empty. Presumably, Hokusai had never seen a copy of *The Spring Dawn Commentary*, so he based his picture on *Kogetsushō*—which, as the quintessential image of *Genji monogatari*, was familiar even to people who had never seen it from ubiquitous depictions like the one in figure 29. Here, in this confused vision of an altogether different book, we see the extent of the power that *Genji monogatari* wielded as an imagined text, embodied in the particular form of its early modern replacement.

The Text in Theory

If the first meaning of "text" in the phrase "Replacing the Text" hinges on the relationship between an object and an idea—a book or another material form that actually exists and the original it replaces, which is imagined through its replacement—the second points to a subjective relationship between a person and a thing.

Beginning in the late 1960s, the word "text" acquired a halo of theoretical connotations in the academic nodes of poststructuralist literary and cultural criticism; by now, this usage has become as familiar as the concept of "reception" in studies of canon formation. "Text" in this partic-

Figure 5 Three women looking out at the sky at dawn, in an illustration by Katsushika Hokusai. (Shakuyakutei Nagane, ed., *Haru no akebono* [privately printed, 1796], 5. Courtesy of Hokusai Museum, Obuse)

ular sense is invoked in referring to all sorts of things—novels, films, paintings, arias, ballets, bodies, names on a blackboard that could be a poem, signed urinals, the totality of being, and the like—once they have been pried from the stiff fingers of dead authors or artists and given an open-ended, never-ending life in the here and now. The concept has been considerably refined over the decades since it first came into use, so that the eternal present of the text is now generally understood as existing within the context of particular interpretive conventions that guide its open-endedness, sanctioning certain kinds of readings but not others.

There is more to the term and to the various inflections it has been given than I can begin to explore here; I would like simply to confirm a basic understanding of the impulse that makes its use so attractive, and to note what I consider a significant drawback to its continued invocation as the default term in referring to the objects of literary criticism. Perhaps the best way to do this is to return to one of the writings that first adumbrated the concept of text as it is now generally used: Roland Barthes's (1915-1980) essay "From Work to Text" (1971). This essay is divided into seven propositions; I quote from the first and last.

> The difference is this: the work is a fragment of substance, occupying a part of the space of books (in a library for example), the Text is a methodological field. The opposition may recall (without at all reproducing term for term) Lacan's distinction between "reality" and "the real": the one is displayed, the other demonstrated; likewise, the work can be seen (in bookshops, in catalogues, in exam syllabuses), the text is a process of demonstration, speaks according to certain rules (or against certain rules); the work can be held in the hand, the text is held in language, only exists in the movement of a discourse (or rather, it is Text for the very reason that it knows itself as text); the Text is not the decomposition of the work, it is the work that is the imaginary tail of the Text; or again, *the Text is experienced only in an activity of production*. It follows that the Text cannot stop (for example on a library shelf); its constitutive movement is that of cutting across (in particular, it can cut across the work, several works).[26]

> This leads us to pose (to propose) a final approach to the Text, that of pleasure. . . . Certainly there exists a pleasure of the work (of certain works); I can delight in reading and re-reading Proust, Flaubert, Balzac, even—why not?—Alexandre Dumas. But this pleasure, no matter how keen and even when free from all prejudice, remains in part (unless by some exceptional critical effort) a pleasure of consumption; for if I can read these authors, I also know that I cannot *re-write* them (that it is impossible today to write 'like that') and this knowledge, depressing enough, suffices to cut me off from the production of these works, in the very moment their remoteness establishes my modernity (is not to be modern to know clearly what cannot be started over again?) As for the Text, it is bound to *jouissance*, that is to a pleasure without separation.[27]

These are slippery passages, and I will not try to do justice to their slipperiness. The crucial point is that the distinction Barthes proposes between the concepts "work" and "text" is ultimately directed neither at works nor at texts, but at authors and readers. The three main questions he asks are: "Who produces the text?" "When is the text produced?" and "Where does the text exist?" And he answers: "The reader," "During reading," and "In reading." Barthes is attempting, in short, to turn the reader into the author.

Barthes gives what might be read as a gloss on these two propositions from "From Work to Text" in another influential essay, "The Death of the Author" (1967), when he suggests that "the modern scriptor is born simultaneously with the text, is in no way equipped with a being preceding or exceeding the writing, is not the subject with the book as predicate; there is no other time than that of the enunciation and every text is eternally written in the *here and now*." Or, again, he writes of "the true place of the writing, which is reading" and argues that "the birth of the reader must be at the cost of the death of the Author."[28]

From a certain perspective, of course, the replacement of the work with the text was necessary, and it has gone a long way in altering conceptions of authorship and readership. At the same time, something seems to have been lost as a consequence, and something more than Michel Foucault, Edward Said, and Stanley Fish have been able to retrieve in their own treatments of textuality. For while Barthes was ultimately most interested in redefining the role of the reader, letting her dance creatively on the author's grave, he somehow got the book mixed up in the deed. In order to insist that writing occurs in reading, Barthes dispenses immediately—in the very first of his propositions, with an almost jarring persistence—with books. The material object, the printed and bound volume "that can be held in the hand" or perch "on a library shelf," the book itself as "a fragment of substance," is all too obviously the product not of the reader's reading, but of other people's labor. Barthes's own mother worked as an ill-paid bookbinder to raise him and his half-brother in the wake of her husband's death a year after Barthes was born.[29] Perhaps for Barthes, the book as a *work* was particularly troublesome in its insistent remoteness, its intransigence—it was too clearly something one "cannot *re-write*." Thus in his writings, the book is buried alongside its author. "The text" is released from its materiality.

And yet, reading Barthes, the text's form continues to haunt us. In his seventh proposition, Barthes complains of feeling cut off "from the production of these works" by writers of earlier ages. The true pleasures of literature are to be found not in consumption, but in production. But Barthes knows that "it is impossible today to write 'like that'" and, no doubt, that it is impossible to get paper like that, and to print like that, and to bind books like that. The work as he defines it is sedimented with history, implicated in both the present and the past, and so it is incapable of being reproduced: it can only be consumed, and the alienated pleasure of consumption can never be an adequate substitute for *jouissance*. All right. Except that by the time "From Work to Text" appeared, Barthes had already published *S/Z* (1970), his intense, scintillating treatment of Honoré de Balzac's story "Sarrasine" *as a text*. Balzac is one of four authors Barthes names at the beginning of his seventh proposition as examples of the sort of writing "I cannot *re-write*." Barthes feels cut off from Balzac's work, then, even after he has engaged with it as a text. The text that is supposed to be *"experienced only in an activity of production"* turns out, in the end, not to have been released from its materiality after all. The text is experienced in an activity of production, but it still "is." The most we can say, then, is that for Barthes, while the materiality of the text may not matter, the text itself is not immaterial.

This is a rather confusing statement. In fact, it seems to encapsulate a common confusion that clings to the concept of the "text" as it has been used for half a century now, and to the notion of "reception," which is so closely bound up with the concept of the text—a connection evoked, for instance, by Haruo Shirane's suggestion that we think of the reception of *Genji monogatari* in terms of "readerly reception" and "writerly reception," which seems to echo the contrast Barthes outlines in *S/Z* and elsewhere between "readerly texts" and "writerly texts."[30] Or, again, here is Hans Robert Jauss, a central figure in the development of reception studies, setting out the concept of reception in "Literary History as a Challenge to Literary Theory" (1967): a literary work, Jauss writes, "is not a monument that monologically reveals its timeless essence. It is much more like an orchestration that strikes ever new resonances among its readers and that frees the text from the material of the words and brings it to a contemporary existence."[31] The work is not a monument, the text rises from its body—yet *the* words linger. *It* still *is*.

When we speak of "the history of the reception of a text," the text is no less "received" because its reception has a history, and it is no less a "text"—in the sense of a fixed sequence of words that is recorded and transmitted using particular technologies, in handscrolls, in books, over the radio and the Internet, and via Nintendo DS handheld game systems—because it is produced as a "Text" in the being of the reader each time it is read, in much the same way a play is produced on stage. There is a profound, confounding tension between the notion of the text as something that exists as an experience, that is made to exist only in the act of its perception, on the one hand, and the notion of the text as some thing that is experienced, that exists out there, in history, on the other. "Every text is eternally written in the *here and now*," Barthes suggests. Endlessly contemporary, seemingly fleeting as time itself, the text is nonetheless simultaneously *eternal*.

This internal incoherence would not have disappeared even had later writers adopted Barthes's occasional, material, typographic marking of "text" and "Text" to differentiate the text as a fixed sequences of words from the Text as something experienced in an activity of production. This becomes clear when we imagine, with Stanley Fish, being *asked* in the context of a classroom, "Is there a text/Text in this class?" And notwithstanding the mileage that textual scholars such as D. F. McKenzie and Jerome McGann have been able to get out of the term, its ambiguous double meaning seems to have contributed to a general tendency, happily fading in recent years, to overlook the materiality of writing, to ignore the demands it places on us as readers, and to pass too lightly over its implications for how we conceive of reading.

This is especially true in the classroom. When a teacher asks a student, "Well, what does the text say?" "the text" sounds like a phantom whose remains can be viewed—"displayed," as Barthes says—in the little coffin of the book, "on a library shelf" or "in the hand," while it itself hovers disembodied overhead, freed "from the material of the words," on some abstract plane apart from history, untouched by editorial practice, unrelated to canonization. Indeed, this "text" seems cut off even from the student reader, who ought, according to the theory, to be experiencing it as an activity of production, because here "what the text says" is densely overwritten by power relations: the text hovering overhead, just out of reach, is the one sanctioned by the interpretive community to which the professor belongs, which the student may or may not be joining. Only those in the know can make the text *say* what it means—everyone else is simply misreading marks on a page. In Stanley Fish's essay "Is There a Text in This Class?" (1979), it is always the student asking the question and the professor who answers. If the professor posed the question, her students might not even realize it was directed at them; she, after all, is the expert who is expected to know how to produce the text. If the professor were to pose the question herself, she would sound, perhaps, like a medium at a séance. *Hello? Are you there? Is there a text in this class?*

The concept of the "text" in various elaborations of this particular Barthesian sense has been very useful, and will go on being useful, in numerous academic nodes. But in the node of literary studies, especially as scholars grow increasingly sensitive to issues of visuality and materiality and to the history of the book, much could be gained from putting some distance between ourselves and this term. What reason do we have anymore to read the pictures in a book, as well as the text, as well as the interactions between the pictures and the text, as a text? Why must we analyze the materiality of the *book* itself as a text? Indeed, doesn't the fact that the book can be analyzed as a text at all tell us something? Perhaps Barthes was correct, in 1967, in asserting that the reader could be born only at the cost of the death of the Author, but in retrospect it seems much less clear that the book had to be buried as well. If anything, the unique materiality of each book, of each copy of each book, and the sense of being "cut off" that it evokes in readers attuned to that sort of thing seems to point toward an understanding of reading as an experience of active, involved production: "The work can be held in the hand," Barthes says, but in reality—since the "work" he is referring to is "a fragment of substance, occupying a part of the space of books"— it *must* be held in the hand. The book, calling to mind other times and other hands, reminds us that our own reading is only one among many: it relativizes its readers. Holding on to this understanding seems more important today than it ever has, as the digital revolution sends books careening by the shelfload into the frozen, untouchable purgatory of cyberspace. And so I would suggest that we turn to the work of textual critics, specifically Peter L. Shillingsburg's influential exploration of the ontology of the work of art in *Scholarly Editing in the Computer Age: Theory and Practice*, to help us to rethink the way in which we refer to the objects of our research. For Shillingsburg, the "work" is an abstraction with no material existence: "From the receiver's perspective a work is the imagined whole implied by all the differing forms of a text that we conceive as representing a single literary creation."[32] A "text," by contrast, "is the actual order of words and punctuation as contained in any one physical form."[33]

This, then, is the second meaning of "Replacing the Text": an effort to back away from our often muddled reliance on the term "text," retaining what it has given us, and to cultivate within the node of Japanese literary studies a specific type of attention to the book as an object and to the embodiedness of the act of reading, of writing, and even of language itself. This approach seems especially fitting in a study that centers on *Genji*, which circulated so long through environments in which copying texts was one manner of reading them—a circumstance that highlights the deep connection between Barthes's rejection of materiality and modern print technology, which made producing books *someone else's work*, not his. The early modern collection of humorous stories *Laugh Yourself Awake* (*Seisuishō*, preface 1623) reports that the linked-verse poet Sōchin "made twenty-three copies of *Genji monogatari* and died as he was making his twenty-fourth, in the midst of the 'Asagao' [The Bluebell] chapter." Another poet, his teacher, composed an elegy: "brush steeped in it heart holding it the dew faded on the bluebell" (*fude ni somi kokoro ni kakeshi chigiri ni ya orishimo kieshi asagao no tsuyu*).[34] For such readers, holding a text in one's heart and steeping one's brush in it were parallel modes of engagement. Contemporary readers no longer make a practice of copying the text of *Genji monogatari*, it is true, but we remain as engaged as ever in its replacement.

Where We Are Headed

Replacing the text. This phrase describes the theoretical channel that gives this study its direction, but the chapters that follow are not about the concept of "replacement" but about replacements; and while this study embodies a theory, it is not structured around one. Broadly speaking, the six main chapters trace a chronological trajectory that starts in the first half of the nineteenth century and continues into the postwar period, occasionally skipping beyond. They are grouped into two parts: "Ninety-Nine Years in the Life of an Image," which focuses on editions of a book published between 1829 and 1928, approaching them from a perspective anchored in the early modern period; and "In Medias Res," which backtracks slightly, commencing in the 1870s, to tell a modern story—one that is simultaneously a continuation of the story begun in part I— about the transnational, translational reinvention of *Genji* as a masterpiece of world literature, and thus as a Japanese national classic. While the study as a whole unfolds chronologically, then, its two parts and its individual chapters are linked in a more tangled manner: they fit together, perhaps, like a Jacob's ladder.

The three chapters in "Ninety-Nine Years in the Life of an Image" center on a single work in an early modern and to some extent modern genre of fiction known as the *gōkan*—literally "combined booklets"—that became an unprecedented best seller and the first genuinely popular replacement of *Genji monogatari* when it was first published in thirty-eight chapters between 1829 and 1842.[35] The work is titled *Nise Murasaki inaka Genji* (*A Fraudulent Murasaki's Bumpkin Genji*); it was written and designed by Ryūtei Tanehiko (1783–1842), a well-known writer of the samurai class, and had pictures, based on Tanehiko's designs, by the celebrated artist Utagawa Kunisada (Utagawa Toyokuni III, 1786–1865). The book's amanuenses and block carvers were master craftsmen, and the book itself is surely one of the most lavish, carefully designed and produced, and visually rewarding publications ever mass-produced in the Japanese tradition.

Inaka Genji is crucial to the history of *Genji*'s canonization in the early modern and modern periods, and also to my idea of how this pivotal moment in literary history might best be narrated. Until recently, the Meiji Restoration of 1868 and Japan's subsequent turn toward the "West"—though strictly speaking the "West" actually lay to the east, since trips in its direction began with a sea voyage from Yokohama to San Francisco—tended to be regarded, at least in Japanese literary studies, as an almost cataclysmic rupture. There were exceptions to this trend: Peter Kornicki, for example, has been limning the continuities between Tokugawa and early Meiji fiction ever since the late 1970s.[36] Over the past decade or so, though, scholars of literature on both sides of both the Pacific and the Atlantic have begun working in a more concerted way to question the familiar narrative of the great upheaval, and to reconsider the transition from the early modern to the modern era in terms of residues and shifts as well as of discontinuities. This is certainly a welcome development. Most often, however, scholarship exploring the connections between early modernity and modernity has been rooted in a theoretical concern with the origins of modernity.

This approach can be productive, of course, but it has its risks. In a provocative study called *Practices of the Sentimental Imagination: Melodrama, the Novel, and the Social Imaginary in Nineteenth-Century Japan*, for instance, Jonathan E. Zwicker suggests that a history of "the long nineteenth century" in Japanese literature will become possible if we accept "an initial wager, a conceptual leap of grouping together—provisionally—under the concept of the novel a set of texts that have traditionally been seen as belonging to two different worlds."[37] Reclassifying works that have conventionally been grouped into distinct genres under the single *modern* rubric of the novel will, the argument goes, allow us to see continuities that we have been missing. Anticipating critics who might point to the enormous shift that took place from the early modern dominance of woodblock printing to a new reliance on movable type in the modern period, Zwicker calls our attention to "a fact so obvious it hardly bears mentioning: whether produced by xylography or typography, we are in fact dealing with books."[38] But what does this mean? Is a book simply a book, regardless of the specific form it takes, and can its material characteristics be so casually discounted? Zwicker's study, whose list of works cited includes several typeset editions of early modern works but only three books actually printed from woodblocks during the early modern period, makes the assumption of bookish universality part of the wager it proposes; my own work can be regarded, in part, as expressing a reluctance to play—as a demonstration of how much we stand to lose if we accept the invitation. The mere fact that the *English language* lets us call something a book or a novel does not obviate the need to look closely at the actual things we are discussing. In truth, there is no guarantee that modern readers will even know an early modern book when they see one—the lacquer-boxed books in figures 5 and 29, for instance—or be able to interpret what they are seeing.³⁹

I would argue that the experience of reading true, tangible early modern woodblock-printed books—not as texts that can be translated without significant change into the bibliographic form of a modern typeset book, but as material objects whose meaning is embodied in their very materiality—must play a role in any attempt to think through the "long nineteenth century." One cannot begin with a theory of the novel and work backward to the facts; books themselves have to be read *as* facts, as objects of knowledge that have the potential to overturn and rearrange the theoretical and interpretive frameworks we bring to them. In the case of early modern popular fiction, it is rarely possible to appeal to accounts by ordinary townspeople of what it was like to read a given book, or listen to it being read, but to some extent books themselves, like genres, guide their readers to interact with them in particular ways, dwelling on certain elements while scarcely noticing others. The clues are still there. The printed pages challenge us to find them, even if it is hard for us, embedded in the anachronism of our belated approach, to know where to look. We need to try, at least, to let early modern books teach us how to read them. This is precisely what I do with *Nise Murasaki inaka Genji*.

Inaka Genji was first published from woodblocks toward the end of the Edo period (1603–1868)—also known as the Tokugawa period or the early modern period. While the blocks were destroyed after the work was banned in 1842, making it impossible to print further copies without going to the considerable trouble and incurring the enormous expense of carving new blocks, the book was repeatedly reissued in typeset editions and was widely read throughout the Meiji period (1868–1912), the Taishō period (1912–1926), and even the early Shōwa period (1926–1989). After *Inaka Genji* emerged as the first broadly popular replacement of *Genji monogatari* as a work of fiction, it ended up being replaced by replacements of itself that gradually ceased to function, in their newly assigned position in the modern literary field, as replacements of *Genji monogatari*. Unfortunately, they no longer functioned as *gōkan*, either. This double devaluation of *Inaka Genji* made room for its replacement, in a larger sense, by a whole new type of replacement of *Genji monogatari* that nonetheless built on a conceptual foundation that *Inaka Genji* had established: the notion of a complete, chapter-for-chapter replacement—intended for a truly popular readership—of *Genji monogatari* as a work of classical fiction. This was the beginning of the modern-Japanese translation, and ultimately of *Genji monogatari*'s reinvention as "literature" in a modern, originally European sense. This complex history of replacement—which is the history not only of *Genji monogatari*'s recanonization but also of the canonization and decanonization of *Inaka Genji* as a masterpiece of early modern popular fiction; of the gradual dismantling of the genre of the *gōkan* itself; of the rise of something like the novel in the narrow sense of the word, denoted in Japanese by the word *shōsetsu*; and of a reorientation of Japanese literature from a focus on an older "world literary system" centered on China to another, newer one centered on Europe—offers an image of history across the Edo-Meiji divide that sets out from an imaginative reconstruction of an early modern rather than a modern perspective, and functions in terms not of simple continuity and rupture, but of continuity through rupture of the sort described by the term "replacement."

This is the broad sweep of "Ninety-Nine Years in the Life of an Image"; each individual chapter on *Inaka Genji* addresses a more particular set of questions. In chapter 1, "A *Gōkan* Is a *Gōkan* Is a *Gōkan*," I try to consider the book, as best I am able, from the viewpoint of a fairly ordinary urban reader, not exceptionally cultivated, during the thirteen-year period when it was first issued. *Inaka Genji* is routinely described as an "adaptation"—or sometimes, I believe incorrectly, as a "parody"—of *Genji monogatari*, and Tanehiko himself clearly conceived of it from the very start in this light. This approach is not inappropriate, then, provided we recognize that when we say one book is an adaptation, or a translation, of another, this is all we are doing: adopting a particular *approach*. Adaptation and translation are, fundamentally, modes of reading.

I am interested in presenting what seems to me a very strong probability: that *Inaka Genji* was not read by the majority of its first readers as a replacement of *Genji monogatari*. Some, notably the cultivated women in the shogun's inner chambers, among whom *Inaka Genji* was all the rage, undoubtedly did appreciate *Inaka Genji*, at least in part, as a replacement of *Genji monogatari*—as did, indeed, the Meiji emperor's wife, Empress Shōken, who reportedly loved both books—but since *Inaka Genji* is already so firmly ensconced in the "adaptation" mode of reading, I do not dwell on this likelihood.[40] I am concerned not with elite readers, but with the townspeople, both women and men, children as well as adults, who constituted the primary audience for works in the *gōkan* genre. There is a tendency to assume that even these ordinary townspeople must have been familiar with *Genji monogatari*, and that their interest in the celebrated classic is what made *Inaka Genji* the best seller it was—that they, too, approached this *gōkan* first and foremost as an adaptation of *Genji monogatari*. In fact, even setting aside the question of whether average townspeople could have afforded a book like *Kogetsushō* or would have had the leisure to plow through its sixty volumes if they borrowed them from a lending library, few could have understood it, since its notes contained numerous *kanji* (Sino-Japanese characters) without glosses in the *kana* syllabary, which formed the core of basic literacy and in which, by and large, *gōkan* were written.

The notion that *Inaka Genji* was popularly read as an adaptation of *Genji monogatari* seems to me to depend on an exaggerated estimation of the breadth of the tale's circulation *as a text* in the early modern period. Thus I present a very different reading of *Inaka Genji*, telling a story in which the best-selling *gōkan* is read at first as a visually and textually sophisticated, thrillingly hybrid, beautifully printed, stylish *book* whose success has little to do with *Genji monogatari*, but over time comes to be subjugated, in the minds of a readership broader than those any previous replacements of *Genji monogatari* had enjoyed, to an image of the classic as "the original" that *Inaka Genji* was now supposed to represent—an image that *Inaka Genji* itself had created. By trying imaginatively to return to the early modern period, starting to write from there rather than from a position that takes for granted *Genji monogatari*'s status as a readily accessible national classic, I am able to trace *Inaka Genji*'s transformation into the first truly popular replacement of *Genji monogatari* as a work of prose fiction and its assumption of the mantle of the tale's prestige. I show, in other words, how *Inaka Genji* created the popular mode of reading that posits a given vernacular work as an adaptation, or a translation, of *Genji monogatari*—how it disseminated the very notion of the tale's replacement for a broadly inclusive audience to such an audience—and thus prepared the way for its own replacement by translations into modern Japanese. At the same time, I show how images of *Inaka Genji*, and images derived from *Inaka Genji*, began to spread in the decades following the book's first publication, thus paralleling my discussion of the global spread of "*Genji* discourse" in part II of this book.

My second chapter on *Inaka Genji*, "Reading Higashiyama," faces in two directions at once. On the one hand, it continues to demonstrate, through a detailed analysis of what I refer to as *Inaka Genji*'s "image-text-book relations," that when we read this book as an adaptation we are adopting only one among many possible approaches to it. This chapter questions the seeming inevitability and naturalness of the application of this mode of reading to *Inaka Genji* by revealing that it is ultimately sanctioned by an understanding of literature thoroughly centered on text. Thus while it may not be entirely inappropriate to view *Inaka Genji* as an adaptation of *Genji monogatari*, it is inappropriate to view the lavishly produced *Inaka Genji*, which has pictures on every page and offers pleasures particular to the *gōkan* form, as only or even primarily an adaptation. Indeed, I would suggest that considering *Inaka Genji* in this way implicates the reader in a sort of solipsism: a failure to recognize traces, unmistakably present in the materiality of the printed book, of reading practices fundamentally different from the almost exclusively textual and intertextual experience that the modern concepts of literature and the novel have long privileged. This is not to say, of course, that early modern Japanese readers innately had some different way of seeing things—it is a question of instruction. Again, books and genres teach us how to read them if we pay attention, and if we are looking in the right place and at the right book. As soon as we turn from a typeset edition of *Inaka Genji* to a woodblock-printed copy of the early modern book, to the *gōkan* as an object, the written text becomes only a part of the picture, and the vision of the work as an adaptation of *Genji monogatari* comes to seem less natural. In this sense, "Reading Higashiyama" stands as a continuation of the argument developed in "A *Gōkan* Is a *Gōkan* Is a *Gōkan*."

Chapter 2 also prepares the ground for the one that follows, "Turning a New Page," which flips from Edo to Tokyo, and in one case Kyoto, to look at several modern editions of *Inaka Genji*. My analysis of image-text-book relations in *Inaka Genji*'s first published form leads me to introduce the concept of bibliographic translation and to use it to chart, through further detailed analysis of a series of modern replacements of the early modern book, the slow, unsteady drift from the writing, printing, publishing, and reading conventions of one age to those of another; from the irrelevance of particularly European and American concepts of "the novel" and "literature" to their gradual reinvention in Japanese in the words *shōsetsu* (fiction, novel, short story, and so on) and *bungaku* (literature).

I mark the unsteadiness of this process—which is, from start to finish, a matter of the *gōkan*'s replacement, both materially and within the contemporary literary field, rather than simply of its disappearance—by introducing the inevitably ambiguous term *yomihon*, which literally describes a "reading book," a work ostensibly centered on its text rather than its pictures, but can also refer to an Edo-period fictional genre that has bibliographic and to some extent generic characteristics distinct from those of the *gōkan*. I contend, in short, that the gradual replacement, over the course of the early decades of the Meiji period, of the *gōkan* by the *shōsetsu*—the eventual replacement, indeed, of all early modern genres of prose fiction by the *shōsetsu*—involved, first of all, a subtle transformation of the relationship among genres within the literary field as it had existed in the early modern period, specifically between the *gōkan* and the *yomihon*. I describe this development, somewhat awkwardly, as the *yomihon*ization of the *gōkan*. The fact that already vague notions of genre (based largely on bibliographic characteristics, and particularly on size) are so obviously in flux during the Meiji period makes the term *yomihon* as I use it here inevitably ambiguous, and this, in turn, makes the whole process somewhat uncertain.

One thing we can say with certainty is that the bibliographic translation of *Inaka Genji* from the material form of the *gōkan* to that of the *shōsetsu*, and from the old genre to the new, involves a shift from the primacy of the picture to the primacy of the text. It is this change that completes the transformation that *Inaka Genji*'s various authors, including its readers, had already begun, turning it from a book into a text and thus into *nothing more than* a popular, inevitably inadequate early modern adaptation of *Genji monogatari*, also conceived of as a text. "Turning a New Page" can be read, then, as a continuation not only of "Reading Higashiyama," but of "A *Gōkan* Is a *Gōkan* Is a *Gōkan*" as well. Ending with a discussion of a typeset edition of *Inaka Genji* published in 1927 and 1928, chapter 3 draws the curtain on the work as it and its genre fade into irrelevance exactly ninety-nine years after the publication in 1829 of its first chapters.

Compared with the looping, loosely interlocking structure of the first part of this study, the three chapters of the second may seem, at least superficially, almost blandly straightforward. But while they may generally follow a neat chronological line from the 1870s into the mid-1950s, they introduce a spatial intricacy by circling the globe, sketching the long and complex process, or the mutually implicated series of processes, by which *Genji monogatari* was re-created first as a masterpiece of "world literature" (as defined in terms of an increasingly hegemonic European world literary system) and only afterward as the quintessential masterpiece of Japan's national literature, where "national literature" is understood as a perceived tradition in which a nation's citizenry actually sees itself participating—whose works are read, or at least *should be read.* As the title of part II, "In Medias Res," suggests, the history these chapters narrate is already under way by the time we enter the scene in chapter 4.

This does not mean, however, that chapter 4 simply picks up where chapter 3 left off, and it certainly does not mean that *Inaka Genji* played a direct role in *Genji*'s canonization outside Japan. It didn't. The connection lies, rather, in the emergence of newspapers, magazines, and other mass media, and the increasingly rapid, global circulation of discourse that they allow—a crucial element in the death of the *gōkan* as a genre that I discuss in chapter 3—and in the fact that much of the discourse about *Genji* and its author that circulates in the West in the closing decades of the nineteenth century can ultimately be traced back to early modern sources. The best example of this, as we will see, is the image of Murasaki Shikibu herself.

The significance of Arthur Waley's English translation of *Genji monogatari, The Tale of Genji*, published in six volumes between 1925 and 1933, has long been recognized. It has in fact been emphasized to such a degree that often it seems to have sprung up out of nowhere. A few scholars have recently turned their attention to a partial translation that preceded Waley's by more than four decades: Suematsu Kenchō's *Genji Monogatari: The Most Celebrated of the Classical Japanese Romances*, issued in one volume in 1882. In chapter 4, "The History of a Romance," I extend this line of research, considering not only the success Suematsu's translation enjoyed as the first English-language replacement of the text of *Genji monogatari*, the role it played in creating an image of the tale for readers outside Japan, and the often-noted political motivations that probably inspired it, but also the discourse that had emerged around *Genji* in the years leading up to the translation's publication, within which and against which Suematsu was consciously working. I explore, in other words, early contributions, long before Waley, to the creation of the global translational loop that turns a literary work into a work of world literature. The chapter closes by following Suematsu from England back to Tokyo, sketching the discourse dealing with *Genji monogatari* in Japanese mass media during the same time period. I suggest that while *Genji monogatari* came to be increasingly widely read after the 1890s, the vision of it as world literature—or, indeed, as literature—did not catch on in Japan as quickly as it did abroad.

It would take Waley to accomplish that—or, rather, two provocative essays about Waley's English translation that Masamune Hakuchō published in 1933. Chapter 5, "From the World to the Nation," centers on these essays and the crucial role that they—and particularly Hakuchō's bold assertion that if *The Tale of Genji* were back-translated from English into Japanese, it would be read in Japan as a classic of world literature—appear to have played in prompting Tanizaki's first translation of *Genji monogatari*, which was indeed successfully marketed as world literature. This observation, which follows on the work of the eminent Tanizaki scholar Chiba Shunji, is only part of a broader argument about a profound shift that occurred in the Japanese literary field during the first decades of the twentieth century toward a new sort of cosmopolitanism, a new understanding of literature as a category that could, at least potentially, incorporate works from all around the globe, including Japan. The chapter traces, in other words, the emergence within Japan not only of an awareness of *Genji* as a work of world literature, and of the emergence of *Genji* itself as what David Damrosch has described as an "effective presence" in the literary field, but also of the possibility of a conception of world literature more extensive than what we might think of as an earlier Sinocentric "world literary system."[41]

The second half of chapter 5 considers the role that Yosano Akiko's first modern-Japanese rendering of *Genji monogatari*, published in 1912 and 1913 as *Shin'yaku Genji monogatari* (*Genji monogatari: A New Translation*), played in the tale's modern recanonization, and then skips ahead a quarter-century to Tanizaki's first translation. Much of the scholarship on Tanizaki's best-selling translation has dealt with the themes of wartime censorship and resistance to censorship, since the text was famously purged of all references, even the most subtle, to anything that might be judged to reflect badly on the imperial household or call into question the unbroken continuity of the imperial line. I take a different approach, setting aside questions of authorial responsibility to consider the larger issue of how Tanizaki's translation was marketed and received, focusing on newspaper advertisements and showing how they strove to frame the tale as world literature. Tanizaki's wartime replacement of *Genji monogatari* finally solidified the discursive framework, I suggest, within which the tale continues to be read, both within Japan and abroad. The notion of *Genji*'s global importance, the sense that this tale best represented Japan as a nation in the eyes of the world, became the key to its domestic success.

The final chapter of this study, "*Genji monogatari*: Translation and Original," returns once more to Masamune Hakuchō, to an essay about *The Tale of Genji* and *Genji monogatari* first published in 1951 and reprinted several times between then and 1955 that wrestles with the nationalist image of *Genji* that Tanizaki's first translation promoted. Between 1951 and 1953, Tanizaki issued a second, uncensored translation of *Genji monogatari* into modern Japanese, which contributed to a major "*Genji* boom": in the 1950s, films, radio dramas, and kabuki plays based on the work were screened, broadcast, or staged almost constantly. Tateishi Kazuhiro has argued persuasively that this spate of popular adaptations represented an attempt to forge a new, postwar national identity divorced from wartime militarism, rooted in an aestheticization of Heian-period court culture as it is seen to be represented in the tale. Hakuchō refers only obliquely to this ongoing phenomenon in his essay, choosing to write instead about how impossibly difficult he finds the classical text and about the glory of Waley's English translation. He subtly undermines the view of *Genji* as the origin of a monolithic, homogeneous "Japanese culture," looking back to an earlier age when, he recalls, no one read *Genji monogatari* as literature, and forward, perhaps, to a time when we—whoever we are—will be able to read the tale in some other way, different from, perhaps even better than, the way we read it now.

The Tale of Genji: Translation, Canonization, and World Literature is a book about many things: about *Genji*; about how we read Japanese literature of different periods and how we understand the relationships between different periods; about world literature; about the history of the study of Japanese literature in English-language contexts; about how we think of literature and continuity, literary history, and literature and community. But if I had to single out one theme, one perspective, that seems, at least to me, to run deepest through it, that theme would be translation. This is a book about *Genji* as translation.

Translation, perhaps, is the paradigmatic form of replacement. At the same time, translation is also a way of knowing and of embodying knowledge. This book not only is about translation, but is shot through, on every page, with translation: translation is central to its methodology. Not only are translated excerpts from primary and secondary sources in multiple languages integral to its arguments, but the very position from which it is written—the relationship of the language in which it is written to the subjects and materials about which it is written—is defined by a deep, inevitable immersion in the practice, the thoughtways of translation. In my conclusion, "Turning to Translation, Returning to Translation," I thus return to the intertwined issues of language and discipline with which I started, to reflect once again on the meaning of writing in English about Japanese literature, to consider the node of English-language Japanese literary studies in a global context, and to suggest that we need to rethink the relationship of translation to what we have been doing all these years, how we have come, and where we are headed.

PART I

❦

Ninety-Nine Years in the Life of an Image

"To be, or not to be, that is the question." And it is an extremely familiar question, of course—so much so that it is tempting to read it as a meta-commentary on the canonicity of the play it calls to mind. For just as Hamlet's survival until the closing lines of act 5 depends on his willingness to keep wrestling with this dilemma, so the play *Hamlet* continues to be recognized as a classic in part because a sufficiently large number of people remain interested in the line "To be, or not to be" and what it represents—Shakespeare's prestige, among other things—and see value in repeating it in various new contexts, not simply on the stage. To a certain extent, *Hamlet* owes its current, seemingly stable position in the English literary canon to this and other sound bites; only when the play stops putting this question to itself—in parodies, advertising copy,

TOUCHSTONE 1

Reimagining the Canon

newspaper headlines, and critical writings—will *Hamlet* finally be dead.

If we had to perform a complete dramatic reading of every literary text we wanted to cite, or at least hold up a copy of the book before we could allude to it, there would be no literary canons. Canons exist, in other words, only because the canonical texts themselves are dispensable; indeed, by the time a canon is established, the texts have already been superseded. A classic, in Mark Twain's oft-quoted phrase, is "a book which people praise and don't read."[1] This is a fairly obvious point, to be sure, and yet theories of canonization have tended to pass somewhat lightly over it, if not ignore it altogether.[2]

Drawing on Pierre Bourdieu's notion of "cultural capital," recent studies of canon formation stress the historical and social production of the value of canonical texts, which is now seldom seen as inherent in the texts themselves. This approach has had a profound impact on the way literary histories are narrated; one might argue, however, that the emphasis it places on canonical texts themselves is misplaced.[3] If the value of a work is theorized as a projection of social interests directly onto a text, then clearly the text must be integral to the process of canonization: without a text, the various authoritative institutions generally understood to be the agents of canonization will have nowhere to assign the value.

The theoretical stance that represents canonization as the projection of value onto texts thus limits the importance of the canon to the few contexts in which canonical texts themselves are actually read—above all, the classroom. But surely canons carry more weight, and live larger lives, than that? *Hamlet* has long since ceased to be Hamlet's favorite haunt. Perhaps, then, we need to reconsider the connection between texts, canons, and value—to acknowledge that canon formation does not depend exclusively, or even for the most part, on the circulation and evaluation of canonical texts, and that canons are not the same as syllabi or even the value-laden readings they inspire.[4]

I am suggesting that canonical works of literature do not remain canonical because they are continually being reproduced—though no doubt in most cases they are—but because they are continually being "replaced," in the technical sense in which I am using this term. The phrase "To be, or not to be" stands metonymically for all of *Hamlet*, as does the image of the Prince of Denmark soliloquizing in the graveyard with poor Yorick's skull in his hand; *In Search of Lost Time* has been reduced to a madeleine; *War and Peace* has been replaced by an impression of its inordinate length. In *Studies of the Novel* (*Chōhen shōsetsu no kenkyū*, 1925), Tayama Katai (1871-1930) lamented that people no longer read the text of *Genji monogatari* itself, contenting themselves instead with adaptations—he cites Ryūtei Tanehiko's *Nise Murasaki inaka Genji* as an example. But, of course, Katai could admonish deluded readers to "go back" to the original text of *Genji monogatari* only because the adaptations had already both certified and advertised their source's status as a classic—because the classic tale had been canonized *in the form of* a series of adaptations broadly defined: *Genji monogatari*'s value was a halo of reflected glory that derived to a large extent from the value people put on images of *Genji monogatari*, and especially, as we will see and as Katai already knew, on *Inaka Genji*.

In this context, the word "image" should be interpreted expansively to include all manner of replacements, from pictures to rewritings, from commentaries to poetic allusions, from "*Genji* names" to the fifty-two "*Genji* incense signs."[5] It is telling that even Katai—who insists that no adaptation (*hon'an sareta mono*) could ever hope to convey "the human emotions, moods, and sensations that are inscribed in such minute detail in the interstices between one written character and the next, one clause and the next"—offers a visual metaphor (another sort of image) when he discusses *Genji monogatari* as a canonical text altered by the long history of its replacement: "The passage of a millennium has imbued the hues and sensations found in the work with a still greater depth. Its colors are like those one sees in old pictures."⁶ Indeed, he describes the irreplaceable text of *Genji monogatari* itself—which he explicitly characterizes as one that must be *read* to be understood, whose value could never be conveyed by a summary—in imagistic terms: there can be no substitute for reading *Genji monogatari*, paradoxically, because "it's all depiction" (*mattaku byōsha de aru*). Katai presents *Genji monogatari*, here, as a series of word-pictures.

If the proliferation of what I am calling "images" of a work is not merely an indication that it has been canonized but also the central process by which its canonization occurs, then studies of canon formation, and by extension research into what I refer to as the "replacement" of canonical works, would surely do well to consider these images. I should stress once more, though, that my invocation of the term "image" is not meant to place undue emphasis on pictures and other visual depictions of canonical texts, significant though they are; I hope to activate a broader range of the word's meanings. My usage is inspired to an extent by Susan Bassnett and André Lefevere, who invoke it in the context of translation studies; still more pertinent, however, is W. J. T. Mitchell's analysis in *Iconology: Image, Text, and Ideology* of "some of the ways we use the word 'image' in a number of institutionalized discourses—particularly literary criticism, art history, theology, and philosophy."⁷ In particular, I am drawing on Mitchell's observation that while speakers of English often assume that "the literal sense of the word 'image' is a graphic, pictorial representation, a concrete material object, and that notions such as mental, verbal, or perceptual imagery are improper derivations from this literal sense," another very different tradition "sees the *literal* sense of the word 'image' as a resolutely non- or even anti-pictorial notion."⁸ This second interpretation, which is said to have its origins in "the account of man's creation 'in the image and likeness' of God," posits that "the true literal image is the mental or spiritual one" or, to press the issue even further, that "the 'true image' is not in any material object, but is encoded in the spiritual—that is, the verbal and textual—understanding."⁹ When I speak of popular images of canonical literature, then, I intend to leave room for the play of both the pictorial and the verbal senses of the word—to include, for instance, both a famous movie still of Laurence Olivier as Hamlet and the question "To be, or not to be?"

The same ambiguity and connotative richness that make "image" so appealing a word to denote the spectrum of texts, practices, and objects that can replace a classic and thus contribute to its canonization make the figure of "image-text relations" a convenient term to use in considering the relationship between a canonical literary text and the replacements through which it is imagined. Mitchell suggests in *Iconology* that words and images stand in a dialectical relationship to one another; the same can be said of canonical texts and the images of them that we produce. Katai criticizes those who think they have grasped what *Genji monogatari* is all about simply because they have read *Inaka Genji*—those who believe that Tanehiko's work offers them an adequate image of *Genji monogatari*—because he believes that no image can ever sufficiently replace the classic. His description of *Genji monogatari*, however, never moves beyond the assertion of its irreplaceable excellence. Like texts and images, *Genji monogatari* and its adaptations are defined in relation to each other. *Genji monogatari*'s unique value comes to be identified precisely in the elements it contains that can never be supplanted by its adaptations, however those elements are defined and redefined over time; the essence of its adaptations, insofar as we view them as adaptations, is said to lie in the fact that they do replace *Genji monogatari*, but only inadequately.

The intertwined histories of *Genji monogatari*'s canonization and *Inaka Genji*'s decanonization in the modern period have made it difficult for even the most cultivated readers today—perhaps especially for the most cultivated readers—to see *Inaka Genji* outside its seemingly objective, stable image-text relationship with the Heian tale. Modern readers find it difficult to see, or even to imagine, what would have been self-evident to any fan of Tanehiko's or Utagawa Kunisada's engrossed in a copy of the latest chapter of *Inaka Genji*: that it was a masterpiece in its own right, and that it was a masterpiece, above all, as a *gōkan*. What precisely makes a *gōkan* a masterpiece, after all? What makes the best *gōkan* stand out above the rest? This question is not easily answered, now that the genre has ceased to exist, and there is no such thing as a recognized canon of great *gōkan*, knowledge of which is generally shared. If we are to learn to appreciate *Inaka Genji* as more than just another point in the endless dotted line that is the history of *Genji monogatari*'s replacement from the early eleventh century to the present, then we must first find a way to forget the modern canon and the status it accords *Genji monogatari*. We must try, little by little, to piece together the elements of greatness that mattered in another age—to imagine our way into another canon.

A Great Book, Not a Great Book

You couldn't escape it: the book had ignited a craze. People papered their walls with prints of its scenes and characters, and wore kimono with patterns it had inspired. Competing publishers copied the style of its covers. Questionable knock-offs appeared. *Nise Murasaki inaka Genji* had emerged as an unprecedented best seller, and it was moving so swiftly that no other work of early modern popular fiction in Japan would ever rival its success. Estimates of its sales per chapter range from an already staggering ten thousand to more than fifteen thousand copies in an age when five thousand was good for a top-class author and another two thousand turned a book into a best seller.[1] Fifteen thousand copies was more than Senkakudō, the major publishing house and bookseller that published *Inaka Genji*, is thought to have sold of all its books combined in prior years.[2] And the actual readership must have been several times larger, even during the period when the book was first published, a few chapters each year between 1829 and 1842: *gōkan* were not all that expensive, but clearly fewer readers bought their own copies than shared with others or rented books from lending libraries.[3] One such library in Nagoya whose catalog has survived stocked five sets of *Inaka Genji*—more than any other *gōkan*, or indeed any other work of fiction.[4]

Observers who left records of those years, and who read *gōkan* consistently enough that they could recognize standouts, agreed that *Inaka Genji* deserved its unprecedented popularity. Even the cantankerous Kyokutei Bakin (1767–1848), an author known to have been bitterly jealous of his rivals, grudgingly conceded that "one has to admit it is a masterpiece."[5] And in his historical and theoretical treatise *A Connoisseur of Fiction in the Native Script* (*Kokuji shōsetsu tsū*, 1849), Kimura Mokurō (1774–1856)—an ardent devotee of both Chinese and Japanese popular fiction—counts *Inaka Genji* among the three paragons of the *gōkan*.[6] Mokurō's praise is particularly noteworthy because of the rearview-mirror perspective it embodies: he was writing in the wake of a series of reforms that had stifled the genre, and after the deaths of three of its most prominent authors, including both Ryūtei Tanehiko and Bakin.[7] Doubtless

CHAPTER 1

A *Gōkan* Is a *Gōkan* Is a *Gōkan*

Inaka Genji *Beyond Parody*

Seeing is forgetting the name of the thing one sees.

Lawrence Weschler,
Seeing Is Forgetting the Name of the Thing One Sees

Mokurō had a sense that the *gōkan*'s heyday had passed; the time to acknowledge its masterpieces had come.

In 1849 *Inaka Genji* was one of the greatest *gōkan* ever published. If one could speak of a "canon" of popular fiction, it unquestionably deserved a place on the list. And while new *gōkan* continued appearing until the late 1880s, none could compete with *Inaka Genji*; if anything, its reputation appears to have increased. In 1883 an advertisement for a movable-type edition of *Inaka Genji* printed as back matter in *The Ryūtei Library* (*Ryūtei sōsho*) explicitly invoked the Chinese comparison that Mokurō had only hinted at, extolling the work not merely as one of the four best *gōkan* of all time, but as "one of the Four Great Literary Marvels of Japan."[8] Although the ad neglected to identify the other titles, it seems safe to assume that they corresponded with those on a list that the novelist Aeba Kōson (1855–1922), a decade later, averred was generally accepted: Bakin's *The Chronicle of the Eight Dogs of the Nansō Satomi Clan* (*Nansō Satomi hakkenden*, 1814–1842), Jippensha Ikku's (1765–1831) *Shanks-Mare on the Eastern Seaboard* (*Tōkaidōchū hizakurige*, 1802–1822), Shikitei Sanba's (1776–1822) *Bathhouse of the Floating World* (*Ukiyoburo*, 1809–1813), and *Inaka Genji*.[9] Of these four works, only *Inaka Genji* was a *gōkan*. Fifty years after its last chapter had appeared, *Inaka Genji* remained the most celebrated work in its genre.

Inaka Genji's fame during its time and beyond would seem to justify a considerable amount of scholarly attention, but in fact surprisingly little has been written about it—much less than has been written about the other three Great Literary Marvels. In part this is due to the popular nature of the genre: from the time the *gōkan* crystallized as an acknowledged form around 1807, its format relegated it to the bottom of the hierarchy of fictional types.[10] Small enough to sit comfortably in the palm of the hand, as the lower forms of fiction usually were, *gōkan* were packed with pictures that covered every page, most occupying full spreads. The text, insinuated into whatever empty spaces were left, was written almost exclusively in the syllabary known as *hiragana*—the core of basic literacy—and was made still easier to read by copyists who limited and standardized their usage of the many *hiragana* forms.[11]

Thus while *gōkan* were clearly enjoyed by both girls and boys, women and men, poor laborers and educated elites, they were habitually described, and to some extent probably were genuinely regarded, as playthings for women and children. The result, as the pioneering scholar Suzuki Jūzō (1919–2010) lamented in his seminal monograph *On Gōkan* (*Gōkan ni tsuite*, 1961), has been that "from an early stage, [*gōkan*] were cast beyond the pale of subjects suitable for research in both literary and art history."¹² Or, again, referring specifically to critical oversight of the pictures in *gōkan* in an essay from 1965: "The facile attitude readers have taken toward *gōkan* in the past has led them to regard the illustrations, which are the single most important feature of works in this genre, as nothing more than supplementary material provided for the amusement of women and children."¹³ For decades, *gōkan* in general and especially their pictures remained largely unstudied, victims of an all-too-literary textual fetishism.

Not only is *Inaka Genji* handicapped by the popular nature of its genre, but it is burdened by a larger, more intractable issue, as Tsuda Mayumi notes in an essay from 2003: "Evaluations of the literary worth of this work will vary greatly," she writes, "depending on whether one places more importance on its relationship to *Genji monogatari* or on its status as a *gōkan*."¹⁴ From the perspective of an ordinary reader, in an age when *Inaka Genji* was still revered as a classic, or even from the viewpoint of an elite aficionado such as Mokurō, this statement would have seemed absurd: What could be more obvious than that a *gōkan* should be enjoyed as a *gōkan*? Times have changed, however, and in the present age it has come to seem absurd not that one might have to be on intimate terms with *Genji monogatari* in order to "get" *Inaka Genji*, but that *Inaka Genji* could ever have been widely appreciated *without* regard to its relationship to the canonical work of which it is said to have been a parody.

The reason for this lies, ultimately, in a restructuring of the Japanese literary canon that took place in the modern period—especially, as this book will show, during the wartime and postwar periods. The effect of this shift has been to divest *Inaka Genji* and its fellow early modern former "popular classics" of their cachet, awarding pride of place instead to the vernacular fiction of the Heian period (794–1185)—above all, *Genji monogatari*. The enshrinement of *Genji monogatari* and other products of the Heian court milieu in a quintessentially national canon of Great Books that are assumed to have influenced the evolution of Japanese culture and aesthetics at all social levels through the ages, if only through a sort of trickle-down effect, has had a profound impact on how we read early modern fiction, including *Inaka Genji*. In her essay, Tsuda allies herself with readers who would place the most importance on *Inaka Genji*'s qualities as a *gōkan*, voicing her discomfort "with the idea of passing judgment on the literary standing of the author or the readers of his time solely on the basis of a simplistic comparison of texts, when no attention has been paid to the context in which *Inaka Genji* was produced."¹⁵ But the canonical weight that *Genji monogatari* has been given, and the largely unexamined assumption that, in one manner or another, the tale has always been an ingredient in the glue that holds the imagined community of the Japanese nation together, have made it seem that the text of the Heian tale *was* the context in which *Inaka Genji* was produced. To the extent that *Inaka Genji* figures at all in Japanese literary history—as opposed to the smaller histories of *gōkan* or of the broader constellation of popular genres known as *kusazōshi* ("grass books" or "stinky books")— it has been consistently described as an adaptation (*hon'an*), or more often as a parody, of *Genji monogatari*. To this day, the only book-length monograph apart from this study to devote more than a chapter to *Inaka Genji* considers its plot, characters, and text solely in relation to those of the Heian tale.[16]

This seemingly natural privileging of *Inaka Genji*'s relationship to *Genji monogatari* over its status as a *gōkan*—of an image of the *gōkan* as a *text* that parodies *Genji monogatari*—places it, even today, in a double bind eerily reminiscent of the one that emerged in 1925 in Tayama Katai's *Studies of the Novel*: the richness and eclecticism of *Inaka Genji*'s pictures and text and even, paradoxically, the extent to which Tanehiko incorporated the classical prose of *Genji monogatari* into his work are overshadowed by the irreplaceable psychological profundities of *Genji monogatari* itself, the canonical weight of which is nevertheless responsible for much of the slight attention Tanehiko's *gōkan* receives.[17] *Inaka Genji* can never be as great as *Genji monogatari*, but neither can it escape being talked about in connection with that classic, and thus, by virtue of its own lesser canonical status, perceived as secondary, derivative, or even lacking. This tendency may have abated somewhat now that *Inaka Genji* is no longer as widely read as it was in earlier periods, but it has not entirely vanished. Even my own treatment of it, in the context of this study of *Genji monogatari*'s replacement into the canons of world and national literature, is a symptom of the bias I am trying to correct.

I have no desire to minimize the significance of *Inaka Genji*'s link to *Genji monogatari*: one aim of this chapter is to counter the mistaken impression that Tanehiko engaged with Murasaki Shikibu's text only superficially and to suggest that this misapprehension is due, at least in part, to the special care Tanehiko took to avoid overplaying an unusual classical connection, and thus seeming discouragingly pedantic in the context of a genre whose raison d'être, from its readers' point of view, was to entertain.[18] At the same time, it is important to recognize that there is much more to *Inaka Genji* than just its relationship to *Genji monogatari* and that a majority of its early modern readers regarded it as a masterpiece in its own right. If we ever hope to get a sense of what made

Inaka Genji the flower of its genre, we must relinquish what this study will show is a surprisingly recent image of *Genji monogatari* as a widely familiar national classic. Indeed, one of the first points this chapter will make is that for a majority of *Inaka Genji*'s early modern readers, *Genji monogatari* almost certainly existed, insofar as it existed at all, as a reflection of *Inaka Genji*, not the other way around.[19]

It is my contention that *Inaka Genji* was not originally read as a parody of *Genji monogatari* and that it was not widely valued—even secondhand, vis-à-vis digests—for its intertextual engagement with the classic Heian text that nonetheless served as its chief inspiration. *Inaka Genji*'s readers savored it, rather, as a rich, playful, erudite mixture of all manner of earlier texts, pictures, and plots; for its text, written in a particular pseudo-dramatic style that Tanehiko himself had created and popularized many years earlier; for the suave sexiness of its main character, Ashikaga Mitsuuji; and, most important, for its visual elements—the sophistication of its image-text-book relations and the stylish, lavish manner in which each chapter was designed, produced, and packaged. *Inaka Genji* was so elegant that readers unfamiliar with the text or even the plot of *Genji monogatari* may well have sensed in its form, more than in its prose or story, the high-class refinement they associated, however abstractly, with the vaguely familiar title of the Heian classic.

At the same time, I argue that sometime during the course of *Inaka Genji*'s original publication history, readers' attitudes toward it underwent a subtle, crucial change: people began not so much to appreciate *Inaka Genji* as a parody or an adaptation of *Genji monogatari*, but at least to think of it as a replacement of an older work and to value it not simply as a brilliant *gōkan*, but as a *gōkan* tinged with the aura of a classic. This development both reflected and was in turn reflected in a shift in Tanehiko's own creative stance. Early on, he had simply been mining *Genji monogatari* as a source for one of his new *gōkan*; by the time he prepared the manuscript for what ended up being the last chapter, *Inaka Genji* was generally recognized as his greatest achievement, and he had decided to keep running with it, turning the book into a bona-fide adaptation of the entire tale. In this sense, and because over the years Tanehiko came to adhere increasingly closely to the text of *Genji monogatari*, *Inaka Genji* can be regarded both as a precursor to the popular translations into modern Japanese that have been a feature of the Japanese literary landscape since the 1880s, and as the book that first induced a truly broad readership in Japan to feel even slightly connected to *Genji monogatari*. *Inaka Genji* made *Genji monogatari*'s canonicity matter outside the circles of the privileged elite.[20]

The epigraph for this chapter, "Seeing is forgetting the name of the thing one sees," is the title of Lawrence Weschler's fascinating biography of the artist Robert Irwin. I chose it because it seems to me that this is precisely what we must do if we hope to reconstruct something of *Inaka Genji*'s former glory: we must stop allowing ourselves to be distracted by the misdirection of its name. We know what *Genji* means today, what it refers to, and it is all too easy to succumb to the tricky solipsism of the present, to assume that those who came before us, and those who will come after, belong to the communities we conjure up around us through our interpretations of such words: to think, that is, that we know, too, what *Genji* meant and what it referred to. The truth is that the past is not something we share with the past, and our knowledge of *Genji* has clouded our vision of the *gōkan*. *Inaka Genji* may not be classed as a Great Book in the current canonical taxonomy, but it was once a Great Literary Marvel; if only we can forget enough of what we know about the name it bears, we may yet learn to see it for the great book it is.

Made in the Image: *Genji monogatari* as *Inaka Genji*

I have been arguing that *Inaka Genji* played a significant role in bringing *Genji monogatari* to the notice of a popular readership in early modern Japan for years now, at conferences, in lectures, and in a previous iteration of some of the material included in this chapter.[21] This suggestion has been greeted with considerable skepticism. One book review that touched on the earlier version of this chapter, for instance, noted that "*Inaka Genji* is merely one instance in a long line of *Genji* 'replacements'" and—taking the *gōkan*'s status as a parody of *Genji monogatari* as an objective, incontestable fact—raised the "obvious question" of "how readers could appreciate the element of parody in Tanehiko's work if they did not already know the text being parodied."[22] The answer to this question is that the question itself is misguided. While well-educated elites surely admired the sheer brilliance and the unobtrusive ingeniousness with which Tanehiko toyed not only with the tale itself, but even with commentaries on it—quoting a passage from *The Rivers and Seas Commentary* (*Kakaishō*, 1362) on a folding screen in one picture, for instance, making it look like calligraphy in classical Chinese by rewriting it, removing the parts written in *hiragana* (figure 6)—most readers simply would not have *seen* those allusions.[23] To them, the gauzy intertextual web was all but invisible. *Inaka Genji* appealed to the widest possible range of early modern readers, and it is a mistake to imagine that our ability, today, to discover so much of *Genji monogatari* in *Inaka Genji* tells us anything at all about what, say, a paper maker, a wet nurse, a maker of roof tiles, or two siblings enjoying the book together might have seen in its pages as they read it through the 1830s, renting new chapters year after year from a local lending library. Or how about a nine-year-old girl whose koto teacher let her read it as a rare treat while she was waiting for her lesson in the 1880s?[24] The obvious question is not "How did they appreciate what we appreciate, in a world that takes *Genji* for granted?" but "What did they appreciate?"

The same review goes on to introduce an argument made by the author of a valuable study of early modern woodblock-printed editions of *Genji monogatari*:

Figure 6 The writing on the screen at the right is a quotation from *Kakaishō*, a *Genji* commentary. (*NMIG*, chapter 14, 12 *ura*–13 *omote*. Courtesy of Waseda University Library, Tokyo)

As Shimizu Fukuko 清水富久子 has already argued, to fully enjoy [the parodic] aspect of *Inaka Genji* readers needed to have some degree of familiarity with *Genji* itself. Shimizu notes that from the seventeenth century onwards, general readers had access to *Genji* in a variety of forms—including printed versions of the original with or without notes, digests, and vernacular translations—and that it is likely that this very familiarity with the original *Genji* was what enabled them to recognize Tanehiko's parodies.[25]

Shimizu, too, as she is paraphrased here, starts from the assumption that *Inaka Genji* is ipso facto a parody and that it was undoubtedly "fully enjoyed" as a parody, and then invokes the trickle-down theory to explain how "general readers" gained the requisite knowledge of "the original *Genji*."[26] This stance is not unique to Shimizu or to the authors of the review; indeed, it stands as a perfect instantiation of the circular logic by which the notion that *Inaka Genji* must have been read as a parody of *Genji monogatari* is sustained. Of course, people enjoyed *Inaka Genji* as a parody: How could it have been otherwise? *Genji monogatari* is a Great Book; everyone read it. Are you sure? Of course we're sure. After all, if people weren't familiar with *Genji monogatari*, how could they have enjoyed *Inaka Genji* as a parody?

Neither is this argument's circularity its only weakness. When *Inaka Genji*'s first chapter was published in 1829, no new edition of *Genji monogatari* had been printed for more than 120 years. The few annotated editions available secondhand in bookstores or in lending libraries—and it is worth noting that the Nagoya library that stocked five full sets of *Inaka Genji* had only a single copy of *Kogetsushō*—would have been not merely unintelligible but illegible to most of *Inaka Genji*'s minimally literate readers, since they were full of cursive *kanji* without *hiragana* glosses and their notes sometimes contained long passages written entirely in classical Chinese.[27] The digests and vernacular translations that Shimizu adduces to explain *Genji monogatari*'s purported familiarity to "general readers," moreover, were essentially a phenomenon of the late seventeenth and early eighteenth centuries.[28] Tanehiko's disciple Ryūtei Senka (Ryūtei Tanehiko II, 1806–1868) stated explicitly in a note to a series of prints based on *Inaka Genji* published from 1852 to 1854 that the very books Shimizu cites "seem old-fashioned from a modern perspective, in terms of both their pictures and their language, and would leave boys and girls accustomed to opulence feeling like they were handling antique dolls."[29] As I will explain in more detail later, Tanehiko—a connoisseur of arcane knowledge relating to the popular culture of previous ages—

includes a number of these titles in a "Complete List of Works Cited" that he offers as a joke (as a parody, in fact) in lieu of a preface to *Inaka Genji*'s third chapter; tellingly, the most recent of the works he cites dates from 1749, and the rest had appeared decades, if not centuries, earlier.

There is, of course, no way to prove conclusively that large numbers of ordinary townspeople were not spending their free moments engrossed in century-old digests of a work that—for some inexplicable reason, assuming it was so popular—had not been published, translated, or rewritten in a contemporary idiom in anyone's living memory.[30] The available evidence suggests, however, that there is truth in what seems to me the commonsensical proposition that they were not and that *Inaka Genji* did indeed come to stand in the eyes of most of its readers as a fleshed-out image of a work that had contributed nothing whatsoever to their entertainment, but whose title they knew and which was perhaps recognizable as a tall lacquered box labeled *Kogetsushō* that was a fixture in the rooms of authors and courtesans, judging from depictions in popular books and prints.[31] It is abundantly clear that women and men who were alive to witness the *Inaka Genji* boom, who were themselves swept up in the fervor, did not share the view prevalent among scholars today that the *gōkan* succeeded as a parody of *Genji monogatari*. They knew what *Genji*'s contemporary ubiquity leads us to forget: it was *Inaka Genji* that made *Genji monogatari*'s canonicity matter to a truly broad, popular readership.

In his 1853 preface to chapter 14 of *Ashikaga Silk: Hand-Dyed Purple* (*Ashikagaginu tezome no murasaki*, 1850-1861), one of a number of sequels to *Inaka Genji*, Ryūtei Senka rejoices in the proliferation of what he calls "*Genji*-wise non-readers of *Genji*" (*Genji yomazu no Genji shiri*): "Ever since my teacher captured the light of the Moon on the Lake [*Kogetsushō*] in his telescope," he writes, "even little dog-beating brats know that there are more Genjis out there than just Yoritomo and Yoshitsune."[32] Yoritomo and Yoshitsune were historical warriors, brothers of the Minamoto clan, or the Genji, familiar from dozens of kabuki plays and works of popular fiction.[33] Senka's point, obviously, is that *Inaka Genji* had, for the first time, made ordinary Edoites aware of the existence of *Genji monogatari* and of that of its male protagonist, Hikaru Genji, if only by association with *Inaka Genji*'s hero, Mitsuuji.

In fact, many of *Inaka Genji*'s readers appear to have labored under the impression that *Inaka Genji* was *Genji monogatari* and that Mitsuuji was Hikaru Genji. Novelist and translator of *Genji monogatari* Enchi Fumiko recollected, "When I first heard the story from my grandmother as a little girl, it was *Inaka Genji*," and described her grandmother telling it to her as she looked at the pictures, identifying the characters for her: "'Mitsuuji is Hikaru Genji,' she would say, and 'Fuji no Kata is Fujitsubo.'"[34] The literary critic Maeda Ai had a similar experience as late as the postwar years, at the tail end of the process of popular recanonization that part II of this study will describe, when even kids like him knew about the tale: "I was always oddly bothered when, after the war, my grandmother told me stories from *Genji monogatari*, and she said Mitsuuji instead of Hikaru Genji."[35] In both cases, *Inaka Genji* provided material for stories that grandmothers, evidently well acquainted with the work, shared with their grandchildren; to a certain extent, as I noted earlier, women and children were indeed the target audience for *gōkan*. It comes as no surprise to find the great haiku poet Naitō Meisetsu speculating in an essay that he began serializing in January 1905—the same year Enchi was born—that "there are probably still grandmothers out there who tell stories about Mitsuuji and Murasaki."[36] Naitō himself explained that knowledge of *Genji monogatari* gleaned from *Inaka Genji* had served him well over the course of his career and made the tale seem "like a path I had walked once before when, much later, I finally read it."[37] And to cite one final example, when the eccentric scholar Kimura Takatarō, in a brief essay about Lord Byron's poem *Parisina* included in a 1923 critical biography and collection of translations of the poet's work, compared "the relationship of Hikaru Genji and the Fujitsubo Consort, or Fuji no Kata, in *Genji monogatari* or *Inaka Genji*" with that between Parisina and Hugo, his description of the plot of "*Genji monogatari* and *Inaka Genji*" in fact applies only to *Inaka Genji*, and it is from *Inaka Genji* that he quotes. Kimura, too, seems to have equated the two works.[38]

An essay serialized from November 1888 to July 1889 by the novelist, playwright, and critic Yoda Gakkai (1834-1909)—also known as the man who taught the author Mori Ōgai classical Chinese—offers a more substantial portrait of the unusually heterogeneous readership *Inaka Genji* garnered and of the process by which the *gōkan* and various products created to capitalize on its popularity propagated an image of *Genji monogatari* as *Inaka Genji* among less-cultivated fans. Gakkai also cites Tanehiko himself as having explicitly stated that his purpose in creating *Inaka Genji* was to encourage ordinary people to read *Genji monogatari*—though Tanehiko may perhaps have been guilty of a certain degree of pious disingenuousness in this regard, or at the very least of a remarkable susceptibility to optimism:

> The prose was largely colloquial at first, in the usual style of popular fiction [*kusazōshi*]. Then, from the third or fourth chapter, Tanehiko gradually began mixing colloquial with elegant language. He noted in

a preface that he was inspired by a somewhat meddlesome, old-womanish desire to make women and children feel curious to read the original book. That said, he kept the elegant and the colloquial from clashing, employing a diction that felt natural and didn't grate on the ear, that was pleasant to read and had an elevated tone, and was easy to understand. As a result, aristocrats and people of high rank took up this book with delight, and for a time it became extraordinarily popular: it wasn't only the ubiquitous prints, there were also votive plaques for shrines and temples, patterns on clothing, fabric pictures on sliding walls paneled with Chinese-style paper—in the end, hardly a surface was left that wasn't decorated with a "Genji picture." Women and children who had never heard of the original understood *Genji* to refer to this book, and there were plenty of people who knew Mitsuuji [the hero of *Inaka Genji*] but had never heard of Hikaru Genji.[39]

It is a telling irony that today woodblock prints in the genre known as "Genji pictures" (*Genji-e*) are frequently introduced by online dealers, and occasionally even in museums, as depictions of characters from *Genji monogatari* when in fact they are almost exclusively based on *Inaka Genji*: in modern times, the canonicity of the vernacular literature of the Heian court makes it seem that "Genji" has always referred to *Genji monogatari*, which is accordingly often referred to simply as "the *Genji*."

Gakkai, who was born in Edo five years after *Inaka Genji*'s first chapter was published and thus seems in a good position to know, indicates that for many of the less-educated townspeople in Edo—this, one suspects, would be a more accurate description of the population he refers to as "women and children"—*Inaka Genji* was the primary referent of the word "Genji." At a certain point, however, the fame of the *gōkan* began to reflect back on *Genji monogatari*. Whether or not Tanehiko actually hoped to encourage readers to tackle the original, and whether or not this had been his hope from the first, he seems to have inspired in many a desire to feel connected to the classic. We may never know when this watershed was achieved, and it was likely less a watershed than a gradual bend in the river, but it was almost certainly well under way by the time Tanehiko announced his decision to adapt the whole of *Genji monogatari*. And by 1894, when the major Meiji-period publisher Hakubunkan issued *The Collected Masterpieces of Tanehiko* (*Tanehiko kessakushū*), a rumbling of interest in *Genji monogatari* that had begun in 1890 (for reasons that will be discussed in chapter 4) had made *Genji monogatari* the primary referent of "Genji," even for the anticipated Meiji audience for Tanehiko's fiction. This is evident from the first lines of the "Brief Biography of Ryūtei

Tanehiko" that opens the collection: "Few are familiar with the titles *The Bamboo Cutter* [*Taketori*] and *The Tale of the Hollow Tree* [*Utsubo*], but when it comes to *Genji monogatari*, hardly anyone, even among women and children, doesn't know the gist of the story. This is not due to the excellence of the work alone; the responsibility lies, rather, with a loyal retainer by the name of Ryūtei Tanehiko who disseminated its name far and wide among the common folk."[40]

Three years later, in the March 1897 issue of *Katei zasshi* (*Home Journal*), a writer who called himself "Old Man Yokutō" (Yokutō Rōjin) made the same point in a manner so explicit, so unambiguous, and so completely in accord with the argument I have been advancing that it is worth quoting at length. Judging from the author's self-description as an "old man," he too, like Gakkai, would seem to have experienced the history he describes firsthand:

> *Genji monogatari*, which people praise as the great treasure of our national literature, as a marvelous rarity without parallel, is said to consist of fifty-four books [*gojūyonjō*], which means, in other words, that it is a voluminous work of fifty-four chapters [*gōjūyonkan*], and even this admirable fact, the very numerousness of its chapters, merits our pride.
>
> How much more worthy, then, are the subtlety of its prose, the skill of its construction, and the perfect accordance of its prose with its construction, how it sparkles with the clear light of a jewel, glows as alluringly as a flower, and so on.
>
> Fitting it is, indeed, that this work has been transmitted as a rarity, praised as a marvel, bandied about through the ages, right down to the present time.
>
> Readers, surely you must know of it! There is a cosmetic product for women, a face-whitening powder, called "Genji Incense." There is a hair oil called "Genji Kyara Incense Oil." There is a crest known as the "Genji Wheel," and another called the "Simplified Genji." Women attendants in the great houses have "Genji names." These are just a few instances, and many more cases of various kinds could be cited of words to which the two characters for "Genji" have been affixed, or of things named directly for the titles of *Genji*'s chapters. Neither is the phenomenon limited to these items: the authors of old miscellanies tell us in great detail of things that existed in the past, including even "Genji Rice," "Genji Soba," "Genji Sweet Bean Soup," and other such products.
>
> The more one looks into it, the more astonishing it is that the use of the word "Genji" has proliferated so widely, and that it all derives,

ultimately, from *Genji monogatari*. But not directly from *Genji monogatari*: there is something that stands in the middle, that has made "Genji" so widely familiar, and that is the work of popular fiction *Inaka Genji*.

Genji monogatari is a book even celebrated experts and great scholars of the national literature struggle to comprehend, and even the most learned are at pains to explicate it—obviously, then, it is not easily understood. It is utterly ridiculous to think that it could be as widely known as it is, among the people of the world.

The fact that it has spread so far is entirely owing to the impact of *Inaka Genji*.

. . .

Truly, if *Genji monogatari* itself is like a treasure of the elegant literary world, *Inaka Genji*, all by itself, stands as the treasure of the colloquial literary world. If Tanehiko had not rewritten *Genji monogatari* as *Inaka Genji* for ordinary people, there is no knowing whether its title would be so widely known as it is.

Yes indeed, the service Ryūtei Tanehiko did *Genji monogatari* by bringing it down a notch, into a familiar time period, is anything but insignificant.

There is, in addition to *Inaka Genji*, a work by Nishiki Bunryū [sic] called *A Tasteful Tale of Genji*, but it is hardly worth speaking of.[41]

A Tasteful Tale of Genji (*Fūryū Genji monogatari*, 1703)—a peculiar six-fascicle patchwork of the first two chapters of *Genji monogatari* and all manner of other texts—is one of the digests from the late seventeenth and early eighteenth centuries that Shimizu Fukuko and others have invoked to explain the assumed familiarity of *Inaka Genji*'s early-nineteenth-century popular readership with *Genji monogatari*, and ordinary townspeople's supposed ability to appreciate the *gōkan*'s close, even minute engagement with the text of *Kogetsushō*. Yokutō Rōjin goes on to say that a work called *Genji monogatari Ferns of Recollection* (*Genji monogatari shinobugusa*) by Kitamura Koshun—the son of Kitamura Kigin, the scholar and poet who edited *Kogetsushō*—"gradually made *Genji monogatari* known among the elevated classes, just as *Inaka Genji* made it known to the general population."[42] Tellingly, although *Ferns of Recollection* was completed early in the Genroku period (1688–1704), it was printed for the first time only in 1834, six years after the publication of *Inaka Genji* had begun.

The trajectory, then, seems crystal clear. In the early years of the Tenpō period (1830–1844), *Inaka Genji* was almost certainly not read by most readers as a replacement for *Genji monogatari*; then, over time, Tanehiko taught them to see the work in this way, and once the equation had been established it became increasingly difficult to consider *Inaka Genji* as anything but a replacement. The modern rise of *Genji monogatari*, through translations both foreign and domestic, as an easily accessible and widely read classic of world and national literature further exacerbated this trend, making it seem that surely everyone in Japan, high and low, has always been familiar with the tale, obscuring from view much of the value of Tanehiko's work, not only as an early vehicle for the spread of an appreciation of its canonicity, but also in its own right, as a *gōkan*. If most of *Inaka Genji*'s first readers were unable to appreciate how it played with *Genji monogatari*, contemporary readers are afflicted with the opposite blindness. In order to understand what the paper maker, the wet nurse, the maker of roof tiles, or that nine-year-old girl killing time before her music lesson might have seen in *Inaka Genji*, we need to forget about *Genji monogatari*.

Or perhaps we just need to sit down and *see* the book. Look at its covers; the innovations it introduced; its characters' fashions and hairstyles; the sexy sagacity of its hero, Mitsuuji. And then reconsider its relationship to *Genji monogatari* and Tanehiko's relationship to *Genji monogatari*, eschewing vague, abstract assertions of *Inaka Genji*'s absolute indebtedness to "the original" in favor of a more rigorous appreciation of *Inaka Genji*'s reworking of *Kogetsushō* that will let us begin to reimagine the *gōkan* as one of the Four Great Literary Marvels of early modern Japan.[43] Maybe then we can appreciate *Inaka Genji* the way Gakkai did when he reread it in 1888, at the age of fifty-four, before he wrote the essay cited earlier. At the time, Gakkai was nearing the end of his first reading of *Kogetsushō*, which he had begun in 1856, at twenty-two, and would finally finish in November 1889; he knew both *Genji monogatari* and *Inaka Genji* more intimately than just about anyone.[44] "When one carefully reads the original before turning to this book, and holds it in mind, comparing the two," he wrote of *Inaka Genji*, "one is struck by the marvelous lightness of touch with which it is written, and the brilliance of the transfiguration, and one finds it ten times more pleasurable than most little books."[45] Indeed, he goes still further in his praise, offering an assessment of *Inaka Genji* whose utter alienness in respect to current discourse about the Japanese literary canon stands as an index of how much we might gain from an attentive, sympathetic reading of this *gōkan*: "While this book was composed using *Genji*'s plot, the gist is naturally quite different, and in terms of its appeal to modern sensibilities and its overall interest it must be judged superior to the original."[46] Once upon a time, it was *natural* to appreciate *Inaka Genji* on its own terms, as a work distinct from *Genji*. Now we need to let the book teach us how to read it that way again.

Designing the Perfect *Gōkan*

In order to imagine what it was like to read *Inaka Genji* when it first came out, and to get a sense of how eye-catching it was as a book, we must, first of all, situate it materially in the context of its genre: we need to know what a *gōkan* was; how *Inaka Genji* improved on certain of the genre's basic elements, pioneering a bold new style; and how that style captivated other designers, other publishers, who made *Inaka Genji* the new model for a long lineage of *gōkan*, putting into circulation what we might think of—in an analogy with the notion of *"Genji* discourse" that will figure prominently in part II of this book—as the *"Inaka Genji* style." The charms with which *Inaka Genji* first seduced its readers were embodied in its form as a book.

The first three chapters of *Inaka Genji*, published in 1829 and 1830 in time for the New Year, as was the convention for works in the genre, were issued in the format common around that time. Each chapter (*hen*) of a *gōkan* consisted of two ten-leaf fascicles (*satsu*) of the "middle size" that were themselves composed of two separate five-leaf booklets (*kan*).[47] The five-leaf booklet had been the basic bibliographic unit of an earlier popular genre, the *kibyōshi*, or "yellowcovers," and the *gōkan* had first come into being when authors and booksellers realized that they could extend the length of the standard three-booklet *kibyōshi* by combining two booklets, making the resulting ten-leaf fascicle the new basic unit, and publishing books that consisted of more than one fascicle, and eventually of multiple two-fascicle chapters.[48] The stitching together of two *kan* to form the longer *satsu* is in fact what gives the genre its name: *gōkan* are literally "combined booklets."

Each two-booklet fascicle in a *gōkan* was provided with front and back covers that were slightly stiffer than the pages inside. The front covers were printed with full-color *nishiki-e* (brocade pictures), composed to form a single scene when the covers of both fascicles of a given chapter, or in some cases three or more fascicles, were placed side by side; the back covers were printed with a solid field of plain black. The inside front cover, or *mikaeshi*, served as a sort of illustrated title page, while the inside back cover, or *okuzuke*, often carried information about the publisher and advertisements for its other publications—and sometimes, reflecting the lopsided demography of the *gōkan* readership, for items such as women's cosmetics and cures for bedwetting.[49]

The first pages of each chapter were devoted to a preface and one or more *kuchi-e* (opening illustrations), also printed in black. *Kuchi-e* are pictures with little, if any, writing that appear in most, though not all, *gōkan*; derived from similar pictures in the *yomihon* (reading books) genre that are known as *shūzō* (the Sino-Japanese reading of the Chinese *xiuxiang*), they are depictions, occupying a full page or a two-page spread, of selections from a given book or of a chapter's characters, attractively posed. Unlike the pictures that accompany the main text of the book—whose lineage can be traced back to the artwork in *kibyōshi*— *kuchi-e*, with their more distinguished pedigree, represent static scenes or frozen moments with a greater degree of compositional sophistication and were frequently enclosed within decorative frames.

As I noted earlier, these bibliographic features, standard in *gōkan* of the period, were shared by the first three chapters of *Inaka Genji*. Beginning with the publication in 1831 of the fourth chapter, however, Tanehiko and his collaborators began to introduce some innovations. One eye-catching experiment first tried in chapter 4 and then retained in subsequent chapters involved the use in the *kuchi-e* of both ordinary black ink (*sumi*) and thin ink (*usuzumi*, which appears gray on the page) printed from a separate block. The use of thin ink—which was commonplace in illustrations for *yomihon* and other genres around the same

(b)

time but was all but unheard of in the less-prestigious *gōkan*—was often eliminated in later printings of *Inaka Genji*, presumably because it required so much effort and added so much to the cost of producing the books. The commercial benefits of retaining this radical innovation, at least in earlier printings of each chapter, must, however, have been thought to justify the added labor: the *kuchi-e* for subsequent chapters sometimes include not one but two separate shades of thin ink.[50]

Indeed, early printings of the *kuchi-e* for chapters 15 and 28 used thin ink in conjunction with light blue ink, another first in *gōkan* printing, while the *kuchi-e* for chapter 5 used thin ink with thick ink (*kozumi*, which yields a darker black). This second experiment failed, evidently because the quality of the paper used in *gōkan* at the time was not good enough for this type of ink to have the desired effect.[51] Neither light blue ink nor thick ink was used in later printings. And finally, in at least two chapters, thin ink was used not only in the *kuchi-e* but also in a picture in the main body of the work: once to represent a face peering into a room through a bamboo blind, and once to represent the ghost of Mitsuuji's mother, Hanagiri, the counterpart of Genji's mother, Kiritsubo, in *Genji monogatari*.[52]

Figure 7 (a) Shinonome, in an early printing, using *usuzumi*, of the *kuchi-e* in chapter 4 of *Nise Murasaki inaka Genji*. (b) Mitsuuji and Tasogare, in an early printing, using *usuzumi*, of the *kuchi-e* in chapter 4. ([a] NMIG, chapter 4, 1 *omote*; [b] NMIG, chapter 4, 1 *ura*–2 *omote*. Both images courtesy of National Diet Library)

(a)

All this talk of special inks and the value of using them comes into focus when one actually examines a few pictures. A comparison of earlier (figure 7) and later (figure 8) printings reveals how much the addition of thin ink contributes to the compositions, and why it would have made *Inaka Genji* stand out among all the other *gōkan* being produced: the thin ink makes the characters' clothing look more solid and adds complexity to the textile patterns (notice the richly detailed handling of the leaves on the outer kimono in figure 7a and the lack of this detail in the later printing, shown in figure 8a), and imbues objects like the fan and mask in figure 7a and the screen showing heaven and hell in figure 7b with an almost palpable depth and weight.[53] In figure 7b, which depicts Mitsuuji and Tasogare—the counterparts of Hikaru Genji and Yūgao in *Genji monogatari*—thin ink has been used to turn the white of the lower half of the page into a billowing fog that encloses the two characters, isolating them from the nebulous gray area behind them and the makeshift screen. The gray gives the picture an added dimension, since without it the screen's hinge—actually just a few pieces of rope, only one of which is visible—marks the illustration's farthest recess, as we see in figure 8b (on the right-hand page of the spread depicted).

(b)

The overall effect of the use of thin ink in this picture is to lend the scene an eerie, otherworldly atmosphere that works with the images of heaven and hell on the screen's two panels to subtly foreshadow the supernatural and faux-supernatural events that will unfold in the course of this chapter. The screen's two panels resonate, moreover, with a passage near the end of chapter 5, in which Tasogare—having slit her own throat with a razor in an effort to protect Mitsuuji from her mother, Shinonome, who has come to try to kill him—sobs, "My mother's demonic appearance reveals, in this world, the form she will take in hell, and makes me see how terrible her suffering will be in the world to come—how sad I am, how sad!" A moment later, after Mitsuuji forgives Shinonome and assures Tasogare that she and he will be reborn on a single lotus blossom in the next world, Tasogare says that, guided by his words, she will gladly die and become a Buddha.[54] The same observations can, of course, be made about the later printing, shown in figure 8b, but in addition to being visually much more appealing, the earlier version, with all its fog and atmosphere, does a far better job of setting the stage for such a reading.

Shades of gray played a role in another pathbreaking innovation introduced in chapter 4 of *Inaka Genji*: the back covers of its two fascicles

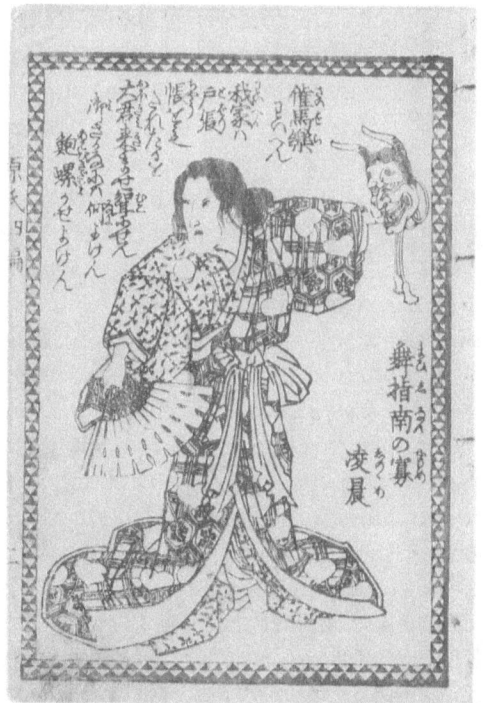

Figure 8 (a) The *kuchi-e* shown in figure 7a, from a later printing of the work, without the *usuzumi*. (b) The *kuchi-e* shown in figure 7b, from a later printing of the work, without the *usuzumi*. ([a] NMIG, chapter 4, 1 omote; [b] NMIG, chapter 4, 1 ura–2 omote. Both images courtesy of the author)

(a)

are no longer plain black or another bland color, as was the case with *gōkan* ever since the genre was created, including the first three chapters of *Inaka Genji*; instead, they feature an elegant, complex design printed with a pale blue or purple-gray ink that includes *Genji* incense signs, evidently randomly chosen, and a floral medallion known as the "floating-warp pattern" (*fusenryō*), which originally derived from China but was closely associated with Heian-period textiles (figure 9).[55] The imposing aura this pattern had is suggested by Kashiwagi's use of a fabric decorated with it, in the "Hashihime" (The Maiden of the Bridge) chapter of *Genji monogatari*, to cover the scroll he leaves behind when he dies, intending it for Genji's wife and his own illicit lover, the Third Princess—not that many of *Inaka Genji*'s readers would have known this.[56]

Figure 9 The first patterned back cover of *Inaka Genji*. (Courtesy of Art Research Center, Ritsumeikan University, Kyoto)

The design of *Inaka Genji*'s back covers was changed at least seven times during the course of the book's Edo-period publication history, and various colors were used. It is hard to overstate the impression of novelty and lavishness that all these patterns would have conveyed to readers long accustomed to plain black covers, particularly since they were always tasteful, subtle, and sophisticated.[57] One of the designs that was used most frequently is a uniform field of gray or light brown that functions as negative space, turning the unprinted areas into white clamshells (figure 10); these shells, which evoke those used in the game "shell matching" (*kai-ōi*), are marked with *Genji* incense signs and the corresponding chapter titles.[58] The back covers of the two fascicles of each chapter that use this clamshell design generally were printed either with different blocks carved with shells marked with different titles and incense signs or with the same

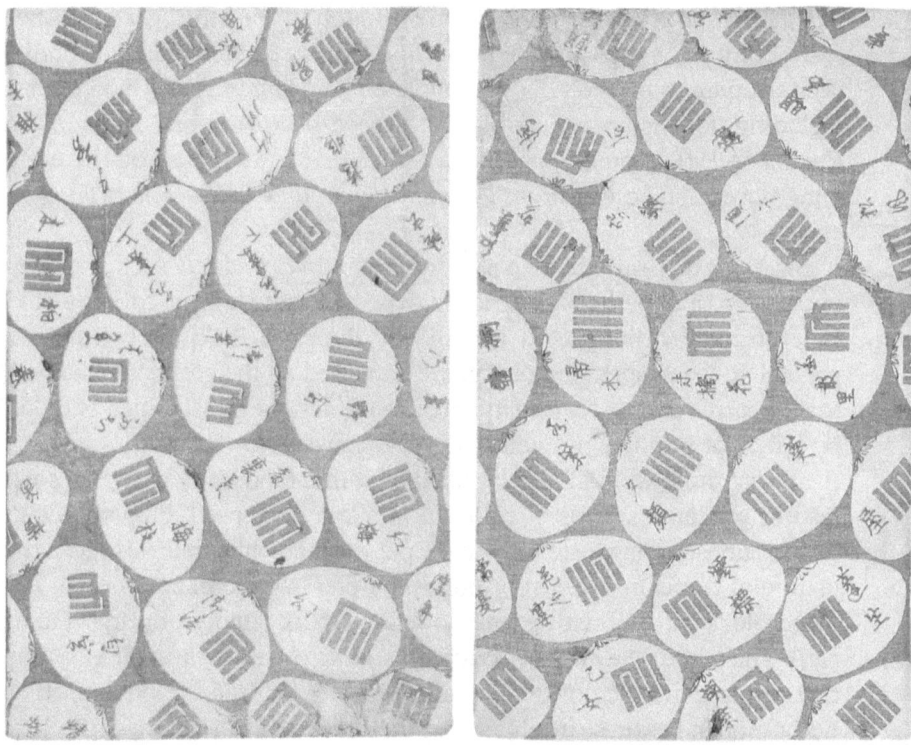

Figure 10 The pattern most often used on the back covers of *Inaka Genji*. Each shell is marked with a *Genji* incense sign and the corresponding chapter title from *Genji monogatari*. (Courtesy of Waseda University Library, Tokyo)

block, but with the paper rotated 180 degrees; the shells form a circle when the two fascicles are aligned, calling to mind the formation in which shells are arranged when the game is played.

The great care with which this design was realized, particularly given that it appeared in a place as seemingly unimportant as a back cover and in a period when the overwhelming majority of such covers were plain black, indicates just how important Tanehiko, Utagawa Kunisada, and especially the man who controlled the purse strings, the publisher Tsuruya Kiemon, considered the material form of *Inaka Genji*. They wanted this book to be, first and foremost, a stylish publication. The extent to which this strategy succeeded is suggested by later imitations: not only did patterned back covers become a standard feature of *gōkan* toward the end of the Edo period, but the clamshell pattern itself was directly copied. This is hardly surprising, to be sure, in *Inaka Genji* sequels such as *Ashikaga Silk: Hand-Dyed Purple* and *Traces in a Rustic Visage* (*Sono yukari hina no omokage*, 1847–1866)—though in the latter *gōkan*, rather disappointingly, the clamshells are not arranged in a circle—but I have seen the pattern even on books completely unrelated to *Genji monogatari*, including, for instance, Bakin's *The Legend of Kinjūrō and Uoko in the Current Style* (*Fūzoku kin'gyoden*, 1829–1833), a *gōkan* based on the early Qing novel *The Legend of Jin Zhong, Cuiyun, and Cuiqiao* (*Jin Yun Qiao zhuan*).[59]

Since *Inaka Genji*'s back covers were so novel and left such a lasting impression, it is perhaps only to be expected that its front covers would be even more striking. This was indeed the case. Risky though it is to generalize when speaking of a genre as varied as the *gōkan*, we can say that as a rule earlier covers exploited to the hilt the possibilities afforded by full-color printing: if a pair of covers showed two characters standing, the background would likely be filled in with a landscape or with a solid field or gradated swaths of color. *Inaka Genji* dispensed altogether with backgrounds, opting instead for a simple, elegant white that was given the texture of crepe, in the best printings, by pressing the paper onto an uninked block—an embossing technique known as "empty printing" (*karazuri*). The white field was flecked with specks of yellow and blue or gray that call to mind the powdered gold and silver foil (*sunago*) often used as decoration in Japanese art, including the covers of classical works such as *Genji monogatari*. The covers of the two fascicles of chapter 1, which show Murasaki Shikibu and Ofuji, the putative author of *Inaka Genji*, are representative (figure 11). The attraction this new style exercised is indicated by the fact that Kunisada would later reproduce many of *Inaka Genji*'s covers almost exactly in his major series of prints, *Lingering Feelings for a Later Genji Collection* (*Genji goshū yojō*, ca. 1857–1861).

And this is just the start. If we broaden our purview to include not just reproductions of *Inaka Genji*'s covers but also the covers for other *gōkan*, we find that echoes of the masterpiece's style reverberated to an almost mind-numbing degree through the whole subsequent history of the genre. It is hardly an exaggeration to say that installments of one or more books with covers in the *Inaka Genji* style, sometimes several at once, appeared every year from the mid-1830s to the late 1870s—though few used textured covers, and many retreated from the simplicity of

Figure 11 The covers by Utagawa Kunisada for chapter 1 of *Inaka Genji*. (Courtesy of National Diet Library)

Figure 12 The covers of chapter 1 of *Edo murasaki fuji no hanatori*, done in the *Inaka Genji* style and featuring a figure with Mitsuuji's characteristic hairstyle. (Courtesy of Waseda University Library, Tokyo)

Inaka Genji's white, filling the background with designs. One of the earliest, *Edo Purple: The Bird in the Wisteria* (*Edo murasaki fuji no hanatori*, 1834), not only mimics the style, but also features a character, Saeda Hisaaki, whose topknot is split in Mitsuuji's trademark "shrimp-tail whisk" (*ebichasen*), invented by Kunisada for chapter 7, published two years earlier (figure 12).⁶⁰ The woman on the right, Asagao, is dressed in a manner reminiscent of that of Ofuji.

Edo Purple is somewhat unusual, though hardly unique, in the extent to which it draws on *Inaka Genji*: its *kuchi-e* is based on one in *Inaka Genji*'s opening chapter, and its first lines echo those of *Inaka Genji*, as do the opening scenes, in which Hanafuji—a combination, perhaps, of *Inaka Genji*'s Hanagiri and Fuji no Kata—plots with her attendants in the garden of Hisaaki's estate in Kyoto, referred to as the "Capital of Flowers," as it is in *Inaka Genji*; one of the servants tries to kill Asagao, Hanafuji's rival, in a hallway; and Hisaaki summons both Asagao and Hanafuji in order to interrogate the latter.⁶¹ All these plot elements are drawn directly from *Inaka Genji*. Tellingly, the author, a certain Fūtei Baryū, claimed to have based the work on "the story Murasaki no Shikibu [sic] left, which ranks all kinds of women," but he drew on only *Inaka Genji*; clearly, the pretended link to *Genji monogatari* did not matter, but the real link to *Inaka Genji* did.⁶² Another early instance of a book with covers in the *Inaka Genji* style, *The Tales of Ise in the Modern Manner* (*Imayō Ise monogatari*, 1835–1838), was evidently deemed to have gone too far in imitating *Inaka Genji* in its first two chapters, judging from a note in a letter that Bakin sent to one of his fans in 1835: "It seems a *gōkan* called *Tales of Ise* or something by Tōri Sanjin was a knockoff of *Inaka Genji*. Issue was taken with it, too, for its inappropriate pictures, and I hear the publisher, Izumiya Ichibē, had to expend a good deal of money to have the matter settled."⁶³ The appearance of two such blatant knockoffs in the course of two years indicates how popular *Inaka Genji* was in the mid-1830s; the fact that all six chapters of *The Tales of Ise in the Modern Manner* continued to be published with covers in the *Inaka Genji* style, even after the publisher was taken to task and required to pay damages, suggests how dominant, and how solidly established, the style had become. This trend would only continue, as an 1848 advertisement in *Traces in a Rustic Visage*'s third chapter indicates: in it, Tsuruya Kiemon notes that "ever since [*Inaka Genji* was published], the books we call *gōkan* have all copied its style, and that remains the case to this day."⁶⁴

The most eloquent indication of the allure of the *Inaka Genji* style is perhaps to be found on the covers of a few books published in the 1870s. Kōeidō, which issued *Edo Purple*, had in fact been in the business of mimicking *Inaka Genji* ever since 1830, the year after the first chapter was released, and continued to publish title after title in the same style through the 1850s, 1860s, and 1870s, evidently pausing only in the wake of the Tenpō Reforms of 1841 to 1843, when *Inaka Genji* was banned at least in part as a rebuke to its lavishness. Kōeidō outdid itself during the 1870s, though, when it produced two sets of covers whose compositions were not simply reminiscent of the *Inaka Genji* style, but actually based directly on particular covers. The first set, from the 1872 second chapter of *A Grove-Warbler Lost in the Grove* (*Yabuuguisu yawata shirazu*, 1871-1872), draws on the covers of chapter 22; the second set (figure 14), even more striking, is from the last chapter of *Heavy Makeup and an Everlasting Shimada* (*Atsugeshō mannen shimada*, 1868-1877) and replicates the covers of chapter 38 (figure 13).[65] The artist responsible for the first of these books used the same imitative technique in his covers for *Three Sake Cups for New Year's Day* (*Kesa no haru mitsugumi sakazuki*), a book based on a tale by the storyteller Sanyūtei Enchō that Seiseidō published in 1872. The covers of chapter 1 of this book (figure 15) were also based loosely on those of chapter 38 of *Inaka Genji*, while the cover for the first fascicle of chapter 3 was based on that for the first fascicle of chapter 35 of *Inaka Genji*.

As one final example of the startling manner in which the *Inaka Genji* style could be adapted, consider Kanagaki Robun's (1829-1894) *A Tale of All Nations Illustrated for Children* (*Osana etoki bankokubanashi*, 1861-1862), which also had pictures by Utagawa Yoshitora. The covers of this book—which incorporate all the elements that *Inaka Genji* had pioneered, including not only the placement of the characters against a plain white ground, the flecks of color intended to suggest powdered gold, and the diagonal arrangement of the title's characters in a style known as "scattered writing" (*chirashigaki*), but even the crepe-like texturing of the paper by the *karazuri* embossing technique—depict, in a startlingly incongruous juxtaposition, the citizens of different Western nations, their clothing shaded with lines and cross-hatching intended to suggest that they have been printed not from ordinary woodblocks, but using the exotic technology of lithography. Figure 16 shows the covers of the second chapter, which recounts the early history of the United States. The man on the first cover (*right*) is George Washington; presumably, the woman on the second (*left*) is Martha Washington. It says quite a lot about how powerful the *Inaka Genji* style was, and about how little bearing *Genji monogatari* was thought to have on its innovations, that it could be put to use three decades after its introduction in depicting foreigners like these.

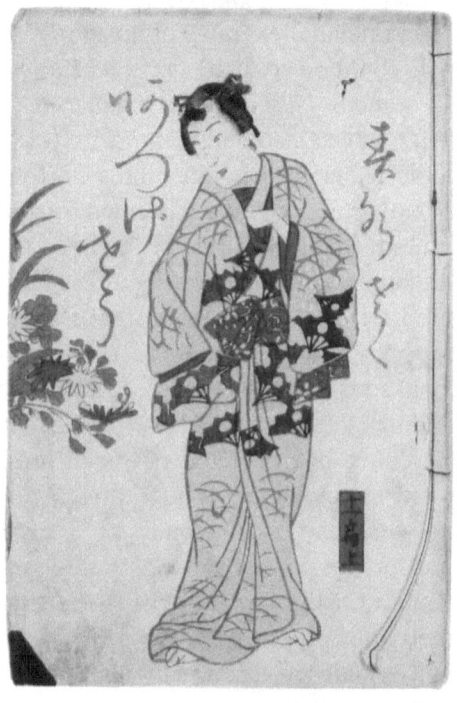

Figure 13 The covers of chapter 38 of *Inaka Genji*. (Courtesy of National Diet Library)

Figure 14 The covers of chapter 11 of *Atsugeshō mannen shimada*, which draw on those of chapter 38 of *Inaka Genji*. (Courtesy of Waseda University Library, Tokyo)

Figure 15 The covers of chapter 1 of *Kesa no haru mitsugumi sakazuki*. The one on the right draws on a cover from chapter 38 of *Inaka Genji*. (Courtesy of Waseda University Library, Tokyo)

Fiction for the Fashionistas

The three covers that were lifted directly from *Inaka Genji* are notable because they reveal both how influential the *Inaka Genji* aesthetic was and for how long—they allow us to gauge the impact of *Inaka Genji*'s innovations on the whole subsequent history of the genre. They also gesture more generally toward one of the modes in which ordinary readers approached *gōkan*. Eiko Kondo has suggested that people would have enjoyed *Inaka Genji* "in much the same way as one nowadays admires photos of interior design and fashion magazines"; upon reflection, one realizes that while three of the characters shown in figures 14 and 15 are posed in essentially the same way as their models in figure 13, so that even the wrinkles in their clothing are alike, the outfits themselves

Figure 16 The covers of chapter 2 of Kanagaki Robun's *Osana etoki bankokubanashi*, done in the *Inaka Genji* style. (Courtesy of Waseda University Library, Tokyo)

are not the same.⁶⁶ Neither is the man's hairstyle in figure 15. The characters have been treated like paper dolls whose clothes and hair can be taken off and changed at will. As it happens, the covers of the first chapters of Tanehiko's *Kantan Travels the Provinces: A Tale* (*Kantan shokoku monogatari*, 1834–1856) play on precisely this kind of attitude toward *gōkan*—this readerly engagement, that is to say, with fashion (figure 17). And in *The Rabbit on the Moon* (*Tamausagi*, 1834?), a *ninjōbon* (book of sentimental fiction) by Tamenaga Shunsui (1790–1843), we find two young women effusing about *Inaka Genji* for this very reason:

> TATSU: Don't you think, Okume, that *With the Script as My Model* and *Inaka Genji* are the best *gōkan*?
> KUME: Well, Tanehiko has always been the best when it comes to *gōkan*.
> TATSU: Actually, just recently, you know, I saw this middle-size book, *The Plum Calendar*, and it sure was good!
> KUME: Oh really? The copy I . . .

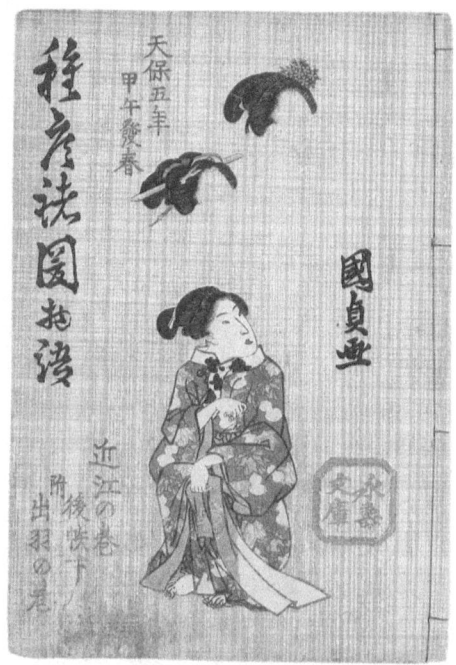 

Figure 17 A cut-out paper doll with her wardrobe on the covers of Ryūtei Tanehiko's *Kantan shokoku monogatari*, "Ōmi no maki," part 2. (Courtesy of Art Research Center, Ritsumeikan University, Kyoto)

TATSU: Yes?

KUME: The copy I saw was just *gorgeously* printed.

TATSU: You know, Okume, you know that girl Ofusa in *The Southeast Garden*? She really looks just like you. Her face, I mean.

KUME: Well her face does, yes, but that Shimada hairdo of hers is just too weird.

TATSU: What! But the hairdos are always pushed up high like that in pictures, don't you think?

KUME: I know, but there are all kinds of wonderful topknots and hairdos in *Inaka Genji*. Come to think of it, just recently this woman hairdresser I know, she was grumbling about that. She said this lady she goes to see all the time, she plopped a copy of *Inaka Genji* down beside her and said, Now I want you to do my hair exactly like *this*. My hairdresser friend didn't know what to do. Oh that Tanehiko, she said, laughing, he just makes my blood boil—why'd he have to go and make a stylish book like that, giving us hairdressers a hard time!

TATSU: It's true, the pictures certainly are well done aren't they?
KUME: You know what my dad says? He says nowadays Kunisada is the greatest *ukiyo-e* artist in all Japan.⁶⁷

Ordinary readers were not likely to leave transcriptions of conversations like this one, of course, so there is no way to confirm that *The Rabbit on the Moon*'s fictional depiction conforms to reality. To the extent that it presents the young women's approach to the book as both reasonable and plausible, however—and in the context there is nothing to suggest that they are being ridiculed or presented ironically—it can at the very least be read as reinforcing a common understanding of how *Inaka Genji* and other *gōkan* were enjoyed.

I noted earlier that *gōkan* sometimes feature advertisements for women's cosmetics; this, too, aligns them with fashion magazines. In chapter 14 of *Inaka Genji*, published in 1835, we encounter a scene in which a woman named Karaginu runs into a servant on the street and the servant tells her, in a less-than-covert instance of covert advertising, that "I'm on my way to pick up some Senjokō, and since Ayanagi says she wants to send some Bigenkō to Mihara, I've got to get some of that, too. Evidently Sakamoto has moved to South Tenmachō, Sanchōme" (figure 18).⁶⁸ Senjokō and Bigenkō were cosmetic products, and Sakamoto was the man who sold them at his store, Sakamotoya, which had indeed recently moved. Tanehiko alludes subtly and brilliantly to this scene in his *kokkeibon* (funnybook) *A Dithering Hokku Contest* (*Tawagoto kuawase*), published in the same year as chapter 14 of *Inaka Genji* with pictures by Utagawa Kuniyoshi. The first page of *A Dithering Hokku Contest* shows a woman sitting and fixing her hair, a few poetry cards spread out before her (figure 19). The writing at the upper right tells us what she is saying: "Hey, if one of the servants is making a trip to Kyōbashi, don't forget to have her pick up some Senjokō. Oh, come to think of it, I hear that Sakamoto's store has moved. It was in that *Inaka Genji* there—could you pass it to me? It's in chapter 14. 'Newly Opened on the West Side of South Tenmachō, Sanchōme.' That would be near Misoya, I guess, that store that sells the hair cords."⁶⁹

This scene in *A Dithering Hokku Contest* appears unremarkable at first glance—the very presence of the advertisement in *Inaka Genji* hints that *gōkan* readers probably did this sort of thing all the time. But it does more than simply mark *gōkan* readers' susceptibility to advertisements; the clever playfulness of Tanehiko's allusion to his own work becomes evident only when we consider the two images side by side. The woman standing at the left on the page from *Inaka Genji* is Karaginu. Her hair is done up in the same style as that of the woman in *A Dithering Hokku Contest*, and the pattern on her kimono appears to be a simplified version of the other woman's as well—a suspicion confirmed by the *kuchi-e* in *Inaka Genji*, in which Karaginu appears, considerably larger, in the same outfit. *A Dithering Hokku Contest* would seem, then, to be offering us an image of Karaginu, asking to see chapter 14 of *Inaka Genji* so that she can refresh her memory not about what she had noticed in the book when she read it, but about what she had heard *inside* it, as one of its characters. This is the sort of subtle gag that only a reader who pays extremely close attention to how characters in a *gōkan* are dressed could be expected to get. Fortunately for Tanehiko, readers of the genre did just that.

Indeed, the gorgeous clothing in *Inaka Genji* would continue to entrance readers long after the fashions themselves faded. We see this, for instance, in Natsume Sōseki's (1867–1916) novel *Autumn Storm (Nowaki*, 1907), when a character attends a concert of Western music for the first time and feels, gazing at the finely dressed women, "as though he were flipping, page after page, through Toyokuni's [Toyokuni III (Kunisada)] *Inaka Genji*, which he had seen as a child."[70] Sōseki was born twenty-five years after the last chapter of *Inaka Genji* was published; *Autumn Storm* appeared when Sōseki was fifty. It says something, surely, that even then he could expect readers to understand what he meant.

The Shining Mitsuuji

If clothes make the man, as they say, then style is not only a matter of clothing: characters, too, can be trendy. Mitsuuji, the hero of *Inaka Genji*, was nothing if not de rigueur, as we have seen in the inheritance of his originally unique topknot by characters in books published a few decades later. Andrew Markus has discussed some of the ways in which Mitsuuji's popularity manifested itself, including a startling instance of "costume play": Matsudaira Naritami, who in 1831 became the eighth daimyo of the Tsuyama fief, reportedly loved dressing up as Mitsuuji and reenacting scenes from *Inaka Genji* with members of his household.[71] It will be worth introducing a few additional examples attesting to Mitsuuji's contribution to the success of *Inaka Genji* and to the creation of an image of *Inaka Genji* that had little, if anything, to do with *Genji monogatari*, for to some extent he, more than anything, came to stand for the book.

In 1836 Kunisada, who realized Tanehiko's sketches for *Inaka Genji*, produced a series of prints called *The Fifty-Three Stations of the Tōkaidō*

Figure 18 A page from *Inaka Genji* showing Karaginu, at the left, walking on the street. Her kimono and hairstyle seem to be the same as those of the woman in figure 19. (*NMIG*, chapter 14, 10 *ura*. Courtesy of National Diet Library)

Figure 19 The first page of Ryūtei Tanehiko's *Tawagoto kuawase*, with an illustration by Utagawa Kuniyoshi. The woman is asking someone to hand her chapter 14 of *Inaka Genji* so she can check the address of a cosmetics shop advertised in its pages. (Courtesy of Art Research Center, Ritsumeikan University, Kyoto)

Road (*Tōkaidō gojūsantsugi no uchi*) that concludes in Kyoto, at the end of the road, with a picture of a woman in Heian-style court dress standing with the palace visible behind her (figure 20). While the figure is not identified, she very closely resembles Murasaki Shikibu as she appears on the cover of the first fascicle of chapter 1 of *Inaka Genji* (see figure 11), right down to the pattern on her outermost kimono and the formal cypress fan she holds; it is as if Kunisada has simply rotated the figure 180 degrees.[72] This invocation of Murasaki Shikibu as a metonym for the Heian court and thus for the city of Kyoto is not unexpected. Two decades later, however, Kunisada would collaborate with Utagawa Hiroshige on a series titled *Fifty-Three Stations from Two Brushes* (*Sōhitsu gojūsantsugi*, 1855) that ends up not before the palace, but at the great Third Avenue Bridge, and replaces Murasaki Shikibu with Mitsuuji and his retainer, Korekichi (figure 21). Today it seems surprising that Mitsuuji could be called on to represent Kyoto in this way, but in 1855 he was at least as popular an icon as Murasaki Shikibu, if not more so.

As it happens, 1855 saw the publication of another book with pictures by Kunisada that gives an even better sense of the extent of Mitsuuji's celebrity, and at the same time reveals a certain troubling aspect of his character that he shares with Hikaru Genji. *An Upwardly Mobile Carp and a Waterfall of Pearls* (*Shussegoi taki no shiratama*) was published as a memorial to the kabuki actor Ichikawa Danjūrō VIII (1823–1854), who had suddenly ended his own life at the age of thirty-two the previous year;[73] the work portrays the dead star in his most famous roles. Mitsuuji, whom Danjūrō had played a few years earlier in the Ichimura Theater's hit *A Kimono Pattern with a Genji Design* (*Genji moyō furisode hinagata*, 1851)—one of two kabuki productions to draw on *Inaka Genji* that year, in a rather unusual competition between two theaters using the same material—was chosen to occupy the very first place in the book (figure 22). We see him lavishly dressed with his trademark topknot and the purple cord that ties it—gray here, of course—holding a folding fan decorated with those familiar flecks of gold. The text, too, is flecked with so many puns and associations that any English translation is bound to be dull by comparison:

ASHIKAGA MITSUUJI

Setting aside the morality of his actions, he is without doubt the greatest gallant of any age past or present. Old and young alike are drawn to him, dote on him, with all their hearts: one need not be an Uji firefly to feel one's body burn with this heartfelt longing. A jewel that glows in the night, the Shining Lord, stretching them out, everywhere, in the country as in the capital, extended just like Genji clouds, catching the light. Even the fabled elixir of immortality the First Emperor sought could hardly have promoted such youthfulness. Here, indeed—ten times over the rank of the pine, whose color remains unchanged for so many millennia, and still his greatness is not exhausted—is a man forever young.[74]

The prose is so concertedly elliptical that it is difficult to decide how much is being said, but the general import is clear: Mitsuuji sleeps around. His behavior may not be entirely admirable, but women everywhere fall for him and get "stretched out"—in Japanese, the verb is *hikihaeru*, which is ordinarily used in talking about cloth and so on but obviously has a different connotation here. The phrase "the rank of the pine" (*matsu no kurai*) in the last sentence is likewise a commonly occurring term for the highest rank of courtesan, the *tayū*.[75] Bearing this in mind, and noticing that the phrase translated here as "ten times over" (*tokaeri mo kasanete*) contains *nete*, from *neru* (to sleep), we arrive at an erotic reading that seems to be the only one that makes any sense in the context: the youthful Mitsuuji is so virile that he can sleep with a courtesan—*Inaka Genji*'s Akogi, played by Fujikawa Hanatomo in *A Kimono Pattern with a Genji Design*—ten times in a row and still be raring to go.

This description of Mitsuuji might seem, on the surface—or rather, just beneath the surface, where the innuendoes pool—a bit overripe, especially since this book was issued as a memorial to the dead Danjūrō. But from a certain perspective, there is something profoundly touching in its insistent eroticism: Mitsuuji is invoked, after all, along with images of youth, popularity, virility, permanence, and longevity, precisely because his character overlaps so perfectly with the image of the actor who played him, now dead by his own hand. Danjūrō VIII was known for his good looks and refinement and was phenomenally popular with women in particular, as evinced by prints issued in the wake of his suicide that show him, or pictures of him, encircled by grieving female fans.[76] If the eroticism carries an elegiac undertone, though, it is due entirely to Danjūrō—Mitsuuji is characterized by eroticism, plain and simple. I remain uncertain whether another possible string of puns in the text, which would make "a jewel that glows in the night, the Shining Lord" (*yakō no tama no Hikaru Genji*) mean something like "the Shining Lord, with family jewels that glow in the night," was really meant to be there or not, but if it was, Mitsuuji's youthful ardor is entirely to blame.

Figure 20 The last print in Utagawa Kunisada's series *Tōkaidō gojūsantsugi no uchi*. A woman resembling Murasaki Shikibu as she is depicted on the cover of chapter 1 of *Inaka Genji* (see figure 11, *right*) stands with the palace in Kyoto behind her. (© Trustees of the British Museum)

Figure 21 The last print in the series *Sōhitsu gojūsantsugi*. Mitsuuji and Korekichi stand in front of the Third Avenue Bridge. (Courtesy of National Diet Library)

I noted earlier that *Inaka Genji* was banned during the Tenpō Reforms at least in part because the authorities considered it too lavish. The book's overt eroticism—the image of profligacy that Mitsuuji so attractively embodied—was surely another factor. Although it is easy to overlook this today, *Inaka Genji* was unusually bold: the very first *kuchi-e* depicting characters from the book, a picture of the shogun Ashikaga Yoshimasa and his concubine Hanagiri, shows the couple fresh from bed, Hanagiri fixing up her hair, and has two captions: the first from *Genji monogatari*—"Sometimes, after sleeping late, he would keep her with him"—and the second from Bai Juyi's (772–846) "Chang hen ge" (Song of Everlasting Pain): "And the nights of spring seemed all too short, / the sun would too soon rise."[77] The reader is left to imagine what the two might have been doing that kept them up so late the previous night. And, indeed, *Inaka Genji* is seldom even this oblique: there is an extraordinary number of pictures of Mitsuuji in bed, often with a woman. One of three such pictures in chapter 6—admittedly, he is sick in one of them—shows him inviting Kotonoha under the covers (figure 23). The text does not even touch on this dalliance, telling us only that Mitsuuji has entrusted Kotonoha with a poem for Kodama, the grandmother of Murasaki—a girl he hopes to take under his wing and raise to be his mistress.[78]

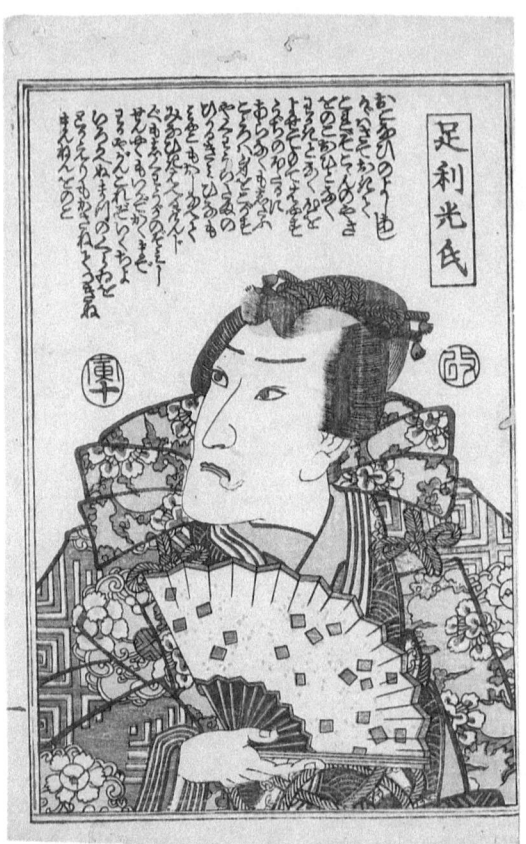

Figure 22 Mitsuuji, as played by Ichikawa Danjūrō VIII. (*Shussegoi taki no shiratama*, fascicle 1, 1 *omote*. Courtesy of Art Research Center, Ritsumeikan University, Kyoto)

Mitsuuji's erotic energies were a defining element of his celebrity, or perhaps his notoriety, and for some readers, at least, this contributed greatly to *Inaka Genji*'s appeal. This is evident in Mitsuuji's appearance in any number of the erotic works known as "spring books" (*shunpon*).

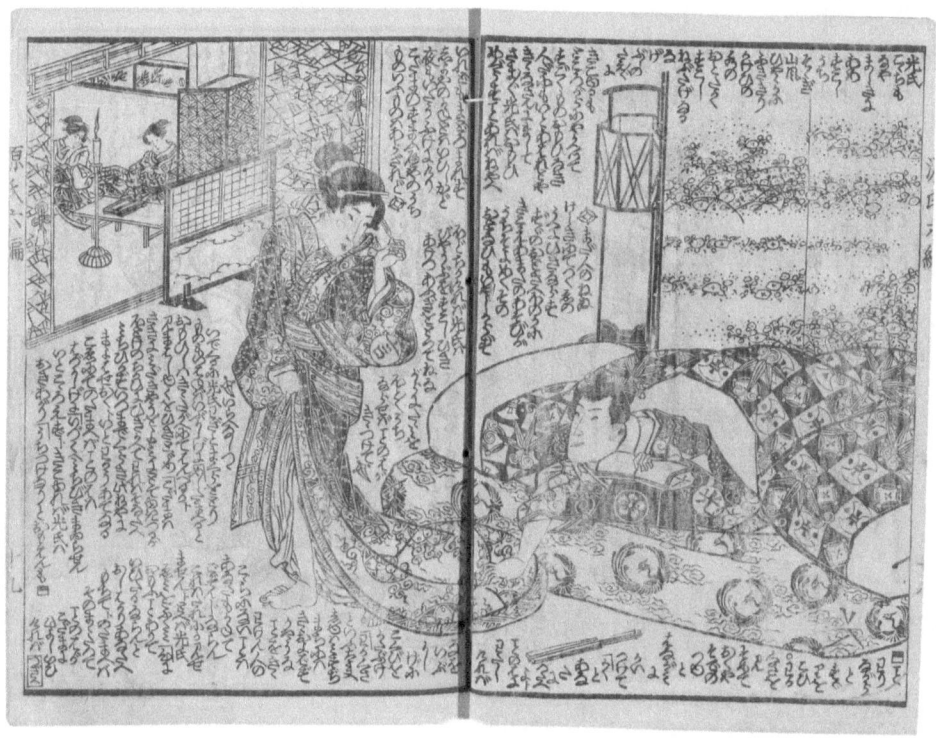

Figure 23 Mitsuuji lures Kotonoha into bed. (*NMIG*, chapter 6, 18 *ura*–19 *omote*. Courtesy of National Diet Library)

The notion that Mitsuuji might have "glowing family jewels," as he would if that pun in *An Upwardly Mobile Carp and a Waterfall of Pearls* is more than just a coincidence, seems less improbable when we find him unveiling "his glistening, shining thing" (*tsuyatsuya to hikaribamitaru ichimotsu*) in one of several explicit spin-offs on *Inaka Genji* that Tanehiko either wrote himself or was at least involved with.[79] But perhaps the most telling indication of the titillating effect that Mitsuuji's busy sex life may have had is found in a portrayal of two of the book's fans that has little in common with the back-and-forth between Okume and Otatsu in *The Rabbit on the Moon*. The picture appears in *A Two-Sided Leaf* (*Konotegashiwa*), an erotic work by Hanagasa Bunkyō with illustrations by Keisai Eisen. This book opens with two pictures featuring a man with Mitsuuji's topknot; the scene relevant here shows a young man and woman grappling (figure 24). Lying on the floor beside them, their covers clearly visible, are the two fascicles of chapter 16 of *Inaka Genji*, newly published

Figure 24 In an illustration by Keisai Eisen, an excited boy lunges at his companion, in apparent confirmation of concern that *Inaka Genji* and books like it would encourage lascivious behavior. (Hanagasa Bunkyō, *Konotegashiwa*, book 2, 2 *ura*–3 *omote*. Courtesy of Ebi Collection, Art Research Center database, Ritsumeikan University, Kyoto)

in 1835, the year before *A Two-Sided Leaf*—and, coincidentally, the same year as *A Dithering Hokku Contest*. The second fascicle has been left open, turned down in mid-read.

This is the sort of thing that helps one understand why *Inaka Genji* not only was banned in 1842 but, as we will see in the third chapter of this book, was first censored and then banned in 1910 and then censored again in 1927 and 1928. And it gets worse, because the characters speak:

"Hey, Oen, how about trying a Mitsuuji, huh? Yow, what are you doing!—hold still. I'm going to teach you something nice, all right? Oh, you're so cute I can't stand it—you're the spitting image of Murasaki in *Inaka Genji*, you know. Shhhhh, be quiet. Wow, is my heart thumping." "Excuse me, you stop that! I don't *want* to. Besides, I hate that Mitsuuji—the big flirt. No, wait, I don't know about this kind of thing, really, what if my mom walks in, she'll find out, and—hey, I'm telling you to stop, will you stop? I'm serious, I'm going to shout! Excuse *me,* you stop that right now!"[80]

One could argue that until shortly before, this teenage couple had been admiring the cleverness with which *Inaka Genji* parodied *Genji monogatari*, and that when the young man endeavors to "try a Mitsuuji" he is really only trying, third-hand, to be Genji. If so, his fancy is subtle indeed. On the surface, at least, that does not seem to be how he, or the young woman with whom he was enjoying the book, appreciated *Inaka Genji*.

The Splendor of Hybridity

When a man gives the celebrated courtesan Otama a *gōkan* in Tōri Sanjin's *sharebon* (book of wit and fashion) *The Legend of Tamagiku, Unexpurgated: A Mirror of the Pleasure Quarters* (*Tamagiku zenden sato kagami,* 1822), she knows exactly what to do with it: "Oh, thank you so much! she said, accepting the booklets from him; then, looking thrilled, she flipped rapidly through to the end of each one, taking in nothing but the pictures."[81] This, evidently, was the procedure. And this, presumably, is how *Inaka Genji* was generally enjoyed: before it was an adaptation of *Genji monogatari*, it was a breathtaking, pathbreaking, luxurious amalgam of eye-catching book design, high fashion, and daring; it was something you just had to see.

So far, we have been approaching *Inaka Genji* from this perspective, in much the same way that Otama would have, focusing on various largely visual elements of the *gōkan* that contributed to its popularity both directly and, through their circulation, independently of the book. But, of course, *Inaka Genji* was not only marvelous to look at, but also an exciting and captivating read, both because of its action-packed plot and because of the exhilarating manner in which it synthesized a diverse array of textual and pictorial elements, of which *Genji monogatari* was only the most famous and important. A haiku by the modern poet Katō Ikuya gives a sense of how *Inaka Genji* drew readers in, portraying it as a literal page-turner, nicely counterbalancing the image of Otama: "Evening chill: flipping so fast through *Inaka Genji*" (*yoizamu ya Inaka Genji no te no hayasa*).[82]

In the remainder of this chapter, I will turn from *Inaka Genji*'s visual elements to issues relating to its text, trying to show how it could be such a page-turner yet at the same time engage so closely with the text of *Genji monogatari*—much more closely, ironically enough, than even those who claim that *Inaka Genji* was read as a parody have recognized. I will touch, too, on Tanehiko's relationship to *Genji monogatari* and on the reasons why the extent of his reworking of the classical text has gone largely unnoticed. Altogether, this will clarify how *Inaka Genji* managed to induce ordinary readers to start caring about *Genji monogatari*'s canonicity, and thus to begin reading Tanehiko's work not only as the most sophisticated and stylish *gōkan* ever, but also as a replacement of *Genji monogatari*.

Briefly, the plot of *Inaka Genji* centers on Ashikaga Mitsuuji, the second son of Ashikaga Yoshimasa (1436–1490), the eighth of the historical Muromachi shoguns—though his name is written with a different graph in *Inaka Genji*. Mitsuuji's mother, Hanagiri, one of Yoshimasa's relatively low-ranking wives, dies after being abused by other members of the shogunal household; Yoshimasa, distraught, considers making Mitsuuji his successor. In order to prevent this departure from the dictates of primogeniture, and to recover a stolen sword, mirror, and poem slip—three objects that embody the authority of Ashikaga rule and thus must be recovered to preserve the stability of the realm—Mitsuuji starts traveling around, acting the part of a playboy, and gathering information about the stolen treasures from women he meets. Yoshimasa, disappointed with his son's profligacy, finally names his first son, Yoshihisa, as his successor. Mitsuuji subsequently engineers the defeat of Yamana Sōzen, the evil figure behind most of the mishaps that occur in the work, including the theft of the treasures. Along the way, there are any number of murders, faked murders, secrets, intrigues, attempted kidnappings, swordfights, supernatural incidents, gruesome suicides, foiled attacks by masked intruders, attempted poisonings, pretended amours, instructive cases of karmic retribution, spirit possessions, intercepted letters, and cases of identity swapping.

Inaka Genji is invariably described as an adaptation of *Genji monogatari*, but even this all-too-brief recounting of its plot should suggest that the center of its interest lies elsewhere. Indeed, the frame of the work—what in kabuki terminology is called the *sekai* (world)—is Higashiyama, a cultural and historical moment named after the district in the east of Kyoto in which Ashikaga Yoshimasa constructed the temple commonly known as Ginkaku-ji (Temple of the Silver Pavilion), to which he retired in 1473. Many of the characters in *Inaka Genji* are loosely based on historical figures, including Yoshimasa and his son Yoshihisa; the evil Yamana Sōzen (Mochitoyo); and Yoshimasa's cunning wife, Toyoshi no Mae, whose historically inaccurate name is written using two characters: 富徽, one borrowed from that of the historical Yoshimasa's actual wife, Hino Tomiko 日野富子, and the other from the Kokiden Consort 弘徽殿女御 in Genji monogatari.

Tanehiko's disciple Ryūtei Senka explained that *Inaka Genji* used the late medieval military tale *Chronicle of the Ōnin War* (*Ōninki*) as its *sekai*, implying that *Genji monogatari* was incorporated as a *shukō*—another kabuki term denoting an innovative take on a common plot or setting, or the incorporation of a new and unexpected element into a familiar framework or cast of characters.[83] In his preface to chapter 15 of *Inaka Genji*, Tanehiko describes "this *Genji*" in similar terms, though he reverses the *sekai* and *shukō*, making *Chronicle of the Ōnin War* the element incorporated into the world of *Genji monogatari*: "Seven years have passed since I first pieced this garment together, patching in *Chronicle of the Ōnin War* where it wouldn't show since it doesn't match the soft, fake purple [*nise murasaki*] exterior."[84] A note in Tanehiko's first draft for one of the chapters also suggests that Tanehiko regarded *Genji monogatari* as a *sekai*: "Because the tale won't fit well into a modern picture book, I have borrowed only the general outline of the story; the finer points have been based on *jōruri*."[85] However the relationship between these two source texts is conceptualized, the view of *Inaka Genji* as a hybrid concoction, half *Chronicle of the Ōnin War* and half *Genji monogatari*, offers a useful corrective to the standard, oversimplified conception of the work as an adaptation of *Genji monogatari*, even on the level of plot.[86]

The canonical weight of *Genji monogatari* has burdened modern readers with an extremely powerful sense that *Inaka Genji* is best read, or perhaps can only be read, as an adaptation of that classic. One effect of this tunnel vision has been to prevent any consideration whatsoever of the *Chronicle of the Ōnin War* connection. I will not be able to redress this imbalance here, but I can at least indicate the nature of the problem by pointing to *Inaka Genji*'s depiction of Yamana Sōzen. He appears as a largely bald man with bushy eyebrows, long sideburns, and a mustache that bristles at the edges of his mouth (see figure 56). Where, one might ask, did this vision of the villain come from? Various prints I have seen suggest that until the publication of *Inaka Genji*, Yamana Sōzen had been presented on the kabuki stage with long hair, either white or black, swept back over his forehead in a hairstyle known as *sōhatsu*.[87] Ichikawa Gentazaemon is shown playing him in this style in Kunisada's series of prints *Portraits of Actors Past and Present* (*Kokon haiyū nigao taizen*, 1862–1863) (figure 25). Clearly, then, Tanehiko was not simply referencing some generally accepted theatrical image of the character, part of a familiar *sekai*. As it happens, Yamana Sōzen is shown in a style strikingly similar to his

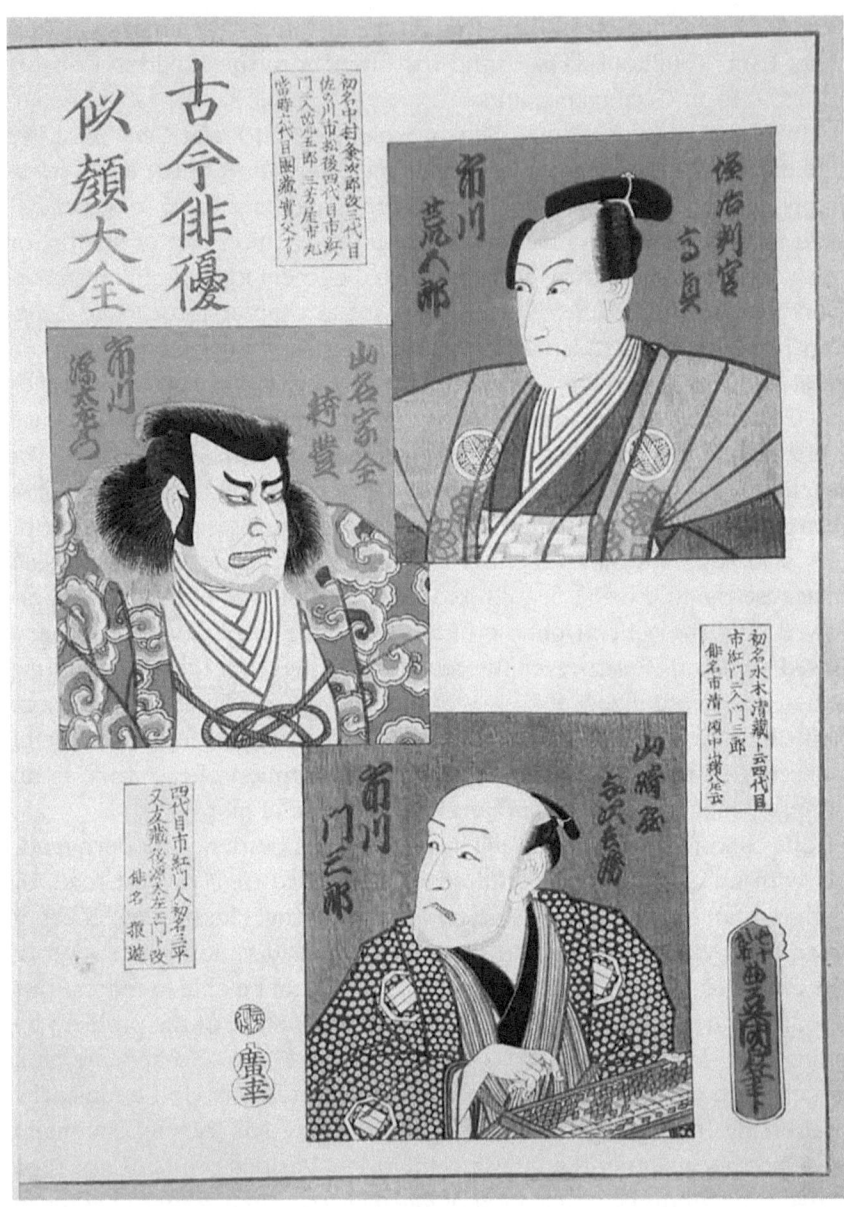

Figure 25 Yamana Sōzen, played by Ichikawa Gentazaemon (*left*), as he was depicted on the kabuki stage before the publication of *Inaka Genji*. (Utagawa Kunisada, *Kokon haiyū nigaoe taizen*. Courtesy of National Diet Library)

Figure 26 Yamana Sōzen (*left*), in an illustration by Keisai Eisen. (Takai Ranzan, *Ehon Ōninki*, book 1, fascicle 1, 9 omote. Courtesy of Art Research Center, Ritsumeikan University, Kyoto)

Inaka Genji appearance in *An Illustrated Chronicle of the Ōnin War* (*Ehon Ōninki*, 1825), a *yomihon* by Takai Ranzan with illustrations by Keisai Eisen (figure 26). This is not to say that this book necessarily inspired Tanehiko; the point, rather, is that a single-minded fixation on *Genji monogatari* has kept anyone from thinking to ask what did.

It is also worth emphasizing how many other epochs in addition to the Higashiyama period and how many other texts beyond *Chronicle of the Ōnin War* and *Genji monogatari* Tanehiko incorporated into *Inaka Genji*. Allusions to the Heian period are scarce but not entirely absent. The first *kuchi-e* in chapter 1, for instance, shows Murasaki Shikibu holed up in Ishiyama Temple preparing to write *Genji monogatari*; she is dressed in the Heian aristocratic style and sits on a Heian-style "raised tatami" (*agedatami*) on an otherwise bare wooden floor (see figure 97). Meanwhile, references to the late medieval period and the first century or so of the early modern period abound. Among these are quotations from, allusions to, or pictorial reproductions of "companion books" (*otogizōshi*), early *kusazōshi*, *nō* plays, puppet plays by Chikamatsu Monzaemon, popular songs, kabuki plots and performative conventions, *kōwakamai* performances, dancing in the Shigayama style, old proverbs, linked verse, poetic texts, and *haikai* poetry, as well as pictures by Hishikawa Moronobu and Nonoguchi Ryūho, pictures in the style of Torii Kiyonobu, and screens by Ogata Kōrin. There is also, of course, an abundance of elements from Tanehiko's own time, including such sophisticated, stylish items as a sizable aquarium, a mechanical fountain, "a kind of drinking vessel known [in Dutch] as a 'kop' [cup] or something," and furnishings imported from the Netherlands, in addition to various made-up props, including one that Tanehiko describes in a note to Kunisada as "another of the usual bogus carriages that don't exist today."[88] As if all this weren't enough, certain episodes have been recycled from Tanehiko's earlier fiction.[89]

Clearly Tanehiko, and presumably his readers as well, reveled in this profusion of references, in the pleasurable dissonance created by the interplay of so many different historical moments, and in the conspicuously fabricated texture of the patchwork narrative space thus called into being. Indeed, he occasionally makes explicit reference to the conflicted, made-up character of this mishmash world. Tanehiko's preface to chapter 16 is so playfully provocative that it is worth quoting in full:

> There were no plum trees in *Songs of Chu*, there were no chrysanthemums in *The Collection of Ten Thousand Leaves*, and there were no prefaces in old *kusazōshi*. There aren't any mosquito nets in *Genji*; neither is there male–male love. Unless hot water counts, there was nothing back then but prayers to do what we do by taking medicine. And even more absent than any of these things are the plot twists of a picture book. As I noted in the preface to chapter 2, I first sketched out a story that would take me as far as "Beneath the Autumn Leaves"; now, contrary to all expectations, I realize that I have paddled my boat all the way to the shores of "Suma" and "Akashi," and since it never occurred to me to prepare for this eventuality, I find myself at a loss, with no wind in my sails, the towrope gone slack. The same thing has happened with the pictures I draw. I totally exhausted my ingenuity just trying to settle on shapes for lamps and screens and armrests; now I have even drawn in "fulling block pillows" and "shared-wing mats," both undreamt-of in the Higashiyama period. And since a sleeping chamber in summer would look rather bleak without a mosquito net, everything in plain view, for the first time I have gone and drawn in a net of hanging cur-

tains in place of the sets of standing curtains found in *Genji*. Best, I thought, to jot out a note explaining myself in this preface-like thing that wouldn't have existed in *kusazōshi* of old.⁹⁰

Behind the standard modest pose, one senses a creative intellect that delights in complicating its awareness of its own fictional inclinations, highlighting even the historicity of the form and presence of the preface itself, which might otherwise seem self-evident. Tanehiko does not feel compelled to "explain himself" in this manner only in his prefaces, either: early in chapter 1, for example, he inserts a note under the feet of a character named Hirugao that reads, "No name is provided in *Genji* for the Kōryōden Intimate. For the time being, then, I will call her Hirugao. I chose this name because it doesn't appear in *Genji*."⁹¹ Later in the same chapter we find, "A note from the author: while I wrote Hirugao into the story as a counterpart to the Kōryōden Intimate, her murder by an unknown intruder is a fabrication all my own."⁹²

Time and again, Tanehiko calls attention to the mixed-up, factually inaccurate, not entirely possible, anachronistic hybridity of the work that he is composing. Indeed, he does the same thing even with his prose style itself, which he describes in his preface to chapter 2—by means of an erudite reworking of a brief exchange in the "Aoi" (Heart-to-Heart) chapter of *Genji monogatari* whose interpretation was long considered one of the book's "three secrets"—as "kabuki, puppet play, and tale, all three rolled into one" (*kabuki, ayatsuri, monogatari, mitsu ga hitotsu ni nattaru*).⁹³ *Inaka Genji* succeeds as well as it does in creating a world of its own not because of the approach it takes toward *Genji monogatari*, but because it does so much, and so well, with so much.

Pedagogical Predilections

At the same time, it is important to note that in the process of marking the points where *Inaka Genji* departs from the facts, Tanehiko also educates his readers, offering tidbits of information few among the *gōkan*'s core audience could be expected to know, often about prestigious topics and works in which they probably ought to be interested. He does this, what is more, in a fashion that can only be described as fun. The first sentence of his preface to chapter 16, which starts with *Songs of Chu* (*Chuci*, ca. third to second century B.C.E.) and *The Collection of Ten Thousand Leaves* (*Man'yōshū*, eighth century) and ends with old *kusazōshi*, may not provide such valuable information, but its witty intermingling of trivia from the linked universes of elegant and vulgar literature is at least nominally instructive. And I would suggest that this technique reproduces in miniature the whole of *Inaka Genji*: the triumvirate of *Songs of Chu*, *The Collection of Ten Thousand Leaves*, and old *kusazōshi* parallels that of kabuki, puppet play, and tale. The dramatic prose style of *Inaka Genji*, modeled on kabuki and *jōruri*, offers a painless introduction to *Genji monogatari*.[94]

This, as Yoda Gakkai explained in the passage I quoted toward the beginning of this chapter, is where *Inaka Genji* derived whatever force it may have had as a pedagogical tool, a vehicle of classic cultivation: if Tanehiko "was inspired by a somewhat meddlesome, old-womanish desire to make women and children feel curious to read the original book," he was also careful to keep "the elegant and the colloquial from clashing, employing a diction that felt natural and didn't grate on the ear, that was pleasant to read and had an elevated tone, and was easy to understand."[95] The elements that Tanehiko worked into his text from *Genji monogatari* do not stand out. The truth is that the book's thoroughly hybrid texture masks startlingly frequent, startlingly lengthy passages of word-for-word translation or even, on occasion, direct quotation from *Genji monogatari*, in the form of *Kogetsushō*, that appear in even the earliest chapters. Very little of the actual classical text of *Genji monogatari* is incorporated into the first fascicle of chapter 1, but a certain amount of translation into the early modern idiom of Tanehiko's age begins to trickle in from the second, particularly in the sections that deal with the continuing ill health and ultimate death of Hanagiri, Mitsuuji's abused mother; the reaction of Hanagiri's mother to her daughter's death; and, above all, the visit that Sugibae, a former maidservant of Hanagiri's, makes to the bereaved mother. The fourth chapter incorporates an astonishing amount of material from *Genji monogatari*, including a stretch of text that blends word-for-word quotation, close translation, not-so-close translation, and completely new invention that runs on for eight double-sided pages in the original woodblock-printed book, or about twelve in a modern typeset edition—almost half the chapter.[96] Tanehiko sometimes changes the order of clauses or otherwise rearranges sentences from *Genji monogatari* in a fashion somewhat reminiscent of Nonoguchi Ryūhō's *Genji in Ten Volumes* (*Jūjō Genji*, 1661), but for a reader closely acquainted with the Heian text, certain passages are still likely to produce an uncanny sense of linguistic déjà vu. Here, for instance, is a passage from the "Utsusemi" (The Cicada Shell) chapter in Royall Tyler's translation of *Genji monoga-*

tari, followed by a passage from *Inaka Genji* in mine. Transcriptions of the corresponding sections from *Kogetsushō* and *Inaka Genji* appear below them.

Ah, thought Genji, I want a look at her sitting across from her partner. He slipped in between the blinds. They had not yet secured the shutter through which the boy had entered, and a gap remained. Genji went to it and peered in toward the west. The nearer end of a screen was folded, and the heat probably explained why a curtain that should have blocked his view had been draped over its stand, so that he could see quite well.

They had the lamp beside them. His first thought was that the one by the central pillar of the chamber, facing away from him, must be she. She seemed to have on two layered, silk twill shifts of a deep red-violet, with some sort of garment over them. Her slender head and slight build left no marked impression, and she was keeping her partner from getting any view of her face. She was also doing her best to conceal her strikingly slim hands.[97]

Ah, thought Mitsuuji, who could just barely make out what Natsuno was saying, I want a look at her playing go. They had not yet secured the little door by the gate, so he slipped secretly inside. Peering into the far room through the blinds that hung over the fence, he saw that the screen had been folded and placed to one side.

They had the lamp beside them. His first thought was that the one leaning against the pillar must be she. She seemed to have on a light blue, single-layered kimono with a red and white lining, the front of which she had pulled tightly together so that she was well covered. Her restrained hairdo and strikingly slim hands struck him as being perfectly ordinary, and she was keeping her partner from getting a look at her face, bending her head down and tucking her chin into the top of her kimono.[98]

さてむかひゐたらんをみバやとおもひて・やをらあゆミいで丶・すだれのはざまにいり給ぬ・このいりつるかうしはまださ丶ねば・ひまミゆるによりて・にしざまにみとをし給へば・このきハにたてたる屏風も・はしのかた・をしたゝまれたるに・まぎるべき木丁なとも・あつければにやうちかけて・いとよくみいれらる・火ちかうともしたり・もやのなかばしらにそばめる人や・わがこゝろかくるとまづめとゞめ給へバ・こきあやのひとへがさねなめり・なにゝかあらんうへにきて・かしらつきほそやかにちいさき人の・も

のげなきすがたぞしたる・かほなどハさしむかひたらん人などにも・わざと
みゆまじうもてなしたり・てつきやせやせとして・いたうひきかくしためり[99]

ミつうぢハ今なつのがいひつることをほのかにきゝごをうつさまを見ばや
とおぼしきりどハそのまゝさゝざれバやをらうちにしのびいりへいにかけた
るすだれよりかなたのざしきを見とをせばびやうぶもかたへにおしたゝみ
火をちかうともしたりはしらのかたによりそふハかの人ならんとよく見るに
みづいろのかたびらならんこうばいねりのうらつけしをまへふかくうちあ
はせかみのかゝりもはでやかならず手ハやせやせとすがたかたちじんぢや
うにしてさしむかふ人にもかほハつましげにあぎとをえりにさしいれてうつ
ぶきがちにもてなしたり[100]

Any number of similar passages occur in chapters 5, 6, 7, and 8. And yet ever since Yamaguchi Takeshi (1884–1932) proposed in 1928 that *Inaka Genji* could be divided into three sections by considering the chapters in terms of "their relationship to the original text of *Genji monogatari*," it has generally been accepted that the work starts in a place quite distant from *Genji monogatari* and gradually inches toward it. It is Yamaguchi's suggestion that

> at first, Tanehiko actually wanted to keep his distance from the original text. But somewhere around chapter 10, he appears to have changed his mind, deciding that perhaps it was not necessary to maintain too great a distance. . . . Even after chapter 10, however, his attitude toward the original was not entirely settled. Tanehiko explains that he decided to introduce fewer elements from kabuki, because he feared he was departing too much from *Genji*. Then, as the chapter numbers moved into the twenties, he adopted a new attitude: he began sticking very close to the original, taking his cues from it. . . . Beginning around chapter 30, we see him attempting, within limits, what amounts to a literal translation of *Genji*, though still he weaves what he writes into his larger scheme. This is particularly true from chapter 38 onward, in the sections based on "Makibashira."[101]

No doubt there is a good deal of truth in this, particularly if we consider the work from a relatively abstract perspective, limiting our view to the level of plot. On the more basic level of the writing itself, however, *Genji monogatari* was there from the beginning.[102] Whether or not Tanehiko truly thought he might be able to prod *Inaka Genji*'s readers to tackle *Kogetsushō* or some other text of *Genji monogatari*, he was subtly introducing them to its language.

Misreading Tanehiko

Although he rarely advertises the pedagogical function of his work—indeed, most of the time he keeps it carefully hidden behind a smoke screen of action and wit—Tanehiko does interrupt his story fairly frequently to assure readers that he has remained faithful to *Genji monogatari*. The two notes I quoted earlier about Hirugao's name and bloody death are perfect examples of this: not only does Tanehiko state in both cases that Hirugao is a counterpart of the Kōryōden Intimate, but he even takes the trouble to explain that he chose the name Hirugao "because it doesn't appear in *Genji*." Tanehiko tries to preserve the integrity of *Genji monogatari* by highlighting a distinction between the text and his own reinvention of it. Even as he strives to make *Inaka Genji* appealing as a *gōkan*, in other words, he is attempting to plant in his readers' minds an image of the classic, to create a place in the popular literary field for the imagined original.

The question arises, then, of why more has not been made of the extent to which the actual text of *Genji monogatari* itself has been incorporated into *Inaka Genji*. To a rather surprising degree, this fact has been either overlooked or passed over by scholars who have written about the work. Indeed, I can think of only two exceptions: Suzuki Jūzō casually remarks in one of his less readily available essays, "When one looks into the manner in which the original has been adapted in the first half of *Inaka Genji*, concealed within its standard *kusazōshi* twists and turns, one discovers that to a startling degree various engaging scenes from the original have been woven into it, and that Tanehiko even tries to work in the language of *Genji* itself."[103] Uchimura Katsushi, meanwhile, points out that "it is unexpectedly easy to lose sight of the fact that, in his own way, Tanehiko had thoroughly digested *Genji* when he wrote his work," and then goes on to address this oversight by conducting a rigorous analysis of Tanehiko's use of *Kogetsushō*.[104] The question remains, however: What makes it "startling" to discover so much *Genji monogatari* in *Inaka Genji*, and what accounts for the "unexpected ease" with which its presence is overlooked?

Part of the reason lies, I think, in the extraordinary influence that Kyokutei Bakin's writings, particularly *Modern Fiction: A Classification of Edo Authors* (*Kinsei mononohon Edo sakusha burui*, preface 1834), have exerted on modern interpretations of early modern literary history. During the modern period, Bakin came to be widely regarded as the greatest author of the second half of the early modern period, and *Modern Fiction*—a hefty collection of sketches and generally catty remarks about those authors who did not have the good fortune to be Bakin himself, composed by Bakin under a pseudonym and circulated in manuscript—includes a particularly belittling description of Tanehiko. Bakin emphasized Tanehiko's supposed lack of scholarship, alleging in particular that *Inaka Genji* was secretly based not on a reading of *Genji monogatari* itself, but on the same earlier reworkings of the tale that Shimizu Fukuko and others say *Inaka Genji*'s core readership must have known. Here is the relevant passage, as translated by Andrew Markus in *The Willow in Autumn*:

> As I think of it, there have been numerous works since the Genroku period to reduce *Genji monogatari* into common language, and to make of it a toy for women and children. Among these are *Onna gokyō*, *Akashi monogatari* in 5 fascicles (printed text from 1681); *Fūryū Genji* (old printed text from mid-Genroku); *Wakakusa Genji* (printed text from 1706); *Hinazuru Genji* (sequel to same); *Saru Genji* (printed text from 1718, a veiled account of the Ejima-Ikushima incident). Doubtless there are others. *Inaka Genji* secretly traces its "parentage" back to these.[105]

Scholars who have dealt with *Inaka Genji* tend to stress the role that Bakin's successful *gōkan* versions of vernacular Chinese fictions, including *A Mooring-Rope of Salvation from Kumbhira's Boat* (*Konpirabune rishō no tomozuna*, 1824-1831) and *A Courtesan's Water Margin* (*Keisei suikoden*, 1825-1835)—both begun in the late Bunsei period (1818-1830), just a few years before *Inaka Genji*—may have played in spurring Tanehiko to attempt a rewriting of his own, but of a Japanese rather than a Chinese story.[106] This argument, which is plausible enough given the rivalry that seems to have existed between the writers, particularly on Bakin's side, tends to stress Bakin's scholarly attainments while devaluing Tanehiko's—the very same approach that Bakin himself adopts in *Modern Fiction*.[107] The subtle bias implicit in this stance is apparent, for instance, in Markus's recapitulation of it in his chapter on *Inaka Genji* in *The Willow in Autumn*:

> Unaccustomed to the scale of the new serial *gōkan*, Tanehiko equally lacked the compendious knowledge of Chinese literature, ancient and modern, that Bakin lorded as his unassailable domain. Not to be bested, Tanehiko probably conceived the idea of a long serial *gōkan* based instead on a Japanese classic—a classic, moreover, already partially assimilated and modernized in a series of Genroku period works with which he was familiar.[108]

Markus later suggests that Tanehiko "commanded at least a good layman's knowledge of select passages" of *Genji monogatari* and points out that he cites the tale in his antiquarian miscellanies, but even so one comes away with the impression that ultimately Tanehiko's interest in the Heian classic was more a matter of convenience and accessibility than anything else.[109] And it is but a short step from here to the harsh evaluation of *Inaka Genji* that another pathbreaking scholar of early modern literature, Nakamura Yukihiko (1911-1998), offers in, unsurprisingly, an essay about *Genji monogatari*'s influence on the literature of the period:

> Ultimately all *Genji monogatari* offered Tanehiko was a means of spicing up his work, holding his readers' interest; the tale did not exert any kind of serious influence upon the work's literary character. It must be counted a terrible pity, both for the original text and for the reader, if anyone at the time believed that by reading [*Inaka Genji*] they were able even to imagine what the original was like.[110]

If negative comparisons with Bakin are one reason why Tanehiko's capabilities as a serious reader of *Genji monogatari* have been questioned, Tanehiko's own approach to the classic is another. I have already discussed his tendency, particularly in earlier chapters of the work, to cloak lengthy passages of more or less word-for-word translation in sensational action; perhaps the best place to turn next in continuing this discussion is the "Complete List of Works Cited" (*zenbu insho mokuroku*) that appears in lieu of a preface at the head of *Inaka Genji*'s third chapter.

NISE MURASAKI INAKA GENJI, CHAPTER 3

COMPLETE LIST OF WORKS CITED

An Outline of The Tale of Genji	A Small Mirror of Genji	Genji in Ten Volumes
Genji for Children	A Hairlock Mirror Genji	A Red and White Genji
A Genji for Little Cranes	A Genji for Little Sprouts	A Genji for Young Bamboo
A Tasteful Tale of Genji	A New Tale of the Lady of the Bridge—also known as *Southeast of the Capital*	

The following *jōruri*:

Genji Visits Sixth Avenue	*Kōkiden Beats Her Rival*	*Lady Aoi*
Kōkiden and the Cormorant-Feather Birthing Hut		A few *nō* plays

A Haikai Genji—I read this casually when I was young, and though lately I have been trying to find a copy I haven't yet succeeded[111]

Various interesting points have been made regarding the titles included in this list. Markus notes that only two of the identifiable works, *An Outline of Genji monogatari* (*Genji monogatari teiyō*, 1432) and *A Small Mirror of Genji* (*Genji kokagami*, ca. 1425?), predate the early modern period, and that all the rest "reflect the important contributions by Matsunaga Teitoku and his disciples to the popularization of the Heian classic."[112] Yamaguchi speculates that a phrase in the preface to Miyako no Nishiki's *A Tasteful Tale of Genji* provided the inspiration for the title *Nise Murasaki inaka Genji*, and suggests that "in various ways, these works determined the attitude Tanehiko took in his adaptation."[113]

Suzuki Jūzō agrees that Tanehiko's attitude toward *Genji monogatari* was heavily influenced by the works on the list, points out that an obtrusively antiquated picture in chapter 5 alludes to one by Okumura Masanobu in *A Genji for Little Sprouts* (*Wakakusa Genji*, 1707), and suggests that Tanehiko's expansion of a subtle allusion by Genji to a popular *saibara* lyric in the "Hahakigi" (The Broom Tree) chapter was based on a similar expansion in *Genji monogatari: A Vulgar Interpretation* (*Zokuge Genji monogatari*, 1721), which does not appear on the list of works cited but was reissued in 1738 under the title *A Genji for Little Sprouts*, which does.[114] In a similar vein, Markus's view that Tanehiko made up his mind to rewrite *Genji monogatari* because the Heian tale was "already partially assimilated and modernized in a series of Genroku period works with which he was familiar" is presumably based on the appearance on Tanehiko's list of the "books of the floating world" (*ukiyozōshi*) *A Tasteful Tale of Genji*, *A Genji for Little Sprouts*, *A Genji for Little Cranes* (*Hinazuru Genji*, 1708), *A Red and White Genji* (*Kōhaku Genji monogatari*, preface 1709), and *A New Tale of the Lady of the Bridge* (*Shin Hashihime monogatari*, preface 1714).[115]

I would suggest, however, that despite the insight these observations would seem to offer into *Inaka Genji*'s genesis, the list has been taken a bit too seriously. It is true, of course, that its printed form resembles that of a bibliography in an antiquarian miscellany and thus inspires a certain amount of trust. But just two chapters later, as part of the preface to chapter 5, Tanehiko provides "A Chart of the Characters in *Nise Murasaki inaka Genji*" (figure 27) that is structured just like the one in *Kogetsushō* (figure 28), for example, except that pictures of lumpy clay dolls have been inserted to represent each of the characters.[116] In his explanation of this figure, Tanehiko remarks that "it would be a hassle to make a new chart, and even if I did no one would look at it," and then goes on to protest, "in copying this thing I'm not playing at scholarship, I'm learning from a play, miming what goes on backstage."[117]

A similarly playful attitude can be ascribed, I think, to Tanehiko's "Complete List of Works Cited." The final work on the list, Takebe Ayatari's *A Haikai Genji* (*Haikai Genji*, preface 1749), is one that Tanehiko read "casually" (*nanigokoronaku*) as a boy, with no intention of doing anything with it, and that he had not seen since. In no sense at all, in other words, can it be described as a "work cited." Indeed, Fujita Tokutarō, who tracked down a handwritten copy of *A Haikai Genji*, ultimately concluded that "it is quite clear the *haikai* poems in *Inaka Genji* were not directly influenced by *A Haikai Genji*."[118] In short, the inclusion of Ayatari's long-lost *Genji* at the very end of the list serves much the same purpose—or at least I would argue that it should—as the in-your-face reference at the conclusion of the preface to chapter 16 to "this preface-like thing that wouldn't have existed in *kusazōshi* of old": it unsettles readers, calling for a sudden reevaluation of the information just provided. Here, too, Tanehiko is fooling around with generic conventions. The list of works cited is intended chiefly as a parody.

Steering Clear of *The Moon on the Lake*

This is not, however, all that is going on in this list. Andrew Markus noted that all but two of the identifiable works it includes were published in the early modern period and can be traced back to Matsunaga Teitoku's efforts to popularize *Genji monogatari* and other classics. If this is the case, one might also expect to see Kitamura Kigin's *Kogetsushō* on it: this was, as I explained in the introduction, one of the most widely circulated and influential texts of *Genji monogatari*, and Kigin was a disciple of Teitoku's. Satō Satoru has demonstrated that Tanehiko's citations of *Genji monogatari* in his antiquarian miscellanies were based on Kigin's text and that Tanehiko was reading it closely, not simply skimming the headnotes.[119] The text of *Inaka Genji* is filled with translations and even startlingly lengthy quotations from *Genji monogatari* whose source is, internal evidence

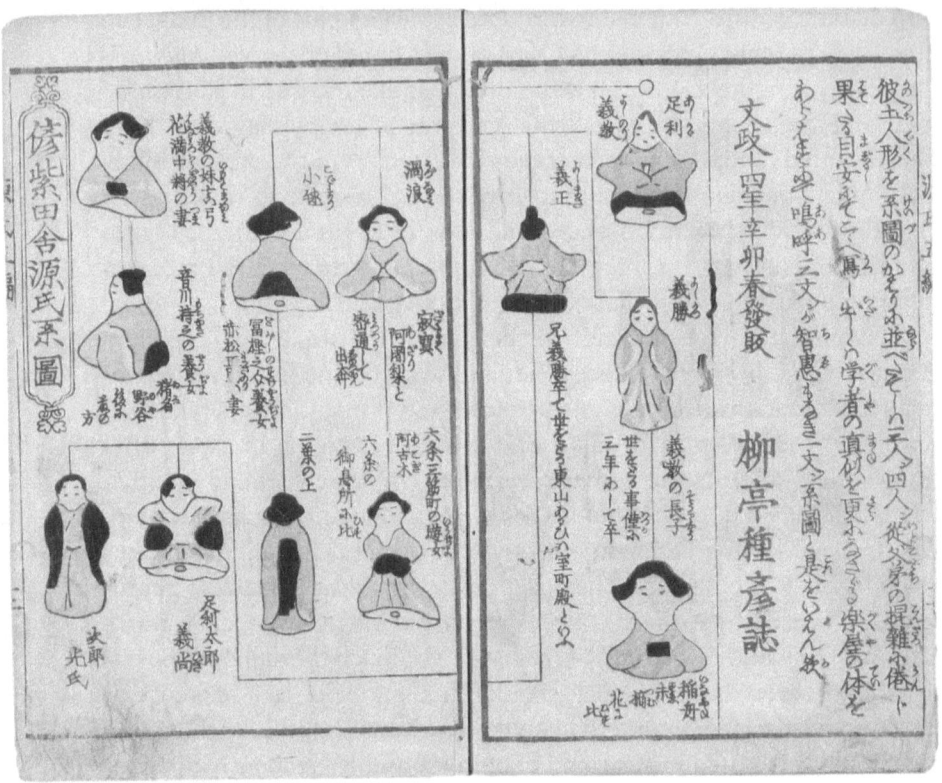

Figure 27 An early printing of Tanehiko's playful genealogy of the characters in *Inaka Genji*, represented by clay dolls. (*NMIG*, chapter 5, 1 *ura*–2 *omote*. Courtesy of National Diet Library)

suggests, *Kogetsushō*; Uchimura Katsushi has shown, moreover, that Tanehiko made good use of the chronology and other elements of this text.[120] In fact, as we saw earlier, Tanehiko's disciple Ryūtei Senka states explicitly in his preface to chapter 14 of *Ashikaga Silk: Hand-Dyed Purple* that *Kogetsushō* was Tanehiko's source for knowledge of *Genji monogatari*, playing on the title of the annotated edition when he wrote that Tanehiko had "captured the light of the *Moon on the Lake* in his telescope."[121] Why, then, doesn't Tanehiko include the text in his list of works cited?

The answer to this question is at least hinted at in the preface to *Inaka Genji*'s first chapter, which introduces Ofuji, an attractive young woman known by the nickname Murasaki Shikibu, the "fraudulent Murasaki [Shikibu]" of the title and the ostensible author of the work:

Someone told this young woman that even if her critical gaze couldn't quite penetrate the depths of the *Rivers and Seas* or take in the entire

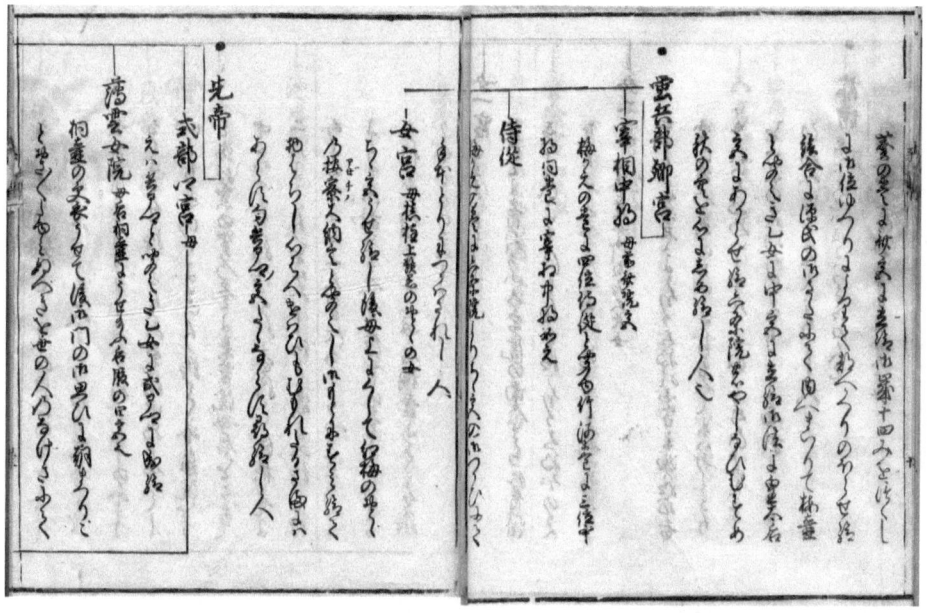

Figure 28 The standard format used in genealogies of the characters in *Genji monogatari*. (Kitamura Kigin, *Genji monogatari kogetsushō*, "Keizu," 10 *ura*–11 *omote*. Courtesy of the author)

expanse of the *Moon on the Lake*, there was always the *Young Sprouts*, which conveniently gathered up the main points. Comparing the *Red and White*, *Little Cranes*, *Hairlock Mirror*, *Small Mirror* and so on would also contribute slightly to her understanding. She should start off, he advised, with *Genji in Ten Volumes*.[122]

When Ofuji goes off to try to purchase these works, however, the clerk has no idea what any of them are and instead presses upon her a number of entirely different titles.

This preface clearly reflects the fact that *Kogetsushō* was widely known in the late 1820s, but at the same time it also assumes that its sixty volumes would have been beyond Ofuji. Indeed, we are explicitly told that "the only books she read were *kusazōshi*."[123] In this, she is probably not unlike many members of *Inaka Genji*'s core readership. Representations of lacquer-boxed copies of *Kogetsushō* appear as a sort of symbolic trope in any number of books and prints, marking either the elegance or the erudition of their owners. A *kibyōshi* by Nansenshō Somahito and Utagawa Toyohiro that was published in 1802 contains a particularly telling example: the story opens with a widower, Tōsaku, making rope as his daughter, Orui, plucks the strings of a koto. "Despite his poverty," the text

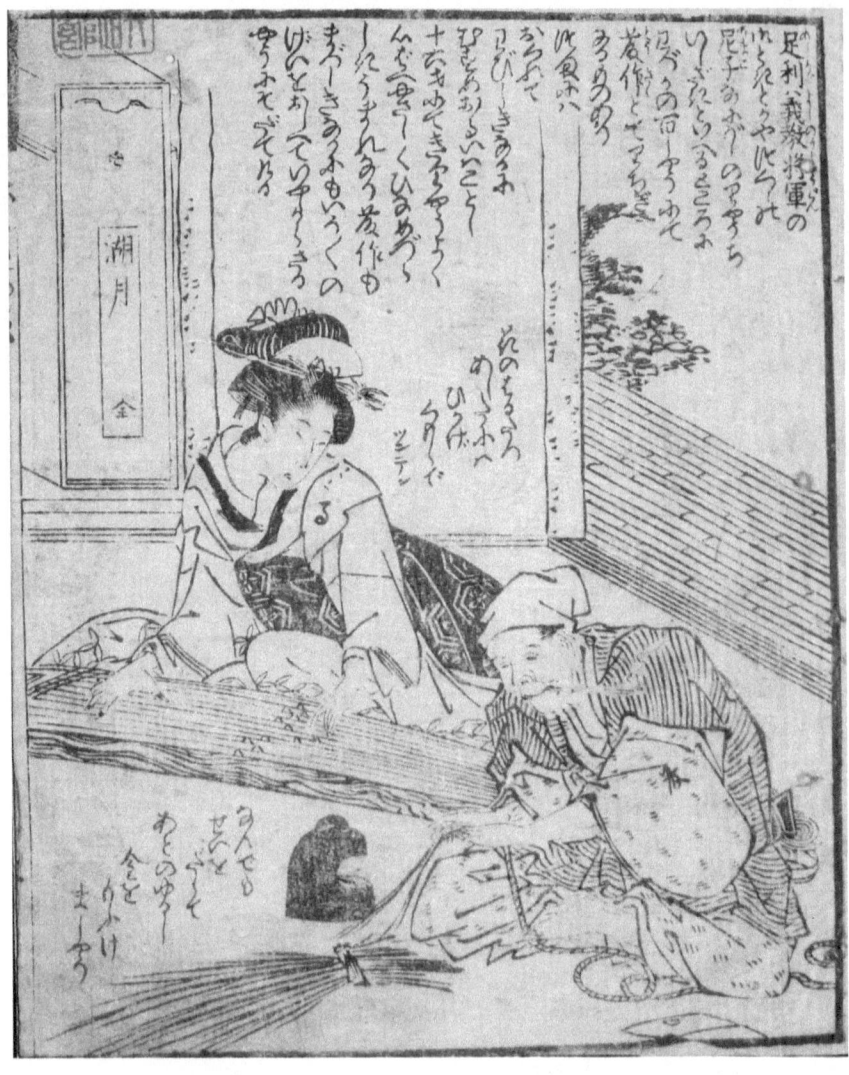

Figure 29 The widower Tōsaku with his cultivated daughter, Orui. A copy of *Kogetsushō* is in the tall box standing in the alcove behind them. (Nansenshō Somahito and Utagawa Toyohiro, *Katakiuchi shigure no tomo* [*Vengeance: A Friend in the Autumn Rain*], fascicle 1, 1 *omote*. Courtesy of National Institute of Japanese Literature, Tokyo)

informs us, "Tōsaku instructed his daughter in all sorts of arts, raising her so that she wouldn't grow up to be coarse."[124] As an unmistakable second symbol of the "arts," along with the koto, a copy of *Kogetsushō* has been drawn in the back of the room (figure 29).[125] Needless to say, it is there precisely because it is a special book, not the sort of thing one would expect to find in such a place or expect such people to be capable of reading. This latter point is borne out by an advance advertisement for *A Tasteful Tale of Genji*, published more than a century before *Inaka Genji*, and by the book's preface, both of which state unambiguously that *Kogetsushō* was itself too difficult for the uninstructed to understand.[126]

Tanehiko may have left *Kogetsushō* out of his "Complete List of Works Cited," then, because, despite the list's stiff academic format, he considered it too pedantic, too scholarly, too special. The latter half of the passage from the preface to chapter 1, by contrast, depends for its humorous effect either on some degree of familiarity on its readers' part with the translations and digests mentioned, or—more likely, it seems to me—on a sense of what books with titles such as these were likely to be.[127] The clerk's mistakes are funny only because he ought at least to recognize the titles, but does not: in other words, the readers must know more about them than the clerk for the joke to succeed. These relatively accessible rewritings put readers' minds at ease, whether or not they had actually encountered the books or would ever be interested in reading them, whereas *Kogetsushō*, the main source of Tanehiko's knowledge of *Genji monogatari*, would most likely have intimidated them.

Remade in the Image: *Inaka Genji* as *Genji monogatari*

In what may well be the most frequently quoted passage in all of *Inaka Genji*, part of the preface to chapter 10, Tanehiko compares his narrative project to a bathhouse where some like it hot and some like it not so hot:

> When I first set about writing this *Inaka Genji* of mine, an elderly friend said to me: You mustn't mess with the story of *Genji* at all, and whenever possible write using the actual words, too, keeping them just as they are. That way you'll give a bit of a helping hand to youngsters who don't read *Genji*. A young friend said to me: Turn the plot of *Genji* on its head, rewrite it all in a kabuki or *jōruri* sort of style. You think there's anyone who isn't reading *Genji*? As I see it, the old man who counseled me to write like *Genji* prefers his bath hot; the one who urged me to write in the kabuki style likes his lukewarm.[128]

Earlier I mentioned Yamaguchi Takeshi's division of *Inaka Genji* into three sections based on the relationship of its text to the text of *Genji monogatari*, each one more "faithful" than the last. Generally speaking, there is no question that this division can be made. But, of course, the whole reason Tanehiko invoked his bathhouse metaphor—in, one should note, the preface to chapter 10, which sits at the end of the block of chapters that Yamaguchi identifies as least closely related to *Genji monogatari*—is that he believed he had been changing his stance all along, pouring more or less of the Heian classic into the mix. On the textual level—"the actual words," in the words of the presumably fictional old friend—the bath had its hot currents right from the beginning.

Tanehiko's bath metaphor resonates nicely with the notion of what I have been calling *Inaka Genji*'s function as a pedagogical tool. The old friend's suggestion that Tanehiko "give a bit of a helping hand to youngsters who don't read *Genji*" is as unambiguous an expression as one could hope for of the role that the incorporation of "the actual words" might be expected to perform. Tanehiko himself not only was a very careful reader of *Kogetsushō* and other images of *Genji monogatari*, but also attended at least one lecture on the tale by Ishikawa Masamochi (1753–1830), author of the commentary *Notes on Genji: A Few Last Drops* (*Genchūyoteki*, date unknown).[129] Indeed, he was interested in other classical texts as well and often alluded to them into his fiction. Suzuki Jūzō points out that *The Pillow Book* is quoted and *Gleanings from Yoshino* (*Yoshino shūi*, colophon 1358) is alluded to in a preface to *Yakko no Koman* (*Yakko no Koman*, preface 1807), an early *yomihon* of Tanehiko's that was also sold under the title *A New Oh If Only I Could Switch Them!* (*Shin torikaebaya monogatari*), an allusion to *Oh If Only I Could Switch Them! A Tale* (*Torikaebaya monogatari*, eleventh–twelfth century); that a record of books in Tanehiko's collection lists copies of *Tosa Diary* (*Tosa nikki*, ca. 935) and *Diary of the Sixteenth Night* (*Izayoi nikki*, 1282), the former of which is mentioned in one of Tanehiko's diary entries and alluded to in *The Straits of Awa* (*Awa no Naruto*, 1807); that Tanehiko wrote in a diary entry that he had been looking over the first book of *The Collection of Ten Thousand Leaves* and quoted a poem from it in *Ōshū's Obsession: A Tale* (*Ōshū shūjaku monogatari*, 1812); and that *Hand-Dyed Gauze Puppets of Times Long Past* (*Mojitezuri mukashi ningyō*, 1813) already contains a reference to the "Momiji no ga" (Beneath the Autumn Leaves) chapter that seems to be based on a reading of *Genji monogatari* itself, presumably *Kogetsushō*, rather than on a digest.[130] Tanehiko also issued a *gōkan* in 1823 that bore the title *A New Tale of the Hollow Tree* (*Shin utsubo monogatari*), alluding to *The Tale of the Hollow Tree* (*Utsubo monogatari*, late tenth century), and opened his *gōkan A Six-Panel Screen of the Floating World* (*Ukiyogata rokumai byōbu*, 1821) in a strikingly un-*gōkan*-like way, with a scene centering on a character's explication of what he argues is a generally misunderstood poem by Saigyō included in *A New Collection of Poems Old and New* (*Shin kokin wakashū*, 1204).[131] All of which is to say that, like his old friend, Tanehiko liked his baths hot.[132] He belonged in the same tub with those who wanted to help the uncultivated youngsters, even if in the end it seemed to him that the best way to be helpful was to heed the voice of the young man who urged him to "turn the plot of *Genji* on its head, rewrite it all in a kabuki or *jōruri* sort of style."

In his preface to chapter 38, the last chapter published before the Tenpō Reforms put an end to Mitsuuji's peregrinations, Tanehiko wrote that "the criticisms once heard to the effect that this flimsy work of mine had no right to *Genji*'s name have, of their own accord, abated somewhat."[133] During the thirteen long years of *Inaka Genji*'s initial publication history, Tanehiko succeeded so brilliantly in educating his readers, in heating up the bath without their even noticing, that he was able to make *Genji monogatari* seem more palatable to more readers—more attractive, even—than it ever had before. By imbuing *Genji monogatari*, or at least the word "Genji," with a new value for a whole new segment of the population—the consumers of Genji pictures, "Genji Kyara Incense Oil," and "Genji Soba"—*Inaka Genji* had become worthy of its namesake. The dialectic of the popular replacement had at last been established. Indeed, insofar as Tanehiko had determined to continue to the end, one might go even further and say that the notion of a modern-Japanese translation for a truly broad popular audience had been born as well. We will see in part II of this book that at least one of the first modern translators was acutely conscious of *Inaka Genji* and the role it had played in making *Genji monogatari* known, to the extent that he saw himself trying to replace *Inaka Genji*. In this sense, *Inaka Genji* can be regarded as having set the stage for the modern recanonization of the classic in whose shadow we remain.

This ended up serving *Genji monogatari* better than it did *Inaka Genji*. In the early years of the Tenpō period, *Genji monogatari* was undoubtedly little more to most of *Inaka Genji*'s readers than a hazily reflected image of this latter work, whose interest, at any rate, lay elsewhere; by the late Tenpō period, the tables were beginning to turn. As Tanehiko himself noted, *Inaka Genji* now had "the right to the name *Genji*," and the ironic result was that the visual splendor and radical hybridity that, more than anything, had distinguished the work, particularly in its early chapters, would gradually start to fade from view.

The fate of *Inaka Genji* in subsequent periods—the creation of new editions of the work in the new, less flexible, less sturdy form of the case-bound book beginning in the late 1880s, in versions that carefully or haphazardly and inexpensively reconfigured the characteristic image-text-book relations of the original woodblock-printed object, reducing the importance of its pictures and other bibliographic elements, transforming its very mechanism as a narrative—will be the subject of chapter 3 of this book. I might note in conclusion, however, that this later publication history completed a process already begun in the Tenpō period, changing *Inaka Genji* from the most visually exciting *gōkan* in the stores—a thrillingly hybrid mishmash, a book that offered its readers access to the celebrated elegance of *Genji monogatari* without making it seem daunting or difficult—into the "Fraudulent Murasaki's Bumpkin Genji" that it was for Tayama Katai in 1925 and for Nakamura Yukihiko in 1953 and that, to a certain extent, it remains even today: a secondary, derivative, necessarily inadequate representation of a classic. An image, not the real thing.

How to Read a *Gōkan*

Chapter 1 called on various types of evidence, both external and internal, to argue that *Inaka Genji* was probably not appreciated by the majority of its early readers as an adaptation of *Genji monogatari*. No doubt, even minimally educated townspeople had some inkling that a work called *Genji monogatari* existed, but at least early on, before *Inaka Genji*'s attractions began to reflect back onto the Heian classic, this link was, at best, one relatively insignificant factor among many that combined to make *Inaka Genji* an unprecedented best seller. The book succeeded not as an adaptation, and still less as a parody of *Genji monogatari*, but as a *gōkan*. Perhaps the young Okume in Tamenaga Shunsui's *The Rabbit on the Moon* identified the true source of its broad appeal when she observed, ever so simply, "Tanehiko has always been the best when it comes to *gōkan*." But what does that mean? What kind of experience did Ryūtei Tanehiko offer his fans? We have considered some of the elements that made *Inaka Genji* stand out from the dozens of *gōkan* released each year as a particularly stylish, sophisticated, sexy publication, even at first glance; now we need to look more closely.

The first chapter of *Inaka Genji* opens with a seductive, rhythmic passage that sets the scene for the beginning of the story: "The 'Palace of Flowers' at the height of its glory, a flower-filled residence on Muromachi Street, in the capital of flowers, high and mighty as the rising sun, to which its written form is related: Higashiyama..."[1] This glittering chain of verbal associations situates readers physically and temporally within the world of the narrative, but also, in a sense, sets

CHAPTER 2

Reading Higashiyama

Image, Text, and Book in Inaka Genji

Despite surprise and terror, for he had heard of such things at least in old tales . . .

Royall Tyler, The Tale of Genji,
"The Twilight Beauty"

Surprised and terrified to actually see such a thing, though he had heard of similar occurrences in old, old tales . . .

Nise Murasaki inaka Genji, chapter 5

むかしものがたりなどにこそ・かゝることハきけと・いとめづらかにむくつけゝれど・
『湖月抄』

むかし〴〵のものがたりにかゝるたぐひハきゝたれどめのまへに見ることハいとめづらかにあやしくて
『僞紫田舎源氏』

the scene for our experience of the book as a whole with a startling metalinguistic gesture, by hinting at a link between the "written form" of the name Higashiyama and the sun. This sudden allusion to a Sino-Japanese character is eye-catching, so to speak, in a genre that seldom evinces much interest in graphology; it is especially startling and suggestive in copies of the chapter in its original woodblock-printed form, in which the *higashi* (east) in Higashiyama is written not with the Sino-Japanese character referred to, but in the *hiragana* syllabary—as is everything in the selection I quoted but the *yama* (mountain) in Higashiyama: はなのみやこのむろまちにはなをかざりしひとかまへはなのごしよとてときめきつあさひののぼるいきほひにもじもえんあるひがし山. In order to make sense of this rather peculiar passage, readers must first mentally draw the character *higashi* 東 from the printed *kana higashi* ひがし, and then break down the character into the pictographs from which it was thought, in Tanehiko's time, to derive: 日 and 木, the first representing "sun" and the second, "tree." Finally, these two pictographs must be recombined—not verbally but pictorially—to form an image of the sun rising through the trees. Only in this manner does the implicit relationship between Higashiyama (Eastern Mountains) and its written form become apparent.

Following these links may not be such a tricky task, given the familiarity of the character in question and the fact that it appears glossed with its reading in a *kuchi-e* on the previous page, but it gives us a taste of the sort of enjoyment we can expect from the experience of reading *Inaka Genji*. Right from its very first sentence, the book's readers are asked, subtly but insistently, to remain on the lookout for hidden signs—words and images whose meaning becomes apparent only when they are read by an eye able to see the textual and the visual as inextricably intertwined.

There has never been any question that pictures were central to the pleasures of the *gōkan*. Otama's reaction upon being presented with a newly published book in *The Legend of Tamagiku*, cited in the previous chapter—"she flipped rapidly through to the end of each [booklet], taking in nothing but the pictures"—was utterly ordinary.[2] But it is not enough simply to say that pictures were important to the *gōkan*. The numerous authors and artists active in the genre had, naturally, different strengths, proclivities, and interests, as well as different notions about the direction their fictions should take; this diversity, along with various fads and generic tendencies, had as much of an effect on pictures as it did on texts. Given this fact, what precisely makes *Inaka Genji* stand out from the crowd? Its pictures are, first of all, noticeably finer than those of most *gōkan*, having been carved and printed with exceptional care. In chapter 1, I stressed the use of thin ink in the *kuchi-e*, but the lavishness did not stop there: the artwork in the main body of the book was also magnificently executed. It features many more indoor scenes than is common, particularly toward the end—a circumstance that stems from Tanehiko's use of *Genji monogatari* as a major source—and these rooms are sumptuously, meticulously realized in every detail, from the pictures and patterns that decorate walls and folding screens to the joints of bamboo fences; from the particular hanging scrolls selected to adorn certain characters' rooms to the grains of different woods used to build the rooms themselves.

Still more remarkable than the incredible detail of the pictures, however, is the sophistication with which Tanehiko and Utagawa Kunisada wove together pictures and text—the mastery with which the two main components of the *gōkan*, verbal and visual, were made to supplement and contradict each other, each conveying information in its own way and at its own pace. *Inaka Genji* stands out among other *gōkan*, including Tanehiko's earlier creations and even his numerous collaborations with Kunisada, for the playful brilliance with which it establishes and stresses *relations* among pictures and words, and for the amount of meaning it packs into both. Indeed, as I indicated in passing in chapter 1, *Inaka Genji* moves beyond image-text relations into what we might call, for lack of a better term, "image-text-book relations." It goes so far as to incorporate into its compositions the materiality of its bookish form, the ink and paper of which both pictures and words consist.

It is significant, I think, that Tanehiko opens *Inaka Genji* with a verbal-visual pun on the very word that identifies the *sekai* (world) within which the narrative unfolds: "Higashiyama" does indeed name the hybrid world that we are about to enter. The obtrusive pun gestures toward a mode of reading that enables a more complex and engaged appreciation of the *gōkan* as a whole, and it is precisely this mode of reading that we must learn to employ in order to see what makes *Inaka Genji* such a truly remarkable book. This chapter centers on an examination of a number of pictures and series of pictures, showing both how they function in visual and material terms and how they participate in the unfolding narrative. I hope that readers will come away with a sense of the particular texture of the pleasures that *Inaka Genji* offers readers—of what to look for in it, of how to look at it, and of its brilliance, not so much as an adaptation or a parody of *Genji monogatari* (though it can certainly be read in that way) but as the most successful best seller that Edo ever saw.

Strategies of a Dream Team

Generally speaking, a distinction can be made between looking at pictures and reading a story, even if the combination of both is what constitutes the act of reading a *gōkan*. There is one pleasure to be had in reading, and another to be had in looking; the two pleasures compliment each other, but they do not necessarily coincide. In *Inaka Genji*, however, the pictures, too, have to be read, and as my example of the implied visual pun embedded in the name Higashiyama suggests, at times its words have to be pictured. The pictures do not represent simply what the writing tells or even what it does not tell; neither does the writing represent simply what the pictures show or fail to show. An important aspect of their relationship is that they do different things in different ways, and do them together; this means, ultimately, that they merge, in the act of reading, more than they do in most other *gōkan*. *Inaka Genji* represents, perhaps, the highest realization of the form's potential. Because to my knowledge no one has ever given detailed readings like those I will be offering of pictures in any genre of fiction published in Edo in the early modern period, certainly not of any *gōkan*, and because I am interested in replacing the simplistic notion of *Inaka Genji* as a textual adaptation of the text of *Genji monogatari* with a reading more attuned to its characteristics as a visual and material object, my treatment of its image-text-book relations will be weighted more heavily toward the pictures.

I chose to begin with a reading of the visual-verbal pun on "Higashiyama," then, less because this type of play is representative of the techniques that Tanehiko uses to tempt his audience to look harder, to focus on visual and sometimes even physical aspects of his work, than because it seems to symbolize the book's image-text relations. Occasionally, Tanehiko invests his characters' names with visual meaning: I noted earlier that the name Toyoshi no Mae makes sense only if readers actually *see* that it is a compound of two *kanji*, the "to" in Hino Tomiko and the "ki" in Kokiden. Another example of a different sort occurs in chapter 19, when Shiraito, one of Toyoshi no Mae's serving women, is struck by "a flash of lightning, straight as the number 1, that charred her bodily to a crisp, changing her from Shiraito to Kuroito," or from "White String" to "Black String."[3] Visual-verbal jugglery of this sort is unusual, however. The bulk of the wordplay in *Inaka Genji* consists of shop-worn, standard-issue "pivot words" (*kakekotoba*) of the sort common in the puppet theater: "Hirugao is stunned, no reply comes to mind, so she lets it drop—her head, that is, hanging, deeply sunk in thought."[4] The pictures are more interesting.

My privileging of pictures over text should not, however, be taken to mean that this chapter is about Kunisada's work rather than Tanehiko's. To be sure, Kunisada's participation was crucial to the project's success. Kunisada, who had debuted as a professional in 1807, just as the *gōkan* was emerging as a genre, rose rapidly to stardom: in 1808 he prepared the artwork for no fewer than thirteen *gōkan*, and within five years he was already being ranked second among print artists after his master, Utagawa Toyokuni (1769–1825).[5] By 1829, when the first chapter of *Inaka Genji* was published, Kunisada was in a class of his own, and his participation in the project was surely a significant factor in its success. The passage in *The Rabbit on the Moon* in which Okume praises Tanehiko as the best *gōkan* author ends with her father's assertion that "nowadays Kunisada is the greatest *ukiyo-e* artist in all Japan"; in the world of the *gōkan*, this was a dream team.

Some sense of the extent to which *Inaka Genji*'s readers appreciated Kunisada's contribution can be gleaned from the extraordinary popularity of *ukiyo-e* belonging to the genre known as "Genji pictures." According to Andreas Marks, an expert on Kunisada's oeuvre, his studio was responsible for eight hundred Genji pictures, including no fewer than thirty-seven diptych and triptych series, only two of which were meant to represent scenes in *Genji monogatari* itself; the rest were efforts to capitalize on *Inaka Genji*'s popularity.[6] Indeed, the origin of the genre can be traced directly to an advertisement in chapter 10, which was sold with temporary covers and title pages when it was released in 1833 because the actual covers were not ready in time, and, as the publisher Tsuruya Kiemon explained, "some of our best customers" were unwilling to wait.[7] A note on the temporary title page of the second fascicle stated that "exquisitely carved and printed" diptych and triptych prints by Kunisada showing "the cherry blossoms at Kurama, the snow at Tadasu, the autumn leaves at Tsūten, and various other beautiful scenes from this *Inaka Genji*" would be ready for purchase by the third month. Advertisements for the series began to be included among *Inaka Genji*'s back matter from chapter 11, issued in 1834.

I noted in the previous chapter that some Genji pictures simply copied *Inaka Genji*'s covers; we will see in this chapter that others were based on *kuchi-e* or scenes from the book. Still others drew on *Inaka Genji*'s sequels or placed its characters in freshly invented scenes. Prints of all these types were so popular that, as Yoda Gakkai explained, "in the end, hardly a surface was left that wasn't decorated with a 'Genji picture.'"[8] Indeed, two prints in this genre were among the earliest *ukiyo-e* to be circulated abroad when they were reproduced in full color, if somewhat clumsily, in Laurence Oliphant's (1829–1888) *Narrative of the Earl of Elgin's Mission to China and Japan in the Years 1857, '58, and '59*, first published in English in 1859 and issued in a second edition the following year.[9] Félix Bracquemond, the painter who is credited with "discovering" Japanese art for European audiences, probably first chanced across the pages from *Hokusai Sketchbooks* (*Hokusai manga*, 1814–1878) that he then shared with his artist acquaintances, sparking the movement now known as Japonism, only in 1862.[10]

Kunisada's visual sensibility and the care with which he fleshed out the splendid, mixed-up world of Tanehiko's Higashiyama had a profound impact on the style in which it was pictured over the course of several decades. At the same time, it is important to remember that the authors—the *sakusha* (literally, "creators")—of *gōkan* guided the artists in their work, providing sketches and directions that were often quite detailed. Tanehiko, who as a samurai with a reasonably good stipend could afford to take the notion of "frivolous writing" seriously, as it were, was particularly meticulous in his designs.[11] This is evident from his manuscripts for *Inaka Genji*, some of which have survived. Figure 30 is Tanehiko's sketch for one of the *kuchi-e* discussed in chapter 1; Kunisada's finished picture is shown in figure 7b. Not only are the two versions quite similar, but Tanehiko has provided notes in red to help Kunisada realize details that he himself did not draw in: his decision to alter the shape of the lantern is one example, but he also points out, for instance, that Tasogare, shown standing on the left, is "the girl introduced at the end of chapter 3. She's about nineteen, looks feisty but she's easily frightened," and comments, "This is the first time I have shown smoking implements in this book." A note on the makeshift screen reads, "A picture of hell. Just a little will be fine if it's too much trouble." Judging from the published picture, Kunisada seems to have been willing to put in the extra effort for this book. Figure 31, meanwhile, is Tanehiko's sketch for one of the pictures in the main body of *Inaka Genji*, Kunisada's version of which is reproduced in figure 32. Again, we see that Tanehiko was ultimately responsible for both the content and the composition.

When we read *Inaka Genji*'s pictures, we are engaging with the products—masterfully realized by Kunisada, as well as by copyists, carvers, and printers—of Tanehiko's particular visual sensibility. He has a certain style, certain preferences. Among the techniques he uses, three seem particularly important and will be the focus of this chapter: his use of pictures to convey information that is at odds with the text or that exceeds what is presented in the text; his use of prefiguration, concealing informa-

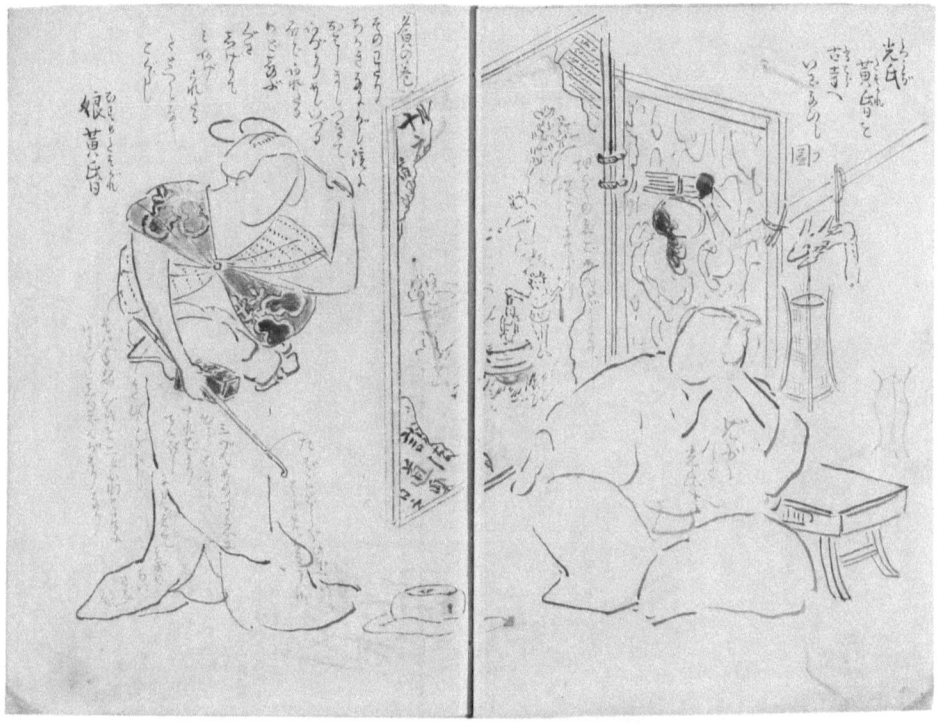

Figure 30 A page from Tanehiko's second, illustrated manuscript for chapter 4 of *Inaka Genji* (3 *ura*–4 *omote*), showing his sketch for the *kuchi-e* shown in figure 7b. (Courtesy of National Diet Library)

tion in pictures that will later be commented on in the text; and his use of what might be referred to as "metapictures," which comment visually on the nature of the pictures that fill *Inaka Genji* and prod the reader toward a greater sensitivity to their workings.[12]

These three techniques sometimes overlap, but each serves a different function. Pictures that show more than the text tells often lend a certain depth to the story, revealing what has been left unsaid or contradicting what actually has been said. They also help keep the work interesting throughout, even when Tanehiko decides to "heat up the bathwater"—for instance, incorporating more material from *Genji monogatari* than most readers might like. Tanehiko himself remarks on the connection between pictorial interest and the slowness of *Genji monogatari*'s plot by *gōkan* standards in a note explaining two pictures in chapter 20 that represent a flashback rather than what is actually taking place, which is simply a long conversation:

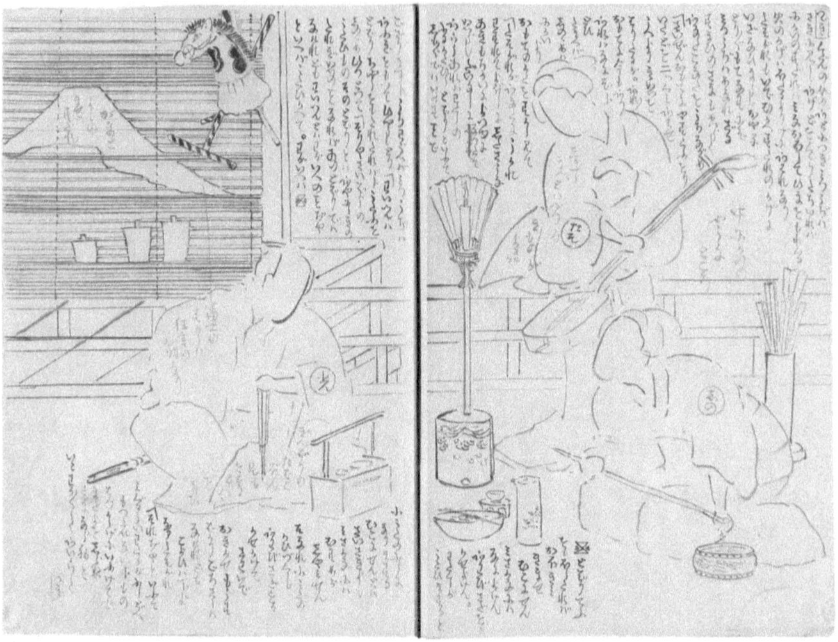

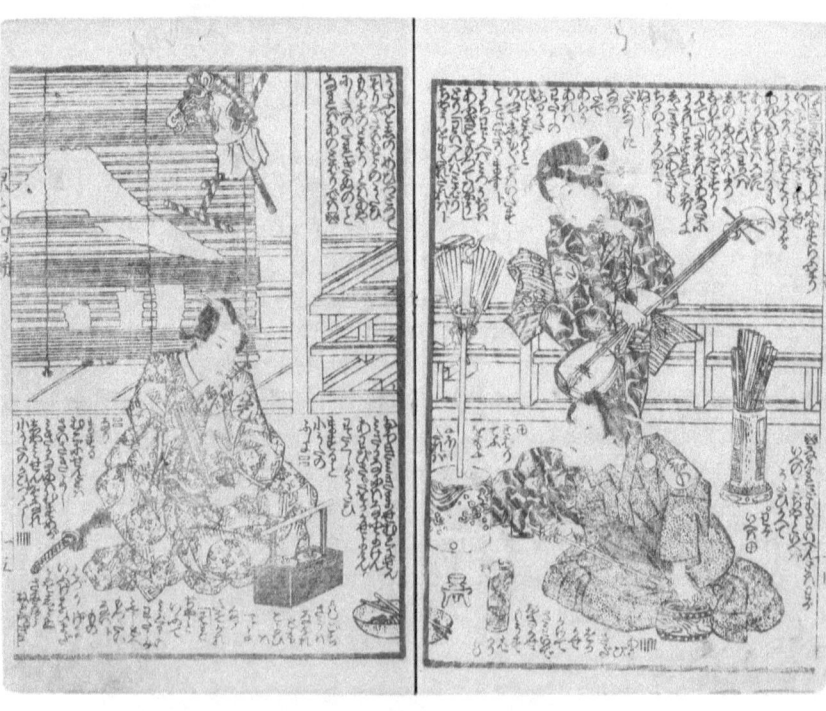

I thought that I would be betraying the sense of this chapter of *Genji* if, finding it cloying, I were to omit the novice's long-winded tale of his love for his daughter, since it has all been written out so exhaustively, so I have presented most of it here, rewriting it all in the vernacular. There's no point duplicating the same picture, though, so I have followed the novice as he recounts past events, directing that the pictures be done in that way.[13]

The point, in other words, is that no reader is going to want to look at two consecutive pictures of people sitting in a room talking. The pictures do not actually present more than the text recounts; they leap to a different narrative level. This is a telling indication of the lengths to which Tanehiko was prepared to go to help members of his core readership, accustomed to non-stop *gōkan* action, overcome their resistance to the slower pace of *Genji monogatari*.

The second technique, which I call "prefiguration," relates directly to the unfolding plot and allows the reader to participate, taking on the role of a detective noticing and interpreting clues, just as Mitsuuji does. The third technique, the metapicture, need not contribute directly to the plot, but helps to encourage precisely the sort of active looking that makes it possible for the reader to read pictures, rather than simply view them, and thus take more pleasure in the book. Since metapictures in *Inaka Genji* have a pedagogical function—it is this pedagogical function that makes them metapictures: they are pictures that teach the reader how to look at pictures, how to read the book in which they appear—it makes sense to begin by looking at a few examples of them. I will then turn to instances of prefiguration, which are more closely related to the particular details of *Inaka Genji*'s plot, and finally to pictures that convey information not given in the written text, which emerge from the woodwork more and more as, learning from the metapictures, the reader begins to look harder.

Metapictures 1: Look at What You Are Reading

The term "metapicture" is somewhat slippery, and the pictures themselves are often rather subtle. They can be particularly easy to overlook

Figure 31 A page from Tanehiko's second, illustrated manuscript for chapter 4 of *Inaka Genji*, showing his sketch for the illustration shown in figure 32. (Courtesy of National Diet Library)

Figure 32 The illustration by Utagawa Kunisada based on the sketch by Tanehiko shown in figure 31. (*NMIG*, chapter 4, 14 *ura*–15 *omote*. Courtesy of National Diet Library)

when one does not have access to a copy of the book in its first published form, since they often exploit its materiality to achieve their full effect. I will begin, then, with a few obvious, even obtrusive examples that work even when reproduced. Instead of making the material form of *Inaka Genji* a meaningful part of their compositions, as do some of the pictures I will discuss later, this first batch of metapictures simply draws readers' attention to the bookishness of the book.

The right-hand page of the spread shown in figure 33, which appears in chapter 32, has been designed in such a way that it seems to have been folded over, allowing a partial view of the page underneath.[14] In the half-seen scene at the top right of this page, Mitsuuji's son Ujinaka is about to entrust a love letter to Sansaku, the son of Mitsuuji's retainer Korekichi. On the left-hand page of the spread, we see Sansaku proffering the letter to his father's sister, the unsuspecting Kofuji. It is not at all uncommon for *gōkan* to depict events taking place at two or more times

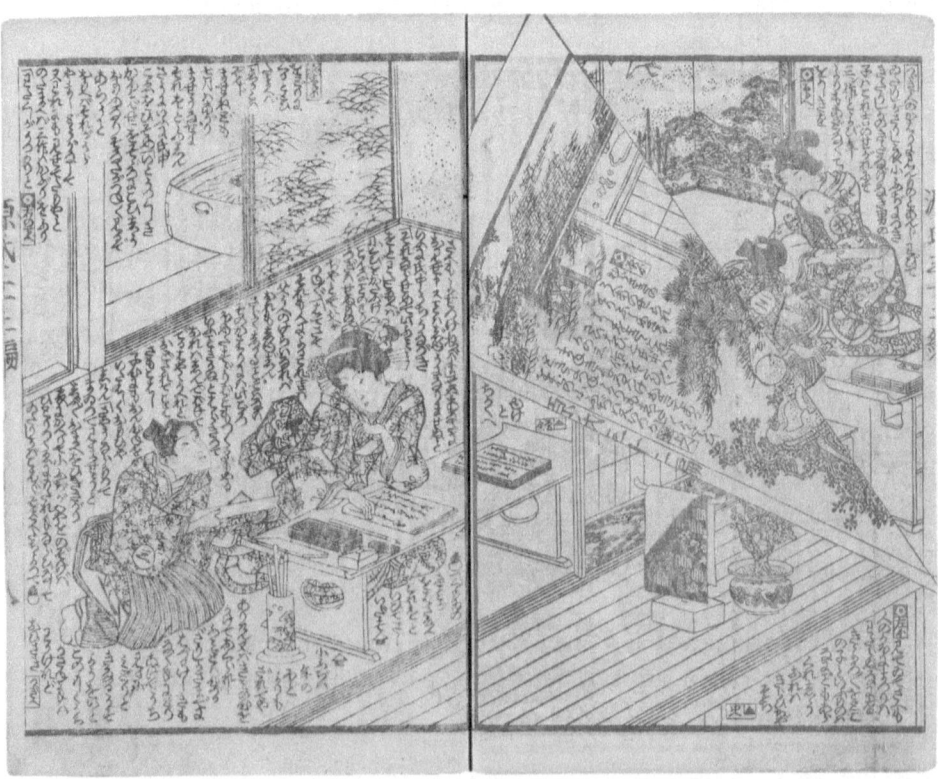

Figure 33 A page printed to look as though it has been folded down. (*NMIG*, chapter 32, 7 *ura*–8 *omote*. Courtesy of National Diet Library)

within a single picture, a technique known as "different times, same picture" (*ijidōzuhō*), which had been around for centuries in Japan, as elsewhere in the world, and occurs frequently—for instance, in illustrated handscrolls of Heian-period tales, including *Genji monogatari*. Tanehiko's fake folded page is an inspired riff on this venerable pictorial tradition, adapted to the form of the bound volume, that takes the technique to a different level: it represents not only more than one time and place in a single picture, but also the manner in which the book as a form is able to represent multiple times and places.

The brilliance of this device, which is as simple as it is startling, lies in the way it incorporates and merges two separate sets of times and places: narrative and readerly. On the one hand, the picture represents two events that occur at different times and in different places within the space of the story; on the other, it calls to mind two distinct times and places in the reader's experience of the work: one before the page is turned, and one after. By suggesting, within a single picture, the movement from the obverse to the reverse side of a page and by correlating this movement with a transition from one time and place to another within the seemingly closed world of the narrative, Tanehiko not only foregrounds the three-dimensionality of the printed page and the two-dimensionality of the picture, but also creates a *relationship* between these two opposed dimensionalities, pictorially illustrating that the movement of a reader's eye across successive pages of the *gōkan*—or, more to the point, the turning of the pages—is what imbues the two-dimensional pictorial space of the narrative with pseudo-three-dimensionality. By the same token, it is the passage of actual time, marked by the turning of pages, that pushes narrative time along its own winding course.

Although the device of the folded page itself is unusual, Tanehiko achieves similar effects by different means throughout *Inaka Genji*.[15] He alludes repeatedly, for instance, both to the material processes of the work's production and to its published form, inducing readers to reflect, if only momentarily, on the physicality of the *gōkan* and the role it plays in the entertainment they are enjoying. The illustrated title page of the first fascicle of chapter 15 offers an example of the first type of allusion, to the production process: it shows three brushes labeled with the names Ryūtei Tanehiko, Senkakudō (the publisher), and Utagawa Kunisada; a water container in the shape of Tanehiko's logo, formed by interlocking the *katakana* ヒ and コ, or *hi* and *ko*, for the "hiko" in his name; an ink stick marked with the chapter's publication date; and an inkstone inscribed with a logo used by Kunisada and other members of the Utagawa school (figure 34). All these objects gesture in a rather obvious way toward the roles that the author, publisher, and artist—and, of course, the objects themselves—played in the production of the book in the reader's hand.[16] Another more ingenious allusion to the production process, significantly included at the very beginning of the book, on the illustrated title page of the first fascicle of chapter 1, subtly links the physical act of creating *Inaka Genji* to that of writing *Genji monogatari*: a note over the picture identifies it as "An Old Inkstone Used by Murasaki Shikibu, a Treasure from Ishiyama Temple in Gōshū" (figure 35).[17]

What I referred to earlier as allusions to the published form of *Inaka Genji* may perhaps be more accurately described as backhanded allusions, since they highlight the form of the *gōkan*—and, as a consequence, the inherently physical nature of the act of enjoying a *gōkan*—by creating the momentary illusion that one is reading a different kind of object. Like

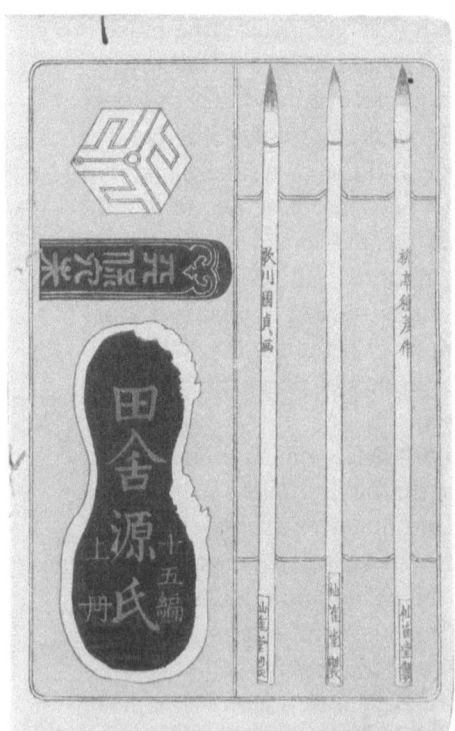 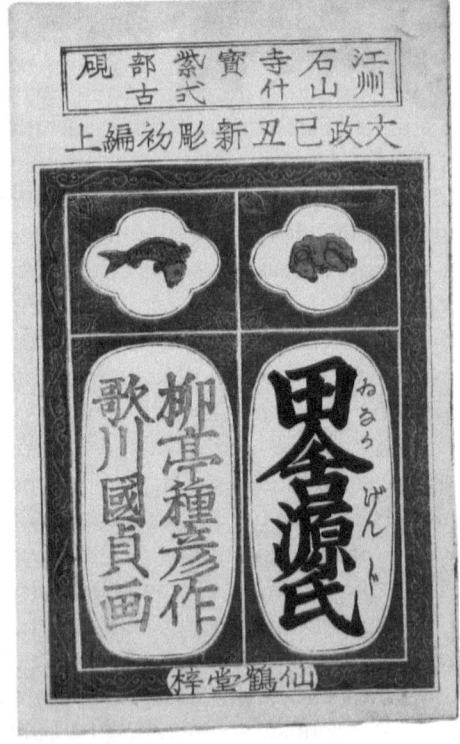

Figure 34 A title page with illustrations of implements used to write or draw. (*NMIG*, chapter 15, inside cover. Courtesy of National Diet Library)

Figure 35 A title page with an illustration based on an inkstone that Murasaki Shikibu was said to have used. (*NMIG*, chapter 1, inside cover. Courtesy of Waseda University Library, Tokyo)

the illustrated title page of chapter 1, showing the inkstone, which both foregrounds the material production of the work and links it to *Genji monogatari*, these pictures perform a double role, simultaneously emphasizing that *Inaka Genji* itself takes the particular historical form of the *gōkan* and indicating that this form functions as a replacement of the older, more elegant format of the illustrated handscroll, in which *Genji monogatari* was often circulated.

A relatively simple example of this technique occurs on the illustrated title page of chapter 30, which shows what *Inaka Genji* might have looked like had it been published as a handscroll, placing the title and chapter number on the cover and using an older, more elegant calligraphic style for the line of text visible at the start of the scroll, which identifies the author, artist, and publisher (figure 36).[18] Figure 37, which appears early in chapter 37, precisely where *Inaka Genji* moves from the "Nowaki" (The Typhoon) chapter of *Genji monogatari* to "Miyuki" (The Imperial Progress), is somewhat more sophisticated, in that the picture makes it appear for an instant as if *Inaka Genji* actually is a handscroll, unrolling to the left, with a title slip that reads "Miyuki no maki" (The Imperial Progress Scroll). The scroll's cover is checkered with the *Genji* incense sign for "Miyuki" and a pattern called *mokkō* or *kamon*, said to be modeled on a cross section of a gourd, often used to decorate handscrolls from the Heian and Kamakura (1185–1333) periods.[19] Here Tanehiko is clearly suggesting that the *gōkan Inaka Genji* replaces not only the handscroll as a form but also *Genji monogatari* itself as a work.

Tanehiko depicts a handscroll for the first time only at the end of chapter 25, in a section that corresponds to the "Eawase" (The Picture Competition) chapter of *Genji monogatari*—the chapter's focus on lavishly prepared scrolls and other forms of illustrated books was presumably what gave him the idea.[20] I argued in chapter 1 that as a result of Tanehiko's cautious, unobtrusively educational efforts to introduce readers to *Genji monogatari*, *Inaka Genji* gradually came to be regarded as a replacement of the Heian classic even by members of its minimally educated core readership, if only in a very rudimentary sense. This point would seem to be borne out by the fact that these visual assertions of interchangeability, which are also attempts to transfer to Tanehiko's *gōkan* something of the elegance and prestige of the handscroll, first appear so late in the work's publication history. It is significant, too, that the image of *Genji monogatari* that Tanehiko chooses to reference is the elegant form of the handscroll, even though it played a relatively small role in the circulation of the tale, which tended from the beginning to be transcribed in booklets. *Kogetsushō*, which was the most influential edition of *Genji monogatari* and

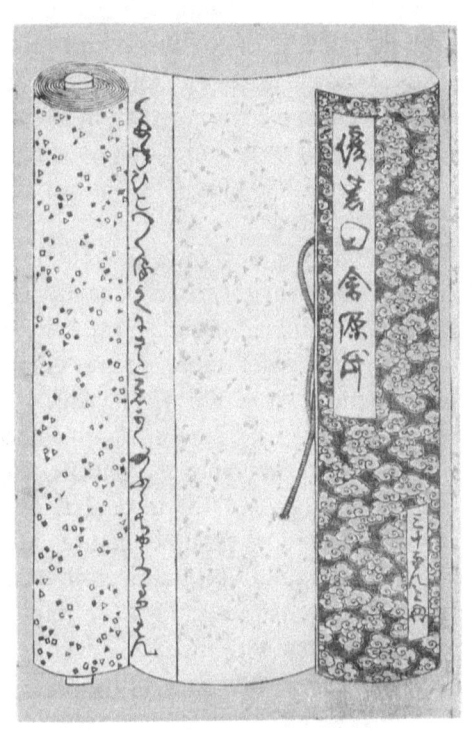

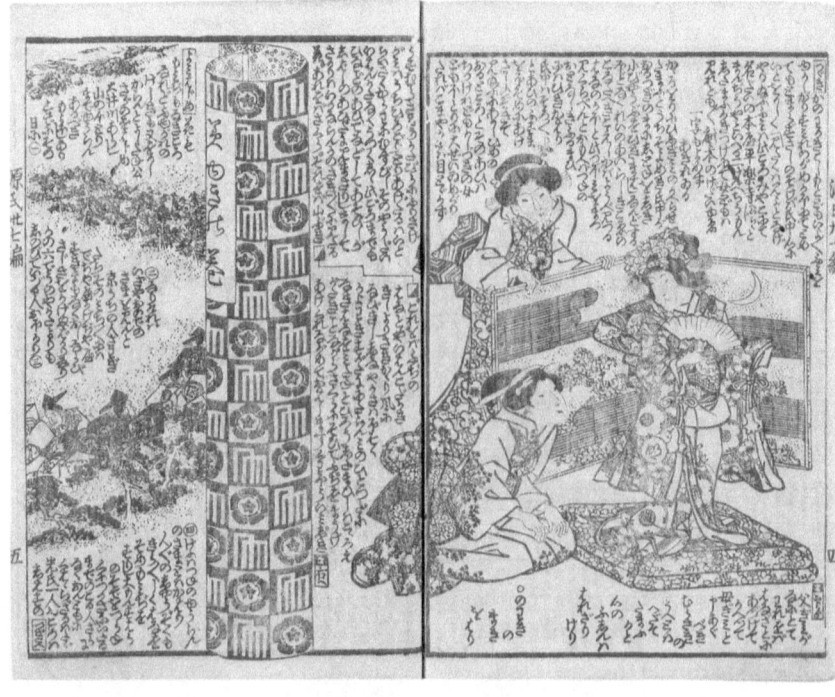

appeared frequently, as we have seen, in prints and popular fiction, particularly in *kibyōshi* but occasionally in *gōkan* as well, is never depicted in *Inaka Genji*. The image of *Genji monogatari* that Tanehiko gives his readers is, truth be told, little more than a fantasy.

Metapictures 2: The Frame and Beyond

By momentarily drawing attention to *Inaka Genji*'s bibliographic form, the pictures of implements for writing and drawing, and of handscrolls, invite a more conscious, attentive enjoyment of the pleasures that the *gōkan* offers; in this, they resemble the fake folded page. Their effect is considerably less sophisticated, however: they do not encourage an awareness of the way the reading process collapses the three-dimensional space outside the work onto the two-dimensional space within it, or of the inevitable link between the passage of time in the reader's world and that in the world of the narrative. I would like now to examine a few of the pictorial devices that Tanehiko uses, at various points throughout *Inaka Genji*, whose effects resemble that of the folded page. Since these techniques often bridge the interior and exterior of the work, importing the three-dimensionality of the printed page into the two-dimensional confines of the printed picture, it is not surprising that they tend to involve frames, the edges of pages, and on occasion even the very thickness of the paper on which the work was printed. First, I will discuss a picture whose frame Tanehiko has highlighted; second, two instances of broken frames; and third, two series of pictures that incorporate into their compositions the thickness of the paper itself. Finally, I will consider two examples of pictures that draw on the physical form of a bound fascicle, not just the materiality of a single page. Some of the pictures I will take up are brilliant not only in the way they play with the physicality of the *gōkan*—that is, as metapictures—but also in the way they interact with the writing on a very high level, and so require us to look at them in some detail and to read them carefully.

Figure 38, which comes from chapter 20, shows an old man and a young woman returning from a trip to gather firewood to sell, lingering

Figure 36 A title page with an illustration of what *Inaka Genji* would have looked like as a handscroll. (*NMIG*, chapter 30, inside cover. Courtesy of Art Research Center, Ritsumeikan University, Kyoto)

Figure 37 A two-page spread that gives the illusion of actually reading a handscroll. (*NMIG*, chapter 37, 4 *ura*–5 *omote*. Courtesy of National Diet Library)

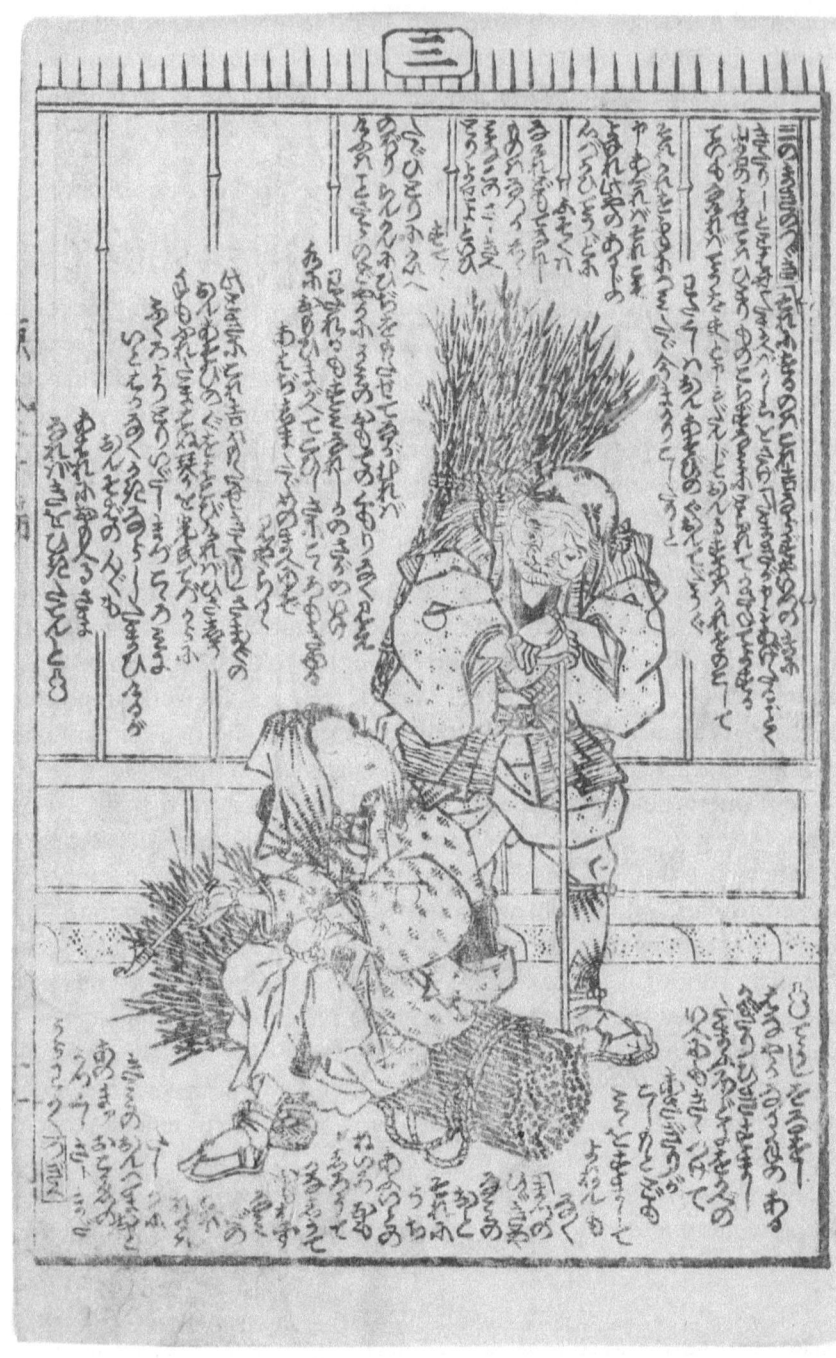

Figure 38 Two "lowly firewood sellers" lingering outside a wall, listening to Mitsuuji play his koto on the other side. (NMIG, chapter 20, 11 omote. Courtesy of National Diet Library)

for a moment outside a wall.²¹ There is no mention of them in the text until the following page, but partway across the top of this one, in a passage that combines direct quotation with more or less freewheeling translation from *Genji monogatari*, Mitsuuji starts quietly plucking his koto, and this knowledge allows the reader to deduce that they are listening to his music—note the man's tilted head, the absorbed look on his face, and the way the young woman is looking up at him, suggesting that they are sharing something even though they do not seem to be talking. We learn on the next page that this is indeed the case. The old man is moved, "though he didn't even know the word 'koto'" and is not really capable of describing what he feels: "Ah, that's a nice sound—sort of sends a shiver down my spine, comes in from the collar. My, it's like the wind on the shore. Keep me from harm, keep me from harm." This scene is rich enough as it is, but what makes it typical of Tanehiko is that there is even more going on than meets the eye, for the whole thing is inspired by a note in *Kogetsushō* that offers two possible interpretations of a word in *Genji monogatari* that is either *shiwafuruhito* (wrinkly old person) or *shiwaburuibito* (lowly firewood seller).²²

What is of particular interest here, though, is not what does not immediately meet the eye but what does: the line of barbs at the top of the page unites the frame enclosing the picture with the wall behind the firewood sellers, making the printed lines feel palpably, confiningly present in a way that frames in *gōkan* ordinarily do not. The three lines at the sides and bottom of the page come to seem like solid borders, just like the one along the top, which actually is a solid border. This is true even though the placement of the boards of the wall behind the two figures implies more space to the left and right: although we can tell that the fence itself extends beyond the frame, the old man and his daughter are caught within it. The slightly claustrophobic atmosphere works subtly to isolate the two "lowly firewood sellers," emphasizing the economic, social, and cultural gaps that separate them from the refined world of the narrative and lending an additional pathos to the scene.

The effect is strengthened by the placement of this picture on the first page of the fascicle, which means that there is nothing next to the two figures but the title page, and by the expansive perspective offered on the following page, which shows Asagiri, the counterpart of *Genji monogatari*'s Akashi no Ue, standing on a hilltop with two attendants, also listening to Mitsuuji's koto (figure 39).²³ Asagiri's connection to Mitsuuji's universe, despite the social gulf she perceives between them, is affirmed four spreads later, in a picture that shows Mitsuuji talking with Asagiri's father in the very same building that she and her two attendants see

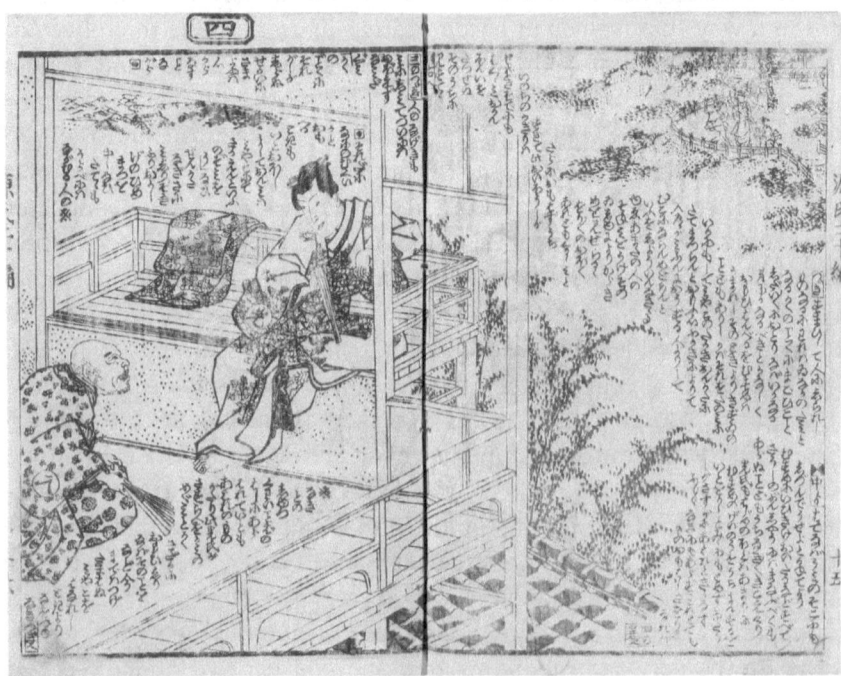

below them as they stand on the hill (figure 40).²⁴ Asagiri and her attendants are just barely visible in the distance in the top-right-hand corner of the second picture. No such connection is available to the firewood sellers outside the wall. The barbs at the top of the picture in figure 38 transform its frame, and hence the page, into a barrier between two classes, two worlds. On an abstract level, then, this marking of the frame achieves the same effect as the depiction of the folded page: the three-dimensionality of the reader's world—of the material page of the *gōkan* itself—is imported into the fictional world that the characters inhabit and is made to bear meaning.

Tanehiko breaks frames as suggestively as he marks them. This is evident from a picture in chapter 19 that shows Mitsuuji standing before a folding screen, aiming a paper-paneled oil lamp, the front of which he has opened to strengthen the illumination, at a woman crouching seductively at the screen's edge (figure 41). In the background—printed smaller and separated from Mitsuuji and the woman by a swath of writing—two retainers peer at the woman, apparently unsure what to make of her.²⁵ This scene corresponds with one at the end of the "Suma" chapter of *Genji monogatari* in which an indistinct figure, presumably the Dragon King, appears and tries to lure Genji into the sea. The woman here, who the retainers speculate is the Dragon King's daughter—"I think they call her the Dragon Girl or something like that"—is actually a powerful mountain priest (*yamabushi*), allied with Yamana Sōzen, who has come all the way to Suma and assumed this form, we later learn, in an effort to corrupt Mitsuuji's pure heart and lure him into a life of unthreatening dissipation.²⁶

The text that accompanies this picture describes a scene somewhat different from the one we are shown. Mitsuuji is said to have "set out his pillow, and seemed to have drifted off to sleep for a moment," when the woman appears, albeit indistinctly, and begins urging him not to attempt to defeat Yamana Sōzen. When "he opened his eyes in his shock at the sight of her sashaying toward him, there was nothing but a dim afterglow, not even a shadow of her form."²⁷ There is a good reason for this discrepancy: in the text, it is easy to have Mitsuuji both sleeping, with his eyes

Figure 39 The two-page spread that follows that shown in figure 38. Note the building in the distance and the curved fence the women stand behind. (*NMIG*, chapter 20, 11 *ura*–12 *omote*. Courtesy of National Diet Library)

Figure 40 Mitsuuji in the building visible in figure 39. The women can be seen standing behind the fence in the upper-right corner. (*NMIG*, chapter 20, 15 *ura*–16 *omote*. Courtesy of National Diet Library)

Figure 41 Mitsuuji seeing a woman who seems to be the Dragon King's daughter. (*NMIG*, chapter 19, 5 *ura*–6 *omote*. Courtesy of National Diet Library)

closed, and seeing, and the woman's supernatural provenance can be indicated by causing her to disappear when he awakes; these effects cannot be achieved in the same way in the picture. In order to imbue the scene with an appropriately eerie, ambiguous atmosphere, Tanehiko depicts Mitsuuji as he probably dreams himself to be, standing, endeavoring to illuminate the mystery before him—presumably in reality he is stretched out on the futon whose corner is visible at the right-hand corner of the picture—and plays with the frame of the folding screen.

The brook painted on this screen can be seen flowing out from underneath the sleeve of the woman's kimono, even though she is crouching past the edge of its last panel. The painted water seems, in other words, to be flowing through her. Alternatively, we might say that she appears to be an extension of the painted surface. Her fusion with the brook is emphasized by the pattern of waves, known as *seigaiha*, with which her kimono has been decorated. In addition to creating an association with water that is entirely appropriate for a woman who is believed to be the daughter of the Dragon King, who lives in the Dragon Palace at the bottom of the sea, this clever pictorial trick indicates that there is some question about her reality—that her figure should not be viewed as belonging entirely to the same plane as that of Mitsuuji and his two retainers.

Like a painted picture, the Dragon Girl is a sort of trick. Furthermore, since the brook is on the front of the screen and would not be visible from the back, her connection to it informs us that the perspective presented in the lower half of this picture is Mitsuuji's. The diagonal ribbon of water itself contributes to this effect by dividing the picture in two, separating Mitsuuji and the woman from the space beyond the screen. We get the sense that the two retainers are not visible to Mitsuuji—and yet at the same time they seem to see the woman, though perhaps not Mitsuuji. All this contributes to the dream-like atmosphere that clings to the lower half of the composition. Meanwhile, the fact that the retainers can see the woman from their position on the other side of the screen, beyond the painted brook, tells us that she is not simply Mitsuuji's dream.

In *gōkan*, certain types of creatures and objects routinely break the frames around pictures: flowing water, mountains, the moon, roofs, weapons, birds, and a variety of supernatural figures such as ghosts, dragons, and snakes. When natural or human-made objects are involved, the broken frame suggests motion, size, height, or the vastness of a landscape. When supernatural creatures are involved, their breaking of the frame highlights their ability to do things that the other characters cannot, such as fly. Here, Tanehiko is drawing on this second convention. Except that he has added an ingenious twist: instead of breaking the frame that encloses the entire picture, as is common, he has broken the frame of a picture within the picture.

Reading further into this pictorial play, we could interpret the not-quite-real, not-quite-not-real woman who crosses the border between two pictorial levels and belongs to both as an allegory of reading: just as the fake Dragon Girl comes into being at the point where the painted screen carries over into the picture that surrounds it, the dreamy worlds that *gōkan* create come into being, as the fake folded page also suggested, only because readers are able to carry information gleaned from each picture, and the text written into it, beyond the boundary of its frame as they turn from one page to the next. This allegorical reading of the composition seems to be supported by its position in *Inaka Genji*—by the pictures that follow it. I noted that there is something unusual about this picture as an instance of frame breaking, because the frame that is broken is within the picture rather than around it, as is usually the case in *gōkan*. Ordinarily, the breaking of a frame gestures toward an intersection of the picture's two-dimensionality with the three-dimensionality of the page on which it is printed and thus of the reader's world: a bird crossing a frame seems capable of flying through the space of the reader's world—the space of the book rather than the space of the narrative—if only to arrive in another picture on another page. Here, the dreaming Mitsuuji is placed in the position of the reader. And as we read on, we find that he continues to occupy this position, at least within the pictures, for some time.

The two pictures that follow this one of the fake Dragon Girl show Mitsuuji looking out the window of his residence in Suma, followed by the scene that meets his eyes: Toyoshi no Mae and her attendant Shiraito standing outside in the rain. These pictures, to which I will return later, are reproduced in figures 50 and 51. The sudden appearance of these two women in Suma turns out to be another dream—and again, as with the Dragon Girl, the dream is partly real. The two women are made visible in figure 51 by a flash of lightning that lights up a sky so black that "it seemed to have been printed with ink"—a clever xylographic variant on the "sky like ground ink" in *Genji monogatari*.[28] The flash explains, perhaps, the darkness under the building. A moment later, Shiraito has been struck and burned to a crisp. The fire spreads to Toyoshi no Mae's sleeve, so Mitsuuji rushes out to extinguish it; when he fails, he rips off the sleeve. Awoken at this point by a loud crash of thunder, he finds that he is still holding the sleeve. We learn later that Shiraito was actually struck by lightning in the capital, that the fire did indeed spread to Toyoshi no Mae's sleeve, and that she was saved when the sleeve mysteriously tore itself off and flew into the air.[29]

The spread that follows figure 51 shows Mitsuuji dreaming of Shiraito's death, holding the torn-off sleeve in his hand; the next picture shows him again either dreaming of or seeing the fake Dragon Girl. In other words, beginning with the scene in which the Dragon Girl first breaks the frame, confusing two levels of pictorial reality, we are presented with a series of five ambiguously real pictures that comes to an end only when, in a scene that bridges the last page of the first fascicle and the first page of the second fascicle of chapter 19, Mitsuuji finally shoots the fake Dragon Girl with an arrow, breaking the mountain priest's spell. It is as though the frame-breaking appearance of the Dragon Girl in figure 41 casts a spell on the pictures of *Inaka Genji* itself, or on Mitsuuji as he is shown in the pictures, and the enchantment is broken only when she is overcome. We might read this series of pictures as an allegory in which Mitsuuji, enchanted by a figure who collapses two levels of pictorial representation, loses himself in a world of dream until he is finally able to pin down the frame-breaking figure, separating dream from reality.

Another instance of frame breaking occurs in chapter 9. The chapter opens with an unusual *kuchi-e* that shows Mitsuuji's father, Ashikaga Yoshimasa, sitting on a cushion on Tsūtenkyō—a bridge long famous for its autumn foliage in the garden of Tōfukuji, a temple in Higashiyama—and looking out at a stage he has built over the water, on which Mitsuuji and his friendly competitor Akamatsu Takanao will later perform the dance "Blue Sea Waves" (Seigaiha), as do Genji and Tō no Chūjō in the "Momiji no ga" (Beneath the Autumn Leaves) chapter of *Genji monogatari* (figure 42).[30] Mitsuuji's older brother, Ashikaga Yoshihisa, who is in line to be the next shogun, stands behind his father; Fuji no Kata, the counterpart of Fujitsubo, kneels at Yoshimasa's left.

What makes this *kuchi-e* unusual is the absence, at the left side of the picture, of one edge of the decorative frame that would normally enclose the entire spread. The thick frames around *kuchi-e* lend them a dignity and weight that help set them apart from the main body of the book, particularly since their patterns usually resonate with the content of the pictures themselves, as is evident from the use of autumn foliage here. We see this, too, in the snake-scale pattern in the frame around the picture of Shinonome in figure 7a, which draws on the conventional association of snakes with ghosts and other transformed humans, and the gourds framing Mitsuuji and Tasogare in figure 7b, which call up both the morning glories in the "Yūgao" (The Twilight Beauty) chapter of *Genji monogatari* and the "crow gourds" that give Mitsuuji a pretext to get acquainted with Tasogare in chapter 4 of *Inaka Genji*, about which I will have more to say later.[31]

The absent edge in the *kuchi-e* in figure 42, suggesting incompleteness, prompts readers to flip the page, maintaining a mental image of the picture in front of them; when they do, they discover that Toyoshi no Mae is standing right behind Fuji no Kata, a stern look on her face (figure 43).[32] The edge of the frame that was missing on the previous page appears here, forming the left-hand border of what has turned out to be a rare three-panel *kuchi-e*.[33] There is something unusual about this border as well, however: it is broken by Takanao's left sleeve, which intrudes from the first page of the main body of the chapter, pushing the third panel of the *kuchi-e* into the background and thus foregrounding its wearer and Mitsuuji, who stands just behind him. The dramatically posed young men are dancing "Seigaiha," the highlight of the day's entertainments.

Viewed in sequence, this series of pictures does a remarkable job of conveying the tensions among the characters, and to a large extent its effectiveness is due to Tanehiko's manipulation of the decorative frame. The first two panels of the *kuchi-e* present us with a scene in which Fuji no Kata, evidently the first to arrive, sits down to exchange a few words with Yoshimasa; unlike Yoshihisa and the reader, she is able to see his face—it is even possible that he is looking back at her. We get a sense, despite Yoshihisa's presence, of the intimacy that Fuji no Kata and Yoshimasa share. Our impression of the scene changes dramatically, however, when we turn the page and an angry Toyoshi no Mae appears, evidently having shown up second: suddenly she is the focus of the picture. Her introduction into the scene makes Yoshihisa, on the previous page, seem less awkward and uncharismatic than he did before, giving him instead an antsy and apologetic air: we notice that Toyoshi no Mae's furious glare seems to be directed at him, her son, and his

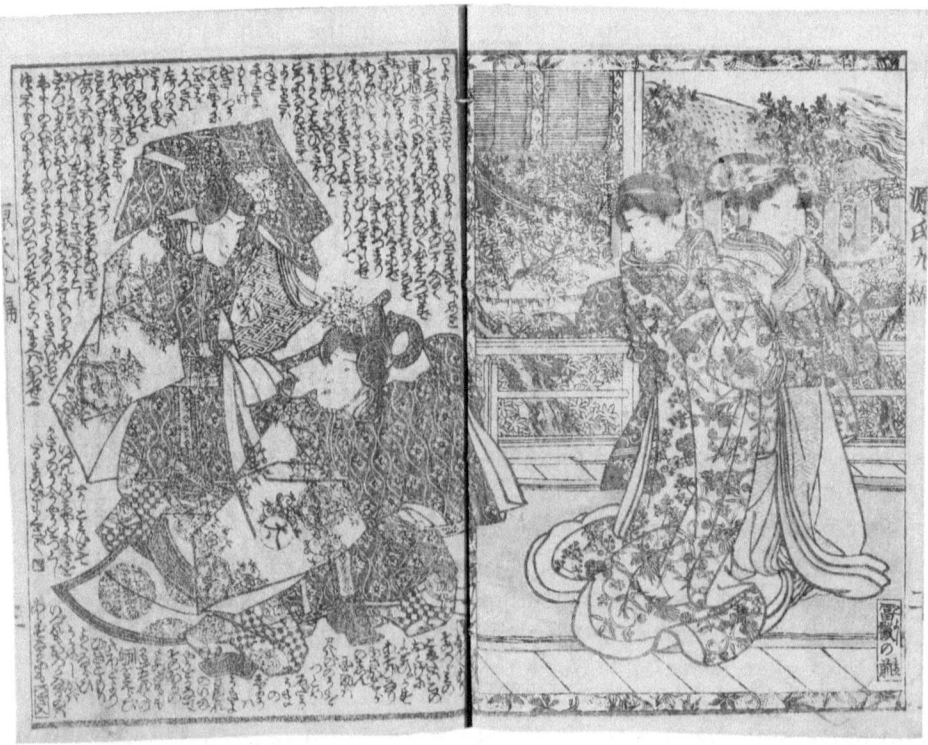

Figure 43 Toyoshi no Mae, standing just behind Fuji no Kata (*right*), and Mitsuuji and Takanao dancing "Blue Sea Waves." (*NMIG*, chapter 9, 2 *ura*–3 *omote*. Courtesy of National Diet Library)

timid look at her. But while she is central to the third panel of the *kuchi-e* and casts a shadow over the entire composition, she is also isolated: although connected to the first two panels by the unusual placement of the decorative frame, which cues readers to reconstruct the three-panel series as a single whole in their minds' eyes, she is simultaneously shut out by her relegation to the back of the page.

Takanao's intrusive sleeve also has the effect of detracting attention from Toyoshi no Mae by literally pushing her into the background. And while Toyoshi no Mae's attendant stands behind her and slightly to the left, when the spread is viewed in its entirety it is the attendant who seems to take precedence, since her gaze does more to structure this spread than her mistress's, which is, in reality, directed off the page at nothing. In breaking the frame, moreover, Takanao's sleeve conflates two separate times, since the scene depicted in the *kuchi-e* takes place before the day's entertainments begin. This allows us to read the puzzled

Figure 42 Yoshimasa, Fuji no Kata, and Yoshihisa on Tsūtenkyō. (*NMIG*, chapter 9, 1 *ura*–2 *omote*. Courtesy of National Diet Library)

gaze of Toyoshi no Mae's attendant as a doubly metapictorial gesture: she is surprised both by the incursion of the main body of the work into the *kuchi-e* in which she herself appears, and by the premature arrival of the future in the present. This perspective of hers, even more than the breaking of the frame, is what gives this series of pictures its instructive force as a metapicture, by showing readers where to look.

It is extremely unusual for a picture from the main body of a *gōkan* to take precedence over a *kuchi-e* in this way—this is the only time it happens in *Inaka Genji*. The effect is all the more powerful because readers know that Mitsuuji is in league with Fuji no Kata and because it is clear that he and Takanao are performing on the very stage that lies empty directly before Yoshimasa in the first spread: in a sense, there is more of a connection between the dynamic figure of the two youths dancing and the scene between Fuji no Kata and Yoshimasa than there is between Toyoshi no Mae and the first picture. It is telling that depictions of this scene in *ukiyo-e*, including both actor prints and Genji pictures, collapse the *kuchi-e* and the picture of the two young men dancing and leave Toyoshi no Mae out of the picture. We see this, for instance, in a print by Kunisada published by Izumiya Ichibē as part of the series *His Figure: Related Copies of Other Pictures* (*Sono sugata yukari no utsushi-e*, 1849–1853) (figure 44).[34]

The complex pictorial presentation of the tensions among Toyoshi no Mae, Fuji no Kata, and Mitsuuji—or, rather, of the manner in which Toyoshi no Mae has been cleverly hemmed in by Mitsuuji and Fuji no Kata—contrasts with the verbal presentation of the scene that opens the first page of the main body of this chapter, on which the two young men are shown dancing:

> The winter day was so short that before one knew it early afternoon had rolled around. At this point, Yoshimasa moved to the seat he had had prepared on Tsūtenkyō, from which he would watch the performances; Toyoshi no Mae sat on his left, and next to her Fuji no Kata, and then a cramped crowd of other women lined up one after the other according to their rank. A folding screen was set up as a divider to Yoshimasa's right, beyond which Yoshihisa was seated, and somewhat further down the bridge Mitsuuji waited, quiet and mature, ready to be of use.[35]

This verbal rewriting places all the characters in the positions appropriate to their rank: Toyoshi no Mae and Yoshihisa are closest to Yoshimasa; Fuji no Kata and Mitsuuji are next. Our reading of this officially

Figure 44 The seventh print in Utagawa Kunisada's series *Sono sugata yukari no utsushi-e*, based on the three-panel *kuchi-e* shown in figures 42 and 43. (© Trustees of the British Museum)

correct portrayal is complicated, however, by the series of pictures we have just seen. The unusual three-panel *kuchi-e* and even more unusual intrusion of the main body of the work into the *kuchi-e* masterfully capture the tensions at the core of the shogunal household; the disjunction between these pictures and the text, which makes no reference to this tension, creates a sense that not everything is being said. The words present only the surface, while the pictures probe deeper. This is one of many instances in which pictures tell us more about what is happening than the prose. In terms of what it accomplishes on an abstract level, this series stands somewhere between the fake folded page and the barbed frame that isolates the firewood sellers: it both incorporates into the composition the movement from one page to the next and uses the materiality of the page as a wall to close off, only partially in this case, what is happening on one side from what is happening on the other.

I mentioned that it is very unusual for one *kuchi-e* to continue beyond a single spread. The shock of the effect is somewhat less in a *gōkan*, however, than it would be in a work printed in the case-bound format that currently dominates the production of literature worldwide. Unlike books in this form, which are created using paper printed on both sides, *gōkan* were made by printing individual sheets on one side only, folding each sheet in half with the printed surface out, stacking the folded sheets, and binding the edges opposite the fold. This format, which is known as *fukurotoji* ("pouch binding," since each folded page forms a pouch), was ideally suited to publications that used cheap, thin paper that could not be printed on both sides and was overwhelmingly the format of choice for printed and even calligraphic works in the Edo period, regardless of paper quality. It is hard, reading a *gōkan*, not to be aware of how it was assembled, and so the idea of linking the three panels of the *kuchi-e* in chapter 9 is more obvious than it would be in an edition of *Inaka Genji* issued in the form of the modern case-bound book: it makes sense that the panel depicting Toyoshi no Mae and her attendant should be connected mentally with the previous panel because they were both printed from a single block on the same side of the same piece of paper. Tanehiko's three-panel *kuchi-e* succeeds so well in part because it exploits the physical characteristics of the *gōkan*.

Tanehiko's awareness of material form is not surprising, considering that books in the early modern period were produced entirely by hand: individuals involved in the first, planning stages of the creation of a new book—the authors and artists—inevitably had to bear in mind the particular constraints placed on them by the woodblock-printing technology they used and the capabilities of the craftsmen who actually created the products. More important, they were able to exploit their heightened awareness of the remarkable freedom that woodblock printing allowed. They could also assume that most of their readers would share this consciousness of form, as we see in a *kibyōshi* by Jippensha Ikku that traces the process by which a book is made: *The Best-Selling Edo Bookseller* (*Atariya shita jihon doiya*, 1802). The publisher in this story ends up having his store mobbed by eager buyers. When he tells them, "We haven't gotten the books bound yet!" someone in the crowd shouts out, "We'll bind them ourselves, just give 'em to us as they are!"[36] As I noted earlier, the same thing happened with chapter 10 of *Inaka Genji*, which was sold with temporary covers that readers were encouraged to replace themselves once the true covers had been printed. In *Inaka Genji*, Tanehiko takes the sensitivity to material form that he shared with his readers to an astonishingly high level. The effectiveness of all the pictures I have analyzed so far stemmed in one way or another from the manner in which they played on the physicality of the *gōkan*. Other pictures work even more directly with the bookishness of the book; it is to these that I turn next.

Metapictures 3: Reading Material

I would like to look first, briefly, at two series of pictures from the main body of *Inaka Genji* that incorporate into their compositions the very thickness of the paper on which they were printed. The first begins early in chapter 1 with a scene inspired by the account, early in *Genji monogatari*, of the cruel pranks played on Kiritsubo by her competitors for the emperor's affections. Figure 45 shows Hanagiri, *Inaka Genji*'s Kiritsubo, standing clad only in her undergarments before the Chinese-style door that leads to the shogun's rooms, having stripped off various items of clothing whose hems were soiled by rotten fish guts strewn across the floor of the hallway by women in the service of her principal rival, Toyoshi no Mae.³⁷ Hanagiri's attendant, Sugibae, is tiptoeing gingerly back in the direction from which she and her mistress came, the soiled clothes over her shoulder, on her way to fetch clean garments. The following spread shows Hanagiri standing by the cedar-plank door through which she and Sugibae had come and through which Sugibae has returned, while Yoshimasa enters at the right through the Chinese-style door seen in the previous picture (figure 46).³⁸ Yoshimasa's presence here is another instance of mixed temporalities, since he does not actually arrive until sometime between 2:00 and 2:30 A.M. and is not mentioned in the text until the next page. At this point, Hanagiri is still alone in the corridor: she has discovered that the Chinese-style door will not open and, hearing Sugibae calling to her, has gone back to the cedar-plank door to listen to what her attendant has to say. The news is bad. Someone, it turns out, has placed a lock on this door, and Sugibae cannot return to the corridor where Hanagiri is waiting. The following spread shows Sugibae crouching on the other side of the door, clean clothes under her arm (figure 47).³⁹

Satō Satoru has suggested that series of pictures like this one represent Tanehiko's importation into the *gōkan* of a visual sensibility inspired by the revolving stage used in the kabuki theater.⁴⁰ Turning the page, moving from the first to the second picture in this series, brings about a ninety-degree shift of perspective much like the rotation of the kabuki stage. The horizontal movement that takes place when we move from the second to the third picture, however, plays not on the kabuki stage but on the material form of the *gōkan* itself. Turning the page takes us from one side of the door to the other: the thickness of the paper comes to represent physically the thickness of the door, and when Hanagiri and Sugibae talk through the door, it is as if they are talking through the page. This series is similar to the three-panel *kuchi-e* discussed earlier, in which the parts of the picture on the obverse and reverse sides of the page were both connected and separated, only here, the thickness of the paper becomes part of the pictures.

The same hallway appears twice more in *Inaka Genji*: once in chapter 11, and again in chapter 37. Interestingly, Tanehiko uses the same trick in chapter 11. First we are presented with a view of the hallway all but identical to that in chapter 1 (figure 48).[41] Mitsuuji is shown flirting with Mihara, the counterpart of *Genji monogatari*'s Gen no Naishi. The following spread shows Yoshimasa standing on the other side of the wall and peering through the blinds at his son (figure 49).[42] The two women nearby, Fuji no Kata and her attendant Tsukasa, do not really enter the scene until later: here, too, the temporalities are mixed. In this sequence, the thickness of the printed page has been used to represent

Figure 45 Hanagiri (*right*) and Sugibae, on her way to fetch clean clothes. (*NMIG*, chapter 1, 6 *ura*–7 *omote*. Courtesy of Waseda University Library, Tokyo)

Figure 46 The hallway shown in figure 45. Hanagiri is talking to Sugibae through the door, while Yoshimasa is just walking into the hall at the back. (*NMIG*, chapter 1, 7 *ura*–8 *omote*. Courtesy of Waseda University Library, Tokyo)

Figure 47 Sugibae talking to Hanagiri through the door shown in figure 46. (*NMIG*, chapter 1, 8 *ura*–9 *omote*. Courtesy of Waseda University Library, Tokyo)

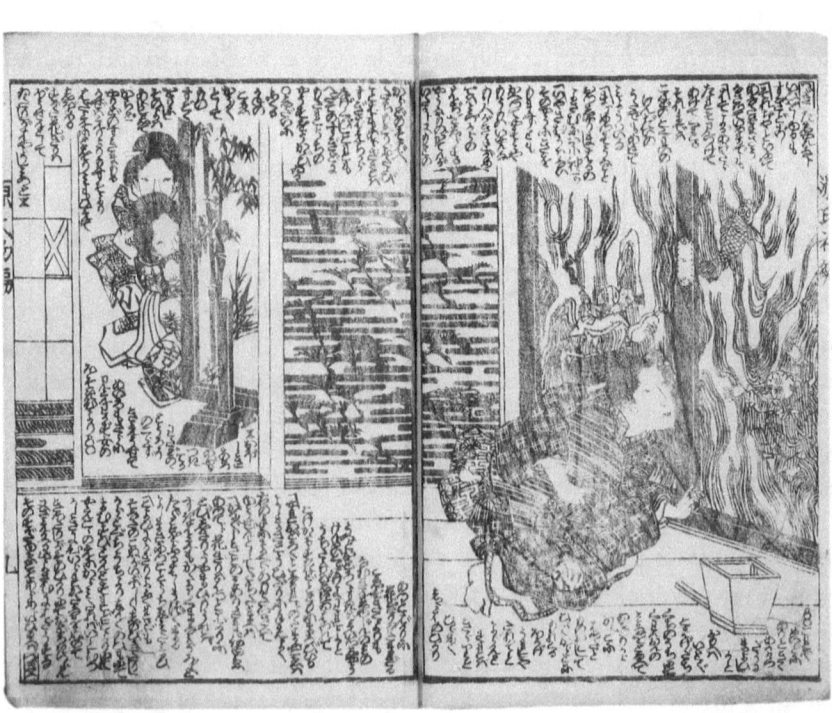

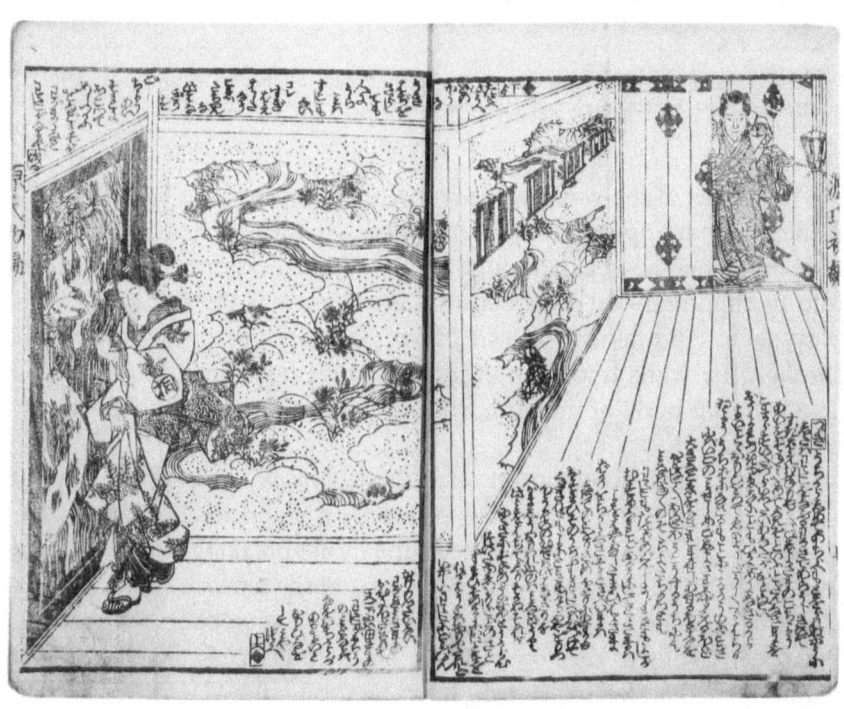

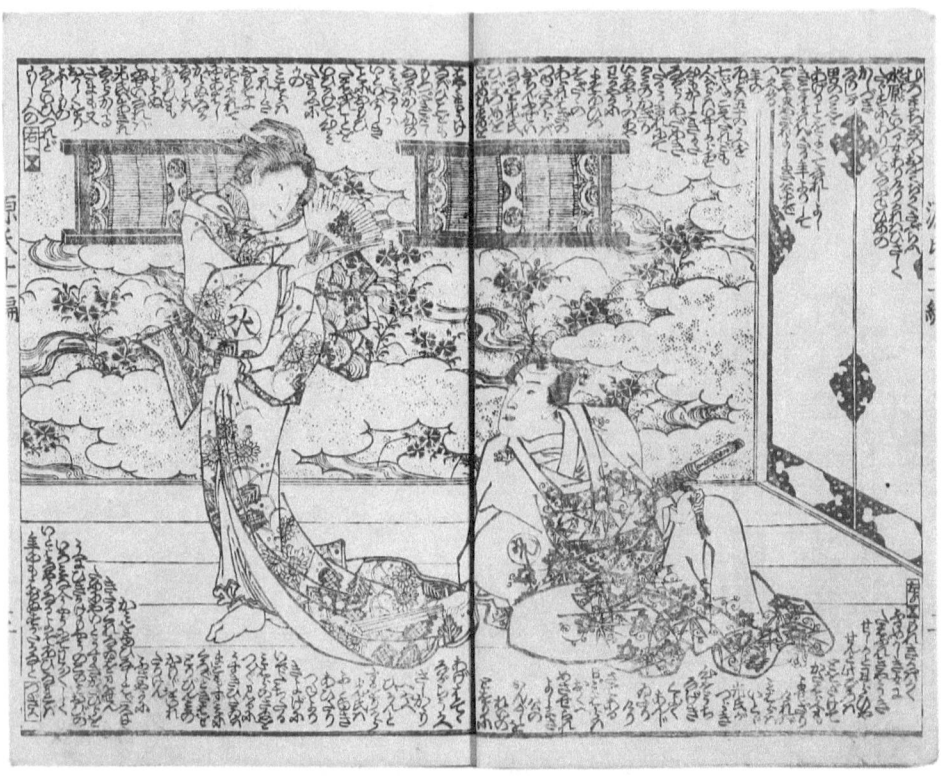

Figure 48 Mitsuuji flirting with Mihara in the hallway shown in figures 45 and 46. (*NMIG*, chapter 11, 2 *ura*–3 *omote*. Courtesy of Waseda University Library, Tokyo)

the thickness of the wall. At the same time, because the hallway is the same one that appears in chapter 1—because the space that Yoshimasa is seeing when he peeks through the blinds is the same one he walked into in chapter 1—we get a sense that the various interior spaces that play such a prominent role in *Inaka Genji* are materially connected through the walls and doors that the pages both show and become. The material body of the book actually seems to constitute the spaces it depicts.

Another, more subtle instance of the technique of using the page to represent the thickness of what is pictured on it appears in chapter 19, in the dream-like sequence that follows the frame-breaking depiction of the fake Dragon Girl discussed earlier. The first of the pictures shows Mitsuuji standing and peeking through a window in the wooden shutters that have been put up to keep out the rain, his attendant Yoshikiyo looking on (figure 50).[43] The folding screen, futon, and oil lamp visible in the back-

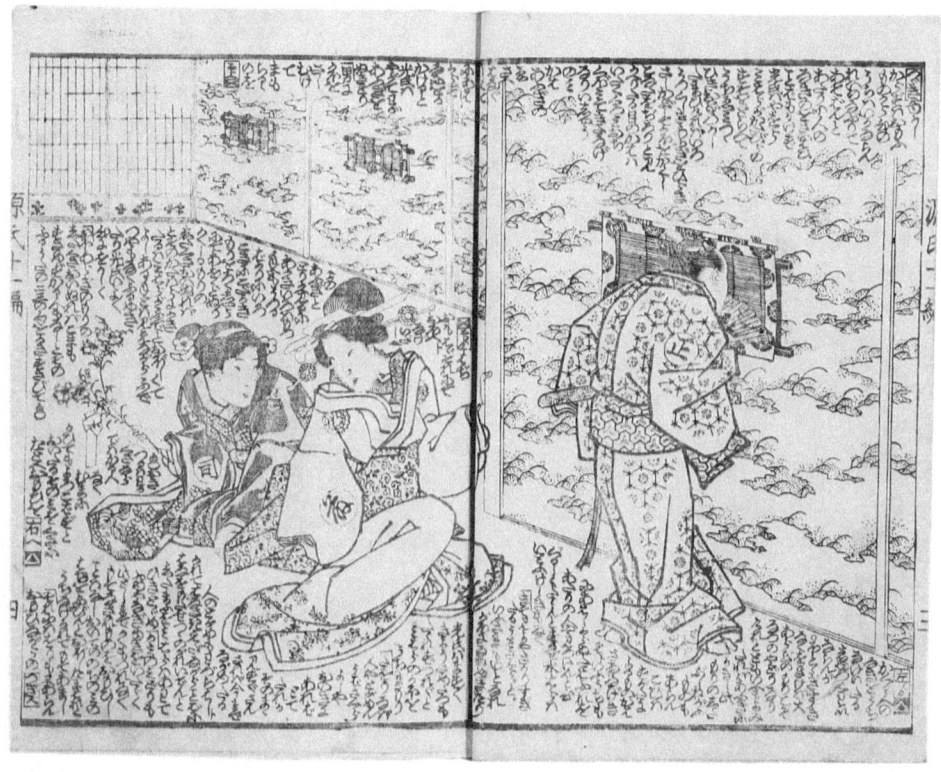

Figure 49 Yoshimasa peering at Mitsuuji and Mihara from the other side of the blinds shown in figure 48. (*NMIG*, chapter 11, 3 *ura*–4 *omote*. Courtesy of Waseda University Library, Tokyo)

ground are, no doubt, the same ones glimpsed in the preceding picture, shown in figure 41, though here they are seen from the other side—the scene has rotated 180 degrees. Flipping the page, we find Toyoshi no Mae and her attendant Shiraito, the woman who, known at that point as Kogiku, came up with the idea of littering the hall with waste to humiliate Hanagiri in chapter 1 (figure 51).[44] Shiraito is holding a knife. This second picture's connection to the first is indicated by the bit of Mitsuuji's sleeve that is visible through the window above the water basin behind Shiraito, and by the glimpse we get through the window on the previous page of the water basin and the branches fanning out over it. Here, again, the thickness of the paper is equated with that of the wall.

I began my discussion of metapictures in *Inaka Genji* with an analysis of a fake folded page, and then considered a picture that highlights its own frame, two instances of frame breaking, and a series of pictures that make the materiality of the printed page part of their compositions.

Figure 50 Mitsuuji looking out the window of his temporary residence in Suma. (*NMIG*, chapter 19, 6 *ura*–7 *omote*. Courtesy of National Diet Library)

By now, it should be clear that all these different types of metapictures engage in some way, directly or indirectly, with the connectedness of each picture with others—with the turning of pages and the mental construction, on the part of the reader, of a whole that encompasses both sides. Like the picture of the fake folded page, they emphasize that it is precisely the movement of the reader's eye across successive pages—the overlapping of the passage of time outside the book with that inside it— that imbues the two-dimensional pictorial space of the narrative with a pseudo-three-dimensionality.

The final sort of metapicture I would like to touch on is one that plays not solely on a page, but on the three-dimensional materiality of the *gōkan* as a bound volume. The first example appears in chapter 2 in a picture that depicts Toyoshi no Mae and Shiraito conspiring to sneak Yamana Sōzen into the palace by hiding him in a chest, sending him in as a present to Fuji no Kata, and then letting him kidnap or kill her as he

Figure 51 Toyoshi no Mae and Shiraito outside the window shown in figure 50. Mitsuuji's sleeve is just visible in the middle of the page. (*NMIG*, chapter 19, 7 *ura*–8 *omote*. Courtesy of National Diet Library)

pleases (figure 52).[45] What is of interest here is Tanehiko's placement of the hinge of the folding door right along the inner edge of the left-hand panel. The door has been printed in such a way that it actually appears to open when the pages are moved. The next example is from a picture in chapter 8 that shows Mitsuuji and a woman named Koben looking at the fans they had agreed to use as signs the previous night (figure 53).[46] Here the corner of the building has been situated along the inner edge of the left panel, just as the hinge of the door is in figure 52. This gives the scene an extra sense of three-dimensionality, making it appear, when a reader holds the book, as if Mitsuuji really is gazing through space at the fan dangling from the bamboo stick, while Koben gazes back at the fan he holds.

By linking the space of the narrative to the materiality of the *gōkan*, these compositions stress in the plainest and most direct manner that the fictional world of *Inaka Genji* is created through a process of reading

Figure 52 Toyoshi no Mae and Shiraito conspiring. The door of the shrine seems to move with the page when the book is opened. (*NMIG*, chapter 2, 12 *ura*–13 *omote*. Courtesy of Waseda University Library, Tokyo)

inextricably bound to the materiality of the published work and to the reader's physical engagement with that material.[47] They remind us that reading is an interactive act and that the book, *this* book, is more than just a text: the pictures are not lively scenes to be interpreted in light of the textual explanations provided, as is frequently the case with *gōkan*, but are themselves packed with information that must be drawn out in order for the world of *Inaka Genji* to come alive, just as the character for *higashi* had to be drawn out of the *hiragana* for *higashi*, and then interpreted pictorially, in order for the very first sentence of the book to make sense. Like that blatant metalinguistic gesture, the instructional metapictures that I have analyzed encourage active, imaginative reading of *Inaka Genji* not as an adaptation, but as an image-text-book.

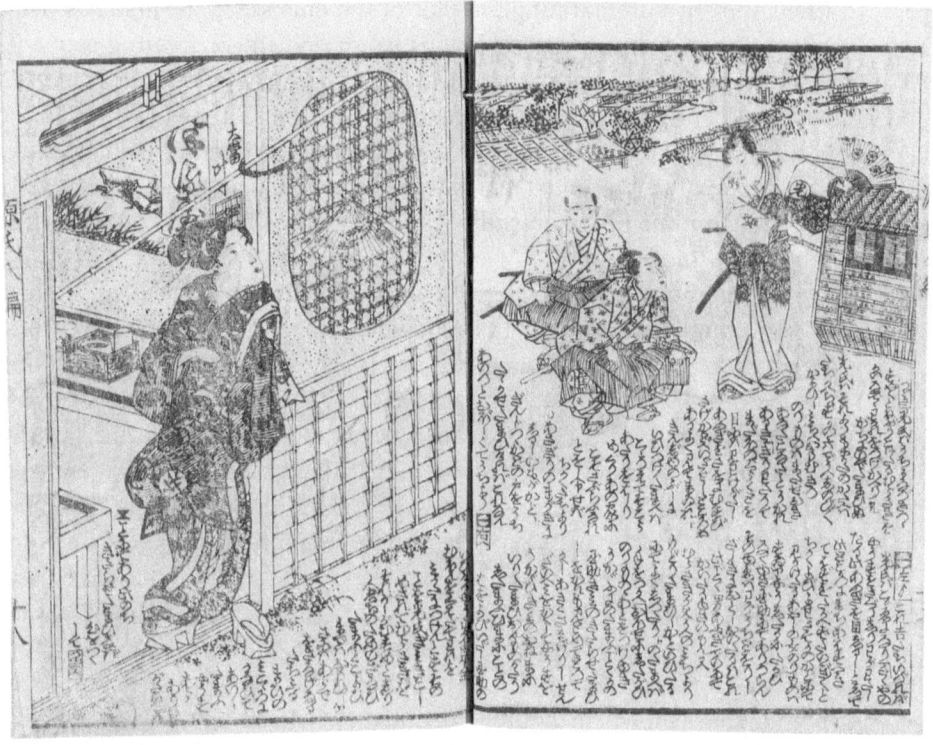

Figure 53 Mitsuuji and Koben noticing the fans. The corner of the building is positioned where the pages come together. (*NMIG*, chapter 8, 17 *ura*–18 *omote*. Courtesy of National Diet Library)

Prefiguration: Reading Practice

The importance of this sort of active interpretive participation is indicated explicitly in chapter 5, when Mitsuuji demonstrates, at the conclusion of one of the most dramatic scenes in the early chapters, his own facility at reading texts into images—a process analogous to drawing an image of the sun rising through the trees from the word "Higashiyama." It will be useful to look somewhat closely at this scene as a case in which the text shows readers how to interpret a picture, makes this sort of brainwork attractive and exciting, and thus points the way toward a mode of participatory reading that enriches the work, as do the various types of metapictures I have been discussing, albeit more subtly. This scene will also serve as an instance of what I have called prefiguration: the pictorial presentation of information that is only later explained in the text.

I will start by summarizing the plot of the episode that Mitsuuji's demonstration of picture reading brings to an end. Incorporating elements from the story of Genji's relationship with Yugao in *Genji monogatari*, it remained one of the most popular in *Inaka Genji* all the way through the Meiji period, largely because it was staged in numerous kabuki plays and frequently represented in prints. For the time being, I will sketch only the basic outline of the episode, since I will consider it in more detail at the end of this chapter.

Mitsuuji has been trying to track down a short sword called Kogarasumaru, another name for the renowned Kogarasu, which was passed down in the Heike clan from eldest son to eldest son for generations after the historical Emperor Suzaku (923–952, r. 930–946) presented it to Taira no Sadamori as a token of gratitude for having killed Taira no Masakado. According to *Kogetsushō*, *Genji monogatari*'s Suzaku emperor corresponds to his historical namesake.[48] This tenuous link to *Genji monogatari* no doubt partly explains the sword's presence here, but in the context of *Inaka Genji* it has a more important meaning: it symbolizes the authority of the Ashikaga shogunate. Without it, Mitsuuji's father, Yoshimasa, is unable to name his successor legitimately. Kogarasumaru was stolen, we later learn, by an impoverished dancing instructor named Shinonome (shown in figures 7a and 8a), whose family was exterminated by Yoshimasa after her father plotted a rebellion. Shinonome's late husband happened to be descended from a long line of ninja and had passed on his family's secret teachings to her. This admixture of poverty, resentment of Yoshimasa, and ninja stealth made Shinonome the perfect candidate for the Kogarasumaru job. She planned to use the gold she was promised as a reward for the sword to have some nice clothes prepared for her beloved daughter, Tasogare (pictured with Mitsuuji in figures 7b and 8b), hoping that this would make it easier for Tasogare to attract a good husband.[49]

Mitsuuji realizes that Shinonome is the thief when Tasogare falls in love with him, prompting her eager mother to welcome him into their recently refurbished house, which had attracted his attention anyway. The story ends tragically when Mitsuuji and Tasogare run off to a dilapidated temple, only to be overtaken by Shinonome, who has been ordered on pain of death, by the same person who urged her to steal Kogarasumaru in the first place, to murder Mitsuuji. Tasogare valiantly slashes her own throat with a razor, thereby distracting Shinonome from her deadly design. Shinonome, stricken with grief, stabs herself in the stomach and launches into a lengthy confession reminiscent of the speeches made at similar moments by characters in kabuki plays.

By the time all this happens, three-quarters of the way through chapter 5, the clever detective Mitsuuji has figured out almost everything he needs to know—the only bit of information he still has to elicit from Shinonome is the identity of the person who convinced her to steal the sword. Shinonome is an honorable thief, however, and there is little hope that she will give up this secret. Unlike his attendant, Nikki Kiyonosuke, who presses him to question her, Mitsuuji realizes this: "Even if I were to ask, how could a tough soul like her, more manly than any man, be expected to tell us outright a name she has sworn not to speak. . . . How about it, Shinonome? Since I've seen this far into your heart already, can't you let me know indirectly, without my asking and without your telling me?"[50] Shinonome responds, in a dramatic moment that calls to mind the dynamic poses struck by characters on the kabuki stage and that later went on to become just such a pose, by lifting, upside down, a bamboo blind that Mitsuuji and Tasogare had taken to shield themselves from the rain (figure 54).[51] The blind has a shape cut out of it that suggests the contour of Mount Fuji.

Naturally, Mitsuuji instantly understands: "Mount Fuji . . . a famous mountain [名山, *meizan*, written in *kanji* in the original publication] unrivaled by any other in Japan, China, or India . . . and when one reads that 'famous mountain' upside down . . . ah, yes, that makes sense, that makes sense."[52] The reader, too, is expected to realize that the word 名山 can be read into the cut-out image of Mount Fuji, and that when this pair of characters is inverted like the blind (they are, of course, printed vertically in the Japanese), this yields 山名, or Yamana, the name of the villain.

The suave hero of *Inaka Genji* offers readers a clear demonstration of the importance of knowing how to read a picture: he shows that pictorial representation can be read and, indeed, will have to be read to keep abreast of the rapidly unfolding narrative of his adventures. Looking at the pictures in *gōkan* and gradually learning the details of what is going on in them from the explanations are two of the pleasures afforded by the genre as a whole—this is what readers do with virtually every picture in *Inaka Genji*. The reading experience this scene offers is, however, significantly different from those that populate most *gōkan*: here, the reader is urged not simply to *look* at a picture and passively wait to have it verbally explained, but to *read* the picture *before* it is explained—to read it the way she would read its explanation. What makes this scene most exciting and captivating is not the demonstration of "reading practice" itself, but the fact that the passage that narrates it appears a full two spreads after the picture showing Shinonome holding up the blind. The gruesome picture of a dying woman sitting in a puddle of her own

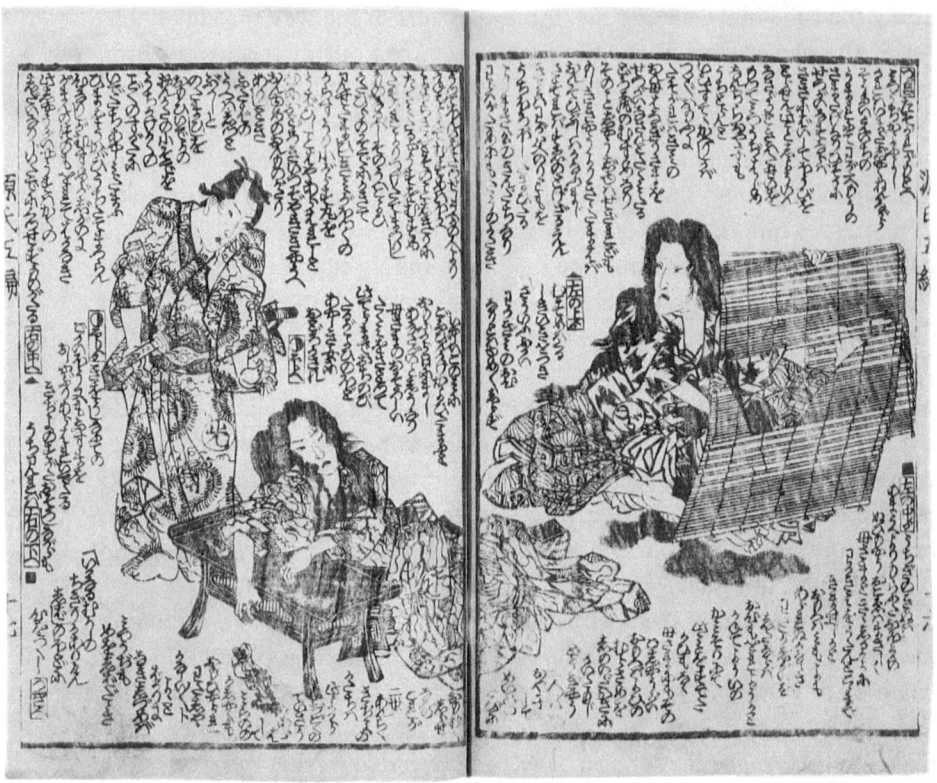

Figure 54 Shinonome holding the bamboo blind upside down for Mitsuuji to see (*right*), while Tasogare leans on a desk, dying. (*NMIG*, chapter 5, 16 *ura*–17 *omote*. Courtesy of Waseda University Library, Tokyo)

blood, using her last remaining energy to hold up a blind and display it, upside down, to Mitsuuji, is offered to the reader first, all on its own, as a riddle crying out to be solved. If the reader has figured out its meaning by the time Mitsuuji provides his interpretation, so much the better; if not, she has now been given an example to follow. This is prefiguration: the picture comes first. In this scene, *Inaka Genji* offers an object lesson in how to read *Inaka Genji*.

The circularity of this formulation is fitting in discussing a work that contains words that must be read as pictures, pictures that must be translated into words, and printed pages depicting printed pages. It is especially appropriate in the context of a treatment of Mitsuuji's identification of Yamana Sōzen as the villain behind Kogarasumaru's disappearance: while Mitsuuji's reading of the characters "Yamana" into a material representation of Mount Fuji first reveals that Yamana Sōzen is the motivating force in one of the overarching stock plots that structures the book as a whole—the search for the missing treasure—Yamana Sōzen is first smuggled into the visual landscape of *Inaka Genji* in a chest said to be full of writing. He leaps pictorially from a chest of words and then appears as a word from a picture. What's more, the series of three spreads that give us our first look at the chest and then show Yamana Sōzen emerging from it serves as an instance of the presentation in *Inaka Genji* of pictorial information that is never explained in the writing and bears no relationship to the plot, but subtly enriches the reading experience.[53]

Earlier, I discussed the picture in chapter 2 that shows Toyoshi no Mae and Shiraito plotting to conceal Yamana Sōzen in the chest and then take it to Fuji no Kata's quarters and let him do as he pleases with her—either kidnap her or kill her on the spot (see figure 52). Figure 55 shows Shiraito kneeling and presenting the chest to Fuji no Kata, who stands at the right of the composition:

> His Lordship [Yoshimasa] will be spending the evening at our quarters, and so, thinking you might find it difficult to while away the hours, my mistress bid me to convey to you that she has packed all sorts of different poetic texts, tales, *kōwakamai*, and *jōruri* into this long chest here, among them *Genji*, the *Ten Thousand Leaves*, *Tales of Ise*, *Shishira*, *Little Ochikubo*, *The Tale of Kyōtarō*, *Yashima*, *Takadachi*, *Wada's Banquet*, *The Splitting of Amida's Chest*, and *Twelve Episodes*. She hopes that you will do her the honor of looking over any of these booklets you should happen to find new and interesting.[54]

The picture that comes next shows Fuji no Kata sitting up on her futon, which has been spread behind the folding screen shown in figure 55, and Mitsuuji about to slip in behind the screen; having gotten wind of Toyoshi no Mae's plot, the two have agreed to fake an affair, hoping that Sōzen will be so disgusted at the thought of a woman being involved with a man who is practically her son that he will stop loving her and leave, which he does. This atmospheric, pseudo-amorous scene corresponds brilliantly to the first meeting between Genji and Fujitsubo in *Genji monogatari*, which is famously passed over in that work, mentioned only in retrospect.[55] The chest remains where it was in the previous picture, eye-catching in its size. The third picture in the series shows Yamana Sōzen, having burst from the chest, holding his undrawn sword under Fuji no Kata's neck as Mitsuuji winces in feigned embarrassment (figure 56).

The detail I would like to focus on in this series of three pictures is the pattern with which the wheeled chest is decorated. It is instantly

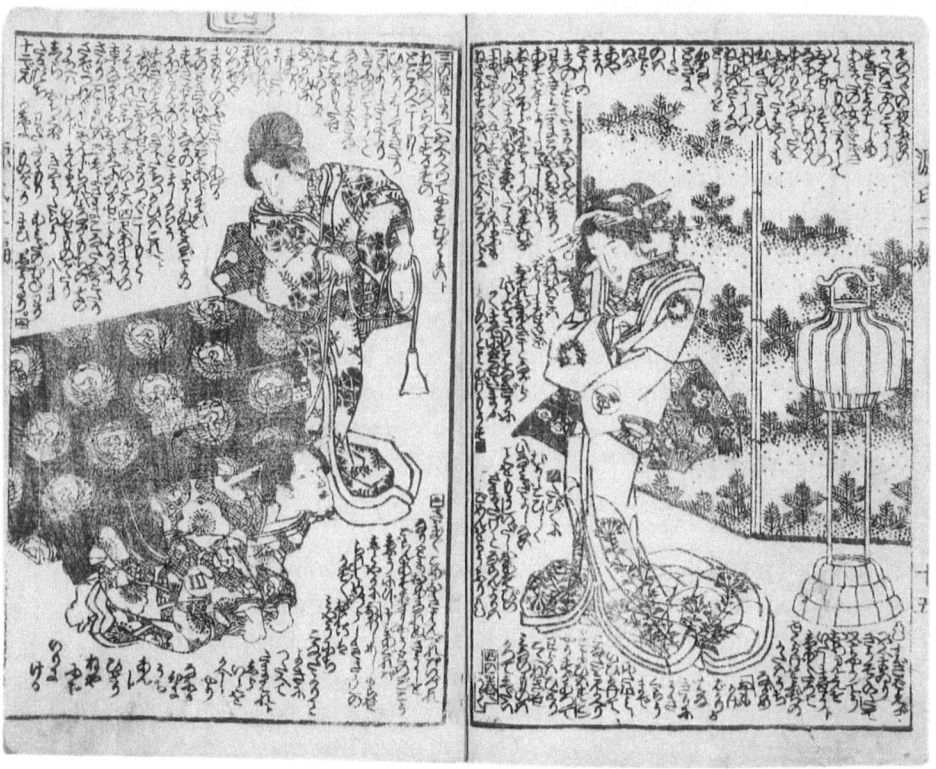

Figure 55 Shiraito and an attendant presenting the chest holding Yamana Sōzen to Fuji no Kata. (*NMIG*, chapter 2, 15 *ura*-16 *omote*. Courtesy of Waseda University Library, Tokyo)

recognizable as the logo of Senkakudō, the combined publishing house and store that issued and sold *Inaka Genji*. While it is not unusual for such advertisements to find their way into the pictures in *gōkan*, they are not generally placed as prominently as this one is, in three spreads in a row. And, of course, there is something special about the context: here the "crane circle" (*tsuru no maru*) logo has been used to decorate not an umbrella or the roof of a palanquin or some other casual prop unrelated to publishing that plays no major role in the plot, but an important chest said to contain *sōshi* (books). The decoration of the chest with Senkakudō's logo is clearly more than a random ad; it is playing on the content of the story and of the chest.

Viewed in this light, it seems significant that the figure who finally emerges from the chest is the brutish Yamana Sōzen, who serves as the driving force behind much of *Inaka Genji*'s plot and is a walking embodiment of the kind of action that keeps readers of *gōkan* entertained.

Figure 56 Yamana Sōzen catching Fuji no Kata and Mitsuuji in the act. (*NMIG*, chapter 2, 17 *ura*–18 *omote*. Courtesy of Waseda University Library, Tokyo)

Moreover, Yamaza Sōzen takes the place of a long list of books, including several of considerable canonical weight, with none other than *Genji monogatari* at its head: the chest that arrives from Senkakudō, which is supposed to contain *Genji monogatari*, actually has something a good deal more exciting inside. Yamana Sōzen's rude intrusion upon the scene can be read, I suggest, as an image of *Inaka Genji* in the process of replacing *Genji monogatari*.

Pictures That Show More: Read What You Are Looking At

So far, I have been analyzing individual passages and pictures in *Inaka Genji*, trying at the same time to demonstrate how each of these artificially isolated moments mirrors, or converses with, others. I have shown that this book creates a complex dialogue between pictures and writing in which words point to pictures and pictures become legible through words, but I have also shown that *Inaka Genji*'s pictures move beyond the text, contradicting, anticipating, and supplementing it. Much of my analysis of the pictures has been dedicated, at least in part, to showing how they encourage readers to adopt a perspective that takes in the whole of *Inaka Genji* not as a text, but as a printed book, a material object. Most of this can be summed up very simply by saying that *Inaka Genji* exploits a variety of sophisticated techniques to make its readers look harder and read more carefully, and with the observation that the pictures in this work are as rich as the written text, especially when they are actively mined for the information they contain. *Inaka Genji* repays the sort of active, participatory reading it urges.

I would like to close this chapter with a reading of the section in which Mitsuuji's discovery of the name Yamana in an inverted Mount Fuji appears. My aim is to give some sense of what the experience of reading *Inaka Genji* as a *gōkan* is like, emphasizing the importance of the pictures and showing that, as my analyses of particular pictures have suggested, there is a key to unlocking the pleasures of Tanehiko's *gōkan*: to realize that for all the complexity and variety of the relationships that obtain between the book's pictures and its text, the pictures are usually read first. The story I will be looking at is the same one I outlined earlier: that of Shinonome's theft of the short sword Kogarasumaru, Mitsuuji's attempts to discover the identity of the thief, his first meeting with Tasogare and the beginning of their amours, his escape with Tasogare to the ruined temple, Shinonome's attempt to murder Mitsuuji, and the suicides of Tasogare and Shinonome.

For our purposes, the episode begins on the spread in chapter 3 covering pages 11 *ura* and 12 *omote* (figure 57).[56] The man on the right is identified—as the characters in *gōkan* usually are, by a small round tag made to look as though it were dyed into the character's clothing—as Nikki Kiyonosuke (the tag, located just below his left elbow, simply says き代 [Kiyo]). Neither the man lying on his back in the middle of the spread nor the cloaked woman standing at the left is identified, the first because he is unimportant and the second because the process of discovering who she is, without any textual aids, will be one of the chief pleasures of reading this section. This picture suggests that Kiyonosuke has successfully captured the woman, but she manages to get away because, hoping to interrogate her, Kiyonosuke attempts to take her alive. All he is able to salvage from the situation is a sleeve that he tears from her kimono.

When Mitsuuji arrives on the scene, Kiyonosuke tells him that the woman got away but left the sword behind in its box; Mitsuuji realizes

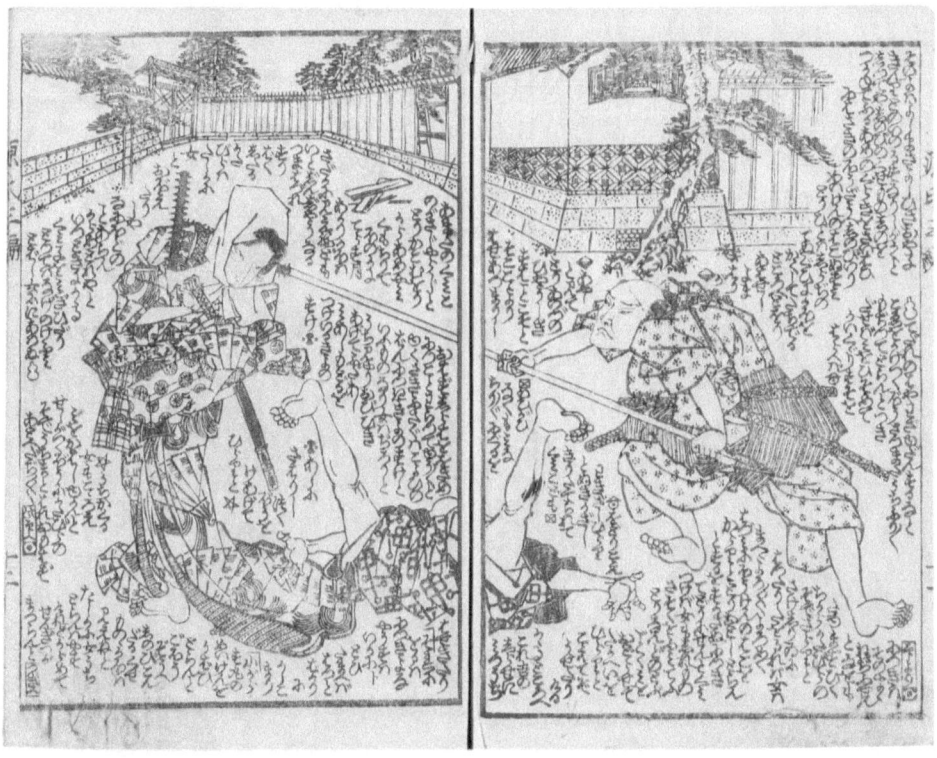

Figure 57 Nikki Kiyonosuke catching the thief who stole the sword Kogarasumaru. (*NMIG*, chapter 3, 11 *ura*–12 *omote*. Courtesy of National Diet Library)

right away that such a clearly experienced thief would have removed the sword immediately after she stole it, saving the empty box to use as a decoy. His suspicions prove correct, of course. And so the hunt for Kogarasumaru begins. Before it has a chance to progress at all, however, Mitsuuji is diverted by a directional taboo into a different episode, based, loosely at first but later extremely closely, on the "Utsusemi" (The Cicada Shell) chapter of *Genji monogatari*. This digression continues for a full eight spreads—a bit under half of the twenty-page chapter. Figure 58 reproduces the spread covering pages 19 *ura* and 20 *omote*; figure 59 shows the single page that comes next (to the left, since pages in *gōkan* are turned from left to right), page 20 *ura*, which concludes the chapter.[57]

In figure 58, we see Mitsuuji heading home after having a bit of an adventure with Karaginu, Kiyonosuke's wife, who is kneeling on the right-hand page. What is of interest in this picture is the trio of crows dipping into view from outside the frame. Kogarasumaru, the name of the sword Shinonome stole, means "Little Crow." Mitsuuji's escapades during the

Figure 58 Mitsuuji taking his leave of Karaginu. The three crows in the upper-left corner call to mind the name of the sword: Little Crow. (*NMIG*, chapter 3, 19 *ura*–20 *omote*. Courtesy of National Diet Library)

Figure 59 The page that follows that shown in figure 58. Tasogare looks up at the crows that are flying toward her on the previous page. (*NMIG*, chapter 3, 20 *ura*. Courtesy of National Diet Library)

second half of chapter 3 ultimately bear fruit in a series of thrilling events and stunning, violent pictures in chapters 15 and 17, but for the time being they seem little more than a distraction from the search for the missing sword, the urgency and interest of which was impressed on the reader by the picture in figure 56, which is much more dynamic and exciting than anything that has happened since then. The crows skimming along the edge of the picture in figure 58 serve as a tantalizing reminder of what has been left hanging in the balance, calling to mind, as they do, the name of the stolen sword. Their leftward, frame-breaking flight is echoed by the gaze of the boy standing to Mitsuuji's left, which encourages the reader to turn the page and see the mystery woman standing there (see figure 59). She is identified, both by a note written in at her right and by the presence on her kimono of the incense sign for the "Yūgao" chapter, as Tasogare, the counterpart of *Genji monogatari*'s Yūgao. Her gaze is aimed in the direction of the crows on the previous page, subtly suggesting that she too is interested or even involved in the theft of "Little Crow." This composition works, incidentally, in the same way as the three-panel *kuchi-e* that I discussed earlier.

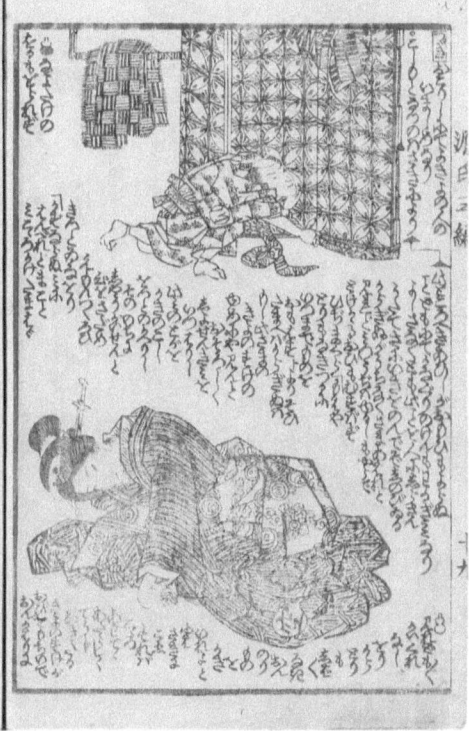

Chapter 4 opens with the *kuchi-e* in figure 7 (and 8), showing Shinonome (identified in the picture by a note to her right) and her daughter Tasogare (their relationship is clarified in a note to her left), so there can be no doubt that the two women will be involved in whatever developments take place in this chapter. But, once again, the Kogarasumaru plot is put on hold while Mitsuuji continues to dally for half the chapter at Kiyonosuke's house. Things get moving only when Mitsuuji happens to become involved with Tasogare after the encounter pictured in the spread covering pages 12 *ura* and 13 *omote* (figure 60).[58] Mitsuuji is leaning rakishly on the top of his palanquin at the left of the picture; his retainer, Korekichi, is accepting the flower that Tasogare holds out to him on a fan, intending it for Mitsuuji. The flower, the text informs us, is a blossom from the *karasuuri* (literally, "crow gourd") vine that climbs the fence. This is clearly a playful *haikai* twist on the *yūgao* (literally, "evening face"; also a gourd-bearing plant) flower, which gives Yūgao her name in *Genji monogatari*, but the reference to crows is even more significant. Keen observers would also notice that the pattern on the strips of cloth laid out to dry at the far right of the picture—in a rather eye-catching

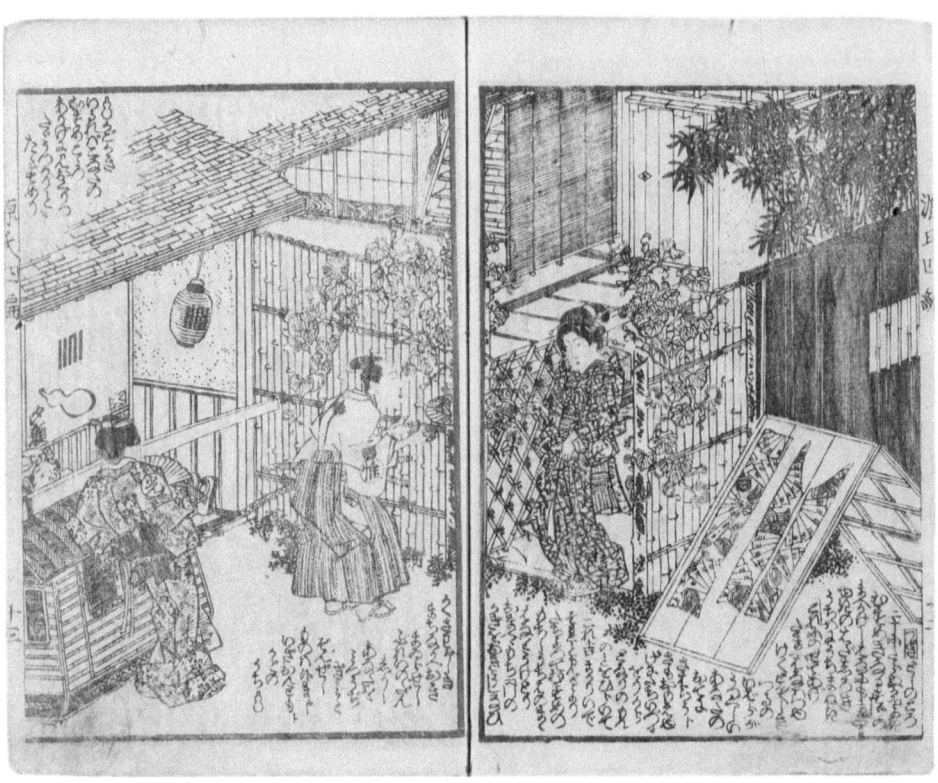

Figure 60 Tasogare passing Korekichi a flower from the "crow gourd" vine to take to Mitsuuji. (*NMIG*, chapter 4, 12 *ura*–13 *omote*. Courtesy of National Diet Library)

spot, particularly because the white drying boards contrast so sharply with the black of the wall and the stand of bamboo behind it—is the same as that on the kimono the thief wears in figure 57. Presumably, the choice of a fan pattern is playing on the use of a fan as the vehicle that in *Genji monogatari*, as in *Inaka Genji*, first links the hero to the young woman in the house, bearing a flower from her to him.

Given the long digression that takes Mitsuuji into Kiyonosuke's house and the passage of a year between the publication of chapter 3 (1830), which includes the picture of the theft of the sword, and that of chapter 4 (1831), the repetition of this fan pattern might easily go unnoticed, even by readers accustomed to noting kimono designs. And while the text accompanying this picture mentions the strips of cloth, nothing of import is said about them until two spreads later, at the beginning of page 13 *ura*, when Mitsuuji casually asks Shinonome about them. The reader's curiosity will certainly be aroused now if she has not yet noticed the pattern, but still nothing has been said explicitly to tie the fabric set out to dry with the kimono worn by the thief; indeed, nothing will be said until the very end of the episode, at the conclusion of chapter 5, when everything is made clear.

Figure 61, which reproduces the spread covering pages 15 *ura* and 16 *omote*, shows Tasogare on the left-hand page, folding the fabric, her eyes turned upward as if she is gazing at Mitsuuji where he sits on the right-hand page.[59] Mitsuuji is actually leaning against a pole on the second floor, however, and the angle of his head suggests that he is probably not visible to Tasogare: he is keeping out of sight, in fact, watching her and noting the pattern on the fabric, surreptitiously. The text on this page describes Mitsuuji whispering something—the reader is not told what—into Kiyonosuke's ear, and Kiyonosuke replying, "Well, if *that's* the case, there can be no doubt! I will take them in myself right away!" Again, it is not made clear *what* is the case; this is still left to the eager,

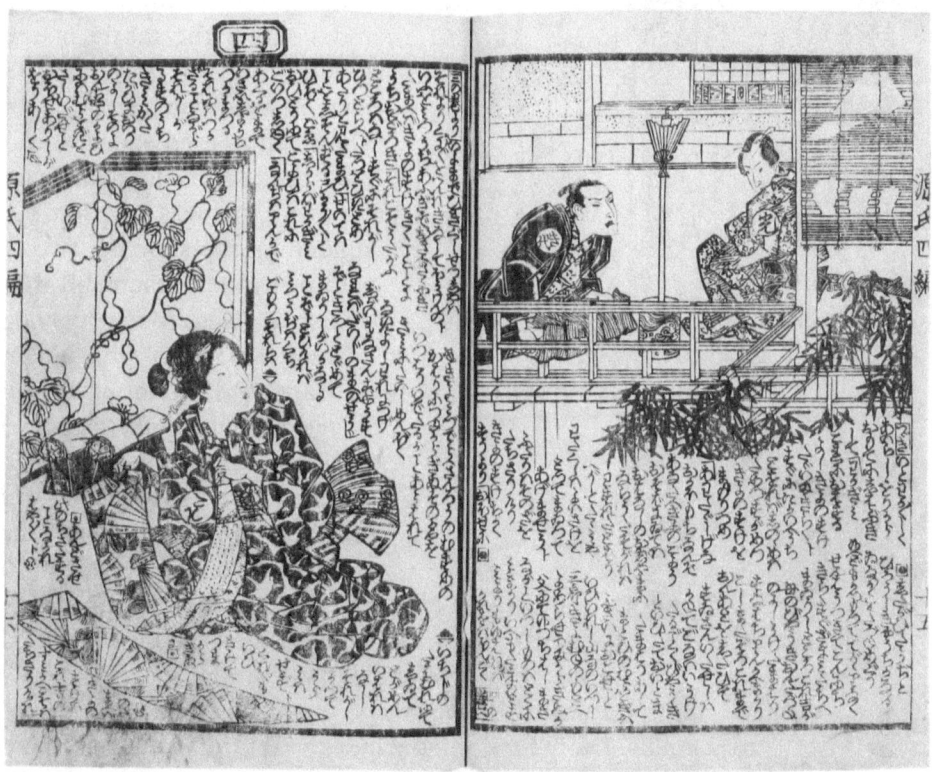

Figure 61 Tasogare folding the fan-patterned cloth as Mitsuuji looks on. (*NMIG*, chapter 4, 15 *ura*–16 *omote*. Courtesy of Waseda University Library, Tokyo)

suspicious imagination. We learn later, on page 13 *ura* of chapter 5, that Kiyonosuke, unobservant bungler that he is, failed to notice the pattern on the strips of cloth until Mitsuuji pointed it out.[60]

After this, the plot develops in ways whose meaning will not become clear until much later; the reader is left hanging yet again, this time for four full spreads. Then, on the very last page of the chapter, as before, flying crows are presented, all alone on a page of text (figure 62).[61] Needless to say, this offers another wordless sign that the search for Kogarasumaru continues. And when Shinonome appears on the very first page of the main body of chapter 5, page 3 *ura* (figure 63), wearing a kimono with a pattern of crows and holding the fabric of the kimono that she is wearing in figure 57, there can be little doubt where things are headed.[62] Mitsuuji confronts Shinonome with the sleeve that was torn from her kimono as she stole the sword, onto which he, presumably, has written a vague poem playing on one in "Yūgao" that might be translated, adapting Royall Tyler's version of the poem in *Genji monogatari*, "Let me then draw near and see whether you are she: Crow Gourd." Here, the word *karasuuri* (crow gourd) would seem to take on another resonance, since *uri* can also mean "seller": "Let me then draw near and see whether you are she: the one who sold Little Crow."

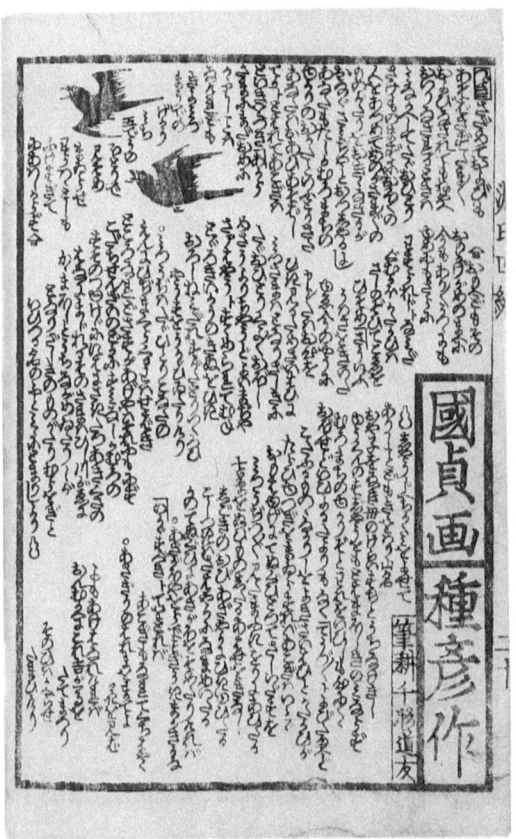

Figure 62 Once again, two crows remind the reader of the stolen sword. (*NMIG*, chapter 4, 20 *omote*. Courtesy of Waseda University Library, Tokyo)

Shinonome is startled by the poem and then feigns calmness. And so the tension builds. Every time Shinonome appears from now on, including when she shows up in disguise at the old temple and tries to murder Mitsuuji—in the clothes and mask shown in the *kuchi-e* in figures 7a and 8a—she is depicted wearing the same crow kimono. Long before her

Figure 63 Mitsuuji confronting Shinonome with the fan-patterned cloth. (*NMIG*, chapter 5, 3 *ura*–4 *omote*. Courtesy of National Diet Library)

identity is finally revealed and she is given a chance to tell her own story in the text—at the old temple, at the end of chapter 5—a variety of subtle visual clues begin turning up in the pictures, giving readers a chance to relish the pleasure of staying one step ahead of the text. And as I mentioned earlier, the tragic climax of this episode comes when Shinonome, bleeding to death, holds up the bamboo blind for Mitsuuji to see, turning it upside down, and again no explanation of this gesture's meaning is provided for two spreads. All we are given is a picture that challenges us to read it.

Curtain Call

In this chapter, I have attempted to engage with *Inaka Genji* as a book, to figure out what sort of reading experience it was designed both to encourage and to reward. *Kogetsushō* played a role in a few of the analyses, but such intertextual connections were never more than frosting on a very rich cake. Indeed, strictly speaking, these links are not quite intertextual at all: *Inaka Genji* offers its readers, including those unfamiliar with the plot of *Genji monogatari*, images of the classic that are almost flamboyantly unreal, untethered to any text. Hardly anyone, after all, would ever see a copy made in the handscroll form like the one depicted in figure 36. What mattered was not the extremely difficult text of *Genji monogatari* itself, in any format, but its replacement through the text of *Inaka Genji*, the pictures, and the intricate dance that the pictures and the text, and even the physical book held in the hand, performed in concert. *Genji monogatari* was made—gradually, for the first time as a popular phenomenon—in the image of an extraordinarily sophisticated *gōkan*.

Needless to say, the readings I have presented here are characteristic of a particular strand of contemporary literary criticism, and it would be no less implausible to argue that either Tanehiko himself or any of his contemporaries might have spoken about *Inaka Genji* in this mode than to presume that the majority of *Inaka Genji*'s readers had anything like the detailed knowledge of *Kogetsushō* or any other text of *Genji monogatari* that they would have needed to appreciate *Inaka Genji* as an adaptation. It is not at all implausible, however, to say that *Inaka Genji*'s core readership was composed of townspeople who were accustomed to reading *gōkan*, who had learned how to enjoy them, and who made the most of what was then still a very special form of entertainment, published annually at New Year. *Inaka Genji*'s readers would, no doubt, have intuitively understood what was going on, without having to verbalize it all. Thus while this chapter may seem rather narrowly focused on the book, on some level it is an attempt to imagine a community of early modern readers who knew what to do with a *gōkan*.

Indeed, that community has left traces of its existence. I noted earlier that the episode dealing with Mitsuuji's search for Kogarasumaru was one of the most popular in all of *Inaka Genji* and that it was frequently enacted on the kabuki stage and represented in *ukiyo-e*, both in actor prints and in Genji pictures. Tasogare figured in the first kabuki play to incorporate *Inaka Genji*, in 1838, and the same episode was staged in its entirety in each of two plays put on in consecutive months by the Ichimura and Nakamura Theaters in Edo in 1851, almost a decade after *Inaka Genji* was banned.[63] It was featured as well in various later plays that drew on *Inaka Genji*, including some that were regularly performed during the Meiji and Taishō periods, notably *A Bumpkin Genji: The Dewy Dawn* (*Inaka Genji tsuyu no shinonome*, 1891)—a retitled excerpt of the

Figure 64 Ichikawa Kodanji IV as Shinonome, in a panel from a triptych by Utagawa Kunisada for the production of *Higashiyama Sakura no sōshi* at the Nakamura Theater in 1851. (Courtesy of Tsubouchi Memorial Theater Museum of Waseda University 6-1546)

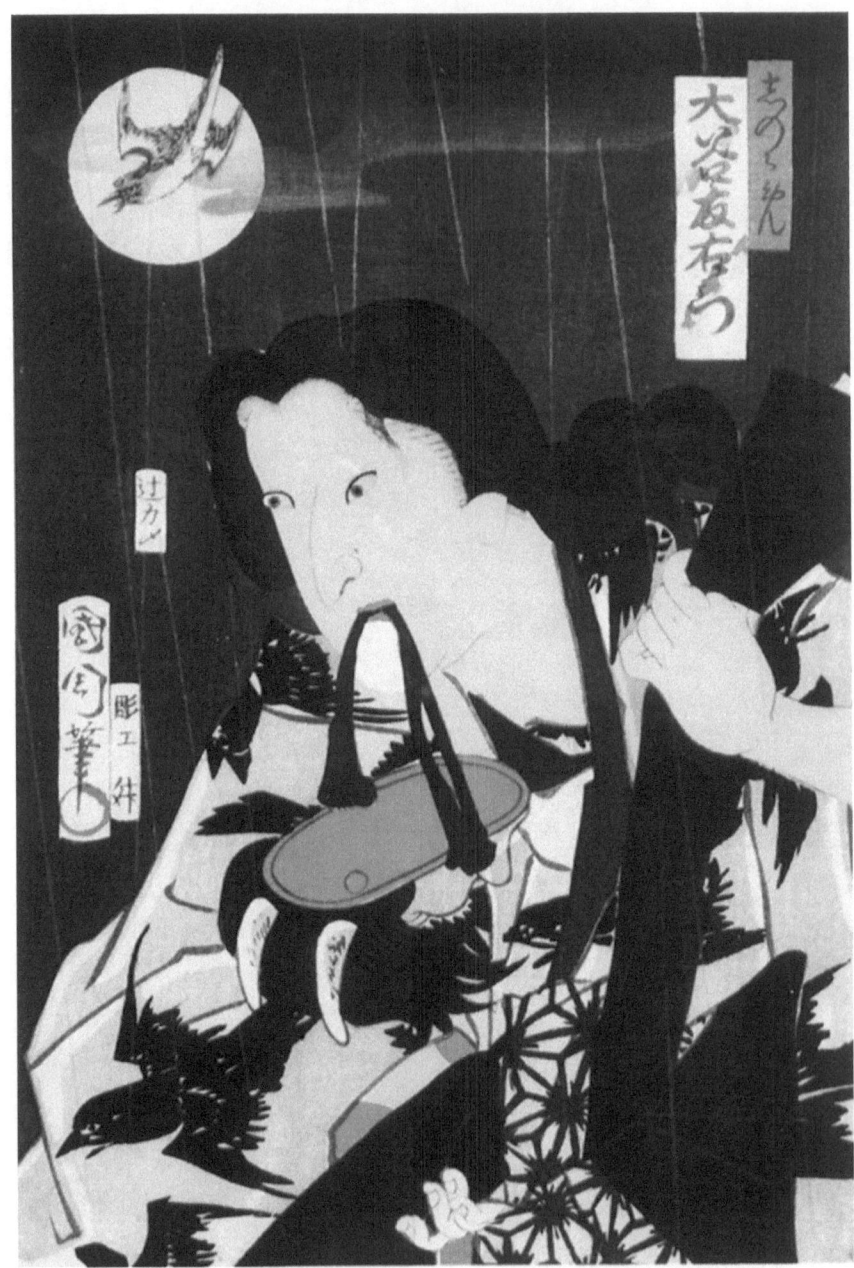

Figure 65 Ōya Tomoemon as Shinonome, in a panel from a triptych by Toyohara Kunichika for the production of *Koi shigure sode ni furudera* at the Morita Theater in 1867. (Courtesy of Tsubouchi Memorial Theater Museum of Waseda University 100-5427)

play first staged at the Ichimura Theater in 1851 that focuses specifically on the encounter between Mitsuuji, Tasogare, and Shinonome at the desolate temple.[64] Almost without exception, posters, playbills, and actor prints created for these plays include the visual signposts that allowed readers of *Inaka Genji* to anticipate the written story.

Among the clues these various publications so assiduously reproduced are the fan-patterned pieces of fabric; Shinonome's crow-patterned kimono; the bamboo blind with the cut-out in the shape of Mount Fuji; and even, in at least one instance, crows flying in the sky. The crows appear on Shinonome's kimono in an elegant triptych created for the first staging of *The Book of the Martyr of Sakura* (*Higashiyama Sakura no sōshi*) in 1851 (figure 64). Both the crow kimono and the crow in the sky are featured, along with the bamboo blind, in a triptych for *A Drizzle of Love Falling Down Temple* (*Koi shigure sode ni furudera*, 1867) (figure 65). The crows on Shinonome's kimono are included in two paintings of the scene at the temple by the artist Kawanabe Kyōsai, even though Kawanabe dispenses with the *aoi*-leaf pattern (which, in *Inaka Genji*, refers to Genji's wife Aoi no Ue) on the outer kimono in one of the two (figure 66).

Figure 66 The climactic scene at the old temple, in a painting by Kawanabe Kyōsai (*Seisei Kyōsai gachō* [*Seisei Kyōsai Picture Album*], vol. 3. Private collection)

The various clues are preserved even more regularly in posters and playbills, which are generally more standardized: a poster for a production of *Eastern Prints of Inaka Genji* (*Inaka Genji Azuma no nishikie*), in 1868, gives a good sense of the general pattern (figures 67 and 68).

Something interesting happened during the 1920s, however: the clues that had been central to *Inaka Genji*—and had for decades been included in prints, posters, and playbills—began to be left out. The change is immediately apparent in two posters created for productions of *A Bumpkin Genji: The Dewy Dawn* at the Imperial Theater, the first in 1917 (figure 69) and the second in 1926 (figure 70): the earlier includes the bamboo blind, and the crows on Shinonome's kimono are easily visible (figure 71); the later is altogether lacking the blind and barely hints at the crow pattern on the kimono (figure 72). A poster for a production of a one-act play simply titled *Inaka Genji*, staged at the Kabukiza in 1921, reveals an even more significant shift (figure 73). None of the clues are even hinted at, but only because the play itself made no use of them. In Motoyama Tekishū's (1881–1958) script, the woman who appears in the guise of a demon is not Tasogare's mother, Shinonome, but Akogi, a courtesan with whom Mitsuuji had been involved (figure 74). Akogi notices Mitsuuji and Tasogare on her way to entertain at a party, and since she happens to be dressed as a demon she decides to stop in and give the couple a scare, only to have Mitsuuji immediately recognize her voice. Akogi then convinces Tasogare to reject Mitsuuji and persuades Mitsuuji to go back home to his wife. The stage directions state specifically that Akogi should appear "in the usual manner, except that her inner kimono is something a bit gaudy—embroidered autumn grasses or something would be fitting."[65]

Motoyama's *Inaka Genji*, which features lengthy exchanges about marriage, infidelity, trust, and jealousy, inherits little more from its namesake than a skeleton: to the extent that it lives as a play, it lives a very "literary" sort of life, in the specifically modern sense that the word *bungaku* had acquired in Japan by this period. No doubt it was only to be expected that the elements that had made Tanehiko's *gōkan* such an incredible success would be stripped away as the literary and theatrical

Figure 67 A poster for the production including *Inaka Genji Azuma no nishikie* at the Morita Theater in 1868. (Courtesy of Tsubouchi Memorial Theater Museum of Waseda University ro22-51-4)

Figure 68 Detail of the upper-left corner of the poster shown in figure 67. (Tsubouchi Memorial Theater Museum of Waseda University)

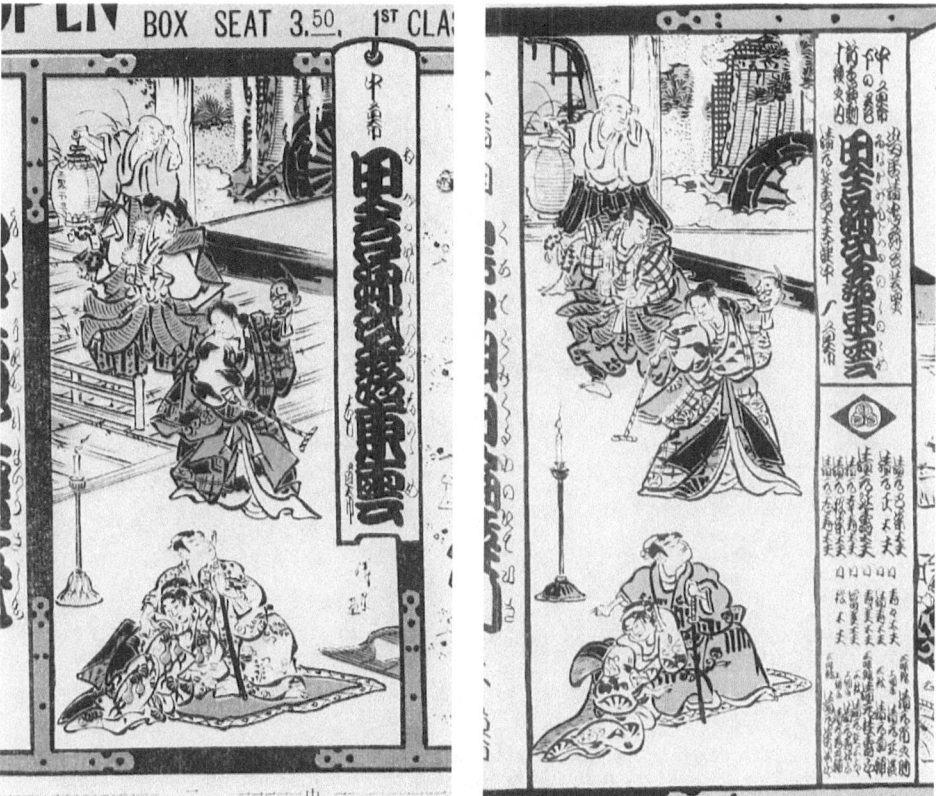

Figure 69 A poster for the production including *Inaka Genji tsuyu no shinonome* at the Imperial Theater in 1917. (Courtesy of Tsubouchi Memorial Theater Museum of Waseda University ro22-55-744)

Figure 70 A poster for the production including *Inaka Genji tsuyu no shinonome* at the Imperial Theater in 1926. (Tsubouchi Memorial Theater Museum of Waseda University ro22-67-9)

Figure 71 Detail of the poster shown in figure 69. (Courtesy of Tsubouchi Memorial Theater Museum of Waseda University)

Figure 72 Detail of the poster shown in figure 70. (Courtesy of Tsubouchi Memorial Theater Museum of Waseda University)

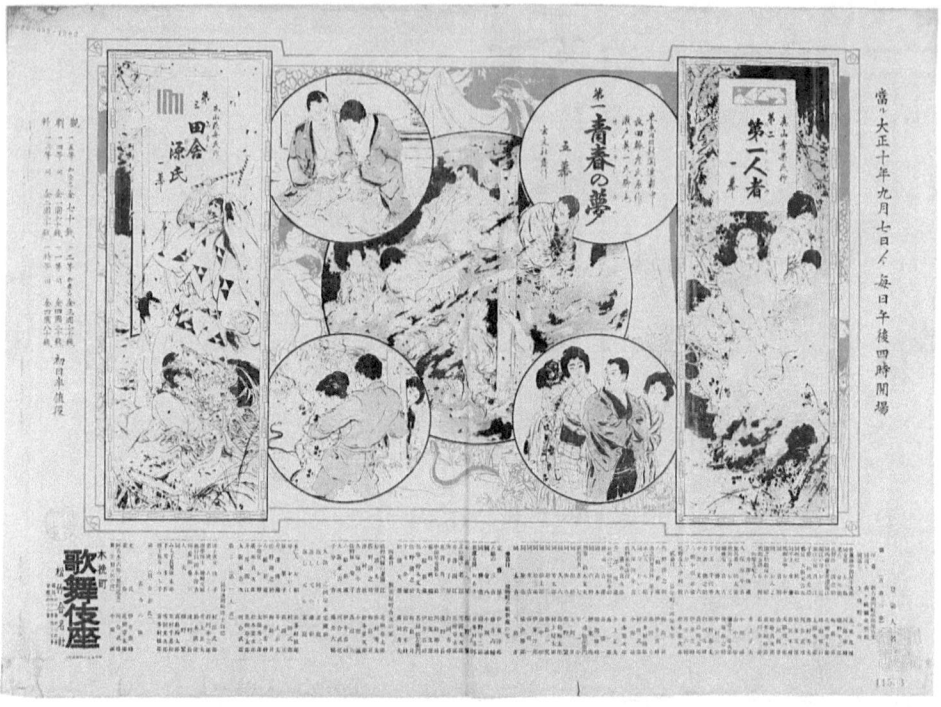

Figure 73 A poster for the production including Motoyama Tekishū's one-act play *Inaka Genji* at the Kabukiza in 1921. (Courtesy of Tsubouchi Memorial Theater Museum of Waseda University ro22-55-1262)

landscape changed. No doubt it was inevitable, too, that this process would affect not only theatrical versions of the story, but *Inaka Genji* itself as a book. In order to have even a shot at survival, it would have to be replaced by new versions of itself that catered to the tastes and expectations of new readers living in a new world. It would have to go on appealing to people who cared about "literature" and no longer had any idea what a *gōkan* was.

The extent to which *Inaka Genji* failed to survive its replacement is indicated by a translation of it into modern Japanese that was published in 1947 by Shuzui Kenji (1899–1983). The cover shows Shinonome dressed in something like the demonic disguise she wears to the old temple, but the artist, Mano Mitsuru (1901–2001), has—predictably, by now—omitted the crows (figure 75). The pattern of *aoi* leaves on a crosshatched background that had originally decorated Shinonome's outer kimono has also been jettisoned in favor of grape leaves on a checked ground. Presumably, Shinonome was chosen to liven up the cover

Figure 74 Detail of the poster shown in figure 73. (Courtesy of Tsubouchi Memorial Theater Museum of Waseda University)

Figure 75 The cover of Shuzui Kenji's *Inaka Genji*, a translation into modern Japanese. Presumably, the figure is intended to represent Shinonome at the old temple. (Courtesy of the author)

because, over the course of innumerable theatrical productions, the scene at the old temple had come to represent *Inaka Genji*, but this scene no longer worked the way it used to. The clues did not really matter. In fact, the clues were not even there. Shuzui's *Inaka Genji* is a translation into modern Japanese of the *text* of Tanehiko's *Inaka Genji*. Not a single picture has been included.

The Death of the *Gōkan*

"To be, or not to be, that is the question." And it is a question that must be repeated. It returns at intervals to the questioner until at last he settles on an answer or until some sea change in the world abroad forces an answer on him.

Translation, the replacement of a text or a book by a new form of itself, has frequently been described in English, in the wake of "The Task of the Translator," Harry Zohn's translation of Walter Benjamin's essay "Die Aufgabe des Übersetzers" (1923) as the "afterlife" of the original. Zohn writes, with Benjamin, of the "potentially eternal afterlife" of great works of art.[1] James Hynd and E. M. Valk offer a different take in their translation of Benjamin's essay, published with the same title and in the same year as Zohn's, writing of "a continuing life that is fundamentally eternal."[2] Is translation a "continuing life" or an "afterlife"? Which metaphor we prefer tells us, perhaps, less about translation itself than about how we conceive of originals and the relationship between originals and translations. In his lecture "Conclusions: Walter Benjamin's 'The Task of the Translator,'" collected posthumously in *The Resistance to Theory* (1986), Paul de Man noted the death that translation as "afterlife" implies: "The process of translation, if we can call it a process, is one of change and of motion that has the appearance of life, but of life as an afterlife, because translation also reveals the death of the original."[3] The phrase "continuing life" carries no such implication. And yet both metaphors suggest that texts can live only one true life. Both metaphors imply that texts have souls that may, if they are lucky, be "received" into everlasting habitations.

There is room for debate about whether *Nise Murasaki inaka Genji* may reasonably be regarded as a translation of *Genji monogatari*. Either way, it is clear that the *gōkan* gave *Genji monogatari* some sort of life in nineteenth-century Japan, different from any it had lived before, recanonizing it through a new medium and in a new form for readers with some prior

CHAPTER 3

Turning a New Page
Bibliographic Translation and the Yomihonization *of* Inaka Genji

knowledge of the classic and making its canonicity relevant for the first time to non-readers who lacked that particular form of cultivation. We saw in chapter 1 how pleased Ryūtei Senka was by the proliferation of what he called "*Genji*-wise non-readers of *Genji*": "Nowadays," he wrote, "even little dog-beating brats know that there are more Genjis out there than just Yoritomo and Yoshitsune."[4] The truth is that there were also more *Genjis* out there than just *Genji monogatari*; if anything, for most ordinary Edoites, *Inaka Genji* and not *Genji monogatari* would have been "the *Genji*." The classic does not have an everlasting soul, unique unto itself: it lives in its replacement. Perhaps we may better conceive of translation, then, and of canonization through translation not in terms of "continuing lives" or "afterlives," but by using a different metaphor: as a series of distinct but connected lives, each carrying and being carried by the karma of its predecessors—translation as reincarnation.

The notion that *Inaka Genji* is a reincarnation of *Genji monogatari* is subtly embedded in its prodigiously polysemous title. The "*nise* Murasaki" in *Nise Murasaki inaka Genji* means, first of all, "a fraudulent Murasaki," and refers to Ofuji, the young woman whom Tanehiko conjures up in the preface to chapter 1 as the *gōkan*'s putative author, depicted on the cover of the chapter's second fascicle (see figure 11). The phrase also clearly plays on the inexpensive "fake purple" (*nisemurasaki*) dye that was a popular substitute for the more pricey "true purple" (*honmurasaki*); in this sense, it may even call to mind the contrast between the bluish "Edo purple" (*Edo murasaki*) favored in Edo and its counterpart, the reddish "Kyoto purple" (*Kyō murasaki*)—and, by extension, the long-standing rivalry between the ancient imperial capital and the newer bureaucratic one: "*inaka* Genji" means "a bumpkin Genji" or "a Genji in the countryside," and the story is set in Kyoto.[5] At the same time, "*nise* Murasaki" may also be read as a pun on "Murasaki II," yielding the meaning "A Bumpkin Genji by Murasaki II" or "A Bumpkin Genji by a Murasaki Living a Second Life." This reading acquires an added resonance when we note that Tanehiko chose to write *nise* using an uncommon character, 偐, whose right half is the "hiko" in "Tanehiko" 種彦: "*nise* Murasaki" visually suggests that Tanehiko, creating his "Bumpkin *Genji*," is Murasaki Shikibu II. Takabatake Ransen (1838–1885) makes the possibility of this reading explicit in his caption to an *ukiyo-e* triptych by Utagawa Yoshitoshi, published in 1884 to commemorate Ransen's assumption of the name Tanehiko III, when he glosses the characters for the "II" in "Murasaki II" 二世紫 as *nise* rather than *nisei*, which would usually be used to denote a successor. Generally when these characters are read as *nise*, they refer to "two worlds" or "two lives" in a Buddhist sense, and allude to the "bond for two lifetimes" (*nise no en, nise no chigiri, nise no yakusoku*) that spouses were thought to share. Tanehiko himself uses *nise* in this same sense in *Inaka Genji*.⁶

If we think of each subsequent replacement, each translation of a text or a book, not as part of a single "continuing life" or "afterlife," but as one in a series of rebirths, then we see that each is subject to its own life course. Perhaps, as de Man suggested, translation reveals the death of the original; but each translation in turn, replacing the original, gives it a new life, and each in turn potentially threatens not just to reveal but to precipitate its predecessor's demise. In this chapter, I consider the gradual process by which not only *Inaka Genji* but the *gōkan* as a genre was essentially killed by translation—by what I refer to as "bibliographic translation," a neologism intended to describe the process by which a book or another object is re-created in a different form for the express purpose of making it accessible to a new audience with new needs or tastes, or to the end product of that process. In this case, I refer to the replacement of *Inaka Genji* as a work and as a book—thirty-eight published chapters in seventy-six woodblock-printed fascicles—by movable-type editions that first began to appear in 1882 and continued to be published fairly regularly until 1953.

In chapter 1, I argued that *Inaka Genji* was able to interest a lowbrow readership in *Genji monogatari*, and thus to emerge as the first truly popular replacement of the classic, precisely because it was so exciting and so attractive as a *gōkan*; this chapter traces the process by which *Inaka Genji* ceased to function as a replacement of *Genji monogatari*—because it ceased to function as a *gōkan*. At the same time, the shifting situation I describe can be viewed as setting the stage for the emergence of the modern-Japanese translation of *Genji monogatari* as a genre in its own right. As author, playwright, and translator of *Genji monogatari* Enchi Fumiko's description of herself in 1986 as "a sort of 'fraudulent Murasaki'" suggests, and as we will see in the following chapter, modern-Japanese translations can be considered replacements of *Inaka Genji* as a replacement of *Genji monogatari*.⁷

The death of the *gōkan* coincided with the birth of the novel in Japan. This was a long-drawn-out affair that involved various attempts—all bound to fail, we see in hindsight—by *gōkan* authors, illustrators, and publishers to adapt their product to the rapidly changing world around them. Two important, linked factors contributed to the demise of this genre and the rise of something like the novel, known in Japanese as the *shōsetsu*: developments in printing and binding technologies, and readers' forgetting of old tastes as they discovered the new pleasures that movable-type publication was best suited to provide—above all, the thrill of timeliness. But while these factors, especially the application of movable type to *gōkan*, unquestionably had a tremendous impact on the genre, the reconfiguration of image–text–book relations they might at first appear to have occasioned was actually a continuation of a trend first initiated in woodblock-printed works. Given the importance of these bibliographic changes, it will be helpful to begin by surveying the material characteristics of *gōkan* originally issued during the Meiji period, particularly in the mid- to late 1870s. Then we will proceed to consider how bibliographic translation helped divest *Inaka Genji* of its canonical value, reducing it to no more than an inadequate textual adaptation of a great classic, dealing the book and, indeed, the genre as a whole a final, fatal blow that erased not only its future but its past glories, leaving men who had once been the authors of *gōkan* no choice but to try their hand at that new fictional form, the novel, or to lay down their brushes and say, "The rest is silence."

The Beginnings of the End

It is poignant, in retrospect, to realize that each new beginning of the end of the *gōkan* must have seemed to publishers and authors at the time like a small step in the right direction. Bibliographic innovations helped create unprecedented short-term best sellers, even though it is clear now that these innovations led the genre into its final decline.

The situation was not promising for *gōkan* in the early 1870s, though in a sense their authors were better off than they had ever been. In July 1872, Kanagaki Robun (1829–1894) and Jōno Arindo (1831–1901) submitted a response to the Ministry of Education's "Three Directives on Teaching" (Sanjō no kyōken), issued in April of the same year as one of three platforms of the Campaign to Promulgate the Great Teaching (Taikyō senpu undō). The directives were rather vague, consisting of injunctions to the designated "educational leaders" (*kyōdōshoku*) to "Respect the gods and love the nation," "Elucidate the logic of heaven and the way of man," and "Place yourselves reverently under the emperor and abide by the will of the court."[8] Educators were to bear these precepts firmly in mind at all times, structuring their whole lives around them. In their response, Robun and Arindo stated their intention to write "in accordance with the goals set out in the Three Directives on Teaching."[9] *Gōkan* had often included pedagogical elements, it is true, and avowals of the need to "encourage virtue and chastise the wicked" had been ubiquitous in discourse about popular fiction, but until 1872 popular authors would certainly never have been officially recognized as educators. The Campaign to Promulgate the Great Teaching thus imbued "frivolous writing" with a prestige that was formerly unimaginable, though only on the condition that authors increase the educational content of their books.

Even had writers not been subject to official pressure, it seems clear that in the pragmatic years of the early 1870s they had little choice but to take their calling seriously. In the same year that the "Three Directives" were issued, Robun published *Roads to the World's Capitals* (*Sekai miyakoji*), a seven-volume introduction to the countries of the world, complete with maps and pictures, that was modeled extremely closely—even in the calligraphic style of its rhythmic and thus easily memorized main text—on Fukuzawa Yukichi's textbook *The Nations of the World* (*Sekai kunizukushi*, 1869). This is particularly striking, given that as recently as the autumn of the previous year, 1871, Robun had "jumped on the coattails of the resounding acclaim with which the world has greeted Professor Fukuzawa's *Ultimate Principles Illustrated* [*Kyūri zukai*, 1868]," writing a rollicking send-up with the punning title *The Cucumber Messenger* (*Kyūrizukai*, 1872).[10] In 1873, Robun was appointed as an "educational leader" by the Kanagawa Prefectural Office and began touring the countryside delivering edifying talks; in 1875, he started a "small newspaper" called *Kanayomi shinbun* (*Kana Newspaper*).

Arindo, too, gave up writing *gōkan* after declaring in his 1872 preface to the final chapter of *In the Willow's Shade: Asazuma in the Moonlight* (*Yanagikage tsuki no Asazuma*, 1870-1872)—whose covers, *kuchi-e*, and pictures, incidentally, imitate those of *Inaka Genji*—that "a history of this sort will seem bizarre enough to begin with, now that the Enlightenment is progressing apace and the world cries out that 'unofficial histories' are an indulgent, unnecessary relic of the past."[11] In his preface to the third chapter of *Otama Pond: How to Wear a Moon-Shaped Comb* (*Otamagaike kushi no tsukigata*, 1874-1877), whose first chapters Arindo wrote in the summer of 1872 but whose publication did not begin until 1874, Tamenaga Shunsui II (Somezaki Nobufusa) explains why he, rather than Arindo, wrote the preface to the second chapter and has now taken over authorship of the book itself: "Recently my literary friend has been so busy with other matters that he hasn't had time to write 'unofficial histories.'"[12] Like Robun, Arindo had become, in Maeda Ai's casually telling phrase, "a newspaper person."[13]

Although the *gōkan* was in trouble in the early 1870s, the situation gradually began to improve: the Campaign to Promulgate the Great Teaching began to peter out during 1874, and in 1877 the Ministry of Education decided to end it. As early as 1878, the genre was beginning to show signs of new life. According to Nakamura Masaaki, the number of new works issued annually jumped from either zero or one between 1872 and 1875 to five in 1876, four in 1877, thirteen in 1878, eighteen in 1879, and twenty-five in 1880. After dipping slightly the next two years, the figure climbed to a high of sixty-two in 1884, and then suddenly dwindled, dropping to two in 1887.[14]

The catalyst for the sudden *gōkan* revival was the re-publication in the genre of an embellished news story—more sensation than news—of *The Life of Omatsu the Singing Beggar* (*Torioi Omatsu no den*), which Kubota Hikosaku serialized in *Kanayomi shinbun* from December 10, 1877, to January 11, 1878. In a preface, Robun wrote in his role as editor (*kōetsu*) of the *gōkan* version, which was titled *A New Tale of Omatsu the Singing Beggar's Adventures at Sea* (*Torioi Omatsu kaijō shinwa*, 1878) and was illustrated by Yōshūsai Chikanobu (Hashimoto Chikanobu), that he had been planning to have Kubota bring the serial to a premature conclusion after its fourteenth installment because "a tale that drifts on and on, as long as 'three strings' of spring mist, is entirely at odds with the aims of a newspaper."[15] Ōkura Magobē, of the publishing house Kin'eidō, suggested that it would be a shame to let such a popular story go to waste and asked for permission to publish it in its entirety. *A New Tale of Omatsu* thus became the first of a series of new *gōkan* that were either based on or almost directly reproduced small-newspaper serials (*tsuzukimono*). The book is reputed to have sold eight thousand copies at a time when two thousand was normal. Some sense of the work's popularity can be gleaned from the fact that in 1877, *Kanayomi shinbun* itself had a print run of nine thousand copies: the *gōkan* sold almost as well as a newspaper.[16]

The surge in *gōkan* publications and sales that began in 1876 and took off in 1878, in the wake of *A New Tale of Omatsu*'s success, does not necessarily mean that the genre was in good health, however. Indeed, I would argue that it was ailing, for two reasons: first, a significant shift was taking place in the *gōkan* publishing schedule that would ultimately make it difficult for the genre to compete with other fictional and semifictional forms, particularly the small-newspaper serial; second, bibliographic innovations were divesting *gōkan* of the rich image–text–book relationships that had been their defining feature.

In Edo, *gōkan* had originally been issued around New Year, though in practice the extent of the publishing season seems to have been fairly loosely defined; toward the very end of the early modern period, they began to appear twice a year, in spring and autumn. Topicality was often a concern, but it was a relatively leisurely topicality—*gōkan* time moved in years, for the most part, not in months or days, and since the popularization in the 1830s of the extended *gōkan*, of which *Inaka Genji* is an early example, readers had grown accustomed to following the arc of a story over the course of years and even decades. The first two volumes of *A New Tale of Omatsu* have an unmistakable New Year air that recalls this customary *gōkan* publishing schedule and suits their release in February, around the lunar New Year. The title page of volume 1 shows a festive arrangement of pine and bamboo (*kadomatsu*) of the kind that people set out before their houses to welcome the New Year god, as well as a paddle and a kite, both associated with New Year celebrations (figure 76).

These are, however, little more than cursory gestures toward an old tradition: what mattered

Figure 76 The title page of volume 1 of *Torioi Omatsu kaijō shinwa*, illustrated by Yōshūsai Chikanobu. (Courtesy of Waseda University Library, Tokyo)

most in the timing of *A New Tale of Omatsu*'s release was not that it accorded with the conventional annual publishing schedule, but that it enabled the *gōkan* to stand not only as a complete work in itself, but as a kind of last installment, a reincarnation, of the story serialized in *Kanayomi shinbun*, which was a *daily* publication—though *The Life of Omatsu* itself had appeared every couple of days, not daily. The importance of this timing is evident in the fact that Ōkura Magobē submitted an application for permission to issue the first two volumes of *A New Tale of Omatsu* on January 18, only a week after the newspaper serial was brought to a premature end.[17] Given the public's evident enthusiasm for the story, it would have made no sense to wait a year, or even a few months, to publish the *gōkan* version. To a large extent, the speed of its publication is what made *A New Tale of Omatsu* a best seller.

The *ungōkan*-like haste with which this book was produced was surely connected to another of its notable characteristics: it does not really look like a *gōkan*, even though it has all the markings of a work in the genre, including such basic bibliographic features as its size; the vividly colored covers of the three fascicles of each volume, which form a single composition; the illustrated title pages; the style of the preface; and the presence of *kuchi-e* in the first fascicle of each chapter or part that depict important characters in attractive poses. The first page of the main body is unusual, for instance, in that it is composed exclusively of text; and while, with two exceptions, all the other pages combine pictures and text, the pictures are comparatively crudely done and present readers with little detail or information about the plot. Figure 77, which comes from volume 2 and shows the boat that picks up Omatsu after she is pushed off a bluff into the ocean, is an extreme if not unusual example of a picture that conveys only a bare minimum of information.[18]

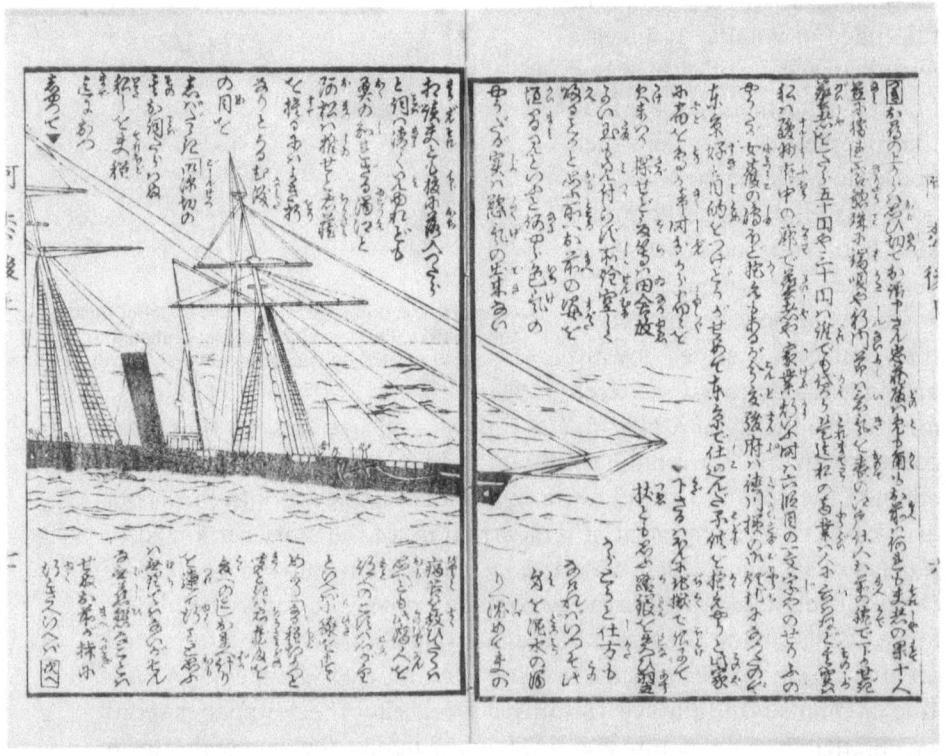

Figure 77 An example of a picture by Chikanobu in *Torioi Omatsu kaijō shinwa* (chapter 2, 6 ura-7 omote) that conveys a minimum of information. (Courtesy of Waseda University Library, Tokyo)

The most jarring discrepancy between *A New Tale of Omatsu* and earlier *gōkan* lies, however, in its text rather than in its pictures. One notices, first of all, that the book was written using a mixture of *kanji* and *hiragana*. Generally speaking, the main text of *gōkan* had been composed almost exclusively in *hiragana*, with only a few easy-to-read characters mixed in here and there; the text of *A New Tale of Omatsu* represents a major departure from established practice. In order to make this new mixed text legible to readers with a limited knowledge of *kanji*, every character or compound of characters was glossed with *hiragana*. Perhaps even more significant, though, is the manner in which the text was laid out on the page: rather than filling the empty spaces in each spread with tight lines of text arranged in any number of distinct, irregularly shaped blobs, as was the case in conventional *gōkan*, the copyist created regularly spaced columns of text, usually twelve or thirteen per page, that extend all the way from the top of the page to the bottom, seeming to pass invisibly through the pictures.

This presentation of a mixed form of writing—incorporating both *kanji* and *hiragana*, in evenly spaced lines that extend, at least implicitly, over the entire page—creates a textual space that looks nothing like earlier *gōkan* but strikingly like *yomihon*, which alternate between full pages of text and pictorial spreads illustrating the story's high points. Indeed, the similarity between the textual format of *A New Tale of Omatsu* and that of *yomihon* extends even further, as we see from a comparison of the first page of the main body of volume 1 (figure 78) with, for instance, that of Bakin's *The Chronicle of the Eight Dogs* (figure 79). The layouts of the two pages are essentially identical: the title and volume numbers are indicated in the first line, at the top right; the author's name—and for *A New Tale of Omatsu* the name of the editor, Robun—is given next, at the bottom; slightly below the top of the page, centered over two lines of text—Kubota and Robun's names in *A New Tale of Omatsu*, a synopsis of the chapter's plot in *The Chronicle of the Eight Dogs*—appear the words "First Installment" (*dai ikkai*). Curiously, it is not clear what this "First Installment" refers to in *A New Tale of Omatsu*: if it was meant to mark the start of the first installment of the serial publication in *Kanayomi shinbun*, one would expect the divisions to have been marked throughout the book. They are not, and the words "Second Installment" never appear.

These peculiarities in the textual layout of *A New Tale of Omatsu*'s pages suggest that while it can still be considered a *gōkan*, its creators had already begun turning their backs on certain fundamental conventions and characteristics of the genre. *Gōkan* published in Edo were characterized by their careful balancing of text with pictures. As a rule,

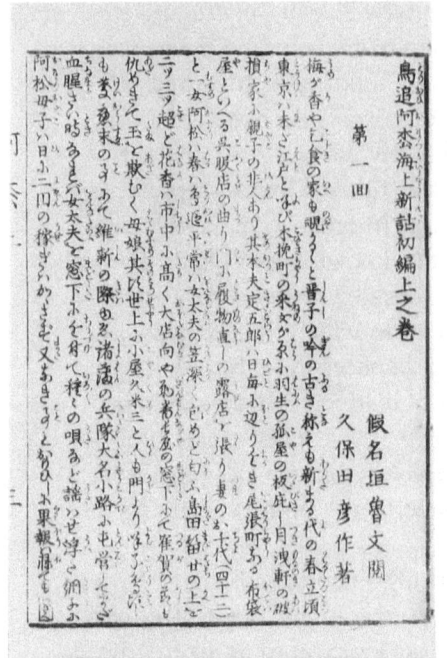 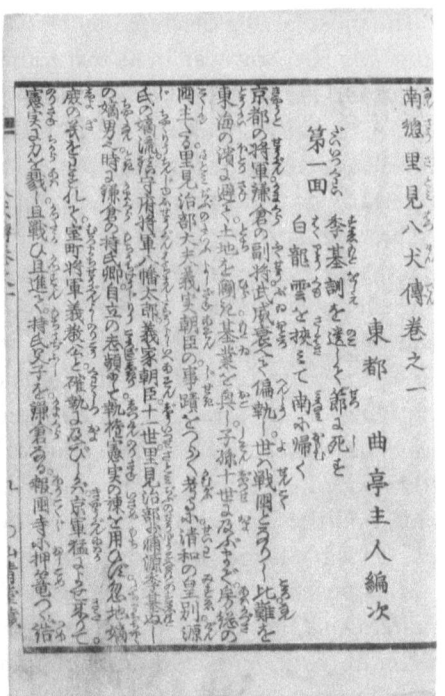

Figure 78 The first page of the main body of volume 1 of *Torioi Omatsu kaijō shinwa* (3 omote). (Courtesy of Waseda University Library, Tokyo)

Figure 79 The first page of the main body of part 1, book 1 of Kyokutei Bakin's *Nansō Satomi hakkenden* (9 omote). (Courtesy of National Diet Library)

the text generally seemed to have been written into the blank spaces in the pictures: the pictures, in other words, structured the pages. Artists were, moreover, frequently given higher billing than authors—even though, as we saw in chapter 2, authors were responsible for preparing sketches and written instructions for artists to work from. In *A New Tale of Omatsu*, on the contrary, the pictures seem almost to be intruding into pages that are fundamentally structured by the regularly spaced lines of text, and while the names Kubota Hikosaku and Kanagaki Robun appear on the kite on the title page of volume 1—along with the title, in the circle at the center, and an abbreviation of the publisher's name—the name of the artist, Yōshūsai Chikanobu, does not (see figure 76). He is named as the book's artist on the wrappers in which the three fascicles of each volume were bound and on one of the title pages in volume 3, and he is identified on the covers specifically as the artist of the covers, but he is hardly given top billing or even equal credit for the work.

A *New Tale of Omatsu* may be regarded, then, as a subtle compromise within the genre of the *gōkan* between the *gōkan* and the *yomihon*; it had taken a considerable first step in the direction of transforming *gōkan* into "reading books." It comes as no surprise to find that an advertisement printed alongside the final newspaper installment of *The Life of Omatsu* actually uses the word *yomihon* rather than *gōkan* to describe the book: "We plan to publish this story separately in the near future as a *gesaku*-style *yomihon*, illustrations added, under the title *A New Tale of Omatsu the Singing Beggar's Adventures at Sea*, and so today, for the time being, we bring this newspaper serialization to an end."[19] In this context, the word *yomihon* need not be taken to denote the genre specifically, especially since the published version of *A New Tale of Omatsu* is clearly not a *yomihon* in the sense in which the genre is usually understood; it may simply mean what it literally says: "a book meant to be read." Either way, the genre now known as the *yomihon* clearly provided a useful model for the reinvention of the *gōkan*, and *A New Tale of Omatsu* was indeed presented as a text-centered work: not a "picture book" (*ezōshi*), as *gōkan* were frequently called during early modern times, but a "reading book" with illustrations that were literally no more than "inserted pictures" (*sashie*), as the pictures in *gōkan* are often called today. Already the text came first.

Time and Type

A New Tale of Omatsu was the first *gōkan* to emerge from a newspaper serial, and thus the first to make such a definitive leap from the slower sense of topicality that had governed earlier works in the genre into the increasingly fast-paced world of Meiji publication, symbolized by the daily newspaper. The basic bibliographic form of the book, however, was in no way unusual for *gōkan* of the time.

This begs the question of when and why the bibliographic shift toward the *yomihon* style first took place. A precise answer to this question would be beyond the scope of this chapter, especially since the history of Meiji *gōkan* is currently being revised by scholars active in Japan. Still, some general observations and speculations can be made. First, *gōkan* published from the early to mid-1870s, such as *In the Willow's Shade: Asazuma in the Moonlight* and *Otama Pond: How to Wear a Moon-Shaped Comb*, have pages that look and read just like earlier *gōkan* (figure 80), while those first published from the late 1870s onward resemble *A New Tale of Omatsu*. Second, the change seems to have begun with a spate of

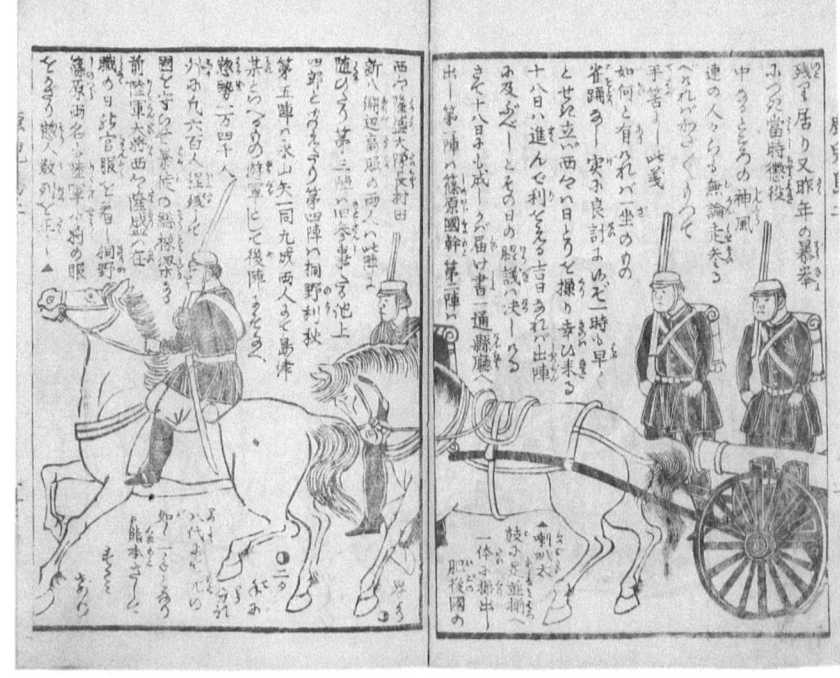

half-documentary works about a number of violent samurai revolts that took place in Kyushu, particularly several that dealt with the Satsuma Rebellion and the life and suicide of its central figure, Saigō Takamori, that began to appear in February 1877, the same month the rebellion broke out. Sasaki Tōru has pointed out that a number of these works were issued simultaneously in two versions, one in a *gōkan* and one in a *yomihon* format, both by the same author and publisher, and suggests persuasively that this overlap likely led to the introduction of *yomihon* characteristics into the *gōkan*. Ōkura Magobē, the publisher of *A New Tale of Omatsu*, applied to the censors for permission to release a *gōkan* about the Satsuma Rebellion the month before *A New Tale of Omatsu* was published, and the two works are very similar in appearance.[20]

Examples of *gōkan* from 1876 to 1877 whose layout closely resembles that of *A New Tale of Omatsu* include *Record of Great Peace in Kumamoto: A Picture Book* (*Ehon Kumamoto taiheiki*, 1876), *Record of the War in Kagoshima: A Picture Book* (*Ehon Kagoshima senki*, 1877), and *The Quest for Sincerity: A Way Back in Dream* (*Tansei yume no fukuro*, 1877). *Record of the War in Kagoshima* is the only one of these three books in which any effort was made to fill the empty spaces with text, and even here the larger size of the writing—necessary to accommodate the mixed *kanji* and *hiragana* prose—imbues the page with the sense of staid, quintessentially textual regularity, not present in earlier works in the genre, that is evident in *A New Tale of Omatsu* (figure 81). The long lines of text play an equally obtrusive role in structuring the spreads in the other two books, though in each the prose is presented in a somewhat different manner: unlike *Record of the War in Kagoshima*, which was written using glossed *kanji* in block style, *Record of Great Peace in Kumamoto* features cursive *kanji* with glosses, while *The Quest for Sincerity* uses cursive *kanji* without glosses. Both of these latter two books were published simultaneously in *yomihon* format.

Through their introduction of movable type into the *gōkan*, two books published at the close of the 1870s further continued the process of what I call the *yomihon*ization of the *gōkan*—the process of shifting the emphasis of the genre from the visual to the textual—which had already been initiated in books first published using woodblock printing, such as *A*

Figure 80 A typical two-page spread in Jōno Arindo's *Yanagikage tsuki no Asazuma* (chapter 5, 5 ura–6 omote). (Courtesy of Waseda University Library, Tokyo)

Figure 81 A typical two-page spread in *Ehon Kagoshima senki* (chapter 2, 10 ura–11 omote). (Courtesy of Waseda University Library, Tokyo)

New Tale of Omatsu. These two books, both issued in 1879 as *gōkan* versions of stories first covered in small newspapers, are Kanagaki Robun's *Takahashi Oden: Tale of a Demon* (*Takahashi Oden yasha monogatari*) and Takabatake Ransen's *Rumors of a Double Life* (*Kōsetsu konotegashiwa*).

Takahashi Oden had been turning up in newspaper stories since she was arrested for murder in 1876; she attracted an enormous amount of attention on January 31, 1879, when she was found guilty, sentenced to death, and beheaded. *Kanayomi shinbun* took up the story the next day, but its serial report broke off after only two installments; on March 3, the publishing house Kinshōdō applied for permission to publish the discontinued story as *Takahashi Oden: Tale of a Demon*. As soon as the following day, an advertisement in *Kanayomi shinbun* touted the forthcoming publication of the book as "an illustrated *yomihon*"; another advertisement on March 10 in *Tōkyō nichinichi shinbun* (*Tokyo Daily Newspaper*) described it in more detail as a "*chūgata* illustrated *yomihon*"—*chūgata* (middle size) described the conventional size of the *gōkan*. Despite these references to the work as a *yomihon*, the book is by and large identical to *gōkan* of the same period, with the exception of its first volume.

Volume 1 of *Takahashi Oden* went on sale on March 14, just eleven days after the paperwork requesting permission to publish the book was filed. Obviously, speed was a primary concern—all the more so because *Takahashi Oden* was not the only *gōkan* dealing with Takahashi's crimes. An advertisement for a competing publication, *Her Name Was Takahashi, the Poisonous Woman: A Brief Account of Her Life; or, Strange Happenings in Tokyo* (*Sono na mo Takahashi dokufu no oden: Tōkyō kibun*), ran on March 12 in *Tōkyō nichinichi shinbun*—the same newspaper that had carried the advertisement for *Takahashi Oden* on March 10—announcing that the first chapter of the book had gone on sale the previous day. New chapters of these two works kept appearing simultaneously, and new advertisements for each kept being placed in the same issues of the same newspapers, until the final chapters were issued in April. In a little more than two months, an astonishing eight chapters of *Takahashi Oden* and seven of *Her Name Was Takahashi* were published. During the 1830s and 1840s, when *Inaka Genji* was published, it would have taken at least two and probably three or even four years for the same number of chapters to appear. With these two books, then, we witness the complete absorption of the *gōkan* into fast-paced newspaper time.[21]

Not surprisingly, contemporary readers were acutely aware of this shifting temporality and its connection to technology and of its effect on the value that readers placed on books. Indeed, this consciousness that something had changed in the early years of the Meiji period lingered on for some time, as we see in a column titled "Books and Movable Type" (Chosho to kappan) that ran in *Tōkyō asahi shinbun* a few decades later, on August 12, 1903:

> Now that the rise of movable type has made publishing so simple, books are no longer as precious as before. In the past, readers used to wait anxiously for the latest installment of works like *The Chronicle of the Eight Dogs* and *Inaka Genji* to appear, one volume at a time, in spring and autumn, and they would go buy them and read them as soon as they came out. Since one could produce the equivalent of only thirty or maybe fifty movable-type pages at any one time, fat books like those you see today would be divided into five or even ten sections, each of which would be issued separately—a very frustrating thing indeed. And yet the works of Bakin, Shunsui, and Tanehiko remain popular with readers today and continue to be incorporated into plays, while those by famous writers from the Meiji period tend to be praised only when they are published, and few continue to be read for long. This is not because their works are inferior to those of the old writers; people have simply taken to treating their books lightly because it is so easy to publish them.[22]

If in 1879 *Takahashi Oden* and *Her Name Was Takahashi* were the first *gōkan* to make the speed with which they appeared such an important element of their appeal, they were also the first to sacrifice the special aura and the long shelf life that *gōkan* of an earlier age had possessed. Timely *gōkan* quickly became outdated.

For my purposes, however, *Takahashi Oden* is more interesting, as it was the first *gōkan* published in Tokyo to make use of movable type. The front and back covers, title page, preface, colophon, and *kuchi-e* of the three fascicles of volume 1 were printed from woodblocks, but the rest of the text, beginning with a foreword sandwiched between the second *kuchi-e* and the first page of the main body, was produced using movable type. The first page of the main body, printed in a mix of glossed *kanji* and *hiragana*, is laid out in the same *yomihon*-like format that was used in *A New Tale of Omatsu* (figure 82). The label "First Installment" means what it says: the second fascicle of volume 1 begins the "Second Installment," the third fascicle begins the "Third Installment," and so on. The text and pictures in volume 1 are completely separated, in *yomihon* fashion—a few pages of text followed by a pictorial spread—and boxed-in explanations of the content of each picture were added, along with labels identifying the important characters, also in a style seen in *yomihon* (figure 83). Yanagawa

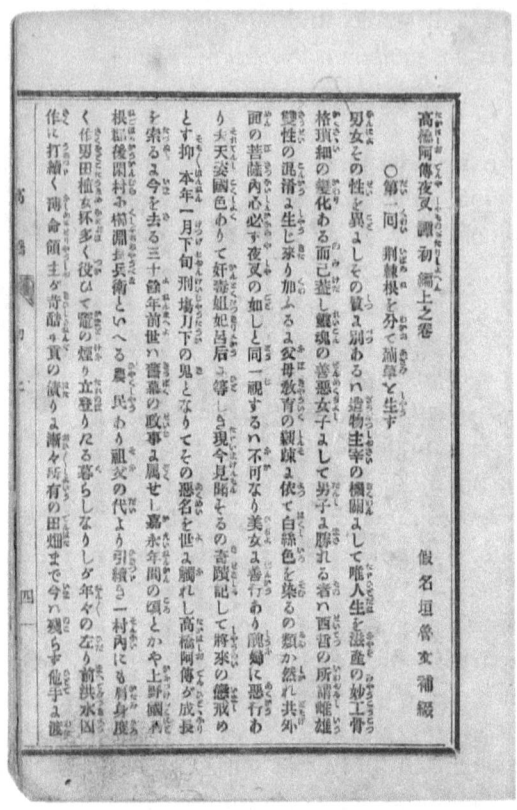

Figure 82 The first page of the main body of volume 1 of Kanagaki Robun's *Takahashi Oden yasha monogatari* (4 *omote*). (Courtesy of Art Research Center, Ritsumeikan University, Kyoto)

Shigenobu's pictures for Bakin's *The Chronicle of the Eight Dogs* (figure 84), for instance, were done in this manner. And as if all this *yomihon*ization were not enough, the title page was designed in a Chinese style, with writing in clerical script (*reisho*) that is reminiscent of a *yomihon* rather than a *gōkan* (figure 85). Comparison with a title page from *The Chronicle of the Eight Dogs* (figure 86) and a more characteristically *gōkan*-esque title page from *A New Tale of Omatsu* (see figure 76) highlights the difference. No doubt the technical difficulty of setting movable type in the negative spaces of the illustrations prompted this extreme movement in the direction of the *yomihon*—as a genre, here, rather than simply as a "book meant to be read." Indeed, printing *Takahashi Oden* using movable type must have proved too time-consuming to allow the publisher to compete with *Her Name Was Takahashi*, which was printed entirely from woodblocks; the second volume was printed from woodblocks and laid out in the same style—half *gōkan* and half *yomihon*—that we saw in *A New Tale of Omatsu*.[23]

The second book I wish to discuss in relation to *yomihon*ization—Takabatake Ransen's *Rumors of a Double Life*, published from September to December 1879—was the first *gōkan* issued in Tokyo whose main text was printed using only movable type, though in recent years it has become clear that experimentation with movable-type *gōkan* had begun

Figure 83 An illustration in volume 1 of Robun's *Takahashi Oden yasha monogatari* (5 *ura*–6 *omote*). (Courtesy of Art Research Center, Ritsumeikan University, Kyoto)

Figure 84 An illustration by Yanagawa Shigenobu in part 4, book 1 of Bakin's *Nansō Satomi hakkenden* (28 *ura*–29 *omote*). (Courtesy of National Diet Library)

高橋阿傳夜刃譚 上篇

仮名垣魯文探旃
守川周之至畫
東京書肆玉松堂梓

八犬傳第六輯

曲亭主人著
柳川重信
溪齋英泉 畫
涌泉堂嗣梓

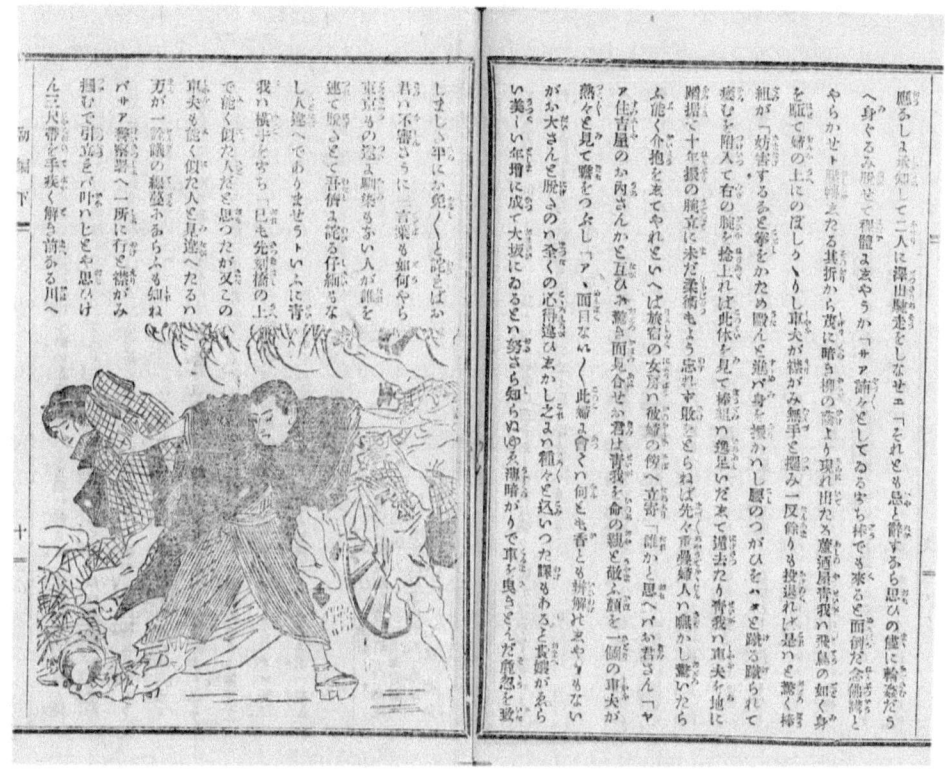

Figure 87 An illustrated spread in volume 1 of Takabatake Ransen's *Kōsetsu konotegashiwa* (10 ura–11 omote). (Courtesy of Waseda University Library, Tokyo)

earlier in the Kyoto and Osaka region.[24] As with *Takahashi Oden*, the front and back covers, title pages, prefaces, colophons, and *kuchi-e* were printed from woodblocks, and movable type was used for only the main text. As with *Takahashi Oden*, the text was printed in both *kanji* and *hiragana*; the text and pictures were not, however, completely separated, as they were in that book: the illustrations first published with *Rumors of a Double Life* when it was serialized in *Hōtan zasshi* (*Redolent Tales: A Magazine*) were cropped and inserted into the text (figure 87). Ironically, the decision not to separate the pictures and the text entirely—presumably

Figure 85 The title page of volume 1 of Robun's *Takahashi Oden yasha monogatari*. (Courtesy of Art Research Center, Ritsumeikan University, Kyoto)

Figure 86 The title page of part 6, book 1 of Bakin's *Nansō Satomi hakkenden*. (Courtesy of National Diet Library)

an attempt to preserve something of the style of the *gōkan*—only made it more obvious than in *yomihon*-style books that the pictures were only illustrations, subordinate to the text.

The three *gōkan* I have considered either helped create or benefited from the revival that took place in the genre around 1878. But the bibliographic experiments that their authors, artists, and publishers conducted as they struggled to survive in a changing climate gradually stripped the genre of the characteristics that had made it unique, moving it closer to the *yomihon*—both as a genre and as a descriptive term for "books meant to be read," in which the text took precedence over the pictures. This jettisoning of the particular image–text–book relations that characterized the *gōkan* in favor of the *yomihon* style would ultimately result in a sort of double abandonment of the genre: first, because the subordination of the pictures to the text undercut one of the main attractions of the *gōkan*; second, because since the *gōkan* had not developed as a primarily textual genre, it would have a hard time competing with actual "books meant to be read"—above all, the new kind of book that would come to be known as the *shōsetsu* (novel). New chapters of a few extended *gōkan* kept appearing in the conventional Edo format through the mid-1880s, but by 1879 the genre had already been dealt a series of near-fatal blows. The poisonous thrust that finally did in the *gōkan* would come when new bibliographic translations of old works, including *Inaka Genji*, began to appear in the 1880s.

The Bibliographic Translation

"It is a great irony," Maeda Ai, a scholar of modern Japanese literature, has observed, "that from 1882 to 1883, precisely at the moment when Edo-style *gōkan* were passing into extinction, the publishing world was being swept up in a revival of 'frivolous writing' from Edo. This revival took two forms: a spate of movable-type transcriptions of woodblock-printed works, and a boom in subscription publishing."[25] The irony that Maeda notes is complemented by a second: it is the revival of "frivolous writing" that ultimately killed the *gōkan*. The movable-type *gōkan* that had started to appear in 1879 had at least been created with the new format in mind—from the outset, the pleasures they offered were primarily topical and textual. This was not the case with early modern *gōkan* bibliographically translated, beginning in 1882, into the *yomihon*ized movable-type format that had by then become standard. In these *gōkan*, in the format in which they had originally been issued, the pictures had come first. The reconfiguration of their image–text–book relations as they were reprinted in movable-type editions, most often made using Western-style paper and bound using the case-binding technique imported from the West, stripped them of much of their interest. It was this above all, I argue, that caused *gōkan* to be nearly forgotten until very recently, even by scholars of early modern literature.

Equally damaging, in the case of *Nise Murasaki inaka Genji*, was that its bibliographic translation from a form that emphasized pictures into a form that emphasized the text—which was part and parcel of the broad popularization of "books meant to be read," particularly the novel—changed the work into an all-too-obviously inadequate replacement of *Genji monogatari*. When Tayama Katai praised *Genji monogatari* in 1925 in terms of "the human emotions, moods, and sensations that are inscribed in such minute detail in the interstices between one written character and the next, one clause and the next" and lamented that people now read "adaptations" such as *Inaka Genji* instead of the original, he was considering *Inaka Genji* first and foremost as a text.[26] Bibliographic translation, in other words, completed the process that Tanehiko himself had initiated, with his unobtrusively pedagogical approach, of turning *Inaka Genji* into a precursor of modern-Japanese translations. In its new guise as a typeset book, however, *Inaka Genji* had become less an elegant, sophisticated, and material replacement than a textual *rewriting* of *Genji monogatari* that no longer functioned very well as a replacement because it no longer possessed the qualities that originally had made it so attractive and entertaining as a *gōkan*. Stripped of the various aspects of its visual and material design that had turned it into an unprecedented best seller and elevated it to the status of a popular classic, *Inaka Genji* became *no more than* a replacement of *Genji monogatari*. The text could be judged, it seemed—or could only be judged—in terms of its relationship to the original of which it was said to be an adaptation, or a parody, and so it came inevitably to seem secondary, inadequate, lacking.

I have already outlined the path that *gōkan* followed as they metamorphosed into "books meant to be read." The rest of this chapter is dedicated to an examination of a selection of movable-type editions of *Inaka Genji* that contain at least some pictures—all but three of the sixteen editions published from 1882 to 1953 do. Not surprisingly, none of the editions manage to accomplish the impossible ideal of an absolute bibliographic translation into a different bibliographic form of the image–text–book relations that characterize the Edo edition; rather than present these books as failures, however, lamenting that they do not work, I consider how they *do* work. My goal, in other words, is to highlight the subtle ways in which the bibliographic translation of *Inaka Genji* changed the character of even the few pictures included in most editions, and to mark what I see as relatively successful attempts to make the pictures function within the bibliographic context of the typeset book. The artists, designers, and publishers responsible for these editions were clearly sensitive to *Inaka Genji*'s bibliographic characteristics, and to a certain extent—limited by the bibliographic and technological conventions of the forms they worked in—they were able to draw on them in their own designs.

This sort of analysis is valuable for a number of reasons. First, it helps clarify the importance of bibliographic form to our perceptions of genre. *Inaka Genji*'s yomihonization may also be discussed in terms of its transformation from a *gōkan* into a so-called early modern novel (*kinsei shōsetsu*), a process that parallels the modern transformation of *Genji monogatari* itself from a *monogatari* (tale, story) first into a romance, and then into a novel—a trajectory that part II of this study traces. This parallelism is perfectly illustrated by an unsigned prefatory note to the 1935 Ichōbon edition of *Inaka Genji*, which states that while *Inaka Genji* "is an adaptation of *Genji monogatari*, as the title indicates," it is such a rich work that "it is fair to describe it as a completely different novel. Thus even those who have read *Genji monogatari* have to read *Inaka Genji*, and those who have read *Inaka Genji* have to read *Genji monogatari*."[27] Here both *Genji monogatari* and *Inaka Genji* are presented as belonging to the same genre, that of the novel. This is not merely a matter of how the works or texts are perceived: both *books* can be read as novels because they were published in a form that accommodates a novelistic mode of reading.

A comparative analysis of different editions of *Inaka Genji* also illustrates how the re-creation of a work from a certain genre into another bibliographic form with its own conventions affects both the work's narrative structure and the particular material manner in which it *means*, thus bringing into sharper relief the concept of bibliographic translation itself. In particular, it helps us see that bibliographic translation is not governed solely by technological constraints: the yomihonization of the *gōkan* began with the woodblock publication of *A New Tale of Omatsu*, rather than with the movable-type publication of *Takahashi Oden*. Bibliographic conventions are precisely that—conventions. There are times when these conventions matter quite a lot; there are also times when they can be bent, imported from one context into another, and thus enabled to keep mattering in translation, as the legions of readers who now read *manga* in English from right to left demonstrate, and as we will see in my analyses of modern editions of *Inaka Genji*.

Typeset Editions of *Inaka Genji*

Year	Publisher or Series	Binding
1882	Moriya Kiyokichi	Pouch binding
1882	Shinshindō	Pouch binding
1888	Ginkadō/Kakuseisha	Case binding
1910	Kibunkai	Case binding
1918	Ehon haishi shōsetsu	Case binding
1927–1928	Nihon meicho zenshū	Case binding

Sixteen full or partial typeset editions of *Inaka Genji* were published between 1882 and 1953. This is too many to consider in detail, so I have limited myself rather strictly, selecting editions from a range of time periods that reveal how *Inaka Genji* continued to change as bibliographic conventions and tastes evolved, as it was translated into new forms that were designed to answer the needs of different readerships and to arouse new desires. Since the period from the late 1870s through the 1880s is so important, witnessing as it did the emergence of new literary forms and the more or less total switch, throughout the Japanese publishing world, to modern Western paper-making techniques and bindings, I begin with three editions from the 1880s.[28] I then skip ahead two decades to consider an edition from 1910, one from 1918, and finally one from 1927–1928. The accompanying table lists the names of the editions, their publication dates, and their bindings. "Pouch binding" is the same *fukurotoji* style used in the original Edo edition of *Inaka Genji*; I use the term "case binding" to refer to the form familiar from the contemporary hardbound book.

Flat Lines: *Inaka Genji* in the 1880s

Three partial editions of *Nise Murasaki inaka Genji* appeared or began to appear in 1882. One was a woodblock publication made by taking apart a copy of the Edo edition and using the pages to carve new blocks—a procedure known as *kabusebori* (cover-and-carve). This was the only way to issue a new woodblock edition of the work, since the original blocks had been confiscated and destroyed when the book was banned during the Tenpō Reforms. The bright covers of this book have an unmistakable Meiji feel, quite different from the quieter tones of the covers of the Edo edition. Otherwise, it is essentially a facsimile.

The second two editions issued in 1882 were printed with movable type. The first of the two, publication of which commenced in May 1882 and continued until at least August 1883, was issued weekly in thin pamphlets of between seven and nine double-sided pages bound in the same pouch-binding format as the Edo edition; published by Moriya Kiyokichi, they were distributed with *Iroha shinbun* (*ABC Newspaper*). In a preface to this edition, Saiga Ryūkō notes that this form of publication had become something of a vogue: "Now that we are progressing along the path of Culture and movable-type printing is all the rage . . . it is by no means uncommon to find magazines arranging to publish masterpieces by writers of old."²⁹ The serial publication of popular classics was an attempt to do for them what *A New Tale of Omatsu* had succeeded so well in doing for the contemporary *gōkan*: to incorporate them into "newspaper time." The extent to which publishing houses were willing to disregard the original format of the works when they did this is apparent from the fact that the length of the individual pamphlets of the Moriya edition of *Inaka Genji*, which are labeled as chapters—"chapter 1" (*daiippen*), "chapter 2" (*dainihen*), and so on—in no way corresponds to that of the chapters of *Inaka Genji*: the first pamphlet of this edition, for instance, breaks off in the middle of a sentence in the second fascicle of chapter 1; when chapter 2 begins, in the second pamphlet, there is no indication that a division originally existed—not even a line break.³⁰ The second typeset edition to appear in 1882, published in Kyoto by Shinshindō, was also bound in the pouch-binding format, although some attention was paid to the divisions in the Edo edition: two chapters were combined in each volume, but the end of one and the beginning of the next are visually identified with a paragraph break in what is otherwise a solid block of text, if not explicitly labeled as such.³¹

The text of the first twenty-one pamphlets of the Moriya edition was printed largely in a mix of *kanji* and *hiragana*, but mostly in the latter; from the twenty-second pamphlet, the concentration of *kanji* increases dramatically, and we begin to encounter a large number of ostentatiously difficult compounds, the "easy readability" of which is guaranteed—as the preface in the first pamphlet promises it will be—only by the presence of *hiragana* glosses beside each character or compound of characters. The word *miyako* (capital) is spelled out in *kana* as ミやこ in the first pamphlet, for instance, but appears in the twenty-seventh pamphlet as 華洛.³² This shift from a relatively easily understood *hiragana*-centered text—though one that still incorporates many more *kanji* than the does Edo edition—to an intentionally, playfully difficult transcription of the original represents an unmistakable shift from a *gōkan* to a *yomihon* textuality: the *yomihon*ization of *Inaka Genji*.

A similar *yomihon*-like style of transcription is used from the outset in the Shinshindō edition, which includes many compounds that ordinary *gōkan* readers of a previous age, at the very least, would have found impossible to interpret without reference to the glosses: two examples just from the first page are 栄輝つ (glorious, splendid), given the reading ときめきつ (to be splendid), and 浮雲 (drifting clouds), glossed as あぶない (dangerous).³³ In his preface to this edition, the editor, Udagawa Bunkai, explains the necessity of this rewriting and the origins of its style in terms that resonate closely with the ideas of bibliographic translation and *yomihon*ization. "Since the book is written in *hiragana*," he writes, referring to calligraphic, woodblock-printed *hiragana*, not the simplified typeset adaptation of the syllabary, "we can only sigh at the great difficulty people of our age have in reading it. And so the publisher at Shinshindō in Kyoto had the notion of rewriting the book in the style of the newspaper serials that are so popular these days and republishing it, binding two chapters of the original under one cover."³⁴ Evidently, people still had no difficulty reading unpunctuated texts: the only punctuation used in either of the two typeset 1882 editions consists of marks indicating the beginning of a quotation, which were common in early modern *gōkan*.

The covers of the Moriya and Shinshindō editions are worth comparing. Although they are very different from each other in style, each reveals an acute consciousness of *Inaka Genji*'s material and visual form and shows that a serious attempt was made to incorporate elements of both, echoing something of the atmosphere of the early modern edition. The front covers of the Moriya edition follow a standard format. Figures 88 and 89 show the covers of pamphlets 8 and 14: the design in the background of each is based on the clamshell pattern I discussed in chapter 1 (see figure 10). In figure 88, the black rectangular box at the right, in which the title and pamphlet number are written, is a variation on the famous inkstone on the illustrated title page of chapter 1 of the Edo edition (see figure 35); the mock genealogy is adapted from that in the preface to chapter 5 of the Edo edition (see figure 27); and the picture is modified from those in the main body of the Edo edition (see figure 43). The artist, Utagawa Yoshiiku, lifted most of his material directly from Utagawa Kunisada's work for the original *Inaka Genji*, and, moreover, took it from different parts of the original edition: it is as if he were collapsing the back cover, title page, preface, and pictures—almost every element of the *gōkan*—onto his covers for the new edition. His decision to frame the title on each cover with a variation on the inkstone that Murasaki Shikibu was said to have used also represents an attempt to reproduce something of the visual wit of the Edo edition.

The artist for the Shinshindō edition, Yamazaki Toshinobu, chose instead to echo the cover of the first fascicle of chapter 1 of the Edo

Figure 88 The cover, by Utagawa Yoshiiku, of pamphlet 8 of the Moriya edition of *Inaka Genji*. (Courtesy of National Diet Library)

Figure 89 The cover, by Yoshiiku, of pamphlet 14 of the Moriya edition of *Inaka Genji*. (Courtesy of National Diet Library)

edition (see figure 11), which depicts Murasaki Shikibu, by making a portrait of her in an entirely different style (figure 90). Again, we see an artist aiming to create a cover that will serve roughly the same function as that of the original edition. The effect is heightened by the use on the back cover of a variant of the same clamshell pattern that inspired Yoshiiku's design for the front cover of the Moriya edition (figure 91).

Neither the Moriya nor the Shinshindō edition includes *kuchi-e*; both editions have illustrations set into the text. One example from each, depicting the same scene, will suffice to show how these illustrations relate to the text in these books—to show, that is, how completely text has triumphed over image. Each of the illustrations is based on the same sequence of pictures in chapter 1 of the Edo edition (see figures 46 and 47). In this sequence, we see Hanagiri listening through the cedar-plank door as her attendant, Sugibae—portrayed on the following page—explains that someone has put a lock on it; Yoshimasa is shown in the background in the first spread, entering the hallway through a Chinese-style door.

Figure 90 The front cover, by Yamazaki Toshinobu, of book 1 of the Shinshindō edition of *Inaka Genji*. (National Diet Library)

Figure 91 The back cover, by Toshinobu, of book 1 of the Shinshindō edition of *Inaka Genji*, with the clamshell pattern. (National Diet Library)

Figure 92 shows Yoshiiku's version of this scene for the Moriya edition; figure 93 shows Toshinobu's for the Shinshindō edition. Yoshiiku's illustration was inserted into the text in the same manner as the illustrations in *Rumors of a Double Life*; the equation of the thickness of the door with that of the paper, which works so well in the Edo edition, has been completely effaced, replaced by a still effective but very different, inescapably flat suggestion of three-dimensionality. This is the only illustration in this edition to be combined with text; perhaps this approach was adopted in an attempt to replicate some of the visual sophistication of the Edo edition. Clearly, both artists tried especially hard to create a sense of three-dimensionality in their illustrations of this scene, but it is also clear that there was a limit to how much they could accomplish without undoing the novelistic balance between image and text that was already becoming standard.

The third edition from the 1880s that I would like to touch on is a book co-published in Tokyo in 1888 by Ginkadō and Kakuseisha, probably

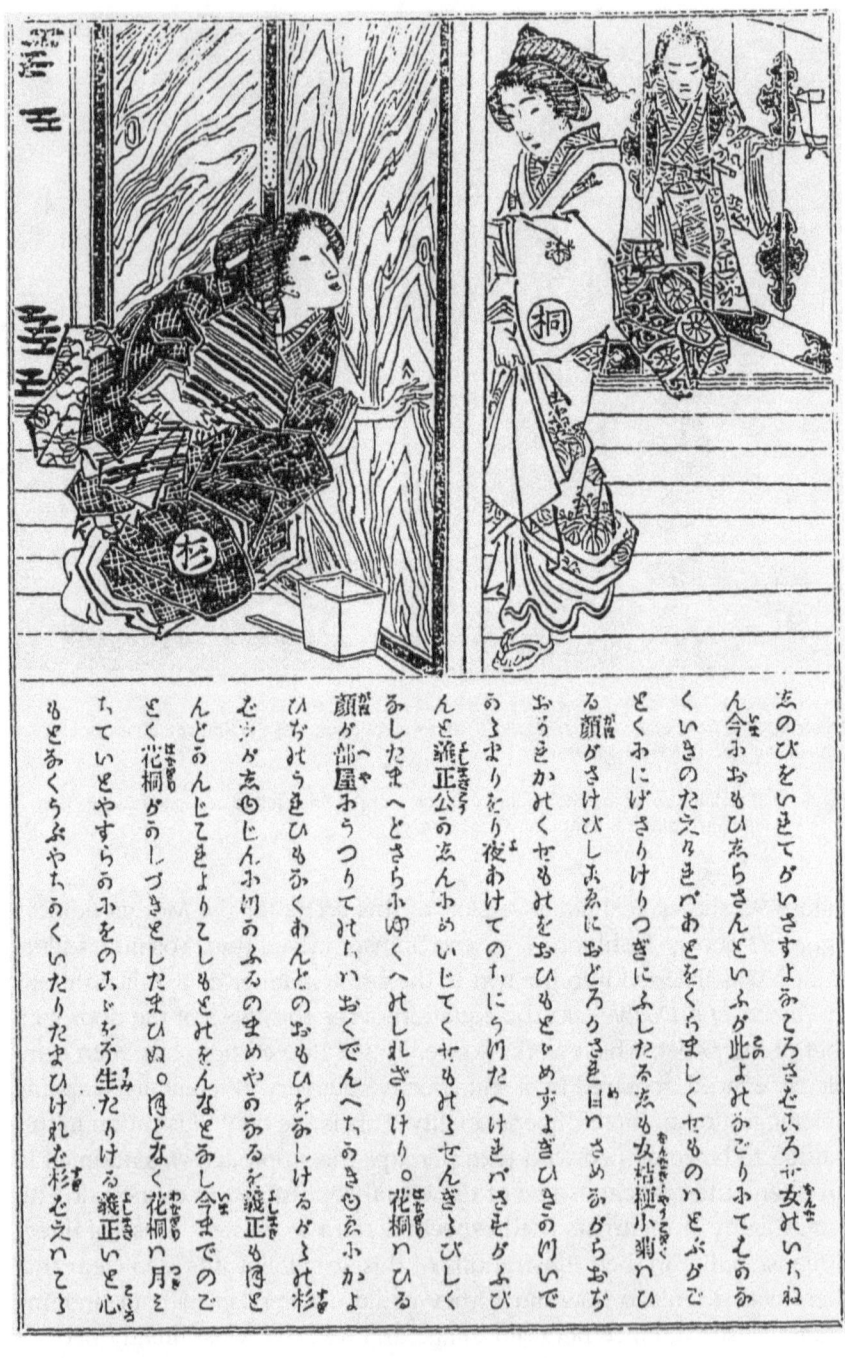

Figure 92 The illustration by Yoshiiku, based on Utagawa Kunisada's picture of the hallway scene, in pamphlet 1 of the Moriya edition of *Inaka Genji* (5 *omote*).(Courtesy of National Diet Library)

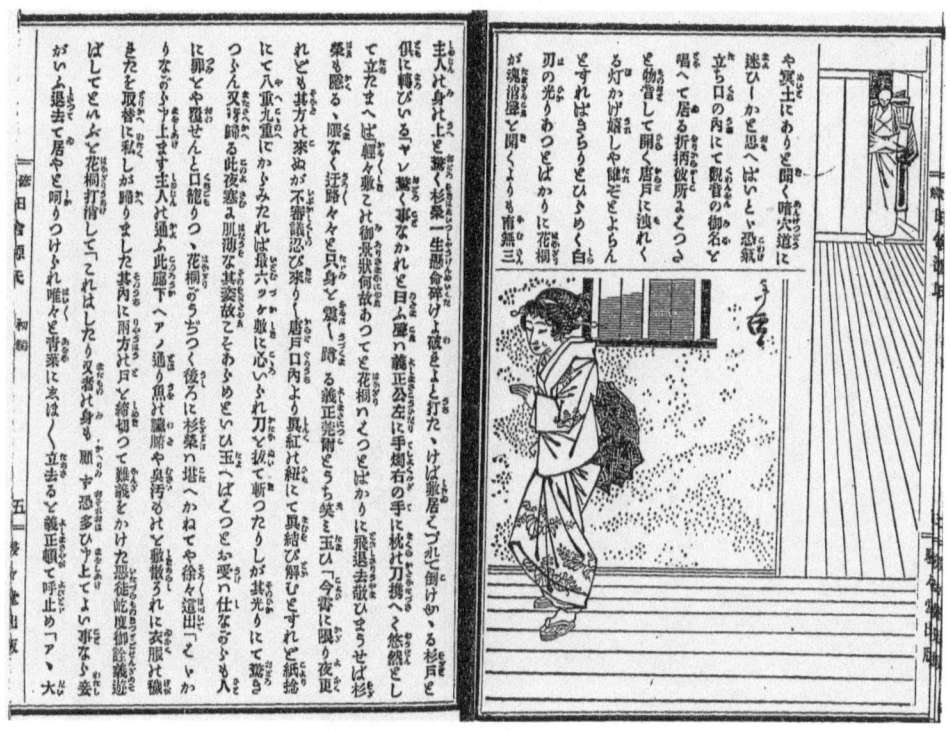

Figure 93 The illustration by Toshinobu, based on Kunisada's picture of the hallway scene, in book 1 of the Shinshindō edition of *Inaka Genji* (main body, 4 *ura*). (Courtesy of National Diet Library)

the first complete movable-type edition of *Inaka Genji*, since the two 1882 publications appear to have been abandoned midway through the story. I have seen a few copies of this edition, in different bindings—some in one volume, some in two. The reason for this variation is unclear and is something about which one would like to know more, particularly since the differences are rather extreme: my own copy of the book was fitted with covers reading *Ise* (as in *The Tales of Ise*) *Murasaki inaka Genji*; another I have seen has lithograph covers—a first for *Inaka Genji*, since those of the Moriya and Shinshindō editions were printed, like the pictures, from woodblocks. The copy I will be discussing is bound in two volumes; the text was printed in the same *yomihon* style used in the Moriya and Shinshindō editions, except that glosses were provided for only a minority of the characters. Here, too, the only punctuation marks included are open quotation marks.

The major pictorial innovation in the 1888 edition was the introduction of thirty-nine single-page, woodblock-printed *kuchi-e* by Ogata Gekkō

Figure 95 Ofuji, the "fake Murasaki," in the second of Gekkō's *kuchi-e* in the 1888 edition of *Inaka Genji* (1:4). (Courtesy of the author)

(1859–1920), based on those in the Edo edition, divided unevenly between the two volumes.[35] All these *kuchi-e* reward careful examination, but in order to keep things simple I will consider only three. The first, which appears on the first page of volume 1, is described in the boxed, inset caption as "A picture of Murasaki Shikibu writing *The Tale of Genji* at the request of Jōtōmon-in during a visit to Ishiyama Temple in Gōshū" (figure 94). The second, which appears on the second page, shows "A modern Shikibu in fake purple, holed up on the second floor of a stonemason's shop to compose *Inaka Genji*" (figure 95). Both pictures are based on *kuchi-e* from chapter 1 of the Edo edition (figures 96 and 97). As we might suppose, given the clever pun on Ishiyama Temple and "stonemason's shop" (*ishiya*) in the second caption, the explanations were taken directly from the Edo edition. This tendency to separate text from image, evident in the use of cartouches for the captions, is indicative of the general shift in image-text-book relations that took place in the course of *Inaka Genji*'s *yomihon*ization, as it was bibliographically translated from

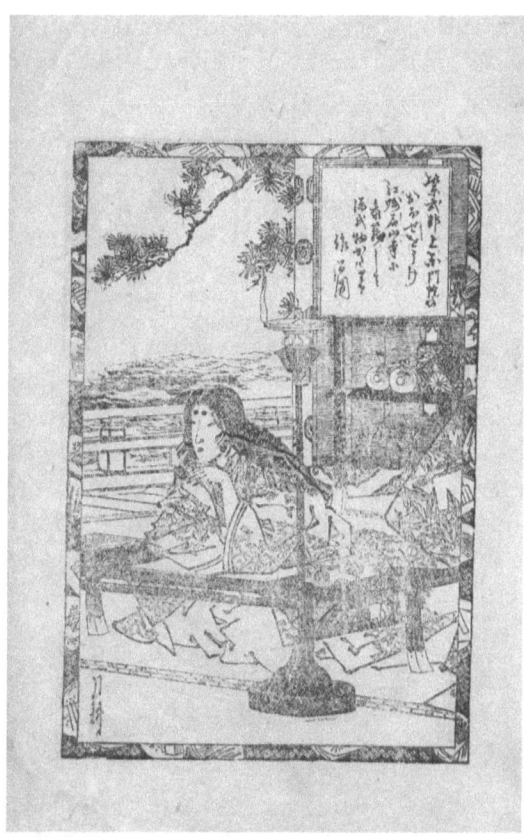

Figure 94 Murasaki Shikibu, in the first of Ogata Gekkō's *kuchi-e* in the 1888 edition of *Inaka Genji* (1:3). (Courtesy of the author)

the form of the *gōkan* to that of the typeset Edo novel as it existed in the 1880s, in which the textual and the visual are no longer so inextricably intertwined.

The segregation of text from image is subtly reinforced by a change in the frames enclosing the pictures themselves. In the Edo edition, both *kuchi-e* are framed in a pattern of autumn foliage—Japanese maple in the first and a variety of leaves in the second—set against a background that suggests cloth dyed using the bind-resist technique *kanokoshibori* (deer-fawn binding, named after the white spots that newborn deer have on their backs). The foliage resonates with the date—the fifteenth of the eighth lunar month, the day of the "moon viewing" (*tsukimi, kangetsu*)—when Murasaki Shikibu is said to have begun writing *Genji monogatari*, inspired by the reflection of the moon on Lake Biwa, and when Ofuji, the "fraudulent Murasaki," started composing *Inaka Genji*.[36] Kunisada's picture of Ofuji clearly marks the date by including behind her—at the top of the spread, straddling both pages—a large table on which are arrayed the various items customarily set out for the moon viewing: a bamboo vase holding stalks of the autumnal grass *susuki*; a tall tray presumably piled with "moon-viewing cakes" (*tsukimi-dango*), though they are obscured by the clouds that hover just beneath the upper border of the picture; and perhaps some *saké*. Gekkō's version includes a barely recognizable vase of *susuki* and provides a glimpse of a few tiny moon-viewing cakes over Ofuji's head; it is far from obvious, however, despite the hovering moon, that this is the evening of the fifteenth. Even assuming that some readers managed to identify the date, they would still have found it impossible to make the seasonal connection between the picture and the frame that is so obvious in the Edo edition, because here that connection does not exist: Gekkō replaced the patterns of autumn leaves with the same clamshell pattern that was used in the 1882 editions. He enclosed every *kuchi-e* in the book, regardless of its content, in an identical frame. Unlike the frames in the Edo edition, then, which are a meaningful element of the scenes being depicted, these frames are separate from the pictures.

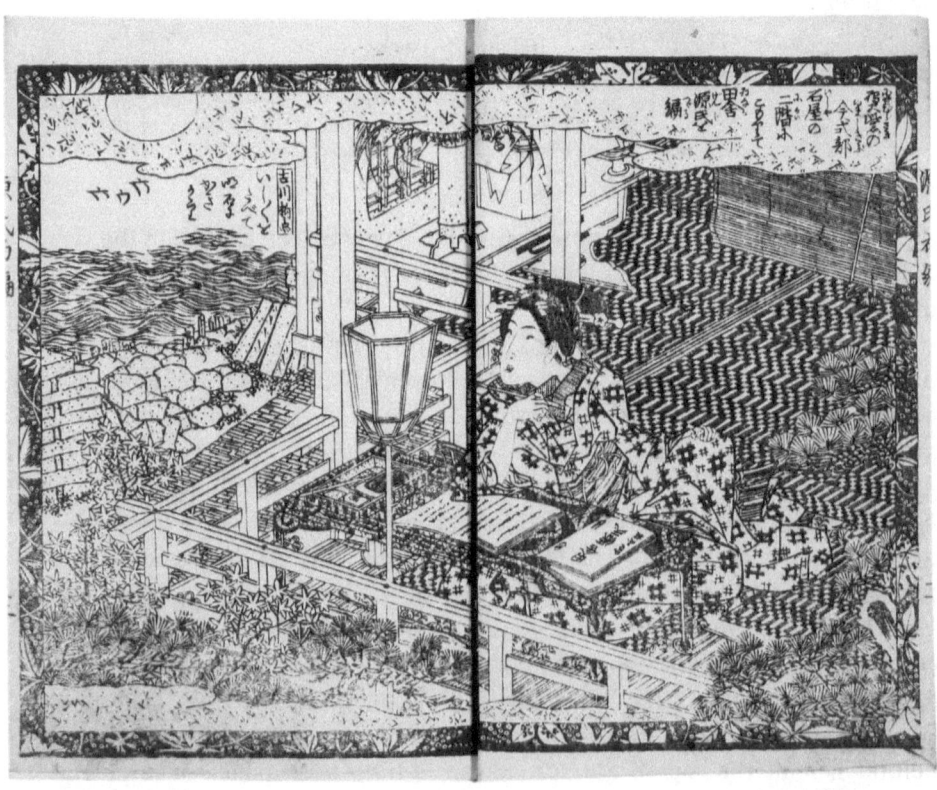

The nature of the difference becomes clearer when we compare another of Gekkō's *kuchi-e* with the picture on which it is based. Gekkō's picture, from the second volume, shows Mitsuuji and Tamakuzu (figure 98); it is based on a *kuchi-e* from chapter 36 of the Edo edition (figure 99). While the stream and grasses in Kunisada's original break through the frame, visibly representing its permeability, the water in Gekkō's picture is entirely contained. In the 1888 edition, the picture and the frame belong to different pictorial levels. The frame is halfway between text and image; it is a boundary that marks the difference between them and between textual and pictorial space. Everything outside the frame, including even the blank space, can be thought of as textual space. The book itself, in other words, is textual space into which the illustrations have been inserted: as I noted earlier, they are literally *sashie* (inserted pictures). This holds true despite occasional instances in which a few lines of text penetrate pictorial space, as they do in figure 98, because the text is not substantial enough to challenge the primacy of the pictorial in the space around it, and is in fact deemphasized still further by the

Figure 96 Murasaki Shikibu, in the first of Utagawa Kunisada's *kuchi-e* in *Inaka Genji*. (*NMIG*, chapter 1, 2 omote. Courtesy of Waseda University Library, Tokyo)

Figure 97 Ofuji, in the second of Kunisada's *kuchi-e* in *Inaka Genji*. (*NMIG*, chapter 1, 2 ura–3 omote. Courtesy of Waseda University Library, Tokyo)

presence of the cartouches, which create their own framed textual space within the larger space of the picture. In essence, the structure of this book can be regarded as a series of nesting spaces: the fundamentally textual space of the book itself is inset with framed pictorial spaces, which are again inset with framed textual spaces.

As a general rule, textual space can be thought of as two dimensional. This brings us back to the four *kuchi-e* depicting Murasaki Shikibu and Ofuji (see figures 94–97). In addition to the stylistic flattening that took place in the transition from the Edo to the Meiji edition—Kunisada's portrait of Murasaki Shikibu draws blatantly on a classical pictorial mode, with its bird's-eye, "no roof" (*fukinukiyatai*) point of view and its non-perspective composition, while Gekkō's is stylistically indistinguishable from all his other pictures—we encounter a sort of conceptual flattening of the printed page itself. When a reader of the Edo edition turns from the picture of Murasaki Shikibu to that of Ofuji, the scene rotates ninety degrees, just like the hallway that Hanagiri and Sugibae are shown walking down in chapter 1 (see figures 45 and 46). Kunisada depicted Murasaki Shikibu sitting with her back to us, the desk on the other side of her and the lamp beyond the desk (see figure 96); Ofuji, though, sits facing us across the desk, and her lamp stands between the desk and us (see figure 97). The scene has turned like a rotating kabuki stage. Here, too, we are made to notice that the movement of our eyes across successive pages of the *gōkan*—the turning of its pages—is what imbues the flat fictional world with pseudo-three-dimensionality. This sophisticated, subtle play on the materiality of the printed work is absent from the 1888 edition. Gekkō turned Murasaki Shikibu (see figure 94) so that she and Ofuji (see figure 95) face in the same direction, reworking the two compositions to make them echo each other in a purely two-dimensional way. Indeed, in most of the copies I have seen of this edition, the two pictures' compositional parallelism is highlighted by their position in the book: they are bound side by side, on facing pages, rather than printed on opposite sides of the same page.

This transformation becomes all the more interesting when we realize that the 1888 edition is the first to have been printed on Western-style paper and made using a case binding, rather than the pouch-binding

Figure 98 Mitsuuji and Tamakuzu, in Gekkō's *kuchi-e* in the 1888 edition of *Inaka Genji* (2:362). (Courtesy of the author)

Figure 99 Mitsuuji and Tamakuzu, in Kunisada's *kuchi-e* in *Inaka Genji*. (*NMIG*, chapter 36, 1 *ura*–2 *omote*. Courtesy of Waseda University Library, Tokyo)

format. As I explained in chapter 2, the obverse and reverse sides of a page in a book bound in the pouch-binding style are really the same side of a single piece of paper that has been folded in half with the printed side out; thus the pictures on each side of a given page are horizontally connected, and it makes sense to align them mentally. Reading a book published in this format, certainly a well-constructed *gōkan*, one has the sense of moving *through* the book—a feeling that is similar on some level, as Suzuki Jūzō has often suggested, to that of reading a handscroll. A scene depicted on one page is transformed into the scene on the next.

This feeling of connectedness is weaker, if not altogether absent, in books bound in the form common today, whose pages are printed on both sides. The surface of a page in a modern "Western-style" book tends, by virtue of its construction—and by virtue of the thoroughly mechanized nature of book production in the modern period, and of the particular reading conventions and sensibilities that have developed within this context—to appear as an island unto itself. If a reader notices that Gekkō's portraits of Murasaki Shikibu and Ofuji are compositionally all but identical, it is because she perceives each one as an isolated image. The transition from Kunisada's sequence of images, designed for a *gōkan* printed in the pouch-binding format, to Gekkō's, designed for a typeset book, is a perfect example of bibliographic translation—all the more so because Gekkō, or whoever was responsible for designing the book, was evidently still trying, by his placement of these two images at the very start of the book, to incorporate into his work some of the pictorial meaning of the Edo edition. Indeed, his depictions of Murasaki Shikibu and Ofuji, with their boxed-in explanatory quotations, take the place even of some of the Edo edition's text: since Tanehiko's prefaces to the chapters were deleted from the 1888 edition, nothing but these pictures informs the reader of the existence of *Inaka Genji*'s ostensible author, the "fraudulent Murasaki."

I noted that the frames around Gekkō's *kuchi-e* suggest that in the 1888 edition the illustrations were inserted into a space that is fundamentally textual. This is especially clear when one compares illustrations from the main body with those from the Moriya and Shinshindō editions. As the depictions of the hallway scene discussed earlier show, the illustrations in these two editions are separated from the text by thin lines, not framed: the pages appear to be divided between pictorial and textual space (see figures 92 and 93). Considerably more space is devoted to the text, it is true, but text and image still seem to exist on the same level. By contrast, in the illustration of the same hallway scene in the 1888 edition (figure 100), as throughout the book, the picture is framed and printed on a page

Figure 100 Hanagiri and Yoshimasa, in Gekkō's *kuchi-e* in the 1888 edition of *Inaka Genji* (1:35). (Courtesy of the author)

all its own, free from text—pages devoted to illustrations do not even have page numbers. The illustrations in this edition are isolated, stuck in, free-floating intruders in a flat, textual world.

Experimentation and Censorship: *Inaka Genji* in 1910

In 1898, the publisher Hakubunkan included *Inaka Genji* in the series New Imperial Library (Zoku teikoku bunko). The format of this book closely resembles the 1888 Ginkadō-Kakuseisha edition and has illustrations by Endō Kōkei that are essentially identical to Ogata Gekkō's for the earlier edition. Twelve years later, in 1910, we see the publication of the first of a limited number of experimental editions of *Inaka Genji* that grapple with the issue of how to translate the entire *gōkan*, pictures and all, into the form of the typeset, case-bound book. Interestingly, 1910 was also the year when the very first edition of *Inaka Genji* to contain no illustrations at all, the Pocket-Size Library (Shūchin bunko) edition published by Sankyō Shoin, appeared—a reminder that the carefully crafted editions examined in this section are exceptions rather than the rule. In general, most new editions of *Inaka Genji* remain focused on the text, incorporating only a few decorative illustrations. This text-centered approach was linked to the progressive naturalization in Japan of text-centered concepts of "literature" and the "novel," of course, but at the same time censorship was also an issue. I discussed *Inaka Genji*'s somewhat bald eroticism, by the standards of its age, in chapter 1, and it seems probable that pictures like the ones I cited then were what Kyokutei Bakin was referring to in a letter to Ozu Keisō dated the tenth day of the eleventh month, 1835—the year chapters 14 through 17 of *Inaka Genji* were issued—when he noted: "The censor had problems with *Inaka Genji*, seeing many questionable elements in its pictures, but Tsuruya laid out quite a lot of money to have a few changes made and the matter was settled."[37] The pictures, as well as the text, remained a problem until at least 1935.

In this section, I consider the Kibunkai (Hollyhock Society) edition, published in 1910 by Yoshikawa Kōbunkan in two volumes that together cover the first eighteen chapters of *Inaka Genji*. This edition is remarkable for the extreme care those involved in its production took in attempting to reproduce as much as possible the visual splendor of the original book. The calligraphy of the title on the cover is Kunisada's, borrowed from two of the Edo edition's covers; the title page of volume 1 represents the inkstone from the title page of chapter 1 of the Edo edition. Sumptuous, full-color woodblock-printed reproductions of all the covers of the chapters in volume 1 were included, inserted before every other chapter, reduced to one-quarter of their original size, and printed on Japanese paper subtly flecked with silver. Volume 2, by contrast, reproduces only the covers of the first two chapters it contains.

Almost all the *kuchi-e* and pictures from the Edo edition appear in this edition, reduced in size and arranged along the bottom of each page without any line separating them from the typeset text above. Since the text that originally filled the blank spaces in the pictures was removed, a reader gets the sense that the typeset text shares the page with the pictures—that this space is both textual and pictorial, as in the original Edo edition. As a result, the text reads as an explanation of the pictures, not the other way around: the pictures in the Kibunkai book are more than just illustrations. The layout of the pages even makes it possible to experience at least a little of the pleasure of the Edo edition's image-text-book relations. The success of this bibliographic translation can be seen, for instance, in the way the effect of the movement from the *kuchi-e* to the first page of the main body of chapter 9 in the Edo edition, which I analyzed in chapter 2, was re-created (figures 42, 43, 101, and 102). The decorative frame that encloses all three panels of the *kuchi-e* in the Edo edition was deleted to maintain a sense of connection between the text and the pictures, except for the side that separates the third panel of the *kuchi-e* from the first page of the main body of the text, in which Mitsuuji and Takano are shown dancing. This one edge was left in place in order to highlight the meaningful intrusion of Takanao's sleeve into the *kuchi-e*.

Perhaps the most remarkable sign of the care with which the Kibunkai edition was designed may be seen in the endpapers of the volumes (figure 103). The pattern was taken from two temporary covers prepared for chapter 10 of the Edo edition when popular demand led publisher Tsuruya Kiemon to release the book before the true covers could be carved and printed (figure 104). These temporary covers are themselves quite sophisticated, comprising an elegant combination of two patterns with auspicious connotations, both associated with Heian-period aristocratic culture: the background of diagonal dotted lines is a version of the "linked seven treasures" (*shippōtsunagi*) design, while the pattern superimposed over it is a "sandbar" design (*suhamagata*).

The Kinbunkai edition is outstanding for its lavish, almost fetishistic attention to the material and visual characteristics of the Edo edition of *Inaka Genji*. Unfortunately, it also stands out as the first modern edition of the work to be censored: only two of the planned four volumes were published. Interestingly, and somewhat ironically from the perspective

偐紫田舎源氏九編

第九編

義政公富徹の前義伺光氏始めとして眤近外様の面々迄
殘る人なく東福寺に集ひければ今日は各自心を屈せず
思ひの儘に酒打ち飲み紅葉狩なすべき旨義政公より觸
られけるにぞ或ひは方丈の座敷に集り或ひは庭に打こ
ぞり莚をはしらせ毛氈を敷連ね酒宴して遊びしが冬の
日の最短くて早書下がる頃になりぬ此時に義政は豫て
棧敷に設け置し通天橋に御座を移され左の方は富徹の
前押並んで藤の方其の外數多の女共處狹しと居流れた
り右の方は光氏は屏風を以て其間を押圍ひ義伺が席と定め少
し下つて光氏は大人しやかにぞ控へける廻廊には諸士
大勢星の如くに列り義政は下知を傳へ準備も最早調
ひつらん夫々と宣へば仰せ畏み候どて何れも衣裳に
綺羅を飾したる舞ごと様々多くあり其鼓
の聲太鼓の音實に世を響かす遊なり遊佐河原之進國助

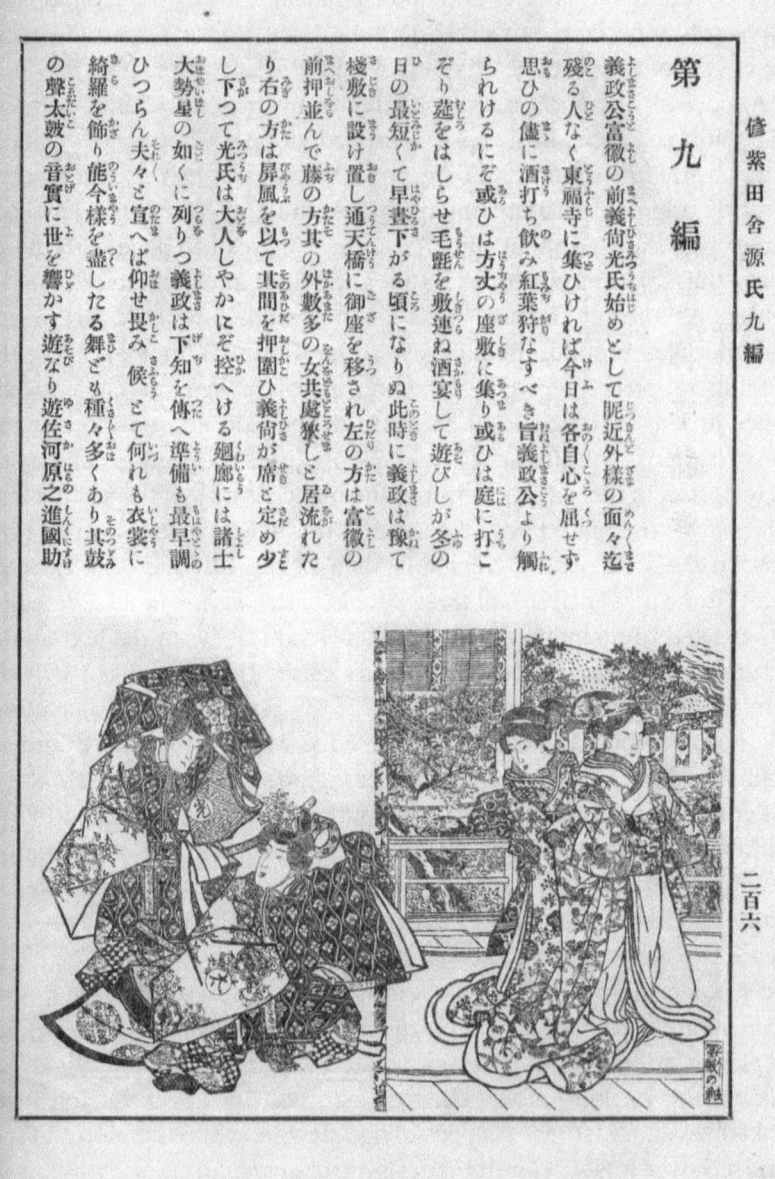

二百六

Figure 102 The scene at Tsūtenkyō, in Kunisada's *kuchi-e*, as reproduced in the Kibunkai edition of *Inaka Genji* (1:106). (Courtesy of the author)

Figure 101 The scene at Tsūtenkyō, in Kunisada's *kuchi-e*, as reproduced in the Kibunkai edition of *Iinaka Genji* (1:105). (Courtesy of the author)

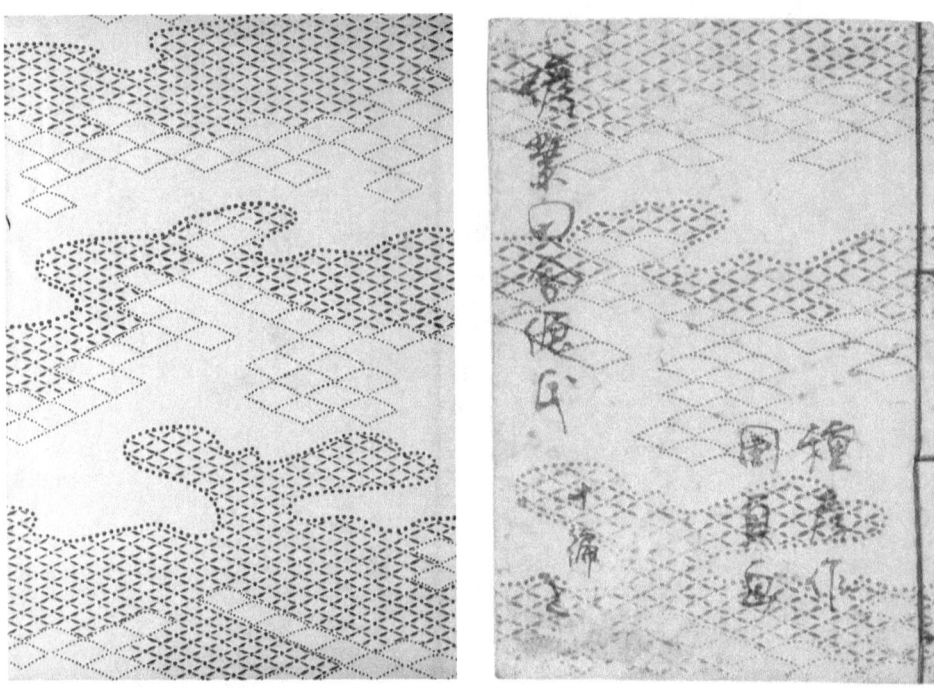

Figure 103 An endpaper from the Kibunkai edition of *Inaka Genji*. (Courtesy of the author)

Figure 104 A temporary cover from chapter 10 of the Edo edition of *Inaka Genji*. (Courtesy of Art Research Center, Ritsumeikan University, Kyoto)

of the book's publisher, it appears that the element of *Inaka Genji* that caught the censor's attention was the same one that Bakin mentioned in his letter to Ozu Keisō and that likely had caused it to be banned in 1842: a comparison of Amenotani Kan'ichi's preface to the first volume with his afterword to the second suggests that it was precisely the experimental, luxurious approach taken in the Kibunkai edition to the visual elements of *Inaka Genji*'s Edo edition—above all, to its covers and pictures—that was principally responsible for its being censored. Both texts are suggestive enough to merit quotation in full; here is the preface to the first volume:

IN PLACE OF A NOTE ON THE TEXT

This work, *Nise Murasaki inaka Genji*, is generally recognized not only as the greatest of all Tanehiko's writings but also as the last true masterpiece of Edo literature. And yet no one realizes that the author of this book took even more pains conceiving the pictures than he did polishing the prose, and it is a rare reader indeed who truly appreciates them. The author, Tanehiko, was what you might call an all-out connoisseur, and came up with fresh ideas for everything from the patterns on characters' clothes to the forms of stone lanterns, oil lamps, bookshelves, folding screens, hibachi, freestanding armrests, and so on. Once, having heard rumors of a stone lantern that might be suitable for this work, he donned his traveling attire and set out on the long road to Utsunomiya to have a look; just thinking about it makes us see why the lingering headache he complains of in the first fascicle of chapter 16 was inevitable, and helps us imagine how very difficult Kunisada's job must have been. Of course, I'm just jotting down a few thoughts that have occurred to me here, thinking that the un-forewarned reader of this work may find that his willow doesn't bend with Tanehiko's wind, causing Kunisada's efforts to vanish like bubbles on the stream.

Spring, Meiji 43 (Year of the Senior Metal-Dog)
In the Kibunkai Building
Amenotani Issaian[38]

Amenotani is perhaps exaggerating when he suggests that "no one realizes that the author of the book took even more pains conceiving the pictures than he did polishing the prose," since in 1910 some readers were still treasuring their copies of the original Edo edition—Enchi Fumiko, born in 1905, would have been reading her family's set with her grandmother around this time, as I noted in chapter 1—but he is not exaggerating much. As we have seen, typeset editions of *Inaka Genji* published since 1882 had departed radically from the image-text-book relations that Tanehiko and Kunisada had so carefully realized, to the extent that by 1910 it had become possible to conceive of a book like the Shūchin bunko edition, which consists entirely of text. Amenotani's preface indicates that this was Kibunkai's motivation for creating an edition that went in precisely the opposite direction, trying to reproduce as much as possible the atmosphere of the Edo edition.

Given the explicit focus on the visual aspects of *Inaka Genji* in his preface, Amenotani's afterword to the second volume comes as something of a surprise:

CONCERNING THE REPRINTING OF VOLUME ONE OF *INAKA GENJI*

A tremendous blow has been dealt to our plans to publish this work in its entirety, owing to the fact that the first volume was greeted with displeasure by the authorities at the Ministry of Internal Affairs. The publisher deeply regrets this, and laments even more that it has ended up committing the not inconsequential sin of betraying the especial good will of its book club members and all its other customers. Of course, if *Inaka Genji* seems to some to be lewd and lowly reading material, this is because these people have done it the disservice of devoting their attention only to the excessive voluptuousness and allure of its pictures, for when it comes to the prose, it is delightfully light and flowing and has, moreover, dignity and elegance, and possesses not the slightest hint of vulgarity. Not only does it represent the true pinnacle of Edo literature, but it is, from what I have chanced to hear, counted among the favorite books of Her Majesty the Empress—something, surely, that gives pause for thought. In a former age it was quite common, particularly among the upper classes, for girls to be made to read the book, perhaps at the urging of their fathers or elder brothers, to aid the cultivation of a meek and mild temperament. But Confucius and Dao Zhi each have their own way of looking at the same candy, and depending on how it is used a good medicine can become a poison—perhaps, then, it is necessary to adapt to changing times and mores. Presuming this is what the authorities at the Ministry of the Interior intended, we will make further amendments to the book and reprint it for release in the near future, thus ensuring that all four volumes of our *Inaka Genji* are made available. Since there is extremely little cause for worry from the second volume on, it seems unlikely to me that we will experience a second crisis of the nature of this book-banning . . . all of which is intended simply to let readers know in advance how, in my view, the situation stands.

(Amenotani Issaian)[39]

In the wake of Kibunkai's brush with the authorities, Amenotani executes a startling about-face: whereas in the first volume he laments the tendency to value *Inaka Genji*'s prose while showing little or no appreciation for its pictures—to treat the book as though it were merely a text—in the afterword to the second he speaks of people doing the book the "disservice" of paying too much attention to its pictures and sings the praises of its prose.

The reference to Empress Shōken's partiality to the book was a cunning way of putting pressure on the censors—in fact, it appears that Kibunkai's invocation of the empress and *Inaka Genji*'s presence in her personal library during its negotiations with the Ministry of the Interior was what persuaded officials to lift the ban, as long as certain adjustments were made.[40] Still more interesting, however, is the suggestion that well-bred girls were often encouraged to read the book: that copies of *Genji monogatari* were frequently included among the items privileged young women took with them when they married is widely known; the possibility that *Inaka Genji* may have served a similar purpose in educating young women, perhaps of a lower class, has not, to my knowledge, been investigated.

At any rate, Amenotani's appeal to class does not seem to have had the desired effect: although an advertisement at the end of volume 2 announces the forthcoming publication of volumes 3 and 4, neither was ever issued. An advertisement at the end of an edition of Jippensha Ikku's *Shanks-Mare on the Eastern Seaboard*, published in 1911 as part of the same Kibunkai series, lists both volumes 1 and 2 of *Inaka Genji* as having been banned, and a note in *Tōkyō asahi shinbun* on July 4, 1910, reports that two hundred bound and twenty-one hundred unbound copies, presumably of the second volume, had been confiscated.[41] The optimistic view that Amenotani expresses in his afterword proved to be misguided, and the edition came to a premature end.

Amenotani notes that he and others involved in the production of the Kibunkai edition of *Inaka Genji* would "make *further* amendments to the book" in accordance with whatever directions they had received from the Ministry of the Interior. The implication, of course, is that changes had already been made—and, indeed, they had been, in a manner that indicates just what aspects of the publication were understood to be inappropriate, certainly on the part of Kibunkai but also, most likely, by the responsible censor at the Ministry of Internal Affairs. In figure 105, from chapter 11 of the Edo edition, we see Takanao acting the part of the angry, jilted lover after discovering Mihara, an "old woman" of fifty-seven or fifty-eight now engaged in Yoshimasa's service, flirting with another man. The other man is his good friend Mitsuuji, who has been involved with her for some time—we encountered the two of them in figure 48. Mitsuuji can be seen crouching behind the folding screen, using it as a shield, ostensibly to hide himself from Mihara's other lover. Comparing this picture

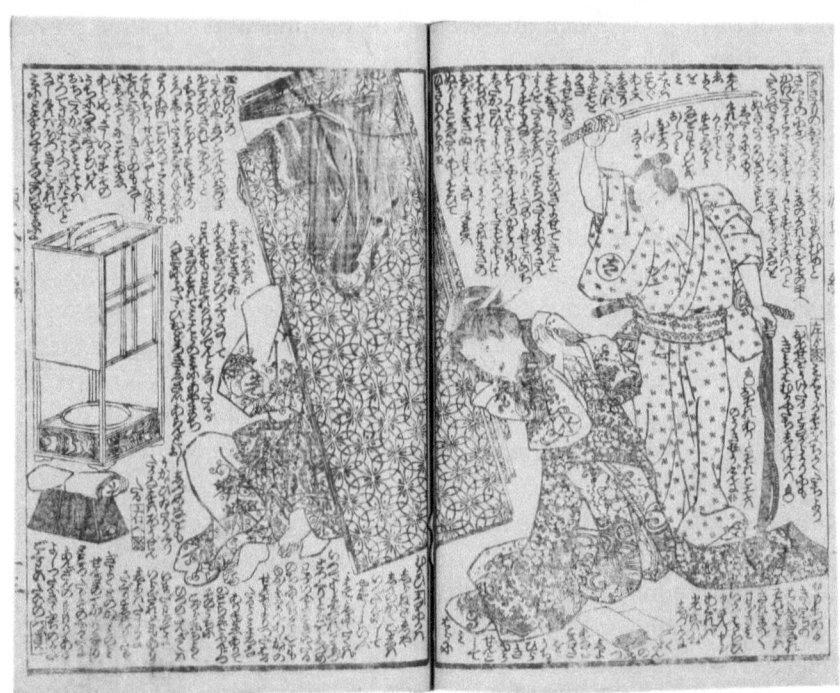

偐紫田舎源氏十一編

騒する水原は誰にも言訳なく死にたれども動徳に身を持たらし所ろ鷲鷗は昔より捩えんる車にも有らん斯許悲いに其中にも光氏君を如何に悲しくて鶉ひく／＼高直が露をおびかへりて光氏君は龍太夫を慇ひて彼も屈風を云へて棚引違ひ顔を蔽し出さんと高直は目を見張瀬々怒れる気色なくも背忍んで来たらんとそ我言ひつる時は云ふまじ返事なく外の男を引入れて最見ふがしの淫奔遊惰情なさるぞ書徳に刀抜持候上れば水原は叱と飛退つてコハ、我君我君とおりろ調滞り顔はしわと哀れと人も傲さんかに御もて恕和て飽気なと櫻たる北壇に梅と櫻の二幅対聖徳君女臓にあられんにも似たる北壇に命を助けんと桜を損合せ伏拝なから娘の中中ら熱くくも其女感人の北中に懸うる如く憾らしく勢から刀を抜たる膽を櫨へ張うに柾書し立出打笑いひつ高直も刀を抜く挙年と微笑ひとにしも押包み急気なりけば刀は達柄に柄年と微笑ひとにしも押包み急気なる

二百七十六

with the one in volume 2 of the Kibunkai edition, we find that Mitsuuji has been erased, leaving the screen precariously balanced on one corner, seemingly in the process of falling over (figure 106). It is not entirely obvious why this decision to delete Mitsuuji was made, particularly since the text states unambiguously that the entire scene is staged, but presumably it was feared that the authorities might object to a picture that *appears* to depict one man flying into a rage on catching his lover in the act with another man or—perhaps more to the point, given the particular antipathy that censors exhibited toward representations of adulterous women— a picture that shows a woman who has obviously been fooling around with two men.[42]

The sexual target of the censorship becomes even more apparent when we compare another set of pictures depicting a later moment in the same scene from the two editions: the pillow that was present in the original, in the very middle of the spread, is gone in the Kibunkai edition (figures 107 and 108). The Ministry of the Interior's specific concern with these implicitly sexual encounters can also be inferred from the fact that a similarly charged scene from chapter 3, showing Mitsuuji pinning down Karaginu's sleeved futon with a pillow, had been left unchanged when volume 1 was published (figure 109). While there is no way to know for sure precisely what sort of guidance the censors may have given Kibunkai, the different approach taken in the first and second volumes suggests the nature of the problem. The same scene that went uncensored in volume 1 of the Kibunkai edition would be censored in 1927, in the Nihon meicho zenshū (Collected Japanese Masterworks) edition edited by Yamaguchi Takeshi (figure 110): here Karaginu and the futon are gone, and an armrest has been substituted for the pillow.

In a sense, that the authorities felt the need to demand the censorship of these pictures is a testament to the success of the bibliographic translation that these editions attempted: if the pictures had seemed to be no more than illustrations of the text, they would surely have deemed it more important to censor the text. The text in the 1910 Kibunkai edition does not appear to have been censored; that in the 1927–1928 Nihon meicho zenshū edition has been.

In chapter 2, I showed that one of the fundamental characteristics of *Inaka Genji*'s image-text-book relations in its original Edo format was

Figure 105 Takanao feigning anger with Mihara while Mitsuuji hides. (*NMIG*, chapter 11, 12 *ura*–13 *omote*. Courtesy of Waseda University Library, Tokyo)

Figure 106 Takanao feigning anger with Mihara in Mitsuuji's absence, in the Kibunkai edition of *Inaka Genji* (2:276). (Courtesy of the author)

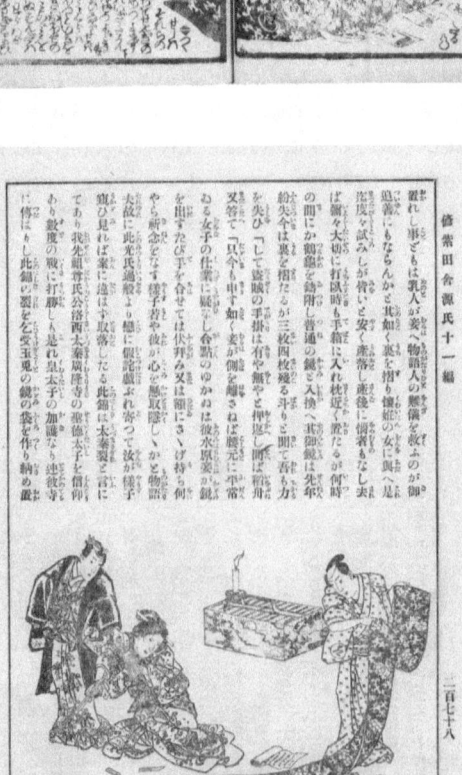

偐紫田舎源氏十一編

二百七十八

that, in the context of the reading experience, the pictures came first. In this chapter, we have seen that in two ways—in terms of the bibliographic development, or death, of the *gōkan* in general and of *Inaka Genji* in particular, and in terms of the censorship of the Kibunkai and Nihon meicho zenshū editions—the pictures also went first.

Last Incarnations: *Inaka Genji* in 1918 and 1927–1928

I would like to conclude this chapter by briefly considering two editions of *Inaka Genji* that can be regarded as heirs to the experimental 1910 Kibunkai version. Each takes a different approach to translating the Edo edition into the form of a typeset book, resisting the continuing trend toward the reduction of its pictures to illustrations and of its insistent three-dimensionality to flatness, and struggling against what we might now describe not as the *yomihon*ization, but as the novelization of *Inaka Genji*. The first is the Ehon haishi shōsetsu (Unofficial Histories with Pictures) edition, published in 1918 by Hakubunkan; the second is the Nihon meicho zenshū edition of 1927–1928. My concern is simply to pinpoint a subtle difference in these two editions' handling of the space of the page, and so to demonstrate that the former is dominated by its text, while the latter is a more or less equal hybrid of text and pictures—as successful an attempt to re-create the experience of reading a *gōkan* as is possible, perhaps, in the modern format of a typeset book—so it should be enough to compare two spreads from each edition with the same spreads from the Edo edition.

The Ehon haishi shōsetsu edition is remarkable as the first typeset version in which the text was inserted into pictures in a style resembling that of the Edo *gōkan*. Needless to say, this was a difficult task, and it was attempted only in places: the book includes a total of seventy-two spreads, five of which were turned into purely pictorial pages, stripped of the text that appears on them in the Edo edition. It was relatively common in books of this period for pages to be framed, and that is the case in this edition. The text never extends as far as the frame, of course, but in theory the frame marks the space within which the text can be printed.

Figure 107 Takanao and Mitsuuji interrogating Mihara. (*NMIG*, chapter 11, 13 *ura* and 14 *omote*. Courtesy of Waseda University Library, Tokyo)

Figure 108 Takanao and Mitsuuji interrogating Mihara—minus the pillow—in the Kibunkai edition of *Inaka Genji* (2:278). (Courtesy of the author)

偐紫田舎源氏 三編

し顔にて、「有難き仕合なりとぞ平伏す光氏は只管に村
痛さ思ひ違へ熱症悶る氣色もなく欄簡拳取亂せし其
中を分入給へば被着打抜ぎて只一人些やかに呶ねた
る上なる衣を押やる途入浴して腹元の来れるならん
と思ふから目も定かには髮やらむ光氏看整姿を窺
「召給ふに依びて夏野がしげりに参りたり水高く生延
し来花咲乱ぬ男郎花詠めとせん悲しやと座に坐し活
給へと聞て発衣心地悪しさは何ともせぬ面もちは
深ゆる心地して起上り戦ひ居る光氏近くすり寄て
ひ昔に、立や戦ひ居られすとり年頭思ひわたりたる心
禋を知らせん池態此家へ方違斯迷湛を待たなばと捨く
言馬へば鬼神も仇まじき御氣配有脳に愛に人ありと
ぞ答へける光氏は詐りて仇心をひき見んと狼狽らを
去給はず、「人達へさは恨めし御身を某見初めしは山

七十四

Figure 111 Mitsuuji and Tasogare on their way to the old temple, in the Ehon haishi shōsetsu edition of *Inaka Genji* (1:92-93). (Courtesy of the author)

This leads to a rather odd phenomenon: we find, in this edition, that even the fully pictorial spreads seem to be haunted by text. Figure 111, showing Mitsuuji and Tasogare making their way through the rain to the old temple, is an example of this. The text that fills the blank spaces above the couple's heads and below their feet in the original pictures has been removed, leaving no text anywhere on the page but the words *Nise Murasaki inaka Genji* at the upper right, the chapter number at the upper left, and the page numbers in the bottom corners. And yet even so, the manner in which the picture was set into the page, within the frame that

Figure 109 Mitsuuji leaning on a pillow, seducing Karaginu, in the Kibunkai edition of *Inaka Genji* (1:74). (Courtesy of the author)

Figure 110 Mitsuuji leaning on an armrest, alone, in the Nihon meicho zenshū edition of *Inaka Genji* (1:118-119). (Courtesy of the author)

marks the outer edge of the textual space, gives the impression that it is subordinate to the text that fills the rest of the book. This image is simply an illustration, even though it stands alone.

This same image-text relationship can be seen throughout the book. Figure 112, which shows a servant named Sayuri batting snow from the branches of a pine tree, is significantly different, for instance, from the same picture in the Edo edition (figure 113). In the *gōkan*, the frames around the pictures mark the theoretical outermost border of the pictorial space, rather than of the textual space, and the pictures are in fact free to break through the border—this breakage is, in fact, what gives this picture its energy, its sense of motion. Here the text was set into the picture. In the Ehon haishi shōsetsu edition, however, the text extends beyond the picture in every direction, and the broom and flying snow that break the frame in the Edo edition were trimmed, as if to keep the picture within a second invisible frame within the frame enclosing the text. The picture is set into the writing.

The Nihon meicho zenshū edition carries the typographical experimentation of the Ehon haishi shōsetsu edition to a breathtaking extreme, mimicking the structure of the *gōkan*, with its mix of text and picture, throughout. Almost every page—and each of its two volumes is approximately eight hundred pages long—has both pictures and text. As figures 114 and 115 indicate, the space of the page appears to belong equally to both picture and text. In the Edo edition, there is never any doubt that the text was written into the pictures, not the other way around; here, the image-text relationship seems perfectly equal—indeed, from the perspective of a reader accustomed to the format of the original Edo edition, *overly* balanced. To a certain extent, the Nihon meicho zenshū edition may, then, be said to have failed. And yet the reading experience it enables is similar enough to that of the now-dead genre of the *gōkan* that it can be taken as an example of what bibliographic translation at its best can accomplish. The snow that breaks the frame in the Edo edition was deleted in the Nihon meicho zenshū edition, just as in the Ehon haishi shōsetsu edition, but even so, in this subtly changed composition, the three small clumps at the upper edge of the picture seem to be flying from the branch in a kind of living sweep, hovering in a space that is neither

Figure 112 Sayuri batting snow from the branches for Mitsuuji, in the Ehon haishi shōsetsu edition of *Inaka Genji* (1:210–211). (Courtesy of the author)

Figure 113 Sayuri batting snow from the branches for Mitsuuji. (*NMIG*, chapter 10, 13 *ura* and 14 *omote*. Courtesy of Waseda University Library, Tokyo)

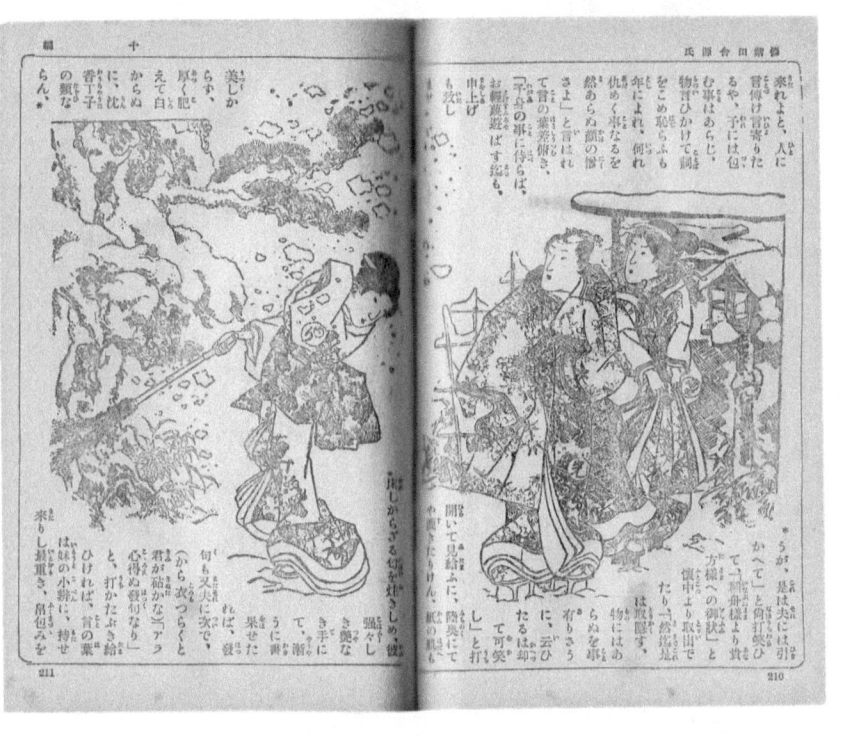

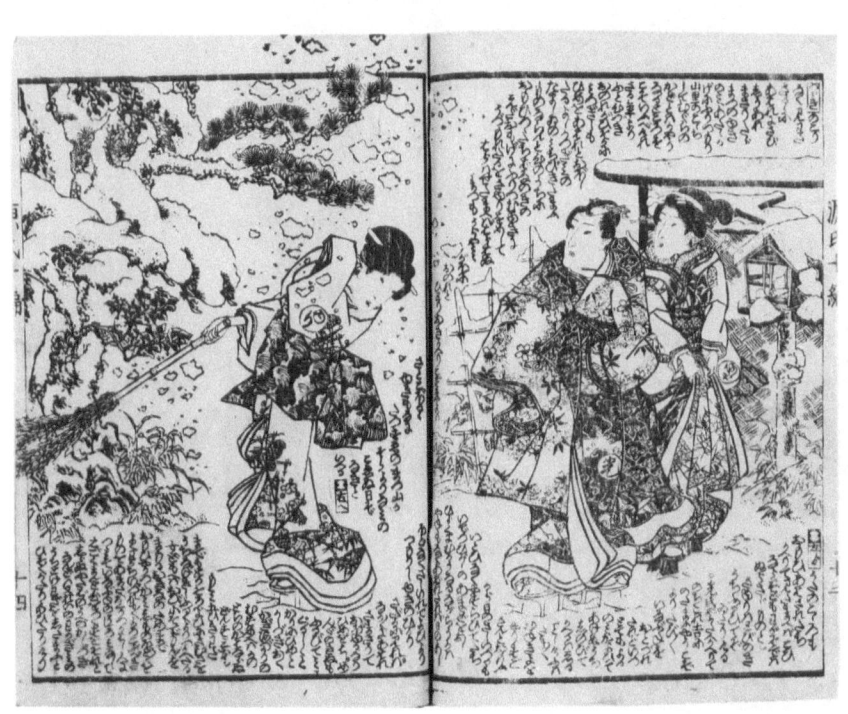

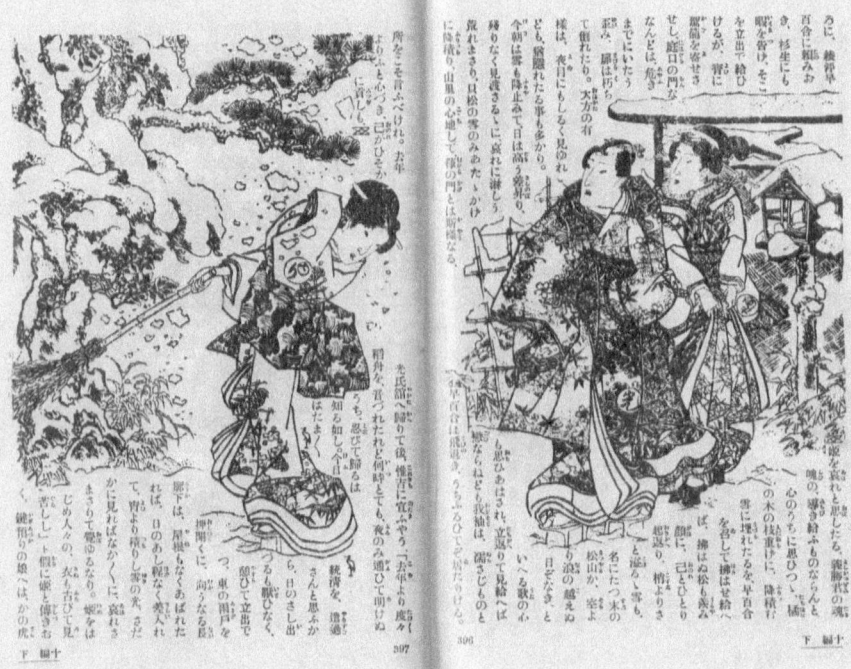

wholly textual nor entirely pictorial—not exactly *gōkan* space, but not exactly novelistic space, either.

The process of bibliographic translation, if we can call it a process, is one of change and of motion that has the appearance of life, but of life in an altogether different reincarnation. This, too, ultimately, is an answer to the question of the *gōkan*'s survival. Except that by this point the *gōkan* was already dead. Even if the Nihon meicho zenshū edition of *Inaka Genji* did read like a modern *gōkan*, it was no longer capable of standing as a replacement of *Genji monogatari*. Already we were living in a new age. Already another history had begun.

Figure 114 Mitsuuji and Tasogare on their way to the old temple, in the Nihon meicho zenshū edition of *Inoka Genji* (1:178-179). (Courtesy of the author)

Figure 115 Sayuri batting snow from the branches for Mitsuuji, in the Nihon meicho zenshū edition of *Inoka Genji* (1:396-397). (Courtesy of the author)

PART II

❧

In Medias Res

On February 11, 2008, *Yomiuri shinbun* (*Yomiuri Newspaper*) ran an editorial titled "*Genji monogatari*: A Masterpiece of World Literature Turns One Thousand."[1] "This, surely, is one masterpiece worthy of the 'World Heritage' name," the article begins, and then goes on to rehearse the standard talking points about its canonical value: "*Genji monogatari* is said to be 'the world's oldest novel'"; "most of us have an image of it as a romantic novel [*ren'ai shōsetsu*] centered on Hikaru Genji, but it is actually a deeply profound work that touches on a variety of themes"; "scholars note that if *Genji monogatari* had not been written, Japanese literary history and the traditional aesthetics of the Japanese people would have developed along vastly different lines." The commonplaces continue as the topic turns to translation: "Perhaps few nowadays read the work in the original. But we can access its charms through numerous translations into modern Japanese by writers such as Yosano Akiko, Tanizaki Jun'ichirō, Enchi Fumiko, and Setouchi Jakuchō." And, of course, as the editorial's author observes, through translations into other media—*manga*, musicals, and the like—and into more than twenty foreign languages.

No new information appears in this editorial. There is nothing even remotely fresh about it. And yet somehow it does not seem at all superfluous; there is a sense of inevitability not only in the content, but also in its publication, early in the year branded as *Genji*'s millennial anniversary. The need is precisely *not* to say something new, but to recognize and reinforce a commonly held image—in the sense in which I have been using the term—of what *Genji* has become in the thousand years since its composition, and to do so in the context of one of the mass media that has helped shape the contours of *Genji* discourse both in Japan and overseas since the 1870s. *Genji* is now celebrated all around the world, including in Japan, as "a masterpiece of world literature," and as the *Yomiuri* editorial notes, it is read and otherwise appreciated almost exclusively in the form of translations, broadly defined to encompass renderings of the original in languages foreign to it—modern Japanese among them—as well as movies, dances, and innumerable other products of the sort Roman Jakobson once placed under the rubric of "intersemiotic translation."[2] The connection between these two defining

TOUCHSTONE 2

The Triangle

Who is there? Me.
Me who? I am me, you are you.
But you take my pronoun,
And we are us.

Marichiko, Untitled poem

characteristics of *Genji*'s existence in the contemporary world—its status as a masterpiece of world literature and its status as a work that endures first and foremost in translation—is clear: "World literature," according to a recent formulation by David Damrosch in *What Is World Literature?*, "is writing that gains in translation."³ But, of course, neither *Genji*'s status as a masterpiece of world literature that survives primarily in translation nor the link between being translated and being world literature is so unforgettably obvious that it requires no reinforcement. We need periodically to be reminded.

In taking stock of the position that *Genji* occupies, then, both in Japan and around the globe, it is not enough simply to acknowledge that it is read around the world, in the form of translations, and that these two situations are related. It is not enough, in other words, to note that versions of *Genji*—full-scale replacements both created and read in a mode first popularized in Japan by *Nise Murasaki inaka Genji*—are continually being produced and circulated. We must also recognize how important it is that *it is known* that *Genji* is read around the world, in the form of translations, and that the two situations are interrelated. Damrosch offers his definition of world literature as "writing that gains in translation" alongside two others: "World literature is an elliptical refraction of national literatures," and "world literature is not a set canon of texts but a mode of reading: a form of detached engagement with worlds beyond our own place and time."⁴ To this trio of useful definitions I would add a fourth: "World literature is a mode of relating to works, whether or not we read them, that is shaped by discourse attesting to their global position."

Tautological though this point may be on some level—world literature is what is said to be world literature—it is crucial. Early in his book, Damrosch comments, "I take world literature to encompass all literary works that circulate beyond their culture of origin, either in translation or in their original language. . . . In its most expansive sense, world literature could include any work that has ever reached beyond its home base."⁵ This perspective is so broad as to exceed the mortal eye—it exists in the eternal gaze, perhaps, of the Great Sphinx of Giza, shown on the cover of *What Is World Literature?*, which Damrosch invokes in the book's final paragraph—and so he narrows it, draws it down from the ethereal precincts of the ideal into the groundedness of the historical by proposing a focus on "actual readers: a work only has an *effective* life as world literature whenever, and wherever, it is actively present within a literary system beyond that of its original culture."⁶ But still, I suggest, this is not quite narrow enough—though in a sense it is also too narrow—because readers and even non-readers are enmeshed in particular histories of reading, given form by communities of readers, and these histories and communities create, in their turn, discourse about world literature.

Damrosch takes the geographical, even individual idiosyncrasies of "whenever, and wherever" seriously, describing the series of case studies that he presents in his book as "my world literature" and noting that "even a genuinely global perspective remains a perspective *from somewhere*."[7] This being the case, surely one might conceive of a literary work, even one in translation, that is "actively present within a literary system beyond that of its original culture" but still is not viewed by some or any of the readers within that system as world literature or even as being of foreign provenance. Conversely, a work may be read as world literature without ever leaving the literary system in which it originated. "Covert" adaptations and translations would be one example of the former that may be imagined even in the context of the modern West; pseudo-translations such as Kenneth Rexroth's "Marichiko" poems are an instance of the latter.[8] It should be noted, too, that *domestic* works can be marketed and read as world literature, as we see from the habit that English-language publishing houses have of advertising the number of languages into which local authors have been translated—and as the promotion of Tanizaki Jun'ichirō's first translation into modern Japanese of *Genji monogatari*, which I discuss in chapter 5, amply demonstrates.

Genji's modern recanonization as a masterpiece of world literature, as writing that has gained in translation, is as much the product of discourse about *Genji*'s global circulation as it is of that circulation itself. Indeed, it is largely a product of the global circulation of discourse concerning *Genji*'s global circulation—along with, of course, the circulation of discourse about *Genji* itself. Consider an example: On January 20, 2008, three weeks before *Yomiuri shinbun* ran its editorial, *New York Times* reporter Norimitsu Onishi opened an article titled "Thumbs Race as Japan's Best Sellers Go Cellular" with the statement, "Until recently, cellphone novels . . . had been dismissed in Japan as a subgenre unworthy of the country that gave the world its first novel, 'The Tale of Genji,' a millennium ago."[9] Less than a month later, on February 16, 2008, an article in *Asahi shinbun* (*Asahi Newspaper*), also about the recent surge in the popularity of cell-phone novels, began: "The cell-phone novel is so popular lately that the *New York Times* reports 'it has become a literary genre of its own in the country of *The Tale of Genji*.'"[10] Neither article has anything to do with *Genji*—though if they had waited a few months, they could have reported, as *Mainichi shinbun* (*Mainichi Newspaper*) did on May 15, 2008, on the appearance of actual cell-phone-novel rewritings of *Genji*.¹¹ But to a large extent, it is precisely this sort of gratuitous global repetition, this looping translation of the same message in contexts often only tangentially relevant to the tale itself, and frequently through mass media circuits, that continually re-creates *Genji* as world literature. At the same time, these translational replacements allow *Genji* to be resituated, within Japanese contexts in particular, as the fountainhead of Japan's *national* literature, which, like all national literatures, is ultimately a by-product of the transnational creation, and continual re-creation, of the concept of literature as a universally applicable category—of the concept, in a certain sense at least, of world literature. This is mirrored in the subtle shift in directionality from "the country that gave the world its first novel" (Japan gives *Genji* to the world) in the *New York Times* to "the country of *The Tale of Genji*" (*Genji* gives Japan to the world) in *Asahi shinbun*.

The sense that "world literature," understood as a world literary system or space, is a product of the historical emergence and spread of a specific notion of literature, and of particular genres such as the novel, has figured prominently over the past decade or so in debates about the meaning of world literature and the way it should be studied. Damrosch's insistence on the plurality of "world literatures"—his repeated reminders that "to understand what world literature is . . . we always need to see *where* it is"—make him rather unusual in this respect, even if his own institutional and geographic location leads him to concentrate "on world literature as it has been construed over the past century in a specific cultural space, that of the formerly provincial and now metropolitan United States."¹² "Provincial" and "metropolitan" correspond reasonably well to the "periphery" and "core" that Franco Moretti invoked in his essay "Conjectures on World Literature," and then expanded by adding the "semi-periphery," or to Pascale Casanova's analogous "dominated" and "dominant" literatures in *The World Republic of Letters*.¹³ In this sense, the exhilarating vision that Damrosch presents as "my world literature" may be seen as lying squarely within the space or system that both Casanova and Moretti map, each in her or his way.¹⁴ But Damrosch is more keen to engage with works of world literature than he is to explain its structure, and where he insists on plurality and recognizes the contingency of his view, Moretti and Casanova insist on singularity: the world literary system is "one and unequal," Moretti contends, while Casanova defines literature "as a unified international field (or a field in the process of being unified)."¹⁵ To an extent, their understanding of world literature resembles Damrosch's first, Sphinxian definition: it is a system, a space, a field that encompasses all literature, everywhere. Essentially, the only limits they place on their maps are chronological: the history of world literary space is the history of the inexorable diffusion of "literature," as it is now understood, from France and England outward.

Casanova traces the nascence of world literary space to Joachim du Bellay's *La deffence et illustration de la langue françoyse* (*The Defense and Illustration of the French Language*, 1549) and tracks its expansion through the nationalist movements in Europe of the late eighteenth and nineteenth centuries into the postwar period of decolonialization.[16] Moretti is less clear about his timeline. In a recent essay, he comments that "between 1650 and 1950 the [English and French] literatures are unquestionably the core of the world literary system," suggesting that he generally concurs with Casanova's periodization.[17] At the same time, he has also proposed a different view of the historicity of world literature, marking the eighteenth century as the turning point:

> The term "world literature" has been around for almost two centuries, but we still do not know what world literature is. . . . Perhaps, because we keep collapsing under a single term *two distinct world literatures*: one that precedes the eighteenth century—and one that follows it. The "first" *Weltliteratur* is a mosaic of separate, "local" cultures; it is characterized by strong internal diversity; it produces new forms mostly by divergence; and is best explained by (some version of) evolutionary theory. The "second" *Weltliteratur* (which I would prefer to call world literary system) is unified by the international literary market; it shows a growing, and at times stunning amount of sameness; its main mechanism of change is convergence; and is best explained by (some version of) world-systems analysis.[18]

Here, interestingly, Moretti proposes that we might speak of two world literatures. But it is hard to help feeling that ultimately he is prompted to do so by a need to wall off what he regards as the unified field of the modern and contemporary world literary system from the diversity that preceded it. In a footnote appended to the third sentence, Moretti concedes: "Speaking of 'local' cultures does not exclude the existence of large regional systems (Indo-European, East Asian, Mediterranean, Meso-American, Scandinavian . . .)." Then he demurs: "But these geographical units are not yet stably subordinated to a single center like the one that emerged in eighteenth-century France and Britain."[19] After observing that "the oldest [literary] spaces" have the greatest autonomy within "the structure of the entire world literary space," Casanova includes a similar note clarifying her reference to "the oldest spaces":

"More precisely, those that have been longest in the space of literary competition. This explains why certain ancient spaces such as China, Japan and the Arab countries are both long-lived and subordinate: they entered the international literary space very late and in subordinate positions."[20] For Moretti, "large regional systems" are just so many apples lined up behind the British and French orange of the "world literary system"; for Casanova, the ancient histories of China, Japan, and the Arab countries are irrelevant: all that matters are when and in what position they joined the international literary space.

The problem with all this is, I hope, almost clear enough to render any comment unnecessary. Both Moretti and Casanova are committed to exploring the inequalities and the Eurocentrism of *"the* world literary space" or *"the* world literary system," but they seem not to have considered the Eurocentrism implicit in *their perception*—their perception *from somewhere*—that there has only ever been one "world literary system," one "world literary space," or perhaps even that literatures all around the world have been so thoroughly subjugated to European literary history that nothing that preceded its coming matters any longer. For this is what the idea of "a unified international field (or a field in the process of being unified)," of *"one* and unequal," implies. Between 1650 and the last two decades of the nineteenth century, at the earliest, Britain and France were most assuredly *not* the core of the "world literary system" that people in Japan would have recognized. And Moretti's claim that no large regional literary system before the one that emerged around France and Britain was "stably subordinated to a single center" merely begs the question of what exactly it means to be stably subordinated and whether, to this day, the entire world has ever really stood in a relationship of stable subordination to a single center. Casanova's suggestion that, to take two cases I am most familiar with, China and Japan remain literarily subordinate because they entered *"the* international literary space" late makes a sort of sense in the context of her argument, focused as she is on relationships among nations, but much of what are now known as Japan, Korea, and Vietnam had already been part of *an* interstate literary space centered around China for centuries before du Bellay, according to Casanova, initiated the formation of world literary space by writing his *deffence*.[21]

In short, there is room to question whether the *appearance*, from Casanova's and Moretti's perspective, of the subordination of peripheries to the center, of the dominated to the dominant, may not be a function of the inability of individuals at the "center" to see that there have been—and perhaps still are, overlapping with the one they see—other "world literary systems" or "world literary spaces." Maybe the history of world literature after the eighteenth century, if we accept Moretti's timeline, is the history of not one but many, sometimes competitive, world literatures: multiple and unequal. Or even multiple and equal *as literatures*, even acknowledging that patterns of circulation of books around the globe have forced on readers in areas that Moretti and Casanova consider peripheral a wider view of world literature than that of readers afflicted by the tunnel vision of the core. Or perhaps multiple and related in ways much too intricate to be described in terms of simple domination and subordination.

In "More Conjectures on World Literature," Moretti revises his earlier argument that Spanish, French, and especially British novels arose autonomously, free from outside interference, while elsewhere novels were a compromise between "foreign *plot*; local *characters*; and then, local *narrative voice*," by acknowledging that "there was no 'autonomous development' in western Europe, and the idea that forms have, so to speak, a *different history* at the core and at the periphery crumbles."[22] What if we were to apply the same insight to Moretti's world literary system itself? What if there was no "autonomous development" of a single, unified world literary system, stably subordinated to France and Britain, that diffused steadily outward, conquering the globe, but rather *numerous* "world literary systems"—each one "worldly" only from an internal perspective—that have formed, shifted, and overlapped over the centuries, their fuzzy borders nestling into one another; and the gradual blending together of these systems, in different concentrations in different regions, as a consequence of the expansion of the world literary system centered on western Europe is what, historically, gave rise to world literature?[23]

This account, which I hope is more nuanced than those Moretti and Casanova have proposed, and certainly reflects more accurately my perspective on world literature as a scholar of Japanese literature—*my* world literature—underwrites my exploration of *Genji*'s recanonization as world literature in the chapters that follow. This will be most apparent in my comparison of Masamune Hakuchō's and Yoda Gakkai's modes of framing *Genji monogatari*'s greatness in chapter 5. At the same time, as I explained earlier, I attempt to fill in what I see as a significant weakness in Damrosch's approach by stressing the role that discourse plays in nudging readers to apply the world literary mode to particular works, whether or not they read them. In brief, I will argue that *Genji*'s contemporary existence may be envisioned as a triangular field delimited by three conceptual lines: *Genji* as a work of world literature, *Genji* as a work that survives almost exclusively in its replacement, and *Genji* as a work that is discursively figured as participating in world literature through its replacements.

The creation of this field has a history, of course. Just as *Inaka Genji* gradually established the mode of reading that allowed a particular work to be viewed as a replacement of *Genji monogatari*, so a series of replacements of *Genji monogatari* occasioned, early on, the transnational circulation of discourse about *Genji*, and then, later, the transnational circulation of discourse about the transnational circulation of *Genji*, which cemented *Genji*'s recanonization as world literature. This elevation of the tale to the status of world literature, both within and without Japan, was also what made it possible to frame it as the wellspring, or at least one among a number of competing candidates for the wellspring, of Japanese literature, of "the traditional aesthetics of the Japanese people," of the Japanese national essence itself, as it was defined and redefined at various points in Japan's modern history. The three chapters in this part, backtracking slightly to begin in the 1870s, trace this complex, globally looping history: the creation of *Genji* discourse, of the *Genji* we all recognize.

Before Our Only Predecessor

Arthur Waley's much celebrated and much criticized English translation of *Genji monogatari*, *The Tale of Genji*, published simultaneously in England and the United States in six volumes between 1925 and 1933, is generally considered to have laid the foundation on which all subsequent replacements of *Genji* in the English-language context, and even beyond it, would build.

To a certain extent, this view is accurate: *The Tale of Genji* represented a new discovery for most of its earliest readers, and with the publication of the translation's first volume, critics began to describe the tale in terms now so familiar as to seem self-evident. Here, for instance, is how Raymond Mortimer opens his rave review, tellingly titled "A New Planet," in the June 20, 1925, issue of the *Nation & Athenæum*:

> It is amusing to wonder which are the twelve finest novels that the genius of man has so far produced. The other day I was stimulated to make a list—no one is likely to agree with it, especially as it includes no novel the interest of which is not chiefly psychological. Here it is: "La Princesse de Clèves," "Clarissa Harlowe," "Les Liasons Dangereuses," "Persuasion," "Adolphe," "Les Illusions Perdues," "La Chartreuse de Parme," "War and Peace," "L'Education Sentimentale," "The Brothers Karamazov," and "A la Recherche du Temps Perdu." If one started to discuss the reasons for such a choice and the other strong candidates, there would be room for nothing else upon this page. But some mathematically minded person may have noticed that only eleven books are included. I suspect that the name of the twelfth is "The Tale of Genji"; and it was reading it which made me attempt this list of its Occidental rivals. Written at the beginning of the eleventh century by a Japanese lady named Murasaki, it is now being translated for the first time.[1]

For Mortimer, Waley's *The Tale of Genji* seems inevitably to have raised the question: What is world literature—or rather, more precisely, what might constitute the canon of world literature? It begs comparison with more familiar masterpieces, above all Marcel Proust's *À la recherche du*

CHAPTER 4

The History of a Romance

Genji *Before Waley*

"Who could have remained indifferent to him, even in the world at large?"

Royall Tyler, *The Tale of Genji*, "Suma"

temps perdu (*In Search of Lost Time*, 1913–1927), still one of the novels to which *Genji* is most frequently likened. "'The Tale of Genji' resembles 'The Arabian Nights' infinitely less," Mortimer argues, "than it does Proust"; and again, "There are moments curiously reminiscent of Proust." He implies that the interest of the work is "chiefly psychological"—one of the notions with which Waley, a friend of Mortimer's, would take issue in his introduction to the translation's second volume, speaking of the work's "rather fallacious air of modernity," but which later readers would tend to accept or even inflate, as Sigmund Freud's student Ruth Jane Mack Brunswick did in 1927 in a brief essay in the *International Journal of Psycho-Analysis* in which she praised the "one might almost say *psychoanalytic*, quality of Murasaki's insight."[2] Mortimer also describes the "civilization that makes the setting for the tale" as "intensely aesthetic," noting that "good taste is a matter of the first importance" to its characters. This emphasis would grow increasingly ubiquitous after George Sansom, another friend of Waley's, summed up his perspective on the entire Heian period in the chapter title "The Rule of Taste" in *A History of Japan to 1334* (1958) and with Ivan Morris's repeated invocations of the same "rule of taste" in *The World of the Shining Prince* (1964).[3]

Clearly, Waley's translation mattered. It and the discourse that grew up around it over the half-century between its publication and that of Edward G. Seidensticker's (1921–2007) translation in 1976 profoundly shaped the way in which contemporary readers, even non-readers, of *Genji* continue to approach the tale—and, as we will see in chapter 5, this includes readers and non-readers in Japan. Indeed, Waley's influence extended beyond the English- and Japanese-language contexts: his translation formed the basis for French, German, Swedish, Dutch, Hungarian, Italian, and Spanish versions of the tale.[4] One might argue, furthermore, that Waley's translation served as the flint that sparked the postwar explosion of Japanese literary studies as a discipline, since it offered several future Japanologists their first image of Japan as anything other than a militaristic menace: when Donald Keene paid 49 cents for a remaindered two-volume copy of *The Tale of Genji* at a Times Square bookstore in the autumn of 1940, he "turned to it as a refuge," relieved that "in the book, antagonism never degenerated into violence, and there were no wars."[5] When Seidensticker published his own translation, he confessed in the introduction, "Arthur Waley's translation of *The Tale of Genji* has been so important to me over the years. . . . It was my introduction to Japanese literature, and its power upon repeated readings—I could not give their total number—has continued to be so great that the process of preparing a new translation has felt like sacrilege."[6] If it seemed like sacrilege for Seidensticker to attempt to replace Waley's work with his own, it is only because Waley's *The Tale of Genji* exercised such a profound and wide-reaching influence on subsequent *Genji* discourse, and on broader discourses about Japanese literature and Japan as a nation, that the translation itself acquired canonical status. Undoubtedly, it was Waley's *The Tale of Genji* that enabled *Genji* to assume gradually—very gradually—its present seemingly stable position in the canon of world literature.[7]

Significant as Waley's translation has been, however, it is possible to overemphasize its role: too much attention to Waley obscures what preceded him. At the end of the paragraph quoted earlier, written in 1925, Mortimer remarks that *Genji monogatari* "is now being translated for the first time." A reviewer writing in the New York journal *Literary Digest International Book Review* made the same point: "[O]nly the first part has been translated, and that only recently."[8] Perhaps this will seem unsurprising, even to those who are aware that in 1882—four decades before Waley began to publish *The Tale of Genji*—the London publishing house Trübner & Company had released a partial translation by a twenty-six-year-old Japanese named Suematsu Kenchō. Suematsu's version has, after all, been all but forgotten. In 1978, a review in *Modern Asian Studies* of Seidensticker's translation described Suematsu's text as "now only a curiosity." Marian Ury, in her essay "The Imaginary Kingdom and the Translator's Art: Notes on Re-reading Waley's *Genji*" (1976), speculated that in the first chapters of his translation, Waley owed "an unadmitted debt to his predecessor," but she still regarded Suematsu's work as little more than an amusing dud written "by an ambitious young Japanese, eager to ingratiate himself," and a treasure trove of "material toward any catalog of Victorian affectations."[9] Seidensticker himself gets the date of Suematsu's translation wrong by twelve years in *Translating Japanese* (*Nihonbun no hon'yaku*, 1983); more surprising still, Terence Barrow errs even further in his introduction to the 1974 Tuttle reprint of the translation itself, mistakenly identifying a reprinting in 1900 as its first publication.[10] Donald Keene—who has observed, "For me, as for all others interested in translating either Chinese or Japanese literature, Waley was our only predecessor"—writes of Suematsu's translation that "it seems to have exercised no influence on Western readers."[11]

To be sure, Suematsu's translation has aged badly. The canonization of Waley's *The Tale of Genji* has lent his work a lovely antique patina; Suematsu's *Genji Monogatari: The Most Celebrated of the Classical Japanese Romances* just seems fusty. But a considerable historical record shows that Suematsu's translation was widely read; that it circulated not only in England and the United States, but in various other countries as well; and that it, rather than Waley's translation, initiated the long process of *Genji*'s canonization as world literature that has created the discursive context within which the tale is now apprehended. The only reason we are not surprised that in 1925 reviewers of Waley's *The Tale of Genji* were unaware of Suematsu's work is that we have learned to regard Waley as "our only predecessor." The truth is that in 1925, ignorance of *Waley's* predecessor was not as forgivable as it might seem today, and when the reviewer in the *Literary Digest International Book Review* snubbed Suematsu, a reader wrote in to point out his mistake:

To the Editor of the International Book Review:

The Review is a dear delight to me, and I am sorry that I am ever called upon to criticize it, especially to the extent of saying that it seems to me that some of your reviewers know no literature excepting Shakespeare, the Lake Poets, and the books published in this country of recent years. One of your writers whom I criticized before, for example, did not know Max Müller. And now we read in the October number a review of Arthur Waley's 1925 translation of "The Tale of Genji," by Lady Murasaki, in which Mr. Louis Moore assures us that "only the first part has ever been translated, and that but recently." Every reader of Oriental literature is familiar with what is known as "the 1882 translation of Genji," made by Suyematz Kenchio, who did into English the first seventeen chapters of the book, which numbers fifty-four chapters. We have had this work in the public libraries for forty years. Waley has translated nine chapters only, though I understand that he intends to make a complete translation to be embodied in six volumes.

New York, October 9, 1925   Ida M. Mellen[12]

One might guess that Ida M. Mellen was some sort of specialist in East Asia, but in fact she was a prominent zoologist, the former chief aquarist of the New York Aquarium, and the author of several books, including *Fishes in the Home* (1927), *The Treatment of Fish Diseases* (1928), and *The Natural History of the Pig: Its Evolutionary Status, Antiquity, Body, Brain, and Behavior, and Its Effect on People* (1952).

Like Mellen's letter to the editor, this chapter is intended to draw attention to a history that has been largely forgotten, but that is nonetheless *our* history—an earlier period in a narrative we ourselves, whoever we are, are entering midway. I start tracing this history not exactly at the beginning, since every beginning has its own prior beginnings, but at least with the emergence of discourse about *Genji* in the days before the work had been translated, or even read, by anyone in Europe or the United States—discourse that continues to circulate, in bits and pieces, even today. I will then consider the effect that Suematsu's *Genji Monogatari* had as a replacement of *Genji* in England, the United States, and, if only tangentially, Europe between its publication in 1882 and the appearance of the first volume of Waley's *The Tale of Genji* in 1925, when the images it put into circulation were subsumed within a fresh outpouring of images of *Genji*. Finally, at the end of this chapter, I consider how we might situate Suematsu's translation in the early history of discourse about *Genji*, academic and popular, in Japan. Taken together, these three parts initiate a revisionist history of *Genji*'s necessarily transnational canonization as world literature, emphasizing not only the significance of the role that Suematsu played in that process, but the crucial importance of mass media and, more generally, the translational and transnational circulation of images of *Genji*. I hope, too, that my treatment of Suematsu and his *Genji Monogatari* will offer readers concerned with Japanese literary studies as a discipline an opportunity to look at its history in a new light, to ask themselves: Who are our predecessors? Who do we want our predecessors to be?

A BEGINNING

First Glimpses of a Tedious Poetess

Genji monogatari was not completely unknown to readers in Europe and the United States, even before the publication of Suematsu Kenchō's translation of its first seventeen chapters in 1882. As early as 1874, the French lawyer Georges Bousquet (1846–1937), who had been invited to Japan in 1872 to serve as a legal adviser to the Japanese government, published an account in the *Revue des deux mondes* (*Review of the Two Worlds*) of a trip he had made in August and September 1873, "from Yédo to Osaka," in the course of which he visited "the little pagoda where the celebrated poetess Murasaki-Shikibu composed the *Genji Mondgatari* [sic], the *Iliad* of Japan."[13] Then, in a brief introductory passage added to an essay first published in August 1874, when it was reprinted in *Le Japon de nos jours et les échelles de l'extrême Orient* (*Japan in Our Day and the Ports of the Far East*, 1877), Bousquet provided what is to my knowledge the first attempted description of *Genji monogatari*'s plot in any language but Japanese, in the context of a discussion of poetry:

> Poetry itself, which never developed any real vigor in the Far East, adopted the breathless rhythms, the false tone of the *Book of Songs*. Even the Sinologists, who can read them in the original, admit that these poetic endeavors testify neither to any loftiness of inspiration, nor to a truly heartfelt lyric enthusiasm. The *kakemono* are inclined to portray poetesses—for women, above all, cultivate the language of the gods—perched upon their heels on the seashore or on the bank of Lake Biwa, in the shade of a blossoming cherry tree, their hair falling freely over their loose robes, a biwa in hand, their writing brushes and their long rolls of paper spread before them, lost in an abstracted reverie.
>
> Most celebrated of all, the beautiful Murasaki would seem to be the painters' favorite subject. Often one sees her prolonging her contemplative meditations until the hour when the sky grows light, a small oil lamp left to burn beside her. But when one looks into her work, the *Gengi Monogatari* [sic], one discovers nothing but a dry chronicle of a civil war that bathed the country in blood for a century, the dispute of the House of Faki with that of the Hei. The effort to encase a plausible meaning, banal though it may be, in the rigid frame of verse sufficed to give it worth and make it famous. Herein lies the secret of such poetic poverty; every flight of inspiration catches on the obstacles posed by an inflexible language; thought fades or pales before taking form, and in the end nothing save the bare skeleton remains.[14]

In chapter 1, I quoted Ryūtei Senka on "*Genji*-wise non-readers of *Genji*": writing in 1853, he rejoiced that "nowadays, even little dog-beating brats know that there are more Genjis out there than just Yoritomo and Yoshitsune."[15] Evidently, Bousquet had not yet caught up. Not only was he confusing *Genji monogatari* with *The Tales of the Heike* (*Heike monogatari*, early thirteenth century), but he does not appear to have known about the Genji at all: "Faki" would seem to be a corruption of Heike, or, as Bousquet would put it, "the House of Hei." Bousquet's summary is about as befuddled, perhaps, as a description of James Joyce's *Ulysses* as the story of a long war between the soldiers of Troy and their enemies, the Trojans.

All this would be merely amusing if Bousquet, an unmistakably non-*Genji*-wise non-reader of *Genji monogatari*, had not gone on to publish a third essay in the October 15, 1878, issue of *Revue des deux mondes* that contained what would become one of the most widely circulated appraisals of *Genji monogatari* in any Western language. The essay, "Le

Japon littéraire" (Literary Japan), traces the history of Japanese literature, dividing it into four periods. Bousquet opens his discussion of the *monogatari*, which he considers "the national genre," by citing "the definition of a Japanese critic"—Kamo no Mabuchi (1687–1769), though he does not name him: "The *monogatari* . . . designates a class of composition that differs from history in that the author makes no attempt to distinguish truth from fiction, contenting himself to reproduce the current tradition respecting the hero."[16] He goes on to introduce the plots of "The Toshikage Scroll" ("Toshikage no maki," the first chapter of *The Tale of the Hollow Tree*, late tenth century), *The Tale of the Bamboo Cutter* (ca. 909), and *The Sumiyoshi Tale* (*Sumiyoshi monogatari*, tenth century); then, at last, he arrives at *Genji monogatari*—although he romanizes the title differently, as he had in 1877:

> Of all the romances the most celebrated by far is the *Gengi monogatari*, in fifty-four books, by the poetess Murasaki Shikibu, who lived in the eleventh century, by our calendar; the hillock where she had a sort of little oratory built for herself, and where she spent long hours contemplating the romantic vista that spread beneath her gaze, is still on view, close by Lake Biwa. Genji is the son of one of the mikado's favorites; nature has so brilliantly endowed him that all Japan is peopled with his amorous conquests; the name of each fresh victim furnishes a new book with its title. It is principally its stylistic qualities, and the development it marked in the formation of the language, that recommends this tedious novel by the Scudéry of Japan.[17]

Madeleine de Scudéry (1607–1701), the author of numerous books, both fiction and nonfiction, was known for her sprawling romances, "*mise-en-abymes* of polite society" that "recount the many adventures of pairs of lovers who endure wars, abductions, shipwrecks and other works of fate but in the end are united in love"[18]—including, for instance, the five-volume, ten-part, thirty-book, 7443-page international best seller *Artamène; ou, Le Grand Cyrus* (1649–1653, translated into English as *Artamenes; or, The Grand Cyrus, an Excellent New Romance*, 1653–1655).[19] Presumably, the similarities that Bousquet imagined between Murasaki Shikibu and Scudéry began with their sex and extended to the length and courtliness of their fictions—though a later French commentator would make the same comparison on the basis of Genji's "good fortune" (*bonheur*), which reminded him of that of Scudéry's heroes.[20]

I said that Bousquet's description of *Genji monogatari* as "this tedious novel by the Scudéry of Japan" (*cet ennuyeux roman de la Scudéry japonaise*) circulated widely. To be precise, it was not Bousquet's phrase itself that was broadcast, but a subtly, significantly misremembered quotation of it that Basil Hall Chamberlain (1850-1935) offered, without citation, in the first edition of his dictionary of Japan, *Things Japanese*, first published in 1890 and reprinted six times in revised editions, the last appearing in 1939. "If the authoress of the *Genji Monogatari*, though lauded to the skies by her compatriots, has been branded by Georges Bousquet as *cette ennuyeuse Scudéry japonaise*," Chamberlain writes, "she surely richly deserves it."[21]

This new rewriting of Bousquet's dismissal—which shifts the locus of tedium from the books to their authors and seems to imply scorn for both women, perhaps for women writers in general[22]—was invoked in turn by W. G. Aston (1841-1911) in his lecture "The Classical Literature of Japan," presented to the Japan Society of London on June 29, 1898: "Du [sic] Bousquet calls the author '*cette ennuyeuse Scudéry Japonaise*,' and Chamberlain endorses his opinion." Aston, however, proceeded to defend Murasaki Shikibu from Bousquet-Chamberlain's attack: "On the other hand, Motoori, who, when every allowance is made for his patriotic prejudices, was no mean critic, has an unlimited admiration for the Genji, and has given reasons for the estimation in which he held it in a work called *Tamano Ogushi*."[23]

When Aston quoted Bousquet via Chamberlain once again in his influential *A History of Japanese Literature* (1899), he extended his—still skeptical—defense of *Genji* even further:

> Japanese critics claim for the *Genji* that it surpasses anything of the kind in Chinese literature, and even deserves to be ranked with the masterpieces of European fiction. None, however, but an extreme Japanophile (the species is not altogether unknown) will go so far as to place Murasaki no Shikibu on a level with Fielding, Thackeray, Victor Hugo, Dumas, and Cervantes. On the other hand, it is unjust to dismiss her summarily with the late M. George Bousquet as "cette ennuyeuse Scudéry japonaise," a verdict endorsed by Mr. Chamberlain. There are in the *Genji* pathos, humor, and an abundant flow of pleasing sentiment, keen observation of men and manners, an appreciation of the charms of nature, and a supreme command of the resources of the Japanese language, which in her hands reached its highest point of excellence. Though never melodramatic, she gives us plenty of incident, and is seldom dull.[24]

A History of Japanese Literature was quite successful: it was reprinted several times in England in Aston's lifetime, and in the United States was reprinted nine times between 1899 and 1937.²⁵ It was also translated into French in 1902 by Henri-D. Davray, and into Japanese in 1908 by Shibano Rokusuke. In Japanese, the phrase *cette ennuyeuse Scudéry japonaise* becomes *kano taikutsu naru Nihon no Sukyuderi*; in the French translation of Aston's book, Chamberlain's misquotation is preserved.²⁶

The success of Aston's specialist treatment of Japanese literature, and his explicit disagreement with Chamberlain, prompted Chamberlain to take a slightly different approach to *Genji* in the fourth edition of *Things Japanese* (1902): he added a footnote to the paragraph in which he had misquoted Bousquet: "Sir Ernest Satow's judgment of the *Genji Monogatari* agrees with ours. . . . Fairness, however, requires that the very different estimate of this work formed by Mr. Aston, the accomplished historian of Japanese literature, should be here cited." Chamberlain proceeded to quote Aston at length, but cunningly undercut Aston's praise by choosing to begin quoting from the words, "I do not profess to have read more than a small part of this portentously long romance."²⁷ Chamberlain himself, of course, offered no such disclaimer.

Bousquet Travels

Between 1878, when Bousquet first spoke of *Genji monogatari* as *cet ennuyeux roman de la Scudéry japonaise*, and 1902, when Chamberlain allied himself with Sir Ernest Satow (1843–1929) and Bousquet (via Chamberlain) in opposition to Aston, the misquoted, subtly misogynist phrase *cette ennuyeuse Scudéry japonaise* had come to serve as the axle around which a minor debate over *Genji*'s literary merits revolved. Traces of this debate soon began, moreover, to seep beyond the porous boundaries of English and French Japanology. In *Die japanische Dichtung (Japanese Literature*, 1904), which drew on Aston's *A History of Japanese Literature*, Otto Hauser reported that Murasaki Shikibu "has been called the Japanese Fraülein von Scudéry, cette ennuyeuse Scudéry Japonaise, but might rather be compared with the kind and simple Marie de France, with perhaps a slight inclination toward Margaret of Navarra."²⁸ It is a bit disconcerting to note that no one ever tracked down Bousquet's original quote and that it continued to be referenced again and again in new contexts by people who had never read the essay in which it appeared. Still more unnerving, however, is that when Chamberlain aligned himself with Bousquet and Satow, he was, evidently without realizing it, concurring with opinions offered by two men who had never read a word of *Genji monogatari*.

Bousquet began his history of the *monogatari* in "Le Japon littéraire," as I noted earlier, by citing "the definition of a Japanese critic." Satow begins the section "Romances" in his long entry on Japanese literature in *The American Cyclopædia*—the earliest essay on the topic in English, to my knowledge, and perhaps in any European language, that might be termed "specialist"—with exactly the same quotation.[29] Bousquet divides the history of Japanese literature into four periods; so, too, does Satow—the only difference being that Satow includes "the age which preceded the introduction of Chinese literature and writing" in the first period, while Bousquet begins his categorization "with the introduction of Chinese writing."[30] And although Bousquet does include Satow's encyclopedia entry in a list of four references at the beginning of his essay, this hardly prepares readers for the discovery that the plot summaries Bousquet provides for the various *monogatari* he mentions consist of word-for-word translations, edited in places, of those provided by Satow.

Bousquet's paragraph on *Genji monogatari* is no exception, except that he has added a few lines to remind his readers of the trip he made to see Murasaki Shikibu's "little pagoda," described four years earlier in the pages of the same journal, and inserted the comparison of Murasaki Shikibu to Scudéry. Here is the passage in *American Cyclopædia* on which Bousquet's paragraph was based:

> Of all these romances the most celebrated is the *Genji Monogatari*, in 54 books, by the poetess Murasaki Shikibu, who flourished at the beginning of the 11th century, the composition of the work being referred usually to the year 1004. It relates the amorous adventures of Hikaru Genji, the son of the mikado's favorite concubine. The titles of the various books into which it is divided are chiefly taken from the names of the women whom he loved. In point of style it is considered to be far superior to all the other monogatari, being far more ornate; but the plot is devoid of interest, and it is only of value as marking a stage in the development of the language.[31]

Obviously, Bousquet was working from Satow's description of *Genji monogatari*, not "looking into" the tale itself—to borrow the phrase he had used the previous year in *Le Japon de nos jours et les échelles de l'extrême Orient*, when he called *Genji* "a dry chronicle of a civil war." And, indeed, Bousquet was not the only one to offer his appraisal of *Genji monogatari* without having read it: by 1874, Satow had already spent several years amassing an extensive collection of Japanese books—the bulk of which, incidentally, Aston borrowed when he was writing *A History of Japanese*

Literature—and had devoted considerable effort to the study of Japanese literary history, but according to his diary, he did not begin to read *Genji monogatari* with his tutor, "old Shiraishi," until July 6, 1881.[32]

Chamberlain may not have realized that neither Bousquet nor Satow had read *Genji monogatari*; then, again, perhaps he had. When Arthur Diósy, the vice chairman of the Japan Society of London, rose to respond to Aston's lecture "The Classical Literature of Japan," he had this to say, according to the published transcript, which presents his comments in the third person:

> In almost every book in Japan reference would be found to the *Genji no Monogatari* [sic] and its authoress Murasaki no Shikibu. The latter appeared to have incurred a good deal of odium on the part of Europeans, as Mr. Aston had stated, but he thought a good deal of that was due to the fact that many of her critics had not attempted to read the work. Some of the books which blamed Murasaki no Shikibu for dullness clearly betrayed the fact that the critics had not read even a translation of the book; they had read in somebody else's book that she was a dull writer, and they simply repeated it. As a matter of fact, however, it was not at all a yellow-backed railway novel or such a work as one would pick up to pass half an hour. A good deal of it would probably be interesting to [the society's] lady members, as it contained elaborate descriptions of costumes, brocades, and embroidery.[33]

If *cette ennuyeuse Scudéry japonaise* had become the axle for a debate about *Genji*'s merits, then, the wheel was spinning in air. But once the phrase had appeared in two works as popular as *Things Japanese* and *A History of Japanese Literature*, it was only natural that it should continue to circulate; and so it did—usually quoted in the supposedly "original" French, but always cited in the mistaken form that derived from Chamberlain's English-language essay. I have mentioned Otto Hauser's *Die japanische Dichtung*; it will be helpful, in order to indicate how widely the phrase circulated, to provide a selection of other examples.

From Gustave Lavieuville's *Essai de psychologie japonaise: La race des dieux* (*Essay on Japanese Psychology: The Race of the Gods*, 1908):

> Beginning in the tenth century we find a very large quantity of very long, very detailed novels of the court in which the elegant, aristocratic, but narrow and frivolous life lived by the emperors and their courtesans is minutely preserved. The *Genji Monogatari* is one of the most celebrated; like many others, it was written by a woman. These

novels—so tedious they are almost impossible for Europeans to read—
depict a small court in which one need not concern oneself with
government, but only with killing time.... The style is long-winded—
Genji Monogatari, 4234 pages—risqué without being indecent; those
Europeans who have had the courage to try and read the book have
described its author as an *"ennuyeuse Scudéry."*³⁴

From Michel Revon's *Anthologie de la littérature japonaise des origines
au XXᵉ siècle* (*Anthology of Japanese Literature from Its Origins to the Twentieth Century*, 1910):

M. Georges Bousquet calls Mouraçaki: *"cette ennuyeuse Scudéry
japonaise."* The phrase has been well served: M. Chamberlain declares
that she "richly deserves" this description (*Things Japanese*, p. 265). M.
Aston (p. 97) and M. Florenz (p. 211) have shown themselves to be less
severe on her. In reality, I believe it would be hard to find among the
literatures of the occident, until a period quite recent, pages of psychology as subtle as those with which the *Ghennji* is, as it were, sewn.³⁵

From Raymond M. Weaver's "The Miscellany of a Japanese Priest,"
published in the *Bookman* (New York) in January 1919:

Japan has produced no Shakespeare, no Chaucer, no Fielding, no Dickens, no Shaw; rather can she boast her Malorys, her Bedes, her Herricks, her anonymous Miracle Plays and her Chronicle Drama. She rates
prime among her classics an epic romance written by the tenth-century
lady-in-waiting, Murasaki Shikibu—a rival in endless sentimental preciosity to Mademoiselle de Scudéry.³⁶

From Oswald White's "A Classic of Feudal Japan," first published in
the *Japan Advertiser* on November 12, 1921; reprinted with the same title
in *Living Age* on January 7, 1922; and reprinted again as the introduction
to White's partial translation of the "Sakaki" (The Green Branch) chapter of *Genji monogatari*, "Parting—A Passage from the *Genji Monogatari*,"
in *Transactions of the Asiatic Society of Japan* in December 1922:

The *Genji Monogatari* is one of the classics of Japanese literature. It is
ranked as a masterpiece by the Japanese themselves but it has not
fared over-well at the hands of foreign critics. Chamberlain says, "If
the authoress of the *Genji Monogatari* . . . has been branded by
Georges Bousquet as 'cette ennuyeuse Scudery [sic] japonaise,' she

surely richly deserves it." Satow agrees, "The plot is devoid of interest; that is, it is only of interest as marking a stage in the development of the language." On the other hand a very different opinion by Aston is quoted in the same passage. . . .

Where authorities of such weight are to be found in opposing camps, the tyro may enroll himself under either flag without fear. I am prepared to subscribe unreservedly to Aston's views.[37]

From Frank Hawley's "Ōbeijin no kenkyū shitaru Nihon bungaku" (Japanese Literature in European Research), published in *Bungei* (*Arts*) in December 1933:

[Chamberlain] suggests that while there are many beautiful verses in the *Ten Thousand Leaves*, they are the sort of thing that serves as material for linguists rather than scholars of literature, products less of poets than of poetasters. He considers the delicate description of the child in the *Tosa Diary*, the plain-spoken satire of the *Pillow Book*, and certain of the poems in *Poems Old and New* to be true literary gems, but when it comes to *Genji monogatari* and Bakin's *Chronicle of the Eight Dogs*, which are generally accorded the most extravagant praise by Japanese and foreigners alike, he says they are rambling and tedious, and agrees with a certain Frenchman who once dubbed Murasaki Shikibu "that enervating Japanese Scudéry" (a woman writer of seventeenth-century France, well known—in a negative sense!—for writing extraordinarily long-winded novels), and he found Bakin's *Chronicle of the Eight Dogs* so flatulent and flaccid that once when someone said to him that it was a very good book, he replied with sarcasm, "Indeed . . . as a sleeping pill!"[38]

From Bruce Lancaster's "Nihongo—The Japanese Language," published in the *Atlantic Monthly* in May 1944:

The need for Americans to learn Japanese in prewar days might have been more apparent had there existed a Japanese literature able to survive export and translation. Many are familiar with the *Genji Monogatari* (about A.D. 1020) of Murasaki Shikibu and may feel that it is but one example of a treasure house as yet untapped. Foreign masters of Japanese are divided on the merits of *Genji*. Sansom calls it one of the great books of the world, and Aston, high among Japanese scholars, agrees with him. Basil Hall Chamberlain heartily endorses Georges Bousquet's comment: "Cette ennuyeuse Scudéry japonaise."[39]

From the entry "Genji Monogatari" in the hugely ambitious nine-volume *Dizionario letterario Bompiani delle opere e dei personaggi di tutti i tempi e di tutte le letterature* (*Bompiani Literary Dictionary of Works and Characters of All Times and All Literatures*, 1947–1950):

> In Europe, when it still had not all been translated, the novel was judged bad by some, for ex. by Bousquet, who called the author: "cette ennuyeuse Scudéry japonaise," while others exaggerated in the opposite direction.[40]

From the entry "Genji Monogatari" in the less ambitious four-volume *Dictionnaire des œuvres de tous les temps et de tous les pays* (*Dictionary of Works of All Times and All Countries*, 1955), evidently translating the Italian citation of the English misquotation of Bousquet's French:

> In Europe, this novel was little appreciated by some: Bousquet, for example, called the author "cette ennuyeuse Scudéry japonaise," while others did not hold back from offering her praise that was often exaggerated.[41]

From Donald Keene's "Seiōjin no *Genji monogatari* no kanshō" (European Appreciations of *The Tale of Genji*), published in *Bungaku* (*Literature*) in Feburary 1954:

> Already in the early Meiji period, *Genji monogatari* was mentioned in Western books. But in those days Europeans had hardly any understanding of the Japanese language of the Heian period, and of course they lacked the knowledge to make a fair assessment of it. For instance, one Frenchman called Murasaki Shikibu "that tedious Scudéry," comparing the author of *Genji monogatari* to an extremely dull woman writer of the seventeenth century.[42]

From the entry "Genji Monogatari" in the Germanizing *Kindlers Literatur Lexikon* (*Kindler's Dictionary of Literature*, 1965–1972):

> Quite different, at first, was the attitude in the West: Basil Hall Chamberlain spoke, with Georges Bousquet, of Murasaki Shikibu as "dieser langweiligen japanischen Scudéry," and Sir Ernest Satow saw in her novel only a historical-linguistic source.[43]

From Edward Seidensticker's "Las libertades de Arthur Waley" (Arthur Waley's Liberties)—not to be confused with the English essay "On Being

Faithful to Murasaki Shikibu"–translated into Spanish by Montserrat Millán, published in *Quimera* in May 1982:

> W. G. Aston, who wrote the first history of Japanese literature in English, admitted that he had not been able to finish it. Sir Ernest Satow was of the opinion that it "only had value as marking a stage in the evolution of the language." Chamberlain's characterization was more optimistic and no less hostile: "If the author of Genji Monogatari, though praised to the skies by her compatriots, has been described by Georges Bousquet as *cette ennuyeuse Scudéry japonaise*, it is surely because she richly deserved it."[44]

And one final example, from Christine Brooke-Rose's novel *Textermination* (1991):

> Orion turns. At the entrance stands a small Japanese lady, startlingly beautiful in a black and blue and gold kimono, with large black and gold pins opening out symmetrically like fanbones from her massively piled black hair. She also holds, open in front of her, a huge black fan with golden cockerels and flying bluebirds on it, although the wintry weather hardly warrants this. Her face is deathly white, her eyelids painted black and downcast, her tiny lips the only red in the general apparition. Behind her, with her, is a strikingly handsome man like a darkfaced archangel, dark-haired, with low-slung lazy eyelids that seem almost purple with fatigue. There is something coarse about the nose, the mouth is too well-fleshed to be strong, the ears are long-lobed like young knurled jackfruit. How does this description enter her head? He has a glittering eye and he's wearing a golden dhoti and red turban. She has no doubt who he is, but murmurs to Orion: Who's he with? The Lady Murasaki?
>
> But Mira, Murasaki Shikibu was an author. I read and reread The Tale of Genji in a tattered Russian translation I found hidden on top of a lavatory tank in my Siberian camp.
>
> You did? The French call her cette ennuyeuse Scudéry japonaise. They would.[45]

More than a dozen examples in six languages, tracing more than a century of unwitting misquotation of a man who had never read *Genji monogatari* and whose low opinion of the work derived from another non-reader, should suffice to give a sense of how *Genji* discourse works: once established, images of the tale often continue to circulate and resonate longer than what might seem, at first, their natural lifetimes, in spheres far removed from those in which they originated. Indeed, this is true of *images of images* of the tale, as well. This, I suggest, is precisely what has happened in the case of Suematsu's translation and the greatly exaggerated reports of its irrelevance.

Naturally, not every image goes on making the rounds for as long as the "ennuyeuse Scudéry" canard has. In an extended essay on the history and techniques of Japanese lacquerware prepared by the Japanese Imperial Commission and published in Paris in *Le Japon à l'Exposition universelle de 1878* (*Japan at the Universal Exposition of 1878*, 1878), for instance, we are instructed that "in 480, a woman, celebrated for her literary works, named Murasaki Shikibu, informs us, in her *Genji Monogatari*, of a new type of lacquer encrusted with mother-of-pearl."[46] This sentence, with its extravagantly incorrect date for *Genji*'s composition, was reproduced as is—minus a comma—when the essay was reprinted in Yokohama the following year in *Les laques et la céramique du Japon* (*Lacquer and Ceramics of Japan*). It was also absorbed more or less unchanged, in a rather clumsy, ambiguously plagiaristic translation, into *Japan: Its History, Traditions, and Religions* (1880), by a former adviser to the Japanese navy, Sir Edward J. Reed: "In 480 a lady, who achieved literary renown, in one of her works* speaks of a novel description of lacquer incrusted with pearl"—the asterisk referring the reader to a footnote that identifies the work as "'Genji Monogatari,' by Mura-saki Shikibu."[47] Reed's book is cited in an entry called "Remarkable Influence of Women upon Literature" in the "Odds and Ends" column of *Routledge's Every Girl's Annual*, where we are told that Murasaki Shikibu, "who lived in 480, . . . wrote the *Genji-Monogatari*, the parent of the Japanese novel, and also much of the poetry of the time."[48] In 1879, the anonymous author of *Le Japon artistique et littéraire* (*Literary and Artistic Japan*) gave the same date for the composition of "*Ghendji Monogatari*."[49] In 1881, Edmond de Goncourt did the same in *La maison d'un artiste* (*The House of an Artist*), perhaps taking his information from Reed, since he, too, romanized the author's name as "Mura-saki Shikibu."[50] The relevant passage in Goncourt's book appears to have been reworked in *Dai-Nippon: O Grande Japão* (*Dai-Nippon: The Great Japan*, 1897), an early book by the Portuguese writer and émigré to Japan Wenceslau de Moraes.[51] After this spate of repetitions, however—all but the last from the years 1878 to 1881—the mistake was noticed and faded.[52]

This may not seem at all surprising, given that the date 480 is more than half a millennium off. But neither Bousquet's description of *Genji* as *cet ennuyeux roman de la Scudéry japonaise* nor Chamberlain's misquotation of this description as *cette ennuyeuse Scudéry japonaise* had any more bearing on *Genji monogatari* or its author than did the baseless date: from a perspective grounded in the material reality of the tale as a text or a book, there is no reason why Bousquet-Chamberlain's unfounded opinion should have circulated for over a century, while the erroneous date faded, for the most part, in only three years. One reason *cette ennuyeuse Scudéry japonaise* circulated so widely and for so long, even though it should have been fairly obvious all along that neither Bousquet nor Chamberlain had read *Genji monogatari*, was perhaps that its status as an attribution of value—in this case, negative value—to the work by means of its author made it the perfect vehicle for further attribution of value, whether positive or negative, to the tale. *Cette ennuyeuse Scudéry japonaise* was a catalyst for the *necessarily* "spinning-in-air" process of *Genji*'s gradual canonization as world literature.

Picturing Murasaki Shikibu

There is, however, a second reason for the long shelf life of the phrase *cette ennuyeuse Scudéry japonaise*: the enormous importance attached, in the early history of *Genji* discourse in Europe and the United States—and in Japan, as the first pictures in *Nise Murasaki inaka Genji* suggest—to the image of Murasaki Shikibu as a woman writer. I will return to this topic when I discuss the impact of Suematsu's translation; here I would like to set the stage by considering Murasaki Shikibu's image as it was presented in English contexts, and as it circulated, early on. The first time Bousquet touched at any length on *Genji monogatari*, he introduced the topic by noting that "the beautiful Murasaki would seem to be the painters' favorite subject," describing a scene that "often one sees": the poet "prolonging her contemplative meditations until the hour when the sky grows light, a small oil lamp left to burn beside her." Marcus B. Huish confirms the familiarity of such pictures during and after the heyday of Japonisme in *Japan and Its Art* (1889),[53] and in *Letters from Japan: A Record of Modern Life in the Island Empire* (1899), Mrs. Hugh Fraser describes the scenery at a Buddhist convent she visited in Komoro in terms of precisely this image, based on a picture she herself owned:

> I have at home a picture of the gentle lady Murasaki Shikibu, who eight hundred years ago retired to just such a spot as this to meditate on the romance which, by command of the Empress, she was to write. It was in August, by the light of the full moon, that she sat all night on

the balcony of a temple between the rocks, far uplifted from earth, and gazing down on Lake Biwa as we here gaze on the distant river. If her temple was like this one, I do not wonder at the power of inspiration which, overflowing her mind, caused her to write the chief incidents of her story on the back of a roll of Buddhist Scriptures, till all the space was covered. Next day, when the sacred frenzy was over, she discovered what she had done, and in time copied out the whole book anew to make reparation.[54]

Images of Murasaki Shikibu were introduced not only through artworks—the prints, paintings, screens, fans, lacquerware, and ceramics that had been entering European and American collections in increasing numbers since the 1860s—and their descriptions, but also by way of textual representations and book illustrations. William Elliot Griffis provides one of the earliest and most influential textual depictions of Murasaki Shikibu in *The Mikado's Empire* (1877), explaining that he is paraphrasing the long-selling *The Greater Learning for Women* (*Onna daigaku*), one of many books detailing proper feminine conduct (*jokunsho*) that helped establish Murasaki Shikibu's image in Japan from the early eighteenth century to at least the late nineteenth:

> Murasaki Shikibu was the daughter of the lord of Echizen. One day a lady of Kamo asked if there was any new entertaining literature or novels, as the empress-dowager wished to read something new. The lady invited Murasaki to write some stories. She, knowing that the great Chinese scholar Shomei completed his collection of the essays of ancient writers by building a high house and secluding himself in it, had a high tower erected at Ishiyama overlooking Lake Biwa, and affording a glorious view of the mountains, especially in the moonlight. There she retired, and one night when the full moon shone upon the waters she was so inspired that she wrote in one night two chapters of the *Genji Monogatari*, a book containing fifty-four chapters in all, which she finished in a few weeks. She presented it to the empress-dowager, who gave it to the mikado. To this day it is a classic.[55]

The Mikado's Empire was widely read, and Griffis's description of Murasaki Shikibu was pressed into service, with or without acknowledgment, as the source for later descriptions. C. A. White cites Griffis as the inspiration for her account in *Classic Literature* (1878).[56] Mary Reed, by contrast, concludes "A Chat About Japanese Dress," published in 1889 in Oscar Wilde's magazine the *Woman's World*, with a description, fittingly purple in its prose, that pretends to be based directly on the "many pretty stories" of Japan but is plainly indebted to Griffis:

> Another little fragment runs on to relate the doings of a lady named *Murasaki*, the daughter of one of the nobles attached to the court, who, being solicited to write, and knowing the value of solitude and a poetic environment, retired—in imitation of some wise sage of the day—to a high tower overlooking the romantic Lake Biwa. In that solitary spot, famed through Nippon for its beauty of mountain fastness and loveliness, she dwelt, waiting for inspiration and ideas. At last these came to her one silent summer night, when everything was hushed and the great pallid moon rising, a ghostlike thing, hung full-orbed, shining wondrously and with exceeding clearness over the dark untroubled waters of the lake, and the everlasting hills just faintly capped with lingering cloud.
>
> The outcome of this seclusion and meditation was the beginning of a book, which the authoress subsequently finished, and which is unto this day regarded as a classic by the Japanese.[57]

Interestingly, while Reed mentions *Genji monogatari* earlier on the same page, she does not give the name of its author; and when she introduces "Murasaki," she refrains from giving the title of the book that *"Murasaki"* wrote: here, it is the mere fact of female authorship that matters, not what the female author authored.

This appears to be the case, as well, in one of the more suggestive representations of Murasaki Shikibu that I have come across—one that combines textual description with pictorial depiction and produces what seems, from a contemporary perspective, a rather odd image of the "poetess." This portrayal, which is included in Edward Greey's children's book *The Wonderful City of Tokio; or Further Adventures of the Jewett Family and Their Friend Oto Nambo* (1882)—a sequel to *Young Americans in Japan; or, The Adventures of the Jewett Family and Their Friend Oto Nambo* (1882)—is remarkable in that it actually thematizes the recognition of Murasaki Shikibu, framing the ability to identify her, to read her image correctly, as a matter of cultural literacy:

> After they had refreshed themselves, Sallie went to her room and brought out a picture, which she exhibited to Oto, saying:
>
> "Will you please tell me what this means? My brothers and I have been arguing about it."

"I know," interrupted Fitz. "That young girl has just parted with her admirer, who has gone off in one of those *fune* (junks), and she is waving good-by to him. I told Sallie so, and she will not believe me."

"You are wrong, this time," said Oto. "The lady was a celebrated poetess, named Mura-saki-shikibu. She lived a long while ago, and wrote the story of the Genji."

"Why does she leave her lamp burning when it is daylight?" said Fitz, in an unconvinced tone. "She is not writing, anyhow."

"She shut herself up in a pavilion and completed the poem in a few days," answered Oto. "Being much absorbed in her occupation, she was not conscious that her lamp was burning long after the sun had risen over the horizon. The picture represents her as saluting the glorious goddess."

"Why did she wear her hair hanging down her back in such an untidy way?" asked the inquisitive boy.

"All poets like to have their locks flowing, when they are composing verses," replied Oto.

Fitz whistled and remarked:

"I told Sallie that the lady was short of hair-pins. I suppose nobody could write poems if they had their hair banged all over, as I used to, when I went to school."

"Fitz, do not be so absurd," said Sallie.

"Boys, are you ready to go to the Ginko?"

They replied in the affirmative, and ordering their *jin-riki-sha*, started from the *yashiki*.[58]

Clearly, Greey wanted his readers to understand, as the children go off with Oto to the bank (*ginkō*), that there is a distinction between those who are able to recognize the woman in the picture that accompanies this passage as Murasaki Shikibu and those who are not (figure 116). It is part of the Jewett children's education—and part of the education of the book's target audience—to learn to recognize Murasaki Shikibu. Yet the picture is ludicrous, and the text describes *Genji monogatari* as a "poem" completed "in a few days" that tells the story not of Hikaru Genji, but of "the Genji"—presumably the Genji clan, the enemy of Bousquet's "House of Faki . . . Hei." *The Wonderful City of Tokio* attaches a sort of cultural capital to the ability to recognize Murasaki Shikibu, then, even as it demonstrates in a rather absurd fashion just how little the content of that recognition matters. Confronted with the oddly gesturing figure on the boardwalk by the leafless, rootless tree, we cannot help recognizing that it is our recognition, ultimately, that makes her who she is and her book a classic.

78   THE WONDERFUL CITY OF TOKIO.

"Will you please tell me what this means? My brothers and I have been arguing about it."

"I know," interrupted Fitz. "That young girl has just parted with her admirer, who has gone off in one of those *fune* (junks), and she is waving good-by to him. I told Sallie so, and she will not believe me."

MURA-SAKI-SHIKIBU, A JAPANESE POETESS.

"You are wrong, this time," said Oto. "The lady was a celebrated poetess, named Mura-saki-shikibu. She lived a long while ago, and wrote the story of the Genji."

"Why does she leave her lamp burning when it is daylight?" said Fitz, in an unconvinced tone. "She is not writing, anyhow."

"She shut herself up in a pavilion and completed the poem in a few days," answered Oto. "Being much absorbed in her occupation, she was not conscious that her lamp was

Figure 116 The "celebrated poetess" Mura-saki-shikibu salutes the sun. (Edward Greey, *The Wonderful City of Tokio; or, Further Adventures of the Jewett Family and Their Friend Oto Nambo* [Boston: Lee and Shepard, 1883], 78. Courtesy of the author)

Figure 117 The back cover of Greey's *The Wonderful City of Tokio*. (Courtesy of the author)

The Wonderful City of Tokio was copyrighted for 1883, but it appears to have been released in the second half of 1882. Certainly, when Greey incorporated the publication data in Japanese into his design for the back cover (figure 117)—a distant descendant of the fake folded page in *Inaka Genji* discussed in chapter 2—he seems to have expected the book to be issued in 1882: "Boston: Lee and Shepard, Publishers, 1882," reads the text on the folded-down flap, and "Edward Greey designed this." There is something suggestive about this timing. In the very same year that Greey saw his image of Murasaki Shikibu—of Americans in Tokyo learning to recognize Murasaki Shikibu—go on the market in the United States, Suematsu Kenchō, a Japanese living in England, was trying to replace precisely such images with one of his own, rooted in his own very different relationships to the tale and its author, and to Japan and Great Britain and the rest of the world. In the end, *The Wonderful City of Tokio* arrived in bookstores only after Suematsu's translation was released, and the older image continued to circulate alongside the new.

THE MOST CELEBRATED OF THE CLASSICAL JAPANESE ROMANCES

Enter Suematsu Kenchō

Suematsu Kenchō was born in 1855 as the fourth son of a village headman. At age eleven, he entered a private academy run by Murakami Butsuzan, a poet and scholar of classical Chinese texts (*kangakusha*). The rigorous training he received in classical Chinese proved helpful after he moved to Tokyo at age seventeen, when he became acquainted with future prime minister Takahashi Korekiyo. Takahashi was then working as a houseboy for G. H. F. Verbeck, a prominent teacher at Kaisei Gakkō, one of the forerunners of Tokyo Imperial University. Suematsu's senior by one year, Takahashi had experienced life abroad—he had gone to San Francisco in 1867 to study, and then unwittingly signed a contract that declared him a "slave."[59] Suematsu was only too happy to teach Takahashi classical Chinese if Takahashi would teach him English. His English lessons began with history: *Peter Parley's Universal History*, a children's book written by Nathaniel Hawthorne and his sister Elizabeth Manning Hawthorne for Samuel G. Goodrich, first published in 1837 and issued in a new edition in 1871. Suematsu was soon proficient enough to join Takahashi in translating articles from the foreign newspapers that Verbeck subscribed to, which they then sold to *Tōkyō nichinichi shinbun*, the largest of the still relatively small "big newspapers" (*ōshinbun*), whose staff Suematsu joined as a translator in 1874.[60]

Months later, Fukuchi Gen'ichirō (Fukuchi Ōchi) took over as editor in chief and president of *Tōkyō nichinichi shinbun*. Fukuchi had accompanied the future three-time prime minister Itō Hirobumi and other politicians on two extended trips overseas and had held a position in the Finance Ministry before he left to take over *Tōkyō nichinichi shinbun*; with these connections, it is hardly surprising that under his stewardship the newspaper tended to cleave to government positions.[61] It was through his work on the paper, and specifically through Fukuchi, that Suematsu came to know Itō, whose daughter he would marry and in whose governments he would serve in a variety of positions. And it was Itō who, in February 1878, sent Suematsu to England, where he would remain until the spring of 1886, serving as an "attaché" to the Japanese legation in London and enrolling in and graduating from Cambridge University, where he studied law, language, and literature.[62] While he seems to have had few official duties, his frequent letters to Itō suggest that he was expected to serve as the elder statesman's eyes and ears abroad.[63] This was not his only unofficial mission, however: on February 9, 1878, the day before his 5:00 A.M. departure from Yokohama, Suematsu was informed, "You are instructed to investigate, when you are free from official business, English and French historiography."[64]

This was Suematsu's situation when he arrived in England: he had considerable training in English and some experience socializing with foreigners; he was intimate with some of the most powerful figures in the Japanese government and in the burgeoning world of mass media; and he had been charged specifically to keep abreast of current events and politics, and to study historiography. Suematsu was well prepared to observe, absorb, and historicize. It was perhaps only to be expected that by the time his translation of the first seventeen chapters of *Genji monogatari* was published in 1882, he would have acquired a nuanced understanding of the various contexts into which he was intervening, political as well as literary, and of the way he might go about changing them. That this was indeed the case is evident from his introduction to the translation.

Introducing *Genji Monogatari*

Previous discussions of Suematsu's *Genji Monogatari* have highlighted two sentences that come near the end of the introduction: "On the whole my principal object is not so much to amuse my readers as to present them with a study of human nature, and to give them information on the history of the social and political condition of my native country nearly a thousand years ago. They will be able to compare it with the condition of mediæval and modern Europe."[65] It goes without saying that this statement is barbed: Suematsu wants his readers to conclude that Heian-period Japan was, if anything, more cultured and civilized than Europe had been until recently or, perhaps, was even in modern times. He wants to help his readers recognize that Japan is not essentially backward, as many of them might think—recall the depth of Aston's condescension in *A History of Japanese Literature* nearly two decades later—and thus, presumably, that it is only fair that the "unequal treaties" that the United States, Britain, France, Russia, and other powers imposed on Japan beginning in 1854 be revised. Japan's foreign minister, Inoue Kaoru, had managed to arrange a series of meetings between representatives of the treaty powers beginning in January 1882, so the matter was completely of-the-moment when Suematsu's translation was published. It was the British foreign minister, moreover, who had thwarted a previous attempt, supported by the United States' representative, to overturn the Tariff Convention of 1866. There was a particularly pressing need to convince the British reading public that Japan deserved better treatment.[66]

That said, I would argue that Suematsu's comparison of Heian-period Japan with Europe and the implicit political message it carried is less important, at least from the perspective of one interested in his attitude to *Genji* and in the development of *Genji* discourse, than his explicit claim that *Genji* is best approached not as a source of amusement, but as a source of *historical* information. Suematsu leads into the comparison, in fact, with a litany of criticisms of the work as fiction:

> The thread of her story is often diffuse and somewhat disjointed, a fault probably due to the fact that she had more flights of imagination than power of equal and systematic condensation, she having been often carried away by that imagination from points where she ought to have rested. But, on the other hand, in most parts the dialogue is scanty, which might have been prolonged to considerable advantage, if it had been framed on models of modern composition. The work, also, is too voluminous.
>
> . . .
>
> The authoress has been by no means exact in following the order of dates, though this appears to have proceeded from her endeavour to complete each distinctive group of ideas in each particular chapter. In fact she had even left the chapters unnumbered. . . . It has no extraordinarily intricate plot like those which excite the readers of the sensational romances of the modern western style . . .
>
> I notice these points beforehand in order to prepare the reader for the more salient faults of the work. On the whole my principal object is not so much to amuse my readers as to present them with a study

of human nature, and to give them information on the history of the social and political condition of my native country nearly a thousand years ago. They will be able to compare it with the condition of mediæval and modern Europe.[67]

Clearly, Suematsu had little confidence that his readers would derive the same sort of pleasure from *Genji* that they took in "sensational romances of the modern western style." In fact, earlier in the introduction, he compares the tale unfavorably with "numerous works of fiction" published in Japan "within the last sixty or seventy years," as well, noting that "when judged as stories, [the recent works] generally excel in their plots those of the classical period."[68]

This is not to say that Suematsu does not value *Genji*, or even that he values it for only its historical content—he is adopting a more subtle stance than that. He sets *Genji* in opposition, after all, to "*sensational* romances of the modern western style" and to recent Japanese fictions by writers whose "status . . . has never been recognized by the public."[69] He makes a distinction, somewhat reminiscent of Tsubouchi Shōyō's discussion of the "true novel" in *The Essence of the Novel* (*Shōsetsu shinzui*, 1885–1886), between romances as they often are nowadays and "true romances," whose value he explains in a passage that draws directly on *Genji* itself:

> The aims which the authoress seems always to have kept in view are revealed to us at some length by the mouth of her hero: "ordinary histories," he is made to say, "are the mere records of events, and are generally treated in a one-sided manner. They give no insight into the true state of society. This, however, is the very sphere on which romances principally dwell. Romances," he continues, "are indeed fictions, but they are by no means always pure inventions; their only peculiarities being these, that in them the writers often trace out, among numerous real characters, the best, when they wish to represent the good, and the oddest, when they wish to amuse."
>
> From these remarks we can plainly see that our authoress fully understood the true vocation of a romance writer, and has successfully realized the conception in her writings.[70]

Suematsu is quoting from the famous passage in the "Hotaru" (Fireflies) chapter of *Genji monogatari* in which Genji lectures Tamakazura on the *monogatari*, first teasing her for "letting yourself get so invested in these silly things, even though part of you knows there is sure to be very little truth in them," and then suddenly changing tack, attempting to win her favor by praising the works in one of his numerous efforts to seduce her.[71] Like many other readers, Suematsu divorces the scene from its context, focusing solely on the second of Genji's two arguments and presenting it as a literary manifesto in which "the aims [of] the authoress" herself "are revealed."[72] He chooses, moreover, to translate words that have nothing to do with any sort of broad vision of "literature" per se, using terms that would resonate with his Victorian readers' understanding of the concept, and their notions of "realism" and "idealism" in particular.[73] This is clear when Suematsu's translation is compared with the relevant passage in *Kogetsushō*—the text of *Genji monogatari* that he used:

日本紀などはたゞかたそばぞかし. これらにこそみちゞしくくはしきこと
はあらめとてわらひ給. その人のうへとて. ありのまゝにいひ出ることこそな
けれ.... よきさまにいふとては. よきことの限をえり出. 人にしたがはんと
ては. またあしきさまのめづらしきことをとりあつめたる. みなかたゞゞにつ
けたる. 此世の外のことならずかし.[74]

> *The Chronicles of Japan* and so on provide only one side of the story. It's in these things here that one really finds the details set out, the ways of the world, he said with a smile. You never see a person described precisely as he is . . . they select only the good points when they wish to present a character as good, and when they want to follow the crowd, they gather up all sorts of startling, wicked things—one way or the other, it's all from this world of ours, and nowhere else.

Suematsu's translation does not always correspond very closely to the Japanese—he unobtrusively skips a few lines, for instance, and the phrase "their only peculiarities being these" seems to have no equivalent in the original—but even in the parts that can be matched up, there are some significant divergences. The Japanese contrasts *The Chronicles of Japan* (*Nihongi*, 720) and other such texts with "these things here"— the fictional stories that Tamakazura is reading—keeping the discussion at the level of particular works whose generic affiliations are left unspecified; Suematsu frames the distinction in terms of an explicit contrast between "ordinary histories" and "romances." Clearly, the choice of the term "romance"—Suematsu's translation has the subtitle *The Most Celebrated of the Classical Japanese Romances*—was meant to suggest the importance of *Genji* to a specifically and characteristically national tradition, to place Genji in a line with King Arthur, Charlemagne, Diderick, and so on.[75] This is the sort of romance he means, I take it, and this is why he contrasts "the true romance" with "the sensational romances" that were then both popular and reviled.[76] The generic opposition of "histories" and "romances" could, likewise, easily be assimilated into a Victorian vision of British literary history: "In the years which followed the Norman Conquest," Anna Buckland writes in *The Story of English Literature*, published the same year as Suematsu's *Genji Monogatari*, "we shall find that our literature is enriched by two classes of works—romances, or the stories of individual life, and chronicles, or stories of the nation's life."[77] And it is perhaps not incidental that this pairing of "chronicles" and "romances" maps equally well onto one of the divisions basic to the early modern Sino-Japanese view of literature that Suematsu grew up with: the split between "official histories" (*seishi*), of which *The Chronicles of Japan* is an example, and various genres of popular fiction known as "unofficial histories" (*haishi, haishi shōsetsu*). Here, in a passage in which "the aims [of] the authoress" are revealed by the mouth of her hero speaking through the pen of her translator, Heian, Victorian, and Tokugawa theories of fiction fuse.

Suematsu's attempt to imbue *Genji* with value as a romance is complemented by his rendering of Genji's explanation of the content of romances: he transforms the Japanese *michimichishiku kuwashiki koto*, an extremely open-ended phrase that I translated as "the details . . . the ways of the world," into the more specific but also more abstract "the true state of society."[78] And while Suematsu may perhaps have thought that he was extrapolating this from the Japanese, he appears to have interpolated the phrase "among numerous real characters," suggesting more explicitly than his base text that the characters in *monogatari* stand in for real, living models—much the way Genji, in his reading, stands in for Murasaki Shikibu. Since *Genji monogatari* is imperfectly realized as a story, then, Suematsu hopes that his readers will appreciate it as a document of social and cultural conditions in Heian Japan, as an example of *historical* romance. "In fact," he suggests, "there is no better history than her story, which so vividly illustrates the society of her time."[79]

One of the Most Talented Women

Suematsu's vision of *Genji* as a historical source—which very clearly reflects the attention he had been giving to the study of historiography since his arrival in London, and which is echoed in his discussion of the potential historical usefulness of local legends in *The Identity of the Great Conqueror Genghis Khan with the Japanese Hero Yoshitsuné* (1879)[80]—colors his introduction, and his translation itself, throughout. Still more important, however, is that his portrayal of "the aims which the authoress seems always to have kept in view" is framed in such a way as to keep "the authoress" herself always in view: the figure of Murasaki Shikibu as a woman writer comes to embody the political and historical functions he wants his *Genji Monogatari* to serve. Of course, this, too, reflects his awareness of the images of the tale and its author that had been circulating since the 1870s, as the first paragraph of his introduction demonstrates:

> *Genji Monogatari*, the original of this translation, is one of the standard works of Japanese literature. It has been regarded for centuries as a national treasure. The title of the work is by no means unknown to those Europeans who take an interest in Japanese matters, for it is mentioned or alluded to in almost every European work relating to our country. It was written by a lady, who, from her writings, is considered one of the most talented women that Japan has ever produced.[81]

Suematsu continues to focus on Murasaki Shikibu for nearly three more pages, or about half the introduction, giving an account of her family and of the meaning and derivation of her name, and then explaining, in more detail than had any previous English-language commentator, the conventional story of how the tale came into being:

> The traditional account given of the circumstances which preceded the writing of the story is this: when the above-mentioned Empress was asked by the Saigu (the sacred virgin of the temple of Ishe) if Her Majesty could not procure an interesting romance for her, because the older fictions had become too familiar, she requested Shikib to write a new one, and the result of this request was this story.
>
> The tradition goes on to say that when this request was made Shikib retired to the Buddhist temple in Ishiyama, situated on hilly ground at the head of the picturesque river Wooji, looking down on lake Biwa. . . . It was the evening of the fifteenth of August. Before her eyes the view extended for miles. In the silver lake below, the pale face of the full moon was reflected in the calm, mirror-like waters, displaying itself in indescribable beauty. Her mind became more and more serene as she gazed on the prospect before her, while her imagination became more and more lively as she grew calmer and calmer. The ideas and incidents of the story, which she was about to write, stole into her mind as if by divine influence. The first topic which struck her most strongly was that given in the chapters on exile. These she wrote

down immediately, in order not to allow the inspiration of the moment to be lost, on the back of a roll of Daihannia (the Chinese translation of Mahāprajñāpāramitā, one of the Buddhist Sūtras), and formed subsequently two chapters in the text, the Suma and Akashi, all the remaining parts of the work having been added one by one. It is said that this idea of exile came naturally to her mind, because a prince who had been known to her from childhood had been an exile at Kushiu, a little before this period.

It is also said that the authoress afterwards copied the roll of Daihannia with her own hand, in expiation of her having profanely used it as a notebook, and that she dedicated it to the Temple, in which there is still a room where she is alleged to have written down the story. A roll of Daihannia is there also, which is asserted to be the very same one copied by her.

How far these traditions are in accordance with fact may be a matter of question, but thus they have come down to us, and are popularly believed.[82]

Immediately after this, Suematsu even comments on the familiarity of visual depictions of Murasaki Shikibu: "Many Europeans, I dare say, have noticed on our lacquer work and other art objects, the representation of a lady seated at a writing-desk, with a pen held in her tiny fingers, gazing at the moon reflected in a lake. This lady is no other than our authoress."[83]

Suematsu was not alone in his perception of how important the figure of Murasaki Shikibu had already become in *Genji* discourse: the publisher of his translation, the large and influential academic press Trübner—just entering its fourth decade in 1882, famous as "the literary intermediary between Europe and the East" since it began to publish *Trübner's American and Oriental Literary Record* in 1865, and since the inauguration, thirteen years later, of its Oriental Series—also capitalized on Murasaki Shikibu's image.[84] The earliest notice of *Genji Monogatari* that I know of, published in the November 19, 1881, issue of the Boston fortnightly *Literary World* and presumably based on information from Trübner, uses precisely this tactic:

—Mr. K. Suyematz, Japanese student in Cambridge, England, is engaged upon a translation into English of the *Genji Monogatari*, the standard classic of the pure old Japanese tongue. It was written in 1004 A.D., by Murasaki Shikibu, a lady at the Mikado's court in Kioto. It is in fifty-four chapters, though the chapters are short. Many of the most popular Japanese pictures on screens, fans, etc, made in Tokio for American export are taken from this classic love-story, which is still a favorite with the Japanese.[85]

When the company first advertised the book in the February 1882 issue of *Trübner & Co.'s Monthly List*, it used the opening of Suematsu's introduction, slightly edited, ending with the observation that Murasaki Shikibu was "one of the most talented women that Japan has ever produced."[86]

More tellingly still, the book itself was designed around the image of Murasaki Shikibu writing at Ishiyama Temple. Near the top of its cover, the title, *Genji Monogatari*, is printed in black, in a standard "Oriental" font meant to evoke the strokes of a calligraphy brush (figure 118). Slightly to the right of center, a silver full moon, surrounded but unobstructed by clouds—though the delicate lines and smudging on the foil suggest that we are seeing it through a haze—hangs over Lake Biwa. The moonlight on the waves has been beautifully captured, lending a sense of tranquility to the scene despite the roughness of the waves themselves, which have been executed in a noticeably woodblock-esque style. Silver foil has been applied, as well, to an outcropping of rock directly below the moon, near the viewer, and, somewhat farther away, to the roof of the building in which, presumably, Murasaki Shikibu sits and looks out.

The image of the author that is only implied in this beautiful and beautifully printed landscape is made visible, incidentally, in a minimally revised edition of *Genji Monogatari* published in Yokohama in 1894. A fold-out picture shows Murasaki Shikibu sitting at her desk and holding a brush (not a pen) in her genuinely "tiny fingers" (figure 119). The angle of the veranda and the subtle delineation of the lake and mountains in the background indicate that the direction from which we are viewing this scene is the same as that from which we admired the one on the cover of the Trübner edition: it is as though, turning from one edition to the next, we have zoomed in on the figure who gave the earlier panoramic perspective its meaning. The object in front of Murasaki Shikibu seems to be a lamp—oddly, she appears to be staring into its flame, rather than out at the moon reflected in the water. In fact, she is not writing, either: her brush is upside down. The picture is signed in the lower-left corner: "Gekkō" for Ogata Gekkō, the artist responsible for the pictures in the 1888 edition of *Nise Murasaki inaka Genji* discussed in chapter 3—one of which, it will be recalled, also depicts Murasaki Shikibu, albeit in a different style (see figure 94).

Figure 118 The cover of the first edition of Suematsu Kenchō's *Genji Monogatari: The Most Celebrated of the Classical Japanese Romances*. (Courtesy of the author)

Figure 119 The frontispiece of the 1894 edition of Suematsu's *Genji Monogatari*. (Courtesy of the author)

Reprints, Rewritings, Reviews

I noted earlier that Suematsu's *Genji Monogatari* is generally thought to have made little, if any, impact when it was published. This assumption would appear to be borne out by the translation's meager sales figures: Rebekah Clements, having examined Trübner's records, reports that a mere 500 copies were printed, of which only 242 were sold in the first decade, while a further 78 were distributed for free.[87] The book itself does not seem to have circulated widely, though as Ida M. Mellen attests, it was available in some public libraries, and some readers would seem to have checked it out.

The truth, however, is that *Genji Monogatari* had an enormous impact, circulating in many different forms and giving rise to an extensive

Genji discourse. No fewer than three new editions were issued in Japan and the United States between 1882 and 1934—the year after the final volume of Arthur Waley's *The Tale of Genji* was published—and it was once retranslated in its entirety: Maximilian Müller-Jabusch rendered it into German as *Die Abenteuer des Prinzen Genji* (*The Adventures of Prince Genji,* introduction 1911), replacing Suematsu's introduction with his own.[88] The German translation is notable for its cover, which may well be the ugliest and most disturbing artwork ever created on a *Genji* theme. The first five chapters were anthologized, moreover, in Charles F. Horne's fourteen-volume *The Sacred Books and Early Literature of the East* (1917). A highly condensed rewriting of much of Suematsu's translation—including "Hahaki-gi (The Broom-like Tree)" and the stories of Genji's interactions with the characters known as Yūgao, Suetsumuhana, and the young Murasaki—was included in Roger Riordan and Tozo Takayanagi's *Sunrise Stories* (1896).[89] Arvède Barine (Louise-Cécile Vincens) also produced a condensed French adaptation—of the first two chapters, "Kiri-tsubo" (The Chamber of Kiri) and "Hahaki-gi," and part of the third, "Yūgao" (Evening Glory)—that appeared in the April 14, 1883, issue of *Revue politique et littéraire de la France et de l'étranger* (*Political and Literary Review of France and Abroad*) and was subsequently included in her *Essais et fantasies* (*Essays and Fantasies,* 1888).[90]

The creation of a new edition or a retranslation of a work requires a considerable investment of energy and capital, of course, and the existence of these works is a sign that *Genji Monogatari* made a powerful impression when it appeared—in an age when Europe and the United States were seized, in the words of an observer writing in 1882, by "the modern craze for things Japanese, which has converted grocer's shops into Japanese art depositories, and flooded the country with penny fans and inferior porcelain"[91]—and that this impression lasted, at least in some quarters. The truth is that Suematsu's translation was widely noticed, especially in England but also to a certain extent in the United States and Europe; and as is frequently the case, reviewers' and other readers' reactions were channeled by its paratexts, particularly its introduction but also its publicity and presumably its design. I have shown that Suematsu and Trübner highlighted the figure of Murasaki Shikibu as a woman writer, making her an image of her work, and that Suematsu argued that *Genji* might best be appreciated not for its story, but as a historical romance affording insight into "the true state of society" in ancient Japan; and sure enough, reviews of the book tend to gravitate to precisely these two points. Indeed, especially from the mid-1890s—spurred in part by the importation and reintroduction of the 1894 edition, issued in Yokohama by Z. P. Maruya, forerunner of the bookstore Maruzen—these two perspectives were increasingly woven together, so that Murasaki Shikibu's fame as a writer came to be cited as a matter of course in treatments of the social position that women had historically occupied in Japan.⁹²

No Better History

I have managed to track down sixteen reviews, and while a few appeared in newspapers such as the *London and China Telegraph* and the *Japan Gazette* that targeted a comparatively small and specialized readership, most ran in well-known and widely read periodicals.⁹³ The *Athenæum*, the *Spectator*, and the *Saturday Review*, for example, were the three most important and highly regarded British weeklies, with the *Athenæum* topping the list.⁹⁴ The reviews of *Genji Monogatari* tend, moreover, to be quite substantial, sometimes nearly twice the length of other long reviews in the same issue. The review in *Notes and Queries* runs to 51 lines, for instance, while the second longest, a notice of William H. Sewell's *The Sexton's Wheel and the Lady Fast: An Ecclesiological Essay*, runs to 30; that in the British edition of *Harper's New Monthly Magazine* runs to 178 lines, compared with 50 for David Christie Murray's *Coals of Fire*, 12 for George Macdonald's *Gifts of the Child Christ*, and 98 for Walter W. Skeat's *A Concise Etymological Dictionary of the English Language*. The review in *Saint James Gazette* is so long that one wishes it were shorter.

Clearly, the publication of *Genji Monogatari* was regarded as an extraordinary literary event. Published a little more than a decade after the formation of the Meiji government, during an age when memories of Tokugawa rule were still fresh enough that Suematsu could address "Jusammi Tokoogawa," to whom he dedicated his translation, as "My Lord," *Genji Monogatari* must have seemed just what *Harper's* said it was: "a genuine novelty."⁹⁵ Perhaps to an extent this explains the reviewers' heavy reliance on Suematsu's introduction: having little, if any, context in which to place the translation, they simply regurgitated what he fed them. Thus we find *Genji Monogatari* described, typically without any acknowledgment that these words were first used by Suematsu, as "one of the standard works of Japanese literature" in both the *London and China Telegraph* and the *Court Journal*; as a "national treasure" in the *London Figaro* and the *Court Journal*; and as "the most celebrated of the classical Japanese romances" in the *Academy*, the *London Figaro*, the *Spectator*, the *Critic*, *Harper's*, and *Englishwoman's Review*. The catchy observation that "there is but one hero, but many heroines," which occurs in *Saint James Gazette*, the *Critic*, and *Harper's*, is another of Suematsu's phrases, as is the praise of Murasaki Shikibu as "one of the most talented women that Japan has ever produced," repeated in the *Court Journal*, the *Critic*, and *Englishwoman's Review*.

And then, of course, there is the evaluation of the romance itself. Again and again, reviewers complain of the flimsy plot but praise the book for its historical value. *Notes and Queries* suggests that "as a mere story, the *Romance of Genji*, like most Oriental fictions, is somewhat insipid; but it offers a curious picture of the state of Japanese society nine hundred years ago, especially as regards the position occupied by women." The *Scotsman* concurs: "The romance itself has little resemblance to the modern type of fiction; it is chiefly interesting from the accurate picture it presents of life in the Japanese Court and capital in the tenth century." The *Manchester Guardian* regrets "that the first English version of a Japanese work made by a native scholar should be of a nature to interest merely the student of court life." Both the *Court Journal* and *Saint James Gazette* seem resolved to ignore the story altogether, focusing instead, in the former, on "the insight into a state of society" and the "complete picture of Japanese life" the tale provides, and observing, in the latter, that "not only are the costumes, rites, and ceremonies, superstitions, folk-lore, and fables of the time constantly illustrated; but the morals, manners, and state of society are reflected with evident and easy sincerity." The *Japan Gazette* says, "The work is valuable as showing us what qualities a work must possess in order to make it classical in Japan; but it has greater value in that it reveals the life of eight centuries ago"; the *Athenæum* repeats Suematsu's quotation of Genji's discourse on fiction in "Hotaru," and then continues to parrot his introduction: "As the translator points out in his preface, there is, as there always is in Oriental romances, a certain want of continuity in the narrative. . . . Nor does he regard it mainly as a work of absorbing interest, but as reflecting a state of society sufficiently interesting to justify its publication in English."

This perspective on *Genji Monogatari* remained influential for decades and, needless to say, was not limited to reviews. In 1886, for instance, the art historian William Anderson referred to "the chapter entitled *É Awasé*, in the *Genji Monogatari*" in *Pictorial Arts of Japan*—a book that Suematsu, an acquaintance of Anderson's, translated into Japanese as *Nihon bijutsu zensho* (1897)—suggesting that the picture competition it describes "undoubtedly was prompted by an actual event that took place within the experience of the author, and goes far towards proving both that the art [of painting] was then held in great esteem, and that the importance of direct study from nature was fully admitted."⁹⁶ This is a typical instance of the manner in which the tale was mined for historical information. Indeed, Suematsu draws on the same chapter in *The Risen Sun*—a book he published in 1905 as part of an effort sponsored by the Japanese government to allay anxiety about the "yellow peril" in Europe and the United States during the Russo-Japanese War—"to show in what sort of relationship pictorial art and society stood towards each other."⁹⁷

Edward Dillon observed in 1894 that the "earliest mention of an incense game is in the *Genji Monogatari*."⁹⁸ Or, for a somewhat different example, here is the critic Paul Mantz referring to *Genji* in *Gazette des beaux-arts* (*Fine Arts Gazette*) in a review of a "retrospective exhibit of Japanese art" curated in 1883 by the *Gazette*'s editor, the well-known art historian and collector Louis Gonse: "We know from a novel that has been translated into English, the novel *Genji Monogatari*," Mantz writes, "that during the 10th century, Japanese society, living in a whirl of pleasures and celebrations, had a passion for all things elegant. It resembled a sort of *cour d'amour* in which men of fashion occupied themselves with poetry, theater, and above all dance."⁹⁹ A footnote refers the reader not to Suematsu's *Genji Monogatari*, but to Arvède Barine's rewriting of its first chapters, which had appeared in *Revue politique et littéraire* the previous month. Even at a double remove, *Genji* was being read as evidence.¹⁰⁰

Perhaps the most telling expression of this tendency is found in *The Sacred Books and Early Literature of the East*, in which Horne uses this quotation as an epigraph for the five chapters of the tale that he includes in the anthology: "Ordinary histories are the mere records of events. They give no insight into the true state of society. This, however, is the very sphere in which romances principally dwell."¹⁰¹ Over the years, these words had come to encapsulate a common vision of *Genji*'s canonical value. *There is no better history*, Suematsu says, *than her story*.

A Women Writer's First Feminist Readers

If the reviews and other publications are consistent in their gravitation toward an appreciation of *Genji Monogatari* as a historical document, they are even more unwavering in their fascination with Murasaki Shikibu, specifically with the image—already familiar from lacquerware and other Japanese imports—of her ensconced in her room at Ishiyama Temple. "It is interesting to be told that the familiar figure of a lady seated at a writing desk and gazing at the moon reflected in a lake is a representation of the authoress," the *London and China Telegraph* tells us. "European readers of Mr. Suyematz's translation, will now be able to understand many of the scenes depicted on the trays and other similar articles from Japan, the figures in which would otherwise be more or less meaningless." The review in *Notes and Queries* commences by noting Murasaki Shikibu's prominence in Japanese art; the one in *Harper's* concludes by wondering if "perhaps we ought to have introduced our notice of the book by the following description given of the authoress: . . . ," and then quoting Suematsu's description of Murasaki Shikibu.

Indeed, the revelation of this previously mysterious woman's identity was judged sufficiently interesting to merit an entry of its own in a column of "Literary Notes" published in the *Critic* on July 1, 1882, about a month before the review of the translation itself. "The lady seated at a writing-desk, holding a pen in her tiny fingers and gazing at the moon reflected in a lake, which we have all seen on Japanese lacquer work and other art objects," the writer tells us, "is supposed to represent Murasaki Shikib [*sic*], the gifted author of 'Genji Monogatari,' a romance which has been read in the Mikado's empire for nearly a thousand years."[102]

Clearly, the attention given to the figure of Murasaki Shikibu when Suematsu's translation was first published derived in part from her familiarity as a decorative motif; but that she was a woman, and that this was true of several classical Japanese writers, also attracted notice—or perhaps it was rather that the notices attracted people's attention to these two facts. It may not be surprising to find *Englishwoman's Review* emphasizing Murasaki Shikibu's sex in its advance notice for the translation, which ran on May 15, 1882: "Messrs. Trübner will shortly publish an English version of the Japanese romance 'Genji Monogatari,' by Mr. Suyematz Kenchio, an attaché of the Japanese legation in London. The author of this work was a woman, as, indeed, were many of the classical authors of Japan."[103] But the *Review* was simply reprinting the material provided by Trübner's publicity staff. The same notice had already circulated widely during the previous months, appearing, for instance, sometimes with slight changes in the wording, in the *Academy* on February 25, in the *Manchester Guardian* on February 27, and even, on March 1, in *Capital and Labour: An Economic, Financial, and Commercial Journal*.[104]

Among the authors of the reviews themselves, *Saint James Gazette*'s is most captivated by the historical circumstance that, as the reviewer puts it, "the literary use of the pure native language [was] in a great measure abandoned to cultivated women." He notes further that "there exists no parallel to the fact that a large proportion of the best writings of the best age of Japanese literature was the work of women." Over time, as the fashion for Japanese lacquer passed, the second type of interest in Murasaki Shikibu, as a woman rather than as a motif, grew increasingly prevalent, and she herself came to be invoked as historical evidence, a positive emblem of the status that women had occasionally enjoyed in ancient Japan and may one day enjoy in the modern world. This trend became particularly noticeable during the 1890s, a decade that saw a remarkable expansion in feminist activities worldwide, as well as the creation of new terms to describe these activities and the people who took part in them, including the word "feminist," which first appeared in print in the *Athenæum* in 1895.[105]

An essay by Alicia Bewicke Little (Mrs. Archibald Little) that appeared in the January 15, 1892, issue of *Englishwoman's Review* represents this emerging "feminist" interest in Murasaki Shikibu. Little, a novelist and well-known writer on Chinese topics who was also one of the founders and the first president, from 1895 to 1906, of the Anti-Foot-Binding Society (Tian Zu Hui, lit. the "Natural Feet Association"), opens this essay, "A Celebrated Japanese Authoress," with an account of a visit to Ishiyama Temple:

> Notwithstanding the intense heat of the hottest summer known in Japan for five and twenty years, I made a point, on a September evening, of visiting the Buddhist Temple at Ishiyama, to which Murasaki Shikib, the authoress of Japan's most celebrated romance, retired for inspiration when the Empress, to whom she had once been Maid of Honour, asked her to write some new romance, the sacred virgin of the celebrated Temple of Ize complaining that she was tired of those already in existence. . . . Above the rocks there is a pretty pagoda, and in front of it, looking over the river, with its long centipede bridge that figures in one of the prettiest Japanese fairy tales, as also over the far-famed Lake Buda [sic], stands the Moon Gazing Arbour. [106]

Little's reference to the "pretty pagoda" recalls Georges Bousquet's account almost exactly two decades earlier of his own visit to "the little pagoda where the celebrated poetess Murasaki-Shikibu composed the *Genji Mondgatari*," but while Bousquet had simply taken in the temple during the course of his sightseeing, Little made a sort of pilgrimage to it, traveling expressly to see the place where Murasaki Shikibu was said to have written her "celebrated romance":

> The arbour itself is like many Japanese moon-gazing stones and arbours, commonplace enough, but the view might fairly be characterized as entrancing, and looking upon it Murasaki is said there and

then to have composed two chapters of her celebrated novel, the *Romance of Genji*, which, for want of other writing materials, she wrote on the back of a roll of a Chinese translation of one of the Buddhist Sutras. To atone for this profanity she is said afterwards to have copied the roll with her own hand, and this, I suppose, was the manuscript in her handwriting I was shown in the Temple. The little room in which she continued her romance is just about six feet square, and so dark one wonders how anyone could write in it. But then this celebrated authoress died in 992 A.D., so perhaps the room, that darkens it, has been built on since. Though to show how well known her book is, the only Japanese schoolboy I have met promptly said: "Oh, yes! I know the *Romance of Genji*, but it is very difficult to understand. In *all* my school there were only six boys who could read it. I was one of the six."[107]

Little's narrative of how Murasaki Shikibu came to write "the *Romance of Genji*" draws so closely on the language of Suematsu's introduction to *Genji Monogatari* that one suspects she must have had a copy of the book beside her as she wrote. This seems even likelier at the end of the essay, when she quotes Suematsu verbatim, although without ever revealing her source: "It now only remains to add that the 'lady seated at a writing-desk, with a pen held in her tiny fingers, gazing at the moon reflected in a lake,' so often to be seen on Japanese lacquer, is Murasaki Shikibu, who died 900 years ago after writing Japan's most celebrated classic romance."[108]

Unlike the author of the *Harper's* review of *Genji Monogatari*, who concludes with the suggestion that "perhaps we ought to have *introduced* our notice of the book" by explaining that Murasaki Shikibu is the lady seen on Japanese lacquerware all the time, Little, writing a decade later, suffers no such doubts. For her, the artistic connection is incidental; it is Murasaki Shikibu the writer and her *Genji* who matter, and Little is interested in them precisely because they allow her to see the history of "the position of women" in a new light:

> Murasaki makes one of her characters say: "Ordinary histories are the mere records of events, and are generally treated in a one-sided manner. They give no insight into the true state of society. This, however, is the very sphere on which romances principally dwell," and it is this that makes her very lifelike romance principally interesting to us—this, and the extraordinarily interesting conversation about women in Chapter II. Unless the translator has unintentionally modernised this conversation, it is well worth the reading for all those interested in the

position of women, for it would almost seem as if men of the present day made precisely the same remarks about women's characters and capacity as Japanese did 900 years ago. How amusing is the description of those women "singularly earnest—too earnest indeed—in the performance of their domestic duty; and such, *with their hair pushed back*, devote themselves like household drudges to household duties." "But there are also women, who are too self-confident and obtrusive. These, if they discover some slight inconsistency in men, fiercely betray their indignation and behave with arrogance. *A man may show a little inconsistency occasionally*, but yet his affection may remain; then matters will in time become right again, and they will pass their lives happily together. . . . And if there should be anything worse than unpleasantness, she should even then complain of it in such a way as not to irritate the man." It must be remembered [these] are young men about the Court talking over the difficulty in selecting the right kind of girl as wife, and it is impossible to believe the talented authoress did not feel some sarcastic bitterness as she imagined these remarks. "There is a time for every thing," says one young man, "and all people, but more especially women, should be constantly careful to watch circumstances and not to air their accomplishments at a time when nobody cares for them. They should practice a sparing economy in displaying their learning and eloquence, and should even, if circumstances require, plead ignorance on subjects with which they are familiar." Does not the nineteenth-century young Englishman say just the same?[109]

One is left wondering whether this type of comparison was among those Suematsu had in mind when he proposed that readers of *Genji Monogatari* might compare the society it portrays with those of medieval and modern Europe. Suematsu was concerned to some extent with women's issues in Japan, as we will see in the last section of this chapter, but his views on women were not always sympathetic: he remarks in his introduction, for instance, that "the concise description of scenery" and "the true and delicate touches of human nature" that abound in *Genji*, especially in the second chapter, "are almost marvelous when we consider the sex of the writer, and the early period when she wrote."[110] Either way, even as Little agrees with Suematsu that Murasaki Shikibu's "very lifelike romance" is interesting principally because of the picture it gives of "the true state of society," she reads it as a feminist, mining it for what it might reveal about the social standing of women both in Murasaki Shikibu's age and in her own, and underscoring the sense of irony, the "sarcastic bitterness," she sees implicit in the discussion of women in the second chapter of the romance, "Hahaki-gi."

Shortly after the passage I have just quoted, Little turns back from the tale to the person of its author as one of a community of similar women, and then gestures toward a still larger transhistorical category. "It seems," she writes, "that at that early period in Japan most of the great writers were women. Those, however, who want carefully accurate information about the women of Japan must henceforth be referred to Miss Bacon's admirable little volume, *Girls and Women of Japan*."[111] Naturally, Alice Mabel Bacon's *Japanese Girls and Women*, first published in 1891, mentions Murasaki Shikibu, too.[112] For both Little and Bacon, the striking prominence of women writers in Japanese literary history, with Murasaki Shikibu as their best representative, had become an essential element in any "carefully accurate" history of Japanese women; by the same token, any treatment of Murasaki Shikibu now inevitably foregrounded women's issues. As I noted earlier, the two main focal points of Suematsu's introduction—*Genji*'s interest as history, on the one hand, and the figure of Murasaki Shikibu, on the other—were now being woven together. The very fact of Murasaki Shikibu's existence had come to be regarded as historical evidence, as having historical interest. And so, from the 1890s on, references to Murasaki Shikibu became all but ubiquitous in treatments of "the woman question" in Japan, whether approving or critical.

The frequency with which and the wide variety of publications within which Murasaki Shikibu began to appear in the wake of Suematsu's translation, if not always as a direct consequence of it, is somewhat startling from a contemporary point of view. In 1890, R. K. Douglas invoked her in the context of a discussion of the education of "Japanese maidens" in an essay called "Progress in Japan," published in the *Edinburgh Review* in July and reprinted in September in the New York weekly *Littell's Living Age*. "That the ignorance of Japanese women was, under the old order of things, deplorable, cannot be denied," he begins. "Of course there were occasionally to be met with girls who, having an intuitive taste for learning, acquired a considerable amount of scholarship, as, for instance, the brilliant authoress of the 'Genji Monogatari'; but these were as rare as flowering aloes, and cannot be said to have affected the general ignorance of their sex."[113] It is worth noting that Douglas assumes that his readers will know of *Genji Monogatari* and know who its "brilliant authoress" was.

She was also invoked in more substantial ways. In an essay titled "The Woman Question in Japan" by Helen E. Gregory-Flecher that ran in *Godey's Magazine* in 1893, for instance, Murasaki Shikibu's existence becomes the linchpin of an entire argument—indeed, of two nested arguments, Gregory-Flecher's and John Stuart Mill's:

> In conclusion I would like to say that the Japanese woman is more than clever. She is absolutely brilliant, when we take her opportunities into consideration. John Stuart Mill in the *Subjection of Women*, in answer to a sneer that they had done nothing in literature, said he had not the slightest doubt that if there were a land where men had not filled the literary field the women would have created the national literature of such a country, and he regretted that he had no method of proving the proposition. It has been proved, however, by the Japanese woman and under strange circumstances. About the fourth century the Japanese borrowed their civilization and adopted the characters of the alphabet from the Chinese. All literary men write in classical Chinese and become thoroughly versed in the literature of that country, just as at one period in England all writers of any pretensions wrote in Norman French. Women were not thought worthy of this higher education and they learned only Japanese, but the great result is that the really national literature, that written in Japanese, is the work of women who are celebrated as poetesses and novelists. The novel considered the finest production of Japanese literature, *Genji Monogatari*, which ranks to-day as a classic[,] was written by a court lady named *Murasaki Shikibu*.[114]

In the same year that Gregory-Flecher's essay was published, Murasaki Shikibu was featured in *Japanese Women*, a book privately printed by the Japanese Women's Commission for the World's Columbian Exposition in Chicago.[115] The following year, Kinza Riugé M. Hirai (Hirai Kinza, Hirai Kinzō, Hirai Ryūge, and so on), a scholar of English literature and a religious activist known for a speech he had presented to the World's Parliament of Religions at the World's Columbian Exposition, contributed a long essay, "The Japanese Life and Customs as Contrasted with Those of the Western World. (With the Treaty Question.)," to the *Journal of the American Geographical Society of New York*. In it, he cited "the fact that we have had many women writers" as evidence "that there has been no prejudice or prohibition against female education, contrary to the popular belief in the Western countries."[116] Naturally, Murasaki Shikibu heads his list of writers. "Women's Literature," an article in the August 23, 1895, issue of the *Atlanta Constitution*, reminded readers of "the rather remarkable fact that the first country in the history of the world to recognize the literary efforts of women was the little kingdom of Japan," and then recounted the story of Murasaki Shikibu's retreat to Lake Biwa—though the source is Griffis's *The Mikado's Empire*, not Suematsu.[117] Murasaki Shikibu appears, along with Mrs. Oura of Nagasaki and Jingu Kogu, in a list of three "eminent women" in the physiognomist Dr. Joseph Simms's rather scattershot "In the Empire of the Mikado: Characteristics, Habits, and Customs of the Japanese People," published in August 1897 in *Frank Leslie's Popular Monthly*.[118] In 1899, the Swiss literary critic Ernest Tissot, elaborating on "the state of indisputable inferiority" into which young women in Japan are raised in "La vie de société au Japon, d'après des auteurs japonais" (The Life of Society in Japan, After the Writings of Some Japanese Authors), an essay published in *Bibliothèque universelle et revue suisse* (*Universal Library and Swiss Review*), explains that this

> is not at all because they are ignorant or lacking in natural abilities. The Japanese woman possesses a charming spirit, but, as one of the classical authors of Nipponese literature, Mme Murasaki Siki-Bu, wrote approximately nine-hundred years ago: "There is time for everything, and everyone, women in particular, must constantly guard against putting their talents on parade when no one wants to see them. In public, women must be extremely frugal with their knowledge and their eloquence; in certain cases, they must even appear ignorant of things they know."[119]

A footnote refers the reader to Suematsu's translation of "le *Roman de Genji*."

In a 1902 obituary for the novelist Samuel Butler, R. A. Streatfeild defends Butler's shocking contention that the *Odyssey* was written by a woman with reference to Murasaki Shikibu: "It has been urged in opposition to Butler's theory that, from the days of Sappho to those of Christina Rossetti, no woman-poet has met with marked success save in works of brief compass and limited scope. Yet it is worth pointing out that a woman wrote the great Japanese classic romance 'Genji Monogatari,' a work which occupies to a certain extent the same position in Japanese literature that the Odyssey occupies in the literature of Greece."[120]

A bit of the episode in "Hahaki-gi"—the second chapter of "the extraordinary novel, *Genji Monogatari*, written by a woman, Murasaki Shikib"— that deals with Shikib-no-jio's affair with the scholar's daughter is quoted in Ethel M. M. McKenna's "The Real Chrysanthemum," published in May 1905 in the *Fortnightly Review*, as evidence that "the young scholars of the Universities were then not too proud to sit at the feet of their professor's daughters and to learn of them."[121] In "The Women of Japan," an essay that ran in the *Forum* in 1906, Adachi Kinnosuke cites Murasaki Shikibu in countering the assertion, by the editor of the *Japan Mail*, that the Japanese woman "is, in fact, totally disqualified to be her husband's intellectual companion."[122] This was considered a forceful enough counterpunch to deserve a note five months later in *Womanhood*: "Adachi Kinnosuke . . . laughs at the idea of his countrywomen being spoken of as the 'mere playthings of men,' or being 'totally disqualified for intellectual companionship.' He retorts that the book 'Genji Monogatari,' which occupies in Japanese literature a place similar to Homer in Greek and Shakespeare in English, was the work of Murasaki Shikibu, a Court lady of rank."[123] On January 2, 1914, a short article in the *Washington Post* called "Women in Japan: High Place Attested by Their Position in State, Religion, and Literature" observed, "The greatest lights in the world of pure Japanese literature are both women—Murasaki Shikibu and Sei Shonagon. Their superb productions—'Genji Monogatari' and 'Makurano Soshi'—are strong proofs of a large measure of liberty and of high position in society enjoyed by women of the time."[124]

This is no more than a sketch of the discourse that developed around Murasaki Shikibu in the wake of Suematsu's translation, especially from the 1890s. I could go on—and no doubt it would be interesting to trace Sei Shōnagon's emergence as Murasaki Shikibu's double over the course of the 1890s and early 1900s—but I think that I have rallied enough evidence to prove my point, which is simply that such a discourse existed and that it developed out of, or at the very least was anticipated by, Suematsu's approach to *Genji* in his introduction and from the publicity strategies that Trübner adopted, which almost certainly also derived from his introduction. And this is an important point—all the more so because it has been overlooked so completely, supplanted by a very different, very truncated understanding of the history of the role of women readers in the development of modern *Genji* discourse.

In July 1925, Virginia Woolf published in *Vogue* a now-famous review of the first volume of Arthur Waley's *The Tale of Genji* that has come to serve as a basic reference point for thinking about Murasaki Shikibu as a woman writer and as a writer read by women. The review has been reprinted in English and even published in Japanese translation; it has been widely cited and discussed, and appears regularly on college syllabi. Just as Waley has come to be regarded as "our only predecessor" as a translator, it has become all too easy to fall prey to the illusion that Woolf is "our only predecessor" as a feminist reader of *The Tale of Genji*.[125] In "Going to Bed with Waley: How Murasaki Shikibu Does and

Does Not Become World Literature," for example, Valerie Henitiuk returns to Woolf—who "as a contemporary of Waley . . . was among the first generation of readers to have access to this text"—to "indulge in a speculative look at a path not taken with regard to the translation history of this great tale, in the interests of suggesting the absent perspective of a potentially ideal translation that we do not and never will have: a version of this masterpiece as read by Virginia Woolf."[126] It is fascinating to imagine what this version might have looked like, even if one is skeptical of the possibility of an ideal translation and whether or not one can imagine Woolf—whose ebullient, elegant take on *The Tale of Genji* is also seeded with garden-variety Orientalisms—producing it. But Woolf was not a woman standing at the *beginning* of a "path not taken." By the time she wrote her review in 1925, Western women and men had been reading *Genji Monogatari* for more than four decades, and reading it as self-described feminists for three; Woolf, who was a little more than a month old when Suematsu's translation hit the shelves, belonged to the second generation of the tale's readers, not the first. She stood at a midway point along the path not taken.

Indeed, already in 1920 we find the lesbian poet Amy Lowell imagining, in her preface to *Diaries of Court Ladies of Old Japan*, something akin to the "ideal translation" that Henitiuk and others imagine Woolf writing: "The Diary proves [Murasaki Shikibu's] dramatic sense, as the 'Genji' would also do could it find so sympathetic a translator."[127] Presumably "so sympathetic" means as sympathetic as Annie Shepley Omori and Dōi Kochi, the translators of the *Diaries*. But considering that Lowell did not simply write "find a translator" as well as her broad familiarity with East Asian literatures in translation, I suspect that it is also a subtle poke at Suematsu. It is rather ironic, in light of the problems that some readers have had with the male gender of all *Genji monogatari*'s translators to date, to note that Lowell was, in fact, the person who recommended Waley's *The Tale of Genji* to Houghton Mifflin, which published the American edition.[128] Or perhaps, considering the matter in a different light, we might note in passing that one of the most often quoted lines in Woolf's review—where she declares that "the Lady Murasaki is not going to prove herself the peer of Tolstoi and Cervantes or those other great writers of the Western world whose ancestors were fighting or squatting in their huts while she gazed from her lattice window at flowers which unfold themselves 'like the lips of people smiling at their own thoughts' "—reads like a reply to Suematsu's suggestion that readers of *Genji Monogatari* might compare the society it depicts with those of medieval and modern

Europe.¹²⁹ The likelihood that Woolf knew nothing of Suematsu's translation does not matter. Like so many other post-Waley readers, she was enmeshed in a history more extensive than she knew.

An Eastern Don Juan

The more we look into the decades of discourse that circulated in the wake of Suematsu's publication of *Genji Monogatari*, the clearer it becomes that many of the central elements of what is generally regarded as twentieth-century, post-Waley *Genji* discourse are actually much older. The review of volume 1 of Waley's translation in the *Literary Digest International Book Review* that I mentioned earlier, for instance—the one that so irked Ida M. Mellen—was titled "Escapades of a Don Juan of Old Japan." The comparison of Genji, and even other characters in the book, with Don Juan recurs so frequently in reviews of *The Tale of Genji*'s six volumes, and so many of these texts were penned by such famous figures, that we might be forgiven for succumbing to the impression that this is where the pairing first emerged: Katherine Angell, the influential first fiction editor of the *New Yorker*, who had joined that magazine's staff a month earlier, described Genji as the "Don Juan of the East" in the *Saturday Review* in September 1925; the same year, the author Francis Bickley wrote in the *Bookman* (London), "To Don Juan, to Casanova, to whatever names have become symbolical in the legend or history of amorous adventure, may be added the name of Genji," and the *Independent* called Genji a "charming, sleepy Japanese Don Juan."¹³⁰ In July 1926, the *Dial* observed that Genji "is Hamlet and Don Juan in one, handsome, irresistible, sensitive, self-accusing, and dressed, on occasion, in a way to make Francis the First and the present Prince of Wales look tawdry."¹³¹ In March 1927, a notice in the *Bookman* (London) of the third volume of *The Tale of Genji* claimed, "There is not much new to be said about the adventures of Prince Genji, the Japanese Don Juan whom Mr. Arthur Waley has revealed to us"—an opinion seconded in April in the *Bookman* (New York), by the conservative political thinker and literary critic Isabel Paterson, who wrote only that the volume "continues the amorous and other adventures of that engaging Japanese Don Juan, Prince Genji."¹³² In a lengthy 1928 review of the fourth volume in the *Bookman* (New York), Conrad Aiken marvels that Murasaki Shikibu "should have given us, in Prince Genji himself, perhaps the most sympathetic and humane and, *ipso facto*, the wisest, portrait of a Don Juan that can be found in literature."¹³³ Waley's Genji stands reflected from every side, as though in a hall of mirrors, as Don Hikaru, creating a sense that this discourse is both self-reflexive and closed.

Yet here, too, Waley's readers were joining a discussion in medias res. *Saint James Gazette*, the *Manchester Guardian*, and *Englishwoman's Review* had likened Genji to Don Juan in their reviews of Suematsu's *Genji Monogatari*, while the *Japan Gazette* had described him as a Lothario. Arvède Barine's rewriting of the first two chapters of Suematsu's translation was titled "Un don Juan japonais." *Sunrise Stories* describes Genji as "a sort of Japanese Don Juan."¹³⁴ In 1897, Francesco de Simone Brouwer published a whole book on Don Juan in Italian, *Ancora Don Giovanni* (*Don Giovanni Again*), in which he introduces the *"Romanzo di Genji"*: "In it are recounted the many conquests and amorous adventures of Prince Genji, who is in all respects the Don Giovanni of our century."¹³⁵ A footnote refers the reader to Suematsu's *Genji Monogatari*. When Frederick Victor Dickins mentions *Genji* in his translation *The Old Bamboo-Hewer's Story* (1888), he gives this citation: "Many chapters of this history of a Japanese Don Juan have been recently translated by Mr. Suyematsu."¹³⁶

One could easily turn up dozens of similar examples. Perhaps I might best conclude, however, by offering one final instance of a display of Genji–Don Juanism that bears an uncertain relationship to Suematsu's translation, but involves a bit of interlingual circulation and thus brings us back to the issue with which I opened this chapter: the global circulation of images of *Genji*. On May 5, 1906, the French writer Léon Charpentier published an essay in *Le Figaro*'s literary supplement, "Un Don Juan dans la littérature japonaise" (A Don Juan in Japanese Literature), in which he shares his discovery that "the legendary type [of Don Juan] is hardly a creation unique to our Occidental literatures" and recounts at length the "characteristic episode" of Genji's adventures with Yūgao, whom he calls "Gloire du Matin" (Morning Glory). Charpentier makes no mention of Suematsu's translation, though he does in a slightly longer version of the essay that appeared eleven days later in *La grande revue*. In Charpentier's telling of the tale, after Gloire du Matin dies, killed by "a sort of flying flame, the spirit of Rokujio," Genji returns to the palace and meets "a young woman, more lovely and charming than any of the women he had encountered so far." Her name was Tayu. "She had a fiancé, poor like her and without a protector. For a smile from her, Genji promised he would give her fiancé honors and fortune. She smiled; she smiled so prettily that her poor fiancé lost everything." After this, Charpentier rushes ahead to the end of Genji's adventures, "until the day when the ambition to govern men entered into him" and he chanced across a charming girl named Violet during a stroll in the countryside at Suma, and she became his wife.[137]

This is a somewhat muddled account of *Genji monogatari*, albeit not as muddled as Georges Bousquet's. But like Bousquet's dismissal, by way of Chamberlain's misquotation, of *cette ennuyeuse Scudéry japonaise*, it was eye-catching, it served a purpose, and it got around. Later in 1906, the Spanish magazine *Cultura española* (*Spanish Culture*) reported that Charpentier had shown that "el tipo legendario de Don Juan no es una creación particular de nuestras literaturas occidentales"—translating the same phrase I translated at the top of the previous paragraph—and said a bit about Charpentier's essay.[138] The article "Don Juan as a Japanese Literary Character," which ran in the July 1906 issue of *Current Literature*, introduced Charpentier's "discovery" to an American audience. The article opens with a reference to an earlier discovery of Charpentier's, news of which *Current Literature* had also reported:

> "Don Quixote," as has recently been shown by a French writer, Léon Charpentier (see *Current Literature*, June), was a Japanese, Oriental creation long before a Western artist conceived and painted him. Now it seems that "Don Juan" also has a Japanese prototype.
>
> The same French writer, who is apparently exploring the ancient and forgotten realms of Japanese legendary lore and romance, announces the discovery of a full-grown Japanese Don Juan. He cannot find anything in the Western character, so long a favorite with novelists, poets, librettists and dramatists, that the Oriental creator of the type did not think of and put into the picture. In fact, the Japanese "Don Juan" is a singularly rich, brilliant, colorful study.
>
> Details of this work are given in an article in the Paris *Figaro*. The Japanese Don Juan is called Genji, and the romance in which his amorous adventures are set forth is entitled "Genji Monogatari." The romance is in fifty-four books or parts, and "seems a trifle long even to the Japanese."[139]

And finally, some seven years later, Eduard Bittcher published an essay in *Der Sammler* (*Collector*) called "Ein Don Juan in der japanischen Literatur" (A Don Juan in Japanese Literature) that was essentially a translation of Charpentier's article.[140]

Welcome to World Literature

I have devoted a fair amount of space to showing that several significant elements of modern and contemporary *Genji* discourse in English and various European languages that are generally assumed to have emerged in response to Waley's *The Tale of Genji* can in fact be traced back further, to the decades following the publication of Suematsu's *Genji Monogatari*. In the end, however, it is less the greater age of these discourses that matters than it is their character, and the fact that they were *circulating*, and circulating in a certain way. When Léon Charpentier "discovers" a Japanese Don Quixote and a Japanese Don Juan, he is in effect postulating a sort of literary equivalency between "legendary types" in Japan and Europe. He sees Genji and Don Juan and their innumerable loves silhouetted in the lamplight of a literary universalism that makes them appear to him as shadows of a single impulse. Europe has its Don Juan, its Don Giovanni, its Lothario; Japan has its Genji. "Here he is, a Japanese Don Giovanni of the tenth century who could pretend to be an ancestor of the Spanish Tenorio," de Simone Brouwer writes in *Ancora Don Giovanni*.[141] These men are related to one another. There is something subtly alluring in this recognition. And so the discovery of a family resemblance is made the subject of articles in Spain, Germany, and the United States—the news gets around. People begin to talk about the fact that people elsewhere are talking about the fact that a figure they had thought local and unique is really just one manifestation of a universal type found even in the most remote of island nations, and his uniqueness and local flavor obtain solely in his deviation from the type. "One has noticed, no doubt," Charpentier writes, "the differences that give Genji and Don Juan their particular character."[142] In this manner, Genji is reborn as "a *sort* of Japanese Don Juan." In this way, *Genji* itself comes to be recanonized as world literature and as a Japanese classic, a local manifestation of the universal type.

This, ultimately, is what we are witnessing when we trace the four decades of discourse about *Genji* that arose in the wake of Suematsu's *Genji Monogatari*. We glimpse it, if only sporadically, in the reviews: the *Japan Gazette*, after commenting "that the nation which preserved for nearly a thousand years the story of the doings of Genji and his companions . . . can have but little good, healthy mental food," goes on to admit that this reflection "would not be quite just; and it may be said that though Boccaccio is classical in Italy, all the Italian classics are not like Boccaccio."[143] *Harper's* notes that *Genji monogatari* "is as well known in Japan as the novels of Le Sage are in Spain, or those of Balzac in

France, or of Thackeray in England."[144] Just as Genji is a different Don Juan, so Murasaki Shikibu is a different Boccaccio, Le Sage, Balzac, Thackeray. In *A History of Japanese Literature*, W. G. Aston countered unnamed Japanese critics who "claim for the *Genji* that it surpasses anything of the kind in Chinese literature, and even deserves to be ranked with the masterpieces of European fiction," asserting that none but an extreme Japanophile "will go so far as to place Murasaki no Shikibu on a level with Fielding, Thackeray, Victor Hugo, Dumas, and Cervantes," but his condescension was rooted in a consciousness that the comparison itself could certainly be made—that each nation has its own list of recognized classics and that the lists are parallel.[145] The previous year, in fact, Aston had opened the talk he delivered to the Japan Society of London, "The Classical Literature of Japan," by arguing explicitly in favor of this world-literary view:

> The foregoing title will probably suggest the inquiry whether the Japanese have any literature which can be justly styled "classical." I venture to answer this question in the affirmative. No doubt the term must be taken with a difference, as is so often the case in connection with "things Japanese." We hardly expect to find in any Eastern country anything like an exact counterpart of the classical literatures of Greece and Rome. But I think it will be found that the essentials are not wanting.[146]

Again, in Samuel Butler's obituary we are informed that *Genji* "occupies to a certain extent the same position in Japanese literature that the Odyssey occupies in the literature of Greece"—a judgment with which Adachi Kinnosuke concurred in 1906: "The position [*Genji monogatari*] occupies in our literature is similar to that occupied by Homer's work in Hellenic literature, and by Shakespeare's works in English literature."[147] Here she is: a Japanese authoress who could pretend to be an ancestor of Fielding, Hugo, Dumas, Cervantes, and Shakespeare. Murasaki Shikibu has taken her place, and *Genji* has taken its place, on the mirrored merry-go-round of images that is world literature.

It is worth noting that those last two quotations were taken from passages that I cited in discussing Murasaki Shikibu's invocation as evidence of the "position of women" in Japan. Ultimately, the circulation of discourse about Murasaki Shikibu as a talented woman, which was underwritten by a new interest in the "universal sisterhood of woman" that developed in the late 1880s and the 1890s—the notion that women in Europe and Japan and everywhere else were no more than different, local variations on a single universal type—was also necessarily implicated in the recanonization of *Genji* as a work of world literature. When Murasaki Shikibu was cited in discussions of the position of women in Japan, it mattered above all that she was recognized as having stature on an international scale. An essay called "The Geisha: A Faithful Study" by the celebrated horticulturalist Reginald J. Farrer, published in 1904 in the recently renamed *Nineteenth Century and After*, demonstrates this connection in the most explicit manner. "The wife," Farrer writes, "belongs to the one class to whom mental charms are not permitted. Japan has produced many female poets and authors—two, indeed, who stand near the world's front rank, Murasaki and Sei Shonagon. But all these have been, at least officially, maidens, or married unhappily, or ladies of glittering Bohemian ways."[148] This argument would have annoyed Adachi Kinnosuke extremely, and yet both men share the recognition that *Genji* is world literature.

It should be obvious that Suematsu's translation, rather than Waley's, initiated the long process of *Genji*'s recanonization as world literature. I noted earlier that three subsequent editions of *Genji Monogatari* were published in Japan and the United States after the first. The second, issued in 1900, was not an edition of the romance per se but an anthology, *The Literature of Japan*, edited by Epiphanius Wilson, that included the whole of *Genji Monogatari* along with Suematsu's introduction. The collection was published by the Colonial Press as part of the second of four volumes dealing with "Oriental Literature" in a series called the World's Great Classics. It would be hard to find more conclusive evidence that already in 1900, at least in English, *Genji Monogatari* was viewed, by some, as one of the world's great classics.

Why, then, has the history of that romance, Suematsu's *Genji Monogatari*, been so thoroughly forgotten? Why is it so easy to forget that Waley stood not at the beginning of the path that has been taken, but midway along it? Why can Donald Keene suggest in his otherwise very perceptive "Japanese Literature in the World" that Suematsu's work "seems to have exercised no influence on Western readers," and then go on to observe, "When the first volume of [Waley's] translation of *The Tale of Genji* appeared in 1923 [sic], the stunned reviewers groped for suitable comparisons with European literature, finding (because it was a court romance) similarities with *Le Morte d'Arthur*, or with Boccaccio because of the many love affairs, or with various other improbable works," without pausing to wonder whether these readers may actually have been repeating the reaction of those who first encountered Suematsu's translation?[149] In fact, a 1925 review in *Punch* unwittingly echoed an even older discourse, likening *The Tale of Genji* to "the aristocratic narratives of Scudéry and La Fayette."¹⁵⁰

The answer, I suspect, lies in the simple fact that Suematsu's translation was superseded as a replacement of *Genji monogatari* by Waley's, just as *Inaka Genji*, which created the notion of the popular replacement of the tale, as well as the desire and the market for works like it, eventually came to be replaced as a replacement by seemingly more faithful translations. And then there is the fact that Waley's translation itself has acquired canonical status: it may be replaced by new translations, but it is never entirely superseded. In her review of Royall Tyler's *The Tale of Genji*, in the *New York Times* in 2001, Janice P. Nimura wrote, "Until recently, English-speaking readers had a choice of two guides: Arthur Waley, who published the first translation of 'Genji' in the 1920's and 30's, and Edward Seidensticker, who delivered the second in 1976."¹⁵¹ Liza Dalby noted in her review of Tyler's translation for the *Los Angeles Times* that "'The Tale of Genji' stepped onto the stage of world literature in the late 1920s with the appearance of Arthur Waley's self-consciously literary translation into English."¹⁵² In both reviews, a discussion of Tyler's new translation occasions a backward glance at the history of *Genji* translations, of *Genji* discourse, of *Genji*'s life in world literature. And in both, Tyler's work elicits a reconfirmation of the canonical status and the enduring historical significance of Waley's, at the expense of Suematsu's.

I wrote in the "Touchstone" to this part that *Genji*'s modern recanonization as a masterpiece of world literature, as writing that has gained in translation, is as much the product of discourse about *Genji*'s global circulation as it is of the tale's circulation—that it is, indeed, largely a product of the global circulation of discourse concerning *Genji*'s global circulation. The continuing presence of Waley in this endless whirl of discourse, and the almost total erasure of Suematsu, indicates once again that when we talk about *Genji*, we are always calling on certain images of the tale and excluding others. In my introduction, I suggested that while the blue, bean-size guide to *Genji monogatari* published in Kyoto in 1749 could be understood as gesturing back toward some notion of an original text of the tale, it did so through the image and the medium of the early modern printed edition. We are caught up in the same mechanics of replacement, and our situation is no different. Whenever we speak of *Genji* today, we imagine it through an image created by the spread of modern translations, above all by Waley's, which did not establish *Genji* as world literature but stabilized its position there—and did so, I argue in chapter 5, by enabling the tale to gain a truly popular readership in Japan. We enter into a world of circulating discourse about *Genji* as world literature, of discourse about *Genji*'s global circulation as world literature, that contains within it a misapprehension, a blindness, an ignorance of its own prehistory. Or perhaps not a blindness, but a blindedness, in the dazzle of the carnival mirrors. It remains to be seen whether the creation of a new narrative can have any effect on such a situation.

SAME TIME, DIFFERENT PICTURE

Not Much of a Beginning

"It seems fair to say," Mitani Kuniaki once noted, "that Tsubouchi Shōyō's *The Essence of the Novel* stands as the point of departure for modern scholarship and criticism on *Genji monogatari*. In Shōyō's assessment, *Genji monogatari* was a 'romance' that 'is best described as a congenial instance of the social *monogatari*, dedicated to the depiction of life among the upper echelons.'" Mitani goes on to cite the well-known dictum with which the chapter "The Focus of the Novel" (Shōsetsu no shugan) begins: "In the novel, human emotions are paramount. Social conditions and customs come next."[153] This bold reframing of the concepts of literature, the novel, and criticism, he suggests, paved the way for modern Japanese interpretations of *Genji monogatari*. Mitani's perspective has been widely echoed in both Japanese- and English-language scholarship.

Once again, we are faced with the question of who our predecessors are. So much outstanding research has been done on the status that *Genji monogatari* occupied in Japan during the Meiji period that it seems almost redundant to add to the pile, but as I bring this chapter to a close I would like to sketch in broad strokes the contours of the situation as I see it, from a perspective focused on *Genji*'s recanonization as world literature. I want to suggest, first, that while Mitani's attention to the modern perspective that Shōyō so compellingly encapsulated in *The Essence of the Novel* is warranted, this perspective did not originate with Shōyō.[154] At the very least, Shōyō was picking up the thread of a discussion that Suematsu had initiated years earlier in London, and in letters and essays he mailed from London to Tokyo, where they were published in *Tōkyō nichinichi shinbun*. Or to be more precise, it could be said that Shōyō was picking up the thread of a transnational, translational conversation that Suematsu himself had *entered into*. That is the first point. The second is that although significant developments took place in Japanese-language *Genji monogatari* discourse during the last decades of the nineteenth century and the first decades of the twentieth, and while Suematsu played a role in bringing them about, these developments were not like those occurring in western Europe and the United States. While in those other contexts *Genji* was being reborn into world literature, in Japan, *Genji monogatari* was hardly even a national classic.

Letters from London

On August 22, 1884, *Tōkyō nichinichi shinbun* published an excerpt from a letter that Suematsu had sent to the paper's publisher and editor in chief—Fukuchi Gen'ichirō, Suematsu's former boss. The excerpt, which deals with painting, includes a number of references to "Eawase" (The Picture Contest) and other chapters of *Genji monogatari*, but it also touches briefly on the interpretation of the romance as a whole. Not surprisingly, Suematsu's stance echoes that developed in the introduction to his translation, in particular the passage in which he cites Genji's narratological seduction of Tamakazura in "Hotaru": "The title of the chapter in which it appears has slipped my mind," he writes, "but it is clear from the passage in which the purpose of the romance is elaborated, by putting the words in Genji's mouth, that *Genji*'s purpose lies in the depiction of human emotions and the tastes of its age."[155] In Japanese, the last phrase reads 源氏ノ主意ハ人情時好ヲ写すニ在ル. This is strikingly close to Shōyō's dictim "In the novel, human emotions are paramount. Social conditions and customs come next," especially in Japanese: 小説の主脳は人情なり。世態風俗これに次ぐ. I am not necessarily suggesting that Shōyō was influenced by Suematsu's letter—indeed, he had finished a draft of *The Essence of the Novel* by the time the letter was published. The point, rather, is that Shōyō's modern appraisal of *Genji monogatari*, like his view of the novel, was already enmeshed in a global discourse by the time he made it public, and that Suematsu played a major role in the establishment and circulation of this discourse in Japan, just as he had in London.

On September 10, 1884, *Tōkyō nichinichi shinbun* ran the first of six installments of Suematsu's long treatise "A Discourse on Poetry and Music" (Kagakuron). Suematsu begins by referring back to his August 22 letter, noting that he had neglected to mention a very important passage in *Genji monogatari* that deals with pictures. He quotes from the "Hahakigi" (The Broom Tree) chapter, "rewriting it in the prose of our time" (*jibun ni kakikae sōrō*), and then turns to William Anderson, the author of *The Pictorial Arts of Japan*, whom he had met the day before:

At the request of the British Library, he has written a book about Japanese art that is now being printed. He told me he frequently cites my English translation of *Genji monogatari*, which I published here two or three years ago. He explained his views to me: "From my observation of Japanese paintings, it seemed to me that Japanese painters devoted their efforts largely to fantastic paintings, or to birds and flowers, and I did not think that they gave much attention to real scenery. Judging from my reading of your translation of *Genji monogatari*, however, this does not appear to have been the case in that period. I have come to this conclusion because where the ways of society are concerned, *Genji* seems to have transcribed the facts. It is interesting to see, for instance, that in the 'Competitive Show of Pictures' chapter, Hikaru Genji's true pictures of Suma come in first."[156]

Here, too, we see *Genji monogatari* being treated as a faithful depiction of "the ways of society," and here, too, this view emerges from what is by now a familiarly uroboric process of translation and back-translation: Suematsu translates into Japanese Anderson's take on Suematsu's English translation of the Japanese *Genji monogatari*. Naturally, Anderson's comments jibe perfectly with, or perhaps echo, Suematsu's own vision of *Genji Monogatari* as outlined in his introduction—an understanding that itself arose, as I noted earlier, in the convergence of a set of theories of fiction that derived from early modern Japan, on the one hand, and England, on the other.

Suematsu continued to make similar observations about *Genji monogatari*'s adherence to social reality in other essays published throughout the 1880s and 1890s, ranging from "Further Thoughts on Poetry, Music, and Painting" (Kagaku kaiga yoron, 1885) to "The Position of the 'Genji Monogatari' in Japanese Literature"—really a reprint of the original introduction to *Genji Monogatari*, with a new introduction to the introduction—which appeared in 1897 in the *Hansei Zasshi*, the English- and sometimes French-language sister publication of *Hansei zasshi* (*Temperance*), forerunner of *Chūōkōron* (*Central Forum*).[157] Sometimes Suematsu refers to *Genji monogatari* in contexts not directly related to the work, and here, too, his attitude remains the same. In the February 26, 1887, edition of *Jogaku zasshi* (*Journal of Women's Education*), for instance, we find a letter Suematsu submitted in response to an essay by the prominent Confucian educator Nishimura Shigeki. Nishimura had stated in the first installment of "Voluntary Marriage" (Danjo aierabu no setsu) that in the past, marriages in Japan had been duolocal, with the husband paying visits to his wife at her parents' house, but that this appeared to have been the custom only for commoners; ranking courtiers and officials brought their wives to live with them at their own residences.[158] Suematsu points out that courtiers did in fact practice duolocal marriage, and cites Hikaru Genji's marriage to Aoi no Ue as his evidence. In this case, *Genji monogatari* serves not simply as an outstanding example of historically informative fiction, but as an actual historical source.[159]

Perhaps it was merely a coincidence that just two weeks after Suematsu's letter was printed in *Jogaku zasshi*, a selection from the "Hahakigi" chapter of *Genji monogatari* in which the Chief Equerry (Sama no Kami) sets out his views on the ideal wife was published in the same journal, ending with a condensation of the very passage that Suematsu rewrote in "A Discourse on Poetry and Music." The selection, translated into a mixed *kana* and *kanji* style deemed appropriate for the journal's readership and titled "Women Classified" (Onna no shinajina), was accompanied by yet another take on the standard representation of Murasaki Shikibu and by what is said to be a sample of her calligraphy (figure 120).[160] Whether this replacement of *Genji monogatari* was inspired by Suematsu's letter is unimportant; what matters is that readers of *Jogaku zasshi* encountered in quick succession his invocation of *Genji monogatari* as a historical source, a translated excerpt from the text, and a picture of Murasaki Shikibu. Suematsu's historical reading came to be superimposed, in a sense, on both Murasaki Shikibu's text and her portrait. Indeed, this is precisely why the sample of her calligraphy was provided—it is a document, an invocation of history. The squiggly lines that mar the writing here and there represent holes left by bookworms and emphasize *this* text's status as a bibliographic translation of an ancient original. Marking the materiality of a bit of old paper imbues even this stylistically modern depiction of Murasaki Shikibu with historical meaning.

Genji monogatari in the Academy

This is one example of the way in which Suematsu's writings on *Genji monogatari* connect with other representations of the work and its author in Japanese mass media. Equally significant, on another level, are the connections one might draw with certain shifts taking place in academic contexts. *Genji Monogatari* was published in London in 1882. This also happened to be the year in which the Course for the Study of the Classics (Koten Kōshūka) was established at what was then called the University of Tokio. The rationale for the creation of this new program is set out in the "Historical Summary" at the beginning of *Tokio Daigaku*

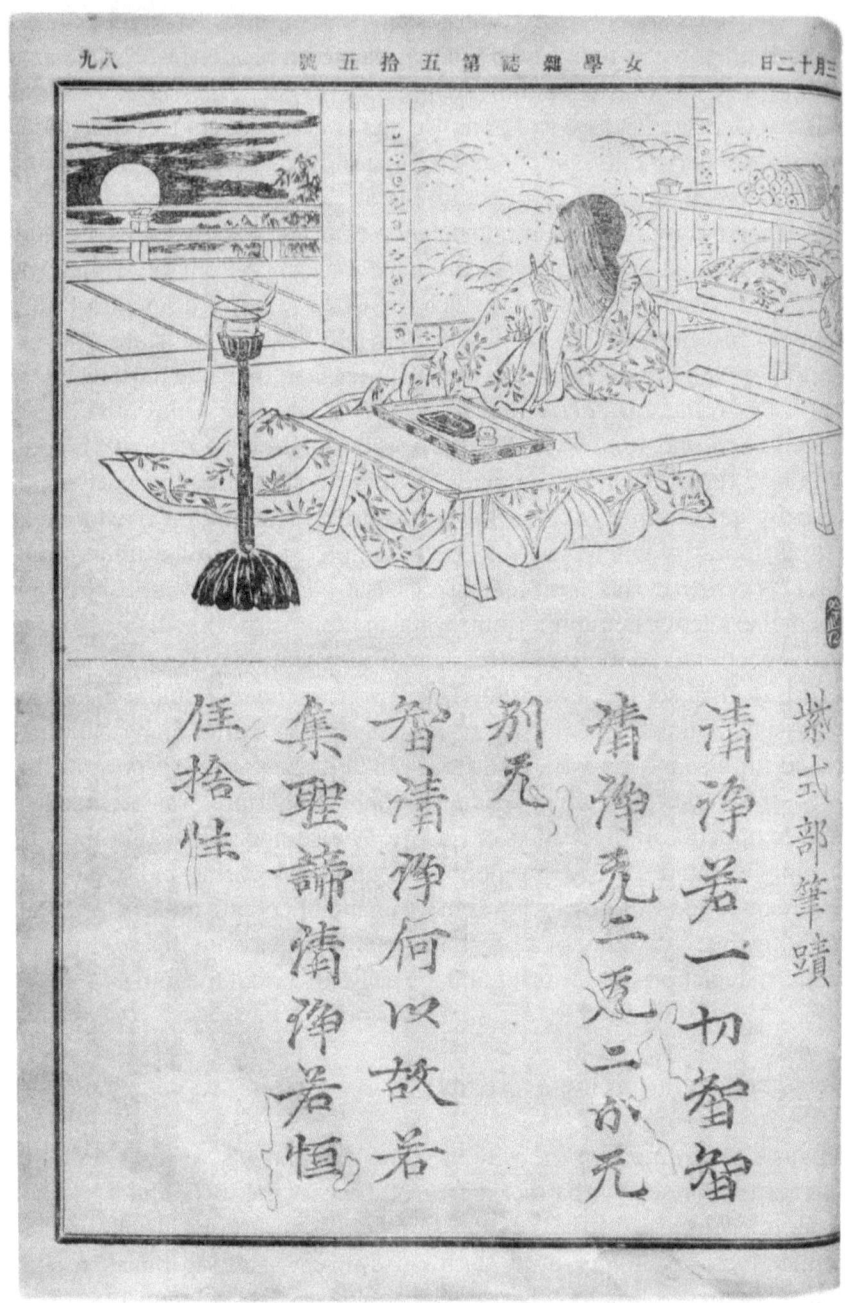

Figure 120 Murasaki Shikibu and what is said to be a reproduction of her calligraphy. ([Murasaki Shikibu,] "Onna no shinajina," *Jogaku zasshi*, March 12, 1887, 89. Courtesy of National Diet Library)

(*University of Tokio*): *The Calendar of the Departments of Law, Science, and Literature, 2542–43 (1882–83)*:

> On the 30th of July, Koten Kōshiū Kua (a course in Japanese classics including ancient laws and history) was established.
>
> In this country there were, and still are, so called Kokugakusha (those who have specifically devoted themselves to the above studies) and they have hitherto been separated into several schools, each pursuing its special branch such as Shintooism, Poetry, etc. Most of the Kokugakusha, being far behind the present times in their progress, afford no assistance to the direct needs of society, and so they are looked upon as almost useless.
>
> Such a state of things, if continued, would have a tendency to cause these studies themselves to be neglected.
>
> Ancient laws, history, poetry and other literary works, however, are of great value to the historians as well as to the student of Sociology, Political Science, Rhetoric, etc., who could not study their respective subjects without reference to the above branches of learning.
>
> Nevertheless, if this present state were to remain for any length of time without improvement, a lack of men who have sufficient knowledge in those studies would be the inevitable consequence, which must be avoided for the sake of the country at large.[161]

A still more explicit statement of the course's purpose appears in the description of the program itself: "The object of this course being to investigate historical facts, old laws, etc., in such a way as to satisfy the direct needs of society, the students are required during the fifth and sixth terms to write an essay on the investigation of some old facts or systems, such as the old system of taxation, old military system, etc."[162] Clearly, this was not a program in the "literary classics" of the sort we might conceive today: classical texts were to be mined for the facts they contained, and their study was expected to answer societal needs in a direct and verifiable manner.

When Suematsu's letters began to appear in *Tōkyō nichinichi shinbun* in August 1884, a year before the first booklet of Shōyō's *The Essence of the Novel*, the thirty-six students admitted to the Course for the Study of the Classics in September 1882, and their juniors in the short-lived course's second and final class, were on summer vacation. *Genji monogatari* was among the works the students in the course to began read in their first year, and if they came across Suematsu's statements on it, they would have found that his understanding of its importance coincided with their university's. Indeed, the same held for students in every course of study in the Department of Literature: students in the Course of Japanese and Chinese Literature studied *Genji monogatari* during their second and third years; students in the Courses of Philosophy, Political Science, and Political Economy studied it in their third.[163] Thus the mid-1880s witnessed the emergence of an intellectual elite trained to approach *Genji monogatari* from a perspective substantially similar to Suematsu's.

Like Suematsu, some of these early students of "the classics" at Tokio University—renamed the Imperial University in 1886 and Tokio Imperial University in 1897—began to think about how *Genji monogatari* might be situated and evaluated vis-à-vis other literatures and to publish essays and books intended for a wide readership that touched on these issues. It is crucial to note, however, that these writings, which constitute a tiny first step along the path toward *Genji monogatari*'s domestic replacement as world literature, were not accompanied by a dramatic shift away from the notion that "there is no better history" than Murasaki Shikibu's story. This overlapping of a nascent world-literary perspective with an enduring historical bent is perfectly illustrated by two articles serialized in *Yomiuri shinbun*, each in four parts and each a condensed version of a lecture, the first by Mikami Sanji (1865-1939) in 1889 and the second by Takatsu Kuwasaburō (1864-1921) in 1895. Both Mikami and Takatsu had enrolled in the newly renamed Course in Japanese Letters (Wabun Gakuka) at Tokio University in 1885—the year before Basil Hall Chamberlain joined the course as a professor of linguistics.[164] In 1890, the year after they graduated, they published the first full-scale history of Japanese literature, *A History of Japanese Literature* (*Nihon bungakushi*).

Mikami's article is introduced as "a discussion of Murasaki Shikibu and Sei Shōnagon" taken from a longer lecture about Japanese literature in general. Mikami begins by noting that *Genji monogatari* and *The Pillow Book* "have long been admired as unparalleled treasures among our nation's literary works," and then explains the value of a comparative perspective: "In discussing the strengths and weaknesses of a thing, its beauties and its faults, insofar as these words are all rooted in comparisons, the more we expand the range of our comparison, the more a given beauty stands revealed in its beauty, and the more clearly we see the nature of each strength revealed as a strength."[165] Then, having noted the enthusiasm with which Japanese art had been received at the Philadelphia International Exhibition in 1876 and the Paris Exposition Universelle in 1878, he moves into a discussion of the relative merits of *Genji monogatari* and *The Pillow Book* in an international context:

People will hardly fault me for suggesting not only that certain passages in these two books, *Genji monogatari* and *Makura no sōshi*, are by no means inferior to Chinese prose, but that certain sections appear more excellent by virtue of the comparison—but what if one should proceed to compare them to the literature of the West, to ask which of these is superior and which inferior?—one must concede that Western writing has its strong points, and in many respects both *Genji monogatari* and *Makura no sōshi* are far indeed from approaching them. And yet the comparison allows their light to shine all the more brilliantly, and we see still more clearly the particular beauties they embody. Indeed our nation, like others, possesses a unique literature, one of which we need not feel ashamed before the world—and naturally the rise and fall of a literature is part and parcel of the fate of the nation. . . . How could anyone born in our Japanese homeland feel anything but reverence for these two women, just as Germans do for Goethe and Schiller, and as the English do for Shakespeare and Milton?[166]

There is no mistaking the world-literary perspective here. At the same time, though, one wonders what the implied answer to that final rhetorical question is: *They couldn't, of course!* or *That's a good question.* Given that in 1889 the work was not available in an affordable, compact form—as I noted in chapter 1, no new text of *Genji monogatari* had been published since a reprint of *Shusho Genji monogatari* was issued in fifty-six volumes in 1706—it was undoubtedly less widely read than Mikami would have liked. *Genji monogatari* may have been generally recognized as a "national treasure," but it was not yet being widely read as a national classic.[167]

Indeed, in the second installment of this article we find Mikami attempting, through a rather humorous deployment of metaphor—a literal re-placement of his authors in the modern world—to help his readers move beyond the notion of *Genji monogatari* as a national treasure and see the two women and their writings in connection to their own lives:

> Sei Shōnagon was very much in tune with the fashions of her day, forever priding herself in her scholarship and failing to keep a handle on housework—describing her in terms of our own time, one might say she resembles a young woman educated at a Christian school who not only thinks nothing at all of standing upon an equal footing with the boys but tries her hand at argumentation, going so far as to insert, here and there, every so often, a bit of English, proclaiming no less than equal rights for men and woman—just such a spirited woman is

she. Murasaki Shikibu, by contrast, is like a wife who, having received an equally exalted education, continues nevertheless to moderate her words and actions in the manner of the *Greater Learning for Women*, obeying the wisdom imparted to her, in her tender years, at her parents' knees.[168]

This zestful presentation of two classical figures in contemporary dress—reminiscent of *Inaka Genji*, steeped in the early modern logic of replacement encapsulated in such terms as *yatsushi* (dressing down), *mitate* (seeing-as), and *imayō* (modernizing)—comes as something of a surprise, given that Mikami had concluded the first installment of his essay by asking how any Japanese could fail to show reverence for these same two women. In fact, the "dressing down" is best understood in connection with that very question: the type of reverence that Mikami has in mind is born, we see, not of a sense of distance and unapproachability, but of proximity and familiarity. In the end, it was a replacement of precisely this sort that would be necessary if *Genji monogatari* was to be recanonized in Japan as world and thus national literature: *Genji monogatari* would have to be presented in a framework that made it seem personally relevant, miraculously modern.

Takatsu's article, published six years after Mikami's under the title "Emotions and Customs in the Age of *Genji monogatari*" (*Gengo jidai no ninjō fūzoku*), is also introduced as an excerpt from a longer lecture, this one delivered to the Shigakukai, or History Study Group.[169] It shows quite clearly how strong the inclination to interpret *Genji monogatari* in historical terms remained:

> Because Murasaki Shikibu was herself on the spot and witnessed those scenes, one finds if one observes *Genji monogatari* closely that, while it records nothing beyond the reign of Emperor Ichijō, it actually does depict realistically the days of the Heian court, when the power of the Fujiwara was at its most extreme; which is to say that *Genji monogatari* can in fact be described as a photograph of its age. For me, drawing on this work, to say this and that about the emotions and customs of that time, as I will now—for me, that is to say, to take up a *monogatari* (a novel, as we would say today), a made-up story, and go on about it, would seem on the face of it to have no bearing whatsoever on the study of history. And yet if one should, just for the sake of it, take up certain facts from within *Genji monogatari* and look for confirmation of them back in those times, a good deal of it will surely ring true.[170]

Takatsu goes on to discuss the lives of both elites and commoners in the Heian capital, touching on various arts, Buddhism, the role women played in politics, and relations between women and men, and closes with a discussion of Murasaki Shikibu's morality and that of her age. The historical approach to *Genji monogatari* remained fundamental in 1895. Indeed, Suematsu's former boss at *Tōkyō nichinichi shinbun*, Fukuchi Gen'ichirō, delivered a lecture titled "On Japanese *Monogatari*" (Nihon no monogatari ni tsuite) to the Shigakukai in 1902 in which he made essentially the same argument about *monogatari*, and *Genji monogatari* in particular, except that rather than focus on the historical dimensions of *monogatari*, he addressed the relevance of *monogatari* to history from a historiographical perspective. "My friends," he concluded, "I would be so bold as to suggest that true history really has no choice but to rely on *monogatari*."[171]

Praised but Unread

So far, I have focused on discourse about *Genji monogatari* in Japanese mass media from the mid-1880s to the mid-1890s and slightly beyond; I have tried to show that Suematsu was among the movers and shakers who first set this discourse in motion. This is important for two reasons. First, it allows us to situate the academic and disciplinary developments that were taking place in the context of the university, changes that have been subjected to much scrutiny in recent years, within a broader discursive field. And second, it lets us see more clearly how—by means of what connections—domestic developments were bound up in larger transnational, translational shifts. It reveals that *Genji monogatari* discourse in Japanese was already starting to overlap with *Genji* discourse in English and other languages.

At the same time, Mikami's article in particular directs our attention toward a crucial element of the situation within Japan that made it more difficult for *Genji monogatari* to be recanonized as a classic of world and national literature domestically than it was abroad. For if, as I suggested at the outset of this part, a work of literature becomes a work of world literature through the circulation of discourse about its global circulation, its image as world literature is also underwritten—or was in the late nineteenth century—by the assumption that it is popular "at home," and presumably not in translation. Again and again in the reviews of Suematsu's translation, it was simply taken for granted that *Genji* was widely read in Japan. The same assumption could not be made within Japan, of course.

In order for *Genji monogatari* to be convincingly presented domestically as a national classic, rather than simply a "national treasure," people actually had to be reading it or at least buying it.

This raises a crucial question: How many people in Japan were reading *Genji monogatari* in the 1880s and 1890s? And more to the point, how many were reading it as literature? The answer, in fact, is that while very few were reading *Genji monogatari* in 1889, when Mikami's lecture was serialized in *Yomiuri shinbun*, many were reading it in 1890 and would go on reading it—in various types of replacements, sometimes in bursts—throughout the Meiji period and beyond. But they were not yet revering it the way the Germans did Goethe and Schiller, and the English did Shakespeare and Milton.

The year 1890 witnessed what might be described as the first in a series of *Genji monogatari* "booms" in Japan—or the second, if we count the long *Inaka Genji* craze that began in the 1830s. A few books related to *Genji monogatari* had already been published in the Meiji period, notably Suzuki Hiroyasu's *A Lecture on Genji monogatari* (*Genji monogatari kōgi*, 1884-1888) and Masuda Ushin's (Masuda Yukinobu) *A New Edition of Murasaki's History; or, A Common Genji monogatari* (*Shinpen Shishi: Ichimei tsūzoku Genji monogatari*, 1888-1904). Suzuki's work was perhaps the first to suggest, using exactly the same phrase that Shōyō would repeat, that *Genji monogatari*'s "larger point" was "the accurate depiction of social conditions and customs" (*setai fūzoku o yoku utsushi*), even though Suzuki explicitly rejected the notion that *Genji monogatari* could be compared with a history.[172] *A New Edition of Murasaki's History* represented the first modern endeavor to "rewrite [*Genji monogatari*] in the prose of our time" (*jibun o motte kore o utsushiaratame*), as Suematsu put it once again in his *kanbun* (all-*kanji* prose) foreword to the work's first volume.[173] But while both these books were given notices in newspapers and attracted a certain amount of attention, they were clearly published in response to a perceived need to make *Genji monogatari* better known, rather than a perceived demand for new texts.

We see this, for instance, in Suematsu's foreword to *A New Edition of Murasaki's History* when he writes: "Extremely numerous are they who have heard stories about the book *Genji*; extremely few are they who have read it."[174] We see it, perhaps, in the inclusion of translated excerpts from seven of the reviews of Suematsu's *Genji Monogatari* in the front of the book "to show how this work has been honored"—the first attempt I have encountered to use discourse about the global circulation of discourse about *Genji monogatari* to enhance its domestic image.[175] We see it in a review of *A New Edition of Murasaki's History* in *Yomiuri shinbun*, which says of *Genji monogatari*: "There are many sections in it that are not easily understood, and it has hardly any readers."[176] And we see it in Masuda's charming preface, in which he recounts what is presumably a fictional encounter with Murasaki Shikibu at Kiyomizu Hall during a walk in Ueno Park one moonlit evening—the combination of the moon and the "clear water" of "Kiyomizu" recalling the Lake Biwa legend—in what turns out to be a dream. It is worth quoting Masuda at some length, not least because his preface reveals the fraught status that *Inaka Genji* was coming to occupy as the notion of the "original text," which it itself had popularized, became increasingly important and because it illustrates so perfectly the dynamics of replacement:

> Embarrassing as it was to have a *monogatari* I dashed off hastily, still in an unpolished form, admired so widely, and then to see it relished so by people even in later times, it is also deeply gratifying. And now to have learned Doctors of a future age clarify, despite all the changes that have transfigured the world, words that grow ever more distant with each passing era, and without altering, even a millennium later, its original form—again and again, I am humbled. And yet, there was a man by the name of Ryūtei something or other who took my tale and transformed it drastically into the style of a later age, so that all the people of the world, even women and girls, knew only the name Mitsuuji, and the august light of Hikaru Kimi hid itself above the clouds, and the moon above Suma and Akashi went dark. Now, in this Great Era ruled by Clarity [*mei ni osamaru* (that is, Meiji)], when His Nine-Fold august Light, so long and distressingly encased in masses of cloud, shines brilliantly forth throughout the world—how I wished there were some way to brush more shine into Hikaru Kimi's light, as well, in keeping with the tenor of the time. But since there was no one I might ask for help, time passed in vain until I heard today that you had come to this building, and I appeared suddenly like this before you, she said. Sure I must be dreaming, I was unable immediately to reply, but then: Ah, alas—your poor, exalted *monogatari*. In all there are no fewer than thirty-some-odd commentaries on it, starting with Koreyuki no Ason's *Endnotes*, expanded upon by Lord Teika, and continuing on to the present day. But none goes beyond picking at words and phrases, explicating terms, these books are no more than toys for scholars and poets; thus, in order to allow Genji's august light to shine brilliantly forth throughout the world, one must first make it easy for even ordinary people to read and understand this *monogatari*. Easily said, but nearly a thousand years have passed

since you inhabited the world, and people today will not likely understand it as it is. It is bound to be difficult to carry out your wishes unless we dye the work again before sending it out into the world, not in the Bumpkin style of that Ryūtei man you mentioned, but in a shade identical to its original purple, I told her, and the woman nodded and said, I entrust it to your brush, and no sooner had I watched her descend the steps than I awoke. The moon had swung low in the sky, and only the sound of the wind in the pines on the peak was clearly audible, blowing past my pillow.[177]

This is an extremely rich passage. One notices, first of all, that while Murasaki Shikibu herself (as channeled by Masuda) confirms my argument in chapter 1 that *Inaka Genji*, and above all Mitsuuji, came to stand in the eyes of "all the people of the world, even women and girls," as an image of *Genji monogatari*, she expresses no gratitude to Tanehiko for extending the canonicity of her *monogatari*. She considers Tanehiko's "transformation" of her writing an imposition and goes so far as to implicitly blame *Inaka Genji* for creating an environment in which "the august light of Hikaru Kimi" had no choice but to "[hide] itself above the clouds." The use of the phrase "above the clouds" (*kumo no ue*), a conventional epithet for the imperial palace, and the repetition of "august light" and "His Nine-Fold august Light" create a parallel between Hikaru Genji and Emperor Meiji, implying that *Inaka Genji* had illegitimately usurped *Genji monogatari*'s position, in much the same way that the shoguns, from a post–Meiji Restoration perspective, had taken power from the imperial line. This is what makes it "in keeping with the tenor of the time" to "brush more shine into Hikaru Kimi's light": the Meiji emperor has regained his rightful place at the head of government, and so it is time for *Genji monogatari* to take its place at the head of the Japanese literary canon. Yet when Masuda responds to Murasaki Shikibu, he speaks in terms that resonate with the "fake purple" (*nise murasaki*) in the title of Tanehiko's work, saying that he will need to "dye the work again before sending it out into the world, not in the Bumpkin style of that Ryūtei man you mentioned, but in a shade identical to its original purple." The whole point of *A New Edition of Murasaki's History*, in other words, is to try to replace *Inaka Genji* with a more "faithful" version of the original that *it* replaced: to remind readers that there are more *Genji*s out there than just *Inaka Genji*.

Perhaps the best evidence that in the 1880s *Genji monogatari* was not yet widely read comes, however, from Mikami Sanji himself, who confesses in the concluding lines of his article on Sei Shōnagon and Murasaki Shikibu that "I have not yet really delved into this book, so I based my appraisal of it solely on a summary."[178] Indeed, even Suematsu admits—in a letter to *Tōkyō nichinichi shinbun* dated August 22, 1884—that he has "yet to read the chapters at the end very carefully."[179] If these two men had not read all of *Genji monogatari*, we can be sure that very few had.

The Boom in 1890

This situation changed dramatically in the autumn of 1890. All of a sudden, for the first time in nearly two centuries, the text of *Genji monogatari* was made newly available in the form of not one but *three* separate typeset editions, with a fourth appearing in 1891.[180] All but one of these are bibliographic translations of Kitamura Kigin's *Kogetsushō*. And their publication was welcomed: *Genji monogatari* became something of a fad—so much so that a "Master Among Clouds" (Unchūshi) was prompted to contribute this prediction to the October 25, 1890, issue of *Yomiuri shinbun*: "*By next summer*: Feverish interest in *old* national literature will abate. We will stop seeing people make such a to-do about *Genji monogatari* and so on."[181]

In part, no doubt, this sudden surge in interest can be explained by the simple circumstance that relatively inexpensive editions had finally become available, and perhaps to a certain extent by the fact that they were relatively easy to read—though the point should not be overemphasized, since the new editions were remarkably faithful to the format of the original woodblock-printed *Kogetsushō*, printing the text, for instance, without paragraph breaks or quotations marks. Their main innovation lay precisely in their use of movable type, and readers were still accustomed to reading at least certain types of woodblock-printed writing. As it happens, Suematsu was among the first to anticipate the effect that the creation of such new editions might have, and to advocate their publication, in *On Japanese Writing* (*Nihon bunshōron*, 1886):

> Consider the various old books of our nation: how many are there in the entire country who can actually read them, and read widely among them; how many are there who can read them and truly understand their character; how many are there who can understand and derive real profit from them—only, it must be said, a small minority of the nation's population. . . . Many types of books will need to be reconfigured into the form of modern writing and printed that way, but with the text

itself unchanged—it is likely that this will increase rather than decrease the profit they yield, by comparison with the older forms. Consider *Genji monogatari*: this book is one of the most flawed among all the books of the East, but in terms of its beauties, too, it is also very rare among the books of the East. In its old form, the number of people who can read it are as few and far between as stars in the morning. If, when it were printed, some new method were used that made its sense immediately apparent, just think how convenient that would be.[182]

Suematsu was undoubtedly right: there was much to be gained from the bibliographical translation of *Genji monogatari*—which is to say of *Kogetsushō*—into the "new form" of the case-bound typeset book, particularly given that by 1888 woodblock-printed books were clearly on the way out.[183] But while this shift certainly played a role in popularizing *Genji monogatari* in 1890, it was not the most significant factor. What mattered most was that the spate of new editions had been "reconfigured into the form of modern writing and printed that way, *but with the text itself unchanged*." The modern-Japanese translations in Suzuki's *A Lecture on Genji monogatari* and Masuda's *A New Edition of Murasaki's History* offered readers access to *Genji monogatari*, but not to its classical language. In 1890, people were interested in precisely this language.

In a recently published essay, "Sounds, Scripts, and Styles: *Kanbun kundokutai* and the National Language Reforms of 1880s Japan," Atsuko Ueda has demonstrated that the late 1880s and early 1890s witnessed a profound shift in the nature of certain debates that had been taking place about the style of Japanese that was most suitable for the modern era. This shift involved a move away from *kanbun kundokutai*—a style that had originally developed as a by-product of a process of translating writing entirely in *kanji*, which is to say *kanbun*, into mixed *kanji* and *kana* prose, but that had emerged as a style of its own—and toward what came to be called *kokubun* (national writing). Over time, Ueda argues, the dichotomy between *kanbun* and *kanbun kundokutai* that had formerly governed language debates was displaced by a new dichotomy between *kokubun* or *kokugo* (the national language), on the one hand, and *kobun* (the old language) or *wabun* (the Yamato language), on the other, even though the process of defining *kokubun* and *kokugo* relied heavily on models for thinking about language that derived from *kanbun* and *kanbun kundokutai*. "In other words, *kokugo* clearly absorbed texts that had *kanbun* ancestry, while erasing *kanbun*'s originary status. This further reinforces the severance of the 'current language' from its *kanbun* 'ancestor.' "[184] In writings by figures such as Sekine Masanao,

Hagino Yoshiyuki, and Ochiai Naobumi, the "current language" was provided with a new lineage that extended back not to all-*kanji* writings modeled on Chinese prose and their translation, but to Heian-period texts written largely in *hiragana* such as *Genji monogatari*. All three of these men had studied in the Course for the Study of the Classics at the University of Tokio, incidentally, and Ochiai was part of the editorial team that prepared one of the editions of *Genji monogatari* that began to appear in 1890.

The shift away from *kanbun* and *kanbun kundokutai* is crucial to the story I have been telling about *Genji monogatari* in Japan. I mentioned earlier that in the first installment of "A Discourse on Poetry and Music," published in 1884, Suematsu included a quotation from "Hahakigi," "rewriting it in the prose of our time" (*jibun ni kakikae sōrō*), and that in his foreword to *A New Edition of Murasaki's History*, published in 1888, he also described Masuda's treatment of *Genji monogatari* as "rewriting it in the prose of our time" (*jibun o motte kore o utsushiaratame*). In the first instance, Suematsu was writing in *kanbun kundokutai*; in the second, he was writing in *kanbun*. This is not particularly striking, perhaps. What *is* striking is the enormity of the difference between the styles of the "rewritings" themselves, each of which Suematsu frames as an instance of *jibun* (the prose of our time): his translation of the excerpt from "Hahakigi" is itself written in *kanbun*, while Masuda's cleaves fairly closely to the style of the original, striving to create what may be considered a modern counterpart of *wabun*, the classical, largely *hiragana* prose in which Murasaki Shikibu wrote. Indeed, Masuda himself views matters in precisely this way, as we see in his "Notes to the Reader" (*hanrei*) about the contents of *A New Edition of Murasaki's History*: "The purpose of this book is to make *Genji monogatari* widely legible to ordinary people. I have thus translated the old language [*kobun*] into the current language [*kinbun*]. Still, not a jot has been either added to or subtracted from the original book in terms of facts or meaning."[185] The "current language" that is "legible to ordinary people" stands here as the modern descendant of Murasaki Shikibu's "old language." And when Suematsu refers to "the prose of our time" in his *kanbun* foreword, writing in a style he had referred to as "the prose of our time" just four years earlier, he might as well be writing in an invisible ink that fades as it dries. The *kanbun* is there, but it is no longer a tenable model for modern writing; it is on its way to becoming a relic of the past.

The rise in interest in prose of the style in which *Genji monogatari* was written was, then, largely responsible for the *Genji monogatari* boom that started in 1890—and, contrary to the prediction of the "Master Among

Clouds," continued to gather momentum rather than fade from view by the summer of 1891. In 1884 Suematsu had been able to translate "Hahakigi" into *kanbun* because the language of *Genji monogatari* was irrelevant to his historical invocation of it; in the 1890s, even as the historical approach continued to dominate, people had become interested in looking anew at the language itself. Indeed, this circumstance is explicitly noted in "On *Genji monogatari*" (*Genji monogatari* ni tsuite), an article by an "Old Man from Yamanote" (Yamanote no Okina) that ran on the front page of *Yomiuri shinbun* on October 7, 1895:

> I have always liked *Genji*. On mornings when I am in some distress, in evenings when I feel sad, I have often read it to distract my thoughts. I have invested my heart in nothing else, really, as I have in *Genji*. These days, ever since the world was swept up in the *wabun* vogue, everyone, even students whose hearts are yet unsettled, makes a show of reading it, and many, though incapable of so much as grasping wherein its meaning lies, offer up utterly incompetent critiques; thus, I have determined to copy out below an extremely simple outline of its general sense from an old book for the edification of the superficial scholarly crowd.[186]

The Old Man proceeds to quote material that seems to derive, in part, from *Notes for the Morning Star* (*Myōjōshō*, ca. 1539–1563) by Sanjōnishi Kin'eda, though he never identifies his source.

Of course, "the *wabun* vogue" (*wabun ryūkō*) was itself a complex phenomenon, and even its supporters could be ambivalent about different elements of *wabun* style. The female gendering of Heian writing—which became so important in English-language discussions of Japanese women and played a pivotal role in the formulation of notions of literary tradition and national subjectivity in Japan during the 1890s—was not always seen as a positive attribute in the context of discussions focused specifically on prose style.[187] Suematsu touched several times on this issue, for instance, beginning in *On Japanese Writing*, where he presents his argument in terms of *kanabumi* (*kana* prose), which is simply another way of saying *wabun*:

> In its old form *kana* prose is, above all, rambling and lacking in energy, tending to make people yawn. No doubt this style is eminently well suited to accounts of travel during the lengthy spring days of the sort Masters of Japanese Studies are prone to write in their many free moments, or to love stories of an age when people plodded from here

to there and back again in ox-carts, but it is hard to make it serve any other purpose. I have treated of this matter already in my "A Discourse on Poetry and Music." Or again, here is what Mr. Yoshiwara Shigetoshi, who has so ably served the Kana Society, once said to me: The reason *kana* prose fared so poorly in later ages is that so many of our old books in *kana* prose are the handiwork of women, and are thus often dawdlingly verbose and devoid of vigor and energy, and scholars of Japanese studies, seeing this, mistook this sort of thing as the model of what *kana* prose should be, and thus went even further and acquired a habit of mimicking the loquacious, dawdling element. It must be said, I think, that he was on to something.[188]

Suematsu makes the same point in "On Literary Styles" (Bunshōron), an essay published in the popular magazine *Taiyō* (*Sun*) in March 1897.[189] And yet at the same moment, he begins, for the first time, to leave behind his former reservations about what he had repeatedly described as "one of the most flawed among all the books of the East" and to position *Genji monogatari* as a classic of world, and thus national, literature.[190] Here he is writing earlier in 1897 in "On Belles Lettres" (Bungaku- bijutsu-jō no iken), also published in *Taiyō*:

> Generally speaking, our historical works of past ages undoubtedly found their models in the Tang dynasty; when it comes to those in a purely literary vein, however, many in those days had already surpassed in their development those of the Chinese—a fact at which one marvels even today. Consider, for example, a book such as *Genji monogatari*. It has been suggested that it was inspired by *Travels to the Caverns of the Immortals* and books of that ilk only because Murasaki Shikibu composed that enormous tome with the burning vigor of a column of flame, with such force she might have written it with a brush as thick as a log; and its structure and its thought, and its passages so wondrously perfect as to deserve, even now, our most enthusiastic praise, cause me to boast before the entire world.[191]

It is surely not a coincidence that Suematsu was writing in the wake of Japan's victory in the Sino-Japanese War (1894–1895), which prompted a revision of Japan's historical relationship to China and its enormous prestige. And as Japan continued to strengthen its position in the international order, and began to revise the unequal treaties, his opinion of *Genji monogatari* kept improving. In January 1904, Suematsu was asked by Prime Minister Katsura Tarō and Foreign Minister Komura Jūtarō to make a trip to Europe, by way of the United States, to try to promote the Japanese cause in the Russo-Japanese War by delivering lectures and publishing.[192] In the United States, he met with President Theodore Roosevelt; in London, he worked with his old language partner Takahashi Korekiyo, now deputy governor of the Yokohama Specie Bank, whom the Japanese government had dispatched to Europe to negotiate loans to fund the war. Suematsu succeeded in his mission, contributing articles to journals and newspapers not only in English but also in French and German, lecturing before numerous societies on topics more or less propagandistic, and publishing two books: *The Risen Sun* (1905) and *A Fantasy of Far Japan; or, Summer Dream Dialogues* (1905), the second of which he sent to the novelist Natsume Sōseki, hoping to have him translate it into Japanese.[193] Not surprisingly, *The Risen Sun*—which deals with matters relating to Japan's history, culture, morals, and military—also includes the chapter "Women's Education," in whose second paragraph Murasaki Shikibu appears.[194] After Suematsu returned to Tokyo in February 1906, he contributed an essay to *Bunshō sekai* (*World of Writing*) called "Japanese and European Writing Viewed in Connection to Translation" (Hon'yakujō yori mitaru Nihonbun to Ōbun), in which he gave his most positive assessment ever of Murasaki Shikibu's prose: "Looking at *Genji monogatari*, in which the thought of the age of *Genji monogatari* is expressed in the language and writing of that time, we find there is nothing at all artificial about it, it is natural, and it is wonderfully done."[195]

Little by little, it was becoming possible—even for a man like Suematsu, whose understanding of *Genji monogatari* had changed very little over two decades—to admire it as something more than a repository of facts. The publication of new editions and the wave of enthusiasm for *wabun* began, ever so slowly, to create the potential for a popular appreciation of *Genji monogatari* in terms of the "thought" it encapsulated: in terms of emotion, spirit, aesthetics, and the supposed absence of artificiality in its prose—the feminine, essentially Japanese "nature" of its language. The Russo-Japanese War and the ensuing rise in popular nationalist sentiment created, moreover, conditions that seemed, even at the time, likely to prompt the discovery of *Genji monogatari* and other old works as national classics.

Divided We Stand

On July 10, 1904, five months to the day after Suematsu set off on his propagandizing mission, the critic and reporter Kakuda Kōkōkakyaku

(Kakuda Kin'ichirō) devoted part of an article on recent literary trends in *Yomiuri shinbun* to precisely this issue: the impact that the war might have on popular awareness of the Japanese classics. Kakuda is now remembered principally for a defense he published in the same newspaper later in 1904 of the poet Yosano Akiko, future translator of *Genji monogatari*, after she published a controversial poem addressed to her brother in the Imperial Army, begging him not to sacrifice his life for the nation.[196] Here is what he had to say about Japanese classics and the war:

THE STUDY OF THE NATION'S CITIZENS' OLD LITERATURE

As the study of [ancient] Greek literature gradually gets under way in our literary circles, I have argued repeatedly that our victories in the war to conquer Russia will engender in our citizens an awareness of the world-wide value of the things we possess at home, and thus call up with regard to literature as well a spirit of self-awareness and self-confidence. This trend is bound eventually to make the study of our old literature thrive. But in order to spread the study of old literature, *we must on this occasion spare no effort in providing notes and commentaries, detailed explications, and thereby giving ancient books a new form, and we must edit the old writing in a new style.* Works such as *Record of Ancient Matters* and *Chronicles of Japan*, for instance, might be published as annotated editions or perhaps as exemplary tales that explain and appraise them in terms of contemporary thought. Works such as *Genji monogatari* and *The Pillow Book* might be edited in a form to make them easy to read, breaking them into sections and paragraphs (though there are already things somewhat along these lines). The legends that appear in *Record of Ancient Matters* and *Chronicles of Japan* and so on—or that do not appear there, being simply recorded as stories in the old gazetteers and other such works—might be idealized, molded, recomposed as poetry. Other tasks would include, no doubt, the inspection of past achievements and the appraisal of historical figures. It is common, in old households, for people to discover things belonging to them in the most unexpected places—in a corner, up against the wall, in a basket—rare treasures whose extraordinary value is only then recognized. Are we not, at this precise moment, on the verge of discovering the treasures we have, here in our own house?[197]

The moment, it seemed, was ripe: war could provide an excuse for the popular rediscovery of the classics through accessible bibliographic translations, which could be mobilized in the creation of a new sense of national unity vis-à-vis the enemy, of national community rooted in the great literary works of the past. And yet it did not happen—not yet. *Genji monogatari* still was not about to be reborn in Japan as a classic of either world or national literature. The most one can say is that the image of *Genji monogatari* as a double classic, global and local, had begun to circulate as a possibility that might someday be realized.

That said, something intriguing was happening during this war. If *Genji monogatari* had not yet begun to function as a "national classic" in the sense in which the term is generally understood—if it was not yet commonly viewed as common property, as both the source and the proof of the constructed reality of national community—it was already beginning to exhibit another, perhaps less obvious characteristic of national literature: now that its readership was growing, it was being read not only by poets and scholars of Japanese literature and the "Old Man from Yamanote," but by people in different situations, with all sorts of different ideas about how the world works and how it ought to work, and about the role that things like literature and nation-states ought to play in it. Even before it came to serve as an emblem of national community, of national identity, *Genji monogatari* had begun to find its way into the fractures that divided that community, that identity.

It is with these fractures that I would like to close: with the images of three men—perhaps not the sort of people one expects to encounter in a book about *Genji monogatari*, but men who are nevertheless linked in complex ways to the trajectory I have been tracing—sharing the experience of reading *Genji monogatari* not as history but as literature, if not as national literature, in the years leading up to and following the Russo-Japanese War. The men are Sakai Toshihiko (1870–1933), Ōsugi Sakae (1885–1923), and Yamaguchi Koken (Yamaguchi Yoshizō, 1883–1920). Sakai was a prominent socialist, a translator of Karl Marx, and one of the founders, along with the journalist Yamaguchi, of the Japanese Communist Party. Ōsugi is best known as a proponent of anarcho-syndicalism and for his murder, along with his lover and six-year-old niece, by a member of the military police. My brief treatment of these men emerges, as we will see, from a startling coincidence and is intended as a sort of coda, to move the discussion from the level of discourse to the level of individual readers of an utterly new type, but at the same time to give a sense of how they may connect, however tenuously, to the larger world of *Genji* discourse. In a sense, this may seem like a digression, a random departure; it is, however, the very randomness of the movement that is so revealing of the changes that were taking place in *Genji monogatari*'s readership, and the literary manner in which readers were slowly beginning to approach the text.

National Literature in the Strangest Places

Sakai Toshihiko moved to Tokyo from Fukuoka in the summer of 1897 to care for his brother, who was dying of tuberculosis. His wife was pregnant, and he needed a job fast. His former boss, Soyano Han'ya—the president of the *Fukuoka nichinichi shinbun* (*Fukuoka Daily News*), who had unsuccessfully run against Suematsu Kenchō for a seat in the National Diet in the first general election in 1890 but was now reconciled with him—sent Sakai to Suematsu with a business card and a borrowed book to return. Suematsu hired Sakai on the spot, asking him to join a committee he headed, with historian and literary critic Yamaji Aizan as his de facto right-hand man, that was gathering material for the monumental *A History of Chōshū in Changing the Mandate* (*Bōchō kaitenshi*, 1921).[198]

Suematsu was a casual, unpretentious person—Aizan described the now Baron Suematsu as "a bit 'person' radical with the *kanji* 'valley' next to it," a combination that yields the word *zoku* (vulgar)—and Sakai immediately took to him. Sakai recalled that, far from making a display of his authority, Suematsu, who tended to dress "rather sloppily in Japanese attire," "sat at the same sort of small desk as everyone else at the head of the rectangle we formed, unsure how best to position his portly body, and frequently sitting cross-legged. For us, 'Dr. Seihyō's testicles' were hardly an unusual sight" ("Seihyō" was Suematsu's nom de plume).[199]

At some point, evidently fairly early in his acquaintance with Suematsu, Sakai borrowed and read a copy of *Genji Monogatari* that his boss had on his study shelf. This seems to have inspired Sakai to read a bit of the original, too—the chapter "Nowaki" (The Typhoon)—right around the same time he was relishing *Les Miserables* in English translation. Evidently deeply moved, he wrote an article summarizing the chapter that ran in *Yomiuri shinbun* on October 25, 1897, under the title "The 'Nowaki' Chapter of *Genji*" (*Genji* Nowaki no maki). The piece closes with these words:

> It seems stupid to be going on about Shikibu's writing at this point, but reading through "Nowaki" just now I was so extraordinarily deeply moved that I wrote down exactly what I felt. Those who know that there are times when one's feeling for the beauty of a piece of poetry or

prose reaches its fullest tide, when one simply cannot bear to remain silent, will not take me to task for doing something pointless.[200]

This is an unmistakably "literary" way of reading *Genji monogatari*, a good deal more appreciative of the language than Suematsu was at this time—not a surprise, perhaps, given that Sakai was not yet twenty when the *wabun* vogue got under way. But, again, there is nothing to suggest that Sakai read *Genji monogatari* as a classic of national literature.

The committee compiling *A History of Chōshū in Changing the Mandate* finished its labors and disbanded two years after Sakai arrived, and he went to work for *Yorozu chōhō* (*Complete Morning Report*); by 1901, he was deeply enough involved in the growing socialist movement that when the Social Democratic Party was banned—within hours of its establishment by Kōtoku Shūsui, a colleague at *Yorozu chōhō*, among others—he went to see the home minister, who had issued the ban.[201] The home minister was none other than Suematsu Kenchō. In October 1903, Sakai quit *Yorozu chōhō* along with Kōtoku Shūsui and Uchimura Kanzō, angry that the mewspaper's founder, Kuroiwa Ruiko, had decided that they could no longer espouse pacifist views as tensions between Japan and Russia escalated. The next month, Sakai and Kōtoku founded their own paper, *Heimin shinbun* (*Commoner's Newspaper*), and continued to agitate against the war even as Suematsu was shipped off to propagandize in Europe.

This is where Ōsugi Sakae enters the picture. Ōsugi, who had introduced himself to Sakai and the *Heimin shinbun* crowd soon after the newspaper was founded, went to Nagoya in the summer of 1904 to stand on street corners, passing out copies of the paper; in April 1905, he began to contribute to its production; in 1906, he and Sakai's sister-in-law Hori Yasuko were married. Then, in January 1908, when the police tried to disperse a meeting of the revolutionary Kin'yōkai (Friday Group) after the conversation turned in the dangerous direction of Thomas More's *Utopia*, Sakai, Ōsugi, and another participant climbed to the roof and began shouting down at passersby. They were arrested, and Ōsugi was sentenced to a month in prison—his third time in jail.[202] In his first letter to his wife from the jail in Ichigaya, dated January 28, he had a request: "Do me a favor and send some books to Yamaguchi, right away. All the English books on that bamboo shelf, on top of the small bookshelf. There are seven, I think. Also *Genji*, the *Lotus Sutra*, *Fujin shinron* [*A New Treatise on Women*], and *Shinkeihō* [*The New Penal Code*]. *Shinkeihō* is just a pamphlet. It should be on the bamboo shelf, too."[203] "Yamaguchi" refers to Yamaguchi Koken, who had been in prison since the previous April.[204] Just a few months earlier, in September 1907, Suematsu had been promoted from baron to viscount, and then, soon after, appointed as tutor to the crown prince of Korea, Yi Ŭn, who was brought to Tokyo in October at the age of ten as a hostage to keep the Korean royal family from interfering as Japan moved toward its official annexation of Korea in 1910.[205] One wonders if Suematsu ever lectured Yi Ŭn about *Genji monogatari*. One wonders what sort of pleasure Yamaguchi took in reading *Genji monogatari* alongside the new penal code in prison, and why Ōsugi, himself in prison, decided to include it among the works he had his wife send. One wonders, too, whether Ōsugi had read Sakai's article about "Nowaki" in *Yomiuri shinbun* or if he had any idea that Sakai had first borrowed *Genji Monogatari* from Suematsu years earlier and read it in English.

In Japan, *Genji monogatari* was not yet a truly national classic, in the sense of a great work seen as belonging to the nation, and to which the nation is thought to belong; neither was it yet regarded as a classic of world literature. But it was moving toward becoming one, both, gradually, in the fractures and the unwitting connectedness of a national, global community.

Toward the Triangle

Earlier I suggested that *Genji*'s contemporary existence might be envisioned as a triangular field delimited by three conceptual lines: *Genji* as a work of world literature, *Genji* as a work that exists first and foremost in translation, and *Genji* as a work that is discursively figured as participating in world literature through translation. I sketched the slow emergence of this field through a transnational, translingual, and translational process of discursive turns and returns whose origins can be traced back to the United States and Europe in the mid-1870s, then back to early modern Japan—and from there, if one is so inclined, through the medieval period to the imagined text of *Genji monogatari* itself and beyond. This chapter commences once again at the very end of the nineteenth century and the dawn of the twentieth and snakes somewhat circuitously toward the moment when the three lines finally clicked into place, creating the field within which *Genji* is now almost inevitably apprehended: the publication between 1939 and 1941, during the final years of World War II, of the first of Tanizaki Jun'ichirō's three modern-Japanese translations of *Genji monogatari*. The story it tells revolves around a figure whose centrality to the history of *Genji*'s recanonization in Japan as both world and national literature is only now beginning to be recognized: the novelist, playwright, critic, and translator Masamune Hakuchō.

For the most part, literary historians tend to portray Hakuchō as a somewhat peripheral figure in the Japanese Naturalist movement and emphasize his penchant for fiction steeped in nihilism, skepticism, and irony. He is also known for what he himself once described as his "worship of the West" (*Seiyō sūhai*)—a phrase whose meaning Tanizaki Jun'ichirō clarified in 1932 when he wrote that "there can't be many authors over forty writing today who are as skeptical of the value of their motherland's traditions and as partial to the literature of the West as Mr. Hakuchō."[1] In terms of both his own literary penchants and the position he has been assigned in literary history, Hakuchō would seem an unlikely candidate for the pivotal role he played in *Genji monogatari*'s modern recanonization. And yet I would suggest that his essays about *Genji*

CHAPTER 5

From the World to the Nation

Making Genji *Ours*

I'm a translation kind of guy.
Yes, I'm a translationperson.

Masamune Hakuchō

are among the most important and provocative in the modern period, and that to a certain extent it was precisely the complexity of the position he adopted in his self-conscious "worship of the West" that allowed him to encounter *Genji* as he did—through English, in Arthur Waley's *The Tale of Genji*—and through this encounter to pave the way for Tanizaki's first translation.

Ironically, Tanizaki's translation became a turning point in the history of *Genji monogatari*'s replacement in modern Japan, and once the tale had rounded the bend, emerging for the first time as a truly popular national classic, Hakuchō's translingually mediated relationship to the tale came to seem twisted, inappropriate. Just as *Inaka Genji* came to be criticized for inadequately embodying the notion of the full-scale popular replacement of *Genji monogatari* that it itself had created, so Hakuchō's "discovery" of *Genji* through its English translation helped establish the seemingly self-evident vision of *Genji* as a national classic that would later be used to criticize him.

If it seems troubling to have to attribute the potency of Hakuchō's provocations to his worship of the West, we might turn to another, more palatable of his self-descriptions: "I'm a translation kind of guy," he writes. "Yes, I'm a translationperson" (*Hon'yakuteki jinbutsu da ne. Hon'yakujin desu*).[2] Hakuchō lived, more self-consciously even than many of his well-read contemporaries, in a translational world. This is apparent as early as Hakuchō's first surviving reference to *Genji monogatari*, in a letter to his younger brother Masamune Atsuo, a future scholar of Japanese literature and co-editor with Yosano Akiko and her husband, Yosano Tekkan, of the 264-volume Library of Japanese Classics (Nihon koten zenshū, 1926–1944).[3] Hakuchō had left his family seat in Okayama and relocated to Tokyo in February 1896, hoping among other things that life in the big city would offer him opportunities to improve his English.[4] The letter, dated November 12, 1897—less than three weeks after Sakai Toshihiko's account of the "Nowaki" (The Typhoon) chapter appeared in *Yomiuri shinbun*—is far from sophisticated, and yet, like Sakai's discovery of "Nowaki," evidently in the wake of his reading of Suematsu Kenchō's English-language *Genji Monogatari*, it subtly reveals how *Genji monogatari* both was and was not being framed in turn-of-the-century Japan, through mass media and translation, as both world and national literature.

Hakuchō reports in the letter that he bought an English-language newspaper on his way home from a class in English conversation and in it found an article on literature. According to this article, if an Englishman were exiled by a tyrant to some desolate island, never to return, and were permitted to take just one book of his choosing, the Englishman would choose Shakespeare; if the same fate befell a Frenchman, he was certain to take Voltaire; and if the man were German, he would take Goethe. What, Hakuchō asks, would a Japanese exile choose?

> Is there any single book that could serve as his companion until his dying day as he lived his life on that desolate island, it seems certain that there is not, even Chikamatsu, comparatively excellent though he may be, does no more than sing the amorous affairs of lowlifes, and while a certain scholar of the national literature has observed that the whole world has been recorded in *Genji*, even so it is nothing but drivel, the story of a pervert, Saikaku is lewd, Ikku and Sanba and their ilk aren't serious, *The Collection of Poems Old and New* is naught but word games, and though at times *The Collection of Ten Thousand Leaves* exhibits a simple honesty that makes it at least worthy of notice still it cannot hold even one-tenth the greatness of the universe, and while there are ten or so works that may be considered nearly equal to a third-rate work in the West (among these third-rate works Chikamatsu would come first, then *The Collection of Ten Thousand Leaves*, *Genji*, two or three works by Bakin, Ikku, Sanba's *Bathhouse of the Floating World*, and the *norito*), in the West there are a few hundred like Shakespeare, who resembled the sea in his immeasurable depth and vastness (his works are almost beyond human), Milton, Dante (these last two wrote about Heaven and Hell), and Goethe, or who stand just one rank below, as Hugo, Macaulay, Byron, Shelley, and Burns. . . . Oh how sad it is to have to admit that there is no one like that in Japan (except for Chikamatsu), and all because people's ideals are so low.⁵

Tanabe Akio points out that it is not entirely clear where the line ought to be drawn between Hakuchō's disappointment with the works he mentions and the opinions expressed in the article, whatever they may have been: it is possible that he is simply parroting what he read.⁶ Indeed, in another letter to his brother, dated April 21, 1898, Hakuchō mentions that while he has been wanting to read *Genji monogatari* and *The Collection of Ten Thousand Leaves* for a long while, he has never had the time.⁷ His dismissal of *Genji monogatari* in the earlier letter as "nothing but drivel, the story of a pervert" is based not on a personal experience of reading it—not on the experience of reading it as one reader in a community of readers—but in a communal vision shared even by nonreaders like him.

And this is significant: Hakuchō, in this letter, stands as a poster child for the young Meiji-born intellectual elite, bilingual, engaging with the world in both English and Japanese, bringing what he learns in English into Japanese, interpreting what he reads in English in terms of its relationship to things Japanese. He agrees implicitly that Japan, like England, France, and Germany, needs a truly national classic—not a national treasure, celebrated but uninteresting, but something that a man, an everyman, might treat as his lifelong companion—but he sees nothing in Japan's history that could possibly fill the bill. His attitude toward *Genji monogatari*, which comes third on his list of works as "nearly equal to a third-rate work in the West," is utterly typical. And in fact, even reading the work does not change his mind: in a letter Hakuchō wrote to his brother in 1899, he says that he has read enough of *Genji monogatari* to know he does not approve. "It is womanish and lewd," he declares, "and I have come to detest it."[8]

Despite his initial dislike, however, Hakuchō continued to return to *Genji monogatari*. In an article on the current theater that appeared in *Yomiuri shinbun* on March 25, 1905, for instance, he refers to the work in the context of a discussion about historical change and cultural difference. After noting that Edo-period kabuki plays would not be able to keep audiences entertained forever, he explains why this is true: "The greatest works will retain their value forever because human emotions have always been the same, all through history and around the globe; the problem is that differences in manners and customs and in the ways emotions are expressed keep ordinary people from really *feeling* this value."[9] *Genji monogatari*, he suggests, is a good example of an "indestructible masterpiece" whose value will always be appreciated by intellectuals, but is bound to be less interesting to ordinary readers than contemporary fiction. *Genji monogatari* may be a treasure, he suggests in 1905, but it is not part of a truly literary national canon.

This brings us to Hakuchō's seminal writings on *Genji*. Between 1926 and 1951, he published four essays that deal expressly and extensively with the tale: "Koten o yonde" (On Reading the Classics, 1926); "Eiyaku *Genji monogatari*" (An English Translation of *Genji monogatari*, 1933); "Futatabi Eiyaku *Genji monogatari* ni tsukite" (Further Thoughts on *Genji monogatari*'s English Translation, 1933); and, some two decades later, "*Genji monogatari*—hon'yaku to gensaku" (*Genji monogatari*: Translation and Original, 1951).[10] The first of these essays, "Koten o yonde," takes up *Genji monogatari*—in this case, the Yūhōdō Library (Yūhōdō bunko) edition, published in four volumes in 1914 and republished in 1926—and the eighteenth-century Chinese classic *The Story of the Stone* (Ch. *Honglou meng*, J. *Kōromu*; also known as *The Dream of the Red Chamber*), which Hakuchō read in a bilingual edition issued in three volumes from 1920 to

1922. The next three essays focus on Arthur Waley's celebrated translation *The Tale of Genji*, which Hakuchō first read in the summer and autumn of 1933, just a few months after the publication in May of its sixth and final volume. These essays are not considered central to Hakuchō's oeuvre, but their importance to *Genji*'s modern recanonization—to the establishment of the triangular frame—makes it worth at least touching on them all, even if it is impossible to do any of them justice.

Before delving into these four essays, however, it will be useful to make a detour. I noted that the first time Hakuchō discussed *Genji monogatari* at length, in "Koten o yonde," he set it alongside *The Story of the Stone*. Early in "Koten o yonde," he reveals what prompted him to tackle these two particular works together: "As a youth, I read a piece in the *Nation's Friend* in which, after including these two titles in a list of his ten favorite books, Yoda Gakkai explained why . . . they were among the greatest literary works of all time."[11] At first blush, this explanation seems straightforward enough, but in fact Hakuchō is misremembering, and doing so in an extremely telling way. In order to make sense of Hakuchō's readings of *Genji*, and to fix them in the larger stream of literary discourse, it will be helpful to consider the reasons for his mistake.

A World Before World Literature

On September 11, 1890, in the midst of the *Genji monogatari* boom discussed in chapter 4, Yoda Gakkai gave a lecture on *Genji monogatari*'s "compositional technique" (*bunpō*) at a literary gathering at Man'yoken, a Western-style restaurant in Kanda. After the lecture, an old friend and fellow activist in the cause of reforming the Japanese theater rose and offered a rebuttal so heated that Gakkai felt obliged first to respond and then to back down, and more than one newspaper covered the exchange.[12] The friend was none other than Suematsu Kenchō. "*Genji* is a fine book," Suematsu said, "but there is nothing in it like this abstruse 'compositional technique' you spoke of. . . . Each volume presents its own pleasures, and they do not form a continuous story. The chronology is so mixed up it that is not even worth discussing. I'd suggest that it was simply a loose collection of volumes dashed off individually that were gathered together at some later point."[13]

After this public belittling of his views by a man twenty-five years his junior but incomparably elevated in his social status—Suematsu had married the daughter of former prime minister Itō Hirobumi the previous year and been elected to the House of Representatives in Japan's first general election just months earlier—Gakkai no longer interacted much with Suematsu. In May 1898, on one of his frequent visits to Ink Cottage, a house in Mukōjima where he had a family with a mistress thirty-one years younger, he discovered that a crew of workers had strung electrical wires through his garden. He wrote to Suematsu, who was then minister of communications, and asked to have the wires taken down. He got no reply. When Gakkai ran into Suematsu in Ueno Park a few months later, Suematsu "didn't recognize me for some time, though he saw me, because he is nearsighted and didn't have his glasses on." Gakkai inquired about the wires, and Suematsu explained that national interests superseded private desires. The next autumn, Suematsu delivered a speech in a town that Gakkai was visiting, and Gakkai encountered his entourage during a stroll. "We parted ways," Gakkai notes in his diary, "without exchanging words."[14] Patrick Caddeau, who has written about the 1890 dispute, is surely right that Gakkai never forgot it.[15]

By 1926, when Hakuchō stumbled into this web of readerly relationships by misremembering what Gakkai had written in *Kokumin no tomo* (*Nation's Friend*), Gakkai had been dead for seventeen years. Considered in this light, it is remarkable that Hakuchō recalled the piece at all and that his memory was even partly correct: Gakkai had indeed included both *Genji monogatari* and *The Story of the Stone* in his response to a survey of prominent writers' favorite books that appeared in 1889 in *Kokumin no tomo*, as Hakuchō says. The response is in the form of a briefly annotated list, however, and does not really compare the two works, except to say that *The Story of the Stone* depicts the glories and decline of a society, and "*Genji* has a hint of that, too."[16]

Most likely, Hakuchō was thinking not of this survey, but of one or both of two essays that Gakkai contributed to *Kokoro no hana* (*Heart's Flower*) in 1902 and 1906, in which he presented a more substantial comparison of the two classics. But throughout these essays, Gakkai adopts the perspective of a scholar of Chinese (*kangakusha*) and frames his discussion of the works solely in terms of a binary relationship between Japanese (*wa*) and Chinese (*kan*) that is incompatible with the sweeping, universalist perspective that Hakuchō remembered him adopting two decades later. Here, for instance, is how Gakkai begins "*Genji monogatari* and *The Story of the Stone*" (*Genji monogatari to Kōrōmu*, 1906):

> I love novels [*shōsetsu*], so ever since I was a child I have read all kinds of books, and as I grew older I began reading "unofficial histories" [*haishi*] in both Japanese and Chinese, and enjoyed discussing them; but of all the works I have read, the two I like best are *Genji* and *The*

Story of the Stone. Scholars of a Kokugaku [Nativist] stripe offer endless interpretations of *Genji*'s exemplary anecdotes, and there are dozens of annotated commentaries, but it seems no one cares to read the book as a novel [*shōsetsu*].

I think *Genji* can be read as a novel, and if you look at it that way, *The Story of the Stone* is a lot like it.[17]

Gakkai takes what he sees as the unusual approach of treating *Genji monogatari* as a "novel" (*shōsetsu*). If this does not appear to be terribly surprising, it is partly because I have Englished the word *shōsetsu* rather than leave it in Japanese. As Gakkai uses the term, *shōsetsu* is more or less synonymous with "unofficial histories" (*haishi*) and takes as its standard works of fiction written in vernacular Chinese, such as *Journey to the West* (Ch. *Xiyouji*, J. *Saiyūki*), *Water Margin* (Ch. *Shuihuzhuan*, J. *Suikoden*), and *The Plum in the Golden Vase* (Ch. *Jinpingmei*, J. *Kinpeibai*), on the one hand, and, on the other, works in genres that emerged in Edo in the late eighteenth and early nineteenth centuries, particularly late *yomihon* and *gōkan*, both of which frequently incorporated plots and characters from Chinese vernacular fiction. Gakkai is reading *Genji monogatari*, in other words, in a self-consciously anachronistic mode, as if the early-eleventh-century tale really belonged to a constellation of popular fictional works produced in Ming- and Qing-dynasty China and Edo-period Japan that he saw as sharing certain features and that were, in fact, historically related.

This was a somewhat fresh perspective in 1906, to be sure, but its freshness has little to do with the vision of literature as world literature implied by the phrase that Hakuchō misattributes to Gakkai: "the greatest literary works of all time." And while Gakkai's privileging of the term *shōsetsu* may betray the influence of changes that had taken place in the understanding of the word since the mid-1880s as a result of the movement to reform Japanese fiction, the increasing availability of translations from Western languages, and the publication of works such as Tsubouchi Shōyō's *The Essence of the Novel*, for Gakkai the word still has a rather different connotation. For Shōyō, *shōsetsu* in its broadest sense encompasses all fiction: everything from the *Iliad* to *Zhuangzi* to Sir Walter Scott's *Rob Roy*, and, in Japan, everything from *Genji monogatari* to the most recent Meiji-period potboilers. In a narrower sense, however, *shōsetsu* is one name among several (*shinsei no monogatari* and *makoto no shōsetsu-haishi* are two other options, and as such he glosses both as "novel") for the final, fully civilized goal of the universal, uni-directional process of fiction's evolution. According to this formulation, the *Iliad* is a myth,

Zhuangzi is a collection of fables, *Genji monogatari* is a romance, and—of course, this is the crux—the true novel has yet to appear in Japan. Either way, Shōyō's *shōsetsu* conjures up a vision of literature that is, at least potentially, global in scope.[18]

Gakkai, who was already fifty-two when the first volumes of *The Essence of the Novel* were published in September 1885, looked out on a more circumscribed fictional world, and his understanding of the term *shōsetsu* derived more heavily from late Edo discourse than did Shōyō's, which represented a translational fusion of European and Edo precedent. Gakkai's invocation of the word *shōsetsu* (and its twin *haishi*) recalls, for example, the definition with which Kimura Mokurō opens *A Connoisseur of Fiction in the Native Script*: "What are *haishi-shōsetsu*? They are what we now refer to as 'reading books' and 'grass books' [*kusazōshi*] and their ilk."[19] Of course, as the qualifying "in the Native Script" in the title implies, "reading books" and "grass books" are the most important genres only in Japan; Mokurō's concept of the *shōsetsu* has a quasi-universalist and, indeed, an evolutionary aspect that seems almost, but not quite, like Shōyō's: as Andrew L. Markus has observed, *A Connoisseur of Fiction in the Native Script* exhibits a "tacit acceptance throughout all discussion that Chinese fiction is normative and the model for what the Japanese *haishi* or *shōsetsu* 'novel' could or should become."[20] In Mokurō's formulation, *shōsetsu* is a category comprising all fiction, but in a world—a world literary system, a world literary space—where all fiction is either Chinese or Japanese, and particularly, in a narrower sense, Japanese and Chinese fiction of the past few hundred years.

For Gakkai, as for Mokurō and other Japanese intellectuals throughout the premodern and early modern periods, the Chinese and Japanese traditions stood in a special, closed relationship. There is a concreteness to Gakkai's vision of the "world" of the *shōsetsu* that is ultimately incompatible with Shōyō's Eurocentric, incipiently global vision: What is a *shōsetsu*? It is, first and foremost, a *yomihon*, a *gōkan*, or a work of Chinese vernacular fiction. *The Story of the Stone* is China's best *shōsetsu*; stretching a point, we might say that *Genji monogatari* is Japan's. There is never any question of Gakkai's bringing a favorite Russian work, or a favorite German work, into the discussion. It is no surprise to note that the list he submitted in response to the *Kokumin no tomo* survey, like nearly half of the published responses, includes only Chinese and Japanese texts, and to find that when he mentions the survey in his diary, he divvies up his responses between China (*Kando*) and "this country" (*honpō*) as though in his mind the rest of the literary map were blank:

"The Chinese works I chose were . . . and the Japanese works were . . ."²¹ Indeed, on one rare occasion when Gakkai writes of the "Kumogakure" (Vanished into the Clouds) chapter in *Genji monogatari* that "this is precisely the sort of gesture you might find in one of these newfangled Western *shōsetsu*"—"Kumogakure" exists only as a title that simultaneously marks Genji's death and the impossibility of describing it—he reveals how little this matters to him by immediately going on to rehearse his familiar comparison of *Genji monogatari* and *The Story of the Stone*.²²

Discovering *Genji* as World Literature

This privileging of the connection between the popular literatures of China and Japan, along with the understanding of the term *shōsetsu* as denoting, above all, a cluster of early modern genres—and connoting, no doubt, the particular physical experience of reading woodblock-printed books, scrutinizing the pictures, smelling the ink, fingering the soft edges of the paper—is exactly what is missing in Hakuchō's recollection of Gakkai's comparison of *Genji monogatari* and *The Story of the Stone*. According to Hakuchō, "Yoda Gakkai explained why they were among the greatest *literary works* of all time." But this is not at all what Gakkai, the *shōsetsu* aficionado, explained; it is, rather, Hakuchō's unconscious rewriting of Gakkai's worldview in terms of his own more fluid vision, in August 1926, of literature and the literary world. His perspective is, of course, decidedly post-Shōyō: if Shōyō's introduction of Europe as a third term into the Japan–China binary spawned a fresh hierarchy, paving the way for a literary "leaving Asia and joining Europe" (*datsua nyūō*) to be accomplished through the perfecting of the Japanese *novel*, Hakuchō's view of fiction hinges on a considerably more flexible notion of *literature* (*bungaku*, a word that does not appear in *The Essence of the Novel*), one able to accommodate works from diverse traditions without necessarily fixing them in a rigid evolutionary hierarchy.²³ Hakuchō misremembers Gakkai's comparison of *Genji* and *The Story of the Stone*, then, because he is trying, without even realizing it, to speak of a time before world literature as he understood it, and to do so from within world literature.

The enormity of the difference between the perspectives of Gakkai and Hakuchō—one of whom lived more than half his life under the Tokugawa regime and was nine years old when Ryūtei Tanehiko died, while the other was born a decade into the Meiji period and was nine when "Aibiki," Futabatei Shimei's celebrated translation of Ivan Turgenev's short story "The

Rendezvous" (Svidanie), was serialized in *Kokumin no tomo*—is clear from the opening lines of Hakuchō's own discussion of *Genji monogatari* in "Koten o yonde":

> At the same time I was struggling through the literal translation of *The Story of the Stone*, I was reading *Genji monogatari* and feeling disgusted with its slipshod, lax, rambling prose. Granted, this is a classical work that appeared in the world a thousand years ago, but I was born in the same country, and I have spent a fair amount of time studying the old language from the time I was young; it seems strange that I feel hatred for this tale, generally thought to be the greatest masterpiece in Japan. But the fact is that I have never before encountered a work so hard to read. I can make my way through the great classics of the West, the *Iliad* and the *Odyssey* and so on, with more interest; but when it comes to *Genji monogatari*, which is considered a national treasure among the literary works of my own country, I can't tell you how many times I have wanted to fling it down. Say what you like about the content, the writing is incomparably bad. The idea of including a book like this in a textbook in this day and age strikes me as absurd. I am sure even *Genji monogatari* would be more interesting when read in an English translation.[24]

This is a fascinating and provocative passage on many levels, but in this context the crucial point is that Hakuchō is situating *Genji monogatari* in the context of a group of "classics" that includes not only Chinese and Japanese works, but the *Iliad* and the *Odyssey* as well—or more generally, in a literary field that encompasses, at least potentially, the entire world. Hakuchō was writing in the "Bungei jihyō" (Current Publications) section of *Chūōkōron* and in these essays he constantly brought together authors from around the globe and from all different time periods: Shakespeare and Saikaku; Zola, Flaubert, Turgenev, and Tōson; Tolstoy, the Gospels, and Confucius. Needless to say, this global perspective was characteristic of the historical moment, just as Gakkai's understanding of the *shōsetsu* reflected *his* age: it is no coincidence that in January 1927, the same month that Hakuchō's essays in *Chūōkōron* were collected in *Bungei hyōron* (*Essays in Literary Criticism*, 1927), the publisher Shinchōsha began to advertise the thirty-eight volumes in the first series of its Library of World Literature (Sekai bungaku zenshū, 1927–1930), the first such collection to be published in Japan.

There is, however, something unexpected in Hakuchō's placement of *Genji monogatari* within this international literary context. Shinchōsha's

Library of World Literature contained only works written in the West, and it would have been as unusual for a reader of *Genji monogatari* to read it the way she read the volumes in that series as it was for Gakkai to approach *Genji monogatari* as a *shōsetsu*—as if, that is to say, it were a late Edo *yomihon*. Hakuchō was so acutely aware of the role that translation played in his intellectual life that he referred to himself as a "translationperson," but to an extent this was typical of Japanese writers of his generation. His suggestion that "even *Genji monogatari* would be more interesting when read in an English translation," though, comes as a bit of a surprise. Hakuchō was not aware, when he wrote "Koten o yonde," that Waley had already published two volumes of *The Tale of Genji*, yet he imagines an English translation to be the vehicle that might make *Genji monogatari* legible to him as literature, allowing it to join "the *Iliad* and the *Odyssey* and so on" in the canon of the world's masterpieces, and thus to become more fully his own as a classic of Japan's national literary heritage.

When the League of Nations commenced operations in 1920, English and French became its two official languages. Beginning in the late 1920s and early 1930s, the deployment of sound-film technology by American movie companies—which had been left with scant European competition in the wake of World War I—set the stage for the gradual spread of English across much of the globe, not only as a language of diplomacy, but as a language of popular culture.[25] Silent film retained its popularity in Japan longer than in Europe, but the beginning of English's worldwide rise to prominence through diplomacy as well as entertainment is undeniably part of the context within which Hakuchō was writing in 1926. Physicist and essayist Terada Torahiko's resigned, good-humored acceptance of English in an essay about talkies, published in 1935, gives a sense of how ubiquitous American films were becoming, and with them the English language: "Talkies are movies that speak, it's true, but you don't have to make them speak just to hear them talk. . . . As for these American films, well, those of us who aren't acquainted with the language find their incessant chattering a bit grating, but I guess that can't be helped."[26] Terada was right, of course: it could not be helped—English was on the march.

And it was this increasingly global English that ultimately provided the impetus for Hakuchō to become more interested in *Genji*, just as it was a translation into English that would eventually make the tale itself "more interesting" for him. In November 1928, Hakuchō and his wife, who had profited enormously from the inclusion of a volume of Hakuchō's fiction in the successful series Library of Modern Japanese Literature (Gendai Nihon bungaku zenshū), set sail for San Francisco, their first stop on what would be a yearlong trip around the world.²⁷ This period abroad, which fulfilled a dream that Hakuchō had cherished for fifty years, brought more than he had anticipated: in Los Angeles, he and his wife were denied housing in an upscale area because they were Japanese, and when they purchased orchestra-section tickets for *The Taming of the Shrew*, they were given seats only at the edge of the last row.²⁸ In the face of such racism, Hakuchō found himself, against all expectation, "daydreaming about the glories of militarism"—a remarkable confession coming from a man so outspoken in condemning the wars he lived through that even the fictional narrator of Ibuse Masuji's novel *Black Rain* (*Kuroi ame*, 1966) recalled him expressing scorn for Hitler in *Yomiuri shinbun* at a time when "everyone else was jumping on the bandwagon."²⁹

And then there was the rediscovery I am concerned with here: his first, secondhand encounter with Waley's *The Tale of Genji*. In a piece written in London that ran in *Yomiuri shinbun* on July 7, 1929—right around the end of the phenomenal two-month run of Japan's first talkie, the Fox Movietone musical short *Marching On* (*Shingun*)³⁰—Hakuchō described how, on a train to Milan, the middle-aged Greek man with whom he and his wife shared a compartment had come to their aid, translating from Italian into English when a customs officer asked about their luggage:

> Now that this experience had brought us together, the man became quite friendly and started talking to me about this and that. When I asked what country he was from, he said he was Greek, that he was interested in Japan, and had read the works of Lafcadio Hearn, who was Greek by blood. . . . This Greek man informed me that he had read *The Tale of Genji* and heartily recommended it. An English translation of *Genji monogatari* seems to have attracted the interest of certain bookish Westerners. In New York a man named Mason, a famous aficionado of Japan, told me, "*Genji* must be counted among the ten greatest literary works of all time." His evaluation was biased, of course; but a lady I met at our hotel in Geneva said the same thing. . . . Personally, I find the work impossible to get through; but perhaps it's understandable that Western readers should be more receptive to Heian-period literature, with its deeper expressions of the nature of human feelings, than to Tokugawa works that depict the twisted lives people lived in those days.³¹

By then, four of the six volumes of Waley's *The Tale of Genji* had been published.³² The fourth of these closed with "Maboroshi" (Mirage), the last chapter in which Genji appears alive and the final of the so-called main chapters (*seihen*); readers had seen enough of Waley's translation to be able to judge it—in language that echoes Hakuchō's misrecollection of Gakkai's survey, but also Waley's preface to *The Tale of Genji*'s first volume—as one of the "ten greatest literary works of all time." In Europe and the United States, Waley's new iteration of *Genji* was finally completing the process that Suematsu's *Genji Monogatari* had initiated four decades earlier, rewriting the romance as a tale and establishing it more firmly, through the vehicle of the English language, as "a masterpiece of world literature."

Hakuchō's curiosity was piqued by what he had heard about the translation, and yet he seems to have made no attempt to obtain a copy. It was not until 1933, just a few months after the sixth and final volume was published, that coincidence placed *The Tale of Genji* in Hakuchō's hands:

> During a stay at the Imperial Hotel, I overhead a foreigner say that he had just finished the recently completed English translation of *Genji monogatari*. He was extraordinarily enthusiastic: "If one were to list up the ten greatest masterpieces in the world," he said, "this tale would certainly be one." Something in the way he praised the tale made it clear that this wasn't just polite nonsense, like when people say they find *kabuki* or *nō* drama so very *interesting*; the man sounded genuinely taken with the work. I couldn't imagine what in *Genji* this foreigner could have found so engaging, but his encomiums struck me so forcefully that I started wanting to read the book—that engaging English translation of *Genji monogatari*—myself. And in the hotel bookshop right in front of me, a smallish place that stocks books for foreigners, I found all six volumes of the translation.[33]

The critic Kobayashi Hideo once noted that apart from Motoori Norinaga, no major literary figure had praised *Genji* as fervently as had Hakuchō.[34] This may come as a surprise, considering the vehemence with which he lambasted the work's prose in "Koten o yonde"—"the writing is like a line of jellyfish, and totally prevents the tale from giving us any true impression of life"—but a glance at the two essays that Hakuchō published after his encounter with Waley's *The Tale of Genji* in 1933 is enough to confirm that Kobayashi was correct.[35] "Eiyaku *Genji monogatari*," which ran in the September issue of *Kaizō* (*Reconstruction*), and "Futatabi Eiyaku *Genji monogatari* ni tsukite," which appeared in three parts on November 15, 16, and 17 in *Tōkyō asahi shinbun* (*Tokyo Asahi Newspaper*), reveal how profound a change Waley's translation had wrought on Hakuchō's view of the tale. "I am feeling more interest than

I ever have in this, the greatest of Japan's classics," he announces at the beginning of "Eiyaku *Genji monogatari*." Then, after recounting his previous struggles with the text:

> I always found it a very boring book—limp and slippery and devoid of anything that might strike a chord in readers' hearts. But now, reading it in English, I find for the first time that I can follow the plot, I understand both the actions and the psychology of the male and female characters, and the narrative and descriptive passages have both become strikingly clear. One has the sense that, apart from specialists in the national literature, very few have read the famous *Genji monogatari* in its entirety with real appreciation—and that includes both authors and lovers of literature. I have the feeling, though, that if this English translation were translated anew into Japanese, it might attract a large and avid readership that would enjoy it as one of the great novels of the world.[36]

It is not going too far, I think, to suggest that in this passage we witness Hakuchō's rediscovery of *Genji* as a masterpiece of world literature. He is joining, as a translationperson, the community of readers that had grown up around *The Tale of Genji*—indeed, an article that ran in the *New York Times* in 1939 welcomes him to the fold, reporting that "a distinguished Japanese novelist and critic said that 'the tale could be better understood and appreciated through Waley's translation than in the original.'"[37] And Hakuchō goes further, gesturing toward the possibility that this community might be extended, translingually, still further: in "Koten o yonde," he had speculated that *Genji monogatari* would be more interesting in an English translation; now that he has read one, he suggests that back-translation would turn *Genji* into a masterpiece of world literature in Japan, as well.

This passage from "Eiyaku *Genji monogatari*" highlights a tension implicit in the idea of the national literary canon. Hakuchō points to the fact that a work can be "famous," and considered important to a nation's literary tradition, without in fact playing any role in the lives of the "authors and lovers of literature" who are, supposedly, the inheritors of that very tradition. This suggests that it requires more than the backing of authoritative figures such as "specialists in the national literature" to imbue a national literary canon with the real power of a perceived tradition. For a canon to become "national" in a manner that includes the present—which is, of course, the whole point of a national literary canon—either the citizenry must be educated to the point where they can read the texts on the list, and enjoy them as works of literature, or the texts themselves must be re-created in a recognizably, approachably literary form. Either way, readers must also be made to see the canon as specifically national: as something that represents, in their own eyes as well as in the eyes of the world, a culture that belongs to them and to which they belong.

These two points have frequently been overlooked by readers of Hakuchō's essays about *Genji*, particularly Japanese "specialists in the national literature," whose status is intimately connected to the canonical value of *Genji monogatari*. The critique "say what you like about the content, the writing is incomparably bad" has been circulating for more than eighty years, being called on to serve as a straw man, a metonymic figure of a deplorable attitude, in much the same manner as the misquoted line of Georges Bousquet's: *cette ennuyeuse Scudéry japonaise*. Except that in Hakuchō's case, it is not simply *Genji*'s value that dismissal of him bolsters, but a sense of national community rooted in a shared language—and, although this sentiment is never articulated in any of the citations I have seen, in the shared feeling that Japanese is threatened by English. "It is utterly laughable to think one can read Waley's translation and praise *Genji monogatari* based solely on that," one critic complains. "You just can't appreciate the flavor of a work from your motherland unless you read it in your mother tongue."[38] Or again, here is Akiyama Ken, an important scholar of *Genji monogatari*, also responding explicitly to Hakuchō: "However different [Heian-period] culture may be from our own, [*Genji monogatari*] can never be placed in the same category with literature in French and English, because of course it is still in the Japanese language."[39]

One may sympathize more or less with this perspective; the point I would like to make is that the presumption on which it relies—that Japanese citizens share a deeper connection to *Genji monogatari*'s language than they do, for instance, to English—is itself, in part, a by-product of Hakuchō's rediscovery of *Genji* as literature through Waley's translation. People had become interested in the language of *Genji monogatari* in the 1890s, it is true, whether or not they could read it; in 1933 the tale itself was all but illegible to non-specialists. This point is nicely made in a column that ran in *Yomiuri shinbun* on September 2, 1933, the day after the official publication date of the issue of *Kaizō* in which "Eiyaku *Genji monogatari*" was printed. The column, which appeared sporadically from August to November 1933, was called "Two Members of the Literary World and Their Prevarications" (Bundan futari anku).

This installment, peculiarly titled "A Discourse on Lowering Electricity Rates" (Dentō nesageron), is presented as a dialogue between two men, Sōkichi (Wavering Tom) and Jiyūjirō (Free John). Sōkichi starts out by asking if Jiyūjirō has read Hakuchō's panegyric on the English translation of *Genji*; Jiyūjirō replies that he has indeed and that he found it "the most novel thing I've seen in quite a while."[40] Jiyūjirō goes on to say that he agrees with Hakuchō rather than Sugimura Sojinkan (Sugimura Kōtarō), whose "Translation or Treason?" (Han'yaku ka hangyaku ka?) ran in the same issue of *Kaizō*. "Generally speaking," Jiyūjirō explains, "it kind of bugs me to hear folks arguing that translation is impossible. . . . That attitude's a bit too pretentious for my tastes, you see."[41] Here is how the conversation ends (Sōkichi is represented in the text by a circle, and Jiyūjirō by a triangle):

△: Hakuchō's view was intriguing. He didn't actually make this point, but you could say that for us, living in modern times, a text like *Genji* that's written in the old language is totally unreadable— it's only after you translate the thing into a foreign language that we can make sense of it, even if we do have to keep consulting the dictionary.

○: In other words horizontal beats vertical . . . you're saying that foreign countries are still closer than the past.

△: Yeah, I'm saying sometimes that might be the case. There's no necessity to keep insisting on tradition, tradition all the time.

○: Ha ha, so it's all about lowering the cost of electricity.

The final sentence, which gives the piece its seemingly non-sequiturial title, contains a pun on the homophones *dentō* (tradition) and *dentō* (electric light), and thus calls up the interpretation: "So it's all about lowering the cost of tradition."

For the participants in this fictional dialogue, the interest in Hakuchō's "Eiyaku *Genji monogatari*" lies not in his frustrated comparison of *Genji monogatari*'s prose with that of its translation—"the original may be concise, but its sentences are like bodies with their heads chopped off, tottering unsteadily this way and that"[42]—but in his affirmation of the possibilities of translation, and in his view of the world as a place where time, not space, creates the most extreme, least bridgeable gaps. Hakuchō speculated that if a translation like Waley's were available in Japan, Japanese readers "would enjoy it as one of the great novels of the world," and one gets the impression that Sōkichi and Jiyūjirō might be among them. In the strange economics of canonization, the less it costs to participate in the act of paying homage to a classic, the more that classic's value rises.

Enter Yosano Akiko

Hakuchō's vision of Japanese readers relishing a back-translation of Waley's *The Tale of Genji* would be realized literally in 2008, when the first volume of Samata Hideki's *Ueirī-ban Genji monogatari* (*The Waley Tale of Genji*) was issued, just in time for the millennial brouhaha.[43] At the same time, it also raises the question of what we are to make of the four-volume, first-ever complete translation of *Genji monogatari* into modern Japanese that the celebrated poet, scholar, and translator Yosano Akiko published in 1912 and 1913: the misleadingly titled *Shin'yaku Genji monogatari* (*Genji monogatari: A New Translation*), which has, in fact, often been compared with Waley's translation. Both adopt a flexible, domesticating approach in their handling of the details, tending at times—particularly in the case of the early chapters of *Shin'yaku Genji monogatari*—to prune and condense, and to rewrite; both remain, to this day, eminently readable.

In *Yosano Akiko and The Tale of Genji*, her persuasive and deeply insightful monograph on the subject of Akiko's professional and personal involvement with *Genji monogatari*, G. G. Rowley notes "the irony that, in the end, it was Yosano Akiko—self-taught, a disciple of no one, and with no ideological axe to grind—who actually achieved what scholars of National Literature had been aiming to do since they published the first moveable type editions of *Genji* in 1890."[44] This is unquestionably true: Akiko created a literary version of *Genji monogatari* capable of suggesting to ordinary, non-specialist readers of Japanese that, as the scholar Sassa Seisetsu put it, *Genji monogatari* was "the unrivaled treasure of our nation and as such, something worth boasting about to all the nations of the world."[45] Indeed, the publication of *Shin'yaku Genji monogatari* stands as a watershed in the history of *Genji monogatari* discourse in Japan, not only because it is the first complete, if somewhat compressed, translation into the modern-Japanese vernacular, but because the discourse that grew up around it helped spread the notion that *Genji monogatari* is unique in the world and that it somehow represents Japan. It contributed materially, that is to say, to the creation of two of the three conceptual lines that delineate the field within which the tale is read today: *Genji* as world literature, and *Genji* as a work that exists first and foremost in translation. It would be another decade until the third line materialized, as reports of the success of Waley's *The Tale of Genji* began to circulate in Japanese newspapers and journals, promoting an image of *Genji* as a work that participates in world literature through translation.[46] It would be another fifteen years after that until Hakuchō and Tanizaki hammered the triangle together.

Akiko's translation—published by Kanao Bun'endō with breathtakingly gorgeous woodblock-printed boxes, covers, end pieces, and illustrations by the Western-style painter and print artist Nakazawa Hiromitsu (1874–1964)—received enthusiastic reviews in major literary magazines and newspapers, and appears to have sold quite well considering that each volume cost 3 yen—enough to pay for a seven-mile ride in one of the six Model-T taxis (*tsujimachi jidōsha*) that began running in Tokyo the same year and triple the price per volume of a two-volume edition of the classical text published in 1912.[47] The best-selling novelist Tokutomi Roka, a good friend of Kanao Bun'en (Kanao Tanejirō), who ran the publishing house Kanao Bun'endō, provides rare, if indirect, evidence of the volumes' brisk sales in a diary entry dated December 2, 1914: "Kanao Bun'en came by. I had a feeling he might drop in to see me sometime soon. The economic downturn has really taken its toll on the man. He keeps getting returns from the country, he said, volume after volume—everything, that is, but *The Stepchild* [*Nasanu naka*, 1913] and *Shin'yaku Genji monogatari*."[48]

Anyone who purchased *Shin'yaku Genji monogatari* would immediately have been struck by its modern, cosmopolitan aura. This was true of its vocabulary, its prose style, the layout of the text, the reworking of the poetry, and above all the narrative structure itself: as Rowley has shown, "Where Murasaki made her narrator both a participant in and an observer of the world of the text through the use of deferential and humilific language, Akiko's paring away of *keigo* marks her narrator as someone 'outside' the world of the text."[49] Kitamura Yuika makes the same point in reference to Akiko's second translation, *Shin-shin'yaku Genji monogatari* (*Genji monogatari: A New New Translation*, 1938–1939), in terms that resonate with my earlier discussion of Gakkai and Hakuchō and their contrasting conceptions of the literary world. "Yosano Akiko catapulted *Genji monogatari*," Kitamura writes, "into the matrix of reception that characterizes the modern novel [*kindai no shōsetsu*]: Author–Work–Reader."[50]

Akiko's translation of *Genji monogatari* into the literary field of late Meiji and early Taishō Japan constituted not only a modern replacement of the classical text, but also a replacement of an old image of *Genji monogatari*, in which the tale was linked to works in the tradition of the Sino-Japanese *haishi-shōsetsu*, above all *Inaka Genji*, with an image of it as part of the broader world of the *shōsetsu*-qua-novel. An air of cosmopolitan modernity inheres in the book's material form as well: its volumes are startlingly heavy, printed on thick *torinoko* paper with gilded edges; the title is printed in gold on the spines; and, most important, there are Nakazawa's delicately colored, beautifully composed woodblock prints. Covering every surface of all four boxes, decorating the covers and spines of each volume, and interspersed at fifty-seven points throughout the book, the prints' compositions, delicate pastel palette, and luxuriant landscapes clearly display the artist's engagement with transnational artistic trends such as Art Nouveau, even as they reference the long history of artistic representations of scenes in *Genji monogatari*.

Consider, for instance, the front covers of *Shin'yaku Genji monogatari*'s first and last volumes (figures 121 and 122). It comes as no surprise to find a depiction of Murasaki Shikibu gazing out over Lake Biwa on the cover of volume 1: here, Nakazawa cleaves quite close to convention. The enormous silver moon, the inclusion of red foliage to suggest the season, the shape of the lattice window behind Murasaki Shikibu, and the type of perspective used all point back to earlier precedents. Yet rather than show Murasaki Shikibu seated inside at a long, low table, Nakazawa has her standing in full view on a veranda—and looking, moreover, decidedly, *realistically* rumpled. This is, in fact, a rather modern Murasaki Shikibu. Unlike most conventional portraits of Murasaki Shikibu, which tend to show her engaged in the act of writing *Genji monogatari*, Nakazawa's depicts her with a book in her hand, reading—a tellingly circular gesture that seems to establish a parallel between Murasaki Shikibu and the reader, almost making it appear that Murasaki Shikibu is inviting her readers to take up their pens and write. And still this is one of the most conventional of Nakazawa's designs: the cover of volume 4 is more typical, with its sleek, stylized take on the clouds ubiquitous in Japanese art; its brilliant repetition, and reversal, of the two pairs of men (Kaoru and Niou and their attendants); its subdued greens, blue, yellow, red, and gray; and its almost overbearing bamboo, which seems like a huge, out-of-control echo of the red Japanese maple on the cover of volume 1.

Something of the effect that *Shin'yaku Genji monogatari* must have had on many of its readers, both through its material form and as a novelistic rewriting of *Genji monogatari*, is suggested by the manner in which Miyamoto Yuriko (1899-1951), an author of proletarian fiction and criticism, responded to it in her youth. When Gakkai and the Meiji empress Shōken read *Genji monogatari*, it made them want to go back and reread *Inaka Genji*; Miyamoto was inspired not to go and read anything, but to write a novel of her own, two of whose characters were called Murasaki and—"using the name of the hero of a tale that is on everyone's lips these days"—Hikaru Kimi, the "Shining Lord."[51] Indeed, Miyamoto was even inspired to copy *Shin'yaku Genji monogatari* as a translation, and as a book: "I imitated it," she wrote in 1935, "by doing a vernacular rewriting of Saikaku's *Nippon eitaigura* [*The Eternal Storehouse of Japan*,

Figure 121 The cover of volume 1 of Yosano Akiko's *Shin'yaku Genji monogatari*. (Courtesy of the author)

Figure 122 The cover of volume 4 of Yosano's *Shin'yaku Genji monogatari*. (Courtesy of the author)

1688] or something, putting a cover on it and binding it—I used to sit around gazing lovingly at that book."[52]

Just as important as the style of *Shin'yaku Genji monogatari* itself, both as a text and as a book, was the manner in which it was promoted. Akiko traveled to Europe from May to October 1912, and before she left she told a newspaper reporter that while she would temporarily suspend other activities during this trip, she planned "to keep working on the translation of *Genji monogatari* that she is now engaged in on the boat and train to Europe, and even while she is traveling in Europe."[53] In her afterword to the fourth volume, Akiko notes that while in France, she visited Auguste Rodin and presented him with copies of volumes 1 and 2. He admired Nakazawa's illustrations, she writes, and told her, "I bitterly regret being unable to read Japanese, but I trust that one day in the future I shall be able to appreciate the thought of this book through the medium of a friend's translation."[54] Both these statements of Akiko's present *Genji monogatari*, in the form of *Shin'yaku Genji monogatari*, as a book that can travel—which is to say, in a rudimentary fashion, as a sort of world literature.

And sure enough, an enormous advertisement announcing the manuscript's completion and the imminent release of the third volume that ran on the front page of *Yomiuri shinbun* on August 19, 1913, invokes the notion not of world literature per se, but of "world art," and appeals explicitly to national pride. A small box at the ad's bottom-right corner reads:

> A Miracle in the History of World Art—*Genji monogatari!*
> Reborn into the Taishō Literary World—*Genji monogatari!*

And the ad copy continues:

> We deem it a MIRACLE of world history and an eternal source of PRIDE for Japanese civilization that in the tenth century, in an age when European art history had as yet nothing worth passing down, the woman poet Murasaki Shikibu appeared in the Extreme Orient and, in the manner of a PURE ARTIST altogether unimpeded by the constraints of tradition, composed the fifty-four chapters of her unprecedented masterpiece of a novel GENJI MONOGATARI, which depicted the emotional daily lives of members of aristocratic society in the ca-

pital of the time without swerving into idealism, writing, quite by coincidence, in the same style referred to in recent times as REALism or IMPRESSIONism. The original text is in the old language, written some thousand years ago, and is by no means easy to read; and while there are commentaries, by and large they offer but twisted interpretations of characters and phrases, and do not convey its true appeal. Not long ago, when Mrs. Yosano AKIKO took up her brush to attempt what none before her ever had, and after long years of arduous labor published two volumes of her SHIN'YAKU GENJI MONOGATARI, all the cognoscenti raved that the tale had found THE BEST POSSIBLE TRANSLATOR. This vast enterprise was made possible only by dint of this woman writer's PROFOUND KNOWLEDGE of the literature and history of the Heian court and her sharp INTUITIVE GRASP of the emotions and mood and of the age. Having returned recently from Europe, she kept adding to the manuscript of her *Shin'yaku*, and now having concluded the two volumes of the third book, she has finished her COMPLETE TRANSLATION. At last, the great woman writer Akiko, A MODERN MURASAKI SHIKIBU, has turned *Genji monogatari* into a masterpiece of a novel IN THE MODERN LANGUAGE capable of being easily appreciated by anyone. In addition, FIFTY-FOUR ILLUSTRATIONS by the great painter NAKAZAWA—all full-color woodblock prints on the highest quality paper, that echo the content in their DAZZLING GORGEOUSNESS, ENTRANCING BEAUTY, and endless variety—enhance the brilliance of this COLLABORATION between TWO BRILLIANT WOMEN of two periods: Heian and Taishō.⁵⁵

Advertisements heralding the publication of the fourth volume—"part three, volume two" (*gekan dai ni*)—took the same approach and used some of the same phrases.⁵⁶

Clearly, *Shin'yaku Genji monogatari* succeeded in making *Genji monogatari* accessible as a modernized classic, replacing it in the Taishō literary field both as a work of global significance and as a work that might best be approached through the medium of translation. Why, then, was it necessary for Hakuchō to wait two decades after its publication to discover the tale, as he did, through *The Tale of Genji*? He was almost certainly aware of the existence of Akiko's *Shin'yaku Genji monogatari*, not simply because of the attention it received—reviews appeared in literary journals such as *Bunshō sekai* (*World of Writing*) and *Shinchō* (*New Tide*), both of which he contributed to in those years and is likely to have at least skimmed on a regular basis, and, as we have seen, the translation was the subject of a substantial publicity campaign that included front-page newspaper advertisements—but also because Kanao Bun'endō published Hakuchō's novel *Ikiryō* (*The Living Spirit*) in 1913, the same year that the second two volumes of *Shin'yaku Genji monogatari* appeared.[57]

The answer is, I think, surprisingly simple. In one of the translation's two forewords, the poet, literary critic, and translator Ueda Bin (1874–1916) lauds Akiko's achievement as "a happy event for the literary world," and suggests that Akiko was "the right person at the right time."[58] Rowley invokes Bin's assertion that it was "the right time" for a colloquial translation of *Genji monogatari* as a starting point for her contextualization of Akiko's work with respect to the less successful efforts of Sassa and other Japanese literary historians, from whose perspective a readable modern-Japanese rendering of *Genji* was in fact long overdue. Seen from a literary rather than a scholarly point of view, however, there is a sense in which Bin's "right time" appears overly optimistic: 1912 to 1913 was, in certain ways, subtly wrong.

Ueda Bin's foreword to *Shin'yaku Genji monogatari* was accompanied by a second one written by Mori Ōgai. The recruitment of these two men made perfect sense for several reasons: Kanao Bun'en had published books by each of them—Bin's *Lectures on Literature* (*Bungei kōwa*) was issued in 1907; *Sabishiki hitobito*, Ōgai's translation of Gerhart Hauptmann's drama *Einsame Menschen* (*Lonely Lives*, 1891), appeared in 1911—and both were intimate enough with Akiko and her husband, Tekkan, to be asked to name their children.[59] This intimacy extended to their writing lives, as well: both Bin and Ōgai had been deeply involved with the magazine *Myōjō* (*Morning Star*), a publication firmly centered around the Yosanos, and when *Myōjō* ceased publication in November 1908, Bin and Ōgai led the way in founding its successor, *Subaru* (*Pleiades*), the inaugural issue of which reached bookstores in January 1909.

The establishment of *Subaru* is now seen as one of the events that precipitated the emergence of the New Romantic School (Shinromanha) and the Aesthetic School (Tanbiha), both potently anti-Naturalist in character. Shimazaki Tōson's *Family* (*Ie*) and Tokuda Shūsei's *Mold* (*Kabi*), two monuments of Naturalist literature in Japan, were completed in 1911, and powerful works in a Naturalist vein by Hakuchō and other writers would continue to appear over the next decade, but in 1912 Bin had the sense that Japanese literature was on the verge of a new departure. It is in precisely this context that I suggest we read his claim that it was "the right time" for Akiko's translation of *Genji monogatari* and his description of its publication as "a happy event for the literary world."

Ōgai, however, was rather less optimistic. "Is it necessary to have *Genji monogatari* translated into the modern vernacular?" he asks at the beginning of his foreword, and continues:

> No doubt it would be fitting for me to try to answer this question, here in the foreword to this book.
>
> When we ask, simply and straightforwardly, whether such a translation is necessary, surely we are asking, to speak more precisely, whether the age requires it. And that is a very difficult question for someone as thoughtless as myself to take up.
>
> So I would like to sidestep that question, approaching the problem of the necessity, or lack of necessity, of this translation from a different angle, so that I can indeed sink my teeth into the matter. I would like, that is to say, to shift the question to the level of my own person.
>
> If someone were to ask me whether I should like to have a text of *Genji monogatari*, translated into the modern vernacular, I would reply, without hesitation, that I do. I feel very keenly the need for a translation of this tale.[60]

Ōgai agrees with Bin that "no one now alive is better suited to translate *Genji monogatari* than Yosano Akiko,"[61] but unlike Bin, who hopes that Akiko's *Genji* will help change the course of Japanese literature, he seems skeptical that the time is right. The problem was, I would suggest, that while the influence of Naturalist theory was beginning to wane, it would take time for people, particularly members of the "literary world" Bin mentioned, to revise their understanding of what counted as literature and, most important, to come to see classical literary works as useful models for a new, perhaps avant-garde literary practice. Writing in 1951, Hakuchō recalled that

> the classics were even more violently shunned in the age of Naturalism [than they had been in the Meiji period]. It goes without saying that *Genji monogatari* and the like were viewed with scorn. Indeed, setting aside the issue of how much or little they thought of the work, I think it would be fair to say that almost no one in the literary world had read it in its entirety.... *Genji monogatari* was something Kokugaku scholars read; it wasn't thought of as something modern literati should be reading.[62]

Even Natsume Sōseki, who looked somewhat askance at Naturalism, wrote in 1910 that "one feels a bit forlorn when one looks back with new eyes at Japan's past. . . . People may point to *Genji monogatari*, Chikamatsu, and Saikaku, seeing in them signs of genius sufficient to illumine our past, but ultimately I find myself unable to muster that species of self-satisfaction."[63] Akutagawa Ryūnosuke, who was involved in the third and fourth series of the journal *Shinshichō* (*New Thought*) and the associated anti-Naturalist "New Thought School," makes the same observation as Hakuchō in his essay "Literary, All Too Literary" (Bungeitekina, amari ni bungeitekina, 1927), except that he is writing not about the earlier heyday of Naturalism, but about the present literary coterie: "I have encountered any number of people who praise *Genji monogatari*. But only two of the writers I associate with actually read the work (even setting aside the question of whether they understood or enjoyed it): Tanizaki Jun'ichirō and Akashi Toshio."[64] Indeed, as late as 1936, Dazai Osamu offered this dubious take on the tale:

> I once saw a newsreel of the sick Trotsky strolling around the city where he would die, Pompeii, seeing the sights. Tears came to my eyes, I was so moved. Our own situation is precisely the same, as we face the classics. I don't think that *Genji monogatari* itself is all that great a work. Doubtless it comes to seem very rare and special as we think of all the gusty, rainy centuries that intervene between it and us, and when we realize that, buried in frost and moss, it still resonates with us here in the twentieth century. No one would praise *Genji monogatari* if you wrote it today.[65]

All of which is to say that Akiko's *Shin'yaku Genji monogatari* was ahead of its time. It was a powerful, brilliantly executed work of literature in its own right, and was well received as such, but the timing of its publication made it difficult for it to do more than initiate the long process of redefining the relationship of Japan's literary present to what was not yet really seen as its past—of replacing *Genji monogatari* in the contemporary literary field and helping ordinary readers learn to see it as a work that represented, in their own eyes and in those of foreign readers, the pinnacle of Japanese literary tradition. It is telling that Miyamoto Yuriko, who was so taken with *Shin'yaku Genji monogatari* in her early teens and who continued to refer to *Genji monogatari* throughout her career, later described her fascination with Akiko's translation and the influence it had exerted upon her as "cute" (*kawaiirashii*).[66] One might argue, perhaps, that in an age when women writers were seldom taken as seriously as their male counterparts, a "COLLABORATION between TWO BRILLIANT WOMEN," as the advertisement quoted earlier put it, was still bound to seem more the stuff of schoolgirl dreams than proper, serious, male literature: in "Koten o yonde," Hakuchō would note that "Murasaki Shikibu was a brilliant woman, but a brilliant woman is still a woman. Her grasp of human nature was shallow."[67]

There is another sense in which *Shin'yaku Genji monogatari*—or, rather, the attempt to promote *Genji monogatari* as a work of global importance—came a bit too early. What reason, after all, did readers have to believe this? It was true that Akiko had made a present of the first two volumes to Rodin, but he could do no more than admire the illustrations and "bitterly regret being unable to read Japanese." Hardly anyone in Japan in the second decade of the twentieth century knew of the existence of Suematsu Kenchō's *Genji Monogatari*, let alone of the considerable success it had enjoyed abroad—even biographies of Suematsu written during his life mentioned the translation in passing, if at all.[68] To speak of *Genji monogatari* as a miracle on a global scale sounded perhaps, as Sōseki had said, like a species of self-satisfaction. Indeed, even the notion that *Genji monogatari* could be regarded as a novel, and enjoyed in the same way as any other work in that genre, would likely have seemed outlandish.

"Literature" as it had been conceptualized in Japan since the mid- to late Meiji period, and above all as it was lived during the heady days of the Taishō period, was always either something that characterized the Western world and had to be created in Japan or something that existed everywhere, at least in potential. This being the case, the best way to introduce a famous unread classic to the nation's citizenry—to induce the majority of the populace to recognize themselves in it and see themselves as its inheritors—was to elevate it through the medium of translation into a *foreign* language, to the status of a work of world literature. It would, perhaps, be going too far to say that the inscription of *Genji* into this translational loop was a necessary condition of its enshrinement as a true national classic, but in the end this is the path that was taken.

The publication of *The Tale of Genji*—described by Raymond Mortimer as "A New Planet" in his review of the first volume—set the ball rolling. It spawned a perfect balance, launching *Genji* into an orbit defined by the dialectical pull between the centrifugal force of world literature and the centripetal force of national literature. When the dancer Doris Humphrey arrived in Japan to tour with the Denishawn Dancers in August 1925, an interviewer reported that "one book never left her side for a moment during the whole long boat voyage to Japan, and that was an English translation of *Genji monogatari*, which is being taken up around the world as a work of Japanese national literature."[69] Someday, Humphrey explained, she hoped to choreograph and perform a dance based on the Uji chapters. The image of Humphrey on the boat, *The Tale of Genji* her constant companion, forms a perfect counterpart to that of Yosano Akiko working on her own translation during her boat and train ride to Europe. The circle these two women drew around the globe shows us *Genji* in the process of its literal, material replacement.

Humphrey's dance, too, when she danced it, would be suspended in the same orbit, a figure of both national and world literature, and would find its own future echoes—in a staging in 1995 at the Japan Society in New York of the dance *The Tale of Genji* by choreographer Saeko Ichinohe, for instance, which featured "a decidedly nontraditional mixed-race cast . . . performing theater and dance that mixed Western contemporary and Asian traditional styles."[70] The rediscovery of *Genji monogatari* as modern literature, a potential source of inspiration for contemporary artistic creation of the sort practiced by dancers as groundbreaking as Humphrey and Ichinohe—the linking, in short, of the present with the past—would be made possible in Japan and persuasive abroad by the circulation, within Japan, of a readable version of the tale marked as something that was more than a local product. This is precisely what Hakuchō was gesturing toward in 1933 when he wrote of *The Tale of Genji* that "if this English translation were translated anew into Japanese, it might attract a large and avid readership that would enjoy it as one of the great novels of the world."

Censoring *Genji monogatari*

And Hakuchō ends up being right, of course. It is the appearance of a steadily increasing stream of translations of *Genji monogatari* into various styles of modern Japanese, and of a wide range of "intersemiotic translations"—beginning in 1951 with a series of successful kabuki plays and continuing with any number of radio dramas, movies, television series, long-selling *manga*, and even cell-phone novels—that finally makes it possible and pleasurable for ordinary non-specialists in Japan to connect to *Genji*. It is translation, in the end, that makes *Genji* "ours."

The particular translation that paved the way for the tale's rapid rise to prominence during the postwar period is the first of Tanizaki Jun'ichirō's three modern-Japanese renderings, published in the midst of the Second Sino-Japanese War, between January 1939 and July 1941: *Jun'ichirō-yaku Genji monogatari* (*Genji monogatari: The Jun'ichirō Translation*), customarily referred to as the "old translation" (*kyūyaku*). The book was published by subscription in twenty-six volumes and sold in two versions: the "popular edition" (*fukyūban*), reasonably priced at 1 yen per volume, and the "collector's edition" (*aizōbon*), issued in a limited run of a thousand copies, each furnished with a custom-made paulownia-wood box signed and stamped by Tanizaki inside its lid, which sold for 80 yen.[71] The popular edition was one of the biggest literary best sellers of 1939: no sooner had the first 150,000 copies of volumes 1 and 2 been printed than Chūōkōronsha, the publisher, was inundated with 50,000 more orders.[72] Sales were so good, in fact, that the wartime shortage of paper made it difficult to respond to the demand for new copies, as newspaper advertisements apologizing for delays in the distribution of the second two volumes reveal.[73] The collector's edition, which soon came to be called the "heirloom collector's edition" (*kahōyō aizōbon*), seems to have sold out in a little more than a month.[74]

Tanizaki's "old translation" is notable for having put *Genji monogatari* on the Japanese literary map as a work that "ordinary people might read in much the way they read an ordinary modern novel," as Tanizaki put it in his preface, describing his aim as a translator.[75] Tanizaki's readers were acutely conscious of the pivotal role that his translation played: Chino Shōshō, a poet and a scholar of German literature who had been associated with both *Myōjō* and *Subaru* and was surely aware of *Shin'yaku Genji monogatari*, observed in *Tōkyō asahi shinbun* in 1939 that as a result of Tanizaki's work, "for the first time, ordinary national citizens [*kokumin taishū*] have been given an opportunity to see for themselves wherein the literary value of this celebrated tale resides."[76] *Jun'ichirō-yaku Genji monogatari* is remarkable, too, for having accomplished this replacement of the tale by means of a veritable blitz of advertising that shrewdly played on the dialectical pull between world and national literature, establishing *Genji monogatari* as the work that best represented Japan to the world. This outpouring of new discourse and the replacement of *Genji monogatari* that it enabled are the focus of my discussion of Tanizaki's work.

It is impossible to discuss this translation, however, without at least touching on its infamy as an example of wartime censorship, or perhaps self-censorship: Tanizaki, working with Yamada Yoshio (1873–1958)—an eminent scholar of Japanese language and literature and one of the editors of the Ministry of Education's manual *Kokutai no hongi* (*Cardinal Principles of the National Entity of Japan*, 1937)—scrupulously expunged every reference to Genji's sexual liaisons with women who were, or would be, intimately involved with an emperor. This includes not only Genji's secret affair with his stepmother, Fujitsubo, which leads to the birth of the future emperor Reizei, but also his relationship with Oborozukiyo, the daughter of the powerful Minister of the Right, who had a good chance of becoming the next empress. Needless to say, the excision of Genji's affair with Fujitsubo obscures the fact that Emperor Reizei is his son, and thus a commoner by birth. Tanizaki also suppressed Genji's attainment of the rank of honorary retired emperor. All three of these changes have profound consequences for the tale and show particularly clearly what I mean when I say that classical texts are not simply "received," but are replaced.

Scholars writing in both Japanese and English have considered the roles of Tanizaki and Yamada in the bowdlerization of *Genji monogatari*. Until recently, the general tendency was to put the bulk of the blame on Yamada, who is routinely described, with good reason, as a "rightist": Ken K. Ito, for instance, suggests that Tanizaki was "willing to go to almost any length in order to translate *Genji monogatari*," including "doing violence to a text that he loved," as he had to do when Yamada "insisted on expunging all references to Genji's act of lèse-majesté."[77] Kobayashi Masaaki takes a similar approach, suggesting that Yamada, who "worked at the front lines of the wartime propaganda machine," was "identified as a proofreader (*kōetsusha*) but in practice also acted as a censor (*ken'etsusha*)."[78] And Eric M. Cazdyn writes that Tanizaki seems to have edited the work "to satisfy the military government and right-wing critics such as Yamada Yoshio."[79]

The notion that Yamada was ultimately responsible for what now seems a rather absurd—and thus all the more chilling—attempt to bend a classical work of fiction to the wartime ideology of "a line of emperors unbroken for ages eternal" (*banseiikkei*) is supported by Tanizaki's own account of his first encounter with the man who would check his work: no sooner had he stepped into Yamada's house in Sendai, Tanizaki writes, than Yamada demanded, in a manner "that could not have been more vehement," that he expunge three of the elements of the tale that were, in the end, eliminated.[80] And blaming Yamada *feels* right because, in part, it allows us to safeguard an image of Tanizaki as an essentially "resistant" writer—to praise his virtues and chastise Yamada for his obvious ideological vices. In an academic climate that highlights the inevitable intermingling of aesthetics, artistry, and politics, it is more comfortable to enjoy the work of a seemingly radical, politically provocative artist than it would be to admire, for instance, the magnificent self-indulgences of a man who may not have cared much what happened to the world as long as he was paid.

Cazdyn, who notes that "concession and collaboration" are indeed "part of the story," presents the figure of the resistant Tanizaki particularly compellingly:

> Tanizaki was surely mindful of the most significant effect of censorship—that it usually foregrounds and highlights precisely what it wishes to expel and bury. In other words, even though Tanizaki's first translation makes no mention of the ascension to the throne by the son born to Genji and his [step]mother, this element (no doubt one that the playful and taboo-transcending Tanizaki would normally seize and exploit) cannot help but pervade the translation despite—or because of—its expurgation.[81]

As Kobayashi points out, Tanizaki actually *marks* the absence of the suppressed sections in both his introduction and his afterword to the "old translation."[82] From a certain perspective, it may even be possible to read a sort of convoluted, Tanizakian pleasure into his subtly contradictory insistence that the cuts both *had* to be made and do not matter at all:

> The truth is that there were, in the plan of the original, elements that it would be improper to transplant just as they are into the modern world, and I have neatly excised all trace of them, and only them. (These elements actually constitute only a tiny portion of the whole and, as Dr. Yamada has noted, even their complete and utter erasure has hardly any influence on the tale's development as a whole, since they are not central to the plot.)[83]

The phrases "I have neatly excised all trace of them" (*kirei ni sakujo shite shimatta*) and "even their complete and utter erasure" (*sono kotogotoku o massatsu shisattemo*) seem almost too cloyingly forthright. They are reminiscent of the masochistic pleasure that Sasuke takes in blinding himself in Tanizaki's novel *A Portrait of Shunkin* (*Shunkinshō*, 1933), ostensibly to avoid shaming Shunkin by witnessing her disfigurement, but also to "see" her old perfection in his mind's eye.[84] Or of the narrator of *The Key* (*Kagi*, 1965), confiding "secrets" to his diary in full, titillating knowledge that his wife will read them there. One detects, perhaps, a hint of staged eroticism in Tanizaki's narrative manipulation of *Genji monogatari*, his willing submission to "the authorities," his open concealment of a scandalous affair.

Maybe this should have made us suspicious. In the end, though, it took the pioneering research of the scholar Nishino Atsushi to question the presumption of Tanizaki's relative innocence. In a series of essays centering on the copy of *Genji monogatari* that Yamada used when he corrected Tanizaki's translation, marking it in the margins with the words *kezureri* (deleted) and *kezuru* (delete), Nishino presents a well-supported and nuanced case against Tanizaki, arguing not that he, rather than Yamada, was alone responsible for censoring *Genji monogatari*, but that he acted as an agent for a broader community that bore collective responsibility:

> *Genji monogatari*'s surrender to the tall tale of the "national entity" was not wholly a consequence of pressure from Yamada. Rather, it was Tanizaki who devoted himself most assiduously to the task of carrying out the deletions, going so far as to make inquiries with the Home Ministry. But if everyone involved expected Yamada Yoshio to perform that role, perhaps Tanizaki simply took it on himself, and did the job more thoroughly. Yamada would later recollect, "There are elements of *Genji monogatari* that were likely to have the book banned on moral grounds if they were openly rewritten in the modern language. This was my biggest concern, right from the beginning, but Tanizaki masterfully excised those elements, and did so in such a way that it all hung together perfectly." . . . Perhaps Tanizaki had just internalized Yamada's intentions, skillfully putting himself in Yamada's place, acting out his role.
>
> At the same time, there is that letter of Tanizaki's: "Even if the authorities gave it a pass, I do think it would be best to head off any troubles that might arise in the world at large with regard to certain sections." When he wrote these words, Tanizaki was not acting on behalf of Yamada Yoshio, or on behalf of the censors. It was "society at large" that concerned him, "even if the authorities gave it a pass." When Tanizaki makes his cuts, fretting about society at large, the censoring subject is no longer Tanizaki or anyone else. The deletions simply happen. No single individual is acting.[85]

The question remains, of course, as to how accurate Tanizaki's assessment of the situation was: perhaps he could have gotten away with more than he did—assuming that he got away with anything. In fact, appealing as it is to believe that Tanizaki was somehow resisting censorship even as he practiced it, the climate in 1939 would not have primed readers to be receptive to his subversive message. If anything, Tanizaki was probably right that bringing the classic in line with wartime ideology rendered it more palatable—not only to the Home Ministry, but to many readers as well. Okazaki Yoshie, who published a stern critique of the first four volumes of the old translation in *Tōkyō asahi shinbun* in May 1939, faulted Tanizaki for "cutting out the spinal cord of this world classic," but nonetheless described the deletions ironically as "a bonus" (*omake*) and observed, "Presumably they made [the translation] still more perfectly suited to a popular readership."[86] He seems to have understood the ameliorative urge behind the censorship, that is to say, even if he himself condemned it.

Neither was this patronizing recognition of the "need" for censorship new. Kobayashi Eiko, who had herself published a modernized version of *Genji monogatari*, spoke approvingly of censorship in 1935 when she recalled an infamous incident in 1933 in which the Tokyo Metropolitan Police suddenly banned a scheduled performance of a theatrical adaptation of *Genji monogatari*. "Young men and women . . . would only have ended up letting themselves go, getting into a lecherous mood," she wrote. "There was a good deal of debate, but personally I'm delighted that the police did us all a favor and put a stop to it."[87] In the end, as Nishino suggests, Tanizaki and his desires matter less than the discursive field that made his translation what it became, even as his translation reconfigured the field.

This dialectical collusion between the pressure brought to bear on *Genji monogatari*—and thus on *Jun'ichirō-yaku Genji monogatari* and any attempt at resistance that it may have embodied—and the effect of Tanizaki's translation on the image of *Genji monogatari* is strikingly expressed in the conclusion to *Murasaki Shikibu* (1943), a study by Shimazu Hisamoto, a prominent scholar of Japanese literature. Not surprisingly, Murasaki Shikibu was the subject of a surge in interest that coincided with the appearance of Tanizaki's translation: the New Year 1939 issue of *Fujin kōron* (*Women's Forum*), published by Chūōkōronsha, included a story by Kamitsukasa Shōken titled "Murasaki Shikibu"; the April 1939 issue of *Ōru yomimono* (*All Reading Material*) featured Yoshiya Nobuko's "Murasaki Shikibu: A Historical Story" (Rekishi shōsetsu Murasaki Shikibu); and in February 1939, Sugita Shōten, the manufacturer of the "medicinal cream" Ammon Papaya, ran a new advertisement claiming that it had been clearing up pimples, freckles, frostbite, and other conditions "since the age of [Murasaki] Shikibu and [Sei Shō]nagon."[88] Shimazu's book meshed with this renewed fascination with Murasaki Shikibu, but presented an image of her different from any we have encountered so far:

> Consider this passage from the "Usugumo" [Wisps of Cloud] chapter, which celebrates the Imperial Line in its unbroken continuity for ages

eternal: "In Cathay there had been innumerable irregularities, some open and some concealed. No example of the kind was to be found in Japan." In these words, expressing the author's absolute conviction, one sees the Japanese spirit spitting in the eye of a great foreign nation—and one sees, too, the flickering of Murasaki Shikibu's national consciousness and idealism. . . . Yes, in her insistence on the centrality of the Imperial House and her self-awareness as a Japanese, Murasaki Shikibu was a good Imperial citizen, a truly Japanese writer. She is counted among the great women of Japanese history, but surely it is also entirely fitting that, in a slightly different sense, more lofty and more impressive, she be described as one of the great women of the Empire. . . . Thus, achieving the highest rank of distinguished service for having achieved world dominance as a literary soldier of Japan, Murasaki Shikibu will live eternally in the hearts of our nation's citizenry as the model of all an Imperial woman should be.[89]

Not only does this passage function as a sort of synecdochical portrait of the discursive field into which Tanizaki's translation replaced *Genji monogatari*, but it borrows one of the translation's techniques. In a sense, Shimazu censors the quotation with which he begins by omitting the next sentence: "And even if something like that happened, how, if it was kept that well hidden, could knowledge of it have been passed on?"[90]

If Shimazu's portrait of Murasaki Shikibu starkly presents the situation that Tanizaki, Yamada, and Chūōkōronsha had to deal with, it also reveals how much the translation had managed to accomplish. In 1913, when Yosano Akiko's *Shin'yaku Genji monogatari* was described in an advertisement as a miracle of world art, there was no reason to believe that many outside Japan would have agreed; three decades later, Shimazu could confidently praise Murasaki Shikibu in the perfective "for *having achieved* world dominance as a literary soldier of Japan" (*Nihon no bungei senshi toshite sekai seiha o nashitogeta*) because now there was evidence. Waley had cemented the tale's position as "one of the dozen greatest masterpieces of the world."[91] At the same time, Shimazu had every reason to assume that readers would accept his description of Murasaki Shikibu as "a *literary* soldier *of Japan*," because *Genji monogatari* had become a national literary best seller. Tanizaki's translation, and the marketing campaign that made it the success it was, led ordinary readers to see *Genji monogatari* in a new light—as "the Tanizaki *Genji*," dialectically suspended between the world and Japan.

Marketing *Genji*

The importance that the publicity department at Chūōkōronsha placed on the idea that *Genji* had a real and verifiable position in world literature, and that Tanizaki's translation would help reinforce that position, is evident in the very first advertisements for *Jun'ichirō-yaku Genji monogatari*. Here, for example, is an announcement of the book's forthcoming publication "on the twenty-third of this month" that was printed in *Tōkyō nichinichi shinbun* on January 2, 1939, as a New Year greeting from Shimanaka Yūsaku (1887–1949), Chūōkōronsha's president:

FELICITATIONS FOR THE NEW YEAR

SHIMANAKA YŪSAKU, PRESIDENT OF CHŪŌKŌRONSHA

As we enter the spring of this third year of glorious successes on the battlefield of the Japan–China Incident, we wish, first of all, to offer our most humble thanks to the loyal and brave officers and men of our army and navy. At present, however, the Incident is advancing from the stage of military conquest to the stage in which we establish order, and the future before us is still fraught with innumerable difficulties and complications. These are the pitifully weak first kicks of a new East Asian culture, the agonies of new shoots budding forth over the dead ashes. How can we, blessed with the good fortune to participate in this sacred war of culture, if only in a minor way, fortify these fragrant buds? It is foolish even to hope that we might push back the onslaught of European and American culture. But surely we have long since awoken from that adoring dream of red-haired foreigners in which we forgot the unique culture of our own nation? Cultural development in this sense must give life to the traditions that flow in our bloodstream, and strive to lift up that which is Japanese, making it that which is of the world.

The fourteenth year of the Shōwa period is indeed a period of great transition in our nation's culture and a period of great discovery for the new East Asian culture. We do not "look into the past in order to know what is new." That which is old and eternally great is itself already new. The fourteenth year of Shōwa is, then, the moment for us to look anew with fresh eyes at our nation's great and unique literature as it becomes the blood and flesh of the new order we are establishing. This is precisely why, at long last, voices have begun crying out for the revival of classical literature. And this is precisely our intention in resurrecting *Genji monogatari*, giving it a modern life. At the dawn of this new spring, our bodies secretly abrim with confidence, we are pleased to share with you this small measure of our ambitions. Nothing could satisfy us more than for you to show us the great kindness of understanding the cause to which we are so sincerely and passionately devoted.

New Year's Day[92]

By publishing Tanizaki's translation of *Genji monogatari*, we are told, Chūōkōronsha hopes to help transform a merely Japanese classic into one that is "of the world," and thus to contribute to the establishment of a new East Asian culture.

This announcement was followed on January 23, the translation's release date, by an advertisement in the same newspaper—reprinted the next day in *Tōkyō asahi shinbun*—that once again stresses the importance of culture, but now also includes references to *Genji monogatari*'s special status as world literature and, finally, proof that *Genji* is being read abroad in translation. A box of text at the lower right declares

> We hope that you, readers, will absorb every last bit of the Tanizaki *Genji*—that you will appreciate it, lose yourself in it, relish this book that is a source of such lofty sentiment as an artistic masterpiece that Japan may hold up with pride before all of humanity, and as evidence of how deeply sensitive to culture we Japanese are. Indeed, we hope you will read this book until it is blackened and falling apart at the seams. That, no doubt, would please Mr. Tanizaki more than anything.

Next we encounter a passage that proclaims, "It is the young and the virile whose future shines the brightest. *Genji monogatari*, heralded as the king of classical literature, the most ancient work of literature in the world, the greatest masterpiece among all extant novels . . . has been resurrected in modern times as a young, virile work of literature." Then, after noting that *Genji monogatari* is regarded by some as "the prototype of realist literature" and by others as "the most outstanding example of symbolist literature," the ad copy continues with the "*Genji* did it first" theme:

> Even the famous *mono no aware*—humanism—is by no means a foreign product. One thousand years ago, Murasaki Shikibu meticulously

crafted Hikaru Genji, the hero of *Genji monogatari*, as a practitioner of humanism. Consider the life of Kashiwagi, who trembles at his sinfulness, or the half of Ukifune's life we see, in which she is judged for her own sins (and note how these approach Tolstoy, Strindberg, and the like in the powerful reality with which they are described). What is that we see shining there? Are those not the tears permitted only to those with an understanding of the universal sense of *aware*?

Finally, at the bottom left, we come to the evidence that *Genji* really is a masterpiece of world literature. First there is the heading:

ALREADY *GENJI* STUDIES IS ALL THE RAGE
AMONG FOREIGNERS

And then the passage:

Genji monogatari is more than simply our nation's greatest novel, it is also one of the most outstanding masterpieces of world literature. Suematsu Seihyō, Aston, and Waley have translated it into English, and now there are plans for Qian Daosun to translate it into Chinese. Presumably, *Genji monogatari* has been so warmly received by foreigners on account of its masterful realistic descriptions, but since Murasaki Shikibu was well versed in matters Japanese and Chinese, Confucianism as well as Buddhism, and since her sense of language was all but perfect and her knowledge of geography and customs profound, the work also affords much material for Japanese studies. The appearance of the Tanizaki *Genji* has spurred foreigners' passion for Japanese studies even more.[93]

It is important to note that the point in this advertisement is not at all that *Genji monogatari*'s greatness was first discovered by foreigners: the tale's status as "our nation's greatest novel" is assumed, and *Genji*'s circulation abroad in translation is cited as proof that it is more than just that. At the same time, however, the image of *Genji* as "one of the most outstanding masterpieces of world literature," the references to Tolstoy and Strindberg, and even the equation of *mono no aware* with humanism help reinforce the notion that *Genji* can be read by ordinary people "in much the way they read an ordinary modern novel."

Many of the advertisements for *Jun'ichirō-yaku Genji monogatari* feature blurbs from writers, scholars, and other figures. One of the most interesting, by Iwanami Shigeo, founder of the bookstore and publisher

Iwanami Shoten, presents the act of reading Tanizaki's work as itself constituting an intervention into international politics, as a means of connecting the national and the global. Indeed, Iwanami goes so far as to reverse Hakuchō's comment about Waley's translation by imagining Tanizaki's translation being translated abroad. The blurb, which begins with the words "*Genji monogatari*, a work that the Japanese race takes pride in before the world," is titled "For a Cultural Japan" (Bunka Nihon no tame ni):

> As the third year of the Japan–China Incident gets under way, Japan's stance continues to be misunderstood by the world, which seems to regard our nation as militaristic and aggressive. Against this background, Chūōkōron's current project is deeply meaningful both socially and internationally. I hope and expect that the appearance of this book will occasion its translation into various languages of the world, and its dissemination, and that this will help give a boost to cultural Japan. At the same time, I deeply hope that this book will be disseminated throughout every corner of our nation, showing not only that Japan had in its past a great work of art, but that people in modern times, too, do in fact take a passionate and serious interest in it, and that even in this troubled moment for our nation a celebrated translation of a classic work like this elicits an outpouring of shared national emotion, and that this knowledge will have some effect in correcting the world's perception of Japan.[94]

Iwanami's linking of the experience of reading and being moved by *Genji* to a vision of "cultural Japan" has the somewhat ironic effect of transforming a seemingly peaceful, private pleasure into a "shared national emotion" (*kokuminteki kangeki*) that itself has a propagandistic purpose. Viewed in another light, however, it also justifies the enjoyment of *Genji* as a form of escapism: Iwanami makes it all right to forget the war. In an age when newspapers were filled with battles, flags, and ads for Hino Ashihei's best-selling *Mugi to heitai* (*Wheat and Soldiers*, 1938) and a flood of imitative titles—*Mud and Soldiers, Flowers and Soldiers, Snow and Soldiers, Saké and Soldiers, Chocolate and Soldiers*—readers were no doubt glad for an excuse to lose themselves in the dream of a peaceful past. One recalls Donald Keene's reaction when he found a remaindered copy of *The Tale of Genji* in Times Square in 1940: "In the book, antagonism never degenerated into violence, and there were no wars."[95]

The idea that *Genji* is both Japan's greatest classic and a masterpiece of world literature remained an almost constant theme throughout

Chūōkōronsha's advertising campaign, appearing so often and in so many forms and in blurbs by so many prominent figures that it would be exhausting to recount them all. Here, then, is a selection, both from Chūōkōronsha's advertising copy and from blurbs:

> One cannot help rejoicing that there is a work among the Japanese classics that so deeply moves the world.
>
> One cannot help rejoicing that there is a work among the Japanese classics that moves people in every country of the world.
>
> I was deeply moved when Tanizaki, who stood on the forefront of the new literature that had overtaken Naturalism, told me of this classical work's worldwide value.
>
> [The characters'] sufferings and how they think, how they live their lives—none of this is any different from today. Search as you may for similar cases, whether in the East or in the West, nothing alters the fact that *there is only one* Genji monogatari *in all the world*.[96]

And finally, a long blurb by the law professor Nakazawa Zennosuke that was printed as part of an advertisement under the title "One Reader's Thoughts" (Ichidokusha no kansō):

> When you discuss literature with a German, he's bound to end up talking about Goethe and Schiller, and if you do the same with an Englishman the discussion inevitably turns to Shakespeare. If you attempted to talk about Shakespeare with a German, however, or mentioned Goethe to an Englishman discoursing on Shakespeare, often he will have no idea who you're talking about—though of course I'm not talking about specialists in literature, here, just ordinary people.
>   Oddly enough, **this gets turned on its head in Japan**. It's not at all uncommon to find that knowledgeable folks who can talk about Goethe and Schiller and Shakespeare and Dostoyevsky don't know the slightest thing about the Japanese classics. There's no doubt—it's a clear case of putting the cart before the horse. It would be understandable if people had read it and then forgotten it. Or if they read it but found it uninteresting—that, at least, makes sense. But it seems more likely to me that the majority of Japanese **haven't even read the products of our ancestors' labor**.

Of course, this isn't exactly without reason. There's **the language problem**. Any number of foreign literary classics can be read quite well enough with a foreign-language education of the sort one gets in school today. And if one takes advantage of translation, which is booming, it becomes possible to enjoy a considerable number of Western masterpieces even in modern Japanese. Ironically, the situation isn't so simple with regard to the Japanese classics. And so, even though here in our own country we have the *Record of Ancient Matters*, to begin with, and the *Great Mirror*, *Tales of Ise*, *Tales of the Heike*, and the *Chronicle of Great Peace*, not to mention *Essays in Idleness*, *Tales of Times Now Past*—we've got all kinds of works, and yet we can't enjoy them, and so we look to foreign works and their translations for a place to let out the emotions we would otherwise pour into them.

So we find ourselves confronted by the problem of translating the Japanese classics into the modern language. This is **an extremely difficult enterprise** for a variety of reasons, but it is also something that absolutely must be done. And this raises the question of what ought to be done first. Not being a specialist in this area I'm not really able to judge for sure, but there's no doubt that *Genji monogatari* **would have to be counted as the first.** It has already been introduced abroad in two or three different forms, so for us not to know the work ourselves is the kind of thing one almost ought to be ashamed of.

Clearly from the perspective of **Japan's national culture**, it is cause for the utmost joy that **Mr. Tanizaki Jun'ichirō has now completed just such a modern-Japanese translation of** *Genji monogatari*, **and that Mr. Yamada Yoshio has checked it**.

Looking now at the two volumes in the first installment, I see that the first volume contains the three chapters "Kiritsubo," "Hahakigi" [The Broom-Tree], and "Utsusemi," while the second contains the two chapters "Yūgao" and "Wakamurasaki" [Young Murasaki]. **The book design and the cover are both great, but the contents are even better.** It's easy to understand, and it feels like *Genji*. The prose has been rendered into the modern language, but it has that elevated style that is the special characteristic of the classics.

I wasn't able to read these two volumes in one sitting, but I'd say it must have taken me a total of **only about three or four hours** over the course of two or three days to read them all the way through. To be able to read five chapters of *Genji* in three or four hours and, what's more, to be able to take real pleasure in reading *Genji*—for a plain old amateur with no particular connection to the classics of our national literature, this is **an astonishing blessing**. At the risk of a slight exaggeration, I think you might well call this **a singular miracle of the Shōwa period.**

It goes without saying that at this moment, as **the sacred war of Asian development** is at last entering the constructive stage, there is an especially pressing necessity for the nation's citizens, who perforce must stand at the core of this project, to reconsider and become more aware of their own culture. Perhaps the translator's motivations for writing this work had nothing to do with the current situation, but from the perspective of its readers this book surely arrived at just the moment when it most needs to be read. Even as I recommend this book to others, I find myself waiting impatiently for another month to pass so that I may continue reading on through all fifty-five chapters.[97]

Six years earlier, in "Eiyaku *Genji monogatari*," Hakuchō had noted that hardly anyone in Japan read *Genji monogatari* and speculated that if Waley's translation were rendered into Japanese, it might attract a large readership that would enjoy it as world literature. Nakazawa's blurb could almost have been written in response. The Japanese, he says, enjoy foreign classics, but not those of their own nation—in fact, they invest emotions in foreign works that should be directed at Japanese classics. The converse of this is that, now that *Genji monogatari* has been translated into the modern language, they will be able to read it in the way they have been accustomed to read foreign classics. In short, Hakuchō's prediction had come true.

Triangulation

The question arises, then, as to whether there was a connection between the prediction and its fulfillment. Did Hakuchō have a direct influence on Tanizaki and the publication of his "old translation"?

Chiba Shunji, one of the foremost experts on Tanizaki, has published an essay in which he takes up precisely this question. He suggests that Hakuchō's writings on *Genji*, particularly the second of his two essays from 1933, "Futatabi Eiyaku *Genji monogatari* ni tsukite," prompted Shimanaka Yūsaku to ask Tanizaki to tackle *Genji monogatari* and influenced Tanizaki himself to take on the project.[98] According to Chiba, the linguist Miyake Takeo, who was then affiliated with the Ministry of Education, first had the idea of publishing a series of modern-Japanese translations of classical works. Shimanaka was interested and decided that Tanizaki would be the ideal translator for *Genji monogatari*, but in the end he was unwilling to commit to publishing the entire series and let another company take it over. Shimanaka was still tempted to ask

Tanizaki to translate *Genji monogatari*, however, and Chiba argues that Hakuchō's praise for *Genji* finally moved him to propose the idea. "I have no doubt," Hakuchō had said, "that now that *Genji* has been introduced through its English translation, it will be enjoyed around the world as a literary work without parallel, in the same way the *Arabian Nights* and *Don Quixote* are treasured by members of the literary establishment around the world, as works unique to the countries that produced them."[99] Chiba's analysis is compelling and suggests that Shimanaka was attracted by precisely the discourses that I have been discussing—about translation and world literature, and about national literature as a by-product of world literature—and that figure so prominently in Chūōkōronsha's advertisements for Tanizaki's translation.

Shimanaka seems to have proposed the *Genji* translation project to Tanizaki when the author visited Tokyo at the end of November 1933. "Futatabi Eiyaku *Genji monogatari* ni tsukite" had been published in *Tōkyō asahi shinbun* on November 15, 16, and 17. And, as Chiba notes, Tanizaki himself had almost certainly read "Eiyaku *Genji monogatari*" when it appeared in the September issue of *Kaizō*, since it was followed by Hakuchō's review of his most recent work: immediately after his discussion of *The Tale of Genji*, Hakuchō takes up Tanizaki's play *Kaoyo* (1933)—the second part of which was printed, moreover, in the same issue of the magazine—and suggests, through repeated comparisons of Tanizaki with the authors of *Genji monogatari* and other Heian works, that it might be best for him not to squander his talent, but to relax and write less. Indeed, Hakuchō goes on to compare the literary spirit of Japanese writers unfavorably with that of "Waley, who spent ten years translating *Genji monogatari* and was able to remain engaged the entire time."[100]

Soon after New Year 1934, Tanizaki had a copy of Waley's *The Tale of Genji* sent to him by Chūōkōronsha and read at least parts of it.[101] In 1935, Tanizaki began his own translation of *Genji monogatari*. Thus, Chiba suggests, "without Waley's English translation Tanizaki's modern-Japanese translation would never have existed, and without Tanizaki's modern-Japanese translation no reevaluation of *Genji monogatari* would ever have taken place."[102] I would not go quite so far, perhaps, since the process of reevaluation had long been under way, and I would add that if the connections that Chiba has made with such care are as solid as they appear, the particular discourses that Hakuchō chose to draw on in his evaluation of Waley's translation are as important as the existence of Waley's translation itself. The significance of Tanizaki's translation, after all, lies in the fact that it enabled *Genji monogatari* to be resituated, within Japan and in the Japanese language, as a "masterpiece of world literature"—in the fact, that is to say, that Tanizaki's translation made Hakuchō's prediction come true. Or to put it in terms of the metaphor that I introduced in chapter 4, when Tanizaki first began translating *Genji monogatari* in 1935, he was already working within the triangular field, though it was still only vaguely defined, and it was the publication of his translation, and the campaign that Chūōkōronsha launched to market it, that finally hammered the three legs of the frame firmly in place.

It would be difficult to overestimate the importance of the emergence of this new perspective on *Genji monogatari*. The entire history of the tale's replacement looked different in its wake. And this, in turn, would affect views of Hakuchō: just as Hakuchō had misremembered Gakkai's statements about *Genji monogatari* because he was trying to remember a time before world literature from within world literature, so Hakuchō's later readers would look back at the essays he wrote before *Genji monogatari* had been repackaged as a true national classic and misread them, because they read them from a perspective that took for granted the status of *Genji monogatari* as a national classic. On February 8, 1939, a blurb by Orikuchi Shinobu, a scholar of literature and folklore, appeared in an advertisement for Tanizaki's translation in *Tōkyō asahi shinbun*: "Not that long ago, no less a figure than the great literary pioneer Mr. Masamune (Hakuchō) was prompted to reevaluate *Genji* by its English translation. That sort of thing is bound to come to a stop now. This thought alone delights me."[103] Interestingly, Yamada Yoshio himself makes a similar point in an essay published in 1948, without mentioning Hakuchō by name:

> This masterpiece was celebrated only in name, and many were unable to read it. Indeed, one famous Japanese literary figure said that he realized what a masterpiece it was only when he read the English translation. If the tale hadn't been translated into the modern language, perhaps others would have ended up writing critical works on it based on its English translation, just as that famous literary figure did. That's how things stood when Mr. Tanizaki's modern-Japanese translation was published.[104]

If the history of *Genji* in the postwar period, beyond the turning point that Yamada identifies, is the history of its triangulation—its continual reinvention, through translation and discourse about translation, as a classic of world and national literature—it is also the history of an almost unacknowledged, almost instinctual effort to push Hakuchō and his English into the background. *Genji*'s contemporary history is, in part, a successful attempt to forget *Genji*'s modern history, its early modern history, and everything before.

Within the Triangle

Early on in "Eiyaku *Genji monogatari*," presumably drawing on the introduction to *The Tale of Genji* that Waley included in volume 2, Hakuchō reports that in the West, Murasaki Shikibu is being compared with Marcel Proust, a writer "with whom contemporary Japan's cutting-edge writers grew utterly infatuated," and suggests that the reason lies in the subtlety with which both *Genji* and *À la recherche du temps perdu* (*In Search of Lost Time*, 1913–1927) succeed in "capturing the subconscious."[105] As a way of drawing this chapter to a close, pointing beyond World War II and even the postwar period, I would like to linger for a moment over this passing comparison of *Genji* to Proust's masterpiece, and Hakuchō's invocation of "contemporary Japan's cutting-edge writers."

Hakuchō is referring to writers such as Yokomitsu Riichi, Kawabata Yasunari, Hori Tatsuo, and Itō Sei, who participated in the short-lived "New Sensibility" (Shinkankakuha) and "New Psychologism" (Shinshinrishugi) movements of the mid-1920s to early 1930s, and were inspired by the artistic creations and theoretical formulations of the European avant-garde. This linking of *The Tale of Genji* with the highly experimental literature of a group of young writers, then in their late twenties and early thirties, functioned, needless to say, as a declaration of *Genji*'s relevance to the present, a recasting of the tale as an ancient work whose literary sensibility was somehow new—not merely modern, but contemporary. Presumably, this sense of *Genji*'s "newness" and potential relevance to readers must have figured in the savvy businessman Shimanaka's decision to push Tanizaki to translate the tale. He had the acumen to realize that a *Genji monogatari* translated by Tanizaki could be the next big thing. This is implicit in the copy for the very first advertisement, in fact, which announces that *Genji* "has been resurrected in modern times as a young, virile work of literature."

But we might also consider Hakuchō's linking of the classic and the cutting edge in another light. At the same time that he is pointing to *Genji*'s newness and potential relevance, he is also holding out the possibility that the young writers on the cutting edge may one day be able to discover an echo of their "New Sensibility" in Japanese tradition, and thus that they themselves may eventually be reinscribed into a tradition reconnected to contemporary Japan by the passage of its classical texts through translation into the canon of world literature. In effect, Hakuchō is opening the door to a reconciliation of the avant-garde with the traditional of the sort that Doris Humphrey had imagined in her dance based on the ten Uji chapters—except that in her case, the tradition was more obviously foreign.

This reinscription, this reconciliation is precisely what the Nobel Prize committee achieved for Kawabata when in 1968 it recognized "his narrative mastery, which with great sensibility expresses the essence of the Japanese mind." And again, it is just this sort of reinscription, through the mechanisms of translation and world literature, that Kawabata himself welcomed in his Nobel Prize acceptance speech, "Japan, the Beautiful, and Myself" (Utsukushii Nihon no watashi, 1968):

> The *Tale of Genji* in particular is the highest pinnacle of Japanese literature. Even down to our day there has not been a piece of fiction to compare with it. That such a modern work should have been written in the eleventh century is a miracle, and as a miracle the work is widely known abroad. Although my grasp of classical Japanese was uncertain, the Heian classics were my principal boyhood reading, and it is the *Genji*, I think, that has meant the most to me.[106]

In Japanese, "the highest pinnacle of Japanese literature" is *Nihon no saikō no shōsetsu*; "such a modern work" is *kindaiteki demo aru chōhen shōsetsu*. The sheer enormity of the change that translation had wrought on the meaning of the word *shōsetsu* since Yoda Gakkai's day could not be more apparent than it is here. And when Kawabata says that *Genji monogatari*'s appearance in the eleventh century "is a miracle," he says more than Edward Seidensticker's English translation does: he calls it *sekai no kiseki*: "a miracle of the world," "a miracle that belongs to the whole world."[107]

It is almost too predictable that when Ibuki Kazuko—Kawabata's editor at Chūōkōron, who had also worked with Tanizaki on his third translation of *Genji monogatari*, *Jun'ichirō-shinshin'yaku Genji monogatari* (*Genji monogatari: The New New Jun'ichirō Translation*, 1964–1965)—visited Kawabata days before he flew to Stockholm, he showed her two sheets of paper on which he had written in very neat handwriting the titles of all fifty-four chapters of *Genji monogatari* and informed her that he was thinking of translating the tale, that "miracle of the world," into modern Japanese.[108] When I quoted the two articles about cell-phone novels from the *New York Times* and *Asahi shinbun* in the "Touchstone" for this part, I noted a change in directionality from "Japan gives *Genji* to the world" to "*Genji* gives Japan to the world"; Kawabata's situation suggests that both these formulations are functions of a third: "the world gives *Genji* to Japan."

It is tempting, especially in an English-language academic context, in a world in which English is becoming increasingly hegemonic, to read Hakuchō's inability to connect with *Genji monogatari*, his extravagant praise of *The Tale of Genji*, and his suggestion that if Waley's English translation were back-translated into Japanese, *Genji* would become popular in Japan as "one of the great novels of the world" as an unconscious betrayal of some deep cultural malaise, as a bitter irony, or even as a subtle form of collaboration with the burgeoning hegemony of the English language. But as chapter 6 will show, Hakuchō the "translation-person" was acutely conscious of the respective positions that the Japanese and English languages occupied in the world. And he knew, as he created his discourse about *Genji*, framing it as a work of world literature whose very existence as literature depends on translation, that this situation was hardly unique to *Genji*. Here is Hakuchō in his fourth and final essay about *Genji*, "*Genji monogatari*—hon'yaku to gensaku" (1951), which is the subject of the following chapter:

> Suppose, for the moment, that Murasaki Shikibu were alive now, and that she had created and published her *Genji monogatari* in something like the form of Waley's translation. In that scenario, she might have been selected to receive the Nobel Prize. But of course there is no way that either the members of the Nobel Prize committee or ordinary lovers of literature would read the original, written as it is in a difficult style unique to Japan, so it would still be read in Waley's skillful translation, and it would be deemed worthy of the prize on the basis of his translation. In that case it would be Waley's *Genji* that was recommended for the prize, and one should not consider the real thing and the translation as one and the same thing. This isn't true only of *Genji*, either. Japanese fiction is not read as it is by the people of the world, and it seems likely to me that when it is translated, the more skillful the translator is, the less like the original the translation will be.[109]

Kawabata's reinscription, and self-inscription, into "Japanese tradition" and the canon of Japanese literature in 1968 is no different, it turns out, from the transnational reinscripton of *Genji* into that tradition in the trio of newspaper articles with which I began this part, and the newspapers were simply repeating, in their turn, Hakuchō's discovery of *Genji* in 1933. This is the repetition, the globally looping translation, within which *Genji* continues to be re-created, again and again, both in Japan and abroad.

The Postwar and Beyond

May 30, 1955. Ten years to the day after Henry L. Stimson, then secretary of war, insisted on scratching Kyoto from the top of the list of potential targets for an atomic bomb, Okada Ikunosuke, professor at the Tokyo University of Fisheries, published an article in *Asahi shinbun* introducing research on one possible "side effect of the peaceful use of nuclear energy." Maguro sashimi wrapped in tin foil and exposed for forty hours to cobalt-60 gamma rays lasted at room temperature, it turned out, for two or three months even in the full heat of summer. "Someday," Okada said, "sashimi will be sold as a sort of preserved food, suitable for taking on excursions."[1]

CHAPTER 6

"*Genji monogatari*: Translation and Original"

Purple Affinities, Once Again

Slogan of the Committee
for the Thousandth Anniversary
of *The Tale of Genji*

A good deal had changed in Japan in the harsh, exhilarating decade since the war had come to an end. At the same time, much had remained the same. Certain elements of postwar life that looked like exhausted, eager repudiations of the past, unambiguous departures from Japan's wartime history, nevertheless inherited old forms. The first postwar boom in the publication of modern-Japanese translations of *Genji monogatari*, still at its height in 1955, was a perfect example. Embodying a quintessentially postwar need to reimagine Japan as a "country of culture" (*bunkakoku*) whose truest traditions were rooted in peace, empathy, and an appreciation of nature, this phenomenon was simultaneously a repetition of the *Genji* boom launched in 1939 by Tanizaki Jun'ichirō's first translation of the tale. One recalls, for instance, Iwanami Shigeo's hope that the great excitement surrounding Tanizaki's first effort would "have some effect in correcting the world's perception" of his country and "give a boost to cultural Japan."[2] The crucial difference between wartime and postwar discourse lay in the fact that, during the war, the propagation of a peaceful vision of the "national polity" had itself served a militaristic purpose, while in the postwar period the effect was anti-militarist. Both during and after the war, the celebration of the tale retained a nationalist coloring, at least in the sense that it helped foster a unified, circumscribed image of Japan and of the Japanese people. If there was something subtly disturbing in this continuity from wartime to the postwar and beyond, however, few seem to have noticed it.

The postwar *Genji* boom had gotten off to an inopportune start in 1947, when most of Japan's population was still struggling to survive, buying what it could afford on the black market, and wringing scarce calories from things that people do not ordinarily eat.³ The first translation to arrive in bookstores was a new edition of poet and scholar Kubota Utsubo's *Genji monogatari: A Modern-Language Translation* (*Gendaigoyaku Genji monogatari*), first published by Kaizōsha in 1939; this was followed in 1948 by the release of Igarashi Chikara's unfinished *Genji monogatari: A Complete Shōwa Translation* (*Genji monogatari: Shōwa kan'yaku*). Momentum continued to build between 1948 and 1955, when four publishers issued no fewer than five editions of Yosano Akiko's second translation of the tale, and Chūōkōronsha published two editions of Tanizaki's second translation: *Genji monogatari: Jun'ichirō shin'yaku* (*Genji monogatari: The New Jun'ichirō Translation*, 1951–1953) and *Shin'yaku Genji monogatari* (*Genji monogatari: The New Translation*, 1955). Three further editions of Tanizaki's second translation would appear in 1956, 1959, and 1961, after which it would be supplanted by a minimally revised third version; Yosano Akiko's second translation continued to be reissued in new forms until as recently as 2008.⁴

Of course, modern-Japanese translations were only one element that contributed to the postwar *Genji* boom. As Tateishi Kazuhiro's insightful work on the "processed culture" of *Genji* in the postwar years has demonstrated, the contours of this boom become clear only when we consider other types of replacements in other media and the interactions among various replacements.⁵ For our purposes, it will suffice to observe that Tanizaki's translation came to be linked, through the person of its translator, with productions in the twin worlds of the kabuki stage and the silver screen. The first volume of *Genji monogatari: Jun'ichirō shin'yaku* went on sale on May 31, 1951, two months after the close of the phenomenally popular production at the Kabukiza, from March 4 to 29, of Funabashi Seiichi's play *Genji monogatari*, for which Tanizaki was called in as a consultant. Tanizaki was also enlisted as a consultant for the first movie version of the tale, Yoshimura Kōsaburō's *Genji monogatari*, which opened on November 2, 1951. This film was named the year's seventh-best movie by the monthly film magazine *Kinema junpō* (*Movie Times*) and made more money than any of its competitors, earning a total of ¥141,050,000.⁶ Tanizaki served as a consultant for five more kabuki plays, based on successive chapters of *Genji monogatari*, that were presented at the Kabukiza in October 1951, May and June 1952, May and June 1954, May and June 1957, and March 1964, as well as for a production of the first of these six plays at the Osaka Kabukiza in November 1951.⁷ Meanwhile, the playwright Hōjō Hideji began to stage his own versions of material from *Genji monogatari* in 1953. Hōjō continued to direct one or more new performances every year until 1961, and sporadically after that. He also scripted eleven radio dramas based on the tale for broadcast on NHK 1 between April 1952 and June 1956.[8]

In the early 1950s, *Genji* was being read, watched, and listened to by more people across Japan than ever before, and in a greater variety of forms and media. The tale was no longer simply a famous classic, or even just a successful translation of a classical text; it had emerged as a minor industry in its own right and as a useful tool in the construction of a new vision of the Japanese nation as a community. The long process of *Genji*'s replacement in popular consciousness that had begun in 1829 with the publication of *Inaka Genji* and continued in the modern period with the appearance of a succession of accessibly literary translations, both at home and abroad, and with the increasingly global circulation of discourse about the tale and its translations, had at long last settled into a magnificent equilibrium. The great, unread classic had become what it remains, essentially, today: a tale that could only ever be read again.

This was the context within which Masamune Hakuchō wrote yet another essay dealing with Murasaki Shikibu's *Genji monogatari* and Arthur Waley's *The Tale of Genji*. First published in the August 1951 issue of *Chūōkōron*, two months after the release of the first volume of *Genji monogatari: Jun'ichirō shin'yaku* and one month before the release of the second, it was unusually widely circulated, appearing not only in the magazine but in three separate editions of a collection called *Reading Notes* (*Dokusho zakki*), the last of which was released, as it happens, on that date exactly a decade after Kyoto escaped destruction, when *Asahi shinbun*'s readership was introduced to the irradiated miracle of sashimi that did not spoil. Or perhaps it would be more accurate to say that this was the context *against which* Hakuchō wrote. In a sense, I will argue, his essay—which veers in unpredictable directions, assuming the shape less of a tightly structured argument than of raw thought—embodies an attempt, or at least an urge, to resist the *Genji* boom and its subtle continuities with the tale's wartime history, to remind readers that the current surge in popularity of all those translations and adaptations of *Genji* did not make *Genji monogatari* "ours."

It is a slippery but provocative essay. And to the extent that our perceptions of *Genji* continue to be informed by the history I have traced, part of which Hakuchō lived through, contributed to, and remembered even as others strove to forget, I believe that we can still learn from him—wherever and whoever we are. In this chapter, I attempt, by highlighting certain of the essay's themes, to clarify the impulse that its seeming formlessness conceals.

As Alien as Gide

The essay, which would be Hakuchō's final major statement about *Genji*, is "*Genji monogatari*–hon'yaku to gensaku" (*Genji monogatari*: Translation and Original). Or perhaps it is not. Although it appeared with this title in *Chūōkōron*, the reprint in *Reading Notes* may, strictly speaking, be untitled: the beginning of the text is marked only with the number 7, indicating that it constitutes the seventh essay of the book's first part. The table of contents for the first part, also called "Reading Notes," lists only the titles of the works discussed in each essay and the page number on which each discussion begins. Essay 7, we are informed, considers "*Genji monogatari*: Original and Translation" (with the "Translation" and "Original" reversed) and *The Brothers Karamazov*. The page number listed next to each of these two titles is the same.

In 1926, Hakuchō had opened "Koten o yonde" with the announcement that he had started to read *The Story of the Stone* and *Genji monogatari* together, but doubted that he would ever finish either one. In 1951, he adopted the same strategy, substituting for the voluminous Chinese classic an equally imposing Russian one. One gets the sense that for Hakuchō, aligning canonical works from different traditions and languages was a way to stoke his interest and to bypass the oppressive, alluring authority of the classic. Although he keeps actual comparison to a minimum and, indeed, hardly touches on *The Brothers Karamazov*, the simple gesture of approaching two masterpieces at once allows him to relativize each and thus explore issues that might not arise if he were simply expounding on a single book, giving himself up to the gravity of its prestige—issues, for instance, such as translation and the mechanics of canonization. Superficially, "*Genji monogatari*–hon'yaku to gensaku" may look like a comparison of two versions of the classic, "translation and original," and to some extent it is, but this discussion overlaps with others.

Hakuchō opens the essay, as he did the ironically titled "Koten o yonde" (On Reading the Classics), by casually situating *Genji* in the broader context of world literature, and then offering readers a confession. Once again, he tells us that he is unable to read the classics:

> "Nowadays, one often sees *Genji monogatari* and collections of Gide's works lined up side by side on bookstore shelves," a man in publish-

ing remarked as we chatted about this and that. "Japanese classics like *Genji* seem to be becoming popular, just as Gide has."

I made up my mind to finish *The Brothers Karamazov*, come what may, so I have been going at it a little at a time, reading a Japanese translation I had on hand. I'm not making much progress, though. I first started reading the book nearly four decades ago, when I got a copy of what was evidently the first English translation, and I have yet to reach the end.

As it happens, even as I continue wrestling with this late-nineteenth-century Russian work, I'm trying to plow my way through a second long novel: that representative Japanese classic, *Genji monogatari*. I was curious to see what sort of impression it would make on me if I approached the original directly, just as it is, without relying on notes, or being harassed by them. I managed to dig up the volumes in the Library of Japanese Classics series, which survived the firebombs, and began reading from the opening lines, the one part of the book that I have had memorized ever since I was a boy: "*Izure no ontoki ni ka, nyōgo kōi amata saburaitamaikeru naka ni ito yangotonaki kiwa ni wa aranu ga, sugurete tokimekitamau arikeri,* etc. etc." But while I started out smoothly enough, I didn't feel the sort of thrill that the author of *Sarashina Diary* did as a girl when her aunt sent her a mountain of fifty-four hand-copied chapters and she completely lost herself in them, forgetting everything else. The voices of all the ordinary people who have given *Genji* its reputation as a dreadful bore rose up in my mind, elbowing aside literary history with its pompous, infinitely effusive assertions of the tale's gorgeousness, splendor, and profundity. So much has changed in our national language, in writing, that after decades spent reading books of all sorts, ancient and new, I am still unable to read with any freedom a novel, a *monogatari*, that a ten-year-old girl most likely skimmed right through. Everything is vague, murky—it's like peering through a fog. I feel as if I'm walking on cobblestones. Each stone may be lovely and elegant on its own, gleaming in all the colors of the rainbow, but we have trouble making our way over the bumps. An annotated text may help one clear the stones one by one, but it starts to get annoying and one loses interest.[9]

Recall that in 1933, writing in the face of wartime censorship—writing, indeed, in one essay, just one week before the Tokyo Metropolitan Police banned a theatrical adaptation of the tale—Hakuchō had given Waley's English-language *The Tale of Genji* an almost incendiary rave review, suggesting that if the translation itself "were translated anew into Japanese, it might attract a large and avid readership that would enjoy it as one of the great novels of the world."¹⁰ Now that such literary translations into modern Japanese had been published and *Genji* really was being enjoyed in Japan as a masterpiece of world literature, neatly fulfilling Hakuchō's prediction, he might have been expected to comment on the tale's newfound popularity. As an admirer of Tanizaki's fiction who had compared Tanizaki with Murasaki Shikibu and Waley in the review of Tanizaki's play *Kaoyo* that followed "Eiyaku *Genji monogatari*" in the September 1933 issue of *Kaizō*, and as a still more dazzled admirer of *Genji*, surely Hakuchō must have read at least one of Tanizaki's translations. So one would think. And yet there is no evidence that he did, and in "*Genji monogatari*–hon'yaku to gensaku" he all but ignores the ongoing *Genji* boom that Tanizaki's versions helped create. Apart from the glancing, roundabout allusion to the tale's popularity in the first paragraph and a passing allusion to Tanizaki's second translation near the end, Hakuchō seems almost studiously to have avoided acknowledging the phenomenon.

Needless to say, this is not because Hakuchō was unaware of it. He could not have escaped the fever of publicity if he had wanted to. A lifelong theater buff, he would go to see one of Funabashi's plays: in the July 1954 issue of the art magazine *Geijutsu shinchō* (*Art Shinchō*), he published a negative review of the third installment, which had been staged in May and June and had covered two of Hakuchō's favorite chapters, "Wakana jō" (Wakana, part I) and "Wakana ge" (Wakana, part II).¹¹ Indeed, Hakuchō was more than just passively aware of the creative energy that *Genji* had inspired; he expressed the hope that affecting art might be born from attempts to fashion dramatic or filmic adaptations in the freewheeling spirit of Waley's translation—"passionately, vividly contemporary" takes on the classic that would have something of the poetry he believed the kabuki star Ichikawa Ebizō IX's Genji and Funabashi's Genji lacked.¹²

So why didn't Hakuchō refer to *Genji*'s multimedia popularity in "*Genji monogatari*–hon'yaku to gensaku" or take up Tanizaki's translation? The answer is implied, perhaps, by the peculiarly abrupt, dangling opening paragraph, with its reference to the works of André Gide. Gide had become popular in Japan in the mid-1920s and rose to considerable prominence in the 1930s—Yokomitsu Riichi cites him and Paul Valéry as the two foreign writers he finds most interesting in his famous "A Discourse on Pure Fiction" (Junsuishōsetsuron, 1935), which is said to have been inspired by Yamanouchi Yoshio's translation of Gide's *Les fauxmonnayeurs* (*The Counterfeiters*, 1925), published earlier the same year.¹³

Gide's star had risen again from the late 1940s through the 1950s, after his acceptance of the Nobel Prize in 1947 and then his death in 1951. His fame at the time can be gauged from the title of a literary history by the Marxist critic Takaoki Yōzō: *A History of European Literary Thought: From Dante to Gide* (*Ōshū bungei shichōshi: Dante yori Jiido made*, 1949). Between 1950 and 1951, Shinchōsha published its seventeen-volume edition of Gide's collected works, which was followed by a spate of competing new translations and new editions of earlier translations. At the same time, there was also a surge in secondary publications that began in the late 1940s and continued through the mid-1950s.

When Hakuchō's acquaintance commented, "Nowadays, one often sees *Genji monogatari* and collections of Gide's works lined up side by side on bookstore shelves," this is the background he had in mind. Hakuchō's interest here, however, and the motive for his, at first glance, quixotic decision to open the essay with this observation lie in the second half of the quotation: "Japanese classics like *Genji* seem to be becoming popular, just as Gide has." In Japanese, ジイドに人氣があるやうに、源氏のやうな日本の古典も人氣が出かかつてるやうです can be read, if a bit aggressively, as suggesting that "*Genji* is becoming popular *in the same manner* as Gide." Later in the essay, Hakuchō goes on to imagine Murasaki Shikibu being awarded the Nobel Prize, just as Gide had been in 1947. Today this may not seem very odd, but in 1951 only two laureates in literature had been selected from outside Europe and the United States: Rabindranath Tagore in 1913 and Gabriela Mistral in 1945. Tagore received the prize for his own translations into English of works originally written in Bengali; Mistral wrote in Spanish. And in 1951, Mistral remained one of only five women to have been honored, compared with forty-two men. Kawabata Yasunari would not become Japan's first recipient of the prize until 1968.

When Hakuchō imagines the Nobel Prize being awarded to Murasaki Shikibu, a Japanese woman who wrote in Japanese, he is indulging, then, in a startling flight of fancy that seems, on the surface, utterly at odds with a sober, objective recognition of the discrimination engrained, judging from the list of awardees, in the very sense of literary excellence on which the Nobel Prize was founded—even if Hakuchō does imagine Murasaki Shikibu being chosen on the basis of a translation into English. And yet, from another perspective, the act of acknowledging the discrimination practiced by the Nobel Prize Committee itself participates in that discrimination, in the sense that it is predicated on an acceptance of the distinctions—West versus East, civilized versus backward, "their authors" versus "our authors"—on which the discrimination is based. Hakuchō is able to imagine Murasaki Shikibu receiving the Nobel Prize, I suggest, because he did not see the world so simply, at least as far as the "Japanese literary tradition" was concerned: in his eyes, it made perfect sense to align Murasaki Shikibu and Gide, because in Japan in 1951, both authors were unquestionably and unambiguously foreign.

Commenting on the difficulty he had connecting to *Genji monogatari*'s Japanese, Hakuchō observes that reading the text was "like peering through a fog." As it happens, he used the exact same metaphor to describe reading Baudelaire in an essay about translation that he wrote in 1931, some two decades earlier.[14] *Genji monogatari* may have been written in Japanese, but its Japanese was not his Japanese—it was as alien to him as French. This intense, almost physical sensitivity to the unbridgeable distance that separates him from the "original" *Genji monogatari* ("I feel," he confesses, "as if I'm walking on cobblestones") is perhaps what inspired that odd first paragraph and what led Hakuchō to avoid mentioning the ongoing *Genji* boom. At a time when Japanese were turning to the tale in various modern guises as the seed of a postwar national identity, a new sense of their community, Hakuchō chose to turn instead, as if to rebuke this urge, to the original and its English translation.

No Great Unifier

In a long passage that immediately follows the one quoted earlier, Hakuchō continues his subtle relativization of the postwar *Genji* boom by turning his gaze toward the past:

> Maybe that's how it is with the classics. Western classics are easy to follow because we read them in translation, but if a contemporary reader were to tackle a work in the original language, just as it is, perhaps the volume, packed with text, would seem like a cobblestone road, irksome to walk on? Matters are worse for people like me who, born in the early years of the Meiji era, enjoyed being buffeted by new winds, imported notions of civilization and enlightenment, and scorned Japan's classical literature. I felt that scorn, at any rate. The same held for young men in the public universities, who took pride in being students at what was then the highest educational level: if one of them, or a group, turned out to be studying the national literature, then he was regarded as a dolt without any aspirations, hopelessly behind the times. If you wanted to study literature, you ought to study English or German literature, or perhaps try your hand at Greek or Latin.

When I was a child—or maybe in the years just before that—there was a sudden surge in respect for Western learning, and Chinese learning and Kokugaku were suppressed. The ideas of Fukuzawa Yukichi and others dominated the world. Fukuzawa's encouragement of Western learning meant, in essence, the importation of a new civilization. This "Western learning" of the early Meiji years is fascinating. Reading a grade-school primer or a basic history of the West or a simple book on economics all counted as Western learning. Pronouncing "one" and "two" in the Keiō Academy style as *ohney* and *tsuoh* could be a first step toward the great profundities of Western learning. The *Analects* and Mencius, *Kojiki* and *Genji* were stale, shopworn remnants of a society in which Chinese learning and Kokugaku still mattered, and could not compete with something as trivial as an imported elementary-school reader.

Looking back now, I am quite taken with this eagerness to smash everything old. The truth is that we can never completely overthrow the old; the mental and spiritual movements of our ancestors continue on as before. But there is something in the act of destroying what we have inherited, no doubt, that makes us humans feel as if night has lifted, conjures the thrill of living. Consider literature: Tsubouchi Shōyō's *The Essence of the Novel* forged a new and modern path by rejecting novels in the "reward the virtuous and punish the wicked" mode of Bakin and others, but the classics were even more violently shunned in the age of Naturalism. *Genji monogatari* and the like were viewed with scorn, that goes without saying. Indeed, even setting aside the issue of what they thought of the work, hardly anyone in the literary world had even read it in its entirety. Japanese novelists weren't reading what is said to be Japan's greatest novel. Rumor had it that Ozaki Kōyō read *Genji* every day while he was writing *Speechless, Wordless,* but I suspected at the time that even he was reading only a given section. I remember that Aeba Kōson, that aficionado of Edo literature, once included *Genji monogatari* in a list of favorite books that he provided in response to a survey by some magazine, and he wrote, "There is a phrase 'Suma *Genji*,' and that's exactly how it was for me with *Genji*: I only read as far as 'Suma,' then made do with *Ferns of Recollection*." That, basically, seems to have been the extent of writers' knowledge of *Genji* back then. *Ferns of Recollection* is a digest of *Genji*. Among my acquaintances, Tayama Katai participated as a *tanka* poet in the Keien group and seems to have had a taste for the national literature, so he may well have read *Genji*, but though I heard him discuss all sorts of works, both old and new, Eastern and Western, on innumerable occasions during our long friendship, he never once mentioned *Genji*. I do know that he was extremely impressed with *The Kagerō Diary*. I doubt Tōson, Shūsei, Hōmei, or any of that crowd read *Genji*. *Genji monogatari* was something Kokugaku scholars read; it wasn't thought of as something modern literati should be reading.[15]

The opening lines of this passage are intriguing, first of all, for their vagueness: it is difficult to say for sure who is reading what in the second sentence. As I indicated in my translation by adding the grammatical subject "we," Hakuchō appears to be speaking in the first clause of other Japanese readers like himself, but it is not clear what language the translations he refers to were written in. Hakuchō often read English translations of literature when Japanese translations were unavailable—this probably had been the case with *The Brothers Karamazov*, since Constance Garnett's English translation had appeared in 1912, and Yonekawa Masao's Japanese version only in 1914—and sometimes even when they were. Hakuchō gives no indication, moreover, where the "contemporary reader" he speaks of hails from, whether Japan or abroad, or what relationship this reader has to the "original language." Here, too, Hakuchō seems to imply that the past and the present are divided by a gulf deeper than any that could stand between two contemporaries.

Hakuchō next takes readers back to a period, distant but still relevant, when *Genji monogatari* experienced the opposite of a boom, having ceased to be considered appropriate reading material for even the cultural elite. This is the first time in his essays on *Genji* that Hakuchō ever recalls this past, and it seems likely that he was spurred to do so by the context against which he wrote: in effect, he is gesturing toward the issue we now think of as "canon formation," invoking history as an explanation for the shifting fortunes of literary works. Calling attention to the lack of interest in *Genji monogatari* as a work of literature during the Meiji and Taishō periods serves to emphasize the historical specificity of the postwar boom, which in turn undercuts the notion that the tale can be regarded as the fountainhead of a clean, linear tradition to which all Japanese are able, at least potentially, to lay claim. This diachronic denial is complimented, moreover, by Hakuchō's synchronic denial of tradition at the start of the essay, when he says, "The voices of all the ordinary people who have given *Genji* its reputation as a dreadful bore rose up in my mind, elbowing aside literary history."

Once Hakuchō has established as a theme the opposition between ordinary readers, including authors, and the authorities who create and disseminate literary history, he shifts his attention to the process of negotiation that takes place between these groups in the construction of language itself. After the passage just quoted, Hakuchō recounts the story of his first encounter with *Genji monogatari* at Waseda University and with *The Tale of Genji* at the Imperial Hotel, and describes his impression of each: "I agreed with everyone else that it was a 'dreadful bore,'" he says of the original, and of Waley's translation, "I felt as though I were being told a dreamlike tale of some foreign land."[16] Then, leaving space between two paragraphs to indicate that he is moving to a new topic, he suddenly launches into an abstract and yet specific meditation on writing:

> We were made to read, and remember, all kinds of writing. Japanese-style Chinese prose of the sort in *The Unofficial History of Japan*; elegant writing in alternating seven- and five-syllable phrases like that in *The Chronicle of the Eight Dogs*; writing in the unmistakably translated style of the Bible. From the Meiji period on, there has been such an extreme confusion of written styles that I had to imitate first one and then another, and through that process create a prose style of my own. Then along came "the unification of speech and writing," in the wake of which writing seemed to have settled, more or less, into a single style, though in fact the tremendous hodgepodge of difference seems only to have increased.[17]

Hakuchō's opposition of "ordinary people" and "literary history" can be boiled down, ultimately, to a simple binary: most people find *Genji monogatari* dull; literary historians invariably place it at the pinnacle of the Japanese literary tradition. His treatment of writing complicates this scheme. Here he is not simply elbowing aside a particular vision of literary tradition, but casually calling into question the very notion of a community of Japanese citizens united first and foremost by their use of a common language. If Murasaki Shikibu's Japanese is not his own, neither are any of the numerous other varieties of Japanese that were in circulation when he was a young boy—at least not automatically. There is no single "Japanese language" available to be inherited, only a jumble of styles. Teachers and other authorities can make us "read, and remember, all kinds of writing," but this is not the same as learning "a language"; authoritative texts can stand as models to be copied, but the pietistic act of copying them is itself productive, a process of replacement. Hakuchō created his own language. Each of us, he suggests, must create a language, cobbling it together bit by bit from the innumerable bits and pieces at hand. And ironically, *genbun'itchi*, the movement to "unify speech and writing"—which aimed, in part, to unify the nation by creating a standard, modern Japanese—only amplified the confusion.

Hakuchō next shifts his focus from the non-unity of the Japanese language to the question of style itself. Here, again, he returns to the issue of community, questioning whether *Genji* has had the unifying force often attributed to it as the pinnacle of Japanese prose:

> *Genji* and other such works seem to have been regarded as the fountainhead and the reservoir of written beauty in the Japanese style, but I wonder if it really has such value. Shakespeare's thirty-odd plays are said to contain more words than any other body of writing in English literature; do the fifty-four chapters of *Genji* bring together so many Japanese words? I suspect that they contain fewer than we think. The tale may be rich in descriptions of flowers, birds, the wind, and the moon, but it deals with a very circumscribed world.[18]

Hakuchō goes on to observe that the descriptions of the passing seasons, from early spring to the end of winter, during the course of the six or seven chapters from "Hatsune" (The First Song of the Year) through "Nowaki" (The Typhoon) or "Miyuki" (The Royal Visit), "suggest that the appreciation subsequent generations of cultured Japanese showed for natural beauty was given its particular form by *Genji*."[19] Shortly afterward, however, he notes that the appreciation of natural beauty is not all there was to Japanese literature. "In the literary arts of the Tokugawa period, with the works of Bakin at their head," he writes, "the glorification of ritual suicide is an ironclad rule. Authors invested their energies in the depiction of all manner of brutal acts."[20] The absence of such brutality in *Genji* was a relief to Hakuchō, and he undoubtedly had the postwar context in which he was writing in mind when he noted that "it is certainly a good thing to become familiar with *Genji*, as an altogether different type of literature."[21]

When Hakuchō offers this positive moral evaluation of *Genji monogatari*, however, he is still standing on the side of ordinary people, rather than with literary history. He suggests, in the face of the ongoing *Genji* boom, that ordinary people can, and should, push aside authoritative visions of community thrust on them from above and improvise their own. Do not read the tale, he says, as the fountainhead of Japanese tradition, of Japanese aesthetics, or of the Japanese language, because it is none of these things. There is no fountainhead, no monolithic, linear tradition. *Genji monogatari* is not a unifying principle. Language is not a unifying principle. If you read *Genji*, take from it what you want, not what you are told you need. Tanizaki had suggested that Hakuchō was unusually skeptical of the value of Japanese traditions; in this essay, at least, Hakuchō reveals himself to be skeptical less of the value of Japanese traditions than of the notion of tradition itself and of a unified community founded in tradition.

In chapter 5, I cited the literary critic Kobayashi Hideo's observation that no major writer except the early modern thinker Motoori Norinaga had been as enthusiastic as Hakuchō in his praise for *Genji monogatari*. This pairing of Norinaga and Hakuchō comes as a considerable surprise: Hakuchō was known, after all, for his "worship of the West," while Norinaga was the most famous proponent of Kokugaku (most often translated as "Nativism" or "National Studies"), a movement that sought to elaborate and propagate an image of Japan as a unique and privileged community largely through the study of old texts and of the language in which they were written. As Susan L. Burns has shown, Norinaga took Kokugaku to a new level by turning "the ancient language of Japan into the privileged signifier of Japanese cultural identity" and making language "the foundation of his discussion of Japan as community."[22] Ultimately, it is precisely this vision that Hakuchō, as enthralled with *Genji* as Norinaga was with *Genji monogatari*, was calling into question.

Translation

Even as Hakuchō develops his indirect critique of the *Genji* boom, he also offers his most direct statements yet on translation. For the most part, this discussion echoes those in his earlier essays: he insists on the distinction between original and translation, not only accepting this difference but welcoming it as a sign of Waley's commitment to a strategy of creative translation superior, in Hakuchō's view, to the sort of translation then dominant in Japan:

> Arthur Waley's *Genji* is not Murasaki Shikibu's *Genji*. No doubt the translator thought he had brought an extraordinary work by a foreign woman writer of great genius to life in the present age, but every translation is, as a matter of course, distinct from the original. Waley's translation, in particular, is completely different in its approach from translations of foreign literature common in Japan today. Strictly speaking, it may well be littered with mistranslations, but that doesn't matter at all when we are dealing with translated novels of this sort; we would do better to consider this work as an original novel by

Waley himself, one that is based on an examination and interpretation of *Genji*.[23]

This willingness to acknowledge the translation as having an existence of its own, apart from but also bound up with the original—to recognize, as I would put it, that the translation functions as a replacement of the original rather than as an instance of its reception—meshes with Hakuchō's reluctance to set *Genji monogatari* on a pedestal fashioned for it by those interested in fostering national unity through the medium of literary history. If every translation is its own book, distinct from the original, then of course all the modern-Japanese translations, kabuki plays, radio dramas, and films that had been appearing since 1947 had to be distinguished from *Genji monogatari*, too, and their popularity should not be taken as a sign that postwar Japan had finally returned to its peaceful, aestheticist roots as a "country of culture."

Although Hakuchō's treatment of *The Tale of Genji* is based on a sense of just how different it is from *Genji monogatari*, something interesting happens when he actually begins to compare the two books. In his earlier essays, Hakuchō did not go into much detail about what separates the translation from the original, in large part because he had found the classical text so maddeningly difficult to read. When he first attempted to plow through the whole book in 1926, he admitted to feeling disgusted with its prose. By the time he sat down to write "*Genji monogatari*—hon'yaku to gensaku" twenty-five years later, he had clearly become a much better reader of classical Japanese. Although his reference to the author of *Sarashina nikki* near the beginning of the essay is intended to highlight the huge distance that still separates him from Murasaki Shikibu's text, it also reveals that he has overcome his former frustration: Hakuchō can now imagine, with sympathy and perhaps even some envy, the delight of a girl who could lose herself so deeply in the work that she forgot everything else. This change allowed him to discover what he likes about *Genji monogatari* and what he does not like about its translation. Something about his appraisals of the two books, however, makes it hard to keep these preferences straight, and this something says a lot, I think, about what *Genji* had become in 1951 and what it remains today. A few quotations should serve to illustrate both the general tenor of his observations and their confusion:

> I think the work should be read as a fairy tale. If the *Arabian Nights* is a fairy tale, so is *Genji*. It skillfully depicts lives of jealousy, suffering, and strife, and does so with a concision unexpected in a woman writer,

and yet it feels as if one is watching it all through a haze; the emotions aren't immediate, but like the sufferings of fairy-tale characters. This is quite different from my sense of the jealousy, suffering, and strife in *The Brothers Karamazov*, which hit me with all the force of reality, though it's all just a product of the author's fantasies. And yet it would be a mistake to suggest that one or the other has taken the correct path as a novel, as literature, or to suggest that one is superior, one inferior. It's fascinating, too, to treat this harsh life, full of hardships, as a fairyland. That, indeed, is literature's raison d'être. Doing with life what is done in *The Twenty-Fifth Hour* and *Darkness at Noon* can't be said, surely, to be the truest and greatest literary path.[24]

The agonized psychologies of Fujitsubo, Genji, Kashiwagi, and the Retired Emperor Reizei also struck me as fairy-tale sufferings, and failed to strike my heart with any sense of immediacy, but when I read Waley's *Genji*, it felt as if he had presented in it, for all to see, the sufferings of modern man. The "ten Uji chapters" were so masterfully transformed into a modern European novel that I lost interest, and felt put off rather than pleased by the fact that it had drifted away from its fairy-tale style, but when I got to "Wakana," parts one and two, and then "Kashiwagi," which comes next, I found these chapters still more engaging than the rest of the book. This, I thought, is the most exquisite description ever. The part where Kashiwagi peeks in at the Third Princess, making use of the Chinese cat, is written with a gentle touch so that the particular scene emerges, all of itself, together with the emotions that overwhelm him, as clearly as could be. The work is filled with descriptions of flowers, birds, the wind, the moon, and portraits of the changing seasons, to the extent that Waley himself settled into a sort of *Genji* mannerism, and one sometimes feels that the same mood just keeps being repeated, but the descriptions of Kashiwagi and the Third Princess are extraordinarily sharp. Reading the section that commences "*Mikichōdomo shidokenaku hikiyaritsutsu, hitoge chikaku yozukite zo miyuru ni, karaneko no ito chiisaku okashige naru o, sukoshi ōki naru neko oitsuzukite, niwaka ni misu no hashi yori hashiriizuru ni, hitobito obiesawagite, soyosoyo to miugoki samayou kehaidomo, koromo no otonai mimi kashikamashiki kokochi su*," it strikes me that the crystal-clear descriptions of the scenes that met this woman author's eyes have no parallel whatsoever. But the differences between languages, and pieces of writing, are a funny thing: when I read Genji's pessimistic reflections in "Wakana" in the classical language of the original, they seem like the reflections of a character in a fairy tale, but when I read them in the English translation, the emotions of the one-time pleasure-loving youth, now an old man, are strikingly immediate. This is a result of the differences between the languages, the writing. I can't get a hold on the agony characters feel, not with any acuteness, when I read the tale as it is, in that *Genji* style. I can only stumble through prose like this: "*Mazu wa omou hito ni samazama okure, nokoritomareru yowai no sue ni mo, akazu oboyuru koto soitaru mi nite suginureba, sore ni kaete ya, omoishi hodo yori wa, ima made mo nagarauru naran to nan omishiraruru.*" It makes me impatient, and it has no real impact on me.[25]

Apparently, a certain English critic described Murasaki Shikibu's style as psychological and placed her in the same line as Proust. When one sees the drifting, nebulous style of the original through the English translation, one certainly might see flickers of something Proustian here and there. You get what you want out of a novel. If you see it as psychological, well, the translation explores psychology with greater clarity than the original, but there are also traces of psychology in the original work's murky ambiguities. And nearly all the poetry has been expunged from the translation—no doubt the translator knew that nothing good would come of trying forcibly to twist into English something that simply couldn't be translated. But these poetry exchanges are part of what makes this novel interesting. The poems take the place of greetings in each scene. They're not intended as poems of truth; they're tossed off, casually murmured. And after they have been composed, the characters say "Ah, that was a bad poem," or "Ah, how sad," or "Ah, how funny," and seem to be sighing or smiling or making sour faces. Places like this, too, give me the sense that this is a fairy-tale world.[26]

Perhaps the most notable, and also the most revealing, element in these quotations is Hakuchō's repeated description of *Genji* as a fairy tale. Hakuchō seems to suggest that *Genji monogatari* has more of this fairy-tale quality—which he associates with the haziness of its language and his own consequent inability to enter "psychologically" into the lives of its characters—than *The Tale of Genji*, whose English he finds clearer, crisper, and more immediately real. Hakuchō would seem to have a preference for literature he can connect with directly, judging from his description of *The Brothers Karamazov* as a novel that struck him "with all the force of reality" and from the concessive form his subsequent praise for *Genji* takes: "*And yet* it would be a mistake to suggest that one or the other has taken the correct path as a novel, as literature, or to suggest that one is superior, one inferior." The fairy-tale quality that Hakuchō perceives in *Genji*—and especially in *Genji monogatari*—is not, it would seem, a positive attribute.

That said, Hakuchō never finished reading *The Brothers Karamazov* forty years earlier, and he is not sure that he will reach the end this time, either. Indeed, he goes so far in his praise of *Genji* as to say that he senses in its treatment of life literature's raison d'être. Perhaps, then, we must distinguish Hakuchō's personal preferences as a reader from the more abstract, theoretical understanding of literature to which he is intellectually committed. He prefers clarity and a sense of immediacy, but as a critic he recognizes the subjectivity of this preference. He is attracted to the sharply delineated, relatively accessible emotional complexities of *The Tale of Genji*, but he also values what he sees as *Genji monogatari*'s shadowy unreality.

To a certain extent, this does seem to be what Hakuchō is saying. Difficulties arise, however, when we move into the second passage. Hakuchō comments that he is put off when Waley's translation loses its fairy-tale feel in the final chapters, becoming too much like a modern European novel. This is interesting, in part, because the last ten chapters of the tale, the "ten Uji chapters" (*Uji jūjō*), have prompted much discussion of Ukifune's supposed modernity as a character, and thus of *Genji monogatari*'s "literary" qualities. In 1914, for instance, Yosano Akiko wrote in a letter to the writer, poet, and lawyer Hiraide Osamu that "Ukifune is the woman I like best. She is a modern sort of person, isn't she, full of inner radiance."[27] The dissatisfaction that Hakuchō feels concerning what he regards, despite his preference for psychologically rich depictions of sympathetic human characters, as the *excessive* modernity of the Uji chapters in Waley's *The Tale of Genji* stems from his sensitivity to the historical gap that separates him so decisively from *Genji monogatari*, and represents a challenge to readers who think they can bridge that distance or, perhaps, do not even notice that it is there. Holding fast to his own position as a modern reader, approaching *Genji monogatari* in the same way he would a modern novel, also means respecting the alterity of the Heian text, acknowledging that the tale will not always be amenable to such an approach because it was not written to answer modern tastes or expectations, in terms of either its plot or its prose style. For Hakuchō, it seems, reading *Genji monogatari* as a modern novel must inevitably entail certain *valuable* disappointments.

A second, still more significant point can be made regarding Hakuchō's reaction to the jarring modernity of Waley's translation of the ten Uji chapters. Oddly, it does not seem to jibe with the distinction that Hakuchō drew between Murasaki Shikibu's and Waley's respective prose styles. If what Hakuchō describes as the fairy-tale quality of *Genji* is primarily associated in his eyes with the murkiness of the classical Japanese text, in contrast to the precise clarity of Waley's *The Tale of Genji*, then what are we to make of his sudden attribution of the same fairy-tale quality to the English text? The solution to this puzzle, I believe, is that despite his acute, minute awareness of the differences between *Genji monogatari* and *The Tale of Genji*, Hakuchō is ultimately unable to keep the two texts entirely separate in his mind.

I noted earlier that Hakuchō's stance toward the classical Japanese text had changed by 1951. His descriptions of the experience of reading no longer convey the sense of angry frustration that permeate his earlier essays, and far from dismissing the tale's prose as "incomparably bad," he now praises it extravagantly, saying that certain passages have "no parallel whatsoever." To be sure, this change was due in part to the greater sensitivity that Hakuchō had developed as a reader of classical Japanese, and of *Genji monogatari* in particular, but his lavish encomiums seem to reflect his experience of Waley's prose, to the extent that it is sometimes impossible to tell which book he is speaking of. After quoting a passage from the classical Japanese, Hakuchō speaks admiringly of the "crystal-clear descriptions of the scenes that met this woman author's eyes," but since he is impressed, ultimately, by the correspondence of the description to the image of the scene he carries in his mind, we cannot help wondering how much his repeated readings of Waley's depiction of the same scene are implicated in the picture. To what extent is Hakuchō admiring Murasaki Shikibu's prose itself, and to what extent is his understanding of her writing illuminated by the clear light of Waley's interpretation? It is all but impossible to say, because on some level Hakuchō appears to have lost the ability to distinguish very rigorously between the two. In 1933, Hakuchō had imagined what it would be like if Waley's translation were translated into modern Japanese, but in 1951, as far as he was concerned, a modern-Japanese version was unnecessary. Reading and rereading *The Tale of Genji* over the course of two decades had turned the classical Japanese text of *Genji monogatari* itself into "one of the great novels of the world." Translation and original had fused.

Indeed, the influence that *The Tale of Genji* exercised on Hakuchō's reading of *Genji monogatari* is apparent even in his description of *Genji* as a fairy tale. In the first footnote in his translation, Waley informs the reader that "this chapter should be read with indulgence. In it Murasaki, still under the influence of her somewhat childish predecessors, writes in a manner which is a blend of the Court chronicle with the conventional fairy-tale."[28] He makes a similar point concerning the tale as a whole in the introduction he included in the second volume of his translation. "It is clear that, if we contrast *Genji* with such fiction as does not exploit the ramifications of the human mind at all (the *Arabian Nights* or *Mother Goose*), it appears to be 'psychological,'" he writes, only to qualify this already tepid statement by observing that "if we go on to compare it with Stendhal, with Tolstoy, with Proust, the *Tale of Genji* appears by contrast to possess little more psychological complication than a Grimm's fairy tale." Then, executing yet another about-face, he says that the tale "does for a definite reason belong more to the category which includes Proust, than to the category which includes Grimm."[29] Mark Morris explains this bewildering volley of prevarications by suggesting that "Waley sought to locate *Genji* at the positive pole of a dichotomy that opposed 'classical' to 'psychological/novel/irregular/Gothic.' [His] concession that *The Tale of Genji* might-sort of-perhaps be spoken of as a 'novel' seems merely his way of praising with faint damns."[30] Viewed in this manner, Waley's perspective sheds light not only on Hakuchō's own shifting description of *Genji* as a fairy tale, but also on his reluctance to place too much emphasis on the tale's exploration of "psychology," and his tentative claim, comparing *Genji* with *The Brothers Karamazov*, that "it would be a mistake to suggest that one or the other has taken the correct path as a novel, as literature."

In chapter 5, I mentioned that *Genji* specialists have tended, over the decades since Hakuchō first began to write his essays on their subject, to brush him aside, to castigate him, as a means of protecting both the sanctity of their academic domain, *Genji* studies, and a comfortable sense of national community rooted in the Japanese language. "However different [Heian-period] culture may be from our own," Akiyama Ken wrote in response to Hakuchō, "[*Genji monogatari*] can never be placed in the same category with literature in French and English, because of course it is still in the Japanese language." But this is precisely the point that Hakuchō was making: the Japanese language itself is a kind of fiction, and if *Genji monogatari* "is still in the Japanese language," its particular iteration of the Japanese language can very easily be placed in the same category with literature in French and English. Hakuchō understood not only that the language in which *Genji monogatari* was written was not his language, that it was not our language, but also that languages do not exist as separate domains and can never be walled off from one another. As a man who had been reading all manner of Japaneses and Englishes all his life, who had lived abroad, and who had discovered a classical Japanese masterpiece not by way of but *in the form of* an English translation, he understood that languages fuse in the person of the polyglot.

Hakuchō knew, as well, that the historical processes of change that take place as a result of the inevitable, interminable interactions of different languages and literatures on a global scale, as in the inaccessible recesses of the individual polyglot's brain, ceaselessly buffet the rock we stand on, here and now, in the ongoing flow of time. He knew that the interpenetration of versions of the same work written in different languages, in different places, at different times, is the reality of world literature, and that this, above all, is what *Genji* had become and what it would remain, no doubt, for the foreseeable future.

Conclusion

Turning to Translation, Returning to Translation

"So that's what lies in wait! But anyone with a memory as blurred as ours is not likely to make it back so far?"

Theodore Weiss,
"The Future of the Past"

This book has traced a vast history, beginning in early-nineteenth-century Edo and pushing ahead, and around the globe, to settle in the postwar era. We have seen how *Nise Murasaki inaka Genji* emerged as the first genuinely popular replacement (adaptation, translation expansively defined) of a tale composed for a narrow aristocratic audience at the Heian court—how *Inaka Genji* in fact created the notion of such a replacement for a popular audience. We have seen how, in the wake of Suematsu Kenchō's *Genji Monogatari* and, most significantly, of Masamune Hakuchō's discovery of Arthur Waley's *The Tale of Genji* and the publication of Tanizaki Jun'ichirō's first modern-Japanese translation, *Inaka Genji* itself was replaced as a replacement of *Genji monogatari* in the popular literary field. And we have seen how—through these repeated replacements over a century and a few decades, through the circulation of discourse about these replacements, and through the circulation of discourse about the circulation of discourse about these replacements—*Genji* came to rest in a position of unparalleled prominence in the firmament of the Japanese literary canon, suspended within the finely balanced centrifugal and centripetal pulls of world and national literature.

My presentation of this history of replacement has been detailed and particular, and while I have endeavored to write in a manner accessible to readers unversed in early modern and modern Japanese literary history, I have tried not to be *too* accessible: by and large, the accommodations I made were cosmetic. I used English more than Japanese titles and provided fewer dates than is common in English-language books on Japanese literature, but I did not simplify my arguments, lard them with references to scholars and theorists who work on materials more familiar in the English-language context, or shy away from dense, involved analyses. In a lecture delivered in 1813, the German philosopher Friedrich Schleiermacher famously proposed that translators have two choices: "Either the translator leaves the writer in peace as much as possible and moves the reader toward him; or he leaves the reader in peace as much as possible and moves the writer toward him."[1] To some extent, the same two paths present themselves to the scholar, particularly to the specialist in a subject foreign to the primary context in which her work will circulate. In writing this book, I tried to adopt something akin to Schleiermacher's second approach, asking readers to wade into the material, to give themselves up to a stream of information somewhat less tamed than much criticism in English. To an extent, I wrote this study, in English, as though I were also writing it in Japanese, always hoping to produce a book that would satisfy an audience of deeply knowledgeable but not always "theoretically inclined" Japanese scholars of Japanese literature for whom I have enormous respect and to whom I am profoundly indebted. But, of course, I was actually writing in English, hoping that my work would interest scholars in other fields.

In the introduction, I touched on the important dual role that the English language plays in this study; I described it as being, in part, a history, in English, of the possibility of writing a history like it in English. Translation, too, has played a dual role in this book, again both as a major element in the transnational, translingual history I have outlined and as an element of the process by which that history came into being. Perhaps the best way to frame the issue is to say that I wrote this book from the perspective not simply of a scholar, but of a scholar-translator, where the scholar-translator is conceived of not simply as a scholar who also translates, but as a scholar whose scholarship, and whose knowledge, is shaped by translation. And because this book is a dual history of the replacement of *Genji monogatari* and the creation, by means of translation, of the possibility of English-language Japanese literary studies as a disciplinary node, I have come, over the course of this project, to see increasingly clearly that scholars in this field are *inescapably* descendents of the early postwar scholars of Japanese literature, whose research often took the form of the translation-plus-introduction. This position has not been easy to occupy, and since the late 1970s, when the translation-plus-introduction came to be regarded as something to be outgrown, many who have written about Japanese literature in English have tried to act as though it was not theirs: they were critics, or critical theorists, not scholar-translators. But for all its discomfort, the position of the scholar-translator has its own particular strengths, if only we can learn better to recognize and to draw on them.

In the pages that follow, rather than weave a conventional conclusion—a look back and a summing up—I would like to reflect on the nature and the position of English-language Japanese literary studies and its relation to translation, drawing on the preceding chapters not so much as a history of the replacement of *Genji monogatari*, but as a history of the emergence of the possibility of that disciplinary node. This conclusion deals, then, less with the arguments I have made than with my methodology, and less with the ground I have covered than with the issue of how we might proceed from here. At the same time, I hope to give a sense of how this study, as an investigation of *Genji*'s early modern and modern canonization, relates to larger scholarly tides.

Turning to Translation

Beginning in the late 1970s, scholars of literature in the United States became interested in the intricacies of canon formation—the compound of processes by which culturally authoritative figures and institutions promote certain texts as "classics" and thus attempt to ensure the continued dominance of their own value systems. In the late 1980s, a highly visible, deeply politicized discussion of the content of "the canon"—which for various reasons was often equated with the reading lists for literature classes—broke out in university English departments and then moved into other, less culturally authoritative departments and programs whose faculties taught and researched canons too marginal, in the North American context, to be described so simply, without any qualifying adjective. Books, chapters, and articles began to appear that considered various "other" canons: the African canon, the canon of *nō* plays, the Spanish canon, the Latin American canon, the Asian American canon, the jazz canon . . .

This mind-boggling expansion seems, in turn, to have helped transform the terms of the central debate. The argument about how or whether "the canon" ought to be opened up to underrepresented groups within the "Western tradition"—and, in particular, what authors to include on the syllabi of courses in English and American literature—has given way to a new discussion of what to do with all those other literatures out there: how to deal with the concept of a global canon, with the reality of the plurality of languages, and with the grand discovery that some are making, apparently for the first time, that even national literatures are multilingual. The movement that Shelley Fisher Fishkin described in her presidential address to the American Studies Association in 2004 as "The Transnational Turn in American Studies," at least as it relates to the gradually multilingualizing study of literature in the United States, looks, from my outsider's perspective, like a welcome backwash from the waves of critical discourse that are constantly surging from the ocean of the English department into the tidal pools of national and regional literary studies.[2]

It is a matter not of theory, but of waking up to the existence of others. "The globalization of English," Paul Jay has written, "is not a theoretical formulation or a political agenda developed by radicals in the humanities to displace the canon. It is a simple fact of contemporary history."[3] Jay is writing not about the English language, but about English literary studies, which he correctly observes "has been at the center of a curricular world organized along the lines of a political map, the borders of which have neatly duplicated those between modern nation-states."[4] What began, then, as a "mirror, mirror on the wall"-style political brouhaha over the United States' representation of its beauties to itself has been transformed by a dawning awareness of "literature's relation to the historical processes of globalization."[5] So, at last, *they* have noticed that "the canon" is just one among many, that the one contains many, and that the many interact as one.

Not surprisingly, the drift in interest in canon formation from the institutional center to the periphery and then, in an altered form, back again toward the center was accompanied by distinct shifts in the emphasis of the work being done. The fierce debate over pedagogy, aesthetic value, representation, and curricular reform was supplanted, in the less visible, less influential contexts of particular national literary studies, by politically minded historical investigations into the modern delineation of national/cultural identities, the transnational establishment of the institution of literature, the spread of the aesthetic concept of culture, and so on. What had begun as a debate about *what to do* evolved, in these other contexts—fields in which there was less point in debating the canons we taught, at least in terms of identity politics and representation, because they were foreign to most of our students and we were foreign to the institutions that first generated them—into a mode of looking at the past and present of literatures, especially at literatures' relationship to the *international* rise of the modern nation-state, the process by which national canons got where they are now.[6] Research of this sort necessarily entailed a transnational, translingual perspective, since the creation of the global idea of the nation-state and its cultural props could be tracked backward only through the confluence of concepts that had emerged in mutually distant places and were elaborated in different languages. And this global viewpoint has led to what might be described, borrowing a nice turn of phrase from Emily Apter, as "the 'comp-lit-ization' of national literatures throughout the humanities."[7] The comp-lit-ization of national literary studies as I understand it—as a border-crossing response to the realization that "literature" (in whatever language) emerged from the fraught, unequal, two-way intricacies of *trade,* that the birth of "literature" (in whatever language) was heralded by the creak of mooring ropes steadying newly arrived ships in old ports—is, I suspect, a large part of what inspired "the transnational turn" in American studies; the turn toward "cosmopolitanism" in English departments; and even, paradoxically, the recent belated turn toward "world literature" in the field of comparative literature.

Contrary to the pronouncements of—to cite just one example—Jonathan Culler in *Comparative Literature in an Age of Globalization,* the American Comparative Literature Association's 2004 Report on the State of the Discipline, I would suggest that, in trying to move beyond its fascinatingly long-lived provincialism, comparative literature has at last begun to participate in a discussion that has been part of the intellectual world of scholars working in national literatures and area studies right from the beginning. Culler proclaims that "comparative literature has triumphed" over national literary studies, from which it was formerly distinguished, "because it did not take it for granted, as did the departments of English, French, Spanish, Italian, Chinese, that a national literature in its historical evolution was the natural and appropriate unit of literary study," and because it "became the site of literary theory, while national literature departments frequently resisted, or at least remained indifferent to, the sorts of theory that did not emanate from their own cultural spheres."[8]

"Literary theory" emanated, of course, from the same European cultural spheres that most scholars in comparative literature consider "their own." And while I cannot speak for "departments of English, French, Spanish, Italian," it is quite clear that Chinese literary studies, certainly studies of modern Chinese literature, never had the option of disregarding the West or the rest of the East the way comparative literature specialists generally disregarded China and the rest of the East, precisely because in the view of scholars of Chinese literature, "literature" and "literary studies" were all too obviously transnational concepts, products of what Lydia Liu has called "translingual practice."[9] And one might note that Culler's very inclusion of Chinese in his list of departments is a further indication of his Eurocentrism, since, as far as I know, no university in the United States or Europe has ever had an independent "Department of Chinese Literature."

A transnational perspective is as inevitable in my own field, Japanese literature, as it is in the field of Chinese literary studies—as this book, particularly its second part, has demonstrated and as a glance at, for instance, the index of Donald Keene's *Dawn to the West: Japanese Literature of the Modern Era* makes abundantly clear: the first entry is *À la recherche du temps perdu* (*In Search of Lost Time*); the second, *À l'ombre des jeunes filles en fleurs* (*Within a Budding Grove*); the third, *ABC Library* (*Iroha bunko*) by Tamenaga Shunsui.¹⁰ Throughout East Asia, at least, "literature" (Mandarin Ch. 文学 *wenxue*, K. 문학 *munhak*, J. 文学 *bungaku*) as it was re-created during modern times has always been world literature; the possibility that national literatures may one day arc into the great flow of world literature, joining what Pascale Casanova has described as "the world republic of letters," was their whole raison d'être; canons were necessarily global and globally intertwined. Heated discussion of "the canon" has simply helped coax some into a greater receptivity to this perspective. The current explosion of interest in world literature emerged, to return to an earlier metaphor, from the fraught, unequal, two-way intricacies of interdepartmental trade, not the "triumph" of comparative literature.

No doubt, I am oversimplifying. The current interest in globalizing the canon is not only an outgrowth of the canon debates. But sometimes those of us who stand at the edge of the great synthesizer we might refer to as "the English department"—or, now that it is beginning to overcome its Eurocentrism, "the comparative literature department"—have to take stock, oversimply, of our situation. The field of Japanese literary studies in the United States has a certain reputation for isolation (or, rather, this is part of our self-image, since our sort of isolation implies a lack of reputation), and it is certainly true that most of us working in this node have little, if any, expectation that our work will be widely read by scholars in other fields, except maybe, rarely, as a source of data. Michael Dutton opened his provocative genealogy of area studies, "Lead Us Not into Translation," with the question, "Why is it impossible to imagine, much less to write, a work like Michel Foucault's *Discipline and Punish* within Asian area studies?" adding, "It is not just about writing such a text but about having it read as something more than a description; having it read for its theoretical significance more generally."¹¹

To a certain extent, this relates to the movement I have been tracing, out to the margins and then back into the center, of interest in canonization: the theoretical argument about *what to do* with "the canon" turned, as the wave streamed into the little pools, into a mode of applied historical investigation; then, as research detailed the interconnectedness of concepts of literature and national literary canons, and of the processes by which both are formed and reformed, a renewed theoretical discussion of *what to do* with world literature broke out in the English and comparative literature departments. They start the debate; we apply their theories; they go on with their theorizing. It is a familiar complaint, a familiar criticism. An all-too-familiar echo of the slogan "Catch up, surpass."

We may also say, however, that the applied historical investigations into canon formation that took place in the rather isolated, marginal contexts of national literary studies, but were necessarily transnationally and translingually oriented, have indeed had "theoretical significance more generally," even setting aside the issue of how given scholarly works are read—that there is, or could be, less to the distinction between debates about *what to do* and applied investigations than there may, at first glance, appear to be.[12] *Inventing the Classics: Modernity, National Identity, and Japanese Literature*, the pathbreaking collection of essays that inaugurated studies of canon formation in the marginal field of Japanese literary studies, may or may not have been read by scholars outside of Asian area studies—it was reviewed by Michele Marra in *Comparative Literature Studies* and advertised in both *PMLA* and *Critical Inquiry*, so it may well have caught the eye of a few non-specialists—but either way, it clearly was inspired by and participated in the wash and backwash of discussion of canons that has been taking place in the United States since the late 1970s. And the very meticulousness and detail that characterize its nine essays allowed it to negotiate a theoretical position of its own, combining reception theory with a more radical constructionist stance that attends to the ways in which discourse reinvents its own object, raising issues relevant to discussions taking place in other fields.

In his much quoted essay "Conjectures on World Literature," Franco Moretti advocates what he calls "distant reading: where distance, let me repeat it, *is a condition of knowledge*: it allows you to focus on units that are much smaller or much larger than the text: devices, themes, tropes—or genres and systems."[13] This term, "distant reading," could to a certain extent be used to describe the methodology of a book like *Inventing the Classics*, with its attention to literary histories and its dedication to a particular type of "secondhand" synthesis of earlier analyses. Moretti, too, draws a distinction between studies of national and world literature, expressing his hopes for the latter. "There is," he writes, "no justification for the study of world literature but this: to be a thorn in the side, a permanent intellectual challenge to national literatures—especially the local literature."[14] But as *Inventing the Classics* and, for that matter, this book's treatments of *Genji monogatari* have illustrated, studies of canon formation that have developed within the context of national literary studies are already "a thorn in the side" of national literatures, and this applied theoretical work continues in its own subtle way to present an intellectual challenge to studies of the local literatures of the United States. From our position on the margins, we—whoever we are—continue to shape the center, even as the center shapes us. The discussion turns and returns.

An interesting parallel can be drawn, I think, between the apparent division of labor in literary studies in the United States into "theoretical work" (the English department, the comparative literature department) and "applied work" (national literature departments and programs, including Japanese literary studies), on the one hand—the division that Dutton laments, but that Culler points to so triumphantly—and, on the other, the apparent division of labor in the context of the global field of Japanese literary studies into "theoretical work" (scholarship in the United States and Europe, "Japanese literary studies," Japanese scholarship that engages with foreign scholarship [*Nihonbungaku kenkyū*]) and "applied work" ("traditional" Japanese-language scholarship [*kokubungaku*], scholarship in the United States and Europe that employs the methods of "traditional" Japanese-language scholarship). Alternatively, we might turn our attention to another related, seemingly clear-cut binary: "theoretical work" (the work critics do) versus "applied work" (the work that is worked on, the subject of "theoretical work"—that is, Japanese literature itself, scholarly editions of which are invariably prepared by scholars in Japan). To some extent, these oppositions do give us an accurate picture of the situation, though the hierarchy they imply—the emphasis placed on "addressing theoretical issues," the notion that Japanese literary studies or East Asian area studies needs scholars able to *Discipline and Punish* like Michel Foucault—is actively rejected by Japanese literary scholars of a traditionalist stripe, above all those who work on premodern literature and who tend to value wide-ranging, detailed, and accurate knowledge of primary sources; the discovery of new archival materials; and the basic ability to read and annotate difficult primary texts more than the ability to offer fresh, inventive, and overtly theoretical perspectives.

While these oppositions may exist on some level, however, such constructed dichotomies also miss the mark. There are three reasons for this. First, so-called traditional Japanese-language scholarship (*kokubungaku*) always draws on foreign scholarship—the philological methods associated with this type of research, epitomized by Ikeda Kikan's *The Tale of Genji Collated*, which I touched on in the introduction, derived largely from Germany, after all, and the invention of "literature" as a global concept is what gave rise to *kokubungaku* in the first place and what reinvented particular works as "national literary classics," as this book has shown with respect to *Genji monogatari*.[15] Second, even the most theoretically oriented scholarship on Japanese literature, at least as it relates to premodern texts, draws on heterogeneous lineages of Japanese scholarship that predate by centuries the invention of "literature" as we know it. And finally, we must remember that "applied work" itself often, if not always, has "theoretical significance more generally." This is particularly true in the case of national literature and area studies departments and programs in the United States that focus on literatures outside Europe, in which research inevitably draws on various methodologies and practices predominant in North America—on, in Culler's words, "sorts of theory that did not emanate from their own cultural spheres."

My discussion of the movement of interest in canonization from the English department to national/regional literature departments and then back into the English and comparative literature departments is a case in point. It was a fairly simple matter for Japanese literary studies to steer clear of the bogged-down dispute over "representation" in the canon so trenchantly critiqued by John Guillory in *Cultural Capital: The Problem of Literary Canon Formation* because, as I observed earlier, Japanese literature is taught in the United States as a foreign literature, not as a mirror of "us readers" and "our" society.[16] It was not a simple matter, however, to know in which direction to steer. The approaches adopted and the issues raised in *Inventing the Classics*—the focus on the relationship of the modern Japanese canon to European formulations of literature during the nineteenth century, on competing genres, on the gendering of Japanese literature, on the relationship among various different languages used in Japan, and on the notion that "there have only been competing canons"[17]—were deeply influenced by the particular historical characteristics of the canons, genres, languages, and transnational relationships that the essays in the collection discuss.

This sounds commonsensical, and it is. But it is worth pausing a moment to consider the implications. There is, as I mentioned a moment ago, a tendency among academics in the United States to place theory and applied work in a hierarchical relationship: the clear, cool waters of abstract theory stream over the pebbles and sands of mundane facts, rolling them into new positions and configurations. If one must have a hierarchy—though it seems better, again, to think in terms of trade, of turns and returns—one ought to place theory on the bottom. Theoretical work channels applied work. The best sort of applied work, in my view, is not an application of theory; it is the application of nitty-gritty facts to theory; it is an attack on theory; it is itself an embodiment of theory. Examples abound. Look at D. F. McKenzie, Mikhail Bakhtin, and Jacques Derrida.

My point, in brief, is that for all the criticisms that have been catapulted back and forth between those who consider themselves "theoretically inclined" and those who insist, with a touch of the craftsperson's pride, that their work is more solid than that, the two camps and their approaches are, in fact, mutually implicated. It is true that some scholars exhibit a marked resistance to theory, but it seems to me that, if anything, over the past decades the theory buffs all but overwhelmed this tendency with their vociferous insistence that "everything is theory," and that it is, perhaps, this assertion that most has to be challenged, even now. At the risk of sounding a bit opaque, it seems to me that we would do well to cultivate the resistance to the resistance to the resistance to theory. We do not need any more triumphs; we have to keep trading, even trading places. Or, rather, we need to bolster our sense of ourselves as members of a discipline that will not allow us, ultimately, to identify so easily with one place or another, or with one place and then another: scholar-translators stand, inevitably, in many places at once and belong fully to none of them.

Scholars based in predominantly English-speaking contexts working on literatures composed in languages other than English, particularly literatures foreign to the cultural spheres of the United States and Europe, have to confront on a daily basis the foreignness of English, of the cultural spheres of the United States and Europe, to the languages and literatures we read and think about. When we write, we must translate. It is not an option for scholars of Japanese literature, for instance, to preserve the quotations we want to discuss untranslated, as comparative literature specialists working on European literatures sometimes do; often we do not even have the option of reproducing the original text in any but its romanized form. We cannot assume that non-specialist readers will even recognize the names of figures who loom as large in our own fields as, for instance, Europeans such as Goethe and Auerbach do in the field of comparative literature—both easily recognizable by their family names alone. And so we must expend precious space *translating* these names, and the titles of works, into cursory explanations. Conversely, when we publish or give lectures in the languages whose literatures we study, we must translate any terms that "did not emanate from [these] cultural spheres."

In the Japanese-language edition of *Inventing the Classics* (*Sōzō sareta koten*), which was published before the English version, the word "canon" is translated three ways: 古典 (koten/kanon), カノン (kanon), and 正典 (seiten). The first of these translations lays the reading カノン (kanon)—a phonetic transcription of the word "canon"—over the word 古典 (koten), which is used in the title and throughout the rest of the book as a match for the "Classics" of the English title, *Inventing the Classics*. Imagine "canon" being translated intralingually as "classics (read ˈkanən)." There is a peculiar contradiction here. To be sure, the English word "canon" contains a similar contradiction: its religious origins bespeak, after all, human recognition of divine, eternal value. But the three-decade history of canonization studies in the United States has overwritten the etymology of the term "canon," giving it a new, specifically literary meaning that allows us to see value as something given rather than recognized. When *Sōzō sareta koten* was released in Japanese, the translator of the introduction had to begin by literally overwriting the Japanese word for "classics" with the Japanese transliteration of "canon": what had to be invented, first of all, was the concept of canonization itself.

The publication of *Sōzō sareta koten* in Japanese was, in this sense, doubly important—but that is simply another way of saying that it was doubly challenging. In the introduction, a creative approach was taken to the thorny problem of the word "canon" by translating it in three ways, one of which calls up the now-submerged etymology of the word in English, contradicting the theoretical orientation of the book. This is great. It gives us a chance to stop and reflect on the theory and practice of canonization studies. Like most research into canonization, *Inventing the Classics/Sōzō sareta koten* is centered, for the most part—as its two titles indicate—on particular canonical texts. It combines a radical constructionist stance with a historical bent that aligns it with reception theory. This is a very productive approach; but at the same time, as I argued at length in the introduction, one cannot help noticing how it stresses canonical *texts* themselves, putting them at the center, treating them as historical givens—entities that are no less "received" because their reception has a history.

There is a telling slippage between the English and Japanese titles of this collection. In the English version, the act of researching the ongoing process of *Inventing the Classics* seems to acquire a theoretical thrust that ghosts the title with a *Re-*: scholarship is itself "reinventing the classics," giving us an opportunity to reconsider *what to do*. The Japanese title, with its perfective *Sōzō sareta* (invented, created, and so on), may be back-translated into English as *The Invented Classics*. Here, scholarship is a matter of historical, archival research into the process by which the classics were invented or, perhaps, into the texts that actually were reinvented as classics, as opposed to those that have been allowed to languish. The tension between these two titles highlights, I think, a subtle, suggestive contradiction that runs through the book itself, in both languages, between method and theory. Noticing this contradiction helps us both to see the strengths of the collection's particular combination of approaches and to figure out how we might ride the wave it created to the next stage by reinventing not the classics, not even the "classics (read 'kanən),'" but the whole concept of canonization as a process that has little, if any, need for classical *texts* themselves. This, of course, is one of the moves this study has attempted to make.

What we are seeing here, in something as simple as the comparison of the titles of two editions of the same book in two different languages, is an opportunity, a strength that is conferred, by the inevitable implication of multilingualism in their work, on scholars engaged in national literary studies outside the spheres in which those studies are regarded as native. The activities of reading and researching in more than one language, and above all the experience of using translations to teach students about literatures they regard, perhaps too easily, as foreign—of constantly having to translate, to compare translations to originals, to talk and think about translations, and sometimes even to produce them—can become, if we allow ourselves to be affected, a thorn in the side of our theorizing.

For scholars like me, based in the United States but engaged in the study of a national literature foreign to the cultural sphere of the United States, translation is omnipresent. The experience of drifting constantly back and forth between two languages, occasionally among a greater number, of feeling languages coursing through our bodies, commingling, forming a solution whose density shifts from one moment to the next—right now, writing this, I am almost all English—never allows us to forget, or never should, the peculiar, both-but-neither position that we occupy at the edge of the English department, washed by its waves of theory, and, in my case, at the edge of Japanese literary studies in Japan, washed by its waves of applied, archival work. Our scholarship, lying in a tidal pool somehow fed by two vast oceans, can act on the immensely valuable applied work of even the most traditionalist scholars of Japanese literature writing in Japanese—or for that matter in other languages—helping to turn the tide of their discussions so that they can return the favor and send new waves through ours; at the same time, it can also act on the valuable theoretical work conducted in English and comparative literature departments in the United States and elsewhere, helping to turn the tide of these discussions so that our own can, in turn, keep moving.

Scholars who are also translators—or translators who are also scholars—and who are eager to be given credit for the contributions they make to their field by translating have long argued that translation is a critical activity. It is, of course, but in most cases it is not the most potent form of critical activity. In some sense, translation is, like the photograph in Roland Barthes's analysis, a "continuous message."[18] Like the photographer's art (and recall how many decades it took for photography to be canonized as art), translation is seldom, if ever, automatic and results in the creation of an utterly idiosyncratic image of its subject that is, however, so perfectly idiosyncratic as to be capable of standing on its own. Critical interpretations are useful, I would contend, precisely because they are partial, incomplete, transparent; translations cover over every word of the text they interpret and—despite the prevailing English-language discourse about translation, which assumes that the ideal translation is transparent and demands that the translator be invisible, as Lawrence Venuti has demonstrated—are opaque.[19] A second critical work comparing the translation with its inspiration is needed to make the translation's critical thrust clear, to enable the original to shine through, to make the translation appear incomplete enough (riddled with enough "loss") that it becomes critically useful.

Scholarly translators of literature would do much better, I suggest, to insist that their work continues to redefine the very contours of the fields in which we work by reinventing the canons we teach and thus gradually redrawing the boundaries within which secondary scholarship (as opposed to the primary scholarship of translation?) is written. We must point out, as I have been trying to do, that their inevitable ties to translation and translingualism are one of the strengths of national literary studies, especially those that deal with literatures, languages, and cultures to which English and the cultural spheres of the United States and Europe are foreign. And we must stress and demonstrate, vociferously and frequently, that translation is an act not only of critical but, more important, of *theoretical* exploration that touches on issues fundamental to contemporary literary studies. Translation is, in fact, more than theoretical—it is a particularly intense form of research, a stream of the best sort of applied work, detailed practice gushing over the pebbles and sands of settled theories, sweeping them into new alignments and configurations. Readers of this book will have noticed that it presents an unusually extensive array of primary materials in translation, beginning with the *Yomiuri shinbun* editorial "On Writing in English" (1888); in part, I hope this will stand as a reminder of the role that translation inevitably plays in a study such as this one.

I suggested earlier that there are moments when we in Japanese literary studies, in East Asian literary studies, in Asian area studies, in area studies, and in national literary studies that deal with languages that are not English must take stock of our situation with respect to other departments. I believe this is such a time. My reasons for thinking this have precisely to do with the dual nature of translation as simultaneously theoretical and applied work; with the inevitability of our connection to translation as an academic activity; with the very welcome surge of interest in translation that we have been seeing recently in various fields, including Japanese literary studies; with the ongoing debates in the disciplines of English and comparative literature about the global canon, globalizing literary studies, globalizing English, the comp lit ization of national literary studies, the transnational turn in American studies, and so on; and with the emergence, over the course of the past three decades or so, of translation studies as a discipline in its own right.

As I see it, all these factors combine to make this the perfect time for scholars in national literary studies—or at the very least Japanese literary studies, which is the one area I know a little bit about—to stop trying to pretend that they do not have so very much to do with translation, that translation is not the defining feature (one of the defining features, perhaps, though it is hard to think of any others) of the field. The spate of conferences and symposiums and panels on translation in East Asia that have taken place over the past few years, and the number of articles, chapters, dissertations, and books now being written and published that deal in one way or another with translation in East Asia, leaves no doubt that our field is already edging slowly in that direction. This is undoubtedly a very good thing. It is one way for us to reach out beyond our isolation. And yet I have a nagging sense that the direction in which we are headed is, somehow, subtly wrong.

Heartening as it is to see this sudden outpouring of interest in translation, I cannot help suspecting that the trend is unrelated to a certain internal necessity that we should perhaps be feeling, collectively, but are not. Are we, in our rush to rethink translation, simply letting ourselves be swept along like a bit of driftwood on the latest theoretical tide to emerge from the English and comparative literature departments? Our own discipline is and has always been inevitably bound up in translation, we live and work in the conjunction of languages, and the experience and act of translating have played a role in the accomplishments of every scholar and in all the scholarship in Japanese literary studies in the English-language academy to date. Translation offers us a chance to break free from the notion that our field is always trying to "catch up, surpass," or even that it has finally caught up: from the perspective of translation studies and the global canon, we have been in the future for a long time. Which is only to say that progress is not a march but a seething—an intermingling of different tides. There was never any catching up to do, and there is no such thing as coming of age.

Returning to Translation

The intertwined histories of translation, translations, and discourse about translation as they pertain to the disciplinary node of Japanese literary studies must, I think, be investigated. Several factors contribute to this necessity. First, there is the circumstance, already alluded to, that Japanese literary studies—most obviously, but not exclusively, in contexts outside Japan—is inevitably bound up with translation.[20] Not only must we translate every passage we quote from Japanese in our writings, but we have to translate important terms specific to one or another of the large academic departments around which we orbit, just as "canon" had to be translated as 古典 (koten/kanon), カノン (kanon), and 正典 (seiten) for the Japanese edition of *Inventing the Classics*, and just as I had to translate the names of early modern genres such as the 合巻 in this book by using both the transliteration *gōkan* and the inadequate, even inaccurate "literal" rendering "combined booklets." More important still, as professors of Japanese literature in an English-reading context, we have to assign translations as texts in most or all of the classes we teach. To a large extent, our syllabi are determined by the availability of translations, and our syllabi shape the future of the field. Murakami Haruki and anime emerged as new subfields within Japanese literary and cultural studies because they became wildly popular in translation, not the other way around. The study of translation, translations, and the history of translation and discourse about translation is necessary, then, if we are to develop a richer understanding and a self-awareness, as a field, of one of the conditions for all our teaching and research.

My second reason for advocating research into the histories of translation, translations, and discourse about translation in our field is, quite simply, that I think if we did look back at these histories, we would find that scholar-translators were saying extremely provocative, interesting things in the 1950s and 1960s—and even, though less often, earlier. The panel "Problems of Translation from Japanese" comes to mind: it was held on March 20, 1964, at the Sixteenth Annual Meeting of the Association for Asian Studies, and its speakers included Ivan Morris, Donald Keene, Howard Hibbet, Edwin McClellan, and Edward Seidensticker.[21] Or there is the searing exchange that took place between Joyce I. Ackroyd and Donald Keene from 1964 to 1965 in the pages first of *Orient/West* and then of the *Journal-Newsletter of the Association of Teachers of Japanese*.[22] Or James Araki's "Japanese Literature: The Practice of Transfer," which introduced both Walter Benjamin's "The Task of the Translator" and the influential translation theorist Eugene A. Nida's notion of equivalence to Japanese literary studies.[23] Or Donald Philippi's thrilling description, emphasizing the perspective of the translator at the moment he or she is translating, of the process of translating Japanese to English: "Translation Between Typologically Diverse Languages."[24] Or Edward Fowler's well-known "Rendering Words, Traversing Cultures: On the Art and Politics of Translating Modern Japanese Fiction.[25]

The list goes on and on, and we could learn a lot from many of the essays it includes. Indeed, much of what was written about Japanese-English translation, particularly in the 1950s and 1960s, is undoubtedly more provocative now than when it was written. In part, this is because scholar-translators in the field appear to have been more conscious then of the role that translation played in their teaching and scholarship, and thus thought and talked more often about it and more deeply; in part, it is because their different assumptions and vocabulary can help relativize and thus denaturalize our own. The concept of "difference in translation," which has been circulating in the field for three decades, becomes unnervingly fresh again the moment it is juxtaposed with the notion of "exoticism in translation," which was a major concern in the 1950s and 1960s.

My third reason for advocating this research is that unless we gain some understanding of the special issues that arise in Japanese–English translation and how they have changed over time, how translation styles and strategies have evolved, and how scholar-translators in the node of Japanese literary studies have discussed their work since at least the 1950s, our knowledge about translation will inevitably be defined to a large extent in relationship to the concerns and perspectives that have emerged in translation studies. Benjamin writes in "The Task of the Translator" that a "real translation" "may be achieved, above all, by a literal rendering of the syntax."[26] This statement can be debated. But if we enter into the debate too soon, without adequately preparing, we run the risk of closing off avenues of thought simply by accepting the terms of the debate. For Benjamin, "syntax" no doubt denoted the arrangement of words into sentences; the arrangement, however, was surely defined along a horizontal, unquestionably European axis. What relevance, one wonders, might the verticality of most Japanese writing have to Benjamin's notion of a "literal"—a metaphor that dies in Japanese—"rendering of the syntax"? Or, rather, how much relevance does "syntax" (and the focus on syntax that has characterized discussions of foreignizing translation strategies) have to Japanese-English translation? Should the term be redefined to make it more relevant to the particular case with which we are concerned? Should it be jettisoned altogether? Questions of this sort are likely to arise, I think, only if we take the trouble to re-create translation studies from within Japanese literary studies. However interested individual members of our scholarly community may be in translation, we are bound to continue repeating old debates, speaking in an ill-fitting, hand-me-down language, unless we cultivate our communal awareness of issues related not to translation as a universal practice—to translation as it is heterogeneously defined in mainstream translation studies—but to translation as it is shaped by its intersection with what we also know, in Japanese, as 翻訳 (hon'yaku).[27]

The past decade or so has seen many panels and symposiums dealing wholly or in part with translation in Japan or broader swaths of East Asia, and the publication of numerous books, dissertations, essays, and articles that draw in one way or another on translation theory or translation studies—most notably, in connection to Japanese, *Translation in Modern Japan*, edited by Indra Levy, which stands as a model for its engagement, through the presentation of key translations, with Japanese-language writings about translation.[28] Positive though this trend is and much as I believe that it should be encouraged, I cannot help feeling that it has emerged for precisely the wrong reasons. Only a full-scale analysis of the sort that I am suggesting we need more of could illuminate the problem fully, but I can at least give a sense of how I see the situation by offering thumbnail sketches of the history of translation studies as a discipline, on the one hand, and of the history of discourse about translation from Japanese, on the other.

The field of translation studies got its name in 1972, when James S. Holmes coined it in a paper called "The Name and Nature of Translation Studies," but the early groundwork for its emergence as a discipline was done during the 1960s. The year 1964 saw the publication of Eugene A. Nida's *Toward a Science of Translating: With Special Reference to the Principles and Procedures Involved in Bible Translating* and the creation of the first translation workshop in the United States at the Writer's Workshop at the University of Iowa, which also began to offer academic credit for literary translations in the same year.[29] In 1965 J. C. Catford published *A Linguistic Theory of Translation: An Essay in Applied Linguistics*, and the National Translation Center was established at the University of Texas at Austin with a grant from the Ford Foundation. In 1968, two translations of Benjamin's "The Task of the Translator" were published: James Hynd and E. M. Valk's in the second issue of *Delos*, the newly founded journal of the National Translation Center—alongside an essay about translating *Genji monogatari* by Edward Seidensticker, as it happened—and Harry Zohn's in *Illuminations*.[30]

Taken together, this series of events and publications in the 1960s can be viewed as the birth of translation studies (though still nameless) as we know it. The young discipline continued to grow in the 1970s as scholars formulated new theoretical models for thinking about the relationship between "source texts" and "target texts" and the roles that translations play in literary evolution and canon formation. In the 1980s, there was a decisive shift from a focus on source texts to a focus on target texts, languages, and cultures; from normative to functionalist theory (*Skopos* theory); and to descriptive translation studies—a movement that André Lefevere and Susan Bassnett describe in *Translation, History, and Culture* as "The 'Cultural Turn' in Translation Studies."[31] By the late 1990s, research on translation had become common in so many fields that it was possible for these scholars to flip their first formulation around, suggesting that "the translation turn in cultural studies is now well underway."[32]

Turning now to Japanese literary studies, we notice first of all that 1964 was the year in which the Association for Asian Studies panel convened and the debate between Joyce I. Ackroyd and Donald Keene began. Keene's "A Reply to Joyce Ackroyd" was printed in the *Journal-Newsletter of the Association of Teachers of Japanese* with this explanation from the editors: "Feeling that the subject of translation is of particular interest to our readers and that Professor Keene's reply should reach the profession, we offer it here."[33] In her reply to Keene's reply, Ackroyd stated explicitly, "My intention was to protest against a theory of translation," and proceeded to argue against the position "that the translator has the right to alter words, meaning, progression of ideas, even the social customs delineated in the story, in order to produce a 'natural' impression."[34] In effect, then, the editors of the *Journal-Newsletter of the Association of Teachers of Japanese* were declaring the importance of translation theory to Japanese literary studies at a time when translation studies did not even exist.

In fact, the panelists anticipated many of the theoretical approaches that translation studies eventually hit on: a version of what is now known as functionalist translation theory, for instance, recurs again and again in the panel. Ivan Morris opened his introductory remarks by arguing that "a literal translation from Japanese or any other language is not only difficult but impossible and indeed a contradiction in terms. The only question is *how* free we should be," and then answered his own question: "This depends on the purpose of the translation."[35] Donald Keene referred to "the basic question: for whose sake is the translation being made?"[36] Edward Seidensticker, too, suggested that there was a "fundamental distinction between a translation aimed at those who have access to the original and one aimed at those who do not."[37] From the perspective of translation studies, these panelists' intense communal awareness of translation and its relationship to culture, language, the economics of publishing, and what we might now call the representation of otherness or difference—an awareness rooted in practice—was far ahead of its time.

During the 1970s, however, as the developing field of Japanese literary studies tried to modernize itself by "catching up" with the industrialized English department, translation gradually began to be thrown over by critical theory. In 1980 the editors of the *Journal of Japanese Studies* printed five papers presented at the symposium "Translation and Japanese Studies," hoping, as Roy Andrew Miller wrote in the introduction, "that they would be able to make at least a preliminary effort toward tracking down the importance of translation in Japanese studies. The key word here is 'preliminary.'" Miller suggested that "perhaps we in Japanese studies are now in the process of evolving a *raison d'être* for translation in which it will eventually be assigned a role somewhat parallel to the lofty position it occupied in the views of the German romantics. Perhaps also we are drawing nearer and nearer to the conclusion that translation itself is *the* discipline of Japanese studies *par excellence*."[38] The participants in this symposium—among whom were Edward Seidensticker, Marleigh Grayer Ryan, Jeffrey P. Mass, Chalmers Johnson, and Dan F. Henderson—wrote again from their perspective as practicing translator-scholars.

Unfortunately, this series of ambitious, thought-provoking essays turned out not to be preliminary, not to herald anything like a new awakening to the importance of translation to Japanese studies. On the contrary, translation appears to have been on the way out for Asian studies as a whole: a prediction made by the editor of the *Journal of Asian Studies* in the "Editor's Note" to the February 1979 issue—that "the study of translation" would soon find more space in the journal—proved to be inaccurate.[39] Interestingly, the editor offered this prediction in the same issue in which Masao Miyoshi's review of Edward Seidensticker's *The Tale of Genji* set the "difference" ball rolling, criticizing Seidensticker's prose for being "as thoroughly English as, say, *Pride and Prejudice*" and, rather peculiarly, suggesting that the problem would be solved if only someone could "render *Genji* into the style of Virginia Woolf."[40]

In the 1980s and early 1990s, a series of review articles and essays—notably, two forceful reviews by Roy Andrew Miller and H. Richard Okada of Helen Craig McCullough's *Brocade by Night: Kokin Wakashū and the Court Style in Japanese Poetry* (1985) and Edward Fowler's review article "On Naturalizing and Making Strange: Japanese Literature in Translation" and "Rendering Words, Transversing Cultures"—engaged with translation from Japanese in a critical manner that could have been productive but may perhaps have had more of a dampening effect than was intended.[41] By 1987, Japanese literary studies had "caught up" with the theoretical English department to the extent that Norma Field could speak of "the ostentatious growth of academic disdain for translation as intellectual activity."[42] At last, the scholar had been liberated from the translator, as if Dr. Jekyll had somehow shaken off Mr. Hyde; critical theory was in the course of being "naturalized," giving us new tools to think about everything but the very conditions of the existence of our field, which we could now blissfully ignore by pretending to be just another English department. Graduate students could no longer be awarded a doctorate for producing an annotated translation with a critical introduction—the sort of work that Michel Foucault, for instance, submitted as his secondary doctoral thesis.[43] Meanwhile, Alfred Birnbaum, a freelance translator with no academic affiliation, was beginning to create his vivacious English translations of Murakami Haruki, preparing the way for what was arguably the most significant shift in English-language Japanese literary studies since Fowler's "reigning triumvirate"—Kawabata Yasunari, Tanizaki Jun'ichirō, and Mishima Yukio—were enthroned as the representative literary figures of modern Japan.[44]

By now it should be fairly clear what troubles me about the recent revival of interest in translation in the node of Japanese literary studies. The problem is that we are, once again, simply letting ourselves be buffeted by waves of theory from the center. Now that cultural studies has made "the translation turn"—now that even the English department has sat up and taken notice of translation—we follow suit. We are still trying to catch up. We are trying to catch up, moreover, by running toward the very spot we were fleeing just a decade ago. This is not the right way to go about making Japanese literary studies a node for translation studies, even if those who are doing it are doing the right thing. We should be looking back at the intertwined histories of translation, translations, and discourse about translation *as they pertain to Japanese literary studies*, trying to re-create translation studies anew from within. We should be building on the theoretical perspectives that translator-scholars *working with Japanese literature* hammered together in the decades before Japanese literary studies started trying to pretend that translation is not all that important. We should be questioning and improving on theories and methodologies that have emerged from translation studies by learning to think better about translation as it intersects with *hon'yaku* from our own perspectives as scholar-translators working with Japanese literature in English as well as in Japanese. We should not, in short, be making "the translation turn"; we should be *re*turning to translation, trying to remember what we once knew so that we will know it still better tomorrow.

Notes

Introduction

1. Mitani Kuniaki, *Genji monogatari shitsukeito* (Tokyo: Yūseidō, 1991), 82.
2. Ibid., 84.
3. SNKBT 20:44; SNKBZ 21:217; *TG* 1:252.
4. *Genji* specialist Nakano Kōichi opens his preface to *Sokushū Genji monogatari ga wakaru!*, a CliffsNotes-style introduction to the tale, with a story that recalls this cartoon, told to him by a friend formerly in the Ministry of Foreign Affairs: "Whenever he went to a country with a traditional culture such as Britain or France and attended a party with his wife, the cultivated wives of that country would come right over and start talking about *Genji monogatari*, as soon as they realized that he and his wife were Japanese" (*Sokushū Genji monogatari ga wakaru!* [Tokyo: Kanki Shuppan, 1999], 3). The Japanese couple (especially the wife, it seems) were always embarrassed by their ignorance of the tale.
5. Mizumura Minae, *Nihongo ga horobiru toki: Eigo no seiki no naka de* (Tokyo: Chukuma Shobō, 2008).
6. Jerome J. McGann, *Black Riders: The Visible Language of Modernism* (Princeton, N.J.: Princeton University Press, 1993), 27.
7. Haruo Shirane, "Introduction: Issues in Canon Formation," in *Inventing the Classics: Modernity, National Identity, and Japanese Literature*, ed. Haruo Shirane and Tomi Suzuki (Stanford, Calif.: Stanford University Press, 2000), 1.
8. Haruo Shirane, "*The Tale of Genji* and the Dynamics of Cultural Production," in *Envisioning The Tale of Genji: Media, Gender, and Cultural Production*, ed. Haruo Shirane (New York: Columbia University Press, 2008), 1.
9. Ibid., 40–41.
10. This is apparent not only from the dual attribution of authorship, but also from the inclusion of passages from *Genji monogatari*, written in the style of a calligraphic manuscript, that are paired with somewhat oversexed translations. See Murasaki Shikibu and Egawa Tatsuya, *Genji monogatari*, 7 vols. (Tokyo:

Shūeisha, 2001-2005). For insightful discussions in English of *manga* and modern-Japanese translations of *Genji*, see Yuika Kitamura, "Sexuality, Gender, and *The Tale of Genji* in Modern Japanese Translations and Manga," in *Envisioning The Tale of Genji*, ed. Shirane, 329-357; and Lynne K. Miyake, "Graphically Speaking: Manga Versions of *The Tale of Genji*," *Monumenta Nipponica* 63, no. 2 (2008): 359-392. For a discussion in Japanese of *Asaki yume mishi*, see Kitamura Yuika, "'Shōjo no yume' no ōkan: *Asaki yume mishi* ron," *Kokusai bunkagaku* 3 bessatsu (2000): 160-146.

11. While the relevant entry in *Murasaki Shikibu nikki* never mentions *Genji monogatari* by name, at least one reference to "a tale" is clearly to it, and most likely the others are as well. There are too many uncertainties about who is doing what and too many debates about textual corruptions to make it useful to translate the passage here, but its basic outline would seem to be as follows: Murasaki Shikibu and presumably the other women in attendance upon Empress Akiko (Shōshi) select and match variously colored papers to be used in preparing beautifully transcribed and bound copies of what seems to be a set of revised "booklets of the tale" already in the empress's possession, each one comprising a chapter. The papers are sent with the booklets and a letter to the chosen calligraphers. As the transcriptions come in, Murasaki Shikibu and the other women order the pages and finish the booklets. One day, in the midst of the excitement, Fujiwara no Michinaga—Akiko's father and a powerful statesman—slips into Murasaki Shikibu's quarters and makes off with what appear to be the unedited first drafts of the "booklets of the tale," which Murasaki Shikibu had hidden there. Michinaga presents these to his second daughter, the future empress Masuko. Murasaki Shikibu finally comments: "All the decently revised copies having been lost, I must surely have acquired a worrisome reputation." It is unclear whether "decently revised copies" refers to the booklets sent out to be copied, which perhaps the calligraphers were not asked to return, or to a second draft of the tale that Murasaki Shikibu made at some earlier point, before she prepared the empress's copy, and that she has since lost track of. Depending on how one interprets this last statement, Murasaki Shikibu mentions either three or four copies of *Genji monogatari* in whose production she was directly involved, all of which were in circulation, and two of which (one revised, one unrevised) ended up in the possession of two empresses. For the passage in the diary, see [Murasaki Shikibu], *Murasaki Shikibu nikki*, ed. Nakano Kōichi, in *Izumi Shikibu nikki. Murasaki Shikibu nikki. Sarashina nikki. Sanuki no Suke no nikki*, ed. Fujioka Tadaharu et al., Shinpen Nihon koten bungaku zenshū 26 (Tokyo: Shōgakkan, 1994), 167-168. For an English translation, see Murasaki Shikibu, *The Diary of Lady Murasaki*, trans. Richard Bowring (London: Penguin, 1996), 32-33.

12. The scene reproduced, from the "Suzumushi" (The Bell Cricket) chapter, shows Genji sitting with the Retired Emperor Reizei, the offspring of his illicit affair with Fujitsubo. The half-erased writing on the bill bears no relation to the picture. Murasaki Shikibu herself appears, in an image taken from the thirteenth-century *Murasaki Shikibu nikki emaki* (*The Diary of Murasaki Shikibu Picture Scroll*), on the lower right of the bill. In 2008, to commemorate the sixtieth anniversary of the Local Autonomy Law, Kyoto Prefecture issued 100,000 1,000-yen coins and 2,050,000 500-yen coins that also featured pictures from *Genji monogatari emaki*.

13. In an entry for the first day of the tenth month of Kankō 5 (1008), Murasaki Shikibu relates an incident that took place during the celebrations on the fiftieth day after the birth of Empress Akiko's son by Emperor Ichijō: Fujiwara no Kintō "looked in and asked 'Tell me, is the young Murasaki around?' I just sat listening, thinking to myself, *Considering that no one even faintly resembling Genji has put in an appearance, how much less likely is it that she would be here?*" This is taken as evidence that male courtiers were already reading *Genji monogatari*. The "millennial anniversary" is thus a celebration less of *Genji monogatari* itself than of the circulation of discourse about *Genji monogatari*. For the passage in the diary, see [Murasaki Shikibu], *Murasaki Shikibu nikki*, 165. For an English translation, see Murasaki Shikibu, *Diary of Lady Murasaki*, 31.

14. The Committee for the Thousandth Anniversary of *Genji monogatari* was established on January 30, 2007, by a number of organizations, including Kyoto-fu, Kyoto City, Uji City, and the Kyoto Chamber of Commerce and Industry, in response to a "call" (*yobikake*) for its creation by Akiyama Ken, Umehara Takeshi, Setouchi Jakuchō, Sen Genshitsu, Donald Keene, Haga Tōru, Murai Yasuhiko, and Reizei Kimiko.

15. Genji Pies were created in 1965 in anticipation of the television drama *Minamoto no Yoshitsune*, which aired the following year. Yoshitsune was a member of the Minamoto clan—that is, a Genji.

16. My account of the activities of the Committee for the Thousandth Anniversary of *Genji monogatari* in this and the following paragraph draws on the wealth of information and statistics collected in *Genji monogatari* Sennenki Iinkai, ed., *Murasaki no yukari, futatabi: Genji monogatari sennenki kōshiki kiroku* (Kyoto: *Genji monogatari* Sennenki Iinkai, 2009). For reproductions of sample newspaper articles and a select list of newspaper articles and broadcasts, see "Shiryōhen (shinbun, terebi)," in ibid., 217–286.

17. "Machi de miru sennenki no shinboru māku, kyarakutā," and "*Genji monogatari* sennenki iinkai rogotaipu shinboru māku no shiyō ni kansuru toriatsukai kitei," both in ibid., 84–85, 164.

18. For a chart listing approximately a thousand events that were "supported" in some way by the Committee for the Thousandth Anniversary of *Genji monogatari*, as well as available attendance figures, see "Shiryōhen (ibento)," in *Murasaki no yukari, futatabi*, ed. *Genji monogatari* Sennenki Iinkai, 171–216.

19. Shimizu Fukuko, "*Genji monogatari* hanpon no honmon," in *Genji monogatari hanpon no kenkyū* (Osaka: Izumi Shoin, 2003), 207–340. Shimizu provides a helpful chart of the lineage of the various texts on p. 291. The title generally read today as *Shusho Genji monogatari* was read *Kashiragaki Genji monogatari* in the early modern period, as Shimizu notes on pp. 17 and 19. The early-seventeenth-century movable-type edition of *Genji monogatari* that I mention is known as the *Den-Sagabon Genji monogatari*.

20. Shimizu makes this point in ibid., 289. Until recently, it was presumed that the *Den-Sagabon Genji monogatari* derived entirely from the Aobyōshibon lineage. Ii Haruki has demonstrated, however, that the three chapters "Hanachirusato" (Falling Flowers), "Tokonatsu" (The Pink), and "Nowaki" (The Typhoon) derived instead from the Kawachibon lineage and that "Yadorigi" (The Ivy) stemmed from a text in the miscellaneous category (*beppon*). See Ii Haruki, "*Den-Sagabon Genji monogatari* no honmon," in *Genji monogatari kenkyū shūsei*,

ed. Masuda Shigeo, Suzuki Hideo, and Ii Haruki, vol. 13, *Genji monogatari no honmon* (Tokyo: Kazama Shobō, 1998), 353–403.

21. Early modern woodblock-printed texts were used as source texts for many modern movable-type replacements of *Genji monogatari* published beginning in 1890, which saw the publication of the first volumes of a spate of new editions, as I will discuss in chapter 4. Annotated editions based on *Kogetsushō* include Fujii Otō, Sassa Seisetsu, Numanami Keion, and Sasakawa Rinpū, *Shinshaku Genji monogatari* (Tokyo: Shinchōsha, 1911, 1914); Miyata Waichirō, *Tōchū taiyaku Genji monogatari* (Tokyo: Bunken Shoin, 1923–1928); and Yoshizawa Yoshinori, *Taikō Genji monogatari shinshaku*, 6 vols. (Tokyo: Heibonsha, 1937–1940). Editions and translations based on *Shusho Genji monogatari* include the widely read Yūhōdō bunko edition of *Genji monogatari*, ed. Mukasa San (Tokyo: Yūhōdō Shoten, 1914); Igarashi Chikara, *Shōwa kan'yaku Genji monogatari* (Tokyo: Seishidō, 1948–1950); and Sanari Kentarō, *Taiyaku Genji monogatari* (Tokyo: Meiji Shoin, 1951–1953).

22. Yamawaki Hatasu, "Ikeda Kikan hakase hencho *Genji monogatari taisei*," *Kokugo to kokubungaku* 34, no. 7 (1957): 59. *Bansui ichiro* actually predates the early modern period as a commentary, having been completed in 1575 by its author, Eikan (Noto no Eikan). During the early modern period, Eikan's commentary was integrated with the text of *Genji monogatari* and circulated widely in print. Yamawaki is referring here to some version of the printed form.

23. "*Kōi Genji monogatari* kankō ni tsukite," in *Genji monogatari kenkyū*, distributed with [Murasaki Shikibu], *Jun'ichirō yaku Genji monogatari*, trans. Tanizaki Jun'ichirō (Tokyo: Chūōkōronsha, 1939–1941), 13:7, 8. We also find this somewhat stern proscription: "From now on, no one who delves into *Genji*, no matter what sort of person he may be, will have any choice but to start from this book. We must emphasize that this is the definitive and the most authoritative edition of the original text of *Genji monogatari*" (7).

24. I will take up Tanizaki's first translation in chapter 5. Tanizaki does not explicitly identify *Kogetsushō* as his source text in his translation, except to note that it was one of the works that Aizawa Tadashi, a young employee at Chūōkōron, had consulted in preparing the genealogy, chronology, and chapter summaries that make up volume 26. When, soon after the war ended, Tanizaki published his translation of a section from the "Sakaki" (The Green Branch) chapter that he had cut from the published book, however, he cited *Kogetsushō* in explaining where the passage appeared in the original. Nishino Atsushi has written a series of essays focusing on a marked-up copy of Kaneko Motōmi's *Teihon Genji monogatari shinkai*—another text that Aizawa consulted—that belonged to Yamada Yoshio, who checked Tanizaki's translation against the original. *Teihon Genji monogatari shinkai* was also based on *Kogetsushō*, although Kaneko collated it with the Kawachibon text, which had recently been discovered by Yamawaki Hatasu. One final bit of evidence: in 1932 or 1933, before the idea for the translation had even been suggested to him, Tanizaki sent a copy of *Kogetsushō* to his third wife, Matsuko, with a letter saying that he felt the tale could have been written for her. For Tanizaki's note about Aizawa, see [Murasaki Shikibu], *Jun'ichirō yaku Genji monogatari*, trans. Tanizaki, 26:202. For Tanizaki's note introducing the self-censored section of "Sakaki," see Tanizaki Jun'ichirō, "Fujitsubo: 'Sakaki' no maki hoi," in *Tanizaki Jun'ichirō zenshū* (To-

kyo: Chūōkōronsha, 1983), 23:241. Tanizaki's presentation of *Kogetsushō* to Matsuko was drawn to my attention by a note in Anthony Hood Chambers, *The Secret Window: Ideal Worlds in Tanizaki's Fiction* (Cambridge, Mass.: Harvard University East Asia Center, 1994), 134n.15. The letter itself is quoted in Tanizaki Matsuko, *Ishōan no yume* (Tokyo: Chūōkōronsha, 1967), 214-215. Regarding the somewhat ambiguous visual reference to early modern texts of *Genji monogatari* in the format of Tanizaki's first translation: the book was issued in two versions, the "popular edition" (*fukyūban*) and the "collector's edition" (*aizōbon*), both with similar covers. The collector's edition came in a horizontal paulownia-wood box of the sort frequently used for calligraphic copies (*shahon*) of *Genji monogatari*; the separately sold box for the popular edition was vertical, like the boxes in which *Kogetsushō* was generally stored.

25. Ibuki Kazuko, *Ware yori hoka ni: Tanizaki Jun'ichirō saigo no jūninen* (Tokyo: Kōdansha, 1994), 22.

26. Roland Barthes, *Image-Music-Text*, trans. Stephen Heath (New York: Hill and Wang, 1977), 156-157.

27. Ibid., 163-164.

28. Ibid., 145, 147, 148.

29. Louis-Jean Calvet, *Roland Barthes: A Biography*, trans. Sarah Wykes (Cambridge: Polity Press, 1994), 18.

30. Shirane, "*Tale of Genji* and the Dynamics of Cultural Production," 9. For instances of Barthes's use of the terms, see Roland Barthes, "I. Evaluation" and "II. Interpretation," in *S/Z*, trans. Richard Miller (New York: Hill and Wang, 1974), 3-6.

31. Hans Robert Jauss, "Literary History as a Challenge to Literary Theory," in *Toward an Aesthetic of Reception*, trans. Timothy Bahti, Theory and History of Literature 2 (Minneapolis: University of Minnesota Press, 1982), 21.

32. Peter L. Shillingsburg, *Scholarly Editing in the Computer Age: Theory and Practice*, 3rd ed. (Ann Arbor: University of Michigan Press, 1996), 43.

33. Ibid., 45.

34. Anrakuan Sakuden, *Seisuishō*, ed. Suzuki Tōzō, Iwanami bunko 30-247-1 (Tokyo: Iwanami Shoten, 1986), 348.

35. I will have more to say about the *gōkan* in the first three chapters of this book; for now, suffice it to say that it is a genre within the overarching category of early modern popular fictional works known as *kusazōshi* ("grass books" or "stinky books," depending on how the word is written and interpreted). The best overview of the genre is still Suzuki Jūzō, *Gōkan ni tsuite*, Bunka kōza shirīzu 9 (Tokyo: Daitōkyū Kinen Bunko, 1961).

36. See, for example, Peter Kornicki, "The Publisher's Go-Between: Kashihonya in the Meiji Period," *Modern Asian Studies* 14, no. 2 (1980): 331-344; "The Survival of Tokugawa Fiction in the Meiji Period," *Harvard Journal of Asiatic Studies* 41, no. 2 (1981): 461-482; *The Reform of Fiction in Meiji Japan* (London: Ithaca Press, 1982); and *The Book in Japan: A Cultural History from the Beginnings to the Nineteenth Century* (Honolulu: University of Hawai'i Press, 2001).

37. Jonathan E. Zwicker, *Practices of the Sentimental Imagination: Melodrama, the Novel, and the Social Imaginary in Nineteenth-Century Japan* (Cambridge, Mass.: Harvard University East Asia Center, 2006), 40.

38. Ibid., 49.

39. Zwicker's recent research, which exhibits an attentiveness to the materiality of print that was largely absent from *Practices of the Sentimental Imagination*, suggests that his expansive use of the term "novel" really was a sort of experimental move, intimately tied to his goals in that book. To that extent, I find the exercise profoundly thought provoking and valuable. Still, there is a reason the names used for early modern genres of fiction in Japan often refer to their material form. Some sense of the difficulties that arise if we accept a wager predicated on discounting the difference between early modern and modern printed works is suggested by Zwicker's discussion of the "frontispieces of each volume" (139) of Kyokutei Bakin's *Fūzoku kin'gyoden* (*The Legend of Kinjūrō and Uoko, in the Current Style*, 1829–1833), a *gōkan* based on the early Qing-period *Jin Yun Qiao zhuan* (*The Legend of Jin Zhong, Cuiyun, and Cuiqiao*). In English, "frontispieces" usually appear opposite the title pages of books; the pictures that Zwicker discusses appear, instead, on the covers of *Fūzoku kin'gyoden*. Perhaps the copy or copies of *Fūzoku kin'gyoden* that Zwicker saw had been taken apart and rebound, given new and plainer covers while the original full-color covers were moved inside the book and placed opposite the title pages to protect them—a common practice with books in this genre. The suggestion that the pictures belong to "each volume" is also misleading. They appear, rather, on the covers *of the individual fascicles* that make up the larger "volumes" or "chapters." Bakin published *Fūzoku kin'gyoden* in a rather complicated manner: from 1829 to 1831, he issued two "chapters" (*hen*), each comprising four fascicles (*maki* or *kan*) numbered one through four; then, in 1833, he issued a further four fascicles as "part two of chapter two" (*gehen no ge*) because, as he explains in the preface to the new addition, "I wasn't finished yet." When the publisher Shōjudō issued a pirated edition of the book from 1837 to 1839—with the prefaces cunningly condensed and rewritten—the new version appeared in five chapters of two fascicles each. *Fūzoku kin'gyoden* is described in Zwicker's list of works cited as having been published in a total of "three volumes," which is correct in a sense—"volume" is a perfectly good translation of the word *hen*, and one could consider "part two of chapter two" a new volume—but if he is going to use the word "volume" as an equivalent of *hen*, then it is incorrect to suggest that the pictures he is talking about are associated particularly with each "volume": in the book's first publication, there are twelve pictures on the twelve covers, not three; and in the reissue, there are five pictures on five covers. These may seem like niggling issues, and to some extent they are; but the world of early modern print is characterized by such complexities, and it is precisely these complexities that belie the suggestion that a book is simply a book and, ultimately, that a *gōkan*, for instance, is a novel. For the quotation from Bakin's preface, see Kyokutei Bakin (text) and Utagawa Kuniyasu (pictures), *Fūzoku kin'gyoden*, 2 chapters in 12 fascicles (Edo: Moriya Jihei, 1829–1833), part 2 of chapter 2, preface *otsu*. This fascicle is numbered in an unusual way: the first half of the preface appears on a page labeled as I have indicated, and the second half is on page 1 *omote*.

40. "While it goes without saying that she enjoyed all branches of arts and learning, having received the education she did, her taste for literature was particu-

larly deep, and she loved to read diaries such as *Taketori, Ise,* and *Tosa* and tales such as *Genji, Eiga,* and *Heike,* and even read *kusazōshi,* and among all these she was particularly fond of *Genji monogatari* and *Inaka Genji,* which she read closely any number of times, and the interesting bits of which she is said to have memorized" ("Kōtaigō heika no goseitoku," part 2, *Yomiuri shinbun,* April 12, 1914).

41. Discussing Johann Peter Eckermann's *Gespräche mit Goethe in den letzten Jahren seines Lebens* (*Conversations with Goethe,* 1835), which recounts Goethe's coinage in 1827 of the term *Weltliteratur* (world literature), David Damrosch notes the wonderful irony that it is "an interesting example of a work that only achieves an effective presence in its country of origin after it has already entered world literature; in a movement that would hardly have surprised Goethe, the book's reception abroad set the stage for its subsequent revival at home" (*What Is World Literature?* [Princeton, N.J.: Princeton University Press, 2003], 32). I will have more to say about "world literary systems" and "world literature" in touchstone 2.

Touchstone 1. Reimagining the Canon

1. Mark Twain, *Following the Equator: A Journey Around the World* (Hartford, Conn.: American Publishing, 1898), 241.

2. If studies of canonization have overlooked this point, important scholars of translation have at least noted it. André Lefevere argues that "rewriting in all its forms occupies a dominant position among the concrete factors" contributing to "the process resulting in the acceptance or rejection, canonization or non-canonization of literary works" (*Translation, Rewriting, and the Manipulation of Literary Fame* [London: Routledge, 1982], 2). See also André Lefevere and Susan Bassnett, "Introduction: Proust's Grandmother and the Thousand and One Nights. The 'Cultural Turn' in Translation Studies," in *Translation, History, and Culture,* ed. Susan Bassnett and André Lefevere (London: Cassell, 1990), esp. 9–10.

3. While Pierre Bourdieu mentions "truncated quotations" as an instance of the sort of "intellectual rumor" that contributes to the constitution of "the 'common sense' of an intellectual generation," his discussion remains centered on "the work of art as an object" or "the work of art as such": "Reading, and *a fortiori* the reading of books, is only one means among others, even among professional readers, of acquiring the knowledge *that is mobilized in reading*" (italics added) (*The Field of Cultural Production* [New York: Columbia University Press, 1993], 32).

4. John Guillory asserts at the outset of his preface to *Cultural Capital,* "Where the debate speaks of the literary canon, its inclusions and exclusions, I will speak of the school, and the institutional forms of syllabus and curriculum. . . . I will argue . . . that it is only by understanding the social function and institutional protocols of the school that we will understand how works are preserved, reproduced, and disseminated over successive generations and centuries" (*Cultural Capital: The Problem of Literary Canon Formation* [Chicago: University of Chicago Press, 1993], vii).

5. Originally, *"Genji* names" *(Genjina)* were given to women in the imperial palace and derived from *Genji monogatari*'s chapter titles. Over time, women in other prominent households began using them as well. In the Edo period, women in the pleasure quarters sometimes invented brand-new *Genji* names, unrelated to the tale. The fifty-two *"Genji* incense signs" *(Genji kō no zu)* were used in an incense-identification game in which twenty-five incense sticks—five each of five varieties—were mixed up and doled out randomly to five teams. Each team had to identify which, if any, of the sticks were the same. A vertical line was drawn for each incense stick, beginning at the right, and horizontal lines would be inserted to connect sticks believed to be the same. The fifty-two possible patterns were matched with chapter titles from *Genji monogatari* (the first and last of the fifty-four chapters were not initially assigned symbols). Teams would announce their results by giving the title corresponding to the pattern obtained. *Genji* incense signs were, and in some quarters still are, frequently used as decorative motifs.

6. Tayama Katai, *Chōhen shōsetsu no kenkyū* (Tokyo: Shinshidansha, 1925), 157.

7. W. J. T. Mitchell, *Iconology: Image, Text, and Ideology* (Chicago: University of Chicago Press, 1986), 9. Lefevere and Bassnett write, "Literature reaches those who are not its professional students much more by way of the 'images' constructed of it in translations, but even more so in anthologies, commentaries, histories, and, occasionally, critical journals, than it does so by means of 'originals,' however venerable they may be, and however much professors of literature and its students who approach it in a 'professional' way may regret this state of affairs" ("Introduction," 9).

8. Mitchell, *Iconology*, 31 (italics in the original).

9. Ibid., 31, 32, 35.

1. A *Gōkan* Is a *Gōkan* Is a *Gōkan*

1. For a discussion of these estimates, see Andrew Lawrence Markus, *The Willow in Autumn: Ryūtei Tanehiko, 1783–1842* (Cambridge, Mass.: Council on East Asian Studies, Harvard University, 1992), 145–146. According to Hamada Keisuke, sales were most brisk in the first five or six days after a *gōkan* was published, continued strong for another two weeks or so, and more or less ended after the New Year. With upward of forty titles appearing each year, the total number of copies of *gōkan* sold would likely have exceeded a hundred thousand. See Hamada Keisuke, "Bakin ni okeru shoshi, sakusha, dokusha no mondai," in *Nihon bungaku kenkyū shiryō sōsho: Bakin*, ed. Nihon bungaku kenkyū shiryō sōsho kankōkai (Tokyo: Yūseidō Shuppan, 1974), 234–236.

2. According to Sōbokuen Shujin, Senkakudō and Tsutaya, the two largest publishers of popular fiction, sold at least ten thousand copies of their books and sometimes as many as thirteen thousand from the winter of each year through the end of the New Year season. It is not entirely clear what time Sōbokuen is speaking of, though he mentions the Bunka period (1804–1818) in the previous paragraph; the books he refers to would seem to be *kibyōshi*. He reports that *Inaka Genji*'s sales "are said to have reached fourteen or fifteen thousand copies" and that it and *Shokoku monogatari* "raised the price of paper

in the capital each time a new chapter was published" (*Edo jidai gikyoku shōsetsu tsūshi* [Tokyo: Kōbunsha, 1927], 126, 129).

3. The price of each *gōkan* chapter rose over time and varied, depending on the author and artist, the quality of the printing, the number of pages in the chapter, and whether the work was new or old. Until 1817, *gōkan* were issued in as many as three forms: "ordinary *gōkan*" (*namigōkan*), "high-quality *gōkan*" (*jōgōkan* or *jōsei gōkan*, which were often issued in wrappers), and "printings on high-quality paper" (*jōshizuri*); after 1817, the last of these three types was no longer produced. In the late Bunsei and early Tenpō periods, an ordinary *gōkan* of twenty pages sold for 110 *mon*; a *gōkan* of the same length in a wrapper (a high-quality *gōkan*) most likely sold for 150 *mon*; an ordinary *gōkan* of thirty pages sold for 150 *mon*; and a high-quality *gōkan* of thirty pages probably sold for 200 *mon*, according to Satō Satoru, "Kusazōshi no zōhon keitai to kakaku: Hanshibongata kusazōshi no igi," *Kinsei bungei* 56 (1992): 57. In a more recent essay, Satō shows that *gōkan* were divided into three categories, with the first being the most expensive and the last the cheapest: *gōkan* by Bakin or Tanehiko with pictures by Utagawa Kunisada; *gōkan* that were by either Tanehiko or Bakin but did not have pictures by Kunisada, or had pictures by Kunisada but were not by Tanehiko or Bakin; and *gōkan* that were not by Bakin or Tanehiko and did not have pictures by Kunisada. See Satō Satoru, "Bunsei-matsu, Tenpō-ki no gōkan ryūtsū to kakaku," *Nihon bungaku* 57, no. 10 (2008): 47. The classic work on lending libraries is Nagatomo Chiyoji, *Kinsei kashihon'ya no kenkyū* (Tokyo: Tōkyōdō Shuppan, 1982).

4. Nagatomo, *Kinsei kashihon'ya no kenkyū*, 159–160. Markus cites Nagatomo on this same point in *Willow in Autumn*, 148.

5. Kyokutei Bakin, letter dated the twenty-sixth day of the fourth month, Tenpō 2 (June 6, 1831), in *Kyokutei shokanshū shūi*, in *Nihon geirin sōsho*, ed. Ikeda Shirōjirō et al. (Tokyo: Rikugōkan, 1929), 9:31. Markus quotes this letter at length in *Willow in Autumn*, 156–158.

6. Kimura Mokurō, *Kokuji shōsetsu tsū*, in *Zoku enseki jisshu* (Tokyo: Chūōkōron, 1980), 1:301. According to Kimura, the three paragons of the *gōkan* genre are *Inaka Genji* and Bakin's *Keisei suikoden* and *Shinpen kinpeibai*. Andrew L. Markus observes that Mokurō's list "is clearly intended to echo groupings of the 'Four Wondrous Works' of Chinese vernacular fiction" ("Kimura Mokurō [1774–1856] and His *Kokuji shōsetsu tsū* [1849]," *Journal of Japanese Studies* 26, no. 2 [2000]: 362).

7. Ryūtei Tanehiko had died in 1842, Tamenaga Shunsui in 1843, and Kyokutei Bakin in 1848. For a discussion of the effect of the Tenpō Reforms on publishing in Edo from 1841 to 1845, see Takayanagi Azuka, "Tenpō kaikakuka ni okeru Edo shuppankai no dōkō," *Kokubun* (Ochanomizu Joshi Daigaku) 92 (2000): 85–94. For a discussion that includes the three major publishing centers, see Minami Kazuo, "Tenpō kaikaku to shuppan tōsei," *Kokugakuin zasshi* 77, no. 6 (1976): 1–18.

8. Takabatake Ransen [Ryūtei Tanehiko III], *Ryūtei sōsho* (Kyoto: Shinshindō, 1883), 1:12.

9. Aeba Kōson, "Bunka-Bunseido no shōsetsuka kōshō," part 1, *Shikai* 13 (1892): 44. Kamei Hideo cites Fukuchi Gen'ichirō as giving the same list in 1875 in a piece in the newspaper *Tōkyō nichinichi shinbun*, in *Meiji bungaku shi* (Tokyo: Iwanami Shoten, 2000), 67.

10. On the dating of the emergence of the *gōkan* as a recognized genre, see Suzuki Jūzō, *Gōkan ni tsuite*, Bunka kōza shirīzu 9 (Tokyo: Daitōkyū Kinen Bunko, 1961), 4-7.

11. On the form writing took in *gōkan* and the role copyists played in establishing it, see Uchida Sōichi, "*Nise Murasaki inaka Genji* no kana jitai: sakusha jihitsu kōhon to hanpon no hikaku kōsatsu," *Machikaneyama ronsō: Bungaku hen* 32 (1998): 15-28; "Ryūtei Tanehiko jihitsu shiryō no kanajitai: kusazōshi kōhon o chūshin ni," *Gobun* 71 (1998): 29-38; and "Bakin *Konpira bune rishō no tomozuna* no kanajitai: hikkō ni yoru hyōki no kaikaku o megutte," *Kokugo mojishi no kenkyū* 5 (2005): 145-168.

12. Suzuki Jūzō, *Gōkan ni tsuite*, 1.

13. Suzuki Jūzō, "*Inaka Genji* no shukō: Gōkan-bon no seikaku," *Kokubungaku kaishaku to kanshō* 30, no. 6 (1965): 47.

14. Tsuda Mayumi, "*Nise Murasaki inaka Genji*," in *Genji monogatari no hensōkyoku: Edo no shirabe*, ed. Suzuki Ken'ichi (Tokyo: Miyai Shoten, 2003), 64.

15. Ibid.

16. Satō Kaneharu, *Genji monogatari nise Murasaki inaka Genji hikaku ronkō* (Tokyo: Yūbun Shoin, 1976).

17. Yamaguchi Takeshi made a similar point in 1926:

> Of course, Tanehiko has been roundly criticized by a certain type of reader for eliminating precisely what makes *Genji monogatari* so wonderful, the psychological description, in his translation of the "Yūgao" [The Twilight Beauty] chapter. From Tanehiko's perspective, however ... clearly he would insist that it is the variety in the pictures that matters, and there is no point at all in looking for such psychological explanations in *Inaka Genji*. ("Ryūtei Tanehiko no kotodomo," in *Yamaguchi Takeshi chosakushū* [Tokyo: Chūōkōronsha, 1972], 4:502)

See also Yamaguchi, "*Nise Murasaki inaka Genji* ni tsuite," in ibid., 392; Suzuki Jūzō, *Nise Murasaki inaka Genji: daiyonpen kaidai*, distributed with *Nise Murasaki inaka Genji: Daiyonpen*, Fukkoku Nihon koten bungakkan, 2nd ser. (Tokyo: Harupu Shuppan, 1978), 9; and Tsuda, "*Nise Murasaki inaka Genji*," 64.

18. Yamaguchi notes that some readers might take the "Complete List of Works Cited" at the beginning of chapter 3 as an indication that Tanehiko could not read *Genji monogatari* itself very well and thus based *Inaka Genji* entirely on later rewritings ("Ryūtei Tanehiko no kotodomo," 504). While Yamaguchi more than once expresses his disagreement with the latter half of this viewpoint (see, for instance, "*Nise Murasaki inaka Genji* ni tsuite," 359, and "Ryūtei Tanehiko no kotodomo," 505), he agrees that Tanehiko's reading of *Genji* may not have been particularly careful or deep: "Of course, it is doubtful just how much he was able to get out of *Genji*" ("*Nise Murasaki inaka Genji* ni tsuite," 361). For a discussion of Tanehiko's background in classical literature, see Suzuki Jūzō, "Gōkanmono no daizai tenki to Tanehiko," *Kokugo to Kokubungaku* 38, no. 4 (1961): 68.

19. Markus recounts a series of anecdotes that illustrate the extent to which this was true in *Willow in Autumn*, 149-150.

20. I should stress that I am arguing that *Inaka Genji* created the notion of the *popular* fictional replacement of *Genji monogatari*—as opposed, for instance, to the digest or guide, which may have aspired to reach readers "all the way down to the roughest mountain girl, the very lowest of the lower ranks," as Okumura Masanobu, the author of the early-eighteenth-century digest *Wakakusa Genji monogatari* put it, but tended to be more explicitly pedagogical and less entertaining than *Inaka Genji*, and enjoyed nowhere near *Inaka Genji*'s circulation. See Okumura Masanobu [Baiō] (text and pictures), *Wakakusa Genji monogatari*, 6 vols. (Edo: Sansendō, 1707), 1:2 omote.

21. Michael Emmerich, "The Splendor of Hybridity: Image and Text in Ryūtei Tanehiko's *Inaka Genji*," in *Envisioning The Tale of Genji: Media, Gender, and Cultural Production*, ed. Haruo Shirane (New York: Columbia University Press, 2008), 211–239.

22. Rebekah Clements and Peter Kornicki, "The Latter Days of the *Genji*," *Monumenta Nipponica* 64, no. 2 (2009): 365n.2, 366. I am indebted to this review for drawing my attention to elements of my argument that needed to be made more explicit.

23. *NMIG*, chapter 14, 12 *ura*; SNKBT 88:485. The source of the quotation would be apparent to anyone familiar with the names of *Genji monogatari*'s major commentaries: the words "*Kakaisho*, preface" appear on the left-hand panel of the screen. As Suzuki Jūzō points out, the passage is cited in *Kogetsushō*; presumably, this is where Tanehiko took it from. See SNKBT 88:465. For the passage, see *KGS*, "Hottan," 4 *omote*; and *GMK* 1:6.

24. I am thinking, here, of a particular modern reader, Hasegawa Shigure, who writes of taking lessons on the two-stringed zither (*nigenkin*) from Osho, the aunt of a friend:

> I went to have my lesson right at noon during summer, but I never got in Osho's way. She might be sleeping, or entertaining a visitor, or the hairdresser might be there, or she might go off to the baths and then come back and start putting on her makeup, but I'd wait until she finished and said, All right, then, let's get started!—hour after hour I'd wait, and the longer I waited the quieter and the happier I became. There was a reason for that: the chest of books at Osho's held more *gōkan* than you could count. And they weren't the sort of things you come across just anywhere. They were so spotless they looked like new, and they were all first printings, so the colored prints on the covers were absolutely magnificent.
>
> "Here you go, Yatchan." When there was no one else around, she even let me look at her treasured copy of *Inaka Genji*. "Because I know you'll be careful with it, Yatchan, and you'll appreciate it. Because you won't just look at the pictures, you'll really read it." (*Kyūbun Nihonbashi* [Tokyo: Iwanami Shoten, 1983], 302–303)

25. Clements and Kornicki, "Latter Days of the *Genji*," 366. Shimizu Fukuko's name is included in Japanese in the review.

26. Clements and Kornicki cite an expanded version of an essay first distributed with the second volume of *NMIG*. Shimizu Fukuko's emphasis differs slightly from the presentation of it here, but if anything she is more direct, if

also rather vague and contradictory, in asserting that *Inaka Genji*'s readers must have been familiar with *Genji monogatari*. She begins her essay by asking "How did [*Inaka Genji*'s] readers come to know the original *Genji monogatari*?" and then goes on to assert, "It is generally accepted that during the Edo period, ordinary people acquainted themselves with *Genji monogatari* not through the original text and commentaries, but through digests and translations. But reading the text of *Inaka Genji*, one begins to think that perhaps its readers may, surprisingly enough, actually have been reading the original text." She immediately undercuts this suggestion, however, by saying, "I think that *some among its readers* had already read *Genji monogatari* in its entirety, while others started reading *Genji monogatari* after being inspired by *Inaka Genji*" (italics added; *Genji monogatari hanpon no kenkyū* [Osaka: Izumi Shoin, 2003], 20). The difference between "its readers" and "some readers" is crucial.

27. On the Nagoya library's holdings, see Nagatomo, *Kinsei kashihon'ya no kenkyū*, 159–160. Markus cites Nagatomo on this same point in *Willow in Autumn*, 148.

28. Shimizu places particular importance on illustrated digests, but the latest works she cites, with the exception of one that postdates *Inaka Genji*, are Okumura Masanobu's *Wakakusa Genji*, *Kōhaku Genji*, and *Hinazuru Genji*, published between 1706 and 1708. See Shimizu, *Genji monogatari hanpon no kenkyū*, 23.

29. Ryūtei Senka specifically mentions "*Fūryū Genji monogatari, Wakakusa Genji monogatari, Kōhaku Genji monogatari*, and so on" (note to Utagawa Kunisada, *Ima Genji nishiki eawase* [Edo: Sanoya Kihei, 1852–1854]).

30. Rebekah Clements provides a list of "translations" made into various forms of Japanese from the eighteenth through the nineteenth centuries in "Mō hitotsu no chūshakusho: Edo jidai ni okeru *Genji monogatari* no shoki zokugoyaku no igi," *Heian bungaku no kochūshaku to juyō* 3 (2011): 40. The most recent translation at the time *Inaka Genji* was published was *Shibun ama no saezuri*, whose five volumes covered as far as chapter 3 of *Genji monogatari* and had been published in 1723. Clements includes in her list a manuscript called *Kogetsushō genkai* that was completed in 1812, but it seems more appropriate to call this book a commentary, and in any event only a single copy is known to have existed.

31. *Kogetsushō* often appears in the rooms of courtesans and male authors, but one rarely encounters images of nonprofessional women reading the book. The only such print I have seen is by Keisai Eisen, showing an obviously very wealthy merchant's daughter, reproduced as *Girl Admiring a Warbler*, in *Reading Surimono: The Interplay of Text and Image in Japanese Prints*, ed. John T. Carpenter (Leiden: Hotei, 2008), 127. Interestingly, the title slip on the volume in the young woman's hands is positioned at the upper left rather than in the center, as was the case with every copy of *Kogetsushō* I have seen, and has *Kogetsushō* written on it, rather than the title of the particular chapter, as one would expect.

32. Ryūtei Senka (text) and Utagawa Kunisada II (pictures), *Ashikagaginu tezome no murasaki* (Edo: Kinrindō, 1853), chapter 14, 1 *omote*.

33. Yoshitsune was by far the more popular of the brothers, and the category is known as "Yoshitsune-mono." Shimazu Hisamoto lists eighteen *kibyōshi*, sixteen *gōkan*, and seventy-two kabuki plays—to sample only the most relevant

early modern genres—among the early modern works he catalogs in *Yoshitsune densetsu to bungaku* (Tokyo: Meiji Shoin, 1935), 96-120.

34. Enchi Fumiko, *Genji monogatari shiken* (Tokyo: Shinchōsha, 1974), 247; Enchi Fumiko et al., *Koten sai'nyūmon* (Tokyo: Kamakura Shobō, 1981), 86.

35. Maeda Ai, "Meicho zenshū to watakushi," in *Yamaguchi Takeshi chosakushū* (Tokyo: Chūōkōronsha, 1972), 5:7-8. My attention was drawn to this essay by Markus, *Willow in Autumn*, 149.

36. Naitō Meisetsu, "Inaka Genji," in *Rōbaikyo zaccho* (Tokyo: Haishodō, 1907), 172. My attention was directed to this essay by Tsuda, "Nise Murasaki inaka Genji," 64.

37. Naitō, "Inaka Genji," 172. Perhaps Naitō's indebtedness to *Inaka Genji* should come as no surprise, since the most famous guide to *Genji monogatari* published specifically for poets, *Genji binkagami* (A Hairlock Mirror Genji, 1660), does not even mention Fujitsubo in its brief summary of the "Kiritsubo" (The Paulownia Pavilion) chapter. See Kojima Munakata and Suzumura Nobufusa, *Genji binkagami*, in *Hihyō shūsei Genji monogatari*, ed. Akiyama Ken et al., vol. 1, *Kinsei zenki hen* (Tokyo: Yumani Shobō, 1999), 37-39. On haikai poets' non-reading of *Genji monogatari*, see Nishida Masahiro, "Edo jidai zenki no Genjigaku," in *Genji monogatari no hensōkyoku*, ed. Suzuki Ken'ichi, 121-130.

38. Kimura Takatarō, *Bairon: Hyōden oyobi shishū* (Tokyo: Tōseidō, 1923), 289-292. "Eccentric" is, if anything, far too mild a word to describe Kimura, who saw a complete identity between the legends in *Kojiki* and *Nihon shoki* and those of ancient Greece, and who argued in *Sekaiteki kenkyū ni motozukeru Nihon taikoshi* (1911-1912) that in ancient times the Japanese people had lived in Asia Minor, Italy, Greece, and Egypt, and had conquered Arabia, Persia, India, and Siam. In the chapter on *Parisina* in *Bairon*, Kimura argues that the poem's plot is identical to that of *Inaka Genji* = *Genji monogatari* and that the etymologies of its characters' names point back to the names of the characters in *Inaka Genji* = *Genji monogatari*: Parisina, for instance, comes from the Latin "Par-isi-noea," while Inanoya (Fuji no Kata's maiden name) comes from "Oena-noea," and both mean "the same as"—that is, the same as the deceased lover each replaces. Thus Byron's poem can be traced back to *Inaka Genji* = *Genji monogatari*, "this novel of ancient India-Japan" (291).

39. Yoda Koji [Gakkai], "Nise Murasaki inaka Genji hyō," part 1, *Shuppan geppyō* 16 (1888): 446.

40. Ryūtei Tanehiko, *Tanehiko kessakushū*, ed. Hakubunkan Hensankyoku, Teikoku bunko 16 (Tokyo: Hakubunkan, 1894), 1. G. G. Rowley cites the scholars Shiota Ryōhei and Hisamatsu Sen'ichi as making the point, independently of each other, that it was Hakubunkan's 1890 Nihon bungaku zensho edition of *Genji monogatari* "that revealed to ordinary Tokyoites the existence of a *Genji* other than Tanehiko's parodic *Nise Murasaki inaka Genji*" (*Yosano Akiko and The Tale of Genji* [Ann Arbor: Center for Japanese Studies, University of Michigan, 2000], 61).

41. Yokutō Rōjin, "Genji monogatari (tsuketari Inaka Genji)," *Katei zasshi* 9, no. 7 (1897): 30-33. *Fūryū Genji monogatari* was actually written by Miyako no Nishiki. Interestingly, *Fūryū Genji monogatari* is also attributed to Nishiki Bunryū in an advertisement included at the end of the first fascicle of two copies of *Sono yukari hina no omokage*'s third chapter that I have seen, one at the

Art Research Center at Ritsumeikan and the other at Waseda University Library. The advertisement is for a work called *Nise Murasaki inaka no shitazome*, which was most likely never published.

42. Yokutō, "*Genji monogatari* (tsuketari *Inaka Genji*)," 33.

43. For an interesting exploration of Tanehiko's use of *Kogetsushō* from the very first pages of *Inaka Genji*, see Uchimura Katsushi, "*Nise Murasaki inaka Genji*ron: sono hōhō o megutte," *Meiji Daigaku Daigakuin kiyō bungaku hen* 21, no. 4 (1983): 15–28. For more about Tanehiko's reading of *Kogetsushō*, see Satō Satoru, "*Genji monogatari* to kinsei bungaku," in *Genji monogatari kōza*, ed. Imai Takuji et al., vol. 8, *Genji monogatari no honbun to juyō* (Tokyo: Benseisha, 1992), 389–390. Mori Senzō, Yamaguchi Takeshi, and others report that Tanehiko possessed an annotated copy of *Kogetsushō* that had belonged to Katō Umaki, a Kokugaku scholar and the grandfather of Tanehiko's wife. This information was first made public by Mizutani Futō in an essay on Ryūtei Tanehiko originally published in 1894; Mizutani says that he got the information from notes left by Sekine Seishi when he died. The truth of this has not, to my knowledge, been confirmed. See Mori Senzō, "Ryūtei Tanehiko (sono ichi)," in *Mori Senzō chosakushū* (Tokyo: Chūōkōronsha, 1970), 1:509; Yamaguchi, "*Nise Murasaki inaka Genji* ni tsuite," 359; and Mizutani Futō, "Ryūtei Tanehiko," in *Mizutani Futō chosakushū* (Tokyo: Chūōkōronsha, 1974), 3:256.

44. According to Gakkai's diary, he began reading *Kogetsushō* on the fourteenth day of the third month, Ansei 3 (April 18, 1856), and finished reading it in early November 1889, only to start reading it from the beginning again. See *GN* 1:97; 8:18.

45. Yoda, "*Nise Murasaki inaka Genji* hyō," 448.

46. Ibid., 446. Gakkai expresses the same sentiment in a diary entry for the eleventh day of the first month, Meiji 4 (March 1, 1871): "I went to Nihonbashi and bought some things. . . . I got both boxes of Ryūtei Tanehiko's *Nise Murasaki inaka Genji*. Frivolous a work though it is, I find it is actually superior to the original in the marvelous way it captures *Genji*'s essence while introducing new twists" (*GN* 3:68).

47. "Middle-size" *chūhon* (or *chūbon*) were so called because they were smaller than *hanshibon* ("half-size books," which are named for the size of paper from which they are made: *hanshi* [half-size paper]) but bigger than *kohon* (or *kobon* [small books]). The following discussion of the bibliographic characteristics of the first and later printings of the Edo edition of *Inaka Genji* draws on Ōtake Yasuko, "Besuto serā no sugata: *Nise Murasaki inaka Genji*," in *Bakin kusazōshi shū geppō* 33 (1994): 5–8, distributed with *Bakin kusazōshi shū*, Sōsho Edo bunko 33 (Tokyo: Kokusho Kankōkai, 1994); Suzuki Jūzō, "Kaisetsu," *SNKBT* 89:757–766; and my own inspection of numerous copies of *Inaka Genji* and other *gōkan* in various collections in Japan. Since *gōkan* and other early modern Japanese books were printed entirely by hand, copies of the same work published at different times are never exactly the same. The most it is possible to say about my description is that in general it should apply to the first printing of *Inaka Genji*; it does not necessarily describe later printings.

48. For a detailed treatment of the *kibyōshi*, see Adam L. Kern, *Manga of the Floating World: Comicbook Culture and the Kibyōshi of Edo Japan* (Cambridge, Mass.: Harvard University Asia Center, 2006). My description of the format of

the *gōkan* is generally applicable, but there were exceptions: Kyokutei Bakin's *Keisei suikoden* (*A Courtesan's Water Margin*), for instance—issued from 1825 to 1835 with pictures provided at various points by Utagawa Toyokuni II, Utagawa Kuniyasu, and Hashimoto Sadahide—was published in chapters of four *satsu*. As an advertisement for the book pointed out, "This means that one chapter of this book is equivalent to two chapters of another book." The ad appears as back matter in the Ritsumeikan University Art Research Center's copy of Ryūtei Tanehiko (text) and Utagawa Kuniyoshi (pictures), *Jimon jidō tawagoto kuawase* (Edo: Senkakudō, 1835).

49. Advertisements for both appear, for instance, in Fūtei Baryū (text) and Utagawa Kagematsu (pictures), *Edo murasaki fuji no hanatori* (Edo: Kōeidō, 1834).

50. Satō Satoru notes that experiments in elaborate printing using thin and thick ink in the *kuchi-e* of *gōkan* occurred briefly during the Bunka period, but that such decorations seem not to have caught on until the Tenpō period, in "Kusazōshi no zōhon keitai to kakaku," 51. Both thin and thick ink were used in the illustrated title pages for chapter 1 of *Inaka Genji*.

51. Suzuki Jūzō, note to *kuchi-e* 3, in SNKBT 88:151.

52. *NMIG*, chapter 16, 17 *omote*, and chapter 17, 2 *ura*; SNKBT 88:561, 574.

53. This screen is actually a makeshift assemblage of a picture of hell and a wooden openwork divider (*ranma*) that shows a heavenly woman (*tennyo*) playing music on the instrument known as the *shō*. Again, though, this is most apparent in early printings, where thin ink is used to mimic the texture of the wood from which the *ranma* was carved.

54. *NMIG*, chapter 5, 17 *omote* and *ura*; SNKBT 88:170. Most of the episode in which this scene appears is included in Ryūtei Tanehiko, *A Country Genji by a Commoner Murasaki*, trans. Chris Drake, in *Early Modern Japanese Literature: An Anthology, 1600–1900*, ed. Haruo Shirane (New York: Columbia University Press, 2002), 801–842.

55. "*Genji* incense signs" (*Genji kō no zu*) were patterns of five vertical lines of varying lengths, some linked by horizontal lines, used in a game in which competing teams tried to identify what permutation of five incenses were contained in a set of five they had been given. Originally, there were fifty-two distinct signs, each of which represented a particular permutation and was named after a chapter of *Genji monogatari*; later, variants of two signs were assigned to the first and last chapters of the tale, which originally had no signs, bringing the total to fifty-four. See also touchstone 1, n. 5.

The *fusenryō* could also be created by floating the weft, so "floating-weft pattern" is an appropriate description as well. The *ryō* in the name—also read *aya*—refers, I believe, to the diagonal orientation of the pattern.

56. KGS, "Hashihime," 42 *omote*; GMK 3:353; SNKBZ 24:164; SNKBT 22:333; TG 2:846.

57. Ōtake says that she has seen only one work printed in the Bunsei period and six printed in the Tenpō period that have patterned rather than plain black covers; the Bunsei-period book was privately printed, not a commercial product, and all the Tenpō-period books were published later than chapter 4 of *Inaka Genji*. See Ōtake, "Besuto serā no sugata," 7. The rapid spread of patterned covers was one of the effects of the Tenpō Reforms, which prohibited the

use of elaborately colored front covers, according to Takayanagi, "Tenpō kaikakuka ni okeru Edo shuppankai no dōkō," 89-90.

58. *Kaiōi*—also known as *kaiawase*, though this was originally a different game—involved searching two groups of shells for matching halves. The person or team to match the most shells won the game. The insides of the shells generally had poems, pictures, or both painted inside them; poems and famous scenes from *Genji monogatari* were particularly popular.

59. Covers with the clamshell design are used on both fascicles of the second chapter of a copy in the collection of Waseda University Library of an unauthorized reprint of Kyokutei Bakin (text) and Utagawa Kuniyasu (pictures), *Fūzoku kin'gyoden*, 5 chapters in 10 fascicles (Edo: Shōjudō, 1837-1839). The covers do not appear to have found their way onto the book from a copy of *Inaka Genji* during rebinding: while the design is closely based on *Inaka Genji*'s covers, they have been sloppily recarved and are unlike those on any copies of *Inaka Genji* that I have seen. I have encountered the same clamshell pattern on other later *gōkan* to whose content they bear no relation.

60. *NMIG*, chapter 38, 1 *omote*; SNKBT 89:638.

61. Fūtei Baryū and Utagawa Kagematsu, *Edo murasaki fuji no hanatori*, 2 *ura*–5 *ura*.

62. Ibid., 1 *omote*.

63. Kyokutei Bakin to Ozu Keisō, letter dated the sixteenth day of the ninth month, Tenpō 6 (November 6, 1835), letter 29, in *Bakin shokanshū*, ed. Shibata Mitsuhiko and Kanda Masayuki (Tokyo: Yagi Shoten, 1993), 4:111. For the book, see Tōri Sanjin (text), Utagawa Sadahide [Gountei Sadahide] (pictures), and Utagawa Kunisada (covers), *Imayō Ise monogatari*, 6 chapters in 24 fascicles (Edo: Izumiya Ichibē, 1835-1838).

64. Keisai Eisen (text) and Utagawa Kunisada (pictures), *Sono yukari hina no omokage* (Edo: Senkakudō and Kinrindō, 1848), chapter 3, back matter.

65. According to the Union Catalog of Early Japanese Books database at the National Institute for Japanese Literature, the first chapter of *A Grove-Warbler Lost in the Grove* was originally published in 1866, with the second through fifth chapters appearing in the Meiji period. The date appended to Sansantei Arindo's preface to the copy of the first chapter that I have seen, in the collection of the Waseda University Library, reads "Manuscript completed 1870, printed 1872." Presumably, this refers only to the preface, which Arindo may have written to accompany a reprint of the first chapter issued to accompany the newly published second through fifth chapters.

66. Eiko Kondo, "*Inaka Genji* Series," in *Essays on Japanese Art Presented to Jack Hillier*, ed. Matthi Forrer (London: Sawers, 1982), 79.

67. Tamenaga Shunsui (text) and Utagawa Kunisada (pictures), *Kōtōshinwa tamausagi* (Edo: Eijudō, 1835?), chapter 1 *jō*, 19 *omote*–21 *omote*. Markus quotes this passage, but takes it from Ishida Motosue's *Kusazōshi no iroiro*, in which it is abridged in a rather misleading manner. See Markus, *Willow in Autumn*, 150-151; and Ishida Motosue, *Kusazōshi no iroiro* (Tokyo: Nansō Shoin, 1928), 306. *With the Script as My Model* is Ryūtei Tanehiko (text) and Utagawa Kunisada (pictures), *Shōhon jitate*, 12 chapters in 69 fascicles (Edo: Eijudō, 1815-1831); *The Plum Calendar* is Tamenaga Shunsui (text), Yanagawa Shigenobu I (pictures), and Yanagawa Shigenobu [Jūzan] II (pictures), *Shunshoku umegoyomi*, 4 chap-

ters in 12 fascicles (Edo: Bun'eidō, 1832-1833); and *The Southeast Garden* is Tamenaga Shunsui (text) and Utagawa Kuninao (pictures), *Shunshoku tatsumi no sono*, 4 chapters in 12 fascicles (Edo: Bun'eidō, 1833-1835).

68. *NMIG*, chapter 14, 10 *ura*; SNKBT 88:481. For an explanation of the scene, see *NMIG*, chapter 14, 15 *ura*-16 *omote*; and SNKBT 88:490.

69. Ryūtei Tanehiko and Utagawa Kuniyoshi, *Jimon jidō tawagoto kuawase*, 1 *ura*.

70. Natsume Sōseki, *Nowaki*, in *Sōseki zenshū* (Tokyo: Iwanami Shoten, 1994), 3:324.

71. Markus, *Willow in Autumn*, 146. Ozawa Keijirō writes that Naritami built three buildings on an estate that he purchased in Negishi after the Meiji Restoration, one in the Japanese style, one in the Chinese style, and one in the Western style: "According to reports of the construction, the two-story building in the Japanese style was as lavish as could be, and it was like looking at the pictures in the popular fictional work *Inaka Genji*" (*Meiji teien ki*, in *Meiji engei shi*, ed. Nihon Engei Kenkyūkai [Tokyo: Nihon Engei Kenkyūkai, 1915], 150).

72. For another picture of Murasaki Shikibu that shares both the same kimono pattern and the fan, see Tayama Takanori, *Hyakunin isshu zue*, 3 fascicles (Kyoto: Nakagawa Tōjirō, 1807), fascicle 2, 129 *ura*. The same image appears in a printing of the book published in Edo in 1822 by Suwaraya Mohē.

73. Danjūrō was thirty-two years old, according to the method of counting used at the time of his death; if he had committed suicide today, he would have been said to be approaching his thirty-first birthday.

74. Utagawa Kunisada [Ichiyōsai Toyokuni] (pictures), *Shussegoi taki no shiratama*, 2 fascicles (Edo: Kikakudō, 1855), 1 *omote*.

75. The anonymous author of the text would seem to be recalling the derivation of the term from a story about the First Emperor of China, who, in addition to searching for an elixir of immortality, bestowed a rank on a pine tree that had sheltered him from the rain. The phrase *tokaeri mo*, which follows immediately after, is also associated with the pine tree or, more specifically, with its famed longevity: pines were said to bloom once in a hundred years, so a "ten-cycle pine tree" would be a thousand years old.

76. For a sampling of a few such images, see D. Max Moerman, "Dying Like a Buddha: Intervisuality and the Cultic Image," *Impressions* 29 (2007-2008): 47-51.

77. *NMIG*, chapter 1, 3 *ura*-4 *omote*; SNKBT 88:9; Bai Juyi, "Song of Everlasting Pain," trans. Stephen Owen, in *An Anthology of Chinese Literature: Beginnings to 1911*, ed. Stephen Owen (New York: Norton, 1996), 442.

78. *NMIG* chapter 6, 18 *ura*-19 *ura*; SNKBT 88:205-206.

79. The quotation appears in *Inaka Genji sumagoto* (*Genji at Ten in the Evening: A Suma Koto*, 1838?) and is cited in Hayashi Yoshikazu, *Edo ehon besutoserā* (Tokyo: Shinchōsha, 1995), 202. While the prefaces to this book and another called *Nise Murasaki Naniwa Genji* (*A Fraudulent Murasaki's Ōsaka Genji*, 1837) are signed "Sanehiko," Hayashi argues convincingly from the roughness of the prose of the main text that *Inaka Genji sumagoto* may have been written by Ryūtei Senka.

80. Hanagasa Bunkyō [Kōshoku Gaishi] (text) and Keisai Eisen (pictures), *Konotegashiwa*, 3 vols. (1836), book 2, 2 *ura*-3 *omote*. I am indebted to Ellis Tinios for directing my attention to the existence of *Konotegashiwa* and to this picture in it.

81. Quoted in Satō Yukiko, *Edo no eiri shōsetsu: Gōkan no sekai* (Tokyo: Perikansha, 2001), 65.

82. Katō Ikuya, *Edozakura: Katō Ikuya kushū* (Tokyo: Ozawa Shoten, 1988), 137.

83. Ryūtei Senka (text) and Utagawa Kunisada II (pictures), *Sono yukari hina no omokage* (Edo: Kinshōdō, 1855), chapter 13, 1 *omote*.

84. *NMIG*, chapter 15, 1 *omote*; SNKBT 88:502.

85. For a transcription, see Suzuki Jūzō, "Kaisetsu," SNKBT 89:774.

86. It is tempting to bring in another term from kabuki: *naimaze*, which denotes the blending in a single script of two separate *sekai*. Sakurada Jisuke I was already making use of *naimaze* in the early 1770s, but the technique was brought to a new level of complexity by Tsuruya Nanboku IV in the Bunka and Bunsei periods, around the same time that Tanehiko started out as an author first of *yomihon* and then of *gōkan*.

87. For a concise description of the character type associated in the theater with the *sōhatsu* hairstyle, see Matsuzaki Hitoshi, *Genroku engeki kenkyū* (Tokyo: Tōkyō Daigaku Shuppankai, 1979), 243–244.

88. For the reference to the Dutch word *kop*, see *NMIG*, chapter 7, 3 *ura*; and SNKBT 88:218. Suzuki Jūzō discovered the note to Kunisada in an excerpt of Tanehiko's second, revised and illustrated, manuscript for chapter 29 that had been inserted into the first, purely textual draft. For a transcription, see Suzuki Jūzō, "Kaisetsu," SNKBT 89:776.

89. According to Suzuki Jūzō,

> For instance, Yamaguchi believes the idea of having an old woman in an *oni* mask attack Mitsuuji, pretending to be the spirit of a living woman—this happens in chapter 5, the counterpart to "Yūgao"—is related to the appearance of a living spirit in *Kantō Koroku mukashi butai*. In fact, there is a scene even more closely reminiscent of this in *Nishiki no obi nazorae mugen* in which the courtesan Kōbai puts on a Hannya mask and menaces a man whispering sweet nothings to his young fiancée. Or again, the idea of having pieces of gold and a letter appear inside a papier-mâché dog, which appears in *Ukiyogata rokumai byōbu*, is cleverly imported into the plot of chapter 10 in *Inaka Genji*, when a secret missive emerges from a papier-mâché dog given along with a doll's house. ("Gōkanmono no daizai tenki to Tanehiko," 69)

Kantō Koroku mukashi butai (1829), *Nishiki no obi nazorae mugen* (1813), and *Ukiyogata rokumai byōbu* (1821) are *gōkan* by Tanehiko. For one of the relevant passages, see Ryūtei Tanehiko (text) and Kitao Shigemasa (pictures), *Kantō Koroku mukashi butai*, 3 chapters in 12 fascicles (Edo: Eijudō and Shunshōken, 1828–1829), chapter 2, 9 *ura*–10 *ura*. This work is reproduced and the text is transcribed in *Ryūtei Tanehiko gōkanshū*, ed. Satō Satoru, Sōsho Edo bunko 35 (Tokyo: Kokushokankōkai, 1995), 416–418, 512–513. For another example, see Ryūtei Tanehiko (text) and Utagawa Toyokuni (pictures), *Ukiyogata rokumai byōbu*, 2 parts in 6 fascicles (Edo: Eijudō, 1821), chapter 1, 11 *ura*–14 *ura*.

90. *NMIG*, chapter 16, 1 *omote*; SNKBT 88:538. The "towrope" (*tsunade no nawa*) is incorporated, presumably, because it appears in Genji's exchange of

poems with the Gosechi Dancer in the "Suma" chapter of *Genji monogatari*; in Tanehiko's preface, the towrope is literally "very long" (*ito nagakute*), but the idea seems to be that he is stuck, at a loss, just like the Gosechi Dancer—hence my translation. See *KGS*, "Suma," 38 *ura*; *GMK* 1:615–16; SNKBZ 21:205; SNKBT 20:35–36; and *TG* 1:247. The reference to hot water is, I would guess, alluding to the scene in which Aoi dies in the "Aoi" (Heart-to-Heart) chapter, during which Genji encourages her to "Drink your hot water" and the onlookers wonder where he has learned such kindness. See *KGS*, "Aoi," 24 *omote* and *ura*; *GMK* 1:457; SNKBZ 21:44; SNKBT 19:310; and *TG* 1:176. As Tyler's translation indicates, the "hot water" here has medicine in it.

91. *NMIG*, chapter 1, 5 *ura*; SNKBT 88:12. The preface to chapter 29 contains another example of this: "Since Denkan's suicide by *harakiri* does not appear in Murasaki Shikibu's script, I've taken my usual liberties" (*NMIG*, chapter 29, 1 *ura*; SNKBT 89:299).

92. *NMIG*, chapter 1, 10 *ura*; SNKBT 88:20. The mere fact that Tanehiko felt the need to include this note shows how limited he expected his readers' knowledge of *Genji monogatari* to be.

93. *NMIG*, chapter 2, 1 *omote*; SNKBT 88:42. The passage in "Aoi" follows the consummation of Genji's marriage to Murasaki. Genji replies to Koremitsu's knowing question, itself a play on words, about how many "baby rat cakes to provide" by asking for "about a third as many" (*mitsu ga hitotsu*) as the "baby boar cakes" they had just been served. See *KGS*, "Aoi," 47 *ura*; *GMK* 1:486; SNKBZ 21:72–3; SNKBT 19:331; and *TG* 1:187.

94. After discoursing at some length in a letter to Ryūtei Senka, dated the third day of the tenth month, 1829, on the use of different combinations of five-, seven-, and sometimes four-syllable phrases to create certain moods, Tanehiko offers a general description of the relationship of his *gōkan* prose style to the style used in *kabuki*:

> The prose I used in *Shōhon jitate* was secretly based in these alternations, but written in a manner that recalled the lines spoken by actors. The style actually used in *kabuki* scripts may work well if one is really going to put on a play and have actors speak the lines, but it proves no use at all when one is writing for children; many of the authors out there aren't aware of this, though, and think everything will turn out fine as long as they write like a play. As a result, no one buys what they write. This is a great secret. It seems as though lines meant to be chanted to music, lines meant to be spoken by actors, and lines meant to be read by women and children ought to be the same, but the truth is that they are extremely different. (Quoted in Satō Satoru, "Ryūtei Tanehiko shokanshū," in *Kinsei bungaku fukan*, ed. Hasegawa Tsuyoshi [Tokyo: Kyūko Shoin, 1997], 768)

95. Yoda, "*Nise Murasaki inaka Genji hyō*," 446.
96. *NMIG*, chapter 4, 6 *ura*–14 *omote*; SNKBT 88:120–132.
97. *TG* 1:48.
98. *NMIG*, chapter 4, 8 *omote*–7 *ura* (the text moves across the top of the two-page spread from right to left and then jumps back to the right, to 7 *ura*); SNKBT 88:121–122.

99. *KGS*, "Utsusemi," 3 *ura*–4 *omote*. In the original, the second *yase* in *yaseyase* is written with a repeat mark (*kurikaeshi*); unfortunately, this is impossible to duplicate in horizontal text. For the corresponding passage in other editions, see *GMK* 1:148; SNKBZ 20:119–120; and SNKBT 19:85–86.

100. *NMIG*, chapter 4, 8 *omote*–7 *ura* (the text moves across the top of the two-page spread from right to left and then jumps back to the right, to 7 *ura*); SNKBT 88:121–122. Here, too, the second *yase* in *yaseyase* is written with a repeat mark (*kurikaeshi*).

101. Yamaguchi, "Nise Murasaki inaka Genji ni tsuite," 370–371.

102. This is not to say that Tanehiko did not stick more or less closely to the text of *Genji* in different chapters or, for that matter, that general trends cannot be identified even at the more basic level of grammar. Analyzing *Inaka Genji* from a linguistic point of view, Fujiwara Miki has demonstrated that Tanehiko avoided the negative ending *nai*, which was common in Japanese spoken in the city of Edo, in favor of the older forms *zu* and *nu*, which were not, and points out that as the work progressed Tanehiko tended to make increasingly frequent use of *zu*, which is the more archaic of the two. See Fujiwara Miki, "Nise Murasaki inaka Genji no kokugogakuteki kōsatsu: kaiwabun kara mita jidaisei to sōsaku ito," *Kagawa Daigaku kokubun kenkyū* 14 (1989): 5–15.

103. Suzuki Jūzō, *Daiyonpen kaidai*, 10.

104. Uchimura, "Nise Murasaki inaka Genjiron," 16.

105. Markus, *Willow in Autumn*, 154–155.

106. *Keisei suikoden*, which was continued after Bakin's death in 1848 by Tanehiko's disciple Ryūtei Senka under the title *Onna suikoden* (*A Woman's Water Margin*, 1848–1851), was issued by *Inaka Genji*'s publisher, Tsuruya Kiemon. While this does not rule out the possibility that Tanehiko hoped *Inaka Genji* would be able to compete with Bakin's works, it does complicate our understanding of what this "competition" may have meant, given the important role publishers played at the time. Takagi Gen has argued that the well-known rivalry between Bakin and Santō Kyōden was staged by Tsuruya Kiemon in an attempt to increase sales; perhaps a similar strategy was being implemented here. See Takagi Gen, "Edo yomihon no keisei," in *Edo yomihon no kenkyū: Jūkyūseiki shōsetsu kō* (Tokyo: Perikansha, 1995), 57–58. Certainly, Tsuruya Kiemon seems to have done an excellent job of promoting both authors: Kimura Mokurō observes that *Nise Murasaki inaka Genji*, *Keisei suikoden*, and Bakin's *Shinpen kinpeibai* (*A New Plum in the Golden Vase*, 1831–1847) were the three most successful *gōkan* ever. See Kimura Mokurō, *Kokuji shōsetsu tsū*, 1:301. Interestingly, the preface to chapter 1 of *Keisei suikoden* begins by noting, "There are those who speak of *Genji* without having read *Genji monogatari*" (Kyokutei Bakin [text] and Utagawa Toyokuni II [pictures], *Keisei suikoden* [Edo: Senkakudō, 1825], chapter 1, fascicle 1, 1 *omote*).

107. For Bakin's well-known comments on *Inaka Genji*, which include the suggestion that the work was secretly based on earlier rewritings of *Genji*, see *Kinsei mono no hon Edo sakusha burui*, in *Kinko bungei onchi sōsho* (Tokyo: Hakubunkan, 1891), 5:44–46. Satō Satoru's series of essays on the relationship of Bakin and Tanehiko and their *kōshō zuihitsu* (antiquarian miscellanies) helpfully clarifies their relationship. See, in particular, Satō Satoru, "Ryūtei Tanehiko: Bakin no egaita Tanehikozō," *Kokubungaku kaishaku to kanshō* 59, no. 8

(1994): 117-121, and "Kōshō zuihitsu no imi suru mono: Ryūtei Tanehiko to Kyokutei Bakin," *Kokugo to kokubungaku* 70, no. 11 (1993): 118-127.

108. Markus, *Willow in Autumn*, 120. It should be noted that in 1829, when the first chapters of *Inaka Genji* appeared, Tanehiko had no idea that he would be able to continue the work as long as he ultimately did, and he certainly did not intend to rewrite the whole of *Genji monogatari*. Indeed, the very concept of the long serial *gōkan* still was not well established: only five chapters of four fascicles each of Bakin's *Keisei suikoden* had appeared at that point, and only four three-fascicle chapters of *Konpira bune rishō no tomozuna* (chapters 6, 7, and 8 of *Keisei suikoden* and chapters 5 and 6 of *Konpira bune rishō no tomozuna* were published in 1829). The only *gōkan* that had continued longer than these two works were Jippensha Ikku's *Kane no waraji*, chapter 18 of which was published in 1828, and Tanehiko's *Shōhonjitate*, chapter 10 of which was published in 1828.

109. Markus, *Willow in Autumn*, 122.

110. Nakamura Yukihiko, "*Genji monogatari* no kinsei bungaku e no eikyō," in *Nakamura Yukihiko chojutsushū* (Tokyo: Chūōkōronsha, 1983), 3:442.

111. *NMIG*, chapter 3, 1 *omote*; SNKBT 88:78. The name usually read as "Kokiden" is read "Kōkiden" in the titles *Kōkiden and the Cormorant-Feather Birthing Hut* (*Kōkiden u no ha no ubuya*, which can also be read as *Kōkiden uwanari uchi*, punning on the meaning *Kōkiden Beats Her Rival*) and *Kōkiden Beats Her Rival* (*Kōkiden uwanari uchi*).

112. Markus, *Willow in Autumn*, 131-132.

113. Yamaguchi, "*Nise Murasaki inaka Genji* ni tsuite," 362-363. Suzuki Jūzō offers some additional possibilities in "Kaisetsu," in SNKBT 89:770.

114. Suzuki Jūzō, *Daiyonpen kaidai*, 8-9. For another allusion to a picture attributed, within the picture, to Nonoguchi Ryūhō, see *NMIG*, chapter 2, 1 *ura*-2 *omote*; and SNKBT 88:41, 43. I might add that while Suzuki's detective work regarding Tanehiko's handling of the *saibara* is impressive, his explanation leaves room for doubt. Suzuki points out that Tanehiko quotes the entire poem, as does *Zokuge Genji*, but then so does *Kogetsushō*. The text that Tanehiko offers is subtly different from that in *Kogetsushō* (the former has *taretareba*, whereas the latter has *kaketaru*, for instance), but it is also subtly different from that in *Zokuge Genji* (which has *taretaru o*). And, indeed, Mitsuuji recites only part of the lyric before Shinonome takes over and "changes it as she sings" (*utaikaete*): in her version, Mitsuuji's *taretareba* becomes *hoshitareba*. In short, Tanehiko could have been referring to *Kogetsushō*. For the relevant passage in *Inaka Genji*, see *NMIG*, chapter 4, 14 *ura*-15 *omote*; and SNKBT 88:133. For the passage in *Kogetsushō*, see *KGS*, "Hahakigi," 36 *ura*; and *GMK* 1:124. For the passage in *Zokuge Genji monogatari*, see Okumura Masanobu (text and pictures), *Zokuge Genji monogatari*, 6 vols. (Edo: Yamaguchi Yagonbei, 1721), 6:18 *ura*.

115. *Wakakusa Genji*, *Hinazuru Genji*, and *Kōhaku Genji* were written and illustrated by Okumura Masanobu as continuations of Miyako no Nishiki's *Fūryū Genji monogatari*; together with *Zokuge Genji monogatari*, which Okumura wrote to replace *Fūryū Genji monogatari*, they cover the chapters from "Kiritsubo" (The Paulownia Pavilion) to "Hana no en" (Under the Cherry Blossoms). *Shin hashihime monogatari* is a rewriting of the last ten chapters of *Genji*, the so-called *Uji jūjō* (ten Uji chapters).

116. *NMIG*, chapter 5, 2 *ura*–3 *omote*; SNKBT 88:148. According to Suzuki Jūzō's annotations in SNKBT, the dolls are *Imado ningyō*. The chart in *Kogetsushō* takes the form common to genealogies of the characters in *Genji* that existed before its publication, the so-called *kokeizu* (old genealogies).

117. The Japanese puns on *gakusha* and *gakuya*. *NMIG*, chapter 5, 2 *ura*; SNKBT 88:148.

118. Fujita Tokutarō, "*Haikai Genji* to *Inaka Genji*," *Kokugo to kokubungaku* 7, no. 3 (1930): 55. Fujita points out in a note at the end of his essay that Hasegawa Kinjirō's *Kaku ya ika ni no ki? (What's Going On Here?*, 1876) also questions the relationship between the two works.

119. Satō Satoru, "*Genji monogatari* to kinsei bungaku," 389–390.

120. Uchimura, "*Nise Murasaki inaka Genjiron*," 15–28.

121. Ryūtei Senka and Utagawa Kunisada II, *Ashikagaginu tezome no murasaki*, chapter 14, 1 *omote*.

122. *NMIG*, chapter 1, 1 *omote*; SNKBT 88:6.

123. *NMIG*, chapter 1, 1 *omote*; SNKBT 88:6.

124. Nansenshō Somahito (text) and Utagawa Toyohiro (pictures), *Katakiuchi shigure no tomo* (Edo: Nishimuraya, 1802), 1 *omote*.

125. For another similar *kibyōshi* depiction of a boxed edition of *Kogetsushō*, also paired with a koto, see Hōseidō Kisanji (text) and Kitao Shigemasa (pictures), *Kisanjin ie no bakemono* (1787), 11 *omote*, reproduced in *Iwasaki Bunko kichōhon sōkan (kinseihen)*, ed. Tōyō Bunko and Nihon Koten Bungaku-kai, vol. 6, *Kusazōshi* (Tokyo: Kichōhon Kankō-kai, 1974), 265. Similar depictions of *Kogetsushō* are common in *kibyōshi*, and while it would be rash to generalize too much, they seem to play a very different role from, for instance, the dismissive reference to the edition a century earlier in "Tsutome no mi ōkami no kiriuri yori wa," the second story in book 7 of Ihara Saikaku's *Shoen ōkagami* (*Kōshokunidaiotoko*, 1684): when two customers disagree about whether a certain phrase appears in *Genji monogatari*, they ask a courtesan to lend them her copy so they can check, only to be sent *Kogetsushō*: "Looking at this book, one of the customers remarked: At any rate, the courtesans in these quarters have come down in the world, too—back in the old days, there wasn't a woman among them who didn't have a set of poetry books in the hand of some celebrated, aristocratic calligrapher" (*Shoen ōkagami* [Osaka: Ikedaya Saburōemon, 1684], book 7, 7 *ura*). For a typeset text, see [Ihara Saikaku,] *Kōshokunidaiotoko*, *Saikakushokokubanashi*, *Honchōnijūfukō*, ed. Fuji Akio et al., Shinpen Nihon bungaku taikei 76 (Tokyo: Iwanami Shoten, 1991).

126. Kawamoto Hitomi, "Kinsei zenki shōsetsu to *Genji monogatari*: *Fūryū Genji monogatari* o chūshin ni," in *Edo jidai no Genji monogatari*, ed. Emoto Hiroshi, Kōza Genji monogatari kenkyū 5 (Tokyo: Ōfū, 2007), 127–128.

127. Most of the works that Tanehiko includes in his list appear, for instance, in the catalog of the Daisō lending library. See Shibata Mitsuhiko, ed., *Daisō zōsho mokuroku to kenkyū: Kashihon'ya Ōnoya Sōbē kyūzō shomoku sakuinhen*, Nihon shoshigaku taikei 27, 2 (Musashimurayama, Tokyo: Seishōdō Shoten, 1983).

128. *NMIG*, chapter 10, 1 *omote*; SNKBT 88:320.

129. Satō Satoru, "Kōshō zuihitsu no imi suru mono," 119. Satō cites Mori Senzō, who cites Sakata Morotō's *Yobe no yūtsuyu*, in "Santō Kyōden itsuji," in *Mori Senzō chosakushū zokuhen* (Tokyo: Chūōkoronsha, 1992), 1:482–487.

130. Suzuki Jūzō, "Gōkanmono no daizai tenki to Tanehiko," 68. Uchimura points out that Tanehiko refers to the "vertical and horizontal" structure of *Genji monogatari* in *Ōshū shūjyaku monogatari*, suggesting that his own storytelling technique is based on this, in "*Nise Murasaki inaka Genji*ron," 20.

131. The character, Aboshi Tamontarō, discourses on the word *tatsu* in Saigyō's famous *shigi tatsu* poem: it should be interpreted, he insists, as meaning "to stand," rather than "to take flight," as is usual. See Ryūtei Tanehiko and Utagawa Toyokuni, *Ukiyogata rokumai byōbu*, part 1, fascicle 1, 5 *ura*.

132. As it happens, Tanehiko really did like his baths hot, as we learn from the "bathhouse incident" in which Tanehiko complained loudly that rustic boors steeping in his local bath had prevailed on the manager to lower the temperature and ended up being thrown into a cold tank of reserve water. See Markus, *Willow in Autumn*, 21-22.

133. *NMIG*, chapter 38, 1 *omote*; SNKBT 89:638.

2. Reading Higashiyama

1. *NMIG*, chapter 1, 4 *ura*; SNKBT 88:10. The first printing of the Edo edition, on which the SNKBT edition is based, leaves out the *yo* in *hana no gosho*; this error was corrected in the second printing, made from new blocks carved after the originals were destroyed in a fire.

2. Quoted in Satō Yukiko, *Edo no eiri shōsetsu: Gōkan no sekai* (Tokyo: Perikansha, 2001), 65.

3. *NMIG*, chapter 19, 13 *ura*; SNKBT 88:662.

4. *NMIG*, chapter 1, 5 *ura*; SNKBT 88:11. Not all of Tanehiko's *kakekotoba* are so unremarkable. In one case, he creates one in the middle of a minimally rewritten passage from *Genji monogatari*, turning "myōgō no ka nado nioi michitaru ni kimi no ōn'oikaze ito koto nareba" into "meikō no nioi mo atari ni Mitsuuji ga oikaze no ito koto nareba." For the sentence in *Genji monogatari*, see KGS, "Wakamurasaki," 12 *ura*; GMK 1:253; SNKBZ 20:211; SNKBT 19:161; and TG 1:88. For the sentence in *Inaka Genji*, see *NMIG*, chapter 6, 16 *ura*-17 *omote*; and SNKBT 88:202.

5. Andrew Lawrence Markus, *The Willow in Autumn: Ryūtei Tanehiko, 1783-1842* (Cambridge, Mass.: Council on East Asian Studies, Harvard University, 1992), 80. Markus provides a concise discussion of the connection between Kunisada and Tanehiko on 79-81. For a more extensive treatment of Kunisada's life and career, see Sebastian Izzard, "Kunisada the Artist," in *Kunisada's World*, ed. Sebastian Izzard (New York: Japan Society, in collaboration with the Ukiyo-e Society of America, 1993), 19-40.

6. Andreas Marks, "A Country Genji: Kunisada's Single-Sheet *Genji* Series," *Impressions* 27 (2005-2006): 60-61. For more on Genji prints and reproductions of numerous examples, see Andreas Marks, ed., *Genji's World in Japanese Woodblock Prints* (Leiden: Brill/Hotei, 2012).

7. The note appears on the temporary title page affixed to the inside of the temporary cover of the first fascicle.

8. Yoda Koji [Gakkai], "*Nise Murasaki inaka Genji* hyō," part 1, *Shuppan geppyō* 16 (1888): 446.

9. The two lithographs appear in Laurence Oliphant, *Narrative of the Earl of Elgin's Mission to China and Japan in the Years 1857, '58, and '59* (Edinburgh: Blackwood, 1859), 1:19; 2:180. The book was translated into French, Italian, Dutch, Polish, and Urdu and reprinted in at least the first two languages; I have seen only the first two of these translations, and the illustrations were not reproduced in either. The print in the second volume appears as a frontispiece in the 1860 American edition, published in New York by Harper & Brothers.

10. Jan Walsh Hokenson, *Japan, France, and East-West Aesthetics: French Literature, 1867–2000* (Madison, N.J.: Fairleigh Dickinson University Press, 2004), 421n.1. On the availability of Japanese prints and printed books in Europe in the nineteenth century, see Phylis Floyd, "Documentary Evidence for the Availability of Japanese Imagery in Europe in Nineteenth-Century Public Collections," *Art Bulletin* 68, no. 1 (1986): 105–141.

11. For a discussion of the value of Tanehiko's stipend and a persuasive assessment of differing opinions about how much he had to rely on his income, see Markus, *Willow in Autumn*, 22–27.

12. My discussion of "metapictures" draws on Mitchell's use of the term. For stimulating readings of a variety of metapictures—all quite different from those I consider, which offer representations of the materiality of pictures rather than of the process of representation itself—see W. J. T. Mitchell, *Picture Theory: Essays on Verbal and Visual Representation* (Chicago: University of Chicago Press, 1994), chapter 2.

13. *NMIG*, chapter 20, 13 *ura*; SNKBT 88:696.

14. *NMIG*, chapter 32, 7 *ura*–8 *omote*; SNKBT 89:422.

15. A second instance of a fake folded page appears in chapter 9 of *Inaka Genji*, but since in this case nothing is happening in the scene partially visible behind the folded page—all we see is a fragment of landscape—it does not achieve the sophistication of the example I have analyzed. See *NMIG*, chapter 9, 13 *ura*; and SNKBT 88:304. Suzuki Jūzō, who would likely have encountered earlier instances of this device, states that he has not, in SNKBT 88:304. The illustrated title page of the second fascicle of Tanehiko's *Keisei seisuiki* (1821) does something similar, making it appear as though a separate title page is peeking out from behind a folded-over table of contents—both written in a calligraphic style typical of *ukiyozōshi*. For an example of a later variation in which a spread is made to look as though a second book, folded back on itself, has been laid down over the first, see Santei Shunba (text) and Utagawa Kunisada II (pictures), *Akegarasu sumie no uchikake* (Edo: Kōeidō, 1867), chapter 3, 3 *ura*–4 *omote*. Part of this spread is incorporated into a rare multi-page *kuchi-e*—something about which I will have more to say later.

16. *NMIG*, chapter 15, fascicle 1, *mikaeshi*; SNKBT 88:500.

17. This inkstone was well known. It appears, for instance, in the section on Ishiyama Temple in Akisato Ritō (text) and Tosa Mitsusada et al. (pictures), *Tōkaidō meisho zue* (Edo: Kobayashi Shinbē, 1797), 2:6 *ura*. Katsushika Hokusai also produced a *surimono* featuring it, which can be seen in Joan B. Mirviss and John T. Carpenter, *The Frank Lloyd Wright Collection of Surimono* (New York: Weatherhill, 1995), 255.

18. *NMIG*, chapter 30, fascicle 1, *mikaeshi*; SNKBT 89:334.

19. *NMIG*, chapter 37, 4 *ura*–5 *omote*; SNKBT 89:605. Suzuki makes the same point about the design in his note to this picture.

20. The first depiction of a handscroll appears in *NMIG*, chapter 25, 18 *ura*–19 *omote*; SNKBT 89:173. For other examples, see *NMIG*, chapter 25, 20 *ura*; SNKBT 89:176; and *NMIG*, chapter 35, 14 *omote*; SNKBT 89:544.

21. *NMIG*, chapter 20, 11 *omote*; SNKBT 88:692.

22. *KGS*, "Akashi," 17 *omote*; *GMK* 1:652; SNKBZ 20:240; SNKBT 20:65. Suzuki cites this note in his explication of the picture, in SNKBT 88:693. The narrator's comment about the old man not knowing what a koto is comes directly from *Genji monogatari*, as do the old man's reference to the wind on the shore and his fear ("Keep me from harm, keep me from harm") of catching a cold. In the latter case, Tanehiko seems to be playing around, reading "kaze o hiku" (to catch a cold) into the phrase "hamakaze o hikiariku" (walking about, blown by the wind on the shore).

23. *NMIG*, chapter 20, 11 *ura*–12 *omote*; SNKBT 88:693.

24. *NMIG*, chapter 20, 15 *ura*–16 *omote*; SNKBT 88:699.

25. *NMIG*, chapter 19, 5 *ura*–6 *omote*; SNKBT 88:650.

26. *NMIG*, chapter 19, 6 *ura*; SNKBT 88:652.

27. *NMIG*, chapter 19, 6 *omote* and *ura*; SNKBT 88:651.

28. For the quotation from *Inaka Genji*, see *NMIG*, chapter 19, 6 *ura*; and SNKBT 88:652. For the quotation from *Genji monogatari*, see *KGS*, "Akashi," 6 *omote*; *GMK* 1:638; SNKBZ 21:227; SNKBT 20:55; and *TG* 1:258.

29. *NMIG*, chapter 19, 13 *omote* and *ura*; SNKBT 88:662.

30. *NMIG*, chapter 9, 1 *ura*–2 *omote*; SNKBT 88:285.

31. For an enlightening discussion of the *urokogata* (snake-scale) pattern, see Tsutsumi Kunihiko, "Jyarinkō: Rekishi, mindan, geinō no hazama nite," *Rijōōrai* 7 (2004): 1–25.

32. *NMIG*, chapter 9, 2 *ura*–3 *omote*; SNKBT 1:286.

33. Only one other three-panel *kuchi-e* appears in *Inaka Genji*, in chapter 19.

34. A similar example of an actor print, also by Kunisada, was published by Tsutaya Kichizō in conjunction with the 1851 performance at the Nakamura Theater of *Higashiyama sakura no sōshi*.

35. *NMIG*, chapter 9, 3 *omote*; SNKBT 88:286.

36. Jippensha Ikku (text and pictures), *Atariya shita jihon doiya*, 2 fascicles (Edo: Murataya, 1802), 9 *ura*–10 *omote*.

37. *NMIG*, chapter 1, 6 *ura*–7 *omote*; SNKBT 88:14.

38. *NMIG*, chapter 1, 7 *ura*–8 *omote*; SNKBT 88:15.

39. *NMIG*, chapter 1, 8 *ura*–9 *omote*; SNKBT 88:16.

40. Satō Satoru, "Nise Murasaki inaka Genji no sashie," in *Kokbungaku kaishaku to kanshō bessatsu: Edo bunka to sabukaruchā*, ed. Watanabe Kenji (Tokyo: Shibundō, 2005), 123–127.

41. *NMIG*, chapter 11, 2 *ura*–3 *omote*; SNKBT 88:358.

42. *NMIG*, chapter 11, 3 *ura*–4 *omote*; SNKBT 88:359.

43. *NMIG*, chapter 19, 6 *ura*–7 *omote*; SNKBT 88:652.

44. *NMIG*, chapter 19, 7 *ura*–8 *omote*; SNKBT 88:654.

45. *NMIG*, chapter 1, 12 *ura*–13 *omote*; SNKBT 88:662.

46. *NMIG*, chapter 8, 17 *ura*–18 *omote*; SNKBT 88:274.

47. For other examples, see *NMIG*, chapter 4, 12 *ura*–13 *omote* (this image is reproduced in figure 60); chapter 6, 1 *ura*–4 *omote*; and SNKBT 88:130, 181, 183. For a particularly good example of another variety of metapicture—the pictorial

representation of an illustrated screen—see *NMIG*, chapter 29, 6 *ura*–7 *omote*; and SNKBT 2:307.

48. *KGS*, "Hottan," 10 *ura*; *GMK* 1:15.

49. The names Tasogare and Shinonome are both taken from poems that Genji presents to Yūgao in the "Yūgao" chapter. Tasogare comes from Genji's first poem to Yūgao: "Yorite koso sore ka to mo mime tasokare ni honobono mitsuru hana no yūgao." Shinonome comes from a later poem: "Inishie mo kaku ya wa hito no madoi ken waga mada shiranu Shinonome no michi." Yūgao also cites the word *tasokare* in one of her poems to Genji. See *KGS*, "Yūgao," 7 *omote*, 22 *ura*, 24 *ura*; *GMK* 1:170, 192, 196; SNKBZ 20:141, 159, 162; SNKBT 19:104, 118, 120; and *TG* 1:58, 65, 66.

50. *NMIG*, chapter 5, 18 *omote* and *ura*; SNKBT 88:172.

51. *NMIG*, chapter 5, 16 *ura*–17 *omote*; SNKBT 88:169.

52. *NMIG*, chapter 5, 19 *omote*; SNKBT 88:173.

53. *NMIG*, chapter 2, 15 *ura*–18 *omote*; SNKBT 88:65–68.

54. *NMIG*, chapter 2, 16 *omote*; SNKBT 88:66. Suzuki suggests that *Shishira* was a mistake on the copyist's part for *Shirara*, and that *Ochikubo* in the Japanese refers to the *otogizōshi Ko'ochikubo*, rather than the classical tale *Ochikubo monogatari*. *Yashima*, *Takadachi*, and *Wada sakamori* are *kōwakamai*; *Amida no munewari* and *Jūnidan* are *kojōruri*. See SNKBT 88:711n.66.

55. In a typically inspired gesture, Tanehiko translates Fujitsubo's famous recollection of the previous meeting, which takes place in chapter 7, so that it refers back to the staged rendezvous in chapter 2. See *NMIG*, chapter 7, 12 *ura*–13 *omote*; SNKBT 88:230.

56. SNKBT 88:93.

57. Ibid., 106–107.

58. Ibid., 130.

59. Ibid., 134.

60. Ibid., 165.

61. Ibid., 142.

62. Ibid., 151.

63. Tasogare appears in a diptych by Kunisada for *Gosho moyō Genji no Edozome*, which was staged at the Ichimura Theater in the third month of 1838, though unfortunately the print suggests little about the play's plot. The diptych is in the collection of the Tsubouchi Memorial Museum at Waseda University.

64. For a text of this excerpt, see *Inaka Genji tsuyu no Shinonome*, in *Meisaku kabuki zenshū*, ed. Gunji Masakatsu, vol. 19 (Tokyo: Tōkyō Sōgensha, 1970).

65. Motoyama Tekishū, *Inaka Genji* (Tokyo: Genji Kai, 1921), 17.

3. Turning a New Page

1. Walter Benjamin, "The Task of the Translator," trans. Henry Zohn, in *Illuminations*, ed. Hannah Arendt (New York: Harcourt, Brace & World, 1968), 71.

2. Walter Benjamin, "The Task of the Translator," trans. James Hynd and E. M. Valk, *Delos* 2 (1968): 80, reprinted in *Translation—Theory and Practice: A*

Historical Reader, ed. Daniel Weissbort and Astradur Eysteinsson (Oxford: Oxford University Press, 2006).

3. Paul de Man, "Conclusions: Walter Benjamin's 'The Task of the Translator,'" in *The Resistance to Theory* (Minneapolis: University of Minnesota Press, 1986), 85.

4. Ryūtei Senka (text) and Utagawa Kunisada II (pictures), *Ashikagaginu tezome no murasaki* (Edo: Kinrindō, 1853), chapter 14, 1 *omote*.

5. Ryūtei Senka supports this reading of the different purples in a note accompanying *Ima Genji nishiki eawase*, a series of prints by Utagawa Kunisada published from 1852 to 1854. According to Senka's interpretation, Tanehiko took his inspiration for the title from the fact that "Musashino has long been famous for its purpleplant [*shisō*]. Even today, people prefer Edo purple [*Edo murasaki*] to Kyoto meadowsweet [*Kyōganoko*]." *Shisō* is variously known as *murasaki-sō, murasaki,* and *Edo murasaki*; *Kyōganoko* refers here to a plant whose name means "Kyoto fawn."

6. *NMIG*, chapter 18, 6 *ura*–7 *omote*; SNKBT 88:616. The pun on "fake purple" and "a bond for two lifetimes" is itself not particularly uncommon, appearing occasionally in *haikai* poetry and elsewhere.

7. Enchi Fumiko, *Uen no hitobito to: taidanshū* (Tokyo: Bungei Shunjū, 1986), 6.

8. Miyake Moritsune, "Sanjō no kyōsoku kankei shiryō," part 1, *Meiji Seitoku Kinen Gakkai kiyō*, n.s., 15 (1995): 91.

9. Okitsu Kaname, *Tenkanki no bungaku: Edo kara Tōkyō e* (Tokyo: Waseda Daigaku Shuppanbu, 1960), 25.

10. Kanagaki Robun (text) and Kawanabe Kyōsai (pictures), *Kyūrizukai* (Tokyo: Bankyūkaku, 1872), 1:1 *omote*. Tanikawa Keiichi has roughly dated Robun's authorship of *Kyūrizukai* from references to it in *Seiyōdōchū hizakurige* and *Aguranabe*, in "Kaidai," in Kanagaki Robun, *Kappa sōden kyūrizukai*, Ripurinto Nihon kindai bungaku 18 (Tokyo: Kokubungaku Kenkyū Shiryōkan, 2005), 95–96. Sasaki Tōru deals with the process of the work's composition in great detail in *Meiji gesaku no kenkyū: Kusazōshi o chūshin toshite* (Tokyo: Waseda Daigaku Shuppanbu, 2009), 17–29. Robun explains the title *Kyūrizukai* with reference to the *kappa*, a mythical creature that lives in rivers and eats cucumbers: "The act of adapting pragmatic and profitable and unmistakably true theories in a useless piece of frivolous fiction has no more value than a *kappa*'s fart: while it may make a lot of noise in the water, once it rises to the surface it turns to froth, and then it's as good as gone" (*Kyūrizukai*, 1 *omote*).

11. Sansantei Arindo (text) and Utagawa Kunisda II (pictures), *Yanagikage tsuki no Asazuma* (Tokyo: Koeidō, 1870), chapter 1, fascicle 1, 1 *omote*.

12. Sansantei Arindo and Tamenaga Shunsui II (text), and Utagawa Kunisada II and Utagawa Kunimasa IV (pictures), *Otamagaike kushi no tsukigata* (Tokyo: Kōeidō, 1878), chapter 3, fascicle 1, 1 *omote*.

13. Maeda Ai, "Meiji shoki gesaku shuppan no dōkō," in *Kindai dokusha no seiritsu* (Tokyo: Iwanami Shoten, 2001), 42. Maeda covers some of the same history I am outlining here, as does Okitsu Kaname—in much greater detail—in his afterword to *Meiji kaikaki bungakushū*, ed. Okitsu Kaname (Tokyo: Tukuma Shobō, 1966), 1:415–434.

14. Nakamura Masaaki, "Bakumatsu, Meiji ni okeru gōkan no tenkai to shuppan," *Nihon bungaku ronkyū* 65 (2006): 12.

15. Kubota Hikosaku (text), Kanagaki Robun (editor), and Yōshūsai Chikanobu (pictures), *Torioi Omatsu kaijō shinwa* (Tokyo: Kin'eidō, 1878), part 1, fascicle 1, 1 *omote*. "Three strings" is another name for the three-stringed instrument generally known as the samisen, which the "singing beggar" Omatsu plays as she walks from house to house asking for money.

16. Maeda, "Meiji shoki gesaku shuppan no dōkō," 48. Maeda's source for the *gōkan* sales figures is an essay by a bookseller: "Ishinrai no shōsetsu," *Waseda bungaku*, May 15, 1897. He seems to have calculated *Kanayomi shinbun*'s print run based on yearly figures provided in *Tōkyōfu tōkeihyō*, which is included in *Meiji nenkan fuken tōkeisho shūsei* (Tokyo: Yūshōdō Firumu Shuppan, 1964).

17. This date appears in the colophons of the first two volumes of the copy at the National Diet Library.

18. Kubota, Robun, and Chikanobu, *Torioi Omatsu kaijō shinwa*, part 2, fascicle 1, 6 *ura*–7 *omote*.

19. *Kanayomi shinbun*, January 11, 1878, in *Fukkoku kanayomi shinbun*, ed. Yamamoto Taketoshi and Tsuchiya Reiko (Tokyo: Akashi Shoten, 1992), 4:6.

20. Sasaki Tōru, "Seinan sensō to kusazōshi: *Torioi Omatsu kaijō shinwa* no shutsugen o megutte," *Kinsei bungei* 69 (1999): 61, 65. Takagi Gen has noted the bibliographic similarities between *gōkan* and a type of *chūhon* (middle-size) *yomihon* known as *kiritsukebon*, in "Makki no chūhon yomihon," in *Edo yomihon no kenkyū: Jūkyūseiki shōsetsu kō* (Tokyo: Perikansha, 1995). But the simultaneous publication of *gōkan* and *yomihon* versions of works dealing with the Satsuma Rebellion seems more likely to have been responsible for the shift in publication style that I have been discussing.

21. This description draws on Maeda, "Meiji shoki gesaku shuppan no dōkō," 49–50.

22. Dekoboko Koji, "Kigo gūgo: Chosho to kappan," *Tōkyō asahi shinbun*, August 12, 1903.

23. It was not unheard of to switch between woodblock and movable-type printing or to produce copies of the same book using both technologies: this happened, for instance, in the printing of Fukuzawa Yukichi's *Gakumon no susume* (1872–1876), some chapters of which were printed from only woodblocks, some with only movable type, and some from both woodblocks and movable type.

24. Sasaki Tōru, "Meiji no kusazōshi: Keihan kappan shōsetsu o chūshin ni," *Kinsei bungei* 66 (1997): 54–66. This essay and "Seinan sensō to kusazōshi" have been collected in Sasaki Tōru, *Meiji gesaku no kenkyū: Kusazōshi o chūshin toshite* (Tokyo: Waseda Daigaku Shuppanbu, 2009).

25. Maeda, "Meiji shoki gesaku shuppan no dōkō," 69.

26. Tayama Katai, *Chōhen shōsetsu no kenkyū* (Tokyo: Shinshidansha, 1925), 157.

27. Ryūtei Tanehiko (text) and Utagawa Kunisada (pictures), *Nise Murasaki inaka Genji*, ed. Sankyō Shoin Henshūbu, 4 vols. (Tokyo: Sankyō Shoin, 1935), preface, 1.

28. According to Yamamoto Kazuaki, so-called Western-style books (*yōsōbon*) began their rapid rise to prominence around 1882, the year in which bookstores first began to specialize in either Japanese- or Western-style books; by 1888 they had largely supplanted Japanese-style books. See Yamamoto Ka-

zuaki, "Kinsei gesaku no 'kindai,'" in *Kinsei to kindai no tsūrō: Jūkyū seiki Nihon no bungaku*, ed. Kōbe Daigaku Bungei Shisōshi Kenkyūkai (Kobe: Sōbunsha Shuppan, 2001), 179–180.

29. Ryūtei Tanehiko (text) and Utagawa Yoshiiku (pictures), *Nise Murasaki inaka Genji* (Yokohama: Moriya Kiyokichi, 1882–1883), pamphlet 1, *mikaeshi*.

30. Ibid., 6 *omote*.

31. Ryūtei Tanehiko (text) and Yamazaki Toshinobu (pictures), *Nise Murasaki inaka Genji* (Kyoto: Shinshindō, 1882), 1:main body, 14 *ura*; 2:main body, 14 *omote*.

32. Ryūtei Tanehiko and Utagawa Yoshiiku, *Nise Murasaki inaka Genji*, pamphlet 1, 1 *omote*; pamphlet 27, 1 *omote*.

33. Ryūtei Tanehiko and Yamazaki Toshinobu, *Nise Murasaki inaka Genji*, 1:main body, 1 *omote*.

34. Ibid., 1:preface, 1 *omote*.

35. The number of *kuchi-e* varies slightly from copy to copy; the most I have seen is forty.

36. *NMIG*, chapter 1, 1 *ura*; SNKBT 88:6.

37. Quoted in Satō Satoru, "Sashie kara mita kinseishōsetsu-shi," in *Iwanami kōza Nihon bungaku-shi*, vol. 10, *Jūkyūseiki no bungaku* (Tokyo: Iwanami Shoten, 1996), 200. On the censorship of *gōkan*, see Satō Satoru, "Gōkan no ken'etsu," *Edo bungaku* 16 (1996): 86–100.

38. Ryūtei Tanehiko (text) and Utagawa Kunisada (pictures), *Nise Murasaki inaka Genji* (Tokyo: Kibunkai, 1910), 1:unpaginated prefatory note.

39. Ibid., 2:480.

40. This is explained in a note from the editors of Kibunkai's magazine *Aoi* published as back matter in the second issue. See Kibunkai Hensanbu, "Kōgō heika no goaidokusho to Aoi Bunko no Inaka Genji," *Aoi* 2 (1910): back matter.

41. "Inaka Genji no hatsubai kinshi," *Tōkyō asahi shinbun*, July 7, 1910. For a note announcing the banning of the first volume, see "*Inaka Genji* hatsubai kinshi," *Tōkyō asahi shinbun*, March 8, 1910. Both notes give the reason as "corruption of public mores" (*fūzoku kairan*). For the advertisement, see [Jippensha Ikku,] *Tōkaidōchū hizakurige*, vol. 1 (Tokyo: Yoshikawa Kōbunkan, 1911). It is unclear whether more than one volume of this work was published.

42. My attention was drawn to the censors' particular concern with images of women adulterers by Jō Ichirō's discussion of Japanese translations of Boccaccio's *Decameron* in *Teihon hakkinbon: Shomotsu to sono shūhen* (Tokyo: Heibonsha, 2004), 173–178.

Touchstone 2. The Triangle

1. "*Genji monogatari*: Sennenki o mukaeta sekaibungaku no kessaku," *Yomiuri shinbun*, February 11, 2008.

2. Roman Jakobson, "On Linguistic Aspects of Translations," in *The Translation Studies Reader*, ed. Lawrence Venuti (London: Routledge, 2000), 114.

3. David Damrosch, *What Is World Literature?* (Princeton, N.J.: Princeton University Press, 2003), 281. In its original context, this definition is printed in italics.

4. Ibid. In their original context, these definitions are printed in italics.

5. Ibid., 4.

6. Ibid. (italics in the original).

7. Ibid., 281, 27. David Damrosch elaborates on his insight that "world literature is experienced differently in different places" (169) in "Comparative World Literature," in *The Canonical Debate Today: Crossing Disciplinary and Cultural Boundaries*, ed. Liviu Papadima, David Damrosch, and Theo D'haen (Amsterdam: Rodopi, 2011), 169–178.

8. Of course, the term "covert translation" implies that translations *should be* marked as translations, which historically has by no means been a universal assumption: Doris Jedamski notes, for instance, that in the Malay Archipelago translations and adaptations often were not marked as such until at least the late 1960s, and cites the "famous early example [of] Lie Kim Hok, who in 1886 combines *Les tribulations d'un Chinois en Chine* (1879) by Jules Verne with the Dutch youth novel *Klaasje Zevenster* by Van Lennep." In 1994, a scholar "discovered that Lie Kim Hok translated whole sections almost literally while omitting other parts completely. . . . Nowhere, however, did he mention the two source texts" ("Translation in the Malay World: Different Communities, Different Agendas," in *Asian Translation Traditions*, ed. Eva Hung and Judy Wakabayashi [Manchester: St. Jerome, 2005], 213–214). For a discussion of Igino Uno Tarchetti's covert translation into Italian of Mary Shelley's "The Mortal Immortal," identified only as "an imitation from the English," see Lawrence Venuti, *The Translator's Invisibility: A History of Translation* (New York: Routledge, 1995), 161–186. For a discussion of Rexroth's hoax, see Emily Apter, "Translation with No Original: Scandals of Textual Reproduction," in *The Translation Zone: A New Comparative Literature* (Princeton, N.J.: Princeton University Press, 2006), 210–225.

9. Norimitsu Onishi, "Thumbs Race as Japan's Best Sellers Go Cellular," *New York Times*, January 20, 2008.

10. Yuri Sachiko, "Keitai shōsetsu kokoro no jitsuyōsho," *Asahi shinbun*, February 16, 2008.

11. "Taikendan kara sōsakumono e, jūdai kara otona e, haba o hirogeru keitai shōsetsu. Dokusha no kyōkan o doko made erareru ka," *Mainichi shinbun*, May 15, 2008.

12. David Damrosch, "Where Is World Literature?," in *Studying Transcultural Literary History*, ed. Gunilla Lindberg-Wada (Berlin: de Gruyter, 2006), 214, and *What Is World Literature?*, 27–28.

13. Franco Moretti, "Conjectures on World Literature," *New Left Review*, January–February 2000, 54–68. Moretti does mention the semi-periphery parenthetically in this essay, but begins to consider its role in earnest only in "More Conjectures on World Literature," *New Left Review*, March–April 2003, 73–81. Pascale Casanova also uses the terms "autonomous" and "heteronomous" in *The World Republic of Letters*, trans. M. B. DeBevoise (Cambridge, Mass.: Harvard University Press, 2004); more recently she has written, "On consideration, however, perhaps the most important opposition is between combative literatures and pacified or non-engaged ones" ("Combative Literatures," trans. Nicholas Gray, *New Left Review*, November 2011, 133).

14. Moretti draws on world-system theory, as elaborated by Immanuel Wallerstein and others, in his analysis of the "world literary system." Casanova

outlines her objection to this term and her reasons for focusing on "spaces of cultural production" and "world literary space" in "Literature as a World," *New Left Review*, January–February 2005, 80–82. In *World Republic of Letters*, she uses the phrase "international literary space."

15. Moretti, "Conjectures on World Literature," 55–56; Casanova, *World Republic of Letters*, 103.

16. Casanova, *World Republic of Letters*, 46–48.

17. Franco Moretti, "World-Systems Analysis, Evolutionary Theory, *Weltliteratur*," in *Immanuel Wallerstein and the Problem of the World: System, Scale, Culture*, ed. David Palumbo-Liu, Bruce Robbins, and Nirvana Tanoukhi (Durham, N.C.: Duke University Press, 2011), 68.

18. Franco Moretti, "Evolution, World-Systems, *Weltliteratur*," in *Studying Transcultural Literary History*, ed. Lindberg-Wada, 120.

19. Ibid.

20. Casanova, "Literature as a World," 83.

21. Casanova cites Japan as one of the literary nations that were "most closed in upon themselves":

> Thus Japan, which was long absent from international literary space, drew upon a very powerful internal tradition, handed down from one generation to another, that was based on a set of models held not merely to be a necessary part of any writer's training, but actually objects of national piety. This cultural context, inaccessible to most foreign readers and extremely difficult to communicate abroad, inevitably favored a national conception of literature. (*World Republic of Letters*, 106–107)

This paragraph stands as a testament to the dangers of what Moretti calls "distant reading."

22. Moretti, "Conjectures on World Literature," 64, and "More Conjectures on World Literature," 79.

23. My argument dovetails nicely with one of the most stimulating, constructive critiques of Moretti's and Casanova's arguments that I have read: Pier Paolo Frassinelli and David Watson, "World Literature: A Receding Horizon," in *Traversing Transnationalism: The Horizons of Literary and Cultural Studies*, ed. Pier Paolo Frassinelli, Ronit Frenkel, and David Watson, Textxet: Studies in Comparative Literature 62 (Amsterdam: Rodopi, 2011), 191–208. Particularly noteworthy responses to Moretti, Casanova, or both include Efraín Kristal, " 'Considering Coldly . . .': A Response to Franco Moretti," *New Left Review*, May–June 2002, 61–74; Alexander Beercroft, "World Literature Without a Hyphen: Toward a Typology of Literary Systems," *New Left Review*, November–December 2002, 87–100; Francesca Orsini, "India in the Mirror of World Fiction," *New Left Review*, January–February 2002, 75–88; and Christopher Prendergast, "Negotiating World Literature," *New Left Review*, March–April 2001, 100–121. Prendergast's and Orsini's essays (the former in a somewhat altered form) and Moretti's "Conjectures on World Literature" were reprinted in *Debating World Literature*, ed. Christopher Prendergast (London: Verso, 2004), 1–25, 319–334, 148–162. It would be interesting to use a statistical analysis of the sort Moretti has pioneered to explore possible relationships between the marginality (from the perspective of

western Europe or the United States) of scholars' areas of specialization—Latin America, South Africa, India, Japan—and their perspectives on world literature. In her essay, Orsini cites Lydia Liu's proposal that we think in terms of "guest" and "host" languages rather than "source" and "target" languages ("India in the Mirror of World Fiction," 81–82; see Lydia Liu, *Translingual Practice: Literature, National Culture, and Translated Modernity—China, 1900–1937* [Stanford, Calif.: Stanford University Press, 1995], 27); Moretti counters, "The culture industry as a 'guest' invited by a 'host' who 'appropriates' its forms. . . . Are these concepts— or daydreams?" ("More Conjectures on World Literature," 80n.15). How one answers Moretti's question will depend to some degree, I suspect, on how little one has to rely on distant reading to imagine "peripheral" perspectives.

4. The History of a Romance

1. Raymond Mortimer, "A New Planet," *Nation & Athenæum: Literary Supplement,* June 20, 1925, 371. Mortimer's musings on "the twelve finest novels that the genius of man has so far produced" were undoubtedly prompted by Waley's preface to the first volume of *The Tale of Genji,* which concluded with the observation, "I have all the time been spurred by the belief that I am translating by far the greatest novel of the East, and one which, even if compared with the fiction of Europe, takes its place as one of the dozen greatest masterpieces of the world" (Lady Murasaki, *The Tale of Genji, by Lady Murasaki,* trans. Arthur Waley [Boston: Houghton Mifflin, 1925], 8). On reviews of Waley's *The Tale of Genji,* see John Walter de Gruchy, *Orienting Arthur Waley: Japonism, Orientalism, and the Creation of Japanese Literature in English* (Honolulu: University of Hawai'i Press, 2003), 125–132.

2. Murasaki Shikibu, *The Sacred Tree: Being the Second Part of The Tale of Genji by Lady Murasaki,* trans. Arthur Waley (Boston: Houghton Mifflin, 1926), 30–31. Waley prefaces his remarks by noting, "One reviewer did indeed analyse the nature of Murasaki's achievement to the extent of classifying her as 'psychological' and in this respect he even went so far as to class her with Marcel Proust"; although Waley does not name him, the "one reviewer" is clearly Mortimer—to whom, incidentally, Waley would dedicate the third volume of his translation. Ruth Jane Mack, "A Dream from an Eleventh-Century Japanese Novel," *International Journal of Psycho-Analysis* 8 (1927): 402–403 (italics added). Mack takes up the passage in the "Aoi" (Heart-to-Heart) chapter in which Lady Rokujo "had the same dream several times": finding herself "in a large magnificent room, where lay a girl whom she knew to be the Princess Aoi," "she had dragged and mauled the prostrate figure, with an outburst of brutal fury such as in her waking life would have been utterly foreign to her" (Murasaki Shikibu, *Tale of Genji,* trans. Waley, 266).

3. George Sansom, *A History of Japan to 1334,* Stanford Studies in the Civilizations of East Asia 1 (Stanford, Calif.: Stanford University Press, 1958), 178; Ivan Morris, *The World of the Shining Prince: Court Life in Ancient Japan* (New York: Knopf, 1964).

4. Kawazoe Fusae, "'Nemureru mori no bijo' no shihanseiki: Sekai de Genji wa dō yomarete kita ka," *Yurīka* 34, no. 2 (2002): 185.

5. Donald Keene, *Chronicles of My Life: An American in the Heart of Japan* (New York: Columbia University Press, 2008), 24–25.

6. Murasaki Shikibu, *The Tale of Genji*, trans. Edward G. Seidensticker (New York: Knopf, 1976), 1:xiv. Seidensticker notes in his memoir that he was not one of those people who was drawn into Japanese literary studies by "a copy of *The Tale of Genji* come upon for almost nothing in a used-book store," but there is no doubt that the work played an important role in his wartime experience of Japan: "During the war I had read Arthur Waley's translation of *The Tale of Genji*, the eleventh-century work which is often called, I think with justice, the first great novel in the literature of the world. I thought it a wonderful thing" (*Tokyo Central: A Memoir* [Seattle: University of Washington Press, 2002], 17, 36).

7. The process was, of course, not only gradual but uneven: in 1937, Herbert E. Fowler could complain that "one misses . . . a sampling of Lady Murasaki's *Tale of Genji*" (review of *World-Literature*, by Ethan Allen Cross, *English Journal* 26, no. 7 [1937]: 593); by 1955, an advertisement run by Brentano's in the October 2 issue of the *New York Times* featuring "64 Books of Distinction at Prices Everyone Can Afford" described *The Tale of Genji* tersely, without beating around the bush: "The Tale of Genji by Lady Murasaki, translated by Arthur Waley. One of the masterpieces of the world. 95¢"; and yet the MLA included the tale in its series Approaches to World Literature, making it the very first Asian work to be admitted, in only 1993, when it published Edward Kamens, ed., *Approaches to Teaching Murasaki Shikibu's The Tale of Genji* (New York: Modern Language Association, 1993).

8. Louis Moore, "Escapades of a Don Juan of Old Japan," *Literary Digest International Book Review* 3, no. 11 (1925): 707.

9. D. E. Mills, review of *The Tale of Genji*, by Murasaki Shikibu, trans. Edward G. Seidensticker, *Modern Asian Studies* 12, no. 4 (1978): 679; Marian Ury, "The Imaginary Kingdom and the Translator's Art: Notes on Re-reading Waley's *Genji*," *Journal of Japanese Studies* 2, no. 2 (1976): 270, 267. Ury's essay, written with her inimitable verve, is well worth reading. Horiguchi Masao goes even further than Ury regarding possible debts to Suematsu, suggesting that both Waley and Seidensticker drew on his translation, though the evidence he adduces seems inconclusive at best. See Horiguchi Masao, "Futatsu no eiyaku *Genji monogatari* jō," *Gekkan kotoba* 3, no. 11 (1979): 16. Midorikawa Machiko, an authority on Waley's translation and on English translations of *Genji monogatari* in general, also suggests that Waley probably consulted Suematsu's translation, in *Genji monogatari eiyaku ni tsuite no kenkyū* (Tokyo: Musashino Shoin, 2010), 49.

10. Seidensticker gives the year as 1894. See E. G. Seidensticker and Anzai Tetsuo, *Nihonbun no hon'yaku* (Tokyo: Taishūkan Shoten, 1983), 223. My attention was drawn to Seidensticker's error by Kawakatsu Mari, "Suematsu Kenchō *Genji monogatari* jobun no shōkai: nihongoyaku oyobi kaisetsu, kaidai," *Rikkyō Daigaku Daigakuin Nihon bungaku ronsō* 5 (2005): 140. For Terence Barrow's mistake, see "Introduction to the New Edition," in Murasaki Shikibu, *The Tale of Genji*, trans. Suematsu Kenchō (Rutland, Vt.: Tuttle, 1974), 9.

11. Donald Keene, "In Your Distant Street Few Drums Were Heard," in *Madly Singing in the Mountains: An Appreciation and Anthology of Arthur Waley*, ed. Ivan Morris (New York: Walker, 1970), 56, and "Japanese Literature in the

World," *Southern Humanities Review* 27, no. 4 (1993): 314. In an essay published in Japanese, Keene has this to say about Suematsu and his translation:

> Suematsu deserves our respect as a pioneer. His translation is quite accurate and there are moments when it even comes close to capturing the quality of the original, but unfortunately his English prose is ponderous and contains too much unnaturally poetic diction, so that at times it annoys its readers, or makes them laugh. At the time it was published, Lafcadio Hearn's *Glimpses of Unfamiliar Japan* and Mitford's *Tales of Old Japan* were being widely read, so one would have expected people to enjoy *Genji* as well, but because his prose was less than fluent very few people seem to have taken any interest in it. ("Seiōjin no *Genji monogatari* no kanshō," *Bungaku* 22, no. 2 [1954]: 1)

12. Ida M. Mellen, "The Tale of Genji," *Literary Digest International Book Review* 3, no. 12 (1925): 828.

13. Georges Bousquet, "Un voyage dans l'intérieur du Japon," *Revue des deux mondes*, January–February 1874, 297, reprinted in Georges Bousquet, *Le Japon de nos jours et les échelles de l'extrême Orient*, 2 vols. (Paris: Hachette, 1877), 1:185. For a discussion of the emergence of Ishiyama Temple as a tourist destination for non-Japanese and the role that Suematsu's translation may have played in this process, see Kawakatsu Mari, "Meijiki ni okeru gaikokujin no Ishiyama-dera kankō—Suematsu Kenchō no sekaihatsu Eiyaku *Genji monogatari* juyō no shiza kara—," *Rikkyō Daigaku Nihon bungaku* 95 (2005): 10–23.

14. Bousquet, *Le Japon de nos jours*, 1:356–357. For the earlier version of the essay, see Georges Bousquet, "Le théatre au Japon, drame et comédie," *Revue des deux mondes*, July–August 1874, 721–760.

15. Ryūtei Senka (text) and Utagawa Kunisada II (pictures), *Ashikagaginu tezome no murasaki* (Edo: Kinrindō, 1853), chapter 14, 1 omote.

16. Georges Bousquet, "Le Japon littéraire," *Revue des deux mondes*, September–October 1878, 755.

17. Ibid., 757.

18. Faith E. Beasely, "Altering the Fabric of History: Women's Participation in the Classical Age," in *A History of Women's Writing in France*, ed. Sonya Stephens (Cambridge: Cambridge University Press, 2000), 71–72.

19. My account of this work's bibliographical composition is based on Madeleine de Scudéry, *Artamène; ou, Le Grand Cyrus* (Paris: Augustin Courbé, 1656).

20. Marquis de la Mazelière, "Vues sur l'histoire du Japon," *La revue de Paris*, March–April 1899, 133. Shortly before de la Mazelière compares *Genji* with the works of Scudéry, he offers this odd and wonderful comment on Japanese writing: "Japanese prose possesses the precision and simplicity that Nietzsche thought possible only in that of the Greek and French languages."

21. Basil Hall Chamberlain, *Things Japanese* (London: Kegan Paul, Trench, Trübner, 1890), 215. It is interesting to note that Chamberlain does not include Suematsu's translation in his list of recommended readings in this edition of *Things Japanese*, but does in the second, published in 1891.

22. Basil Hall Chamberlain expresses his opinion of women and their writing less obliquely in an essay read to the Asiatic Society of Japan on March 18,

1885: "Most of the Classical Prose is 'feminine' prose in the most disparaging sense that can be given to that term" ("On the Various Styles Used in Japanese Literature," in *Transactions of the Asiatic Society of Japan* [Yokohama: Meiklejohn, 1885], 8:97).

23. W. G. Aston, "The Classical Literature of Japan," in *Transactions and Proceedings of the Japan Society, London* (London: Kegan Paul, Trench, Trübner, 1899), 4, part 4:281.

24. W. G. Aston, *A History of Japanese Literature* (New York: Appleton, 1899), 96–97.

25. Peter F. Kornicki, "William George Aston (1841–1911)," in *Britain and Japan, 1859–1991: Themes and Personalities*, ed. Sir Hugh Cortazzi and Gordon Daniels (London: Routledge, 1991), 71.

26. W. G. Aston, *Nihon bungakushi*, trans. Shibano Rokusuke (Tokyo: Dainippon Tosho Kabushiki-gaisha, 1908), 197, and *Littérature japonaise*, trans. Henry-D. Davray (Paris: Armand Colin, 1902), 93.

27. Basil Hall Chamberlain, *Things Japanese*, 4th ed. (London: Murray, 1902), 293. The note remains in the fifth and sixth editions, though in the sixth Chamberlain adds a paragraph at the end: "Arthur Waley's beautiful English version in six volumes will henceforth enable the cultivated European reader to form his own opinion on the matter,—so far, that is, as any literary opinion can be founded on a translation." He goes on to say that "of late years we have come to doubt whether we thoroughly understood the exceptionally difficult text" (*Things Japanese*, 6th ed. [London: Kegan Paul, Trench Trübner; Kobe: Thompson, 1939], 319–320).

28. Otto Hauser, *Die japanische Dichtung* (Berlin: Bard, Marquardt, 1904), 44. The phrase *cette ennuyeuse Scudéry Japonaise* is in roman type in the original.

29. Ernest Satow, "Japan, Language and Literature of," in *American Cyclopædia*, ed. George Ripley and Charles A. Dana (New York: Appleton, 1874), 9:557. Satow prepared the part of the entry that deals with literature; J. C. Hepburn wrote about the Japanese language. Aston delivered his first lecture on Japanese literature the following year, at a meeting of the Asiatic Society of Japan held on June 30, 1875. For a transcript, see W. G. Aston, "An Ancient Japanese Classic (The 'Tosa Nikki,' or Tosa Diary)," in *Transactions of the Asiatic Society of Japan*, reprint of the 1st ed. (Yokohama: Meiklejohn, 1884), 3, part 2:109–117.

30. For the two writers' respective periodizations, see Satow, "Japan, Language and Literature of," 564; and Bousquet, "Le Japon littéraire," 748–749.

31. Satow, "Japan, Language and Literature of," 559.

32. *The Diaries and Letters of Sir Ernest Mason Satow (1843–1929): A Scholar-Diplomat in East Asia*, ed. Ian C. Ruxton (Lewiston, N.Y.: Mellen, 1998), 139. On Satow's book-collecting activities, see Peter F. Kornicki, "Ernest Mason Satow (1843–1929)," in *Britain and Japan, 1859–1991*, ed. Cortazzi and Daniels, 80–81. Aston thanks Satow for the use of his library at the end of his preface to *A History of Japanese Literature*.

33. Aston, "Classical Literature of Japan," 286.

34. Gustave Lavieuville, *Essai de psychologie japonaise: La race des dieux* (Paris: Augustin Challamel, 1908), 51–52.

35. Michel Revon, *Anthologie de la littérature japonaise des origines au XXe siècle*, 5th ed. (Paris: Delagrave, 1923), 177. The reference to Aston is, of course,

to *A History of Japanese Literature*; Florenz refers to Karl Florenz, *Geschichte der japanischen Litteratur* (Leipzig: Amelang, 1906).

36. Raymond M. Weaver, "The Miscellany of a Japanese Priest," *Bookman* (New York), January 1919, 590.

37. Oswald White, "A Classic of Feudal Japan," *Living Age*, January 7, 1922, 49.

38. Frank Hawley, "Ōbeijin no kenkyū shitaru Nihon bungaku," *Bungei* 1, no. 2 (1933): 16-17.

39. Bruce Lancaster, "Nihongo—The Japanese Language," *Atlantic Monthly*, May 1944, 104.

40. "Genji Monogatari," in *Dizionario letterario Bompiani delle opere e dei personaggi di tutti i tempi e di tutte le letterature* (Milan: Bompiani, 1947-1950), 3:568.

41. "Genji Monogatari," in *Dictionnaire des œuvres de tous les temps et de tous les pays* (Paris: Société d'Édition de Dictionnaires et Encyclopédies, 1955), 2:444.

42. Keene, "Seiōjin no *Genji monogatari* no kanshō," 1-5.

43. "Genji Monogatari," in *Kindlers Literatur Lexikon*, ed. Gert Woerner (Zurich: Kindler, 1965-1972), 3:603.

44. Edward Seidensticker, "Las libertades de Arthur Waley," trans. Montserrat Millán, *Quimera* 19 (1982): 36, and "On Being Faithful to Murasaki Shikibu," in *This Country Japan* (Tokyo: Kodansha, 1979).

45. Christine Brooke-Rose, *Textermination* (New York: New Directions, 1992), 67-68.

46. La Commission Impériale Japonaise, ed., *Le Japon à l'Exposition universelle de 1878* (Paris: Commission Impériale du Japon, 1878), 65.

47. Sir Edward J. Reed, *Japan: Its History, Traditions, and Religions with the Narrative of a Visit in 1879* (London: Murray, 1880), 2:33. Much of the text in this section is translated directly and without specific acknowledgment from *Le Japon à l'Exposition universelle de 1878*. Reed states in his preface to volume 1, "It is obvious that the historical portions of this work must be mainly the results of compilation" and mentions in particular that he has "made free use of the works composed by officers of the imperial Japanese government for presentation at the various foreign exhibitions of Japanese arts and manufactures" (v). He has hardly, however, "been scrupulously careful to cite his authorities, and to give exact quotations where that could be done" (v). Ironically, the title page of the work specifies, "The Right of Translation is reserved." For the same passage in the Japanese reprint of the essay on lacquer, see La Commission Impériale Japonaise, ed., *Les laques et la céramique du Japon* (Yokohama: Commission Impériale Japonaise, 1879), 4. The same section was also reprinted as "Les laques du Japon" and signed by "Maëda, Commissaire général du Japon à l'Exposition universelle de Paris," in *La revue scientifique de la France et de l'étranger* 2, no. 50 (1878): 1173-1178.

48. "Odds and Ends," *Routledge's Every Girl's Annual* 27 (1880?): 240.

49. *Le Japon artistique et littéraire* (Paris: Alphonse Lemerre, 1879), 6.

50. Edmond de Goncourt, *La maison d'un artiste* (Paris: Charpentier, 1881), 2:310.

51. Wenceslau de Moraes, *Dai-Nippon: O grande Japão* (Lisbon: Imprensa Nacional, 1897), 100.

52. Edward Gilbertson points out explicitly in a chapter on "Lacquer" how unreliable *Le Japon à l'Exposition universelle de 1878* is, noting in particular, "The author . . . makes the authoress, Murasaki Shikibu, live about 500 years before her real date" (Burlington Fine Arts Club, *Catalogue of Specimens of Japanese Lacquer and Metal Work Exhibited in 1894* [London: Burlington Fine Arts Club, 1894], xxxviii–xxxix).

53. Murasaki Shikibu, Marcus B. Huish observes, "receives frequent notice at the hands of the artists, as she sits in the moonlight in the temple of Ishi-yama-dera overlooking Lake Biwa, and composes the great romance of the Genji Monogatari" (*Japan and Its Art* [London: Fine Art Society, 1889], 100).

54. Mrs. Hugh Fraser, *Letters from Japan: A Record of Modern Life in the Island Empire* (New York: Macmillan, 1899), 1:300.

55. William Elliot Griffis, *The Mikado's Empire* (New York: Harper, 1877), 210–211.

56. C. A. White, *Classic Literature: Principally Sanskrit, Greek, and Roman with some account of the Persian, Chinese, and Japanese in the form of Sketches of the Authors and Specimens from Translations of their Works* (New York: Holt, 1878), 423.

57. Mary Reed, "A Chat About Japanese Costume," in *The Woman's World*, ed. Oscar Wilde, facsimile of the 1889 edition (New York: Source Book Press, 1970), 2:560.

58. Edward Greey, *The Wonderful City of Tokio; or, Further Adventures of the Jewett Family and Their Friend Oto Nambo* (Boston: Lee and Shepard, 1883), 77–79. A similar scene involving the children's failure to recognize "a large painting, which represented a lady washing a book in a curiously shaped tub that had two pairs of handles" appears in *Young Americans in Japan; or, The Adventures of the Jewett Family and Their Friend Oto Nambo* (Boston: Lee and Shepard, 1882). Fitz asks his host, the poet Katayama Denshichi, "Is that—a picture of—your—amiable lady, sir?" only to be told that it is not: "[I]t represents the famous poetess, Onono Komachi (Miss Small-city of the Small-field)" (308).

59. For an account of Takahashi's colorful life during this period and beyond, see Richard J. Smethurst, *From Foot Soldier to Finance Minister: Takahashi Korekiyo, Japan's Keynes* (Cambridge, Mass.: Harvard University Asia Center, 2007).

60. With 7,430 subscribers in 1874, *Tōkyō nichinichi shinbun* was one of only two "big newspapers" with more than 3,000 subscribers. See James L. Huffman, *Creating a Public: People and Press in Meiji Japan* (Honolulu: University of Hawai'i Press, 1997), 64. My account of Suematsu's early life draws on the first chapter of Tamae Hikotarō, *Seihyō Suematsu Kenchō no shōgai* (Fukuoka: Ashi Shobō, 1985), which incorporates extended quotations from Takahashi Korekiyo's autobiography, *Takahashi Korekiyo jiden* (Tokyo: Chikura Shobō, 1936).

61. Huffman, *Creating a Public*, 52, 72.

62. Suematsu is described, presumably by himself, as an "attaché to the Japanese legation in London" on the title page of *GM*. For an excellent account of Suematsu's time in Britain, see Margaret Mehl, "Suematsu Kenchō in Britain, 1878–1886," *Japan Forum* 5, no. 2 (1993): 173–193.

63. Mehl, "Suematsu Kenchō in Britain," 174.

64. The date and time of Suematsu's departure is given in Tamae Hikotarō, "Suematsu Kenchō zaiei tsūshin," *Nihon rekishi* 517 (1991): 75. For the text of the additional assignment, see Tamae, *Seihyō Suematsu Kenchō no shōgai*, 57.

65. *GM*, xvi. The significance of Suematsu's juxtaposition of Heian-period Japan and Europe is noted, for instance, in Kawakatsu Mari, "Suematsu Kenchō *Genji Monogatari* kankō no ji ni miru shuppan jijō: Igirisu ni taisuru bunka imeeji sōsaku to Tokugawa Akitake," *Nihon kindai bungaku* 73 (2005): 7, and *Meiji kara Shōwa ni okeru Genji monogatari no juyō* (Osaka: Izumi Shoin, 2008), 44–45; Gruchy, *Orienting Arthur Waley*, 121; Gaye Rowley, "Kokka aidentitī to kanon keisei: Meijiki ni okeru *Genji monogatari* no yakuwari," *Nihon kindai bungaku* 71 (2004): 231; Tomi Suzuki, "*The Tale of Genji*, National Literature, Language, and Modernism," in *Envisioning The Tale of Genji: Media, Gender, and Cultural Production*, ed. Haruo Shirane (New York: Columbia University Press, 2008), 244–245; and Rebekah Clements, "Suematsu Kenchō and the First English Translation of *Genji monogatari*: Translation, Tactics, and the 'Women's Question,'" *Japan Forum* 23, no. 1 (2011): 29–30.

66. Michael R. Auslin, *Negotiating with Imperialism: The Unequal Treaties and the Culture of Japanese Diplomacy* (Cambridge, Mass.: Harvard University Press, 2004), 198–199.

67. *GM*, xv–xvi.

68. Ibid., xv.

69. Ibid.

70. Ibid., xii–xiii.

71. *KGS*, "Hotaru," 16 *omote*; *GMK* 2:426–427; *SNKBZ* 33:210–211; *SNKBT* 20:438; *TG* 1:461.

72. For insightful discussions of this scene in the "Hotaru" chapter that do highlight the erotic context, see H. Richard Okada, *Figures of Resistance: Language, Poetry, and Narrating in The Tale of Genji and Other Mid-Heian Texts* (Durham, N.C.: Duke University Press, 1991), 219–229; and Edwin A. Cranston, "Murasaki's 'Art of Fiction,'" *Japan Quarterly* 18, no. 2 (1971): 207–213. For a discussion of medieval interpretations of the passage, see Thomas Harper, "Medieval Interpretations of Murasaki Shikibu's 'Defense of the Art of Fiction,'" in *Studies on Japanese Culture*, ed. Saburo Ota and Rikutaro Fukuda (Tokyo: Japan PEN Club, 1973), 1:56–61.

73. For a discussion of the concepts of "realism" and "idealism" as they were taken up by British critics, see Sharon Marcus, "Comparative Sapphism," in *The Literary Channel: The Inter-National Invention of the Novel*, ed. Margaret Cohen and Carolyn Dever (Princeton, N.J.: Princeton University Press, 2002), 251–285.

74. *KGS*, "Hotaru," 17 *omote* and *ura*; *GMK* 2:428–429; *SNKBZ* 22:212; *SNKBT* 20:439; *TG* 1:461.

75. "As Arthur is the centre of British romance and Charlemagne of French romance, so Diderick is the central figure of the German minnesingers" (E. Cobham Brewer, *The Reader's Handbook of Allusions, References, Plots, and Stories*, 3rd ed., corrected and enlarged [London: Chatto and Windus, 1882], 252).

76. An advertisement in *Publishers' Weekly* for the children's magazine *St. Nicholas* indicates why Suematsu would not have wanted *Genji* to be associated with the "sensational romance," which existed as a genre in its own right in this period: "Boy Lost!—What a thrilling cry is this?" the main body of the ad begins,

How it vibrates along the heart-strings of every parent, and thrills through a whole city! And yet it is of hourly occurrence. A hundred thousand boys, in homes of culture and refinement, are every year *lost* by reason of the poison of bad books, and bad sensational romances. Almost every week a boy is found at some railway station with a revolver in one pocket and a sensational story paper in the other, having run away from home to lead a life of adventure. ("The St. Nicholas Library" [advertisement], *Publishers' Weekly*, Christmas number, 1875, 821)

77. Anna Buckland, *The Story of English Literature* (London: Cassell, Petter, Galpin, 1882), 20.

78. The adjective *michimichishi*, which is evidently being used here to characterize the *monogatari*, is used by Tō Shikibu no Jō (the "Fujiwara Aide of Ceremonial" in Royall Tyler's translation) in the "Hahakigi" (The Broom Tree) chapter when he relates the tale of his well-educated, garlic-eating former lover: in that context, however, it is to the more difficult passages of the canonical Chinese texts that the word refers. See *KGS*, "Hahakigi," 29 *omote*; *GMK* 1:111; SNKBZ 20:86; SNKBT 19:57; and *TG* 1:33. Tyler translates the phrase *michimichishiku kuwashiki koto* subtly and brilliantly as "truly rewarding particulars" (*TG* 1:461); Seidensticker makes due with "the details" (Murasaki Shikibu, *Tale of Genji*, trans. Seidensticker, 1:437); Waley gives "the most minute information about all sorts of people's private affairs" (Murasaki Shibiku, *A Wreath of Cloud: Being the Third Part of The Tale of Genji by Lady Murasaki*, trans. Arthur Waley [London: George Allen & Unwin, 1927], 255).

79. *GM*, xiv.

80. For an account by Suematsu of his historiographical studies in England, based on a notebook he kept at the time, see Suematsu Kenchō, "Rekishi kenkyūhō ni tsukite," parts 1 and 2, *Shigaku zasshi* 17, no. 8 (1906): 1–19; no. 9 (1906): 31–48. Discussions of local "stories" and the care with which they must be used appear throughout Suematsu's privately printed treatise on Genghis Khan, *The Identity of the Great Conqueror Genghis Khan with the Japanese Hero Yoshitsuné: An Historical Thesis* (London: Collingridge, 1879).

81. *GM*, ix.

82. Ibid., xi–xii.

83. Ibid., xii. For an insightful discussion of Suematsu's depiction of women in *Genji monogatari*, see Rebekah Clements, "Suematsu Kenchō-yaku *Genji monogatari* ni okeru 'josei,'" *Heianchō bungaku kenkyū* 16 (2008): 70–60. Clements offers a much needed correction to Mari's "Suematsu Kenchō *Genji monogatari* jobun no shōkai," which presents an argument about the same issue based on misunderstandings of Suematsu's preface.

84. For the description of Trübner & Company as "the literary intermediary between Europe and the East," see William Heinemann, "Nicholas Trübner," *Bibliographer* 5, no. 6 (1884): 173. On the importance of the "Oriental Series," see A. H. Sayce, "In Memorium: Nicholas Trübner," *Trübner's American, European, and Oriental Literary Record*, n.s., 5, nos. 3–4 (1884): 33–35. A large selection of obituaries from Europe and the United States, including the one from the *Bibliographer*, are reprinted in this issue.

85. Untitled notice of *Genji Monogatari*, by Suyematz Kenchio, *Literary World* (Boston, Mass.), November 19, 1881, 424.

86. "Genji Monogatari: The Most Celebrated of the Classical Japanese Romances," *Trübner & Co.'s Monthly List*, February 1882, 13. The advertisement ran in almost exactly the same form in the March and April issues, and then again in May, this time with quotes from reviews in the *Scotsman*, the *Academy*, and the *London and China Telegraph*. The only discrepancy between the texts of the ads themselves is that the February printing describes the book as "Vol. 1," while the later printings do not. In his dedication, which is signed "Nov. 1881," Suematsu refers to the volume as "the first installment of my translation." The rapid disappearance of the "Vol. 1" from the ad seems to suggest that Trübner, taking Suematsu at his word, planned to continue with the project and that it was Suematsu himself who decided to abandon it.

87. Clements, "Suematsu Kenchō and the First English Translation of *Genji monogatari*," 41-42. Evidently, Trübner's records cover only as far as 1892.

88. The three reprints are, or are found in, [Murasaki Shikibu,] *Genji Monogatari: The Most Celebrated of the Classical Japanese Romances*, trans. Suyematz Kenchio (Yokohama: Maruya, 1894); Epiphanius Wilson, ed., *Japanese Literature* (London: Colonial Press, 1900); and [Murasaki Shikibu,] *Genji Monogatari*, vol. 1, *Kiri-Tsubo, Hahaki-Gi, Woots-Semi*, trans. Kenchio Suyematz (Tokyo: San Kaku Sha, 1934). In more recent times, as we have seen, Tuttle has reissued the translation. For the German version, see Murasaki Shikibu, *Die Abenteuer des Prinzen Genji*, trans. from Suematsu Kenchō's English translation by Maximilian Müller-Jabusch (Munich: Langen, ca. 1912). I have relied for the date of this undated work on Oskar Nachod, *Bibliographie von Japan, 1906-1926 [-1937]* (Stuttgart: Hiersemann, 1970). Mitani Kuniaki mentions a Dutch retranslation of Suematsu's English in "Meiji-ki no *Genji monogatari* kenkyū," *Kokubungaku: Kaishaku to kanshō* 48, no. 10 (1983): 53. I have been unable to find any evidence that this book ever existed and suspect that he was referring to a brief essay in an art magazine by M. W. de Visser, "De *Genji Monogatari*," *Oude Kunst*, January 15, 1918, 106-111.

89. Roger Riordan and Tozo Takayanagi, *Sunrise Stories* (New York: Scribner, 1896).

90. Arvède Barine, "La haute société japonaise au Xe siècle: Un don Juan japonais," *Revue politique et littéraire de la France et de l'étranger*, April 7, 1883, 460-465, and "Un don Juan japonais," in *Essais et fantasies* (Paris: Hachette, 1888), 243-277.

91. Henry N. Shore, "Remarks on the Character and Social Industries of the Inhabitants of China and Japan," *Journal of the Society of Arts* 30 (1882): 631.

92. A notice in the April 16, 1898, issue of the *Dial* states that one Thomas Whittaker was selling the "Second edition, revised" of Suematsu's *Genji Monogatari*, which is the Maruya edition. See "List of New Books," *Dial*, April 16, 1898, 270. The *New York Times* reviewed this edition on April 16, 1898–the paper's first review of *Genji*, since the first edition had received only a publication notice in its April 8, 1882, issue. For an account of the history of Z. P. Maruya and Maruzen, see Olive Checkland, "Maruzen and the Foreign Book Trade," in *Japan and Britain After 1859: Creating Cultural Bridges* (New York: Routledge Curzon, 2003), 59-72.

93. Previously, only six reviews had been discovered. Rebekah Clements discusses all six, and argues that one in *Saint James Gazette* was by W. G. Aston, in "Yōroppa ga hajimete *Genji monogatari* ni deatta toki: Suematsu Kenchō-yaku *Genji Monogatari* Eiji sinbunhyō no shōkai o megutte," in *Heian bungaku no kochūshaku to juyō*, ed. Jinno Hidenori and Yokomizo Hiroshi (Tokyo: Musashino Shoin, 2008): 1:173–170; Valerie Henitiuk discusses four in "A Creditable Performance Under the Circumstances? Suematsu Kenchō and the Pre-Waley *Tale of Genji*," *TTR: Traduction, terminologie, rédaction* 23, no. 1 (2010): 41–71. The reviews, which will be reprinted in a forthcoming issue of the Italian translation studies journal *Testo a fronte* devoted to *Genji monogatari*, are as follows: unsigned review of *Genji Monogatari*, by Suyematz Kenchio, *London and China Telegraph*, March 28, 1882, 271; G. Barnett Smith, "New Novels," *Academy: A Weekly Review of Literature, Science, and Art* (London), April 1, 1882, 227; unsigned review of *Genji Monogatari*, by Suyematz Kenchio, *Notes and Queries: A Medium of Intercommunication for Literary Men, General Readers, Etc.*, April 8, 1882, 279–280; unsigned review of *Genji Monogatari*, by Suyematz Kenchio, *Scotsman*, April 8, 1882, 11; unsigned review of *Genji Monogatari*, by Suyematz Kenchio, *London Figaro*, April 19, 1882, 11; unsigned review of *Genji Monogatari*, by Suyematz Kenchio, *Court Journal*, April 29, 1882, 485; unsigned review of *Genji Monogatari*, by Suyematz Kenchio, *Spectator*, April 29, 1882, 571; unsigned review of *Genji Monogatari*, by Suyematz Kenchio, *Nation*, May 4, 1882, 386–387; unsigned review of *Genji Monogatari*, by Suyematz Kenchio, *Saturday Review*, June 3, 1882, 707; unsigned review of *Genji Monogatari*, by Suyematz Kenchio, *Saint James Gazette*, June 7, 1882; unsigned review of *Genji Monogatari*, by Suyematz Kenchio, *Critic* (New York), July 29, 1882, 201; unsigned review of *Genji Monogatari*, by Suyematz Kenchio, *Japan Gazette* (Yokohama), August 11, 1882, 61; [R. R. Bowker,] "Editor's Literary Record," *Harper's New Monthly Magazine* (European edition), August 1882, 470–472; unsigned review of *Genji Monogatari*, by Suyematz Kenchio, *Manchester Guardian*, September 8, 1882, 7; unsigned review of *Genji Monogatari*, by Suyematz Kenchio, *Athenæum*, September 26, 1882, 360–361; and unsigned review of *Genji Monogatari*, by Suyematz Kenchio, *Englishwoman's Review* (London), November 15, 1882, 517–519. Since most of the reviews are short, I will not provide subsequent citations. One further review that, while not of *Genji Monogatari*, is nonetheless interesting in this connection is a short piece about Madame Yukio Ozaki's *Romances of Old Japan* by "A. D. W."—that is, Arthur David Waley. In it, Waley snipes that "Part of the 'Genji' has been wretchedly translated by Suyematsu, but the task is a gigantic one. The methods of the now fashionable Proust appear cursory when compared with those of Lady Murasaki, the authoress of this encyclopædic romance, which has been computed to consist of more than twelve hundred thousand words" ("Japanese Tales," *Athenæum*, December 26, 1919, 1398).

94. Ellen Miller Casey, "Weekly Reviews of Fiction: The 'Athenaeum' vs. the 'Spectator' and the 'Saturday Review,'" *Victorian Periodicals Review* 23, no. 1 (1990): 8–12.

95. The identity of "Jusammi Tokoogawa" ("a Tokugawa of the third rank") is uncertain. Mehl suggests that he was Tokugawa Yoshinori, in "Suematsu Kenchō in Britain," 187–188; Kawakatsu asserts that he could only be Tokugawa Akitake (1853–1910), in "Suematsu Kenchō *Genji Monogatari* kankō no ji," 1–4;

Ōuchi Hidenori agrees that Akitake is a strong candidate, but argues that Tokugawa Iesato (1863-1940) is a more likely possibility, in "Suematsu Kenchō no eiyaku," in *Genji monogatari no gendaigoyaku to hon'yaku*, ed. Kawazoe Fusae, Kōza Genji monogatari kenkyū 12, (Tokyo: Ōfū, 2008), 12-15; and Clements reports that Noboru Koyama of the Cambridge University Library also regards Akitake as the most likely choice, in "Suematsu Kenchō and the First English Translation of *Genji monogatari*," 44n.3.

96. William Anderson, *The Pictorial Arts of Japan* (London: Lowe, Marston, Searle, and Rivington, 1886), 24.

97. Baron Suyematsu, *The Risen Sun* (London: Constable, 1905), 211. Suematsu goes on to quote at some length from the "Ye-awase" (The Picture Contest) chapter and then continues with a quotation from "Hahaki-gi" that illustrates the "notions as to what a picture should be that were entertained by the gentry of this epoch" (215-216). For background on the "yellow peril" and Suematsu's activities during the Russo-Japanese War, see Robert B. Valliant, "The Selling of Japan: Japanese Manipulation of Western Opinion, 1900-1905," *Monumenta Nipponica* 29, no. 4 (1974): 415-438.

98. Edward Dillon, "A Neglected Sense," *Nineteenth Century* 35, no. 206 (1894): 576n.2.

99. Paul Mantz, "Exposition de l'art japonais," *Gazette des beaux-arts* 27, no. 5 (1883): 403.

100. This is not a surprise, perhaps, since Barine observes in the first paragraph of the introduction to her rewriting that "the state of society is depicted with such truth that it is regarded as the best historical work to consult about that distant time" ("La haute société japonaise au Xe siècle," 460).

101. Charles F. Horne, *The Sacred Books and Early Literature of the East*, vol. 13, *Japan* (New York: Parke, Austin, and Lipscomb, 1917), 229. Horne has modified the quotation slightly. He includes a second epigraph as well, taken from Suematsu's introduction: "No country could have been happier than was ours at this epoch."

102. "Literary Notes," *Critic*, July 1, 1882, 177.

103. "Foreign Notes and News," *Englishwoman's Review*, May 15, 1882, 240.

104. "Philology Notes," *Academy: A Weekly Review of Literature, Science, and Art* (London), February 25, 1882, 142; "Literary and Other Notes," *Manchester Guardian*, February 27, 1882, 7; "Literature and Art," *Capital and Labour: An Economic, Financial, and Commercial Journal* (London), March 1, 1882, 86.

105. Barbara Caine, *English Feminism: 1780-1980* (Oxford: Oxford University Press, 1997), xv, 134.

106. Alicia Bewicke Little, "A Celebrated Japanese Authoress," *Englishwoman's Review*, January 15, 1892, 58-59.

107. Ibid., 59.

108. Ibid., 61-62.

109. Ibid., 59-60.

110. *GM*, xv.

111. Little, "Celebrated Japanese Authoress," 60.

112. Alice Mabel Bacon, however, alludes to Murasaki Shikibu only in a note: "Many of the classics of Japanese literature are the works of women. Among these distinguished writers can be mentioned Murasaki Shikibu, Seishō

Nagon, and Iséno Taiyu, all court ladies in the time of the Emperor Ichijō (about 1000 A.D.). . . . The Emperor gathered around him talented men and women, but the great works that remain are, strange to say, mostly those of women" (*Japanese Girls and Women*, rev. and enlarged ed. [Boston: Houghton Mifflin, 1902], 118–119).

113. R. K. Douglas, "Progress in Japan," *Edinburgh Review*, July 1890, 66–67; [R. K. Douglas,] "Progress in Japan," *Littell's Living Age*, September 27, 1890, 790.

114. Helen E. Gregory-Flecher, "The Woman Question in Japan," *Godey's Magazine*, September 1893, 332–344.

115. Japanese Women's Commission, "Murasaki Shikibu," in *Japanese Women* (Chicago: McClurg, 1893), 43–45. See also the picture on 38, which may well be of Murasaki Shikibu.

116. Kinza Riugé M. Hirai, "The Japanese Life and Customs as Contrasted with Those of the Western World. (With the Treaty Question.)," *Journal of the American Geographical Society of New York* 26, no. 1 (1894): 139–140.

117. Elizabeth A. Hines, "Women's Literature," *Atlanta Constitution*, August 23, 1895.

118. Dr. Joseph Simms, "In the Empire of the Mikado: Characteristics, Habits, and Customs of the Japanese People," *Frank Leslie's Popular Monthly*, August 1897, 178.

119. Ernest Tissot, "La vie de société au Japon, d'après des auteurs japonais," part 1, *Bibliothèque universelle et revue suisse* 13, no. 37 (1899): 100.

120. R. A. Streatfeild, "Samuel Butler," *Monthly Review*, September 1902, 143.

121. Ethel M. M. McKenna, "The Real Chrysanthemum," *Fortnightly Review*, May 1905, 864.

122. Adachi Kinnosuke, "The Women of Japan," *Forum* 38, no. 1 (1906): 142.

123. "Adachi Kinnosuke," *Womanhood* (London), December 1906, 26.

124. "Women in Japan," *Washington Post*, January 2, 1914, 6. The article is said to have been reprinted from the *Japanese Society Bulletin*.

125. For the first publication of the review, see Virginia Woolf, "The Tale of Genji: The First Volume of Mr. Arthur Waley's Translation of a Great Japanese Novel by the Lady Murasaki," *Vogue*, July 1925, 53, 80. For an English reprint, see Virginia Woolf, "The Tale of Genji: The First Volume of Mr. Arthur Waley's Translation of a Great Japanese Novel by the Lady Murasaki," *Literature East/West* 11, no. 4 (1967): 424–427. A Japanese translation of the review was published in 1952, during the first postwar *Genji* boom discussed in chapter 6: Virginia Woolf, "Genji monogatari o yonde," trans. Abe Tomoji, *Fujin kōron* 38, no. 1 (1952): 118–121. The translation has been reprinted in *Hihyō shūsei Genji monogatari*, ed. Akiyama Ken et al., vol. 4, *Kindai no sōken* (Tokyo: Yumani Shobō, 1999), 388–392.

126. Valerie Henitiuk, "Going to Bed with Waley: How Murasaki Shikibu Does and Does Not Become World Literature," *Comparative Literature Studies* 45, no. 1 (2008): 45, 41. Henitiuk refers to Suematsu's translation in passing, but accepts the received wisdom that it did not circulate widely. Her stimulating essay reads like a reply to Masao Miyoshi, who "idly dreams what might have happened had Woolf learned to read Japanese, or, better still, had she translated *The Tale of Genji*!" in "Translation as Interpretation," *Journal of Asian Studies* 38, no. 2 (1979): 301. Needless to say, she is not alone in her privileging

of Woolf: Mark Morris goes further, suggesting that "Virginia Woolf was the first important writer—female or male—to call attention to the tale" ("Tale of Genji, The," in *The Cambridge Guide to Women's Writing in English*, ed. Lorna Sage [Cambridge: Cambridge University Press, 1999], 615).

127. Amy Lowell, "Introduction," in *Diaries of Court Ladies of Old Japan*, trans. Annie Shepley Omori and Kochi Doi (Boston: Houghton Mifflin, 1920), xxvi.

128. S. Foster Damon, *Amy Lowell: A Chronicle, with Extracts from Her Correspondence* (Boston: Houghton Mifflin, 1935), 670. As Henitiuk writes, "Translations of a foreign, orientalized culture can operate as a form of Western aggression and colonization, appropriating the Other for its own purposes. This effect is aggravated several times over when a Japanese court lady writing women's lives and women's selves a millennium ago is rendered for an English-language audience only by men, and men who possess varying motivations as her mediators" ("Going to Bed with Waley," 41).

129. Woolf, "Tale of Genji," 53. I am not the first to have noticed this echo. See G. G. Rowley, "Literary Canon and National Identity: *The Tale of Genji* in Meiji Japan," *Japan Forum* 9, no. 1 (1997): 7.

130. Katherine Angell, "The Don Juan of the East," *Saturday Review of Literature*, September 5, 1925, 99–100; Francis Bickley, "A Japanese Masterpiece," *Bookman* (London), October 1925, 32; "New Books in Brief Review," *Independent* (New York), August 5, 1925, 192.

131. "The Sacred Tree," *Dial*, July 1926, 80.

132. "The Bookman's Table," *Bookman* (London), March 1927, 333; Isabel Paterson, "The New Season in Fiction," *Bookman* (New York), April 1927, 161.

133. Conrad Aiken, "Flower of Old Japan," *Bookman* (New York), December 1928, 479.

134. Riordan and Takayanagi, *Sunrise Stories*, 95.

135. F. de Simone Brouwer, *Ancora Don Giovanni* (Naples: Stabilimento Tipografico Pierro e Veraldi, 1897), 8. The passage continues with some charming descriptions of Genji:

> He too goes in search of the eternal feminine, which in its infinite variety becomes the object of his thoughts, his desires, the pivot around which his life unfolds. Bold and fiery, he possessed in common with Don Giovanni a disdain for obstacles, an inconstancy, a contempt for all morality, and the power of seduction and great success. Endowed with a heart ever ready to love, and affectionate towards women, grateful and sincere in the first rush, fate nevertheless makes him irresistibly unfaithful and drives him to new love.

136. Frederick Victor Dickins, *The Old Bamboo-Hewer's Story* (London: Trübner, 1888), 37.

137. Léon Charpentier, "Un don Juan dans la littérature japonaise," *Le Figaro* (literary supplement), May 5, 1906, 1–2, and "Un don Juan dans la littérature japonaise," *Le grande revue*, May 16, 1906, 351–363. Charpentier must have had some source beside Suematsu's translation, not only because he gets the story wrong, but also because he expands an allusion to a poem (Genji's question to

Koremitsu about the flowers blooming on the fence at the beginning of "Yūgao" [The Twilight Beauty]) that is not expanded in Suematsu's translation.

138. "Mosaico," *Cultura española* 3 (1906): 757.

139. "Don Juan as a Japanese Literary Character," *Current Literature*, July 1906, 56. The Japanese Don Quixote is Minamoto no Yorimitsu. See "A Japanese 'Don Quixote,'" *Current Literature*, June 1906, 615.

140. Eduard Bittcher, "Ein Don Juan in der japanischen Literatur," *Der Sammler* 41 (1913): 2–5. My attention was drawn to this essay by Armand E. Singer, *A Bibliography of the Don Juan Theme: Versions and Criticism*, West Virginia University Bulletin 54, no. 10-1 (Morgantown: West Virginia University Press, 1954), 128. I am indebted to Kerim Yasar for helping me acquire Bittcher's essay.

141. Brouwer, *Ancora Don Giovanni*, 8.

142. Charpentier, "Un don Juan dans la littérature japonaise," 2.

143. Unsigned review of *Genji Monogatari*, by Suyematz Kenchio, *Japan Gazette*, 61.

144. [Bowker,] "Editor's Literary Record," 471.

145. Aston, *History of Japanese Literature*, 96–97.

146. Aston, "Classical Literature of Japan," 274.

147. Streatfeild, "Samuel Butler," 143; Adachi, "Women of Japan," 142.

148. Reginald J. Farrer, "The Geisha: A Faithful Study," *Nineteenth Century and After* 55, no. 326 (1904): 632–633.

149. Keene, "Japanese Literature in the World," 314–315.

150. "Our Booking Office (by Mr. Punch's Staff of Learned Clerks)," *Punch; or, The London Charivari*, July 1, 1925, 721.

151. Janice P. Nimura, "Courtly Lust," *New York Times Book Review*, December 2, 2001.

152. Liza Dalby, "When Poetry Mattered," *Los Angeles Times*, October 21, 2001.

153. Mitani, "Meiji-ki no *Genji monogatari* kenkyū," 53. The word "social" in the first quotation from *Shōsetsu shinzui* is glossed in *katakana* in Mitani's essay, and I have translated the sentence accordingly; in the editions I have consulted, the word is glossed in *hiragana* as *sewa* here, though it is glossed as "social" elsewhere. For the quotations in *Shōsetsu shinzui*, see Tsubouchi Shōyō, *Shōsetsu shinzui*, 9 fascicles, facsimile reproduction in *Seisen meicho fukkoku zenshū* (Tokyo: Nihon Kindai Bungakukan, 1982), fascicle 4, 29 *ura*; fascicle 2, 19 *ura*. For the same quotations in a more readily accessible edition, see Tsubouchi Shōyō, *Shōsetsu shinzui*, in *Tsubouchi Shōyō-shū*, ed. Inagaki Tatsurō, Meiji bungaku zenshū 16 (Tokyo: Chikuma Shobō, 1969), 22, 16.

154. Atsuko Ueda has dedicated an entire book to showing that *Shōsetsu shinzui* was part of a larger epistemological shift of the sort I am describing, not its origin: *Concealment of Politics, Politics of Concealment: The Production of "Literature" in Meiji Japan* (Stanford, Calif.: Stanford University Press, 2007).

155. Suematsu Kenchō, "Ronzetsu," *Tōkyō nichinichi shinbun*, August 22, 1884.

156. Suematsu Kenchō, "Kagakuron 1," *Tōkyō nichinichi shinbun* (late edition), September 10, 1884. For a more readily available reprinting, see Suematsu Kenchō, "Kagakuron," in *Meiji geijutsu-bungaku-ron shū*, ed. Hijikata Teiichi,

Meiji bungaku zenshū 79 (Tokyo: Chikuma Shobō, 1975), 49. The book commissioned by the British Museum—the texts of the essay say "Gosochisshi Mūjiamu" but presumably the "goso" was an amanuensis's or compositor's misreading of Suematsu's handwritten "buri"—was William Anderson, *Descriptive and Historical Catalogue of a Collection of Japanese and Chinese Paintings in the British Museum* (London: Longman, 1886). For the relevant passage, see 13–14.

157. Suematsu Kenchō, "Kagaku kaiga yoron," *Tōkyō nichinichi shinbun* (late edition), February 7, 1885. This essay ran in four installments (not three, as suggested in the Suematsu Kenchō chronology in *Meiji geijutsu-bungaku-ron shū*) on February 4, 5, 6, and 7, 1885, always in the late edition. Baron Suematsu, "The Position of the 'Genji Monogatari' in Japanese Literature," *Hansei zasshi* 12, no. 11 (1897): 10–17.

158. Nishimura Shigeki, "Danjo aierabu no setsu," *Jogaku zasshi*, February 5, 1887, 200; February 12, 1887, 7–8; February 19, 1887, 30–31. "Voluntary Marriage" is the translation given in the journal's English-language table of contents.

159. Suematsu Kenchō [Seihyō], "Suematsu Kenchō-kun yori no shokan," *Jogaku zasshi*, February 26, 1887, 49.

160. [Murasaki Shikibu,] "Onna no shinajina," translator unidentified, *Jogaku zasshi*, March 12, 1887, 87–90. The first page has been mispaginated as 78. The passage, parts of which have been condensed, corresponds to *KGS*, "Hahakigi," 7 *omote*–16 *ura*; *GMK* 1:73–88; *SNKBZ* 20:63–70; *SNKBT* 19:39–45; and *TG* 1:25–27.

161. *Tokio Daigaku (University of Tokio): The Calendar of the Departments of Law, Science, and Literature, 2542–43 (1882–83)* (Tokyo: Maruya, 1883), 8–9.

162. Ibid., 83.

163. Ibid., 77.

164. Mikami Sanji, "Mikami Sanji ryakunenpu," in *Meiji jidai no rekishi gakkai: Mikami Sanji kaikyūdan* (Tokyo: Yoshikawa Kōbunkan, 1991), 245. For Mikami's recollections of his time in the Course in Japanese Letters, see "Bungakubu gakusei jidai," in ibid., 29–41.

165. Mikami Sanji, "Sei Shōnagon to Murasaki Shikibu," part 1, ed. Itō Kenkichi, *Yomiuri shinbun* (morning edition), May 22, 1889.

166. Ibid.

167. The lack of any new editions of *Genji monogatari* between 1706 and 1890 is noted in G. G. Rowley, *Yosano Akiko and The Tale of Genji* (Ann Arbor: Center for Japanese Studies, University of Michigan, 2000), 23. For an excellent overview of the status *Genji monogatari* occupied in Japan before the Meiji period and then during the Meiji period, in the years leading up to the publication of Yosano Akiko's translation in 1912 and 1913, see ibid., chapters 1 and 3.

168. Mikami Sanji, "Sei Shōnagon to Murasaki Shikibu," part 2, ed. Itō Kenkichi, *Yomiuri shinbun* (morning edition), May 24, 1889.

169. Takatsu Kuwasaburō, "*Gengo* jidai no ninjō fūzoku," part 1, *Yomiuri shinbun* (morning edition), October 14, 1895. The anonymous editor's introduction to this article states that Takatsu gave the lecture at Hitotsubashi Daigaku on October 12 and that "I excerpt a little bit here, just as I heard it." A different text of what is either the same lecture—perhaps transcribed from Takatsu's text, perhaps

differently delivered, perhaps just "differently heard"—or a similar lecture was published in two parts in the journal of the Shigakukai, in which the date of the lecture is given as October 14. See Takatsu Kuwasaburō, "Gengo jidai no ninjō fūzoku," parts 1 and 2, Shigaku zasshi 6, no. 11 (1895): 6–20; no. 12 (1895): 1–13.

170. Takatsu, "Gengo jidai no ninjō fūzoku," part 1.

171. Fukuchi Gen'ichirō, "Nihon no monogatari ni tsukite," Shigaku zasshi 13, no. 6 (1902): 1–14.

172. Suzuki Hiroyasu, Genji monogatari kōgi, ed. Kurokawa Mayori, transcribed by Ogushi Takashi (Tokyo: Yanagawa Umejirō/Chūgaidō, 1884), part 1:1 ura, 4 omote.

173. Suematsu Kenchō, "Shinpen Shishi jo," in [Murasaki Shikibu,] Shinpen Shishi, trans. Masuda Ushin (Tokyo: Seishidō, 1888), 1:7.

174. Ibid.

175. [Murasaki Shikibu,] Shinpen Shishi, 1:5.

176. "Saikin shuppansho," Yomiuri shinbun, August 17, 1888.

177. [Murasaki Shikibu,] Shinpen Shishi, 1:1–4. Genji monogatari Endnotes (Genji monogatari okuiri) is by Fujiwara no Teika, not Koreyuki, whose commentary is known as Genji shaku.

178. Mikami Sanji, "Sei Shōnagon to Murasaki Shikibu," part 4, ed. Itō Kenkichi, Yomiuri shinbun (morning edition), May 26, 1889.

179. Suematsu Kenchō, "Ronzetsu," Tōkyō nichinichi shinbun, August 22, 1884.

180. The four editions are [Murasaki Shikibu,] Genji monogatari kogetsushō, original notes by Kitamura Kigin, ed. and annotated by Oda Sugao, 8 vols., Kōsei hochū kokubun zensho seihen 1–8 (Osaka: Kokubunkan, 1890–1891); [Murasaki Shikibu and Kitamura Kigin,] Zōchū teisei Genji monogatari kogetsushō, ed. Inokuma Natsuki, 8 vols. (Osaka: Tosho Shuppan, 1890–1891); [Murasaki Shikibu,] Genji monogatari, ed. Ochiai Naobumi, Konakamura Yoshikata [Ikebe Tōen], and Hagino Yoshiyuki, 5 vols., Nihon bungaku zensho 8–12 (Tokyo: Hakubunkan, 1890–1891); and [Murasaki Shikibu and Kitamura Kigin,] Teisei zōchū Genji monogatari kogetsushō, ed. Inokuma Natsuki, 8 vols. (Osaka: Sekizenkan, 1891). It is interesting to note that all but one of these editions were published in Osaka. The second of the two editions prepared by Inokuma Natsuki is essentially identical to the first; oddly, both contain the same foreword by Reizei Tamemoto identifying Tosho Shuppan as the publisher, even though the calligraphy is slightly different—suggesting that Tamemoto retranscribed the text for the second edition. The text and some of the notes of the Hakubunkan edition appear to be based on Kogetsushō, but the annotations have been drastically reduced; only enough information is provided to make the text legible. My copy of the Sekizenkan edition contains marginal glosses and grammatical notes written in red that continue, tellingly, only through the first pages of the second chapter, "Hahakigi."

181. Unchūshi, "Yogen," Yomiuri shinbun (morning edition), October 25, 1890. Unchūshi is the Japanese reading of Yunzhongzi, the name of a Taoist immortal who figures in the Ming novel Fengshen yanyi (The Investiture of the Gods). I have been unable to figure out whose pen name this might be.

182. Suematsu Kenchō, Nihon bunshōron, in Meiji geijutsu-bungaku-ron shū, ed. Hijikata, 75.

183. On the timing of the replacement of woodblock-printed books by typeset books, see Yamamoto Kazuaki, "Kinsei gesaku no 'kindai,'" in *Kinsei to kindai no tsūrō: Jūkyū seiki Nihon no bungaku*, ed. Kōbe Daigaku Bungei Shisōshi Kenkyūkai (Kobe: Sōbun Shuppan, 2001), 179–180; and Iwakiri Shinichirō, "Meijiki no insatsu to shuppan: Kindai bungeisho sōtei no hensen o chūshin ni," in *Nihon no moji bunka o saguru: NichiFutsu no shiten kara*, ed. Christophe Marquet et al. (Tokyo: Bensei Shuppan, 2010), 408–411.

184. Atsuko Ueda, "Sound, Scripts, and Styles: *Kanbun kundokutai* and the National Language Reforms of 1880s Japan," in *Translation in Modern Japan*, ed. Indra Levy (London: Routledge, 2011), 157.

185. [Murasaki Shikibu,] *Shinpen Shishi*, 1:15. Ironically, in light of the point I am making here, the opposition between *kobun* and *kinbun* derives from, or at the very least echoes, the distinction that came to be made in Han-dynasty China between *guwen* and *jinwen*.

186. Yamanote no Okina, "*Genji monogatari* ni tsuite," *Yomiuri shinbun* (morning edition), October 7, 1895. The importance of the *wabun* vogue to *Genji monogatari*'s popularity in 1890 is confirmed by an advertisement for a *wabun*-letter-writing manual called *Futsūbun taigo Wabun shōsoku zensho* that was included as back matter in the last volume of the 1890 Kokubunkan edition of *Genji monogatari*. The advertisement notes that "*wabun* is so much in vogue that one hardly need comment on the phenomenon" and suggests that readers will benefit from consulting 570 sample letters from various classical sources, including *Genji monogatari*, that the book reproduces, along with translations into "ordinary prose" (*futsūbunshō*).

187. For discussions of gender ideology in the construction of "national literature studies" in Japan, see Tomi Suzuki, "Gender and Genre: Modern Literary Histories and Women's Diary Literature," in *Inventing the Classics: Modernity, National Identity, and Japanese Literature*, ed. Haruo Shirane and Tomi Suzuki (Stanford, Calif.: Stanford University Press, 2000), 71–95; and Tomiko Yoda, "Gender and the Nationalization of Heian Literature," in *Gender and National Literature: Heian Texts in the Constructions of Japanese Modernity* (Durham, N.C.: Duke University Press, 2004), chapter 2.

188. Suematsu, *Nihon bunshōron*, 71.

189. Suematsu Kenchō, "Bunshōron," *Taiyō* 3, no. 5 (1897): 43. The translation "On Literary Styles" is taken from the magazine's English-language table of contents.

190. For the quotation about *Genji monogatari* being "one of the most flawed" books of the East, see Suematsu, *Nihon bunshōron*, 75. For another instance, see Suematsu, "Shinpen Shishi jo," 6.

191. Suematsu Kenchō, "Bungaku-bijutsu-jō no iken," *Taiyō* 3, no. 1 (1897): 63–64.

192. Valliant, "Selling of Japan," 422.

193. For a partial list of Suematsu's publications and lectures, see Ian Nish, "Suematsu Kencho: International Envoy to Wartime Europe," in Ian Nish and David Steeds, "On the Periphery of the Russo-Japanese War," part 2, LSE STICERD Research Paper, no. IS/05/491, May 2005, 15–17, http://sticerd.lse.ac.uk/dps/is/is491.pdf. This essay drew my attention to the fact that Suematsu met with Theodore Roosevelt and collaborated again with Takahashi Korekiyo.

On Suematsu's request to Natsume Sōseki, see Kimura Ki, "Genji monogatari saisho no eiyakusha," *Bungaku* 44, no. 5 (1976): 123.

194. Suyematsu, *Risen Sun*, 155. The essay was reprinted from Alfred Stead, *Japan by the Japanese: A Survey by Its Highest Authorities* (London: Heinemann, 1904). As I noted earlier, *The Risen Sun* also includes an excerpt from "Ye-awase" in the chapter "Arts and Letters."

195. Suematsu Kenchō, "Hon'yakujō yori mitaru Nihonbun to Ōbun," *Bunshō sekai* 1, no. 10 (1906): 3.

196. For a discussion of the controversy, including Kakuda's role in it, see Steve Rabson, "Yosano Akiko on War: To Give One's Life or Not—A Question of Which War," in "Yosano Akiko (1878–1942)," special issue, *Journal of the Association of Teachers of Japanese* 25, no. 1 (1991): 45–74.

197. Kakuda Kōkōkakyaku [Kennan], "Fūtōgo," *Yomiuri shinbun*, July 10, 1904, *getsuyō furoku*. The italics represent emphasis marks in the original.

198. Sakai Toshihiko, *Sakai Toshihiko-den* (Tokyo: Kaizōsha, 1926), 215–217.

199. Ibid., 226, 216, 220.

200. Yūbunshi [Sakai Toshihiko], "Genji Nowaki no maki," *Yomiuri shinbun*, October 25, 1897, *getsuyō furoku*. For information about Sakai's move to Tokyo, his encounters with Suematsu, and his reading of *Genji Monogatari* and the "Nowaki" chapter of *Genji monogatari*, I have relied on Sakai, *Sakai Toshihiko-den*, esp. part 6.

201. F. G. Notehelfer, *Kōtoku Shūsui: Portrait of a Japanese Radical* (Cambridge: Cambridge University Press, 1974), 67; Donald Keene, *Emperor of Japan: Meiji and His World, 1852–1912* (New York: Columbia University Press, 2002), 685.

202. My sketch of Ōsugi's career draws on Thomas A. Stanley, *Ōsugi Sakae, Anarchist in Taishō Japan: The Creativity of the Ego* (Cambridge, Mass.: Council on East Asian Studies, Harvard University, 1981), chapters 3 and 4.

203. Ōsugi Sakae, "Gokuchū shōsoku," in *Ōsugi Sakae zenshū*, ed. Akiyama Kiyoshi et al. (Tokyo: Gendaishisōsha, 1965), 13:279.

204. Koken had been sentenced to prison on April 13, 1907, for having published "Fubo o kere" (Kick Your Parents!), *Heimin shinbun*, March 27, 1907. He was sent to prison on April 25. On the "Fubo o kere" incident and Koken's subsequent imprisonment, see Tanaka Hideo, *Yamaguchi Koken shōden* (Tokyo: Karin Shobō, 2006), 274–283, 285–291.

205. Herbert P. Bix, *Hirohito and the Making of Modern Japan* (New York: HarperCollins, 2000), 35. In September, Yi Ǔn's father, Kojung, had dispatched three envoys to The Hague to protest the fact that Japan had made Korea a protectorate without consulting him. His protests were ignored: evidently, since Korea was now a protectorate of Japan, the Japanese government would have had to lodge the protest.

5. From the World to the Nation

1. Tanizaki Jun'ichirō, "Masamune Hakuchō no hihyō o yonde," in *Tanizaki Jun'ichirō zenshū* (Tokyo: Chūōkōronsha, 1982), 20:401–402.

2. Quoted in Kobayashi Hideo, *Kobayashi Hideo taiwashū* (Tokyo: Kōdansha, 1966), 55.

3. The Yosanos stopped working on the series in 1928, midway through the publication of the second of six series. See G. G. Rowley, *Yosano Akiko and The Tale of Genji* (Ann Arbor: Center for Japanese Studies, University of Michigan, 2000), 144-146.

4. Hakuchō cited three reasons for his move to Tokyo; the other two were his fascination with the "Master of Theater" (*gekisei*), Ichikawa Danjūrō IX, and his desire to deepen his understanding of Christianity and the Bible. See Tanabe Akeo, *Hyōden Masamune Hakuchō* (Tokyo: Gakugei Shorin, 1977), 25, 36; and Takahashi Yasuo, *Masamune Hakuchō: Otogibanashi, Nihon dasshutsu ni itaru made* (Tokyo: Chūsekisha, 1981), 117.

5. Masamune Hakuchō, letter 6, in *MHZ* 30:257-258.

6. Tanabe, *Hyōden Masamune Hakuchō*, 46.

7. Masamune Hakuchō, letter 8, in *MHZ* 30:259.

8. Masamune Hakuchō, letter 11, in *MHZ* 30:263.

9. Masamune Hakuchō, "Shōsetsugeki to shirōto shibai," in *MHZ* 24:23.

10. Masamune Hakuchō, "Koten o yonde," *Chūōkōron* 41, no. 8 (1926): 130-138, reprinted in *Bungei hyōron* (Tokyo: Kaizōsha, 1927) and in *MHZ* 23:131-137; "Eiyaku *Genji monogatari*," *Kaizō* 15, no. 9 (1933): 194-204, reprinted in *Waga saikin no bungaku hyōron* (Tokyo: Kaizōsha, 1934) and in *MHZ* 23:466-470; "Saikin no shūkaku: Eiyaku *Genji monogatari* o yomu," parts 1-3, *Tōkyō asahi shinbun*, November 15-17, 1933, reprinted as "Futatabi Eiyaku *Genji monogatari* ni tsukite," in *MHZ* 22:185-190; and "*Genji monogatari*—hon'yaku to gensaku," *Chūōkōron* 66, no. 8 (1951): 131-137, reprinted in *MHZ* 21: 499-508. One other essay in addition to these four deals at some length, though not exclusively, with Waley's *The Tale of Genji*: first published in *Bungei shunjū*, October 1, 1933, it is reprinted as "Karuizawa nite," in *MHZ* 27:213-219. My translation of "Koten o yonde" will be appearing in Thomas Harper and Haruo Shirane, eds., *Reading The Tale of Genji: Sources from the First Millennium* (New York: Columbia University Press, 2014); a translation of "*Genji monogatari*: hon'yaku to gensaku" is forthcoming in *Monumenta Nipponica* 68, no. 1 (2013).

11. Masamune, "Koten o yonde," 130; *Bungei hyōron*, 153; *MHZ* 23:132.

12. Gakkai refers to Suematsu as an "old friend" in a diary entry for July 9, 1886 (Meiji 19). See *GN* 6:346. The debate between Gakkai and Suematsu was covered in "Gakkai Koji ōi ni Seihyō itsujin to zessen," *Kokumin shinbun*, September 15, 1890; and "Suematsu Kenchō-shi to Yoda Hyakusen-shi no daigekiron," *Yomiuri shinbun*, September 15, 1890.

13. *GN* 8:113-114.

14. On Ink Cottage (Bokusui Bessho) and Gakkai's mistress Fukushima Suika, see Imai Gen'e, "Suika no shiika," *Gobun kenkyū* 76 (1995): 1-12. On Gakkai's discovery of the power lines, his letter to Suematsu, and his two subsequent meetings with Suematsu, see *GN* 10:473-474; 11:35-36, 190.

15. Patrick Caddeau, "Yoda Gakkai and Suematsu Kenchō: A Debate over the First Translation of *Genji* into English," in *Kaigai ni okeru Genji monogatari no sekai: Hon'yaku to kenkyū*, ed. Ii Haruki, Kokusai Nihon bungaku kenkyū hōkokushū 3 (Tokyo: Kazama Shobō, 2004), 141-149, and *Appraising Genji: Literary Criticism and Cultural Anxiety in the Age of the Last Samurai* (Albany: State University of New York Press, 2006), 147-154.

16. Tokutomi Sohō, ed., "Shomoku jisshu," supplement to *Kokumin no tomo* 48 (1889): 641.

17. Yoda Gakkai, "*Genji monogatari* to *Kōrōmu*," in *Hihyō shūsei Genji monogatari*, ed. Akiyama Ken et al., vol. 3, *Kindai no hihyō* (Tokyo: Yumani Shobō, 1999), 50.

18. My discussion of *Shōsetsu shinzui* draws in particular on the preface, "*Shōsetsu shinzui* shogen," and second chapter, "Shōsetsu no hensen." See Tsubouchi Shōyō, *Shōsetsu shinzui*, facsimile reproduction in *Seisen meicho fukkoku zenshū* (Tokyo: Nihon Kindai Bungakukan, 1982), 1:*jo* 1 omote–2 ura, 7 omote–10 ura; 2:11 omote–19 ura. For a detailed discussion of the history of the term *shōsetsu*, see Tomi Suzuki, *Narrating the Self: Fictions of Japanese Modernity* (Stanford, Calif.: Stanford University Press, 1996), 16–23.

19. Kimura Mokurō, *Kokuji shōsetsu tsū*, in *Zoku enseki jisshu* (Tokyo: Chūōkōron, 1980), 1:297.

20. Andrew L. Markus, "Kimura Mokurō (1774–1856) and His *Kokuji shōsetsu tsū* (1849)," *Journal of Japanese Studies* 26, no. 2 (2000): 369.

21. It is worth noting that most respondents to the 1889 survey were reading European works either in the original or in translation. My discussion of Gakkai is not meant to suggest that a nascent concept of "world literature" focused on a European conception of literature did not exist in 1906: Mikami Sanji and Takatsu Kuwasaburō mention *ueruto riteratsūru* (*Weltliteratur* [world literature]) at the beginning of a chapter on national literature in *Nihon bungakushi* (1890), and scholar of Japanese literature Haga Yaichi (1867–1927) had published *Sekai bungakusha nenpyō* (*A Chronology of World Literary Figures*) in 1892. See Mikami Sanji and Takatsu Kuwasaburō, *Nihon bungakushi*, Meiji Taishō bungakushi shūsei 1 and 2 (Tokyo: Nihon Tosho Sentā, 1982), 25; and Haga Yaichi, *Sekai bungakusha nenpyō* (Tokyo: Fuzan-bō, 1904). The importance of publications of this sort should not, however, be overestimated. Haga's chronology is hardly a chronology of world "literature" as the category is understood today, or even as Hakuchō understood it in 1926: Murasaki Shikibu appears in his list, but so, in the 1904 second edition, does the political philosopher Herbert Spencer. Neither is Haga's mental map of the world so different from Gakkai's: like Shōyō, he simply brings in the West as a third term, giving his chronology a three-tiered layout: Japan is at the top, China is in the middle, and the West is at the bottom.

22. It is significant, too, that the title of the essay uses the term *haishi*, once again, as an equivalent of *shōsetsu*. For the quotation, see Yoda Gakkai, "Haishi ni arawaretaru josei," *Bungei kurabu* 11, no. 5 (1905): 189.

23. "Datsua-ron" (On Leaving Asia), the editorial by Fukuzawa Yukichi that inspired the slogan "leaving Asia and joining Europe," ran in *Jiji shinpō* on March 16, 1885, just six months before the first three booklets of *Shōsetsu shinzui* were published. The observation that "literature" does not appear in *Shōsetsu shinzui* is taken from Suzuki, *Narrating the Self*, 195n.58. Shōyō does use the compound *bungaku* itself in a different sense: it appears twice in the phrase *bungaku no shihyō* (a model for learning how to write), as noted in Tomi Suzuki, "Nihon bungaku to sekai bungaku: *Genji monogatari* to kindai Nihon," in *Kaigai ni okeru Genji monogatari*, ed. Haruo Shirane, Kōza Genji monogatari kenkyū 11 (Tokyo: Ōfū, 2008), 196–197.

24. Masamune, "Koten o yonde," 131; *Bungei hyōron*, 159; *MHZ* 23:135.

25. David Crystal, *English as a Global Language* (Cambridge: Cambridge University Press, 1997), 79, 90.

26. Terada Torahiko, *Terada Torahiko zen zuihitsu shū* (Tokyo: Iwanami Shoten, 1992), 419.

27. The date of Hakuchō and his wife's departure, November 28, appears in the notes to "Kaigai nite no aru hi aru yoru," in *MHZ* 27:495. Gendai Nihon bungaku zenshū, a thirty-seven-volume series issued between 1926 and 1928 by the publisher of *Kaizō*, sparked a boom in enpon (1-yen books) that continued until the early 1950s. Hakuchō notes that royalties from this series funded his travels with his wife in "Enpon no koto nado," in *MHZ* 28:382–383.

28. Masamune, "Kaigai nite no aru hi aru yoru," 93–94.

29. *Masamune Hakuchō: Bundan-teki jijoden/bundan gojūnen*, ed. Nakajima Kawatarō, Sakka no jiden 5 (Tokyo: Nihon Tosho Sentā 1994), 164; Ibuse Masaji, *Kuroi ame* (Tokyo: Shinchōsha, 1966), 309–310, and *Black Rain*, trans. John Bester (Tokyo: Kodansha International, 1969), 282.

30. On *Marching On*, see Joseph L. Anderson and Donald Richie, *The Japanese Film: Art and Industry*, expanded ed. (Princeton, N.J.: Princeton University Press, 1982), 74. May 9 is given as the starting date for the run in Kokubungaku Henshūbu, ed., *Meiji Taishō Shōwa Fūzoku bunkashi* (Tokyo: Gakutōsha, 1994), 148.

31. Masamune Hakuchō, "Ni san no kenbun," in *MHZ* 27:113–114.

32. The publication dates for the six volumes of Waley's *Genji* were as follows: *The Tale of Genji*, May 1925; *The Sacred Tree*, February 23, 1926; *A Wreath of Cloud*, February 8, 1927; *Blue Trousers*, May 1928; *The Lady of the Boat*, June 1932; and *The Bridge of Dreams*, May 1933. See Francis A. Johns, *A Bibliography of Arthur Waley*, 2nd ed. (Atlantic Highlands, N.J.: Athlone Press, 1988), entries A11, A12, A13, A15, A21, A22.

33. Masamune, "*Genji monogatari*—hon'yaku to gensaku," 132–133; *MHZ* 21:501.

34. Kobayashi Hideo, "Norinaga no *Genjikan*" (lecture, September 25, 1972, Nagoya Chūnichi Hōru), in *Kobayashi Hideo kōenshū*, vol. 5, *Zuisō nidai Motoori Norinaga o megutte* (Tokyo: Shinchō Kasetto & CD, 2004).

35. Masamune, "Koten o yonde," 134, 135; *Bungei hyōron*, 159, 161; *MHZ* 23:135.

36. Masamune, "Eiyaku *Genji monogatari*," 194; *MHZ* 23:466.

37. Edward Larocque Tinker, "New Editions, Fine & Otherwise," *New York Times*, December 24, 1939.

38. Furuta Hiromu, "Ueirī no eiyaku *Genji monogatari* ni tsuite," in *Genji monogatari no eiyaku no kenkyū*, ed. Furuta Hiromu et al., Hikaku bungaku kenkyū sōsho 4 (Tokyo: Kyōiku Shuppan Sentā, 1980), 221.

39. Akiyama Ken, "*Genji monogatari* gendaigoyaku no hōhō: Nidome no chōsen kara," in *Ima Genji monogatari o dō yomu ka*, ed. Murofushi Shinsuke (Tokyo: Ōfu, 1995), 28–29.

40. "Bundan futari anku: dentōryō nesage ron," *Yomiuri shinbun*, September 2, 1933.

41. This essay is reprinted as Sugimura Kōtarō, "Han'yaku ka hangyaku ka," in *Sojinkan zenshū* (Tokyo: Nihon Hyōronsha, 1937), 10:190–202.

42. Masamune, "Eiyaku *Genji monogatari*," 196; *MHZ* 23:468.

43. Murasaki Shikibu, *Ueirī-ban Genji monogatari*, 4 vols., trans. from Arthur Waley's English translation by Samata Hideki (Tokyo: Heibonsha Laiburarī, 2008–2009).

44. Rowley, *Yosano Akiko and The Tale of Genji*, 71.

45. Sassa Seisetsu et al., eds., *Shinshaku Genji monogatari* (Tokyo: Shinchōsha, 1911), 3, cited in Rowley, *Yosano Akiko and The Tale of Genji*, 66.

46. The first volume of Waley's translation was published in May 1925. August saw the publication of "Shinkō sen to suru Nihon bungaku no hon'yaku," part 2, "Murasaki Shikibu no *Genji monogatari* chikaku kansei sareru ichidai meiyaku," *Yomiuri shinbun*, August 18, 1925. Excerpts from the *Spectator*'s review of the first volume were translated in "Eiyaku *Genji monogatari* Eishi *Supekutēta* hyō," parts 1 and 2, *Yomiuri shinbun*, September 25 and 26, 1925. For two early reviews originally written in Japanese, see Takagi Ichinosuke, "*Genji monogatari* no Eiyaku," *Kokugo to kokubungaku* 2, no. 10 (1925): 183–193; and Igarashi Chikara, "Vērī-shi no *Eiyaku Genji monogatari* o yomu," *Waseda bungaku* 243 (1926): 2–19.

47. Three yen was the original list price for *Shin'yaku Genji monogatari*. Advertisements in *Yomiuri shinbun* on August 19 and November 17, 1913, reveal that the price per volume was reduced over time to 2 yen and 50 sen, and then to 1 yen and 50 sen; a notice in *Yomiuri shinbun* on March 25, 1914, announces that "for a limited time only" Kanao Bun'endō would offer *Shin'yaku Genji monogatari* and twenty other titles "to general readers at a price so low it's as good as wholesale." For taxi rates, see Shigenobu Yukihiko, *Takushī: Modan Tōkyō minzokushi* (Tokyo: Nihon Editā Sukūru Shuppanbu, 1999), 37. The edition that was sold at 1 yen per volume was [Murasaki Shikibu,] *Genji monogatari*, ed. Ikebe Yoshikata [Ikebe Tōen], Motoori Toyokai, et al., *Kōchū kokubun sōsho*, 2 vols. (Tokyo: Hakubunkan, 1912).

48. Quoted in Ishizuka Jun'ichi, *Kanao Bun'endō o meguru hitobito* (Tokyo: Shinjuku Shobō, 2005), 136.

49. Rowley, *Yosano Akiko and The Tale of Genji*, 96. For a meticulous and insightful analysis of *Shin'yaku Genji monogatari*, see chapters 5 and 6.

50. Kitamura Yuika, "*Genji monogatari* no saisei: Gendaigoyakuron," *Bungaku* 3, no. 1 (1992): 45. For a masterful analysis of the position of the narrator in modern-Japanese translations of *Genji monogatari* by Yosano Akiko, Tanizaki Jun'ichirō, and Enchi Fumiko, see Kitamura Yuika, "*Genji monogatari* no hen'yō: Gendaigoyakuron," *Kindai* (Kōbe Daigaku *Kindai* Hakkōkai), December 1988, 67–83. This essay is identified as "part 1," but regrettably no sequel has yet appeared.

51. I touched on Empress Shōken's love of *Genji monogatari* and *Inaka Genji* in the introduction. Miyamoto's novel, which remained unfinished and unpublished until it was included in her collected works, is called "Nishikigi." For the quotation, see Miyamoto Yuriko, "Nishikigi," in *Miyamoto Yuriko zenshū* (Tokyo: Shin Nihon Shuppansha, 1981), 28:151. Miyamoto Yuriko waxes nostalgic about her encounter with *Shin'yaku Genji monogatari* and her composition of "Nishikigi" in "Mukashi no omoide," in *Miyamoto Yuriko zenshū* (Tokyo: Shin Nihon Shuppansha, 1981), 17:307.

52. Miyamoto Yuriko, "Yukue fumei no shojosaku," in *Miyamoto Yuriko zenshū* 17:417.

53. "Pari e," *Yomiuri shinbun*, May 1, 1912.

54. Yosano Akiko, "Shin'yaku Genji monogatari no nochi ni," in [Murasaki Shikibu,] *Shin'yaku Genji monogatari*, trans. Yosano Akiko (Tokyo: Kanao Bun'endō, 1913), 4:7, cited in Rowley, *Yosano Akiko and The Tale of Genji*, 73.

55. Advertisement for *Shin'yaku Genji monogatari*, *Yomiuri shinbun*, August 19, 1913.

56. See, for instance, advertisement for *Shin'yaku Genji monogatari*, *Yomiuri shinbun*, November 5, 1913.

57. For a list of eight reviews in major newspapers and literary journals, see Rowley, *Yosano Akiko and The Tale of Genji*, 87n.46.

58. Ueda Bin, foreword to [Murasaki Shikibu,] *Shin'yaku Genji monogatari*, trans. Yosano Akiko (Tokyo: Kanao Bun'endō, 1912), 1:1. For Rowley's discussion of what made Akiko "the right person at the right time," see "*The Tale of Genji* in the Meiji Period," in Rowley, *Yosano Akiko and The Tale of Genji*, chapter 3.

59. For a discussion of the Yosanos' relationships with Ōgai and Bin, see Rowley, *Yosano Akiko and The Tale of Genji*, 82–84.

60. Mori Rintarō, foreword to [Murasaki Shikibu,] *Shin'yaku Genji monogatari*, trans. Yosano, 1:1.

61. Ibid., 4.

62. Masamune, "*Genji monogatari*—hon'yaku to gensaku," 132; MHZ 21: 500–501.

63. Natsume Sōseki, "Tōyō bijutsu zufu," in *Sōseki zenshū* (Tokyo: Iwanami Shoten, 1995), 16:306–307.

64. Akutagawa Ryūnosuke, "Bungeitekina, amari ni bungeitekina," in *Hihyō shūsei Genji monogatari*, ed. Akiyama et al., 3:102.

65. Dazai Osamu, "Koten ryūtōdabi," in *Dazai Osamu zenshū* (Tokyo: Chikuma Shobō, 1977), 10:73.

66. Miyamoto, "Mukashi no omoide," 307.

67. Masamune, "Koten o yonde," 135; *Bungei hyōron*, 161; MHZ 23:136.

68. See, for instance, Ogiwara Zentarō, *Teikoku hakushi retsuden* (Tokyo: Keigyōsha, 1890); Hanabusa Yoshitarō and Yamamoto Genta, *Nihon hakushi zenden* (Tokyo: Hakubunkan, 1892); Toyabe Sentarō, *Meiji jinbutsu hyōron* (Tokyo: Hakubunkan, 1900); and Kayahara Rentarō, *Jinbutsu hyōron* (Tokyo: Seinen Zusho Shuppan Kyōkai, 1901).

69. "*Genji monogatari* o itsuka wa butō ni suru: Tenishōn butōdan-chū no hanagata Hanfurē-jō," *Yomiuri shinbun*, August 30, 1925.

70. Jennifer Dunning, "Dance Review: Japan's Traditional Tastes," *New York Times*, March 4, 1995.

71. For a more detailed description of these two books and an analysis of fifteen editions of Tanizaki's three translations and the publishing strategy they embodied, see Tateishi Kazuhiro, "Tanizaki Jun'ichirō-yaku *Genji monogatari* no shuppan senryaku," in *Genji monogatari no gendaigoyaku to hon'yaku*, ed. Kawazoe Fusae, Kōza Genji monogatari kenkyū 12 (Tokyo: Ōfū, 2008), 227–262. The two versions of the "old translation" are described on 229.

72. For initial sales figures, see "Sasuga wa dai Tanizaki," *Yomiuri shinbun*, February 3, 1939. In romanizing the title of this essay as "dai Tanizaki" rather than "ō Tanizaki," I am drawing on Koyano Atsushi, *Tanizaki Jun'ichirō-den: Dōdōtaru jinsei* (Tokyo: Chūōkōronshinsha, 2006), 11–13. The figure of 50,000

additional orders comes from Shiozawa Minobu, *Shōwa besuto serā sesōshi* (Tokyo: Daisanbunmeisha, 1988), 64–65.

73. An advertisement in *Yomiuri shinbun*, April 4, 1939, explains the reasons for the delay; an advertisement in *Yomiuri shinbun*, April 16, 1939, announces that the next two volumes, 3 and 4, are finally ready for distribution.

74. The first two volumes of *Jun'ichirō-yaku Genji monogatari* went on sale on January 13, 1939; an advertisement in *Yomiuri shinbun*, February 22, 1939, announces that the heirloom collector's edition has already sold out; and subsequent advertisements mention only the popular edition.

75. [Murasaki Shikibu,] *Jun'ichirō yaku Genji monogatari*, trans. Tanizaki Jun'ichirō, 26 vols. (Tokyo: Chūōkōronsha, 1939–1941), 1:5.

76. Chino Shōshō, "Koten no gendaigoyaku," *Tōkyō asahi shinbun*, April 3, 1939.

77. Ken K. Ito, *Visions of Desire: Tanizaki's Fictional Worlds* (Stanford, Calif.: Stanford University Press, 1991), 186.

78. Kobayashi Masaaki, "Wartime Japan, the Imperial Line, and *The Tale of Genji*," trans. Michael Emmerich, in *Envisioning the Tale of Genji: Media, Gender, and Cultural Production*, ed. Haruo Shirane (New York: Columbia University Press, 2008), 293. This essay brings together material from essays that Kobayashi, one of the first scholars to deal with *Genji monogatari*'s wartime troubles, published in Japanese. See Kobayashi Masaaki, "Shōwa jūsannen no *Genji monogatari*," *Kokubungaku* 44, no. 5 (1999): 25–31; "Senjō no *Genji monogatari*," *Kokubungaku* 45, no. 14 (2000): 43–49; "Wadatsumi no *Genji monogatari*: senjika no junan," in *"Miyabi" isetsu: Genji monogatari to iu bunka*, ed. Yoshī Miyako (Tokyo: Shinwasha, 2002), 183–228; "Shōwa senjika no *Genji monogatari*," in *Genji bunka no jikū*, ed. Tateishi Kazuhiro and Andō Tōru (Tokyo: Shinwasha, 2005), 78–97; "Banseiikkei mondai to senjika *Genji monogatari* ni tsuite," *Rikkyō Daigaku Nihon bungaku kenkyūjo nenpō* 4 (2005): 14–23; and "Tatakau *Genji monogatari*: Han Banseiikkei-ron," *Nihon bungaku* 56, no. 1 (2007): 11–23.

79. Eric M. Cazdyn, *The Flash of Capital: Film and Geopolitics in Japan* (Durham, N.C.: Duke University Press, 2002), 97.

80. Tanizaki Jun'ichirō, "Ano koro no koto (Yamada Yashio tsuitō)," in *Tanizaki Jun'ichirō zenshū* (Tokyo: Chūōkōronsha, 1969), 23:357. In Tanizaki's account, the three elements Yamada objects to are Genji's affair with Fujitsubo, the fact that their child becomes emperor, and the fact that Genji rises to the rank of honorary retired emperor. In actual fact, Tanizaki also erases all traces that Genji is sexually involved with Oborozukiyo: when her father walks in on them at the end of the "Sakaki" (The Green Branch) chapter, for instance, he discovers only a sheet of paper with Genji's handwriting, rather than a sheet of paper, a violet sash, and then finally Genji himself in dishabille. See [Murasaki Shikibu,] *Jun'ichirō-yaku Genji monogatari*, trans. Tanizaki, 4:155–157.

81. Cazdyn, *Flash of Capital*, 98. Kobayashi Masaaki makes the same point: "By carrying out the deletions and rewritings and, at the same time, by repeating his claim of their irrelevance to the work in both the preface and the colophon, Tanizaki sketches a sort of negative view of the taboo that was placed on the *Genji* by the wartime government" ("Wartime Japan," 293).

82. Kobayashi Masaaki, "Wartime Japan," 293.

83. Tanizaki Jun'ichirō, "Jo," in [Murasaki Shikibu,] *Jun'ichirō-yaku Genji monogatari*, trans. Tanizaki, 1:6.

84. Tanizaki Jun'ichirō, *Shunkinshō*, Shinchō bunko 150 (Tokyo: Shinchōsha, 2003), 66.

85. Nishino Atsushi, "Hai o yoseatsumeru: Yamada Yoshio to Tanizaki Jun'ichirō-yaku *Genji monogatari*," in *Kindai bungaku ni okeru Genji monogatari*, ed. Chiba Shunji, Kōza Genji monogatari kenkyū 6 (Tokyo: Ōfū, 2007), 156–157.

86. Okazaki Yoshie, "Tanizaki *Genji*-ron, part 4, Jūrin sareta geijutsuteki kyōchi," *Tōkyō asahi shinbun*, May 26, 1939, and "Tanizaki *Genji*-ron," part 1, "Dainikai haihon made tsūdoku shite," *Tōkyō asahi shinbun*, May 23, 1939. For the other two parts, see Okazaki Yoshie, "Tanizaki *Genji*-ron," part 2, "Sokonawareta genbun no in'ei, ganchiku," *Tōkyō asahi shinbun*, May 24, 1939, and "Tanizaki *Genji*-ron," part 3, "Tsūzokuteki ni chōshizuita sanbun," *Tōkyō asahi shinbun*, May 25, 1939. For a response to Okazaki, see Nagao Takeo, "Tanizaki *Genji* ni kisu," *Tōkyō asahi shinbun*, June 7, 1939.

87. Kobayashi Eiko, *Genji Ise monogatari shinkenkyū* (Tokyo: Shinbunkan, 1935), 136–137. Kobayashi's "modern rendering," *Genji monogatari kasshaku* (1924), is not a "modern Japanese translation" in the usual sense: she simply made the classical text easier to read by rewriting it using as many glossed *kanji* as possible. For discussions of the banning of the 1933 play, see Kobayashi Masaaki, "Wartime Japan"; and Samuel L. Leiter, "Performing the Emperor's New Clothes: *The Mikado*, *The Tale of Genji*, and Lèse majesté on the Japanese Stage," in *Rising from the Flames: The Rebirth of Theater in Occupied Japan, 1945–1952*, ed. Samuel L. Leiter (Lanham, Md.: Lexington Books, 2009), 125–171. Interestingly, *Genji Ise monogatari shinkenkyū* is included among a number of books donated to the Durham University library by Arthur Waley, who was presumably sent it by an acquaintance in Japan. See Midorikawa Machiko, *Genji monogatari eiyaku ni tsuite no kenkyū* (Tokyo: Musashino Shoin, 2010), 208n.20.

88. Kamitsukasa Shōken, "Yomikiri shōsetsu: Murasaki Shikibu," *Fujin kōron* 24, no. 1 (1939): 226–237; Yoshiya Nobuko, "Rekishi shōsetsu Murasaki Shikibu," *Ōru yomimono* 9, no. 4 (1939): 376–393; advertisement for Amon Papaya, *Tōkyō asahi shinbun*, February 15, 1939.

89. Shimazu Hisamoto, *Murasaki Shikibu* (Tokyo: Seigodō, 1943), 246–249. In order to maintain a link with Kobayashi Masaaki's "Wartime Japan," I have based my translation of the passage from "Usugumo" on *TG* 1:357. Needless to say, Tanizaki himself expunges the entire incident, from the prelate's and Genji's conversations with Emperor Reizei to the emperor's reading of the history books and promotion of Genji. For the start of the passage that would have included the deleted pages, see [Murasaki Shikibu,] *Jun'ichirō-yaku Genji monogatari*, trans. Tanizaki, 7:101.

90. For a very different interpretation of the same passage from *Genji monogatari* that includes the line that Shimazu omits (quoted here in Royall Tyler's translation), see Kobayashi Masaaki, "Wartime Japan," 288–299.

91. Murasaki Shikibu, *The Tale of Genji, by Lady Murasaki*, trans. Arthur Waley (Boston: Houghton Mifflin, 1925), 8.

92. Shimanaka Yūsaku, "Kyōga shinnen," *Tōkyō nichinichi shinbun*, January 2, 1939.

93. Advertisement for *Jun'ichirō-yaku Genji monogatari*, *Tōkyō nichinichi shinbun*, January 23, 1939.

94. Advertisement for *Jun'ichirō-yaku Genji monogatari*, *Tōkyō asahi shinbun*, February 2, 1939. Iwanami's blurb appears again in an advertisement in *Tōkyō nichinichi shinbun*, February 5, 1939.

95. Donald Keene, *Chronicles of My Life: An American in the Heart of Japan* (New York: Columbia University Press, 2008), 24-25.

96. Advertisement for *Jun'ichirō-yaku Genji monogatari*, *Tōkyō nichinichi shinbun*, January 26, 1939; advertisement for *Jun'ichirō-yaku Genji monogatari*, *Tōkyō nichinichi shinbun*, January 29, 1939; advertisement for *Jun'ichirō-yaku Genji monogatari*, *Tōkyō nichinichi shinbun*, February 5, 1939; advertisement for *Jun'ichirō-yaku Genji monogatari*, *Tōkyō nichinichi shinbun*, February 27, 1939. The first, second, and fourth ads ran, sometimes in slightly different forms, in *Tōkyō asahi shinbun* on January 30, February 2, and February 28, 1939.

97. Advertisement for *Jun'ichirō-yaku Genji monogatari*, *Tōkyō asahi shinbun*, January 22, 1939. The same advertisement appeared in *Tōkyō nichinichi shinbun*, January 23, 1939. Advertisements for Tanizaki's old translation routinely refer to *Genji monogatari*'s "fifty-five" chapters because they include "Kumogakure," which consists of only a title and is thus generally not counted.

98. Chiba Shunji, "Kindai bungaku no naka no *Genji monogatari*," in *Kindai bungaku ni okeru Genji monogatari*, ed. Chiba. I outline the section of Chiba's argument relating to Tanizaki's "old translation" later, but there is much more to the essay than this. See also Mizukami Tsutomu and Chiba Shunji, eds., *Zōho kaiteiban Tanizaki sensei no shokan: Aru shuppansha shachō e no tegami o yomu* (Tokyo: Chūōkōron, 2008), 345-351.

99. Masamune, "Saikin no shūkaku," part 2; *MHZ* 22:188.

100. Masamune, "Eiyaku *Genji monogatari*," 201; *MHZ* 23:473.

101. Tanizaki Jun'ichirō quotes Waley's translation in *Bunshō dokuhon* (Tokyo: Chūōkōronsha, 1934).

102. Chiba, "Kindai bungaku no naka no *Genji monogatari*," 22.

103. Advertisement for *Jun'ichirō-yaku Genji monogatari*, *Tōkyō asahi shinbun*, February 8, 1939. The same blurb appeared in an advertisement in *Tōkyō nichinichi shinbun*, February 9, 1939.

104. Yamada Yoshio, "*Genji monogatari* to Tanizaki Jun'ichirō," *Furusato* 2, no. 1 (1948): 15.

105. Masamune, "Eiyaku *Genji monogatari*," 195; *MHZ* 23:467.

106. Kawabata Yasunari, *Japan, the Beautiful, and Myself*, trans. Edward G. Seidensticker (Tokyo: Kodansha International, 1969), 47-46.

107. Ibid., 31.

108. Ibuki Kazuko, *Kawabata Yasunari: Hitomi no densetsu* (Tokyo: PHP Kenkyūjo, 1997), 65-73.

109. Masamune, "*Genji monogatari*—hon'yaku to gensaku," 136-137; *MHZ* 21:507.

6. "*Genji monogatari*: Translation and Original"

1. For an account of the meeting at which Stimson insisted on removing Kyoto from the list, see Len Giovannitti and Fred Freed, *The Decision to Drop the Bomb* (New York: Coward-McCann, 1965), 40-41. On everlasting sashimi, see

Okada Ikunosuke, "Genshiryoku sakkin ikaga: Sashimi wa sankagetsu motsu," *Asahi shinbun*, May 30, 1955.

2. Advertisement for *Jun'ichirō-yaku Genji monogatari*, *Tōkyō asahi shinbun*, February 2, 1939.

3. John W. Dower paints an eloquent portrait of this period in *Embracing Defeat: Japan in the Wake of World War II* (New York: Norton, 1999).

4. For an annotated chronology relating to the various editions of Tanizaki's three translations of *Genji*, see Ikeda Yazaburō, "Tanizaki *Genji* nendaiki," part 3, "*Kyūyaku 'Tanizaki* Genji' *no kankō*," and "Tanizaki *Genji* nendaiki," part 4, "*Shin'yaku* kara *shinshin'yaku* made," both in *Hihyō shūsei Genji monogatari*, ed. Akiyama Ken et al., vol. 5, *Senjika hen* (Yumani Shobō, 1999). For a more extensive list of the editions, with pictures of some of the boxes and covers, see the "Tanizaki Jun'ichirō" section of Tateishi Kazuhiro's information-packed online database, *Genji monogatari kakō bunka dētābēsu*, http://homepage3.nifty.com/genji_db/; for a more detailed discussion of the different versions, see Ibuki Kazuko and G. G. Rowley, "'The Tanizaki *Genji*': Inception, Process, and Afterthoughts," in *The Grand Old Man and the Great Tradition: Essays on Tanizaki Jun'ichirō in Honor of Adriana Boscaro*, ed. Luisa Bienati and Bonaventura Ruperti (Ann Arbor: Center for Japanese Studies, University of Michigan, 2009), 25–52. For an extensive list of the editions of Yosano Akiko's translation, also with pictures of some of the boxes and covers, see Tateishi Kazuhiro, "Yosano Akiko," in *Genji monogatari kakō bunka dētābēsu*. My count of Yosano Akiko's books includes two editions not yet on this list: *Genji monogatari*, trans. Yosano Akiko, 2 vols., Nihon kokumin bungaku zenshū 3 and 4 (Tokyo: Kawade Shobō, 1955, 1956), and the electronic edition "*Genji monogatari* + chottodakebungaku," created for the Nintendo DS handheld game system.

5. See, for instance, Tateishi Kazuhiro, "*Genji monogatari* no kakō to ryūtsū: Biteki ōchō gensō to seisa no hensei," *Genji kenkyū* 5 (2000): 127–146, and "Eigaka sareta *Genji monogatari*" and "Kabuki to Takarazuka-geki no *Genji monogatari*," both in *Genji bunka no jikū*, ed. Tateishi Kazuhiro and Andō Tōru (Tokyo: Shinwasha, 2005).

6. Tateishi, "Eigaka sareta *Genji monogatari*," 127. Tateishi Kazuhiro, "Kabuki," in *Genji monogatari kakō bunka dētābēsu*. "Eigaka sareta *Genji monogatari*" offers an excellent discussion of the various film and anime versions of *Genji* produced over the last half-century.

7. Tateishi, "Kabuki." For an excellent discussion of kabuki and Takarazuka adaptations of *Genji*, see Tateishi, "Kabuki to Takarazuka-geki no *Genji monogatari*." See also Matsui Toshiaki, "Sengo kabuki ni hana hiraita *Genji monogatari*," and Ishibashi Ken'ichirō, "Kabuki de atsukawarete kita *Genji monogatari*," both in *Bessatsu taiyō: Kabuki Genji monogatari* (Tokyo: Heibonsha, 2001).

8. For a list of these radio dramas, see Tateishi Kazuhiro, "Rajio dorama," in *Genji monogatari kakō bunka dētābēsu*. For an overview of the various replacements of *Genji* that were circulating in the early postwar period and beyond, see Tateishi, "*Genji monogatari* no kakō to ryūtsū." For a longer introduction, see Uesaka Nobuo, *Genji monogatari tenshō: Engekishi ni miru* (Tokyo: Yūbun Shoin, 1987).

9. Masamune Hakuchō, "*Genji monogatari*—hon'yaku to gensaku," *Chūōkōron* 66, no. 8 (1951): 131; *MHZ* 21:499.

10. Masamune Hakuchō, "Eiyaku *Genji monogatari*," *Kaizō* 15, no. 9 (1933): 194; *MHZ* 23:466.

11. For the text of the review, see Masamune Hakuchō, "Kabuki no *Genji monogatari*," in *MHZ* 24:597–599.

12. Ibid., 597–598.

13. Yokomitsu Riichi, "Junsuishōsetsuron," in *Yokomitsu Riichi zenshū*, vol. 12 (Tokyo: Kawade Shobō, 1956).

14. Masamune Hakuchō, "Koten no gendaigoyaku," in *MHZ* 23:354.

15. Masamune, "*Genji monogatari*—hon'yaku to gensaku," 131–132; *MHZ* 21:499–501.

16. Masamune, "*Genji monogatari*—hon'yaku to gensaku," 132, 133; *MHZ* 21:501.

17. Masamune, "*Genji monogatari*—hon'yaku to gensaku," 133; *MHZ* 21:502.

18. Masamune, "*Genji monogatari*—hon'yaku to gensaku," 133–134; *MHZ* 21:503.

19. Masamune, "*Genji monogatari*—hon'yaku to gensaku," 134; *MHZ* 21:503.

20. Masamune, "*Genji monogatari*—hon'yaku to gensaku," 134; *MHZ* 21:504.

21. Masamune, "*Genji monogatari*—hon'yaku to gensaku," 134; *MHZ* 21:504.

22. Susan L. Burns, *Before the Nation: Kokugaku and the Imagining of Community in Early Modern Japan* (Durham, N.C.: Duke University Press, 2003), 67.

23. Masamune, "*Genji monogatari*—hon'yaku to gensaku," 133; *MHZ* 21:502.

24. Masamune, "*Genji monogatari*—hon'yaku to gensaku," 134; *MHZ* 21:503–504. *The Twenty-Fifth Hour* is the English title (Rita Eldon's translation) of a novel by the Romanian writer Virgil Gheorghiu, which was translated into Japanese via the French by Kawamori Yoshizō and published in 1950 under the title *Nijūgoji*. *Darkness at Noon* is the English title of a novel by Arthur Koestler, originally written in German but first published in an English translation (subsequently translated back into German) by Daphne Hardy; the Japanese translation of this English translation, *Mahiru no ankoku* by Okamoto Seikei, was published in 1950.

25. Masamune, "*Genji monogatari*—hon'yaku to gensaku," 113–114; *MHZ* 21:504. In Japanese "making use of the Chinese cat" is *Karaneko o ayatsutte*. It is not entirely clear what Masamune is thinking of here, since Kashiwagi is simply a spectator to the incident.

26. Masamune, "*Genji monogatari*—hon'yaku to gensaku," 136; *MHZ* 21:506–507.

27. Quoted, in Gaye Rowley's translation, in Royall Tyler and Susan Tyler, "The Possession of Ukifune," *Asiatica Venetiana* 5 (2000 [2002]): 177. This essay, which uses Yosano Akiko's quotation as its epigraph, gives a sampling of statements by scholars who agree, and offers a powerful counterargument. For a more readily accessible version of the essay that does not include the epigraph, see "Genji and Suzaku (2): The Possibility of Ukifune," in Royall Tyler, *The Disaster of the Third Princess: Essays on the Tale of Genji* (Canberra: Australian National University E Press, 2009), 97–129. This book, which is to my mind among the best about *Genji* in English or Japanese from recent decades, is available as a free downloaded from the ANU E Press Web site: http://epress.anu.edu.au/third_princess/html/frames.php.

28. Murasaki Shikibu, *The Tale of Genji, by Lady Murasaki,* trans. Arthur Waley (Boston: Houghton Mifflin, 1925), 2.

29. Arthur Waley, "Introduction," in Lady Murasaki, *The Sacred Tree: Being the Second Part of The Tale of Genji by Lady Murasaki,* trans. Arthur Waley (Boston: Houghton Mifflin, 1926), 30.

30. Mark Morris, "Desire and the Prince: New Work on *Genji Monogatari*—A Review Article," *Journal of Asian Studies* 49, no. 2 (1990): 292.

Conclusion

1. Friedrich Schleiermacher, "On the Different Methods of Translating," trans. Susan Bernofsky, in *The Translation Studies Reader,* ed. Lawrence Venuti, 2nd ed. (London: Routledge, 2004), 49.

2. Shelly Fisher Fishkin, "Crossroads of Cultures: The Transnational Turn in American Studies—Presidential Address to the American Studies Association, Nov. 12, 2004," *American Quarterly* 57, no. 1 (2005): 17–57. Marc Shell and Werner Sollors, eds., *The Multilingual Anthology of American Literature: A Reader of Original Texts with English Translations* (New York: New York University Press, 2000), which Fishkin cites as an example of the transnational turn in American studies, was marketed in part as a belated response to the canon debates, which, the back cover copy notes, "largely ignored . . . indigenous American works written in languages other than English."

3. Paul Jay, "Beyond Discipline? Globalization and the Future of English," *PMLA* 116, no. 1 (2001): 33.

4. Ibid., 32.

5. Ibid., 33.

6. My point is not that there is no need to change the canon of Japanese literature as it is taught in English—this is, in fact, one of the most important things translators do—or that attempts have not been made to do so in ways influenced by identity politics: Phyllis Birnbaum, ed. and trans., *Rabbits, Crabs, Etc.: Stories by Japanese Women* (Honolulu: University of Hawai'i Press, 1982); Yukiko Tanaka, ed., *To Live and to Write: Selections by Japanese Women Writers, 1913–1938* (Seattle: Seal Press, 1987); Stephen J. Miller, ed., *Partings at Dawn: An Anthology of Japanese Gay Literature* (San Francisco: Gay Sunshine Press, 1996); translations and discussions of fiction by Korean-Japanese and Japanese-Brazilian writers; and so on can all be viewed in this light. But the canon debates that broke out in the English department were focused on the relationship of "our" society to "our" literature, and this relationship does not obtain when the literature being taught comes from somewhere else. Transforming the canon of Japanese literature into English has had an effect on images of Japan in English-reading contexts, but there was never any likelihood that this would have a direct impact on, for instance, the culture and society of the United States, as many canon reformers hoped their work would. All this is clear from the fact that the most significant challenges to the canon of Japanese literature in English have been along the lines that Edward Fowler outlined—the introduction of works by popular writers such as Murakami Haruki and Yoshimoto Banana, and more recently translated *manga* and anime—in "Rendering Words,

Traversing Cultures: On the Art and Politics of Translating Modern Japanese Fiction," *Journal of Japanese Studies* 18, no. 1 (1992): 1-44.

7. Emily Apter, *The Translation Zone: A New Comparative Literature* (Princeton, N.J.: Princeton University Press, 2006), 41.

8. Jonathan Culler, "Comparative Literature, at Last," in *Comparative Literature in an Age of Globalization*, ed. Haun Saussy (Baltimore: Johns Hopkins University Press, 2006), 238, 237, 237.

9. Lydia Liu, *Translingual Practice: Literature, National Culture, and Translated Modernity—China, 1900-1937* (Stanford, Calif.: Stanford University Press, 1995), esp. 1-42.

10. Donald Keene, *Dawn to the West: Japanese Literature of the Modern Era* (New York: Holt, Rinehart and Winston, 1984), 1253.

11. Michael Dutton, "Lead Us Not into Translation: Notes Toward a Theoretical Foundation for Asian Studies," *Nepantla: Views from South* 3, no. 3 (2002): 495.

12. Here I am offering my own versions of arguments that have been circulating for years. See, for instance, Andrew Gordon, "Taking Japanese Studies Seriously," in *The Postwar Development of Japanese Studies in the United States*, ed. Helen Hardacre (Leiden: Brill, 1998), 387-405; and Alan Tansman, "Japanese Studies: The Intangible Act of Translation," in *The Politics of Knowledge: Area Studies and the Disciplines*, ed. David Szanton (Berkeley: University of California Press, 2004), 184-216.

13. Franco Moretti, "Conjectures on World Literature," *New Left Review*, January-February 2000, 57.

14. Ibid., 68.

15. On Ikeda's broad familiarity with English-, French-, and especially German-language textual criticism, see Peter Kornicki, "Ikeda Kikan and the Textual Tradition of the *Tosa nikki*: European Influences on Japanese Textual Scholarship," *Revue d'histoire des textes*, n.s., 3 (2008): 263-282. My gratitude to Gaye Rowley for drawing my attention to this article.

16. John Guillory, *Cultural Capital: The Problem of Literary Canon Formation* (Chicago: University of Chicago Press, 1993), esp. "Canonical and Noncanonical: The Current Debate," 3-82.

17. Haruo Shirane, "Curriculum and Competing Canons," in *Inventing the Classics: Modernity, National Identity, and Japanese Literature*, ed. Haruo Shirane and Tomi Suzuki (Stanford, Calif.: Stanford University Press, 2000), 220.

18. Roland Barthes, *Image-Music-Text*, trans. Stephen Heath (New York: Hill and Wang, 1977), 17. "The Photographic Message" and "Rhetoric of the Image" have a lot to say metaphorically, I think, about translation.

19. See, for instance, Lawrence Venuti, *The Translator's Invisibility: A History of Translation* (New York: Routledge, 1995), and *The Scandals of Translation: Toward an Ethics of Difference* (New York: Routledge, 1998).

20. It is interesting to note that scholars of Japanese literature active in Japan are given credit for the form of translation known as *honkoku*: the rewriting of calligraphic manuscripts or xylographic texts in typescript versions, which often involves the addition of punctuation (itself a highly subjective form of interpretation) and *kanji*, in cases where the original texts are written mostly in either *katakana* or *hiragana*. Learning to translate in this way plays a much

larger role in graduate training in Japan, indeed, than learning to translate into English does in any graduate program in Japanese literature I know of in the United States.

21. The essays presented at the panel were published, along with a response by James Araki, in *Journal-Newsletter of the Association of Teachers of Japanese* 2, nos. 1–2 (1964).

22. Joyce I. Ackroyd, "Can Japanese Be Translated?" *Orient/West* 9, no. 5 (1964): 67–72; Donald Keene, "A Reply to Joyce Ackroyd," *Journal-Newsletter of the Association of Teachers of Japanese* 2, no. 3 (1964): 19–22; Joyce I. Ackroyd, "A Reply to Donald Keene," *Journal-Newsletter of the Association of Teachers of Japanese* 3, nos. 1–2 (1965): 13–20.

23. James Araki, "Japanese Literature: The Practice of Transfer," *Monumenta Nipponica* 31, no. 1 (1976): 77–85.

24. Donald Philippi, "Translating Between Typologically Diverse Languages," *Meta* 34, no. 4 (1989): 680–685.

25. Fowler, "Rendering Words, Traversing Cultures."

26. Walter Benjamin, "The Task of the Translator," trans. Henry Zohn, in *Illuminations*, ed. Hannah Arendt (New York: Harcourt, Brace & World, 1968), 79.

27. If I seem to have drawn on surprisingly few books and essays in translation studies, this is the reason. It is not that I do not find the work already being done in translation studies stimulating and valuable; it is that I have not found it *necessary*. Eva Hung and Judy Wakabayashi write that "'non Western' translation traditions . . . offer the opportunity to refurbish Translation Studies in the West and critique it from an outside perspective. An implicit idea underlying this book is that ideas and practices of translation in different cultures are not necessarily a replica of translation elsewhere, so Western models and theories of translation cannot simply be applied uncritically to other contexts" (introduction to *Asian Translation Traditions* [Manchester: St. Jerome, 2005], 1). I agree.

28. Indra Levy, ed., *Translation in Modern Japan* (New York: Routledge, 2010). Within the field of translation studies itself, Judy Wakabayashi has been most active in considering translation as it relates to Japanese. Four recent collections that have tried to prepare the way for a broader engagement with translation practices in Asia are Hung and Wakabayashi, eds., *Asian Translation Traditions*; Ronit Ricci and Jan van der Putten, eds., *Translation in Asia: Theories, Practices, Histories* (Manchester: St. Jerome, 2011); Martha P. Y. Cheung, ed., *An Anthology of Chinese Discourse on Translation*, vol. 1, *From Earliest Times to the Buddhist Project* (Manchester: St. Jerome, 2006); and Leo Tak-hung Chan, *Twentieth-Century Chinese Translation Theory: Modes, Issues, and Debates*, Benjamins Translation Library 51 (Amsterdam: John Benjamins, 2004). Three important books that have helped move translation studies past its Eurocentrism are Marilyn Gaddis Rose, ed., *Beyond the Western Tradition*, Translation Perspectives 11 (Binghamton: Center for Research in Translation, State University of New York at Binghamton, 2000); Theo Hermans, ed., *Translating Others*, 2 vols. (Manchester: St. Jerome, 2006); and Maria Tymoczko, *Enlarging Translation, Empowering Translators* (Manchester: St. Jerome, 2007).

29. James S. Holmes, "The Name and Nature of Translation Studies" was reprinted in an expanded form in *Translated! Papers on Literary Translation and Translation Studies*, ed. James S. Holmes (Amsterdam: Rodopi, 1988), 67–80;

Eugene A. Nida, *Toward a Science of Translating: With Special Reference to the Principles and Procedures Involved in Bible Translating* (Leiden: Brill, 1964); Edwin Gentzler, *Contemporary Translation Theories*, 2nd rev. ed. (Clevedon: Multilingual Matters, 2001), 5.

30. J. C. Catford, *A Linguistic Theory of Translation: An Essay in Applied Linguistics* (London: Oxford University Press, 1965); Walter Benjamin, "The Task of the Translator," trans. James Hynd and E. M. Valk, *Delos* 2 (1968): 80, reprinted in *Translation—Theory and Practice: A Historical Reader*, ed. Daniel Weissbort and Astradur Eysteinsson (Oxford: Oxford University Press, 2006); Edward Seidensticker, "A Decade or So for *Genji*," *Delos* 2 (1968): 126–131.

31. André Lefevere and Susan Bassnett, "Introduction: Proust's Grandmother and the Thousand and One Nights. The 'Cultural Turn' in Translation Studies," in *Translation, History, and Culture*, ed. Susan Bassnett and André Lefevere (London: Cassell, 1990), 1.

32. Susan Bassnett, "The Translation Turn in Cultural Studies," in *Constructing Cultures: Essays on Literary Translation*, ed. Susan Bassnett and André Lefevere (Clevedon: Multilingual Matters, 1998), 136.

33. Keene, "Reply to Joyce Ackroyd," 19.

34. Ackroyd, "Reply to Donald Keene," 13, 15.

35. Ivan Morris, "Notes on Literary Translation from Japanese into English," *Journal-Newsletter of the Association of Teachers of Japanese* 2, nos. 1–2 (1964): 1.

36. Donald Keene, "Problems of Translating Decorative Language," *Journal-Newsletter of the Association of Teachers of Japanese* 2, nos. 1–2 (1964): 11.

37. Edward Seidensticker, "The Reader, General and Otherwise," *Journal-Newsletter of the Association of Teachers of Japanese* 2, nos. 1–2 (1964): 21.

38. Roy Andrew Miller, "Symposium: Translation and Japanese Studies: Introduction," *Journal of Japanese Studies* 6, no. 1 (1980): 2, 4.

39. "Editor's Note," *Journal of Asian Studies* 38, no. 2 (1979): 229.

40. Masao Miyoshi, "Translation as Interpretation," *Journal of Asian Studies* 38, no. 2 (1979): 300, 302. This suggestion is echoed in Valerie Henitiuk, "Going to Bed With Waley: How Murasaki Shikibu Does and Does Not Become World Literature," *Comparative Literature Studies* 45, no. 1 (2008): 40–61.

41. Roy Andrew Miller, "Review: No Time for Literature," *Journal of the American Oriental Society* 107, no. 4 (1987): 745–760; H. Richard Okada, "Translation and Difference: A Review Article," *Journal of Asian Studies* 47, no. 1 (1988): 29–40; Edward Fowler, "On Naturalizing and Making Strange: Japanese Literature in Translation," *Journal of Japanese Studies* 16, no. 1 (1990): 115–132.

42. Norma Field, "The Guest Mavin," *SWET Newsletter* 37 (1989): 13, quoted in Fowler, "Rendering Words, Traversing Cultures," 19.

43. The introductory portion of Foucault's translation-plus-introduction thesis has been published in English translation as Michel Foucault, *Introduction to Kant's Anthropology*, ed. Roberto Nigro, trans. Roberto Nigro and Kate Briggs (Los Angeles: Semiotext[e], 2008).

44. Fowler, "Rendering Words, Traversing Cultures," 8.

Index

Numbers in italics refer to pages on which illustrations appear.

À la recherche du temps perdu (*In Search of Lost Time*; Proust), 237–238, 358, 387–388
ABC Library (*Iroha bunko*; Tamenaga Shunsui), 388
Abenteuer des Prinzen Genji, Die (*The Adventures of Prince Genji*; Müller-Jabusch, trans.), 270, 444n.88
Ackroyd, Joyce I., 397, 400
actor prints, 89, *90*, 134, 160
Adachi Kinnosuke, 281, 287, 288
adaptations, 44, 46, 89
advertisements, 39, 43, 184; for Ammon Papaya "medicinal cream," 347; in *gōkan*, 61, 76, 150; "One Reader's Thoughts," 353–355; for Suematsu's translation, 267, 444n.86; for Tanizaki's translation, 350–352; for Yosano's translation, 336–337
Aeba Kōson, 48, 371
Aesthetic School (Tanbiha), 338
"Aibiki" (The Rendezvous; Turgenev; Futabatei, trans.), 323–324
Aiken, Conrad, 283–284
Aizawa Tadashi, 408n.24

Akamatsu Takanao (character in *Inaka Genji*), 131, *132*, 134, 215, 216, 218
Akashi monogatari, 98
Akashi Toshio, 340
Akiko (empress of Japan), 406n.11, 407n.13
Akiyama Ken, 329, 381
Akutagawa Ryūnosuke, 340
Amenotani Kan'ichi, 212, 213–215
American Cyclopœdia, The, 246
anarcho-syndicalism, 310
Ancora Don Giovanni (*Don Giovanni Again*; Simone Brouwer), 284, 286, 448n.135
Anderson, William, 272, 291–292
Angell, Katherine, 283
anime, 397, 464n.6
annotated editions, 10, 14, 54, 408n.21
Anthologie de littérature japonaise des origines au XXe siècle (*Anthology of Japanese Literature from Its Origins to the Twentieth Century*; Revon), 248
Anti-Foot-Binding Society (Tian Zu Hui; Natural Feet Association), 275

antiquarian miscellanies (*kōshō zuihitsu*), 99, 424n.106
Aoi no Ue (character in *Genji*), 163, 293
Apter, Emily, 386
Arabian Nights, 238, 356, 376, 381
Araki, James, 397
Arblay, Madame d' [Fanny Burney], 5
area studies, 387–391, 395
art history, 45, 49, 336
Artamène; ou, Le Grand Cyrus (*Artamenes; or, The Grand Cyrus, an Excellent New Romance*; Scudéry), 243
Arthur (mythic British king), 263, 442n.75
Asagiri (character in *Inaka Genji*), 125, 126, 127
Asahi shinbun (newspaper), 231, 232
Ashikaga Mitsuuji (as character in *Inaka Genji*), 51, 55–56, 64, 88, 221, 425n.114; censored images of, 215, *216*, 217, *218*; as counterpart of Genji, 64, 77, 80–81, *83*, 84, 84–87, *85*; Dragon King's daughter and, 127–130, *128*; flirting scene with Mihara, 138, *140*; hairstyle of, 60, *69*, 70; in kabuki, 165; looking at fans with Koben, 143, *145*; mother of, 63, 94; as musician on koto, 124, *125*; peeking through window, 140, *142*; with Tamakuzu, 203, *204*; theft of Kogarasumaru and, 146–147, *148*, 152–159, *154*, *155*, 160
Ashikaga Silk: Hand-Dyed Purple (*Ashikaginu tezome no murasaki*; Ryūtei Senka), 55, 67, 102
Ashikaga Yoshihisa, 131, 132, 134
Ashikaga Yoshimasa, 84, 88, 89; as character in *Inaka Genji*, 84, 88, 131, 132, *133*, 134, 137, 138, *139*, 140, *141*, 146, 149, 196, *198*, *207*
Association for Asian Studies, 397, 400
Aston, W. G., 244, 245, 246–247, 351, 439nn.29,32; condescending attitude of, 261; on *Genji* as masterpiece, 287

Athenæum (literary journal), 271, 274, 275
Auerbach, Erich, 392
author, death of the, 27, 30
Autumn Storm (*Nowaki*; Sōseki), 77

Bacon, Alice Mabel, 278, 446n.112
Bai Juyi, 84
Bakhtin, Mikhail, 391
Balzac, Honoré de, 28, 286–287
banknotes, *Genji* and, 11, 406n.12
Barine, Arvède [Louise-Cécile Vincens], 270, 273, 284, 446n.100
Barrow, Terence, 239
Barthes, Roland, 26–30, 394
Bassnett, Susan, 45, 400, 412n.7
Bathhouse of the Floating World (*Ukiyoburo*; Shikitei), 48, 317
Baudelaire, Charles, 370
Bellay, Joachim du, 233, 234
Benjamin, Walter, 171, 397, 398
Best-Selling Edo Bookseller, The (*Atariya shita jihon doiya*; Jippensha), 136
bibliographic translation. *See* translation: bibliographic
Bickley, Francis, 283
binding technologies, 18, 173; case, 191, 193; pouch, 136, 193, *194*, 206
Birnbaum, Alfred, 402
Bittcher, Eduard, 285
Biwa, Lake, 5, 242, 243, 280; Ishiyama Temple and, 265, 267, *268*; Murasaki Shikibu gazing on, 254, 333, *334*
"Black Cat" Yamato Transport, 12
Black Rain (*Kuroi ame*; Ibuse), 326
"Blue-Covers" (Aobyōshibon) lineage, of *Genji*, 20, 407n.20
Boccaccio, Giovanni, 286, 287, 288
Book of the Martyr of Sakura, The (*Higashiyama Sakura no sōshi* [kabuki play]), *161*, 163
"Books and Movable Type" (*Chosho to kappan* [newspaper column]), 185
Bourdieu, Pierre, 11, 43, 411n.3

Bousquet, Georges, 241–247, 249, 253, 275, 285, 329
Bracquemond, Félix, 114
Britain (England), 6, 7; diffusion of "literature" from, 233; Suematsu's translation in, 240; "unequal treaties" of, with Japan, 261; Victorian vision of literary history in, 264; world literary system and, 233–234
Brocade by Night (McCullough), 401
Brooke-Rose, Christine, 251
Brothers Karamazov, The (Dostoyevsky), 366–367, 372, 377, 378–379, 381
Brunswick, Ruth Jane Mack, 436n.2
Buckland, Anna, 264
Buddhism, 172–173, 253, 264–265, 299, 351
Bumpkin Genji: The Dewy Dawn, A (*Inaka Genji tsuyu shinonome* [kabuki play]), 160, 163, 165, *166*
bungaku (literature), 36, 323, 455n.23
Bungei hyōron (*Essays in Literary Criticism*; Hakuchō), 324
Bunka period, 412n.2, 419n.50
Bunsei peirod, 98, 419n.57
Bunshō sekai (*World of Writing* [literary journal]), 337
Burns, Susan L., 375
Butler, Samuel, 280, 287
Byron, Lord, 56, 317

Caddeau, Patrick, 320
calligraphy/calligraphic transcriptions, 10, 14, 121, 406n.11, 409n.24; attributed to Murasaki Shikibu, 293, *294*; "Blue-Covers," 20; classical Chinese, 52; *fukurotoji* (pouch binding) format and, 136; "Oriental" font in evocation of, 267, *268*
Calvino, Italo, 1
Campaign to Promote the Great Teaching (Taikyō senpu undō), 174–176
canonization, 17, 288, 388, 406n.11; as academic study, 8, 10, 393; canon formation, 24, 45, 372, 385, 388, 400; decanonization, 17, 34; hypercanonization of *Genji*, 14; institutions as agents of, 43; as projection of value into texts, 44; reception of canonized texts, 9; Suematsu's translation and, 241; translation as reincarnation and, 172. *See also* recanonization
canons/canonicity: classroom syllabi and, 44, 411n.4; of English literature, 43; globalization and, 388; national literature and, 328–329; translation of "canon," 392, 397; "Western tradition" of, 385; of world literature, 359; world literature and, 383
Casanova, Pascale, 232–235, 388, 434n.13, 435n.21
Catford, J. C., 399
Cazdyn, Eric M., 344–345
cell-phone novels, 231–232, 342, 359–360
censorship, 39, 209, 212, 342–348, 433n.42
Cervantes, Miguel de, 244, 287
Chamberlain, Basil Hall, 245, 249, 250, 252–253, 438n.21; as professor at Tokio University, 296; on Waley's translation, 439n.27; women writers dismissed by, 244, 438n.22
"Chang hen ge" (Song of Everlasting Pain; Bai Juyi), 84
Charlemagne, 263, 442n.75
Charpentier, Léon, 284–285, 286, 448n.137
"Chat About Japanese Dress, A" (Reed), 254–255
Chaucer, Geoffrey, 248
Chiba Shunji, 39, 355, 356
Chikamatsu Monzaemon, 5, 92, 317, 340
China, 5, 34, 234, 275; classical language of, 56, 259, 279; classical literature of, 318; comparative literature and, 387; First Emperor of, 421n.75; vernacular fiction of, 98, 321
Chinese learning, 7, 371

Chino Shōshō, 343
Chronicle of the Eight Dogs of the Nansō Satomi Clan, The (*Nansō Satomi hakkenden*; Bakin), 5, 7, 185, 373; canonical status of, 249; as one of Four Great Literary Marvels of Japan, 48; textual format of, 179, *180*; translation of, 6; Yanagawa Shigenobu's pictures for, 185–186, *187*
Chronicle of the Ōnin War (*Ōninki*), 89
Chronicles of Japan, The (*Nihongi*), 263, 264, 309
Chūōkōron (journal), 292, 324, 365, 366
Chūōkōronsha (publisher), 343, 347–350, 352, 353, 356–357; Kawabata's editor at, 359; postwar editions of Tanizaki's translation and, 364; publicity department of, 349
Classic Literature (White), 254
"Classic of Feudal Japan, A" (White), 248
"Classical Literature of Japan, The" (Aston), 244, 247, 287
"Classics Day," 15–17
Clements, Rebekah, 269, 416n.30
Collected Masterpieces of Tanehiko, The (*Tanehiko kessakushū*), 57–58, 417n.40
Collection of Ten Thousand Leaves, The (*Man'yōshū*), 92, 94, 106, 249, 317
Colonial Press, 288
colonialism, 4, 8
commentaries, 321, 416n.29
Committee for the Thousandth Anniversary of *Genji monogatari*, 12, 13, 14, 16, 363, 407n.14
Communist Party, Japanese, 310
companion books (*otogizōshi*), 92
comparative literature, 390, 391, 392; global canon debate in, 396; "triumph" of, 387, 388; world literature in, 387
"Conclusions: Walter Benjamin's 'The Task of the Translator'" (de Man), 171
Confucius, 214, 324

"Conjectures on World Literature" (Moretti), 232, 389, 435n.23
Connoisseur of Fiction in the Native Script, A (*Kokuji shōsetsu tsū*; Mokurō), 47, 322
Course for the Study of the Classics (Koten Kōshūka), 293, 295, 305
Courtesan's Water Margin, A (*Keisei suikoden*; Bakin), 98, 424n.106, 425n.108
"crane circle" (*tsuru no maru*) logo, 150
"Crossroads of Cultures: The Transnational Turn in American Studies" (Fishkin), 385, 464n.2
Cucumber Messenger, The (*Kyūrizukai*; Robun), 175, 431n.10
Culler, Jonathan, 387, 390, 391
cultural capital, 11, 43, 256
Cultural Capital: The Problem of Literary Canon Formation (Guillory), 391
cultural studies, 9, 17, 397, 400, 402

Dai-Nippon: O Grande Japão (*Dai-Nippon: The Great Japan*; Moraes), 252
Dalby, Liza, 289
Damrosch, David, 39, 230, 232, 235, 411n.41
Dante Alighieri, 317
Darkness at Noon (Koestler), 377, 463n.24
"Datsua-ron" (On Leaving Asia; Fukuzawa), 455n.23
Davray, Henri-D., 245
Dawn to the West (Keene), 387
Dazai Osamu, 340
de Man, Paul, 171, 173
"Death of the Author, The" (Barthes), 27
Deffence et illustration de la langue françoyse, La (*The Defense and Illustration of the French Language*; Bellay), 233, 234
Den-Sagabon Genji monogatari, 407nn.19–20
Derrida, Jacques, 391
Diaries of Court Ladies of Old Japan (Omori and Doi), 282

Diary of the Sixteenth Night (Izayoi nikki), 106
Dickens, Charles, 5, 248
Dickins, Frederick Victor, 284
Dictionnaire des œuvres de tous les temps et tous les pays (Dictionary of Works of All Times and All Countries), 250
Diderick (minnesinger), 263, 442n.75
difference, representation of, 401
digests, 54, 105
Dillon, Edward, 273
Diósy, Arthur, 247
Discipline and Punish (Foucault), 388, 389
"Discourse on Lowering Electricity Rates, A" (Dentō nesageron; Hakuchō), 329–330
"Discourse on Poetry and Music, A" (Suematsu), 305
"Discourse on Pure Fiction, A" (Junsuishōsetsuron; Yokomitsu), 368
Dithering Hokku Contest, A (Tawagoto kuawase; Tanehiko), 76–77, 79
Dizionario letterario Bompiani (Bompiani Literary Dictionary), 250
Dōi Kochi, 282
"Don Juan as a Japanese Literary Character" (literary journal article), 285
"Don Juan dans la littérature japonaise, Un" (A Don Juan in Japanese Literature; Charpentier), 284–285
"Don Juan in der japanischen Literatur, Ein" (A Don Juan in Japanese Literature; Bittcher), 285
Don Quixote (Cervantes), 285, 286, 356
Dostoyevsky, Fyodor, 353
Douglas, R. K., 278
Dragon Girl (character in Inaka Genji), 127–130, *128*, 140
Dream of the Red Chamber, The (Chinese classic), 318
Drizzle of Love Falling Down Temple, A (Koi shigure sode ni furudera [kabuki play]), *162*, 163

Dumas, Alexandre, 26, 244, 287
Dutton, Michael, 388, 390

Eastern Prints of Inaka Genji (Inaka Genji Azuma no nishikie [kabuki play]), *164*, 165
Edo (Tokugawa) period, 33, 37, 321, 323; "Genji names" in, 44, 58, 412n.5; readers of Genji in, 416n.26; ritual suicide in, 374
"Edo purple" (Edo murasaki), 172, 431n.5
Edo Purple: The Bird in the Wisteria (Edo murasaki fuji no hanatori; Fūtei), 70, 419n.49
Egawa Tatusya, 11, 15
Eikan (Noto no Eikan), 408n.22
"Eiyaku Genji monogatari" (An English Translation of Genji monogatari; Hakuchō), 318, 327–328, 330, 355, 356, 358, 368
Eldon, Rita, 463n.24
Eliot, George, 5
"Emotions and Customs in the Age of Genji monogatari" (Gengo jidai no ninjō fūzoku; Takatsu), 298–299, 450n.169
Enchi Fumiko, 55–56, 173, 213, 229
Endnotes (Koreyuki no Ason), 301
Endō Kōkei, 208
England. See Britain (England)
English language, 33, 238, 246, 316, 381; "Classics Day" proclamation in, 15–16; globalization of, 4, 325, 386, 396; Japanese literary studies in, 2, 40, 384; League of Nations and, 325; writing in, 2–8
Envisioning The Tale of Genji (Shirane, ed.), 9
eroticism, 81, 84, 85, *85*, 208
Essaie de psychologie japonaise (Essay on Japanese Psychology; Lavieuville), 247–248
Essais et fantaisies (Essays and Fantasies; Barine), 270
Essence of the Novel, The (Shōsetsu shinzui; Shōyō), 262, 290, 295, 321–322, 323, 371, 449n.153

Eurocentrism, 234, 322, 387, 388, 466n.28
Europe, 286, 327, 392, 395; avant-garde movements in, 358; craze for things Japanese in, 270; *Genji* discourse in, 253; "yellow peril" anxiety in, 273

Fall of the Japanese Language in the Age of English, The (*Nihongo ga horobiru toki: Eigo no seiki no naka de*; Mizumura), 7
Fantasy of Far Japan; or, Summer Dream Dialogues, A (Suematsu), 308
Farrer, Reginald J., 288
Faux-monnayeurs, Les (*The Counterfeiters*; Gide), 368
feminism, 275–283
Field, Norma, 402
Fielding, Henry, 244, 248, 287
Fifty-Three Stations from Two Brushes (*Sōhitsu gojūsantsugi*; Kunisada and Hiroshige, illus.), 80, 83
Fifty-Three Stations of the Tōkaidō Road (*Tōkaidō gojūsantsugi no uchi*; Kunisada, illus.), 77, 80, 82
films, 342, 364, 368, 376
Fish, Stanley, 27, 29
Fisher, Ed, 3, 4
Fishkin, Shelley Fisher, 385, 464n.2
Flaubert, Gustave, 324
foreigners, depictions of, 71, 74
Foucault, Michel, 27, 388, 390, 402
Fowler, Edward, 398, 401–402
Fowler, Herbert E., 437n.7
France, 5, 6, 233–234, 261
Fraser, Mrs. Hugh, 253–254
French language, 6, 245, 247, 308, 325, 381
Freud, Sigmund, 238
"From Work to Text" (Barthes), 26–28
Fuji, Mount, 5, 147, 148, 152, 163
Fuji no Kata (character in *Inaka Genji*), 56, 70, 130, 134, 138; conspiracy against, 142, 149; maiden name of, 417n.38
Fujitsubo (character in *Genji*), 149, 430n.55

Fujiwara clan, 298
Fujiwara no Kintō, 407n.13
Fujiwara no Michinaga, 406n.11
Fujiwara no Teika, 15
Fukuchi Gen'ichirō (Fukuchi Ōchi), 259–260, 299
fukurotoji (pouch binding) format, 136, 193, 194, 206
Fukuzawa Yukichi, 175, 371, 432n.23
Funabashi Seiichi, 364, 368
"Further Thoughts on Poetry, Music, and Painting" (*Kagaku kaiga yoron*; Suematsu), 292, 293, 450n.157
Fūryū Genji (Nishiki), 98, 425n.115
fusenryō (floating-warp pattern), 66, 419n.55
Futabatei Shimei, 323–324
"Futatabi Eiyaku *Genji monogatarai* ni tsukite" (Further Thoughts on *Genji monogatari*'s English Translation; Hakuchō), 318, 327, 355, 356
Fūtei Baryū, 70
"Future of the Past, The" (Weiss), 383
Fūzoku kin'gyoden (*The Legend of Kinjūrō and Uoko, in the Current Style*; Bakin), 410n.39

Gakkai (Yoda Gakkai), 56–58, 60, 94, 235, 357, 418n.46; on *Genji* as novel, 320–321, 323; on "*Genji* pictures," 113; Suematsu and, 319–320, 454n.12
Gakumon no susume (Fukuzawa), 432n.23
Garnett, Constance, 372
Gavronsky, Serge, 9
Geijutsu shinchō (*Art Shinchō* [magazine]), 368
"Geisha: A Faithful Study, The" (Farrer), 288
Genji (fusion of original and translations in imagination), 2, 30, 32, 38, 376–382
Genji (Hikaru Genji; character in *Genji*), 55–57, 63, 146, 229, 377; censored sexual liaisons of, in Tanizaki's translation, 343–344, 459n.80; as Don Juan, 283–285,

286; duolocal marriage of, with Aoi no Ue, 293; in "Hotaru" chapter, 262–263; as humanist, 351; Meiji Emperor and, 302; as millennial anniversary official character, 13; Mitsuuji as counterpart of, 64; in "Suzumushi" chapter, 406n.12
Genji (Minamoto) clan, 55, 256, 407n.15
Genji discourse, 1, 61, 236, 310; Genji as Don Juan, 283–285, 286; global spread of, 35, 231; in Japanese, 290–291; mass media and, 229; Suematsu's translation and, 241, 261, 269–270; Tyler's translation and, 289; Waley's translation and, 239; women readers in development of, 281
Genji for Little Cranes, A (*Hinazuru Genji*), 98, 99, 100, 425n.115
Genji for Little Sprouts, A (*Wakakusa Genji*; Okumura), 98, 99, 100, 415n.20, 416n.28, 425n.115
Genji in Ten Volumes (*Jūjō Genji*; Nonoguchi), 94
Genji incense signs, 44, 58, 107, 154, 412n.5; game of, 419n.55; handscroll in *Inaka Genji*, 121, 122; shell patterns and, 66, 67
Genji monogatari (Egawa, trans.), 11, 15, 405n.10
Genji monogatari (Murasaki Shikibu), 6, 50–51, 91, 215, 399; "bean-size" illustrated guide to, 11–12, *12*, 18, *19*, 20, 23, 289; canonicity/canonization of, 8, 15, 46, 49, 55, 171–172, 385; cartoon about, *3*, 3–4, 8, 405n.4; censorship of, 342–348; commentaries on, 52, *53*, 321, 416n.29; as fairy tale, 379, 380; first Western encounters with, 241–247; genealogy of characters in, *103*, 426n.116; general readers' familiarity with, 54, 109; "Genji names" and, 44, 58, 412n.5; hiragana writing of, 305; as imagined text, 23; *Inaka Genji* and, 52–60, 105–108; lack of interest in, during Meiji and Taishō periods, 372; millennial anniversary of, 2, 7, 12–17, 229; nationalism and, 307–310; *Nihon bungaku zensho* edition of, 417n.40; as novel, 322, 325; as oldest novel, 229; "original text" of, 10, 14, 96, 301, 408n.23; in popular imagination, 20; popularization of, 101; recanonization of, 290, 298, 315; rereading of, 1; as romance, 263–264, 288, 322, 442n.76; textual transmission of, 18; theatrical adaptations of, 347, 364–365, 367, 368; "three secrets" of, 93; transformation of, from tale to romance and novel, 192; typeset editions of, 303–308, 451n.180, 452n.186; as unread text, 44, 245, 251, 299–303. *See also specific characters*
CHAPTERS OF: "Aoi" (Heart-to-Heart), 93, 423n.93; "Asagao" (The Bluebell), 31; "Eawase" (The Picture Contest), 121, 291, 292; "Hashihime" (The Maiden of the Bridge), 14, 66; "Hatsune" (The Warbler's First Song), 374; "Hotaru" (Fireflies), 262–263, 272, 291; "Kiritsubo" (The Paulownia Pavilion), 270, 354; "Kumogakure" (Vanished into the Clouds), 323; "Maboroshi" (The Seer), 326–327; "Miyuki" (The Imperial Progress), 121, 374; "Momiji no ga" (Beneath the Autumn Leaves), 131; "Nowaki" (The Typhoon), 121, 311, 316, 374; "Sakaki" (The Green Branch), 248; "Suma," 127, 371, 423n.90; Uji chapters (Uji jūjō), 359, 377, 379, 425n.115; "Usugumo" (Wisps of Cloud), 347–348, 460n.89; "Utsusemi" (The Cicada Shell), 94–95, 153, 354; "Wakamurasaki" (Young Murasaki), 354; "Yūgao" (The Twilight Beauty), 21, 109, 131, 154, 270, 354, 430n.49. *See also Genji monogatari*: "Hahakigi" (The Broom Tree)

"HAHAKIGI" (THE BROOM TREE), 100, 270, 278, 291, 293, 305, 443n.78; feminists' interest in, 280; in Suematsu's translation, 306; in Tanizaki's translation, 354
AS MASTERPIECE OF WORLD LITERATURE, 8, 31, 37, 39, 310, 312; catalyst for canonization of, 253; discovery of, as world literature, 323-330; entry of, into world literature, 286-290; imagined community of Japanese nation and, 3; Japanese nationalism and, 307-308; reminders of status of, 230; Tanizaki's translation and, 352-353, 357; in translations, 229
MODERN-JAPANESE TRANSLATIONS OF, 21, 34, 39, 107, 229, 342, 354, 359; in postwar period, 363-365, 376, 380
REPLACEMENT OF, 10-17, 31, 33-34, 35, 44-45, 160; in postwar period, 365; Tanizaki's translation and, 316, 348; "Women Classified" selection, 293, *294*; world literature and, 235-236, 289
Genji Monogatarai (Suematsu, trans.), 8, 239-241, 286, 316, 327, 383; canonization of *Genji* as world literature and, 288-289; cover of first edition of, 267, *268*; critical reviews of, 271-273, 284, 299, 300, 445n.93; feminist readers of, 273-283; focus of, on Murasaki Shikibu, 264-267 "Hahakigi" chapter in, 270; "Hotaru" chapter in, 262-263, 272, 291; introduction to, 260-264, 292; Japanese academy and, 293; as little-known work, 341; publisher's advertisement for, 267, 444n.86; reprints of, 269-271; role of, in image of tale outside Japan, 38; supposed irrelevance of, 252
Genji monogatari (play; Yoshimura), 364
Genji monogatari: A Complete Shōwa Translation (*Genji monogatari: Shōwa kan'yaku*; Igarashi, trans.), 364

"Genji monogatari: A Masterpiece of World Literature Turns One Thousand" (newspaper editorial), 229
Genji monogatari: A Modern-Language Translation (*Gendaigoyaku Genji monogatari*; Kubota Utsubo, trans.), 364
Genji monogatari: A Vulgar Interpretation (*Zokuge Genji monogatari*), 100, 425nn.114-115
Genji monogatari: Juni'ichirō shin'yaku (*Genji monogatari: The New Jun'ichirō Translation*; Tanizaki, trans.), 364, 365
"*Genji monogatari* and *The Story of the Stone*" (*Genji monogatari* to *Kōrōmu*; Gakkai), 320-321
Genji monogatari Ferns of Recollection (*Genji monogatari shinobugusa*; Kitamura Koshun), 59, 371
"*Genji monogatari*—hon'yaku to gensaku" (*Genji monogatari*: Translation and Original; Hakuchō), 318, 360, 366-380
Genji monogatari Millennial Anniversary Matcha Baumkuchen, 12-13, 14, 23
Genji Nostalgia (music album), 12
"*Genji* names," 44, 58, 412n.5
"*Genji* pictures" (*Genji-e*), 57, 107, 113, 160
Genroku period, 59, 98, 100
Germany, 5, 6, 7, 286; language of, 6, 308
Gheorghiu, Virgil, 463n.24
Gide, André, 367, 368-370
Girls and Women of Japan (Bacon), 278, 446n.112
Gleanings from Yoshino (*Yoshino shūi*), 106
globalization, 386
Goethe, Johann Wolfgang, 6, 297, 300, 317, 353, 392, 411n.41
"Going to Bed with Waley" (Henitiuk), 281-282, 447n.126
gōkan, 31, 33, 123, 409n.35, 410n.39; audience for, 35; bibliographic translation and, 190-193; Chinese

vernacular fiction and, 321; death of, 38, 171–174, 190, 225; decline of, 174–181, *177*, *178*; dismantling of, 34; emergence of, 48; *fukurotoji* (pouch binding) format of, 136; hand printing of, 418n.47; *ijidōzuhō* (different times, same picture) in, 118–119; as *kusazōshi*, 50, 56, 92, 93, 94, 97, 101, 103, 322, 409n.35; as long serials, 98, 425n.108; as masterpiece, 46; metapictures in, 123, 127, 129–130; physicality of, 136, 142, 143–144; prices of, 47, 413n.3; sales figures for, 47, 412n.1; successful, 424n.106; townspeople as readers of, 160; versions of Chinese fiction and, 98; written text and, 36; *yomihon*ization of, 37, 179–181, *182*, 183–186, *186*, *187*, *188*, *189*, 189–190, 194. See also *Inaka Genji*: as *gōkan*

Goncourt, Edmond de, 252

Goodrich, Samuel G., 259

Gosechi Dancer (character in *Genji*), 423n.90

Greater Learning for Women, The (*Onna daigaku*), 254

Greey, Edward, 255, 256, 258, 259

Gregory-Fletcher, Helen E., 278–279

Griffis, William Elliot, 254, 255, 280

Grimm, Brothers, 381

Grove-Warbler Lost in the Grove, A (*Yabuuguisu yawata shirazu*), 71, 420n.65

Guillory, John, 391, 411n.4

Haga Yaichi, 455n.21

Hagino Yohiyuki, 305

haikai (poetry), 92, 101, 155

Haikai Genji, A (*Haikai Genji*; Takebe), 101

haiku (poetry), 87

Hakubunkan (Meiji-period publisher), 57, 208, 219, 417n.40, 451n.180

Hamada Keisuke, 412n.1

Hamlet (Shakespeare), 43, 44, 45

Hanagasa Bunkyō, 85, 421n.80

Hanagiri (character in *Inaka Genji*), 70, 84, 88, 137; death of, 94; images of, *138*, *139*, 196, *198*, *207*

Hand-Dyed Gauze Puppets of Times Long Past (*Mojitezuri mukashi ningyō*; Tanehiko), 106

handscrolls, 121, *122*, 123, 206

Hansei zasshi (*Temperance* [magazine]), 292

Hardy, Daphne, 463n.24

Hasegawa Kinjirō, 426n.118

Hasegawa Shigure, 415n.24

Hashimoto Sadahide, 419n.48

Hauptmann, Gerhart, 338

Hauser, Otto, 245, 247

Hawley, Frank, 249

Hawthorne, Elizabeth Manning, 259

Hawthorne, Nathaniel, 259

Heavy Makeup and an Everlasting Shimada (*Atsugeshō mannen shimada*), 71, 72

Heian period, 40, 91, 329; court of, 49, 57, 80, 298, 337; decorated handscrolls of, 121; Japanese language of, 250; medieval Europe compared with, 260–261; and "rule of taste," 238; vernacular fiction of, 49

Heike clan, 146

Heimin shinbun (*Commoner's Newpaper*), 312

Henderson, Dan F., 401

Henitiuk, Valerie, 282, 447n.126

Her Name Was Takahashi, the Poisonous Woman (*Sono na mo Takahashi dokufu no oden*), 184, 185, 186

Hibbet, Howard, 397

Higashiyama district/period, 88, 91, 109–110, 114, 145

Hino Ashihei, 352

Hino Tomiko, 89, 112

hiragana syllabary, 48, 449n.153, 466n.20; Heian-period texts written in, 305; in *Inaka Genji*, 52, 53, 54, 144; mixed with *kanji*, 179, 183, 194; Murasaki Shikibu's use of, 305; woodblock printing of, 195

Hirai, Kinza Riugé M., 279

His Figure: Related Copies of Other Pictures (*Sono sugata yukari no utsushi-e*; Kunisada, illus.), 134, 135
Hisamatsu Sen'ichi, 417n.40
Hishikawa Moronobu, 92
historiography, 260, 264
history, 4, 16, 27, 273; nonexistence of objective, 2; romances and, 263–264
History of Chōshū in Changing the Mandate, A (*Bōchō kaitenshi*), 311, 312
History of European Literary Thought, A (*Ōshū bungei shichōshi*; Takaoki), 369
History of Japan to 1334, A (Sansom), 238
History of Japanese Literature, A (Aston), 244–245, 246–247, 261, 287, 439n.32
History of Japanese Literature, A (*Nihon bungakushi*; Mikami and Takatsu), 296
Hōjō Hideji, 365
Hokusai Sketchbooks (*Hokusai manga*), 114
Holmes, James S., 399
Hōmei, 372
Homer, 281, 287
Hori Yasuko, 312
Horne, Charles F., 270, 273, 446n.101
Hōtan zasshi (*Redolent Tales: A Magazine*), 189
Hugo, Victor, 244, 287
Huish, Marcus B., 253, 441n.53
Humphrey, Doris, 341–342, 359
Hung, Eva, 466n.27
Hynd, James, 171, 399

Ibuse Masuji, 326
Ichijō (emperor of Japan), 298, 407n.13, 446n.12
Ichikawa Danjūrō IV, *161*
Ichikawa Danjūrō IX, 454n.4
Ichikawa Danjūrō VIII, 80, 81, *84*, 421n.73
Ichikawa Ebizō IX, 368
Ichikawa Gentazaemon, 89, *90*

Ichimura Theater, 80, 160, 430n.63
Ichinohe, Saeko, 342
Iconology: Image, Text, and Ideology (Mitchell), 45, 46
Identity of the Great Conqueror Genghis Khan with the Japanese Hero Yoshitsuné: An Historical Thesis, The (Suematsu), 264, 443n.80
Igarashi Chikara, 364
Ikeda Kikan, 20–21, 390
Ikiryō (*The Living Spirit*; Hakuchō), 338
Iliad (Homer), 321, 324, 325
Illustrated Chronicle of the Ōnin War, An (*Ehon Ōninki*; Takai and Keisai), 91, *91*
Illustrated Mirror of The Tale of Genji in Album Form, An (*Genji monogatari ekagamichō*), 12, 14, 23
Illustrated Tale of Genji, An (*Eiri Genji monogatari*; Yamamoto, illus.), 18, 20
Ima Genji nishiki eawase (Kunisada, illus.), 431n.5
image-text(-book) relations, 36, 190, 222; bibliographic innovations and, 176; bibliographic translation and, 191; definition of, 45–46; *Inaka Genji* and, 51, 108, 111; movable-type editions and, 191
"Imaginary Kingdom and the Translator's Art, The" (Ury), 239
Imperial Theater (Tokyo), 165, 166
"In the Empire of the Mikado" (Simms), 280
Inaka Genji (*Nise Murasaki inaka Genji* [*A Fraudulent Murasaki's Bumpkin Genji*]; Tanehiko), 31–36, 44, 185, 333, 365; banned during Tenpō Reforms, 71, 84, 86, 160; bibliographic translations of, 190, 191–193; and canon of Great Books or Four Great Literary Marvels, 48, 49, 52, 54, 60; canonization and decanonization of, 34; "A Chart of the Characters" in, 101, *102*; clamshell patterns on back covers of, 66–68, *67*, 196, *197*;

"Complete List of Works Cited" in, 55, 99-101, 105, 414n.18; fame and popularity of, 47-52; fashion and, 60, 72, 73, 73-77, 75, 78; hybridity and, 87-89, 90, 91, 91-93, 107; image-text relation of, to *Genji*, 46; made and remade in image of *Genji*, 52-60, 53, 105-108; Mitsuuji as counterpart of Genji in, 77, 80-81, 83, 84-87; as parody, 50, 51, 52, 54; pedagogical elements in, 93-96, 106; plot of, 88, 150; prefiguration in, 114, 117, 145-151, 148, 150, 151; sales figures for, 47, 412n.2. *See also kuchi-e; specific characters*
  AS GŌKAN, 48, 60, 108, 121, 177; as perfect *gōkan*, 61-68, 62-63, 64-65, 66, 67, 69, 70-71; pictures in, read before text, 151-159, 153, 154-155, 156, 157, 158, 159; reading of, 109-111; *yomihon*ization of, 192, 194, 200
  METAPICTURES IN, 114, 117; frame of picture and beyond, 123, 124, 125, 126, 127-136, 128, 132, 133, 135; looking and reading, 117-121, 118, 122, 123; reading material, 137-138, 138, 139, 140, 140-144, 141, 142, 143, 144, 145
  AS REPLACEMENT FOR *GENJI*, 52, 60, 121, 151, 173, 236, 383, 415n.20; bibliographic translation and, 191; criticism of, 316; popularization of *Genji* in Japan and, 230; world literature and, 289
  TYPESET EDITIONS OF: Ehon haishi shōsetsu, 193, 219, 221, 221-222; Ginkadō/Kakuseisha, 1, 193, 197, 205, 207, 208; Kibunkai, 193, 208-209, 210, 211, 212, 212-215, 216, 217, 218, 219, 220; Moriya, 193-197, 196, 198, 206; Nihon meicho zenshū, 193, 217, 219, 220, 222, 223, 224, 225; Pocket-Size Library, 208; Shinshindō, 193-197, 199, 206

Inaka Genji (play; Motoyama), 165, 168

Inaka Genji (Shuzui, trans.), 168, 169, 170
Inaka Genji sumagoto (Ryūtei Senka?), 421n.79
Inokuma Natsuki, 451n.180
Inoue Kaoru, 261
Internet, 28
Inventing the Classics (Shirane and Suzuki, eds.), 9, 389, 391, 392-394, 397
Irwin, Robert, 52
"Is There a Text in This Class?" (Fish), 29
Ishida Motosue, 420n.67
Ishikawa Masamochi, 106
Ishiyama Temple, 91, 120, 200, 441n.53; Bousquet's description of, 241; Little's visit to, 275; in Suematsu's translation, 265, 267, 268
Ito, Ken K., 344
Itō Hirobumi, 259-260, 319
Iwanami Shigeo, 351-352, 363
Iwanami Shoten (publisher), 352
Izumiya Ichibei (publisher), 70, 134

Jakobson, Roman, 229
Japan: academic interest in *Genji* in, 293, 295-299; as "country of culture," 363, 376; cultural history of, 9; English-language knowledge about, 4; imagined community of, 3, 50; "international literary space" and, 234, 435n.21; Ministry of Education in, 174, 175-176; postwar national identity of, 40; turn of, to the "West," 32
Japan: Its History, Traditions, and Religions (Reed), 252
"Japan, the Beautiful, and Myself" (Utsukushii Nihon no watashi; Kawabata), 359
Japan and Its Art (Huish), 253
Japan Society, 342
"Japanese and European Writing Viewed in Connection to Translation" (Hon'yakujō yori mitaru Nihonbun to Ōbun; Suematsu), 308

Japanese language, 2, 3, 238, 318, 329; classical, 10; *genbun'itchi* (unify speech and writing) movement, 373-274; Japanese Empire and, 6, 7-8; modern, 21, 39, 107, 168, 170; national community rooted in, 381; reforms of 1880s and, 304-305; translations in viewpoint of, 10. See also *hiragana* syllabary; *kanji*
"Japanese Life and Customs as Contrasted with Those of the Western World, The" (Hirai), 279
Japanese literary studies, 2, 30, 241, 384, 394; canonization and, 391; division of labor in, 390; establishment of, as academic field, 4; in global context, 4, 40; Meiji-period turn to the "West" and, 32; Nida's equivalence notion and, 397-398; in postwar period, 238; reputation of, for isolation, 388; translation and, 396, 397, 400, 402, 465n.20; translation studies and, 399
Japanese literature, 22, 37-38, 58, 238, 370, 384, 464n.6; canon of Great Books or Four Great Literary Marvels in, 48, 49, 52, 54, 60; in English translation, 4, 40; "long nineteenth century" in, 32; orientation of, to China and Europe, 34; women writers and, 274, 279; world literature and, 232
"Japanese Literature: The Practice of Transfer" (Araki), 397
"Japanese Literature in the World" (Keene), 288
Japanese Women (Japanese Women's Commission), 279
Japanische Dichtung, Die (*Japanese Literature*; Hauser), 245, 247
Japon à l'Exposition universelle de 1878, Le (*Japan at the Universal Exposition of 1878*), 252, 440n.47, 441n.52
Japon artistique et littéraire, Le (*Literary and Artistic Japan*), 252

Japon de nos jours et les échelles de l'extrême Orient, Le (*Japan in Our Day and the Ports of the Far East*), 241, 246
"Japon littéraire, Le" (Literary Japan; Bousquet), 242-243, 246
Japonisme, 114, 253
Jauss, Hans Robert, 28
Jay, Paul, 386
Jingu Kogu, 280
Jippensha Ikku, 48, 136, 215, 317, 425n.108
Jogaku zasshi (*Journal of Women's Education*), 292, 293
Johnson, Chalmers, 401
Jōno Arindo, 174, 175
Jonson, Ben, 5
jōruri, 89, 94, 105, 107
Journal of Asian Studies, 401
Journal of Japanese Studies, 401
Journal-Newsletter of the Association of Teachers of Japanese, 397, 400
Journey to the West (Ch. Xiyouji, J. Saiyūki), 321
Jun'ichirō-shinshin'yaku Genji monogatari (*Genji monogatari: The New New Jun'ichirō Translation*; Tanizaki, trans.), 359
Jun'ichirō-yaku Genji monogatari (*Genji monogatari: The Jun'ichirō Translation*; Tanizaki, trans.), 22, 342-355; Hakuchō's influence and, 355-361; "heirloom collector's edition" of, 343, 459n.74; marketing of, 349-355, 461n.97

kabuki, 92, 96, 105, 107, 416n.33; confession speeches in, 146; *gōkan* prose style and, 94, 423n.94; historical change and, 318; Ichikawa Danjūrō VIII, 80, 81, 84, 421n.73; in postwar period, 40, 376; revolving stage used in, 137, 205; Tanizaki's translation and, 364; terms from world of, 88, 89, 422n.86; theft of Kogarasumaru as theme in, 160, 161, 162, 163, 164, 165, 166-167, 168, 169
Kabukiza, 165, 364

Kagerō Diary, The, 372
Kaizō (journal), 368
Kaizōsha (publisher), 364
kakekotoba (pivot words), 112, 427n.4
Kaku ya ika ni no ki? (What's Going On Here?; Hasegawa Kinjirō), 426n.118
Kakuda Kōkōkakyaku (Kakuda Kin'ichirō), 308–309
Kamakura period, 121
Kamitsukasa Shōken, 347
Kamo no Mabuchi, 243
kana syllabary, 35, 110, 293, 306, 307
Kanagaki Robun, 71, 174, 175, 431n.10; gōkan revival and, 176; A New Tale of Omatsu and, 179, 180
Kanao Bun'endō (publisher), 332, 338
Kanayomi shinbun (newspaper), 175, 176, 177, 184, 432n.16
kanbun kundokutai writing, 304–305
Kane no waraji (Jippensha), 425n.108
Kaneko Motōmi, 408n.24
kanji (Sino-Japanese characters), 35, 54, 112, 147; adoption of, in Japan, 279; as kanbun, 304, 305; mixed with hiragana (kana), 179, 183, 194, 293, 304
Kantan Travels the Provinces: A Tale (Kantan shokoku monogatari; Tanehiko), 74, 75
Kantō Koroku mukashi butai (Tanehiko), 422n.89
Kaoyo (Tanizaki), 356, 368
Karaginu (character in Inaka Genji), 76–77, 79, 153
katakana syllabary, 119, 449n.153, 466n.20
Katei zasshi (Home Journal), 58
Katō Ikuya, 87
Katō Umaki, 418n.43
Katsura Tarō, 307–308
Katsushika Hokusai, 23
Kawabata Yasunari, 358, 359–360, 369, 402
Kawachibon text, 408n.24
Kawamori Yoshizō, 463n.24
Kawanabe Kyōsai, 163, 431n.10
Keene, Donald, 238, 250, 352, 387, 438n.11; debate with Ackroyd, 397,
400; on Suematsu's translation, 288
Keisai Eisen, 85, 91
Key, The (Kagi; Tanizaki), 345
Kibunkai (Hollyhock Society), 208
kibyōshi (yellowcovers), 61, 62, 103–104, 104, 123, 136, 426n.6
Kimono Pattern with a Genji Design, A (Genji moyō furisode hinagata [kabuki play]), 80, 81
Kimura Mokurō, 47–48, 49, 322, 424n.106
Kimura Takatarō, 56, 417n.38
Kindlers Literatur Lexikon (Kindler's Dictionary of Literature), 250
Kin'eidō (publisher), 176
Kinshōdō (publisher), 184
Kiritsubo (character in Genji), 63, 137
Kitamura Kigin, 18, 23, 59, 101, 303
Kitamura Koshun, 59
Kitamura Yuika, 332
Kobayashi Eiko, 347
Kobayashi Hideo, 327, 375
Kobayashi Masaaki, 344, 345, 459n.81
Koben (character in Inaka Genji), 143, 145
robun (old language), 304, 452n.185
Kodama (character in Inaka Genji), 84
Kōeidō (publisher), 70–71
Kogarasumaru (Kogarasu [name of sword]), 148, 152; crow symbolism of, 153–154, 154, 155, 158; as symbol of Ashikaga shogunate, 146
Kogetsushō (The Moon on the Lake Commentary; Kitamura Kigin), 20, 23, 54, 106, 146, 416n.30; absence of, from Inaka Genji, 121, 123; bibliographic translations of, 303, 304; excluded from Tanehiko's "Complete List of Works Cited," 101–105; Inaka Genji and, 59, 60, 94, 95, 96, 101–105, 104, 160, 418n.43; similarity of "bean-size" Genji guide's cover to, 18, 19; as source text for Tanizaki's translation, 21–22, 408n.24; Suematsu's translation and, 263; townspeople's access to, 35

Kokiden Consort (character in *Genji*), 89
kokubun (national writing), 304
Kokugaku (Nativism, National Studies), 295, 339, 372; annotated commentaries on *Genji* and, 321; language as signifier of identity and, 375; suppression of, 371
kokugo (national language), 304
Kokumin no tomo (*Nation's Friend* [journal]), 320, 322, 324
Kokutai no hongi (*Cardinal Principles of the National Entity of Japan*), 343
Komura Jūtarō, 307–308
Kondo Eiko, 73
Korea, 7, 234, 313, 453n.205
Korekichi (character in *Inaka Genji*), 80, *83*, 118, 155, *156*
Koreyuki no Ason, 301
Kornicki, Peter, 32
"Koten o yonde" (On Reading the Classics; Hakuchō), 318, 319, 324, 325, 328, 341, 366
Kōtoku Shūsui, 312
Kotonoha (character in *Inaka Genji*), 84, *85*
kōwakamai (recitative dance), 92, 149, 430n.54
kozumi (thick ink), 63
Kubota Hikosaku, 176, 179
Kubota Utsubo, 364
kuchi-e (opening illustrations), 61–63, *62–63, 64–65*, 70, 77, 419n.50; eroticism in, 84; frame breaking in, 131, *133*, 134; in Kibunkai edition of *Inaka Genji*, 209; Murasaki Shikibu depicted in, 91; in *A New Tale of Omatsu*, 178; picture from main body of *gōkan* and, 134; in *Takahashi Oden*, 185; Tanehiko's sketches for, 114, *115, 116*; thin ink in, 111; three-panel, 131, 135, 136, 137, 154, 429n.33; in typeset editions of *Inaka Genji*, 196, 199–203, *200, 201, 202, 203, 204, 205–206, 207*; in *Willow's Shade*, 175
Kuroiwa Ruiko, 312

kusazōshi ("grass books" or "stinky books"), 50, 56, 92, 93, 94, 97, 101, 103, 322, 409n.35
Kusazōshi no iroiro (Ishida), 420n.67
Kyokutei Bakin, 5, 6, 68, 317, 410n.39; death of, 47, 413n.7; on *Inaka Genji*, 47, 70, 208, 232; influence of, on interpretations of literary history, 96–97; popularity of, 185; ritual suicide glorified by, 374
"Kyoto purple" (*Kyō murasaki*), 172

Lacan, Jacques, 26
Lacques et la céramiques du Japon, Les (*Lacquer and Ceramics of Japan*), 252, 440n.47
Lancaster, Bruce, 249
Laugh Yourself Awake (*Seishuishō*), 30
Lavieuville, Gustave, 247–248
"Lead Us Not into Translation" (Dutton), 388
Lecture on Genji monogatari, A (*Genji monogatari kōgi*; Suzuki Hiroyasu), 300, 304
Lectures on Literature (*Bungei kōwa*; Ueda Bin), 338
Lefevere, André, 45, 400, 411n.2, 412n.7
Legend of Jin Zhong, Cuiyun, and Cuiqiao, The (*Jin Yun Qiao zhuan*), 68, 410n.39
Legend of Kinjūrō and Uoko in the Current Style, The (*Fūzoku kin'gyoden*; Bakin), 68, 420n.59
Legend of Tamagiku, Unexpurgated: A Mirror of the Pleasure Quarters (*Tamagiku zenden sato kagami*; Tōri), 87, 110
Letters from Japan (Fraser), 253–254
Levy, Indra, 399
"Libertades de Arthur Waley, Las" (Arthur Waley's Liberties; Seidensticker), 250–251
Library of Japanese Classics (*Nihon koten zenshi*; Yosano and Yosano, eds.), 316, 367, 454n.3
Library of Modern Japanese Literature (*Gendai Nihon bungaku zenshū*), 325, 456n.27

Library of World Literature (Sekai bungaku zenshū), 324–325
Life of Omatsu the Singing Beggar, The (*Torioi Omatsu no den*; Kubota Hikosaku), 176, 177, 181
Lingering Feelings for a Later Genji Collection (*Genji goshū yojō*; Kunisada, illus.), 68
Linguistic Theory of Translation, A (Catford), 399
"linked seven treasures" (*shippōtsunagi*) design, 209
literacy and cultural literacy, 35, 48, 255–256
"Literary, All Too Literary" (Bungeitekina, amari ni bungeitekina; Akutagawa), 340
literary criticism, 17, 24, 26, 45, 160
literary history, 40, 229, 247, 367, 376, 383; Bakin and, 97; British, 264; European, 234, 369; Hakuchō and, 315, 372, 373, 374; *Inaka Genji* and, 32, 50; women writers in, 278
"Literary History as a Challenge to Literary Theory" (Jauss), 28
literature, 36, 323, 387, 412n.7; case-bound format for, 135; globalization and, 386; invention of, 391; nationalism and, 5; production of, 27. *See also* Japanese literature; world literature
Literature of Japan, The (Wilson, ed.), 288
Little, Alicia Bewicke, 275–278
Lowell, Amy, 282

Maeda Ai, 56, 175, 190
magazines, 38
Mahiru no ankoku (*Darkness at Noon*; Koestler; Okamoto, trans.), 463n.24
Maison d'un artiste, La (*The House of an Artist*; Goncourt), 252
Manchuria, invasion of, 7
manga, 10–11, 15, 192, 229, 342, 406n.10, 464n.6
Mano Mitsuru, 168
Mantz, Paul, 273
Marching On (*Shingun* [film]), 326–327

Marks, Andreas, 113
Markus, Andrew, 77, 98–99, 100, 101, 322
Marra, Michele, 389
Masamune Atsuo, 316
Masamune Hakuchō, 7, 38–39, 235, 315–319, 331, 342; *Genji monogatari* as world literature and, 323–330; last essay on *Genji* by, 365–382; postwar *Genji* boom and, 370–372; on style and language, 372–375; on translation, 375–382; on Waley's translation, 40, 355, 360; on "worship of the West," 316; writings on *Genji* by, 318–319
Masao Miyoshi, 447n.126
Mass, Jeffrey P., 401
mass media, 2, 38, 241, 260, 293, 299
"Master Among Clouds" (Unchūshi), 303, 305–306, 451n.181
Masuda Ushin (Masuda Yukinobu), 300–302, 305
Matsudaira Naritami, 77
Matsunaga Teitoku, 100, 101
Mazelière, Marquis de la, 438n.20
McClellan, Edwin, 397
McCullough, Helen Craig, 401
McGann, Jerome, 8, 17, 29
McKenna, Ethel M. M., 280–281
McKenzie, D. F., 17, 29, 391
Meiji period, 33, 37, 57, 146, 271, 323; classics shunned in, 339; *Genji's* reputation in Europe and, 250; *Genji's* status in, 290, 372; *gōkan* in, 174, 184; kabuki in, 160; "literature" conceptualized in, 341; "Western learning" in, 371; writing styles and, 373
Meiji Restoration, 32
Mellen, Ida M., 240, 269, 283
metapictures. *See Inaka Genji*: metapictures in
Mihara (character in *Inaka Genji*), 78, 138, *140*, 215, *216*, 218
Mikado's Empire, The (Griffis), 254, 280
Mikami Sanji, 296–298, 300, 302–303
Mill, John Stuart, 279
Millán, Montserrat, 251
Miller, Roy Andrew, 401

Milton, John, 6, 297, 300, 317
Minamoto (Genji) clan, 55
"Miscellany of a Japanese Priest, The" (Weaver), 248
Mishima Yukio, 402
Mistral, Gabriela, 369
Mitani Kuniaki, 1, 4, 290, 449n.153
Mitchell, W. J. T., 45, 46
Miyake Takeo, 355
Miyamoto Yuriko, 333, 340, 457n.51
Mizumura Minae, 7
Mizutani Futō, 418n.43
Modern Fiction: A Classification of Edo Authors (*Kinsei mononohon Edo sakusha burui*; Bakin), 97, 98
Mold (*Kabi*; Tokuda), 338
Moore, Louis, 240
Mooring-Rope of Salvation from Kumbhira's Boat, A (*Konpirabune rishōno tomozuna*; Bakin), 98, 425n.108
Moraes, Wenceslau de, 252
"More Conjectures on World Literature" (Moretti), 235
Moretti, Franco, 232–235, 389, 434nn.13–14
Mori Ōgai, 56, 338–339
Morita Theater, 162
Moriya Kiyokichi (publisher), 193–197
Morris, Ivan, 238, 397, 400
Morris, Mark, 381
Morte d'Arthur, Le (Malory), 288
Mortimer, Raymond, 237–238, 239, 341, 436n.1
Motoori Norinaga, 21, 244, 327, 375
Motoyama Tekishū, 165
movable-type editions, 20, 32, 183, 408n.21; of *Inaka Genji*, 48, 173; readers' new pleasures and, 173–174; woodblock printing and, 186, 189, 432n.23
Mugi to heitai (*Wheat and Soldiers*; Hino Ashihei), 352
Müller, Max, 240
Müller-Jabusch, Maximilian, 270
Murakami Butsuzan, 259
Murakami Haruki, 397, 402, 464n.6
Murasaki Shikibu, 5, 86, 287–288, 341; as avatar of fantasy Japan, 3; calligraphy attributed to, 293, *294*; diary of, 11, 12, 16, 406nn.11–12, 407n.13; different versions of *Genji* and, 11, 14–15, 406n.11; feminists' discovery of, 273–283; inkstone said to be used by, 120, *120*, 428n.17; Japanese academic interest in, 296–299; Japanese language and, 373; Masuda's fictional encounter with, 301–303; in modern literary imagination, 7; as Nobel Prize winner, 7, 360, 369, 370; Ofuji as "fraudulent Murasaki," 102, 201, 206; Proust compared with, 358, 378; Scudéry compared with, 241–245, 246, 248, 249–253, 285

IMAGES OF, 38, 68, *69*, 80, *82*, 91; by Kunisada, *202*, 203, 205; by Ogata Gekkō, *201*, 202–203, 206, 267; in Shinshindō edition of *Inaka Genji*, 196, *197*; on *Shin'yaku Genji monogatari* cover, 333, *334*; in Suematsu's translation, 267, *269*; as woman writer in *Genji* discourse, 253–256, *257*, 258–259

"Murasaki Shikibu" (Kamitsukasa), 347
Murasaki Shikibu (Shimazu), 347–348
"Murasaki Shikibu: A Historical Story" (Rekishi shōsetsu Murasaki Shikibu; Yoshiya), 347
musicals, 229
Myōjō (*Morning Star* [magazine]), 338, 343

Naitō Meisetsu, 56, 417n.37
Nakamura Masaaki, 176
Nakamura Theater, 160, 161
Nakamura Yukihiko, 99, 108
Nakano Kōichi, 405n.4
Nakazawa Hiromitsu, 332–333
Nakazawa Zennosuke, 353–355
"Name and Nature of Translation Studies, The" (Holmes), 399
Nansenshō Somahito, 103
Narrative of the Earl of Elgin's Mission to China and Japan in the Years

1857, '58, and '59 (Oliphant), 114, 428n.9
national literature, of Japan. *See* Japanese literature
National Translation Center, 399
nationalism, 39, 233, 363
Nations of the World, The (*Sekai kunizukushi*; Fukuzawa), 175
Nativism. *See* Kokugaku
Natsume Sōseki, 77, 308, 339–340, 341
Naturalism, 315, 338, 340, 371
New Collection of Poems Old and New, A (*Shin kokin wakashū*), 106
New Edition of Murasaki's History, A (*Shinpen Shishi*; Masuda), 300–302, 304, 305
New Imperial Library (Zoku teikoku bunko), 208
New Oh If Only I Could Switch Them! A (*Shin torikaebaya monogatari*; Tanehiko), 106
"New Planet, A" (Mortimer), 237–238
New Plum in the Golden Vase, A (*Shinpen kinpeibai*; Bakin), 424n.106
"New Psychologism" (Shinshinrishugi) movement, 358
New Romantic School (Shinromanha), 338
"New Sensibility" (Shinkankakuha) movement, 358
New Tale of Omatsu the Singing Beggar's Adventures at Sea, A (*Torioi Omatsu kaijō shinwa*; Yōshūsai, illus.), 176, *177*, 177–181, *178*, 432n.15; gōkan incorporated into "newspaper time" by, 194; woodblock printing of, 183–184, 192; *yomihon*-like textual format of, 179, *180*, 183, 185
New Tale of the Hollow Tree, A (*Shin utsubo monogatari*; Tanehiko), 106
New Tale of the Lady of the Bridge, A (*Shin Hashihime monogatari*), 99, 100, 425n.115
newspapers, 38, 43; serials in, 176, 181. *See also specific newspapers*
NHK (Japan Broadcasting Corporation), 12, 365

Nida, Eugene A., 397–398, 399
Nihon bijutsu zensho (*Pictorial Arts of Japan*; Anderson; Suematsu, trans.), 272
"Nihongo—The Japanese Language" (Lancaster), 249
Nijūgoji (*The Twenty-Fifth Hour*; Gheorgiu; Kawamori, trans.), 463n.24
Nikki Kiyonosuke (character in *Inaka Genji*), 147, 152–153, *153*, 155–157, *159*
Nimura, Janice P., 289
ninjōbon (books of sentimental fiction), 74
Nippon eitaigura (*The Eternal Storehouse of Japan*; Saikaku), 333
Nise Murasaki inaka Genji (*A Fraudulent Murasaki's Bumpkin Genji*). See *Inaka Genji*
Nise Murasaki inaka no shitazome, 418n.41
Nise Murasaki Naniwa Genji (*A Fraudulent Murasaki's Ōsaka Genji*; "Sanehiko"), 421n.79
Nishiki Bunryū (Miyako no Nishiki), 59, 99, 417n.41, 425n.115
Nishiki no obi nazorae mugen (Tanehiko), 422n.89
nishiki-e (brocade book covers), 61
Nishimura Shigeki, 292
Nishino Atsushi, 345–346, 347, 408n.24
nō, 92
Nobel Prize in Literature: Gide and, 369; Kawabata and, 359, 369; Murasaki Shikibu and, 7, 360, 369, 370
Nonoguchi Ryūho, 92, 94
Norimitsu Onishi, 231
Notes for the Morning Star (*Myōjōshō*; Sanjōnishi), 306
Notes on Genji: A Few Last Drops (*Genchūyoteki*; Ishikawa), 106
novel, 36, 232; "autonomous development" of, 235; birth of, 173; Genji as oldest, 229; theory of, 32. *See also shōsetsu*

"'Nowaki' Chapter of *Genji*, The" (*Genji* Nowaki no maki; Sakai), 311–312, 313

"Ōbeijin no kenkyū shitaru Nihon bungaku" (Japanese Literature in European Research; Hawley), 249
Ochiai Naobumi, 305
Odyssey (Homer), 324, 325
Ofuji ("fraudulent Murasaki" of *Inaka Genji*), 172, 201; images of, 68, 69, 70, *200*, *203*, 205, *206*; *Kogetsushō* and, 102–103
Ogata Gekkō, 199–200, 201, 203, 205–206, 267
Ogata Kōrin, 92
Oh If Only I Could Switch Them! A Tale (*Torikaebaya monogatari*), 106
Okada, H. Richard, 401
Okada Ikunosuke, 363
Okamoto Seikei, 463n.24
Okazaki Yoshie, 347
Okumura Masanobu, 415n.20, 416n.28, 425n.115
Ōkura Magobē, 176, 177, 183
Old Bamboo-Hewer's Story, The (Dickins, trans.), 284
"Old Man from Yamanote," 306, 310, 452n.186
Oliphant, Laurence, 114
Olivier, Laurence, 43, 45
Omori, Annie Shepley, 282
"On Being Faithful to Murasaki Shikibu" (Seidensticker), 251
"On Belles Lettres" (Bungaku-bijutsu-jō; Suematsu), 307
"On *Genji monogatari*" (*Genji monogatari* ni tsuite; "Old Man from Yamanote"), 306, 452n.186
On Gōkan (*Gōkan ni tsuite*; Suzuki Jūzō), 48–49
"On Japanese *Monogatari*" (Nihon no monogatari ni tsuite; Fukuchi), 299
On Japanese Writing (*Nihon bunshōron*; Suematsu), 303–304, 306–307
"On Literary Styles" (Bunshōron; Suematsu), 307
"On Naturalizing and Making Strange" (Fowler), 402

"On Writing in English" (Eibun o motte chojutsu suru koto [newspaper editorial]), 4–8, 10, 16, 395
"One Reader's Thoughts" (Ichidokusha no kansō; Nakazawa Zennosuke), 353–355
Onna gokyō, 98
Orient/West (journal), 397
Orientalisms, 282
Orikuchi Shinobu, 357
Ōshimabon, 20, 21
Ōshū's Obsession: A Tale (*Ōshū shūjyaku monogatari*; Tanehiko), 106, 427n.130
Ōsugi Sakae, 310, 312–313
Otama Pond: How to Wear a Moon-Shaped Comb (*Otamagaike kushi no tsukigata*; Jōno Arindo), 175, 181
Oura, Mrs., 280
Outline of Genji monogatari, An (*Genji monogatari teiyō*), 99, 100
Ōya Tomoemon, 162
Ozaki Kōyō, 371
Ozawa Keijirō, 421n.71
Ozu Keisō, 208, 212

Palm-Size Tale of Genji, The (*Shōchū Genji monogatari*), 11
Parisina (Byron), 56, 417n.38
parody, 50, 51
"Parting—A Passage from the *Genji Monogatari*" (White), 248–249
Philippi, Donald, 397
philosophy, 45
Pictorial Arts of Japan, The (Anderson), 272, 291–292
Pillow Book, The (*Makura no sōshi*; Sei Shōnagon), 23, 106, 249, 281, 296–297, 309
Plum Calendar (Tamenaga Shunsui), 74–75, 420n.67
Plum in the Golden Vase, The (Ch. *Jinpingmei*, J. *Kinpeibai*), 321
Portrait of Shunkin, A (*Shunkinshō*; Tanizaki), 345
Portraits of Actors Past and Present (*Kokon haiyū nigao taizen*; Kunisada, illus.), 89, *90*

postage stamps, *Genji* and, 12
poststructuralism, 24
Practices of the Sentimental Imagination (Zwicker), 32, 410n.39
prefiguration, 7, 114, 145–151, *148*, *150*, *151*
printing technologies, 173
"Problems of Translation from Japanese" (conference panel), 397
"Progress in Japan" (Douglas), 278
Proust, Marcel, 237–238, 358, 378, 381, 436n.2, 445n.93
puppet plays, 92, 94, 112

Quest for Sincerity: A Way Back in Dream, The (*Tansei yume no fukuro*), 183

Rabbit on the Moon, The (*Tamausagi*; Tamenaga Shunsui), 74–76, 109
radio, 40, 342, 365, 376
reading: "adaptation" mode of, 34; "death of the author" and, 27, 30; embodiedness of, 30; history of, 1–2; readers as authors, 27; reading practice, 147; subjectivity of interpretive experience of, 17
Reading Notes (*Dokusho zakki*), 365, 366
"Real Chrysanthemum, The" (McKenna), 280–281
realism, 263, 350
recanonization, 14, 17, 34; of *Genji*, 231, 290, 298, 299; of *Inaka Genji*, 34. See also canonization
reception, 9–10, 11, 14, 17, 24, 28
Record of Ancient Matters, 309, 354
Record of Great Peace in Kumamoto: A Picture Book (*Ehon Kumamoto taiheiki*), 183
Record of the War in Kagoshima: A Picture Book (*Ehon Kagoshima senki*), 182, 183
Red and White Genji, A (*Kōhaku Genji monogatari*), 99, 100, 425n.115
Reed, Sir Edward J., 252, 440n.47
Reed, Mary, 254–255
Reizei (emperor of Japan), 344, 377, 460n.89

Reizei Tamemoto, 451n.180
"Rendering Words, Traversing Cultures" (Fowler), 398, 402
"Rendezvous, The" (Svidanie; Turgenev), 323–324
replacement, 10–17, 20, 30; of canonical works, 45; complexity of process of, 21, 22–23; as continuity through rupture, 34; history of, 383; translation as paradigmatic form of, 40; *yatsushi* (dressing down), *mitate* (seeing-as), and *imayō* (modernizing) as, 298
"Reply to Joyce Ackroyd, A" (Keene), 400
Resistance to Theory, The (de Man), 171
Revon, Michel, 248
Rexroth, Kenneth, 231
Rin' (music group), 12
Riordan, Roger, 270
Risen Sun, The (Suematsu), 273, 308
Rivers and Seas Commentary, The (*Kakaishō*), 52, 415n.23
Rob Roy (Scott), 321
Rodin, Auguste, 336, 341
Roosevelt, Theodore, 308, 452n.193
Rowley, G. G., 331, 332, 338, 417n.40
Rumors of a Double Life (*Kōsetsu konotegashiwa*; Takabatake), 184, 186, *189*, 189–190
Russia, 261
Russo-Japanese War, 273, 308
Ryan, Marleigh Grayer, 401
Ryūtei Library, The (*Ryūtei sōsho*), 48
Ryūtei Senka (Ryūtei Tanehiko II), 54, 55, 242, 421n.79, 424n.106; on *Chronicle of the Ōnin War*, 89; on reading of different purples, 431n.5; on Tanehiko's use of *Kogetsushō*, 102
Ryūtei Tanehiko, 31, 34, 44, 46, 50, 60; bathhouse metaphor of, for *Inaka Genji*, 105; canonicity of *Genji* and, 302; death of, 47, 323, 413n.7; education of readers by, 93–96, 106; *gōkan* by, 106, 109, 422n.89; knowledge of past popular culture, 54–55; material form of books and,

Ryūtei Tanehiko (*continued*)
136; misreading of, 96–101;
Murasaki Shikibu's text and, 50,
88, 96–97, 414nn.17–18, 424n.102;
as Murasaki Shikibu II, 172; note to
Kunisada on period objects, 92,
422n.88; parody in work of, 52, 54;
partnership with Kunisada on
Inaka Genji, 112–115, *115*, *116*, 117,
213; pictorial devices used by, 123;
playful allusions to own work,
74–77; popular interest in *Genji*
and, 56–57, 58, 423n.92; popularity
of, 185; prefaces to chapters of
Inaka Genji, by, 89, 92–93, 206,
423n.91. See also *Inaka Genji*

Sacred Books and Early Literature of the East, The (Horne), 270, 273
Said, Edward, 27
Saiga Ryūkō, 194
Saigyō, 106, 427n.131
Saikaku, 324, 333, 340
Sakai Toshihiko, 310, 311–312, 316
Samata Hideki, 331
"sandbar" (*suhamagata*) design, 209
Sanjōnishi Kin'eda, 306
Sankyō Shoin (publisher), 208
Sansantei Arindo, 420n.65
Sansom, George, 238, 249
Santō Kyōden, 424n.106
Sanyūtei Enchō, 71
Sarashina Diary (*Sarashina nikki*), 367, 376
"Sarrasine" (Balzac), 28
Saru Genji, 98
Sasaki Tōru, 431n.10
sashie (inserted pictures), 203
Satō Satoru, 101, 137, 419n.50
Satow, Sir Ernest, 245, 246–247, 249, 439n.29
"scattered writing" (*chirashigaki*), 71
Schiller, Johann, 6, 297, 300, 353
Schleiermacher, Friedrich, 383–384
Scholarly Editing in the Computer Age (Shillingsburg), 30
Scott, Walter, 5, 321
Scudéry, Madeleine de, 243, 246, 248, 289, 438n.20

Second *Genji monogatari* International Forum, 14
Seeing Is Forgetting the Name of the Thing One Sees (Weschler), 47, 52
Sei Shōnagon, 23, 281, 288, 296–298, 302, 347
Seidensticker, Edward G., 289, 359, 397, 399, 401; on Bousquet's description of Murasaki Shikibu, 250–251; on translation and access to original, 400–401; Waley's influence and, 238, 437n.6
"Seiōjin no *Genji monogatari* no kanshō" (European Appreciations of *The Tale of Genji*; Keene), 250
Seiseidō (publisher), 71
sekai (world), 88, 89, 111, 422n.86
Sekine Masanao, 304
Senkakudō (publisher), 119, 150, 151
Setouchi Jakuchō, 229
Shakespeare, William, 5, 240, 248, 281, 287, 353; global perspective on literature and, 324; as icon of English-language literature, 317; number of words in plays of, 374; prestige of, 43; reverence for, 297, 300; translation of works of, 6
Shakuyakutei Nagane, 25
Shanks-Mare on the Eastern Seaboard (*Tōkaidōchū hizakurige*; Jippensha), 48, 215
Shaw, George Bernard, 248
shell-matching game (*kai-ōi*), 66
Shibamoto Yuki, 15
Shibano Rokusuke, 245
Shikitei Sanba, 48
Shillingsburg, Peter, 17, 30
Shimanaka Yūsaku, 349, 355–356, 358
Shimazaki Tōson, 324, 338, 372
Shimazu Hisamoto, 347, 416n.33
Shimizu Fukuko, 20, 54, 59, 98, 407n.19, 415n.26
Shinchō (*New Tide* [literary journal]), 337
Shinchōsha (publisher), 324–325
Shinonome (character in *Inaka Genji*), 65, 146, 153, 425n.114, 430n.49; crow-patterned kimono of, 158,

159, 162, 163, *163*, 165, *167*; in kabuki, *161*, *162*, 165, 168, *169*; print image of, with and without *usuzumi* ink, *63*, *65*; theft of Kogarasumaru by, 152, 156, 158–159, *159*
Shinshichō (*New Thought* [journal]), 340
Shinshindō (publisher), 193–197
Shin-shin'yaku Genji monogatari (*Genji monogatari: A New New Translation*; Yosano Akiko, trans.), 332
Shin'yaku Genji monogatari (*Genji monogatari: A New Translation*; Yosano Akiko, trans.), 331–333, 336–341, 348; front covers of, *333*, *334*, *335*; price of, 332, 457n.47
Shin'yaku Genji monogatari (*Genji monogatari: The New Translation*; Tanizaki, trans.), 364
Shiota Ryōhei, 417n.40
Shiraito (character in *Inaka Genji*), 141, 142, *143*, *144*, 149
Shirane, Haruo, 9–10, 28
Shōhonjitate (Tanehiko), 423n.94, 425n.108
Shōken (empress of Japan), 34, 215, 333, 457n.51
Shomei, 254
shōsetsu (fiction, novel, short story), 36, 37, 173, 190, 320–321; change in, 359; as cluster of early modern genres, 323; early modern, 192; "unofficial histories," 264, 321, 322, 332; Western, 323
Shōwa period, 33, 349, 354
Shuzui Kenji, 168, 169, 170
Simms, Joseph, 280
Simone Brouwer, Francesco de, 284, 286
Sino-Japanese War, First (1894–1895), 307
Sino-Japanese War, Second (1937–1945), 342, 349, 352, 355
Six-Panel Screen of the Floating World, A (*Ukiyogata rokumai byōbu*; Tanehiko), 106, 422n.89, 427n.131
Skopos theory, 400

Small Mirror of Genji, A (*Genji kokogami*), 99, 100
Sōbokuen Shujin, 412n.2
Sōchin, 30–31
Sokushū Genji monogatari ga wakaru!, 405n.4
songs, popular, 92
Songs of Chu (*Chuci*), 92, 94
sound-film technology, 325
"Sounds, Scripts, and Styles" (Atsuko Ueda), 304
Southeast Garden, The (Tamenaga Shunsui), 75, 420n.67
Soyano Han'ya, 311
Sōzō sareta koten (*Inventing the Classics*; Shirane and Suzuki, eds.), 392–394
Spain, 286
Speechless, Wordless (Ozaki), 371
"spring books" (*shunpon*), 84
Spring Dawn (*Haru no akebono*; Hokusai, illus.), 23, *25*
Spring Dawn Commentary, The (*Shunshoshō*), 23
Stimson, Henry L., 363
Story of English Literature, The (Buckland), 264
Story of the Stone, The (*Honglou meng*), 318, 319, 320–321, 322, 323, 324, 366
Straits of Awa, The (*Awa no Naruto*), 106
Streatfeild, R. A., 280
Strindberg, August, 351
Studies of the Novel (*Chōhen shōsetsu no kenkyū*; Tayama), 44
Subaru (*Pleiades* [magazine]), 338, 343
Suematsu Kenchō, 8, 38, 239–241, 383, 437n.9, 438n.11; Gakkai and, 319–320, 454n.12; *Genji* discourse in Japan and, 291–293, 299; introduction to *Genji* translation by, 260–264, 292; Japanese academy and, 293, 295–299; Japanese nationalism/empire and, 307–308, 312–313; life of, 259–260, 441n.62; on Murasaki Shikibu, 265–267; Sakai and, 311; on typeset editions, 303–304

Suematsu Seihyō (Suematsu Kenchō), 351
Sugibae (character in *Inaka Genji*), 94, 137, *138*, *139*
Sugimura Sojinkan (Sugimura Kōtarō), 330
Sugita Shōten, 347
sumi (black ink), 62
Sumiyoshi Tale, The (*Sumiyoshi monogatari*), 243
Sunrise Stories (Riordan and Tozo), 270, 284
Suzaku (emperor of Japan), 146
Suzuki, Tomi, 9
Suzuki Hiroyasu, 300
Suzuki Jūzō, 48–49, 106, 415n.23, 422nn.88–89; on reading *gōkan* like a handscroll, 206; on Tanehiko's use of *Genji* text, 97
syntax, 398
S/Z (Barthes), 28

Tagore, Rabindranath, 369
Taira no Masakado, 146
Taira no Sadamori, 146
Taishō period, 33, 160, 337, 341, 372
Takabatake Ransen (Ryūtei Tanehiko III), 172, 184, 186
Takagi Gen, 424n.106, 432n.20
Takahashi Korekiyo, 259, 452n.193
Takahashi Oden, 184
Takahashi Oden: Tale of a Demon (*Takahashi Oden yasha monogatari*; Robun), 184, *185*, *186*, *187*; printing technologies and, 186, 192; title page of, *188*
Takai Ranzan, 91
Takaoki Yōzō, 369
Takatsu Kuwasaburō, 296, 298–299
Takebe Ayatari, 101
Takeda Izumo, 5
Tale of All Nations Illustrated for Children, A (*Osana bankokubanashi*; Robun), 71, 74
Tale of Genji, The (dance; Ichinohe, choreographer), 342
Tale of Genji, The (Seidensticker, trans.), 238, 401

Tale of Genji, The (Tyler, trans.), 94–95, 237, 289, 443n.78
Tale of Genji, The (Waley, trans.), 38–39, 270, 286, 325, 373, 383; back-translation of, 331; canonical status of, 289; critical reviews of, 237–238, 239, 240, 283, 436nn.1–2; Hakuchō's essays on, 319, 326–328, 352, 355, 360, 365, 379–380; Hakuchō's review of, 367–368; influence of, 237–239, 437n.6; popular readership in Japan and, 289; success of, 331; Tanizaki and, 356; Woolf's review of, 281–282; "worship of the West" and, 316
"The Tale of Genji + A Little Bit of Literature" (*Genji monogatari + chottodakebungaku* [video game]), 13
Tale of Genji Collated, The (*Kōi Genji monogatari*; Ikeda, ed.), 20, 21, 22, 390, 408n.23
Tale of Genji Compendium, The (*Genji monogatari taisei*; Ikeda, ed.), 20–21
Tale of Genji Jeweled Comb, The (*Genji monogatari tama no ogushi*; Norinaga), 21, 244
Tale of Genji Museum, 12
Tale of Genji Picture Scroll (*Genji monogatari emaki*), 11, 406n.12
Tale of Genji with Headnotes, The (*Shusho Genji monogatari*), 20, 21, 407n.19
Tale of the Bamboo Tree, The, 243
Tale of the Hollow Tree, The (*Utsubo monogatari*), 106, 243
Tales of Ise, The (*Ise monogatari*), 199, 354
Tales of Ise in the Modern Manner, The (*Imayō Ise monogatari*; Tōri), 70
Tales of the Heike, The (*Heike monogatari*), 242, 354
Tamenaga Shunsui, 74, 109, 185, 388, 413n.7, 420n.67
Tamenaga Shunsui II (Somezaki Nobufusa), 175
Tanabe Akio, 317
Tanikawa Keiichi, 431n.10

Tanizaki Jun'ichirō, 21–22, 229, 231, 315, 340, 408n.24; censorship of *Genji* and, 344–348, 459nn.80–81; fiction of, 368; first *Genji* translation by, 39, 342–348, 355, 363; Hakuchō's influence and, 355–361; kabuki and, 364; in "reigning triumvirate" of Japanese literary figures, 402; replacement of *Genji* and, 316, 383; second *Genji* translation by, 39–40, 364; third *Genji* translation by, 359; Waley's translation and, 39, 331

"Task of the Translator, The" (Die Aufgabe des Übersetzers; Benjamin), 171, 397, 398, 399

Tasogare (character in *Inaka Genji*), 64, 65, 114, 131, *221*, 430n.49; as counterpart of Yūgao, 154; death of, 146, *148*, 152; in kabuki, 160, 165, 430n.63; print image of, *64*; theft of Kogarasumaru and, 152, 154, *155*, 157, *157*

Tasteful Tale of Genji, A (*Fūryū Genji monogatari*; Nishiki), 59, 99, 100, 105, 417n.41

Tateishi Kazuhiro, 40, 364

Tayama Katai, 44, 46, 108, 191, 371

Teihon Genji monogatari shinkai (Kaneko), 408n.24

Tenpō period, 59, 71, 84, 107, 108, 419n.57

Terada Torahiko, 325

text and textuality, 27, 36; canonization and, 44; as imagined original, 17–18, 20–23; primacy of, over pictures, 37, 196; in theory, 24–31; *yomihon*ization of *gōkan* and, 179. *See also* image-text(-book) relations

Textermination (Brooke-Rose), 251

Thackery, William Makepeace, 5, 244, 287

theology, 45

Things Japanese (Chamberlain), 245, 247

"Three Directives on Teaching" (Sanjō no kyōken; Ministry of Education), 174, 175

Three Sake Cups for New Year's Day (*Kesa no haru mitsugumi sakazuki*), 71

time (temporality), representation of passage of, 137, 138, 142

Tissot, Ernest, 280

Tokio (Imperial) University, 293, 295–296, 305

Tokuda Shūsei, 338, 372

Tokugawa Akitake, 445n.95

Tokugawa Iesato, 446n.95

Tokugawa Yoshinori, 445n.95

Tōkyō asahi shinbun (newspaper), 185, 343, 347, 350, 356; advertisement for Tanizaki's translation in, 357; on censorship of *Inaka Genji*, 215

Tōkyō nichinichi shinbun (newspaper), 259, 260, 291, 295, 303, 349, 441n.60

Tolstoy, Leo, 324, 351, 381

Tōri Sanjin, 70, 87

Torii Kiyonobu, 92

Tosa Diary (*Tosa nikki*), 106, 249

"Toshikage Scroll, The" (Toshikage no maki), 243

Tosho Shuppan (publisher), 451n.180

Toward a Science of Translating (Nida), 399

Toyohara Kunichika, 162

Toyoshi no Mae (character in *Inaka Genji*), *132*, 132–134, 136, 141; conspiring with Shiraito, 142, *144*; standing in rain, *130*, *143*

Tozo Takayanagi, 270

Traces in a Rustic Visage (*Sono yukari hina no omokage*; Keisai), 67–68, 70

"Translating Between Typologically Diverse Languages" (Philippi), 398

Translating Japanese (*Nihonbun no hon'yaku*; Seidensticker), 239

translation, 2, 230, 315, 316, 383–384; as "afterlife" of original, 171; back-, 39, 292, 331, 393; covert, 231, 434n.8; "difference in translation," 398; dual nature of, 395–396; "exoticism in translation," 398; functionalist translation theory, 400; intersemiotic, 229; Japanese literature in English, 4; original

translation (continued)
    fused with, 380; as paradigmatic form of replacement, 40; photography compared with, 394–395; "pietistic" and "cannibalistic," 9–10; as reincarnation, 172; as replacement, 10–17, 230; return to, 397–403; scholar-translators, 384, 394, 398, 401, 403; similarity of languages and, 6; translation studies, 396, 398, 399, 401, 466nn.27–28; "translation turn," 400, 402, 403; type-, 8, 10, 21; vernacular, 54
    BIBLIOGRAPHIC, 36, 37, 173, 174, 190–193, 195, 206, 217, 225, 293; of *Kogetsushō*, 303, 304; rediscovery of classics through, 309–310
Translation, History, and Culture (Lefevere and Bassnett), 400
"Translation and Japanese Studies" (symposium), 401
Translation in Modern Japan (Levy, ed.), 399
"Translation or Treason?" (Han'yaku ka hangyaku ka?; Sugimura), 330
transliteration, 10
Trübner (publisher), 239, 266, 267, 269, 270, 281
Tsubouchi Shōyō, 262, 290, 291, 295, 300, 323; classics rejected by, 371; vision of *shōsetsu* as all fiction, 321–322
Tsuda Mayumi, 49
Tsuruya Kiemon (publisher), 67, 70, 113, 208, 209, 424n.106
Turgenev, Ivan, 323–324
Twain, Mark, 43
Twenty-Fifth Hour, The (Gheorgiu), 377, 463n.24
Two-Sided Leaf, A (*Konotegashiwa*; Hanagasa and Keisai), 85–86, *86*
Tyler, Royall, 94–95, 158, 237, 289, 443n.78

Uchimura Kanzō, 312
Uchimura Katshushi, 97, 102
Udagawa Bunkai, 195
Ueda, Atsuko, 304, 449n.154
Ueda Bin, 338
Ueirī-ban Genji monogatari (*The Waley Tale of Genji*; Samata, trans.), 331
Ujinaka (character in *Inaka Genji*), 118
Ukifune (character in *Genji*), 1
ukiyo-e (pictures of the floating world), 113, 134, 160, 172
ukiyozōshi (books of the floating world), 100, 428n.15
Ultimate Principles Illustrated (*Kyūri zukai*; Fukuzawa), 175
United States, 5, 7, 232, 286, 288, 386; academic theory in, 391; canonization studies in, 393; craze for things Japanese in, 270; *Genji* discourse in, 253; Japanese literary studies in, 4, 388; literary studies in, 385; literatures foreign to cultural sphere of, 392, 394, 395; local literatures of, 389; relation of, with Japan, 2; Suematsu in, 308; Suematsu's translation in, 240; translation workshop at University of Iowa, 399; "unequal treaties" of, with Japan, 261; Waley's translation in, 327
Unofficial History of Japan, The (*Nihon gaishi*; Rai San'yō), 373
Upwardly Mobile Carp and a Waterfall of Pearls, A (*Shussegoi taki no shiratama*; Kunisada, illus.), 80, 85
Ury, Marian, 239, 437n.9
usuzumi (thin ink), 62–63, 64, 111
Utagawa Hiroshige, 80
Utagawa Kuninao, 421n.67
Utagawa Kunisada (Utagawa Toyokuni III), 31, 46, 67, 68, 111, 420n.67; actor portraits by, 89, *90*, 429n.34; in *Autumn Storm*, 77; kabuki and, 161, 430n.63; logo used by, 119, *120*; partnership with Tanehiko on *Inaka Genji*, 112–115, *115*, *116*, 117, 213; typeset editions of *Inaka Genji* and, 195
Utagawa Kuniyasu, 410n.39, 419n.48
Utagawa Kuniyoshi, 79
Utagawa Toyohiro, 103

Utagawa Toyokuni, 113
Utagawa Toyokuni II, 419n.48
Utagawa Yoshiiku, 195, 196, 197, 198
Utagawa Yoshitora, 71
Utagawa Yoshitoshi, 172

Valéry, Paul, 368
Valk, E. M., 171, 399
Venuti, Lawrence, 395
Verbeck, G. H. F., 259
"Vie de société au Japon, d'après des auteurs japonais, La" (The Life of Society in Japan, After the Writings of Some Japanese Authors; Tissot), 280
visuality, 29
Voltaire, 317
"Voluntary Marriage" (Danjo aierabu no setsu; Nishimura), 292–293

wabun (Yamato language), 304, 305, 306–307, 312, 452n.186
Wakabayashi, Judy, 466nn.27–28
Waley, Arthur, 8, 38, 40, 237–239, 351; creative translation by, 375–376; Genji as masterpiece and, 348; on Mortimer's review of his translation, 436n.2; as "only predecessor" translator, 281; preface to first volume of Genji translation by, 327; on Suematsu's translation, 445n.93
Wallerstein, Immanuel, 434n.14
Washington, George and Martha, 71, 74
Water Margin (Ch. Shuihuzhuan, J. Suikoden), 321
Weaver, Raymond M., 248
Weiss, Theodore, 383
Weschler, Lawrence, 47, 52
Western-style books (yōsōbon), 206, 432n.28
What Is World Literature? (Damrosch), 230
White, C. A., 254
White, Oswald, 248
Who from a Restless Dream (Asaki yume mishi; Yamato), 10–11
"Why Read the Classics?" (Calvino), 1

Willow in Autumn, The (Markus), 98
Willow's Shade: Asazuma in the Moonlight (Yanagikage tsuke no Asazume; Jōno Arindo), 175, 181, 182
Wilson, Epiphanius, 288
With the Script as My Model (Tanehiko), 74, 420n.67
"Woman Question in Japan, The" (Gregory-Fletcher), 278–279
Woman's Water Margin, A (Onna suikoden; Ryūtei Senka), 424n.106
women, 57, 81, 94, 272, 299; cosmetics advertisements in gōkan and, 61, 76; in court society, 34; female gendering of Heian writing, 306; as feminist readers of Genji, 273–283, 287–288; Genji adaptations and, 98; "Genji names" of, 44, 58, 412n.5; as readers of gōkan, 34–35, 48–49, 56; as writers, 244, 255, 438n.22
"Women Classified" (Onna no shinajina), 293, 294
"Women in Japan" (newspaper article), 281
"Women of Japan, The" (Adachi), 281
"Women's Literature" (Hirai), 279–280
Wonderful City of Tokio, The (Greey), 255–256, 257, 258, 258–259, 441n.58
woodblock printing, 32, 33, 53, 106; constraints of, 136; kabusebori (cover-and-carve), 193; movable type and, 186, 189, 303, 432n.23; shift from visual to textual, 183–184; Sino-Japanese characters in, 110
Woolf, Virginia, 281–283, 401, 447n.126
world literary system, 233, 434n.14; Eurocentric, 37, 234; plurality of, 234, 235; Sinocentric, 34, 39, 234
world literature, 286–290, 296, 366, 411n.41, 455n.21; canon of, 237–238, 359; in comparative literature, 387; definition of, 230, 232–233; historicity of, 233;

world literature (continued)
  Japanese academic interest in
  Genji and, 297; national literature
  and, 343, 388; polyglot and, 382;
  translation and, 38, 230. See also
  Genji monogatari: as masterpiece of
  world literature
World of the Shining Prince, The
  (Morris), 238
World Republic of Letters, The
  (Casanova), 233
World War I, 325
World War II, 315, 358

Yakko no Koman (Tanehiko), 106
Yamada Yoshio, 348, 354, 408n.24;
  censorship of Tanizaki's
  translation and, 343, 344, 346; on
  Hakuchō and Tanizaki's
  translation, 357
Yamaguchi Koken (Yamaguchi
  Yoshizō), 310, 312, 453n.204
Yamaguchi Takeshi, 96, 100, 105–106,
  414nn.17–18
Yamaji Aizan, 311
Yamamoto Kazuaki, 432n.28
Yamamoto Shunshō, 18
Yamana Sōzen (character in Inaka
  Genji), 88, 89, 90, 91, 127, 152;
  smuggled in chest, 142, 149,
  150–151, 150, 151; as villain, 147,
  148–149
Yamanouchi Yoshio, 368
Yamato Waki, 10–11
Yamawaki Hatatsu, 408n.24
Yamazaki Toshinobu, 195, 196
Yanagawa Shigenobu, 185–186,
  420n.67
Yi Ŭn, 313, 453n.205
Yokomitsu Riichi, 358, 368
Yokutō Rōjin ("Old Man Yokutō"),
  58–59
yomihon (reading book), 36–37, 62, 91,
  106, 325; Chinese vernacular
  fiction and, 321; chūhon or chūgata
  (middle-size), 184, 432n.20;
  decline of gōkan and, 179, 181; as
  important genre only in Japan,
  322; speed of publishing, movable
  type, and, 183–186, 186, 187, 188,
  189, 189–190
Yomiuri shinbun (newspaper), 229,
  231, 296, 309, 318; advertisement
  for Yosano's translation in,
  336–337; on Genji as fad, 303;
  Hakuchō's writings in, 326,
  329–330; Mikami's lecture in, 300;
  "On Writing in English" in, 4–8,
  10, 16, 395; Sakai's article in,
  311–312, 313, 316
Yonekawa Masao, 372
Yorozu chōhō (Complete Morning
  Report), 312
Yosano Akiko, 39, 229, 309, 316,
  330–333, 336–342, 463n.27;
  millennial anniversary of Genji
  and, 13; postwar editions of
  translations by, 364
Yosano Akiko and The Tale of Genji
  (Rowley), 331
Yosano Tekkan, 316
Yoshidaya Zengorō, 11
Yoshikawa Kōbunkan, 208
Yoshikawa Shigetoshi, 307
Yoshimoto Banana, 464n.6
Yoshimura Kōsaburō, 364
Yoshinaga Minoru, 21
Yoshitsune-mono, 416n.33
Yoshiya Nobuko, 347
Yōshūsai Chikanobu (Hashimoto
  Chikanobu), 176, 178, 180
Young Americans in Japan (Greey),
  255
Yūgao (character in Genji), 64, 146,
  155, 270, 422n.89
Yūhōdō Library (Yūhōdō bunko), 318

Zohn, Harry, 171, 399
Zola, Emile, 324
Z. P. Maruya (publisher), 271,
  444n.92
Zwicker, Jonathan E., 32, 410n.39

GPSR Authorized Representative: Easy Access System Europe, Mustamäe tee 50, 10621 Tallinn, Estonia, gpsr.requests@easproject.com